THE ROUTLEDGE COMPANION TO HUMANISM AND LITERATURE

The Routledge Companion to Humanism and Literature provides readers with a comprehensive reassessment of the value of humanism in an intellectual landscape. Offering contributions by leading international scholars, this volume seeks to define literature as a core expressive form and an essential constitutive element of newly reformulated understandings of humanism.

While the value of humanism has recently been dominated by anti-humanist and post-humanist perspectives which focused on the flaws and exclusions of previous definitions of humanism, this volume examines the human problems, dilemmas, fears, and aspirations expressed in literature, as a fundamentally humanist art form and activity. Divided into three overarching categories, this companion will explore the histories, developments, debates, and contestations of humanism in literature, and deliver fresh definitions of "the new humanism" for the humanities. This focus aims to transcend the boundaries of a world in which human life is all too often defined in terms of restrictions—political, economic, theological, intellectual—and lived in terms of obedience, conformity, isolation, and fear.

The Routledge Companion to Humanism and Literature will provide invaluable support to humanities students and scholars alike seeking to navigate the relevance and resilience of humanism across world cultures and literatures.

Michael Bryson is Professor of English at California State University, Northridge. Among his books are two on the English poet John Milton, *The Tyranny of Heaven: Milton's Rejection of God as King* (2004), and *The Atheist Milton* (2016), as well as two books on world literature from the ancient to the modern, *Love and its Critics* (2017), and *The Humanist (Re)Turn: Reclaiming the Self in Literature* (2019). He is the editor of the Literature in the Humanities section of the open access journal *Humanities*, and has published widely on American, English, and World literatures.

ROUTLEDGE LITERATURE COMPANIONS

Also available in this series:

THE ROUTLEDGE COMPANION TO AUSTRALIAN LITERATURE
Edited by Jessica Gildersleeve

THE ROUTLEDGE COMPANION TO JANE AUSTEN
Edited by Cheryl A. Wilson and Maria H. Frawley

THE ROUTLEDGE COMPANION TO LITERATURE AND CLASS
Edited by Gloria McMillan

**THE ROUTLEDGE COMPANION TO THE BRITISH AND NORTH AMERICAN
LITERARY MAGAZINE**
Edited by Tim Lanzendörfer

THE ROUTLEDGE COMPANION TO LITERATURE AND EMOTION
Edited by Patrick Colm Hogan, Bradley J. Irish and Lalita Pandit Hogan

THE ROUTLEDGE COMPANION TO YAN LIANKE
Edited by Riccardo Moratto and Howard Yuen Fung Choy

THE ROUTLEDGE COMPANION TO KOREAN LITERATURE
Edited by Heekyoung Cho

THE ROUTLEDGE COMPANION TO HUMANISM AND LITERATURE
Edited by Michael Bryson

For more information on this series, please visit: www.routledge.com/Routledge-Literature-
Companions/book-series/RC4444

THE ROUTLEDGE COMPANION TO HUMANISM AND LITERATURE

Edited by Michael Bryson

NEW YORK AND LONDON

Cover image: Mostafameraji, CC0, via Wikimedia Commons

First published 2022
by Routledge
605 Third Avenue, New York, NY 10158

and by Routledge
4 Park Square, Milton Park, Abingdon, Oxon, OX14 4RN

Routledge is an imprint of the Taylor & Francis Group, an informa business

© 2022 selection and editorial matter, Michael Bryson; individual chapters, the contributors

The right of Michael Bryson to be identified as the author of the editorial material, and of the authors for their individual chapters, has been asserted in accordance with sections 77 and 78 of the Copyright, Designs and Patents Act 1988.

All rights reserved. No part of this book may be reprinted or reproduced or utilised in any form or by any electronic, mechanical, or other means, now known or hereafter invented, including photocopying and recording, or in any information storage or retrieval system, without permission in writing from the publishers.

Trademark notice: Product or corporate names may be trademarks or registered trademarks, and are used only for identification and explanation without intent to infringe.

Library of Congress Cataloging-in-Publication Data
A catalog record for this title has been requested

ISBN: 978-0-367-49411-7 (hbk)
ISBN: 978-0-367-49412-4 (pbk)
ISBN: 978-1-003-04600-4 (ebk)

DOI: 10.4324/9781003046004

Typeset in Bembo
by codeMantra

CONTENTS

List of Figures	*ix*
List of Contributors	*xi*
Introduction: The Old Argument: Humanism and Anti-Humanism *Michael Bryson*	1

PART I
Theoretical Perspectives on Humanism   **9**

1 "We Are Ourselves the Entities to be Analyzed": Heidegger on Being Human *Robin M. Muller*	11
2 Frantz Fanon: Postcoloniality and New Humanism *Deepa Jani*	31
3 Edward Said and Humanism *Masoud Farahmandfar*	50
4 "A Different Kind of Humanism": Edward Said's Césairian Critical Humanism *Sauleha Kamal*	60
5 Sloterdijk's Love Letter on Humanism *Daniel Adleman*	73
6 The Animal Turn as a Challenge to Humanism *Krzysztof Skonieczny*	86

Contents

PART II
Literary Perspectives on Humanism, East and West   **99**

7   Mapping Indic Humanism(s) in Vedic Medical and Post-Vedic
Tāntric Epistemologies   101
Abhisek Ghosal

8   Reformative Aspect of *Bhasha* Literatures and Aging in India:
Old Age, Body and Locale in Hindi Short Stories   114
Saurav Kumar

9   Humanistic Approaches in Hindi Literature: From Medieval
to Modern Times   124
Prachi Priyanka

10   Headhunting and Native Agency in Lundayeh Oral Literature:
A Humanist Perspective   146
Kavitha Ganesan and Shaffarullah Abdul Rahman

11   Woman is the Measure of All Things: Authoritarianism and
Anti-Humanism in the Criticism of Anglo-Saxon Poetry   173
Michael Bryson

12   Humanism and Universal Values in European Medieval Literature:
Freidank's *Bescheidenheit* and *Sir Gawain and the Green Knight*   191
Albrecht Classen

13   The Circulation of Atheism in Early Modern England:
Marlowe, Greene, and Shakespeare   209
Peter C. Herman

14   Surrogacy and Empire in *The Man-Plant* and Eighteenth-Century
Vernacular Medical Texts   229
Danielle Spratt

Contents

PART III
Digital Humanisms   **249**

15 Digital Humanities and the Humanistic Tradition: Situating Digital
Humanism   251
Mauro Carassai

16 Beyond the Algorithms: On Performance and Subjectivity in *Detroit:*
Become Human   282
Nizar Zouidi

Index   289

FIGURES

10.1	The highlighted area depicts the Lundayeh "ancestral homeland" in Borneo	147
10.2	The floorplan (schematic) of a longhouse	148
10.3	Cross-section of a longhouse	149
10.4	Southeast Asian tribal cosmology	151
10.5	Headhunting as reality maintenance	151
13.1	Published references to atheism 1574–1606	211
13.2	Map created at Early Modern Map of London, dir. Janelle Jenstad https://mapoflondon.uvic.ca/index.htm	215
13.3	Portrait of Elizabeth I by Marcus Gheeraerts the Younger https://commons.wikimedia.org/wiki/File:Elizabeth_I_portrait,_Marcus_Gheeraerts_the_Younger_c.1595.jpg	220
15.1	Storyspace screenshot. Searching for the name "Beer" in the Storyspace version of the Dickens Web [Landow and Kahn 1992]	258
15.2	A Topic Model of the PMLA collection in which "topics" are visualized as bubbles of words (Reproduced by Permission of Andrew Goldstone, Rutgers University, author of the DFR Browser)	265

CONTRIBUTORS

Daniel Adleman is an Assistant Professor of Writing and Rhetoric at the University of Toronto, where he teaches A Brief History of Persuasion, Digital Rhetoric, and Writing for Social Change. He is the co-founder of the Vancouver Institute for Social Research (VISR) and the University of Toronto's Franklin Lecture Series. His recent articles can be found in *Cultural Studies*, *Cultural Politics*, and *Canadian Review of American Studies*. Daniel is currently co-authoring a book on rhetoric's uncanny relationship with psychoanalysis for Routledge.

Michael Bryson is Professor of English at California State University, Northridge. Among his books are two on the English poet John Milton, *The Tyranny of Heaven: Milton's Rejection of God as King* (U. Delaware Press, 2004), and *The Atheist Milton* (Ashgate, 2012/Routledge 2016), as well as two books on world literature from the ancient to the modern, *Love and its Critics* (Open Book, 2017), and *The Humanist (Re)Turn: Reclaiming the Self in Literature* (Routledge, 2019). He is the editor of the Literature in the Humanities section of the open access journal *Humanities*, and has published widely on American, English, and World literatures.

Mauro Carassai is Associate Professor of Liberal Studies and English at California State University Northridge where he teaches courses in digital humanities, literary theory, and interdisciplinary studies He was a Brittain Postdoctoral Fellow at Georgia Institute of Technology in 2014–2015 and a visiting Fulbright at Brown University in 2007–2008. His research combines literary theory, philosophy of language, and digital literatures within the larger frame of American literatures and American studies. His scholarly work has been published in journals such as *Culture Machine*, *LEA Almanac*, *DHQ*, and *ADA—A Journal of Gender Media and Technology*. He co-edited a double issue for the *Digital Humanities Quarterly* titled "Futures of Digital Studies" and he is currently at work on a manuscript exploring problems and perspectives in configuring an *Ordinary Digital Philosophy*.

Albrecht Classen is University Distinguished Professor of German Studies at the University of Arizona, Tucson. He has currently published 115 scholarly books on German and European medieval and early modern literature, most recently *Freedom, Imprisonment, and Slavery in the Pre-Modern Time* (2021) and Tracing *the Trails in Medieval Literature* (Routledge, 2021). In his other recent books, he explored the history of toleration and tolerance (2018 and 2020), prostitution in medieval literature (2019), the topics of the forest and of water in medieval literature (2015 and 2018), magic and magicians (2017), and the Paradigm Shift in the late Middle Ages (2019). He is the

xi

editor-in-chief of the journals *Mediaevistik* and *Humanities*, and serves on many different boards of international journals dedicated to the Humanities.

Masoud Farahmandfar is Assistant Professor of English literature at Allameh Tabataba'i University in Iran. His research interests include postcolonial studies, Orientalism, and historical fiction, and he has given talks and has published several books and articles related to these subjects.

Kavitha Ganesan is Senior Lecturer at Universiti Malaysia Sabah and has been primarily working on Malaysian Literature in English with a particular interest in female life-writing. Her current research interest is in areas related to postcolonial indigenous studies.

Abhisek Ghosal is currently working as a Senior Ph.D. Research Scholar at the Department of Humanities and Social Sciences, Indian Institute of Technology, Kharagpur, India. His research interests include Critical Theory, Continental Thinking, South Asian Literature, and Indic Studies, among others. He has widely published articles in different flagship journals.

Peter C. Herman has published, among other books, *Unspeakable: The Literature of Terrorism from the Gunpowder Plot to 9/11, Critical Concepts: Literature and Terrorism*, and *Destabilizing Milton: "Paradise Lost" and the Poetics of Incertitude.* He is currently working on a project called "Early Modern Others," and he teaches at San Diego State University.

Deepa Jani is Assistant Professor of English at SUNY Old Westbury, specializing in Postcolonial Literatures and Critical Theory. Her articles are published or forthcoming in *Commonwealth Essays and Studies, Forum for Modern Language Studies, Research in African Literatures*, and an edited collection on Postcolonial Studies. She is completing her book manuscript, "J. M. Coetzee: Language, Ethics, and the Critique of Humanism."

Sauleha Kamal is a Ph.D. candidate and Overseas Research Scholar at the University of York, researching empathy and the literary marketplace in the context of human rights and politics in post-9/11 South Asian narratives. She is an alumna of the University of Cambridge, and Barnard College, Columbia University, where she studied English and Economics. Her scholarly work, essays, and fiction have appeared in various places including *Postcolonial Text, The Atlantic*, and *Catapult*. She was a writer-in-residence at Yaddo in 2019.

Saurav Kumar is UGC Junior Research Fellow in the Department of English, Banaras Hindu University, Varanasi, India. He has recently submitted his Ph.D. thesis titled "Fiction as Gerontological Resource: A Critical Study of Select Novels." His areas of interest are literary and cultural gerontology, post-structuralism, transcultural humanities, and vegan studies. His recent publications include research articles in *The Gerontologist* and *Indian Journal of Gender Studies* (forthcoming), chapters in the volumes *Transcultural Humanities in South Asia: Critical Essays on Literature and Culture* (Routledge 2022) and *The Routledge Handbook of Vegan Studies* (2021), and an English translation of a Hindi story, "Palang," in *Indian Literature* (2021), the bimonthly journal of Sahitya Akademi.

Robin M. Muller is Associate Professor of Philosophy at California State University, Northridge, where she teaches broadly in 19th- and 20th-century philosophy. Her Ph.D. from The New School for Social Research is in Philosophy, and her MA in Theoretical Linguistics is from University College London. She specializes in phenomenology, especially at its intersections with the human sciences, and has published several articles on the French phenomenologist Maurice Merleau-Ponty. She also has research interests in the history of philosophy of race and has a forthcoming article about the philosophical significance of slave narratives.

Prachi Priyanka finds her interest in intertextuality and visual culture, Indian literature, Partition narratives, and Victorian studies. She has two books to her credit: *Thistle & Weeds* (2016) and *Caste, Class and Gender in Modern Indian Literature* (2021). Currently, she is Assistant Professor in the Department of English, School of Humanities and Social Sciences, Sharda University, India.

Shaffarullah Abdul Rahman is a Senior Lecturer at Universiti Malaysia Sabah (UMS). His main research focus on the philosophical study of tranquility in Western, Indian, and Chinese philosophies during the classical period; the renewals in philosophy of religion; and the meta-philosophical questions concerning the purpose of philosophy.

Krzysztof Skonieczny is assistant professor at the Faculty of "Artes Liberales," University of Warsaw, where he is a member of the Techno-Humanities Lab. His interests include political philosophy, psychoanalysis, posthumanities, and animal studies. He is the author of *Animals and Immanence. A Conceptual Inquiry* (Routledge 2020) and the co-editor (with Szymon Wróbel) of *Atheism Revisited. Rethinking Modernity and Inventing New Modes of Life* (Palgrave Macmillan 2020).

Danielle Spratt is Professor of English at California State University, Northridge, where she teaches classes on eighteenth-century literature, the history of science and medicine, satire, Jane Austen, and public humanities. With Bridget Draxler, she is the author of *Engaging the Age of Jane Austen: Public Humanities in Practice* (2018).

Nizar Zouidi is Assistant Professor of English Literature at the University of Hail, Saudi Arabia, and at the University of Gafsa, Tunisia. Zouidi edited a book on the representations of evil in literature and media and authored several articles on the subject. He is currently studying writing for video games.

Introduction

The Old Argument: Humanism and Anti-Humanism

Michael Bryson

It is among our oldest arguments—a debate between two ancient Greeks: Protagoras and Plato. Their dispute formed the outlines of an ongoing conflict between those for whom the significance of a human life is to be found *in* that human life, and those for whom such significance or meaning is to be found *anywhere except* that life: outside the individual, outside the realm of a world accessible through the senses and the direct experience of life in all its tactility, difficulty, and (occasional) joy.

Protagoras, especially in light of his famous dictum πάντων χρημάτων μέτρον ἐστὶν ἄνθρωπος[1] [*pánton chremáton métron estìn ánthropos*—of all useful things, the measure is humankind], can be seen as our first identifiable humanist, in the sense that his argument locates the standard of value *inside* human experience, life, and judgment, making individual human beings the best arbiters of where value is to be found. Plato, on the other hand, is our first anti-humanist, locating the standard of value *outside* that same human experience, life, and judgment.[2]

For Plato, and those who follow in the tradition of thought he has come to represent, "all that is given in experience counts as a hindrance and a barrier to be broken through."[3] For a modern (and non-Platonic) thinker, however, the situation is different: the *a priori* structures of thought that take the Forms, or the dictates of a theology, or what Lyotard calls a grand narrative (of whatever stripe) to be the measure of all things are themselves the hindrance and the barrier to be broken through.[4] And it is especially difficult, especially important, to break through that barrier when it takes something like the following form: *the meaning of a human life, and the significance of the existence of the human species, must always be found in some value/idea/source/environment external to that individual life and to that collective existence.* In Plato, that form of thinking is expressed most directly in the *Laws*, in the idea that *God* is the measure of all things (an idea that the later Roman church was only too happy to promulgate): "ὁ δὴ θεὸς ἡμῖν πάντων χρημάτων μέτρον ἂν εἴη μάλιστα, καὶ πολὺ μᾶλλον ἤ πού τις, ὥς φασιν, ἄνθρωπος"[5] [Now for us, God is the measure of all useful things, in the highest degree, much more than is any man they speak of]. In nationalist forms of thought, this manifests in much the same way: the nation (as an abstraction) is the measure rather than its citizens or any individual citizen ("Ask not what your country can do for you—Ask what you can do for your country"). In what might be termed "corporatist" thought, the corporation, the enterprise, the business (and in academic terms, the university, college, or department) is the measure rather than the individual worker or the workers as a collective. This is the ideological assumption behind the idea that it is a necessary thing to be "a team player," or "a stakeholder" (in somewhat more modern jargon) on the individual level. But this is also what is behind the idea that the human species must find the value of its own existence in various forms of political organization, economic practice, theological doctrine, or even ecological adaptation.

DOI: 10.4324/9781003046004-1

The key ingredient in all these forms of thought (and myriad others) is the fundamental idea that *you*, *I*, and *we* are not the measures (or measurers) of what is useful, beneficial, desirable, or even necessary. That measure, that standard, that deciding factor and deciding agency always-already resides outside, in something or someone to which we are eternally called to submit. What matter, then, if that eternally-external measure is God, or the State, or the Party, or the Corporation, or even (as some contemporary thinkers would have it) the Environment? The central idea remains— *you, I, we, do not measure. We are measured unto.* And it is this state of being measured unto—reduced and silenced before that deciding factor/agency—that comprises the shared DNA, if you will, of the various anti-humanist forms of theory and practice that decenter the living human (collective or individual) in favor of abstractions, systems, or even non-human forms of life. It has been fashionable, especially among thinkers whose formative years were clouded by the Nazi occupation of France in the mid-1940s,[6] to speak of the death (or the end) of Man, and the decentering and depriviliging of the human perspective and experience (as if we could have any other), but behind the various statements of such a position inevitably lies the humbug, the snake-oil, the old misanthropic idea that of all entities in the universe, the only one that does not count is the human being.

In the face of this kind of thinking, Protagoras' full declaration stands as a radically pro-human (and perhaps the original humanist) manifesto: "πάντων χρημάτων μέτρον ἐστὶν ἄνθρωπος, τῶν μὲν ὄντων ὡς ἔστιν, τῶν δὲ οὐκ ὄντων ὡς οὐκ ἔστιν"[7] [Of all useful things the measure is humankind: of those that are, that they are; and of those that are not, that they are not]. But is it ἄνθρωπος in the collective sense (the human species) or in the individual sense (the particular human being) to which Protagoras is referring? Arguments such as Plato's (in the *Thaetetus* especially) try to shoehorn Protagoras' dictum into the latter sense, in an attempt to portray his idea as a form of relativism which undermines all objective truth. But this, as F. C. S. Schiller has cogently argued, is neither a necessary nor even a coherent way of understanding Protagoras' famously ambiguous utterance. As Schiller argues:

> we do not know its exact context and scope, and so can interpret it in various ways. But, however we understand it, it is most important and suggestive, and, *in every way but one*, it is a fundamental truth. That one way, of course, is Plato's.[8]

For Schiller, the "great mistake" is to regard either interpretation as "exclud[ing] the other."[9] The individual can, in some sense, be the measure of all things, but so also can humanity in the collective sense: "Man [...] is the measure also in the generic sense of man."[10]

But the definitions of humanism at work in much recent postmodern/post-humanist theory ignore all of this—*when they are not actively promoting the very attitudes that humanism has long opposed*. We have, of late, too-quickly and too-facilely abandoned the various ideas that inform what has been called humanism in the modern era: 1) the "instrumental" tradition that places "Man" at the center of the world (insisting that humans can, through an objective knowledge of nature, shape nature to human ends—Descartes, Bacon, etc.); and 2) the "idealist" tradition (famous, for example, from Kant's *Critique of Pure Reason*) in which it is argued that the world exists meaningfully only insofar as it is reflected upon by and in human thinking; and also 3) the "dialectical" tradition (a kind of left-Hegelian position) in which it is maintained that the world is what it is at least partially through the influence and interaction of humans, and humans are what they are, in turn, through interaction with and influence from the world. Postmodern and post-humanist rejections of Humanism tend to conflate the first two positions, and then oppose the straw-man conflation while giving short shrift to the third position. This results in jumping to all kinds of extremes. For example, Slavoj Žižek argues that human subjectivity is a lie, that the "first lesson of psycho-analysis is that this 'richness of inner life' is fundamentally fake."[11] Eileen Crist argues ominously for "contracting humanity's scale and scope,"[12] while Stefanie Fishel declares that "we

Introduction

have never been wholly human, biologically or otherwise," and maintains that the category of the "human" is merely a repressive product of "the Enlightenment project."[13] Behind all of this lies the insistence of Frantz Fanon that we must "put an end to this narcissism according to which [Man] imagines himself different from other 'animals.'"[14] *Post-humanism* often seems like *anti-humanism* with a fresh coat of theoretical paint.

Indeed, at their outer limits, anti-humanist arguments against humanism can often seem like little more than stalking horses for eliminationism[15] or tyranny.[16] Even the less problematic among such arguments confuse means and ends. In arguing against a capitalized and industrialized world as the results of *humanism* they reflect a basic misunderstanding of the aims of humanistic inquiry and points of view.[17] Capitalism is a fundamentally anti-humanistic (and literally anti-human) enterprise, seeking to subordinate human life in the mass to the building of great wealth for the few (what is fundamentally "humanist" about an Amazon fulfillment center, or a Chinese sweatshop operation that produces iPhones and other Apple products?). Marx pursues a profoundly humanist argument, when he contends that the only essential value in any of the commodities produced in an industrialized world is that which can be measured in *human labor*, which represents "the eternal natural condition of human life."[18] Of all useful things, again, humanity is the measure of value. As Nietzsche argues "Whatever has value in the present world does not have it of itself [...] but was given and gifted that value, and we were those givers and gifters! Only we made the world that concerns people!"[19]

In the face of such arguments, the anti-humanists have been (and are) those among us who would decenter human beings from their own standards of value—those who would insist that we look outside individual human experience to the Forms, to God(s), to the Party, to Nature abstracted into a kind of deity to be valued in itself (rather than as an environment that enables and supports a healthy and thriving human experience), to Economies of production and consumption raised to the level of an implacable Moloch who demands endless blood sacrifice and yet is never appeased. The term itself has revealing origins, coming from Louis Althusser's egregious (and willful) misreading of Marx:

> From a strict theoretical standpoint, one can and must then speak openly of *a theoretical anti-humanism of Marx*, and see in this *theoretical anti-humanism* the condition of absolute (negative) possibility of (positive) knowledge of the human world itself, and its practical transformation. We can only *know* something about men on the absolute condition of reducing the philosophical (theoretical) myth of man to ashes.[20]

Years later, in his autobiography, Althusser admitted that he had rewritten Marx in order to make the German thinker's work more compatible with his own French ideas. This rewriting:

> gave a particular form to my exposition of Marxist theory, hence, among many specialists and activists, the feeling that I had fabricated a Marx of my own, quite foreign to the real Marx, an imaginary Marxism (Raymond Aron). I readily admit this [...]. Yes, I realize that I fabricated a philosophy for Marx that was different from vulgar Marxism, but as it provided the reader with a no longer contradictory but coherent and intelligible exhibition, I thought that the objective had been achieved and that I had also "appropriated" Marx by giving him back his demands for consistency and intelligibility.[21]

Marx's thinking could not have been more different than the distorted image of it promulgated by Althusser:

> Applied to man, if one wants to judge all human deeds, movements, relationships, etc. according to the principle of utility, it is first a question of human nature in general and then of human nature, which has been historically modified in every epoch.[22]

For Marx, human nature existed, not as a myth, but as a concrete fact in the world, one that was variously impacted by the conditions of different historical ages, but an ineradicable fact nonetheless, and one specifically *not* to be reduced to ashes. The anti-humanists among us, in the manner of Althusser, have long argued that humanity (thinly-disguised in the critical formulation of *le mythe* [...] *de l'homme* that *is* to be *réduire en cendres*) should be decentered, marginalized, and forced to make way for *something or someone* other than itself. Always last on the list, in an anti-humanist universe of two things, humanity would be second. In such a universe of ten things, humanity would be tenth. For the anti-humanists—from Plato to Althusser and the anti-humanists of the present day—human life is to be sacrificed to some greater standard of value, whether that be the truth and reality of the Forms, the imperious will of a god, or the benefit of a planet that will long outlive us no matter what we do. The inescapable impression left by much of this work is not just deterministic, but misanthropic, as if the so-called Wisdom of Silenus (that it would be better for "people to die as soon as possible"[23]) were now the reigning ethos in the academic anti-humanist world.[24]

The Routledge Companion to Humanism and Literature pursues a course correction to much of the recent discourse surrounding humanism, with contributions from around the world—including voices and perspectives from non-Western authors who have too often and too long been marginalized—all of which collectively aim at reformulated working definitions of humanism as a response to an increasingly troubled age. Why is this book necessary? Because something crucial is being forgotten/elided in current discussions of the flaws and exclusions of Humanism: the idea that Humanism began as (and in many ways remains) a perspective that reflects an urgent need to free ourselves from physical and intellectual tyranny. Originally, this manifested in the desire to escape both death and the domination of the gods. From that perspective, ancient Mesopotamian and Levantine works like *Gilgamesh*, *Atrahasis*, and *Job* are humanist, as they focus on human concerns, place humanity in opposition to mortality and the gods, and, in the case of *Atrahasis*, serve as the oldest example we have of the "figure that stands up for humans against the gods" motif later made famous in the Promethean legends. Humanism, seen in this light, is a focus on specifically *human* problems, dilemmas, fears, aspirations, areas of knowledge and ignorance, etc. That focus often stems from a desire to transcend the limitations of a theistic, tyrannical, or otherwise limiting context that enforces the idea that human life is about accepting limits, about obedience, isolation, wanting less, accepting less, and doing/thinking/being what one is told before one finally dies. Seen through this lens, the contributors to this volume make clear that medieval Anglo-Saxon and German poets are asserting and/or engaging with what might be called "humanist" values, as are the authors of sixteenth-and seventeenth-century English plays; the authors of eighteenth-century English medical texts; medieval and modern Indian authors and texts; the modern singers of traditional (Malaysian) Lundayeh oral tales; modern European philosophers like Jean-Paul Sartre, Martin Heidegger, and Peter Sloterdijk; critics and theorists like Frantz Fanon and Edward Said; and the innovative theorists and practitioners of the emerging field(s) of digital humanism. Even those who critique and oppose the humanist tradition—scholars such as Rosi Braidotti and Donna Haraway, for example—can be seen as arguing for an expansion of values (much like those found in the tradition they oppose) to those (human or animal) who have been excluded therefrom.

The emerging thread of this collection is a kind of Saidian idea of a humanism redefined to widen its parameters as far as possible, on the grounds that the typically-conceived version of humanism was really just European humanism in disguise (and sometimes not even bothering with a disguise). Sylvia Wynter has rightly pointed out that the concepts of the human, and humanity, that we too often take for granted are built on exclusion, emerging from a "humanist strategy of returning to the pagan thought of Greece and Rome for arguments to legitimate the state's rise to hegemony, outside the limits of the temporal sovereignty claimed by the papacy," which provided "a model for the invention of a by-nature difference between 'natural masters' and 'natural slaves,' one able to replace the Christian/Enemies-of-Christ legitimating difference."[25] The lines

Introduction

of thought pursued in the present volume propose countering a false or exclusive humanism of the kind Wynter decries, not with anti-humanism or post-humanism, but with an attempt at something like *a genuinely inclusive humanism that is ever striving to be more inclusive still*, what Paul Gilroy refers to as a "radically nonracial" and "willfully ungendered humanism," and even a "pragmatic, planetary humanism" that "exhibits a primary concern with the forms of human dignity [...] accompanied by a belated return to consideration of the chronic tragedy, vulnerability, and frailty that have defined our species."[26] In pursuit of this new form of humanism, Gilroy calls for "a principled, cross-cultural approach to the history and literature of extreme situations in which the boundaries of what it means to be human were being negotiated and tested minute by minute, day by day."[27] As Edward Said has argued, "Humanism is the only—I would go so far as saying the final—resistance we have against the inhuman practices and injustices that disfigure human history."[28] Perhaps this resistance can be best understood in the words of Terence (an African slave who became a free man and one of the most influential dramatists of the ancient Roman world): *homo sum, humani nihil a me alienum puto* [I am human, nothing human is alien to me].[29] The old humanism made too many things that are human alien to it, and an expanded/reformulated humanism is an attempt to more closely live up to that Terentian ideal, by reconnecting the flawed, incomplete, but necessary humanist project to the original sense of a need to escape from tyranny, seeking new (and recovering old) understandings of literature as a fundamentally humanist art form and activity.

Literature is among the most important elements in a reformulated set of definitions and understandings of humanism, which aim to enhance empathy, not strive for domination, to include, not exclude, emphasizing connection and interdependence between humans, and between humans, other animals, and the environment. As Cicero reminds us, literature can serve, and often has served, as part of those "arts by which the young are accustomed to humanity,"[30] helping us to "regulate our studies," not by external dictates, or in reference to values outside ourselves, but by "the measure of our own nature."[31] This, as Robin Headlam Wells argues, is

> one of the chief justifications for the study of literature: imaginative contact with other minds in periods or cultures remote from our own helps us to appreciate that our common humanity is more important than the ethnic and religious differences that continue to create so much havoc in the modern world.[32]

Postmodernism and anti-humanism have pointed out the flaws and exclusions in previous definitions of humanism, but as Wells suggests, "[i]t's time we got over our misplaced embarrassment about human nature and recognised anti-humanism for what it really is."[33] The project pursued in the following chapters, seeking to define literature as a core expressive form and a core constitutive element of newly-reformulated understandings of humanism, can point us toward that necessary correction.

Bibliography

Althusser, Louis. *L'avenir dure longtemps*. Paris, Stock/Imec, 1992.

Althusser, Louis. "Marxisme et humanisme." In *Cahiers de l'Institut des Sciences Économique Appliquées* 20 (1964), 109–133. Article reprinted in *Pour Marx*, 1965.

Behrent, Michael C. "Can the Critique of Capitalism be Antihumanist?" *History and Theory* 54 (3), 372–388.

Cicero. *Pro Archia. Post Reditum in Senatu. Post Reditum ad Quirites. De Domo Sua. De Haruspicum Responsis. Pro Plancio.* Edited by N. H. Watts. Loeb Classical Library 158. Cambridge: Harvard University Press, 1923.

Cicero. *De Officiis. Or On Duties*. Edited by Walter Miller. Loeb Classical Library 30. Cambridge: Harvard University Press, 1913.

Crist, Eileen. "Reimagining the Human." *Science* 362 (6420), 1242, 1244. doi: 10.1126/science.aau6026

Crutchfield, Parker. "Compulsory moral bioenhancement should be covert." *Bioethics* 33 (1), 112–121.

Crutchfield, Parker. "'Morality pills' may be the US's best shot at ending the coronavirus pandemic, according to one ethicist." *The Conversation*. August 10, 2020. https://theconversation.com/morality-pills-may-be-the-uss-best-shot-at-ending-the-coronavirus-pandemic-according-to-one-ethicist-142601.

Fanon, Frantz. *Peau Noire, Masques Blanc*. Paris: Éditions du Seuil, 1952.

Fishel, Stefanie. *The Microbial State: Global Thriving and the Body Politic*. Minneapolis: University of Minnesota Press, 2017.

Gilroy, Paul. *Against Race: Imagining Political Culture Beyond the Color Line*. Cambridge: The Belknap Press of Harvard University Press, 2000.

Gomperz, Theodore. *Greek Thinkers: A History of Ancient Philosophy*. Vol. 3. London: John Murray, 1905.

Lyotard, Jean-François. *La Condition postmoderne. Rapport sur le savoir*. Paris: Éditions de Minuit, 1979.

Marx, Karl. *Das Kapital: Kritik der politischen Oekonomie*. Erster Band, Buch 1: Der Produktionsprocess des Kapitals. Hamburg: Verlag von Otto Meissner, 1867.

Nietzsche, Friederich. *Die Fröliche Wissenschaft*. Leipzig: Verlag von E. W. Fritzsch, 1887.

Plato. *Laws*, Volume I: Books 1–6. Edited by R. G. Bury. Loeb Classical Library 187. Cambridge: Harvard University Press, 1926.

Plutarch. *Moralia*, Volume II. Edited by Frank Cole Babbitt. Loeb Classical Library. Cambridge: Harvard University Press, 1928.

Said, Edward. *Orientalism*, 25th Anniversary Edition. New York: Knopf-Doubleday, 2014.

Savulescu, Julian and Ingmar Persson. *Unfit for the Future: The Need for Moral Enhancement*. Oxford: Oxford University Press, 2012.

Schiller, F. C. S. *Studies in Humanism*. New York: Macmillan, 1907.

Sextus Empiricus. *Against Logicians*. Edited by R. G. Bury. Cambridge: Loeb Classical Library, Harvard University Press, 1935.

Terence. *The Woman of Andros. The Self-Tormentor. The Eunuch*. Edited by John Barsby. Loeb Classical Library 22. Cambridge: Harvard University Press, 2001.

Van Berkel, Tazuko A. "Made to Measure: Protagoras' *Metron*." *Protagoras of Abdera: The Man, His Measure*. Edited by Johannes M. Van Ophuijsen, Marlein Van Raalte, and Peter Stork. Leiden: Brill, 2013, 38–67.

Wells, Robin Headlam. *Shakespeare's Humanism*. Cambridge: Cambridge University Press, 2005.

Wynter, Sylvia. "Unsettling the Coloniality of Being/Power/Truth/Freedom: Towards the Human, After Man, Its Overrepresentation—An Argument." *CR: The New Centennial Review* 3, (3) (Fall 2003), 257–337.

Zizek, Slavoj. *First as Tragedy, Then as Farce*. London: Verso, 2009.

Notes

1 Quoted in Sextus Empiricus, *Against Logicians*. Edited by R. G. Bury (Cambridge, MA: Loeb Classical Library, Harvard University Press, 1935), 7.60. All translations in this chapter are my own.

2 As Tazuko A. Van Berkel argues, Protagoras may well be describing humanity, not merely as the measurer but also as "the 'measuring unit' of everything, that *in terms of what* all things are measured" ("Made to Measure: Protagoras' *Metron*." In *Protagoras of Abdera: The Man, His Measure*. Edited by Johannes M. Van Ophuijsen, Marlein Van Raalte, and Peter Stork [Leiden, Brill, 2013], 59.)

3 Theodore Gomperz. *Greek Thinkers: A History of Ancient Philosophy*. Vol. 3 (London: John Murray, 1905), 88.

4 "Le recours aux grands récits est exclu; on ne saurait donc recourir ni à la dialectique de l'Esprit ni même à l'émancipation de l'humanité comme validation du discours scientifique postmoderne. Mais […] le 'petit récit' reste la forme par excellence que prend l'invention imaginative, et tout d'abord dans la science" (Jean-François Lyotard. *La Condition postmoderne. Rapport sur le savoir* [Paris: Éditions de Minuit, 1979], 98).

   [The recourse to the grand narratives is excluded; we cannot, therefore, resort to the dialectic of the Spirit or even to the emancipation of humanity as a validation of postmodern scientific discourse. But […] the "little narrative" remains the form par excellence that imaginative invention takes, and first of all in science.]

5 Plato. *Laws*, Volume I: Books 1–6. Edited by R. G. Bury. Loeb Classical Library 187. (Cambridge: Harvard University Press, 1926), 716c, 294.

6 For perhaps the definitive work on this topic, see Tony Judt, *Past Imperfect: French Intellectuals, 1944–1956*. (Berkely: University of California Press, 1992).

7 Quoted in Sextus Empiricus, *Against Logicians*. Edited by R. G. Bury (Cambridge: Loeb Classical Library, Harvard University Press, 1935), 7.60.

Introduction

8   F. C. S. Schiller. *Studies in Humanism* (New York: Macmillan, 1907), 33.

9   Ibid.

10 Ibid., 34.

11 Slavoj Zizek. *First as Tragedy, Then as Farce* (London: Verso, 2009), 40.

12 Eileen Crist. "Reimagining the Human." *Science* 362 (6420), 1242, 1244. doi: 10.1126/science.aau6026

13 Stefanie Fishel. *The Microbial State: Global Thriving and the Body Politic* (Minneapolis: University of Minnesota Press, 2017), 101–102.

14 "faire admettre à l'homme qu'il n'est rien, absolument rien—et qu'il lui faut en finir avec ce narcissisme selon lequel il s'imagine différent des autres « animaux »" (Frantz Fanon. *Peau Noire, Masques Blanc* [Paris: Éditions du Seuil, 1952], 17–18).

15 See, for example, the Voluntary Human Extinction Movement, represented online at http://www.vhemt.org/

16 See the work of Parker Crutchfield on the biochemical manipulations he calls *Moral Enhancement*. Crutchfield follows in the footsteps of Julian Savulescu and Ingmar Persson, two Oxford researchers who argue in their 2012 book, *Unfit for the Future: The Need for Moral Enhancement* (Oxford: Oxford University Press) that human morality evolved for living in small communities, and needs to be enhanced through biotechnology in the modern world. In a recent scholarly article, Dr. Crutchfield argues that "[n]ot only should moral bioenhancement be compulsory, it should also be covert, conducted without the knowledge of those who are being enhanced" ("Compulsory Moral Bioenhancement Should Be Covert." *Bioethics* 33 (1), 113). Elsewhere, in a popular forum, Crutchfield framed the question as one of forcing a resistant population into compliance over the issue of COVID-19 vaccines: "To me, it seems the problem of coronavirus defectors could be solved by moral enhancement: like receiving a vaccine to beef up your immune system, people could take a substance to boost their cooperative, pro-social behavior. Could a psychoactive pill be the solution to the pandemic?" ("'Morality pills' may be the US's best shot at ending the coronavirus pandemic, according to one ethicist." *The Conversation*. August 10, 2020. https://theconversation.com/morality-pills-may-be-the-uss-best-shot-at-ending-the-coronavirus-pandemic-according-to-one-ethicist-142601. Accessed September 7, 2021)

17 As Michael C. Behrent argues, in an analysis of Foucault's thinking about Adam Smith, for Foucault and so many who follow him, "[o]nce one considers human beings as subjects of interest, it becomes impossible to have any a priori knowledge of society, the totality of individual interests being unknowable." ("Can the Critique of Capitalism be Antihumanist?" *History and Theory*, 54 (3), 384.) From an anti-humanist (Foucauldian) perspective, even considering human beings "as subjects of interest" gets in the way of understanding the systems and structures that oppress so many *actual human beings*. A more perverse form of analysis of the world in which humans live, move, and have their being can scarcely be imagined.

18 Der Arbeitsprocess […] ist zweckmässige Thätigkeit zur Herstellung von Gebrauchswerthen, Aneignung des Natürlichen für menschliche Bedürfnisse, allgemeine Bedingung des Stoffwechsels zwischen Mensch und Natur, ewige Naturbedingung des menschlichen Lebens und daher unabhängig von jeder Form dieses Lebens, vielmehr allen seinen Gesellschaftsformen gleich gemeinsam. (Karl Marx. *Das Kapital: Kritik der politischen Oekonomie*. Erster Band, Buch 1: *Der Produktionsprocess des Kapitals* [Hamburg: Verlag von Otto Meissner, 1867], 171.)

    [Labor […] is an expedient activity for the production of use value, the appropriation of nature for human needs, the general condition of the metabolism between man and nature, the eternal natural condition of human life and therefore independent of every form of this life, rather all its forms of society together.]

19 "Was nur Werth hat in der jetzigen Welt, das hat ihn nicht an sich […] sondern dem hat man einen Werth einmal gegeben, geschenkt, und wir waren diese Gebenden und Schenkenden! Wir erst haben die Welt, die den Menschen Etwas angeht, geschaffen!" (Friederich Nietzsche. *Die Fröliche Wissenschaft* [Leipzig: Verlag von E.W. Fritzsch, 1887], 301.)

20 "Sous le rapport strict de la théorie, on peut et on doit alors parler ouvertement d'un *anti-humanisme théorique de Marx*, et voir dans cet *anti-humanisme théorique* la condition de possibilité absolue (négative) de la connaissance (positive) du monde humain lui-même, et de sa transformation pratique. On ne peut *connaître* quelque, chose des hommes qu'à la condition absolue de réduire en cendres le mythe philosophique (théorique) de l'homme." (Louis Althusser. *Marxisme et humanisme*. In *Cahiers de l'Institut des Sciences Économique Appliquées* 20 (1964), 109–133. Article reprinted in *Pour Marx*, 1965, 225–249, this quote from 236).

21 "donna une forme particulière à mon exposé de la théorie marxiste, d'où, chez nombre de spécialistes et de militants, le sentiment que j'avais fabriqué un Marx à moi, bien étranger au Marx réel, un

marxisme imaginaire (Raymond Aron). Je le reconnais volontiers […] Oui, je me rends bien compte que j'ai comme fabriqué une philosophie pour Marx différente du marxisme vulgaire, mais comme elle fournissait au lecteur une exposition non plus contradictoire mais cohérente et intelligible, je pensai que l'objectif était atteint et que je m'étais aussi « approprié » Marx en lui rendant ses exigences de cohérence et d'intelligibilité." (Louis Althusser. *L'avenir dure longtemps*. [Paris, Stock/Imec, 1992], 214.)

22 "Auf den Menschen angewandt, wenn man alle menschliche Tat, Bewegung, Verhältnisse usw. nach dem Nützlichkeitsprinzip beurteilen will, handelt es sich erst um die menschliche Natur im allgemeinen und dann um die in jeder Epoche historisch modifizierte Menschennatur." (Karl Marx. *Das Kapital: Kritik der politischen Oekonomie*. Erster Band, Buch 1: *Der Produktionsprocess des Kapitals* [Hamburg: Verlag von Otto Meissner, 1867], 596–597, n. 64.)

23 "τὸ γενομένους ἀποθανεῖν ὡς τάχιστα" (In Plutarch, *Moralia*, Volume II. Edited by Frank Cole Babbitt. Loeb Classical Library [Cambridge: Harvard University Press, 1928], 178). As Nietzsche recounts the advice of Silenus to King Midas: "Das Allerbeste ist für dich gänzlich unerreichbar: nicht geboren zu-sein, nicht zu sein, nichts zu sein. Das Zweitbeste aber ist für dich—bald zu sterben" [The best thing is completely out of reach for you: not to have been born, not to exist. But the second-best thing is for you—to die soon] (*Die Geburt der Tragödie aus dem Geiste der Musik* [Leipzig: Verlag von E.W. Fritzsch, 1872], 11–12).

24 See Alan Weisman for an illustration of an extreme version of this thinking. Weisman imagines a world in which human beings have become extinct, where "a Homo sapiens-specific virus—natural or diabol-ically nano-engineered—picks us off but leaves everything else intact." Considering the terrible effects of the COVID-19 virus around the world since late 2019/early 2020, such a vision is horrific. (Alan Weisman. *The World Without Us* [New York: Thomas Dunne Books, 2007], 4.)

25 Sylvia Wynter. "Unsettling the Coloniality of Being/Power/Truth/Freedom: Towards the Human, Af-ter Man, Its Overrepresentation—An Argument." *CR: The New Centennial Review* 3, (3) (Fall 2003), 297.

26 Paul Gilroy. *Against Race: Imagining Political Culture Beyond the Color Line* (Cambridge: The Belknap Press of Harvard University Press, 2000), 15–17.

27 Ibid., 18.

28 Edward Said. *Orientalism*, 25th Anniversary Edition (New York: Knopf-Doubleday, 2014), xxix.

29 Terence. (From *Heautontimorumenos* or *The Self-Tormenter*.) Quoted from *The Woman of Andros. The Self-Tormentor. The Eunuch*. Edited by John Barsby. Loeb Classical Library 22. (Cambridge: Harvard University Press, 2001), l.77, 186.

30 "artibus quibus aetas puerilis ad humanitatem informari solet" (Cicero, *Pro Archia Poeta Oratio*). In Ci-cero. *Pro Archia. Post Reditum in Senatu. Post Reditum ad Quirites. De Domo Sua. De Haruspicum Responsis. Pro Plancio*. Edited by N. H. Watts. Loeb Classical Library 158. (Cambridge: Harvard University Press, 1923), 3.2–3, 10.

31 "studia nostra nostrae naturae regula metiamur" (Cicero, *De Officiis*, 1.110.31. In Cicero. *On Duties*. Edited by Walter Miller. Loeb Classical Library 30. Cambridge: Harvard University Press, 1913, 112).

32 Robin Headlam Wells. *Shakespeare's Humanism*. Cambridge: Cambridge University Press, 2005, 202.

33 Ibid.

PART I

Theoretical Perspectives on Humanism

1

"We Are Ourselves the Entities to be Analyzed"

Heidegger on Being Human

Robin M. Muller

Introduction

My aim in this chapter is to clarify the status of human Being (as distinct, perhaps, from *the* human being) in a number of key figures in 20th-century Continental thought: What is or is not "humanist" about the literary philosophy of the French existentialists? About the revolutionary politics of Fanon? About Heidegger's interrogation of Being as lived out in the everyday—that is, by those who build and seek shelter, write poetry and do logic, feel the pangs of fear and the crush of boredom, live and die? I'll answer these questions by focusing on how the human being traditionally appears to the objectivizing perspective of Western metaphysics—an argument I draw out through Heidegger. I'll then show that running through Heidegger's work is an attempt to make sense of a human *way of being* obscured by these traditional conceptualizations. Finally, by emphasizing the distinctions that Heidegger draws between his own project and that of the existentialists—whom he dismisses as "metaphysical"—I show where Heidegger's considered view is consistent with some putatively "anti-humanist" strands of Continental thought, even as it continues to center human Being. In part, for this reason, Heidegger suspects that we might do well to do away with these terms.[1]

I develop this argument in two parts. The first follows Heidegger to motivate the place of humanism in the wider tradition of Western metaphysics. I begin by explaining what Heidegger thinks is wrong with that tradition, centering my discussion on *Being and Time*. More precisely, I offer a close analysis of how, for Heidegger, metaphysical inquiry traditionally unfolds, and what it obscures. The main thread I hope to bring out in this discussion is that Heidegger sees metaphysics as aligned, generally speaking, with the sciences—in fact, that it is "scientistic" and its perspective too narrow. In doing this, I also bring into view what I call Heidegger's "adverbial" conception of human Being—that is, the claim that there is a human *way* of being that must be considered on its own terms. In the second line of argument, I explain in what sense "humanism" is metaphysical, centering on the *Letter on Humanism*. Given that Heidegger's critique of metaphysics will align closely with his criticisms of science, it is perhaps surprising that one of Heidegger's targets in the *Letter on Humanism* is Sartre. Sartre's existentialism, after all, is founded in part on the idea that a certain scientific perspective on human behavior, and on what the human being *is*, obscures human freedom. I try, however, to reconstruct Heidegger's argument in a way that makes clear how his criticisms of existentialist humanism and metaphysics fit together. I also try to show in this discussion how other strands of humanism, both in the Continental tradition and in the history of philosophy, are ensnared by it. To that end, I conclude with some remarks about the impact of Heidegger's criticisms on later 20th-century thought.

DOI: 10.4324/9781003046004-3

Before I begin, I should acknowledge a number of ways in which the strategy I adopt here needs defending. First, there is great diversity within the existentialist tradition, so in this sense, singling out Sartre as its exemplar risks missing the broader significance of existentialist thought—or even existentialist humanism. It also risks being somewhat unfair to the existentialist tradition, since many of the objections we might pose to Sartre are answered by other existentialist thinkers (Merleau-Ponty is, perhaps, one prominent example). I emphasize Sartre, however, because his is the position against which Heidegger situates himself in his *Letter on Humanism*. The charge that existentialism is metaphysical turns, for instance, on Heidegger's objection that Sartre's famous invocation of the existentialist slogan ("existence precedes essence"), adapted from Heidegger's own words in *Being and Time*, misrepresents what the word "existence" means in the human case. Exploring how Sartre understands the phrase is thus important for assessing the charge that existentialism remains firmly rooted within the conceptual framework of Western metaphysics—precisely the framework that Heidegger subjects to critique.

Second, as we will see, "humanism" is an expansive, perhaps ambiguous term in the history of Western thought, and Continental philosophy in particular. We find in the scholarly literature, for instance, references to both the humanism and the anti-humanism of Nietzsche, of Judith Butler, of Fanon. Foucault, who is consistently anti-humanist, only dates the "humanism" he rejects to the late 19th century, and Merleau-Ponty defends a Marxist humanism purged of materialist metaphysics in order to critique all other humanisms. Even in Sartre's 1945 lecture—entitled *Existentialism is a Humanism*—we find him distinguishing his own "humanistic" centering of the human being as the source of creative power and meaning from a kind of self-laudatory humanism expressed in the swells of pride that would tether the lunar footfalls of Neil Armstrong or the record-shattering sprints of Jesse Owens to the achievements of "mankind." If there is a terminological ambiguity at work, then it risks making difficult the broader task I have set for myself here—opening from a narrow textual debate onto the status of humanism in Continental thought more generally. Nevertheless, it remains that many of the above figures explicitly position themselves on one side of another of a "humanist" divide. If we can clarify what is being either embraced or rejected in these positionings, this may provide some insight into the broader landscape of Continental thought.

The last point is this: As I noted above, I have centered Heidegger as the critic of humanist metaphysics in part because of the broader impact of his *Letter* on Continental thought. For this reason, my choice to begin with *Being and Time* may strike some readers as peculiar, and the path through his "destruction" of metaphysics is a circuitous route to the later critique. But the early text brings into relief a concern that remains essential to Heidegger's thought—and without which, I think, the argument of both texts risks being misunderstood. As he argues in the *Letter*, for instance, the argument of *Being and Time* is "against humanism" precisely because humanism "does not set the *humanitas* of man high enough."[2] Emphasizing the earlier discussion therefore puts us in the best position to appreciate how Heidegger was—and remained—a thinker of human Being, even (or especially) as he holds traditional conceptions of the human up for critique.

The Project of *Being and Time*

In *Being and Time*, Heidegger seeks to revive a question that has, on his view, been largely forgotten. He invokes it first as a problem of obscurity: Using a passage from Plato's *Sophist*, he reminds us that we human beings, we philosophers, "used to think we understood" what is meant by the expression "being," and yet "have now become perplexed."[3] The opening pages trace from this moment of perplexity a sweeping history of Western metaphysics, wending from ancient philosophy through modernity to the doorstep of the 20th century.

At least intuitively, the forces of this history should propel our understanding of Being in the direction of clarity. That is, with advancements in the natural, physical, and human sciences, our picture of the fundamental nature of reality should be sharpened, with the result that we become less "perplexed." But Heidegger argues that these press in the opposite direction. The history of philosophy, in his reconstruction, largely *covers over* the question of Being, burying its meaning in obscurity. The task of the opening chapters of *Being and Time* is to figure out how to reformulate that question and so to unearth a fundamental ontological problem—what is meant by the expression "Being"?—that had somehow been skipped over. This requires disentangling the practice of "philosophy" from the traditional methodologies of the sciences and through this, Heidegger argues, demands the "destruction" of metaphysics.

As I have already noted, Heidegger locates "humanism" with the metaphysical tradition. He reasons, then, that it, too, ought to be a casualty of the latter's destruction. But the specific charge Heidegger levels against metaphysics—its *forgetting* of Being—is surprising. For millennia, philosophers have posed metaphysical puzzles and have endeavored to describe the conditions of possibility of all things, even as they acknowledge—in Aristotle's phrasing—that "Being is said in many ways."[4] What I first want to bring out here, then, is the idea that—by announcing the need to "destroy" metaphysics, and in a sense to retrace the steps of the history of philosophy back to Plato—Heidegger has in his sights, not the value of philosophy as a form of human inquiry, but a certain conception of philosophical inquiry that distorts, and sometimes fails even to bring into view, the very thing it is meant to clarify. Humanism, Heidegger argues, reproduces this error and thus fails to bring into view our own "humanity." Motivating this later critique involves reconstructing what is "wrong" with metaphysics in the first place.

Re-Formulating the Question of Being

If Heidegger's goal in *Being and Time* is to "reformulate" the question of the meaning of Being, the task cannot simply be to pose the question "What is Being?" again, as if we had somehow, improbably, stopped asking it since the time of the Greeks. Instead, we must better understand how traditional formulations of the question miss the mark. In Heidegger's approach, this involves getting clear on what is involved in the practice of questioning to begin with, since he takes seriously that any "inquiry" is a complex, purposive activity in which the form of the question is as important as its content.

To make this clear, Heidegger starts by identifying four "constitutive factors"[5] in any question, each of which interacts with the others in important ways. Specifically, the activity of questioning always involves:

(A) a *questioner*, the one who says, "I wonder";
(B) something that the question, or the questioner's wonder, is *about*;[6]
(C) something that the questioner "interrogates"[7] with her question (that is, some "who" or "what" that the questioner interacts with, turns over in thought, analyzes, dissects); and
(D) "something that is to be found out by the asking"[8]—that is, some sense of what is to be clarified through the questioning process and that therefore sets its satisfaction condition.

Inasmuch as philosophy is something like the activity of questioning as such, it includes, of course, a number of specific inquiries. Metaphysics—the study of Being—is among these. So understood, we could say of metaphysical inquiry, at least in its traditional formulation, that it has a structure of the following type: In metaphysical inquiry,

(A) a metaphysician inquires
(B) about Being, by interrogating
(C) beings, or entities with the ultimate goal of discovering
(D) what Being is.

But when the question is put this way, a concern should immediately arise. Notice, for instance, that in (D), the question utilizes "being" in its verbal form: The questioner asks what Being *is*. In order to even understand the question she is posing, Heidegger notices, she has to already have at least some vague sense of what the verb "being" means. To put this somewhat differently, the question at the center of metaphysical inquiry seems to *presuppose* at least some understanding of "being." The problem Heidegger identifies is that our "intuitive" understanding of what the verb "is" means is not, in fact, what metaphysics ends up designating with the expression "being." If he is right about this, then what metaphysics ends up saying something *about*—(B)—is not Being in general, but one very narrow *way of* being that the metaphysician conceptualizes in a fundamentally distorting way.

This certainly poses a problem for the fate of metaphysics. But Heidegger quickly realizes that it is not a uniquely metaphysical problem. Some understanding of "being"—that is, of the meaning of the verb "to be"—is presupposed in any inquiry whatsoever. As Heidegger puts this, "we always conduct our activities in an understanding of Being," even if we "do not *know*"—as Plato warned—"what 'Being' means."[9]

It is not always easy to grasp why Heidegger might say this. On the one hand, a question's relationship to Being is sometimes grammatically explicit: What *is* a quantum? Where *are* my house keys? How *is* the soup? These questions confront the same puzzle, even if they aren't obviously questions *about* Being: what does "being" mean? On the other hand, a question's relationship to Being is often implicit: What understanding of "being," for instance, shapes questions about where I want to live, whether I want children, or what shoes to wear? To make clear how Heidegger connects these sorts of cases, I want to work through each of his "structural items"[10] in turn. As I will try to bring out, while Heidegger's primary point of contrast will be between "existential" and "theoretical" or "scientific" analysis, he turns his attention to a range of ways in which we engage in "inquiry" in order to bring into view both how an intuitive understanding of "being" *always* shapes human activity and how metaphysics obscures what human activity reveals about Being in general. I'll return to summarize how these point toward the "error" of humanism.

Every Question Has a Questioner

Let's begin with the idea that every question has a *questioner*, since this is the most intuitive among what Heidegger calls a question's "constitutive factors."[11] (In fact, Heidegger does not even name this factor explicitly in this section[12] of the text, though it becomes a key component of his argument as it develops.)

Three factors emerge as significant for Heidegger here. The first is that the questioner in any inquiry is always a *human questioner*. Rocks and rivers do not ask about the environment in which they are located or why they exist, but the question "What is life?" is posed by the living biologist; "What is the fundamental nature of the physical universe?" is formed in the throat of the physicist; and "What is human culture?" is posed by the anthropologist at a certain moment in human history. The second point Heidegger notices is that each of these questions "implicates" the questioner in some way: Life, after all, includes *human* life; the physical universe includes the physicist's *physical body*, and human culture includes the culture that produces the practice of anthropology. Philosophy, of course, is no different: A philosopher who poses questions about Being, after all, is a philosopher who *exists*.

Heidegger strives to consolidate these insights by introducing the neologism "Dasein." For my purposes, we can say that "Dasein" is roughly coextensive with "human Being." The term remains untranslated in the English-language literature, however, because it has no obvious equivalent. The reason is that Heidegger chooses the term "Dasein" to express an essential *structural* feature of the human "way of being," which is the fact that, for us, our existence *matters*. A moment ago, I put this point by saying that the human inquirer (say, the biologist, the anthropologist, the metaphysician) is implicated in—and so is concerned with—questions about Being, whereas the stone and the river are not. The term "Dasein," for Heidegger, is a way to talk about human beings in light of this self-reflexive concern.

But *how*, exactly, do we concern ourselves with Being? If we accept, for instance, that existence does not matter to a stone, do we really want to go so far as to say that an *animal* lacks concern for whether or not it *is*—for instance, whether it lives or dies? To answer these questions, it helps to turn our attention to Heidegger's third point, which is that Dasein always interprets or understands itself *as being* a certain way.

Consider a human being engaged in the activity of research. If she takes herself to be engaging in scientific inquiry, she will do so *as a scientist*—indeed, of a particular kind. Moreover, her interpretation of herself as a particular sort of scientist—to put this differently, her sense of what it means *to be* the kind of researcher she is—is evident in the way that she carries out her work. The literary theorist, after all, does not try to analyze *Don Quixote* under a microscope any more than the mathematician seeks the "moral" of 2 + 2 = 4. To do so would be inconsistent with what it means *to be* a literary theorist or a mathematician. When Heidegger talks about our self-reflective existence, he has this in mind. Our actions have the character they do, he argues, because of who or what or how we take ourselves *to be*. Of course, the ways in which we interpret ourselves are not limited to professional titles: The father who stands up at the PTA meeting might ask about the curriculum *as a concerned parent*, I may wonder about the location of the changing room *as a woman*, and we might question the limits of our responsibilities—to animals, to the environment—*as human*.[13] We can therefore restate Heidegger's insight like this: Every question, whether it is about the origins of the universe or the opening hours of the grocery store, is shaped or guided—even if only in some general or unarticulated way—by whatever or whomever the inquirer is taking herself *to be*. And metaphysical questions are no different: Inasmuch as metaphysics is a discipline within the field of philosophy, when the metaphysician poses the question "What is Being?",[14] she does so as a practitioner of that field and thus "within some understanding" of what *being a metaphysician* means. Notice, however, that there is a peculiar result here: At least with respect to understanding what the "being" of "being-a-metaphysician" means, the metaphysician is in no better position than is any human questioner going about any other everyday human activity.

Every Question is About Something

I have said so far that metaphysicians "conduct [their] activities in an understanding of Being" in the sense that, in order to engage in metaphysics, a metaphysician has to know what "being-a-metaphysician" means. Let us now turn to the second factor Heidegger identifies: What is asked *about* in the inquiring activity.

On a certain framing, "what is asked about" in any field of study is the *object* of the inquiry. So understood, every field of inquiry has an object proper to it: The biologist poses questions about Life, the anthropologist Human Culture, the physicist the Physical Universe. Part of what makes any scientific inquiry systematic and "objective," then, is that some understanding of its object is shared among its practitioners. If that shared conception is called into question—for instance, when the discovery of arsenic-metabolizing bacteria potentially revolutionized the concept of Life—the object nevertheless remains accessible to and evaluable by the relevant scientific community. In this sense, the sciences are not *subjective* because they do not take into account, or depend on, features particular to the subject who poses the question. And metaphysics, as a systemic inquiry with an "object" proper to it, is a science. What distinguishes it from the other sciences is only that it is *broad*. That is, where the specific sciences interrogate some region, some portion, of Being, the metaphysician is interested in Being in general. On this conception, we could say of metaphysics what the philosopher Wilfrid Sellars later says of the discipline of philosophy as a whole: that it seeks "to understand how things in the broadest possible sense of the term hang together in the broadest possible sense of the term."[15]

To this point, it has been helpful for us to try to capture what it means for a question to be "about" something by referring to the *object* of inquiry. But it is important to flag where this formulation risks being misleading. Colloquially, after all, objects are physical things, and not all questions are about things we can reach out and touch. I might, for instance, walk into an art studio and inquire *about painting* or interrogate the guidance counselor *about a career in philosophy*. Even the objects of scientific study aren't objects in this colloquial sense: I cannot hold Life in my hands or stand in front of the Human as such.

Now, this is hardly a problem from the perspective of the scientist. She need only say that her object ("Life," or "the Human") is an abstract, general category—not a *thing*, but a *concept*. Since concepts are scientifically evaluable inasmuch as they manifest in physical beings, the biologist studies the concept of Life through living things, the anthropologist the Human through human cultures, and so on. A scientist will, by consequence, be able to speak of the "essence" of her object in the same way that she speaks of the essence of particular beings: If there are properties and characteristic patterns of activity, for instance, that hold across each of the entities that are studied by her science (if we discover that human beings throughout history are rational, or social, or political, or mortal), she will conclude that these properties define the Human as such. But it is less clear how a list of properties makes sense of the "objects" of my inquiry into "painting" or a "career in philosophy." Painting, for instance, is an activity that one must know *how to* do in addition to knowing *about* in some abstract way. A "career in philosophy" is neither an "entity" nor a concept with essential properties, so much as a loose network of associations that includes, *inter alia*, a person's commitment to a certain kind of formal education, professional recognition by her peers, signed contracts, grant proposals, attendance at conferences, and so forth. It is here, for Heidegger, that the status of metaphysics *as a* science is most troubling. The "error" of the history of metaphysics, Heidegger argues, is that its practitioners have assumed that *to be* means "to be a thing or a concept with properties." The result is, first, that philosophers have generally talked about Being as if it were *a being*—the most universal or abstract or general sort of being, to be sure, but a being nonetheless. It is, second, that the metaphysical conception of Being—that is, where "being" means *Being-an-entity*—makes it difficult to make sense, among other things, of the understanding of "being" expressed in the activity of *doing philosophy*.

This point turns out to be essential to Heidegger's destructive project, so let me offer two examples to draw out what I take it to mean. Let's first consider a biologist, whose "object" in Heidegger's sense is "Life." As a scientist, the biologist will interpret this object (that is, "Life") as a concept that defines certain entities as *living* in light, perhaps, of their capacity to carry out a kind of metabolic process, or because they are a self-containing chemical system. Given this understanding, she will pursue her inquiry by, say, analyzing cellular processes or assessing how microorganisms thrive under differing atmospheric conditions. These are the "entities" she interrogates. Now, certainly, this process illuminates her object of inquiry. But it does so in a radically different way than when the question "What is Life" is posed, for example, by the victim of colonial oppression, who is committed perhaps to some interpretation of Life as flourishing. This is in part because her different interpretation of Life directs the political subject toward, *inter alia*, the form of suffering endured by her fellow human beings, or toward the ways in which the conditions of possibility of human happiness are preserved and withheld by the law. If she were urged to turn her attention to cellular processes, she would respond by saying, "that is not what I *mean* by living."

In one sense, this points to the rigor or seriousness of science. As I have said, what makes science systematic and objective is that every scientific community shares at least some general interpretation of their object of inquiry and of the method of access appropriate to it, even while the practitioners acknowledge that this interpretation can be revolutionized by new discoveries. A different way to put this, though, is to say that, in any kind of inquiry—and science is only one example here—our intuitions about the "object" of inquiry circumscribe some range of appropriate responses. This is why the question "What is Life?" posed in the pages of a biochemistry textbook will yield quite different answers than when it is posed by the ethicist hunched over a tray of embryos, the cancer patient, the enslaved human being. The insight Heidegger makes is that any one of these answers is "true." What makes it true, however, is not a function of its absolute correspondence to some feature of the world. Instead, what makes it 'true' is the way in which it clarifies the intuition that prompted the question in the first place. The fact that the biologist can understand the political subject's objection—"that is not what I *mean* by living"—as expressing a different sort of anxiety, and not an error, is evidence that she already "knows" this.

With this criticism in mind, let's now consider an example of what I'll call classroom metaphysics. Imagine a philosophy professor who drags a chair to the front of the classroom with the charge that her students should tell her what it *is*. She might try this with a range of entities (What is a poem? What is a fungus? What is a mathematical theorem?). But when she does this, she is urging them to answer in a certain way: The response she wants, for instance, is not that the chair is like the one that used to be in my grandmother's sitting room; that it is a relief to my aching feet; that it is old, or uncomfortable; the product of an exploitative labor process; or that it is useful for propping open the doorway—though, to be clear, these are possible ways for the chair *to be*. The answer she is looking for is that the chair is a certain sort of object whose essential properties distinguish it from whatever it is not. If her students were to answer in any other way, she would say to them: "That is not what I *mean*."

What emerges through these examples is the peculiar paradox of metaphysical inquiry: on the one hand, metaphysics is supposed to be the broadest science inasmuch as it poses questions about Being in general. On the other hand, its perspective on Being is blinkered and narrow, permitting consideration only of beings as they show themselves to the questioner in a certain way: Metaphysics, in other words, is organized or guided in advance by a rather narrow assumption about what "Being" really means (in much the same way that biology is guided by a narrow range of possible understandings of what "Life" means). It does this, moreover, by design. "Philosophy," Heidegger acknowledges, "is hounded by the fear that it loses prestige and validity if it is not a science."[16] In renewing the question of Being, the goal is to free philosophy from this fear, to cease limiting philosophical inquiry to the narrow scientistic perspective of metaphysics. Heidegger calls this new pursuit—which he thinks could genuinely bring the plural possibilities of Being into view—"fundamental ontology."

Every Question "Interrogates" Some Being(s)

We have seen so far how an understanding of Being is, for Heidegger, implied in any activity, including the activity of doing philosophy, and that this understanding is made evident in the character of the activity itself. For example, when I pose a question of any kind, I necessarily take myself *to be* a certain sort of questioner, and this prescribes where I go looking for answers: If I am a biologist, I know that I will have to seek out the common properties of Life among *living beings*, whereas if I am an anthropologist, I will interrogate, *inter alia*, *human beings*. These are the entities any given science "interrogates."

Now, in the context of the sciences, there is sometimes the impression that different "regions" of Being are cordoned off in some way. Heidegger reminds us, however, that the entities interrogated by the sciences often overlap. Being *alive* and being *human*, for instance, are both potentially ways for the same entity—say, a physical body—to *be*. This is why I have been stressing the importance of the questioner's own self-interpretation. Who or what a questioner takes herself to be

("I am a biologist," "I am an anthropologist") determines in what light the same entity appears to her. As a biologist, I will be drawn to beings inasmuch as they are living, as an anthropologist, inasmuch as they evidence cooperative human activity, and so on. Neither of these is more or less "true" of the interrogated being than the other. Thus, none of them can be the "final" answer. This same point applies beyond the University walls. There are multiple ways for a human being *to be human*, for instance, and the way centered by the anthropologist may be different than what is understood by the poet or the dictator. Again, Heidegger is not interested in adjudicating among these potentially conflicting interpretations. Instead, it is the *fact* that Being expresses itself in a range of modes—many of which are inaccessible to the methods of traditional metaphysics or the sciences—that interests him.

One effect of Heidegger's interest here is that it opens up a much looser sense of what counts as a "philosophical" question. This is my second point. We have already seen, for instance, that scientific inquiry—inquiring into the meaning of Life, or the essential properties of the Human—is not the only form of questioning. In fact, scientific questions share something structurally in common with much more basic, practical questions like: what should I have for lunch? How does this apple taste? What time does the store close?—questions that are part of an everyday human life. In fact, these questions are *more* a part of our everyday life than questions of science, including *for* the scientist (even the biologist must choose her breakfast cereal). The hesitation in taking these questions seriously, of course, is that these are not the sort of things we are used to grouping under the heading of "inquiry." (There is no "philosophy" of choosing our breakfast cereal, except, perhaps, in the loosest sense.)

I have so far tried to justify the idea that these genuinely *do* count as inquiry, at least insofar as their structure is concerned. What interests Heidegger, as we have seen, is that these questions always draw on an implicit understanding of Being: When I am confronted, for instance, with the choice of breakfast cereal, a certain understanding of my being is in the background for me inasmuch as I take *being healthy* or *being indulgent* to be possibilities for me. Likewise, when I wonder how the apple tastes, I am already operating within an understanding of the ways an apple can be. A concern for its taste, after all, means that I interpret it as something *to be eaten* and not *to be thrown* at the raccoon who is rummaging through the garbage can. This is why Heidegger reasons that Dasein "in its average everydayness" always operates within an understanding of Being. He means by this, first, that a human being, *qua* Dasein, always takes herself *to be* some way, and, second, that her way of being locates her in an environment that matters to her because *it is* a certain way. On close inspection, moreover, this understanding would seem to be both more basic and more expansive than the understanding of "being" presumed by the sciences. After all, to grasp that *to be eaten* and *to be thrown* are ways for apples to be, just as to grasp that *to be healthy* and *to be indulgent* are ways for humans to be, is to have at the root a conception of what it means *to be* whose possibilities are not limited to the physical presence of existing entities to which objectively observable properties attach.

This is, as it were, bad news for metaphysics. A moment ago, recall, I said that the metaphysician is in no better position than the average everyday human being going about her everyday life—at least with respect to grasping implicitly what it means *to be*. We can now sharpen this to say that the metaphysician is quite a bit worse off than the average everyday human, inasmuch as the latter can understand herself in a plurality of ways over the course of her day (she *is* a concerned parent, a frustrated grocery shopper, and so on), whereas the metaphysician confines herself by design to considering "being" in the sense of Being-an-object. To work our way out of this predicament, we need as philosophers some method for analyzing Being in light of the various ways in which beings can appear. Such a method would free us to renew the question of Being while enabling us to raise what Heidegger calls our "pre-ontological understanding" to something explicit. He argues that that method is phenomenology.

A full consideration of Heidegger's modification of phenomenology would take us too far afield. For my purposes, however, what matters is that Heidegger turns to phenomenology as his method of analysis because phenomenology is concerned with how things *appear*.[17] "Appearance," in this context, is not meant in the sense of "mere" appearance. Indeed, phenomenology is not interested in whether or not things are showing up in the *right* way at all, as if this could be discovered absent some context of appearing to a certain kind of observer. Instead, phenomenology is concerned with how things show up in light of different interests. Since we have seen that the scientific observer is "interested" in objects only in a narrow sort of way—and not, for all that, as they appear in her everyday life—phenomenology involves returning to analyze a range of experiences without pre-committing to the idea that things really *are* the way that they appear to the objectizing attitude of the sciences.

We have still left open the question of what "entity" the phenomenologist should interrogate. But the answer has wended its way through the analysis so far. Recall that Heidegger introduced the term "Dasein" to express the fact that when a human being engages in any sort of activity, she does so "within" some understanding of Being. It is in light of this understanding of Being that things appear to her in a particular way. While one of Dasein's possible activities is the practice of science, in which case things appear to her as certain *kinds* of entities with certain objective properties, Dasein is also, potentially, the healthy eater, the frustrated grocery shopper, the parent to the curious child, the woman who asks about painting. In fact, our way of slipping in and out of each of these ways of being—without, for all that, losing the *fact* of being reflexively concerned with Being—is what leads Heidegger to conclude that "we are ourselves the entities to be analyzed."[18] The point I want to underline at this point is only that "we" are to be analyzed, for Heidegger, not with attention to *what makes us human*, but to the ways in which Being is expressed through human activity. What he is trying to bring out, in other words, is the implicit conception of "being" that is "carried along" by the anthropologist as she excavates the ruins, by the cancer patient as she confronts her own mortality, by the NASA scientist as she is stunned by the beauty of the universe, by the person who is waiting for the streetcar in the rain.

Something is Intended in Every Question

It is worth returning at this point to Heidegger's initial observation: Metaphysics has forgotten Being. We have seen that traditional metaphysics hypostasizes Being, as if it were a general or abstract entity, *a being*. In doing so, metaphysics has historically posed the question of Being in a way that prevents actually clarifying what it means *to be* in the first place. By focusing on the activity of *doing* metaphysics—as an example of inquiry more generally—Heidegger has been able to draw out the way in which every human being carries within herself some "pre-ontological" understanding of the meaning of the phrase "to be." It is this pre-ontological understanding of the meaning of "being" in all its plurality that is "intended" by fundamental ontology: to renew the question of Being, Heidegger argues, we must interrogate the way in which the environing world appears to us in light of our average everyday concerns. To do this, we must take up the posture, not of *philosophers* in the narrow sense of the technical practitioners of metaphysics, but of *phenomenologists*.

As we pursue this sort of project—what Heidegger calls the "existential analysis of Dasein"—we discover a peculiar inversion of traditional metaphysics: Metaphysics interrogates *entity after entity* in order to discover among them some singular sense of Being. Heidegger, by contrast, interrogates a single entity—Dasein in its average everydayness—in order to discover the plural expressions of Being within which Dasein lives. In this process, as I now want to show, phenomenology "accomplishes" the destruction of metaphysics. Specifically, the process of describing Dasein *in the activity of existing* turns out to be revelatory of multiple ways of being that cannot be made explicit in traditional philosophical vocabulary. Since this argument is developed over the course of most of *Being and Time*, I'll spend some time briefly reconstructing it here. I'll then open this up to a discussion of Heidegger's critical assessment of "humanism."

Heidegger's Existential Analysis

Imagine that I am asked to describe myself, and I answer that "I am a philosopher." In one sense, the phrase "I am a philosopher" is an appropriate description of *what* I am. It is not a description of my essence, to be clear. But it expresses some features of my identity that I acquired through hard study and a bit of professional luck. It is the feature I announce, for example, on my business card or in response to the relevant sort of question at a cocktail party, at an interdisciplinary conference, at the customs checkpoint. At the same time, however, the very fact that the phrase tells a person *what* I am also distorts what it is to be a philosopher. The reason is that to be a philosopher is not simply to be an entity (say, a human being) who possesses certain characteristics, or even who lays claim to certain qualifications or professional obligations. It means to participate in certain activities: to *do* philosophy or to engage in the activity of research *as a philosopher*. Since this sense of what it means to be a philosopher is carried along as I engage in philosophical activities, the way in which I *am* a philosopher is quite different than the way in which this piece of furniture I am sitting on *is* a chair or indeed the way in which any other sort of entity *is*.

Already, Heidegger wants us to flag two points here. The first is that a conflation seems to have crept into the vocabulary of traditional metaphysics. Recall that earlier I described metaphysics as the broadest science—and thus one not confined to any region of entities. The metaphysician is not only concerned with living things or human beings, in other words, but with everything that *exists*. We have also seen, however, that the metaphysician only interprets things in light of their objective properties. An implicit assumption of traditional metaphysics is therefore that everything that *is*, exists in more or less the same way: everything that *is*, is an existing being with some set of properties essential to it that differentiate it from what it *is not*. We have just seen, however, that the philosopher *is* a philosopher in a fundamentally different way than the chair *is* a chair. Heidegger flags this difference (imperceptible to the metaphysical "way of seeing") by saying that only *Dasein* exists. This is not a way of consigning other sorts of things to the field of the imaginary; it is simply meant to signal that human existence—*qua* existence—is related to Being in the way that the chair (like the river or the rock) is not.

To be fair, traditional metaphysics gives us resources to *try* to describe this difference. We could say, for instance, that human beings and chairs are both, in a certain sense, objects, but that the former is an object of a special kind: She is, for instance, a body endowed with consciousness, or a soul, or with the capacity for rational self-reflection, and this special property or endowment enables her to be oriented toward her own existence in a way that the chair, which lacks that endowment, is not. This distinction separates the world into subjects and objects, distinguished from one another by their properties. But Heidegger's second warning is that were I to describe myself in the manner of traditional metaphysics—say, by ascribing properties to myself as if I were an entity distinguished by my possession of rational consciousness—this precludes full consideration of *who I am*.

This point deserves sharpening. What, exactly, is obscured? To answer this, let's return to what I am doing when I do philosophy. Like any academic discipline, doing philosophy involves, among other things, engaging in specific activities: I write, for instance, I teach, and so on. (Philosophy may "begin in wonder," but it is very much a practical activity.) When I engage in one of its characteristic activities, however—say, when I sit down to write—the best way to describe what I am doing is not to say that I am a subject set against a world of objects. For example, while in order to write I must position my body at the desk and so adopt a certain spatial orientation to the objects in my surroundings, the *activity* of writing, the doing of philosophy, is chiefly directed toward the paper I am writing. Its "object" is the end result of the project I'm engaged in. What is more, inasmuch as I am oriented toward a project and not a physical object, even the physical "objects" in the room do not really turn up for me in light of their objective properties. For instance, the desk and the screen to which my line of sight is directed do not really seem to me to be objects with determinate properties, but practical possibilities for fulfilling my role as a philosopher: The desk is *to be written at*, the keyboard *to be typed on*, and so on. When this means is that, when I attend to the *doing* of philosophy, neither I (as the agent) nor the paper (as my goal) are neatly captured by the classical language of subject and object.

In what sense does this recognition open, or clarify, an understanding of Being? One answer is that when I am doing philosophy in the way I just described, I discover that my orientation to my surroundings is not especially well described as an objective spatial relation in which I am *in* the world as one object among others. This is because what I am doing, and how I do it, is shaped by a singular goal: To continue with the paper I am writing. If I look closer, moreover, I will see that the activity of doing philosophy involves me in a network of meaningful social and practical relations. By involving myself in the activity of writing, for instance, I place myself in relation to my university; to my community of fellow philosophers; to each of the previous drafts I have abandoned over the weeks. In this sense, the activity of writing is guided not only by a practical aim—to finish the paper—but by the fact that I take myself to participate *as a philosopher* in a certain community and history. To put this more directly, my activity is guided by my understanding of myself *as being a philosopher* in the social, historical, and practical sense, and this is why the environment shows up to me in the way that it does. When I fill in my profession on a customs form, then, I am not announcing some contingent feature of my identity. I am announcing one of my possible ways of being.

For Heidegger, this shift—from an entity's properties to its possibilities, or possible ways of being—transforms traditional philosophical vocabulary. When Heidegger says, for instance, that the human being is *Being-in-the-world*, he means by this not that the human is some entity spatially situated in a physical environment—an object-among-objects, like water *in* a cup, or a cup *in* the room. He means that she is immersed in an environment that is saturated with meaning and possibility for her, given who or what she takes herself *to be*. This environment is a "world." When I say that I am *in* academia, then, or I speak of "the world" of philosophy, it is these senses (and not some determinate spatial position or some specific set of entities) I am signaling. Recall in this context that Heidegger has reserved the word "existence" for this (human) manner of immersion in a (meaningful) world. This is why he says that only human beings *exist*.

Now, I have so far tracked the way in which my sense of myself *as a philosopher* impacts how I engage in philosophical activity, and how this opens up a broader sense of what it means *to be a* philosopher. But being-a-philosopher is not the *only* way for me to be. Like any individual, I come to understand myself and my existence (even in a single moment) in terms of a network of overlapping areas of concern and obligation. My understanding of myself as a philosopher, for instance, which perhaps shapes how I am at the present moment, may recede to the background if I organize myself around a different mode of self-understanding. When I walk my dog, for example, I will position myself with respect to a different community and history, and that may put me at odds with my understanding of myself as a philosopher. Even so, these ways of being—*as* a philosopher and *as* a dog-owner—can overlap in the course of everyday experience: my being a dog-owner, for example, can impact my way of being a philosopher, and vice versa, since performing one role can involve a privative relation—as when the dog's need for play interrupts my writing process—or a positive relation to the other, as when I use the occasion of his walks to reflect on my work.

So, what is the lesson here? Importantly, there are two directions to take this insight. I have so far walked through one of these possibilities by teasing out what, for Heidegger, is illuminated by a phenomenology of everyday life. I have shown, for instance, that everyday human existence—which we can see by attending to everyday activity—is carried along and shaped by an understanding of "being" that does not fit neatly with the rejected metaphysics. Through this, Heidegger discovers the way in which the human being exists *in a world*. If we hew closely to this reading, what is significant in *Being and Time* is that the world in which Dasein exists is not chiefly understood as a collection of determinate objects nor Dasein as "a subject," and this reveals something striking about human existence. For instance, it reveals that human existence is best made sense of in light of the ways in which the world is *meaningful* to me.

This is the path pursued by the existentialist tradition, and Sartre in particular, who finds in the pages of *Being and Time* the outline for an epic drama of human existence—one that promises to make *philosophical* the minutiae of everyday life: Waiting for the streetcar, walking the dog, selecting a breakfast cereal, mourning a friend. As we will see in a moment, part of the humanism of the existentialist tradition is the way in which this thread of *Being and Time* is picked up. But this is not, I want to underline, how Heidegger conceives of his own project; for example, what is of interest to Heidegger about human existence is not that I, as a particular individual, modulate my existence in a way that I navigate between modes, that I slip in and out of different ways of being as I carry out the project of a life. What is of interest is the fact that my ways of being—for instance, of being a philosopher and being a dog-owner—involve a common structure: each is guided by a certain way of being concerned for my own Being, a certain concern for *who* and not just *what* I take myself to be. To put this more directly, Heidegger's interest in everyday human existence is an interest in bringing this concernful mode of Being into view and showing that *this* and not my rationality, or my sociality, or my having a soul, or consciousness, is the essence of being human. What this means is that Heidegger, for all the existential drama of *Being and Time*, is not interested in human existence *as such*. Its question is how Being must be structured such that human ways of being can bring it into view. Using Heidegger's own taxonomy, we can therefore chart the project of *Being and Time* like this: For Heidegger, engaging in the project of fundamental ontology involves: (A) a questioner, who inquires *as a phenomenologist* about (B) the Being of Dasein, which she pursues (C) by interrogating *human beings engaged in the activity of existing*. She does this, however, not in order to understand human existence as such; she does this because *through* the analysis of Dasein she is able, potentially, to bring (D) the meaning of Being itself into view.

So, what does this have to do with Heidegger's objection to humanism? One possible answer is that humanism is simply concerned with a different sort of aim. As I want to argue now, however, Heidegger's objections are not just about a difference in aim. His concern is that the history of humanism inherits the narrow perspective of Western metaphysics. As he puts this, "every humanism is either grounded in a metaphysics or is itself made to be the ground of one."[19] Let me turn to that criticism now.

Humanism and Metaphysics

One of the threads running throughout my discussion has been that traditional metaphysics is "scientistic." In this context, that term expresses the belief that entities can be understood *as they really are* only when they are investigated from the objectivizing perspective of the sciences. We have seen, however, that the sciences interrogate entities with respect to their properties, whereas Heidegger has argued that Being-an-object-with-properties is only one possible way for things to be. Since, moreover, Being-an-object-with-properties turns out to be a rather unusual way for beings to be for us (and, when the "object" is Dasein, fundamentally *distorts* its way of being), Heidegger concludes that the perspective adopted by metaphysics (as well as by the specific sciences) does not get to anything "fundamental" about what it means for an entity *to be*. In fact, it does not even pose the question of the meaning of Being in the first place. To renew that question—and thus grasp what "being" means—Heidegger argues we must clarify the "pre-ontological intuition" that is implicitly in the background as Dasein goes about the business of everyday existence. It is in everyday life, after all, that we discover that the mode of Being-an-object-with-properties is only one of Being's possible expressions. Our aim should be to bring other possibilities into view. The method for doing this is phenomenology.

When we begin from this point, the charge that humanism is metaphysical is ambiguous. On the one hand, that sort of objection could mean simply that humanism has historically been *wrong* about what a human being *is* (that is, Heidegger's charge could well be that the history of humanism is the history of error and that it inherits this error in some way from the history of metaphysics). But this is not exactly his position: "Humanists," he allows, have historically had meaningful and *true* insights into what it means to be human. Instead, the problem with humanism for Heidegger is its method. By *presuming* what it means to be human, and using metaphysical concepts and language to express this, humanists have historically failed to think "in the direction of" man's *humanity*. The previous discussion serves as a way to focus on this charge. The question remains open as to whether something like a phenomenological humanism could be possible—a humanism in which we could renew the question of the human in a meaningful and pluralistic way.

Let me turn now to the text in which the connection between humanism and metaphysics is made explicit. As is well known, Heidegger's critical discussion about humanism is centered in a 1946 letter—published as the *Letter on Humanism*—that Heidegger wrote in response to the French philosopher Jean Beaufret. The question animating the letter is how philosophers might "restore meaning" to the word "humanism."[20] That question is, potentially, fraught with tension in the wake of the Second World War—and in this sense is especially resonant as posed to Heidegger, who was himself a member of the Nazi party and had been banned from University teaching in Germany. The narrower context of the letter, however—that is, what seemed to Beaufret to make the question urgent—is that the French philosopher Jean-Paul Sartre had recently given a public lecture at the Club Maintenant in Paris entitled "Existentialism is a Humanism," in which he both defended existentialist philosophy from a series of criticisms recently leveled against it, and connected that philosophy, and his defense of it, to Heidegger.

Taken together, the historical context sets a complicated task for Heidegger. On the one hand, his goal in the letter is to guard himself against the charge that—in rejecting the "humanist" label, he welcomes the barbaric and cruel. For all Heidegger's concern to reject certain terms, then—"existentialism," "humanism"—he shares this "defensive" goal with Sartre. On the other hand, however, Heidegger wants to distinguish his position from Sartre's, whom he accuses of fundamentally misunderstanding the critique of metaphysics. These two threads wend together in a way that sometimes makes the precise target of Heidegger's account obscure.

Heidegger starts his discussion, for instance, by defining a "humanism" of values. In this context, "humanism" expresses a concern that human beings be humane, and so it takes seriously the freedom of the human being to be *inhumane*.[21] This kind of ethical humanism also urges the movement of human culture and individual human behavior toward a particular ideal. We call this an "ethical" humanism, then, inasmuch as it expresses this ideal in the form of an "ought." As Heidegger puts this, humanism in the sphere of values is loosely understood as the idea that "man" must "become free for his humanity and find his worth in it."[22] He tells us that we find this kind of ethical framing in the redemptive narratives of Christianity, where our "humanity" emerges from the status of human beings as "children of God"; in the early history of the Roman Republic, where the striving for civic virtue was supposed to differentiate barbarous from "civilized" peoples; and more recently wending its way through Hegel and Marx, where the historical elevation of human beings over their animal nature is supposed to open the sphere of social recognition in which human beings come to see one another as deserving of dignity and as potential referents of rights. While these arguments differ widely, of course, Heidegger lumps them together in order to show how each charts—at the level of individual behavior and of world-historical development—the "progress" of human beings in the direction of *humanity*.

As I have underlined, Heidegger is careful to say that when he positions himself against these narratives, he does not mean to take the side of the *inhumane*.[23] On his view, there is nothing implicitly wrong in the striving for civic virtue, in finding humility before (and redemption through) God, or in the struggle for recognition and human rights—nor anything admirable about their opposites. I will return in a moment to some of the ways in which the values of humanism outlined here have historically functioned in service of human cruelty, but adjudicating this discussion is not Heidegger's concern. Even so, the worry is apt. Sartre's own spirited defense of existentialism the year before, for instance, had been centered on its alignment with these humanist values: While existentialism is atheist, Sartre argues, this is not a harbinger of a kind of moral chaos or consignment to a world without meaning; while existentialism emphasizes human anguish, it does not prevent meaningful action or lead to "quietism or despair"[24]; while it centers the human individual, it does not make unintelligible something like cooperative, transformative action; and—last—while it often *seems* to celebrate the dark, the cruel, the selfish (one thinks here of the murderer who wanders the pages of Camus' *Stranger*, of the damned souls of Sartre's *No Exit*), it is in fact an "optimistic" philosophy that "makes human life possible."[25] Indeed, Sartre argues that existentialism is optimistic precisely *because* it centers on the idea that the human being is free to be cruel or kind, humane or inhumane. To attribute human behavior or the pursuit of certain values to human nature—that is, to some natural or causal factor—would be the pessimistic view.

Put this way, of course, Heidegger needn't disagree. But as I want to bring out, he and Sartre differ widely in how to defend the values of ethical humanism in the first place. What, for instance, is their ground? And in what sense is this *existentialist?*

To answer the first of these questions, Heidegger argues that, historically, any ethical humanism has been pursued on the basis of certain assumptions about what it means to be human in the first place. For example, humanists have traditionally begun from the position that to be human is to be a rational (or political, or social) animal.[26] In Heidegger's view, this means that humanists have largely presumed that it is the human possession of some specific property that makes the human being *free* to be cruel or kind. Moreover, these assumptions about "the essential nature of the Human" among the early "humanists" were taken to be "obvious".[27] While the specific contents of humanist positions have therefore differed—debates about "human nature" have occupied philosophers since the time of the Greeks—Heidegger argues that each share a common structure: in the background of every humanism is the idea that there is some property, essential to human beings, the possession of which frees them to pursue, *inter alia*, civic virtue, a relationship to God, or cooperative social activities. This is one sense in which humanism is *metaphysical*. It utilizes the language of human essence and human nature—and situates these terms within the wider context of historical human progress in a human world. Moreover, it does so "with regard to an already established interpretation of nature, history, world, and the ground of the world, that is, of beings as a whole"[28]—rather than remaining open to other interpretive possibilities.

But Sartre's existentialist humanism rejects these essentializing definitions. As he is careful to underline in his lecture, there is no human nature at all; human freedom is a fact, a condition.[29] We might be inclined, then, to say that Sartre avoids endorsing the kind of humanism that Heidegger targets as metaphysical, especially because his argument centers on the idea that what distinguishes us from other sorts of objects is that we are uniquely self-creating—a human life is a *project*. In fact, he claims to get this point from Heidegger. To assess this view, however, it is worth zeroing in on *why* Heidegger thinks humanism prevents understanding what it means to be human.

Consider the classical definition of the human as a rational animal. As it is usually understood, the predicate "rational" is supposed to pick out what makes the human unique, what is distinctive

Heidegger on Being Human

of the human being *qua* human. The assumption, as Heidegger reads it, is that, absent this special property, "man" shares his animality with oxen and dogs. The idea the human being *is* an animal, in other words, is not held up for question.[30] As a political matter, the rootedness of "the human" in "the animal" has historically been a means of oppression and exploitation. For example, by making human freedom and dignity, *qua* human, contingent on the possession of rationality (and, of course, reserving for a certain narrow category of "rational animals" the power to recognize a fellow human being as having a rational consciousness), it has long been possible to deny rights to women, to indigenous persons, to the enslaved, without this being inconsistent with a certain understanding of *humanist* ideals. The ambivalence of thinkers like Fanon (and, following him, the rich traditions of Afro-pessimism and black nihilism) about the possibilities of "humanism" to ground any kind of emancipatory politics are, in part, founded on this fact.[31] But Heidegger's point is not that it is *wrong* to grasp human beings through the lens of their place in the animal kingdom. His point is that being-a-rational-animal is how human beings appear to a certain kind of zoological perspective, whereas this perspective does not reveal anything especially interesting about the human capacity for "humanity." The view that the human is a special kind of animal, in other words, *prevents* consideration of what is supposed to be the very center of a humanism of values. The reason is that "metaphysics," as Heidegger says, "thinks of man on the basis of *animalitas* and does not think in the direction of his *humanitas*."[32]

Let's return with this in view to Sartre. Given this context, we might respond on behalf of Sartre by saying that thinking in the direction of "humanity" and not on the basis of "animality" is precisely what existentialism tries to do. And perhaps it does this more forcefully. After all, Sartre's existentialist humanism outright rejects (rather than wants to leave open) essentializing definitions of the human. The reason is that Sartre sees existentialism as prompting us to the reflective rejection of the pessimistic frameworks of the natural and human sciences. The result is a humanism, he argues, that urges us to think the specific excellence of human beings without supposing that some shared predicate attaches to all mankind. (This is why, in his novel *Nausea*, he uses the narrator to rail against a certain kind of Comtean humanism that preaches the "religion of humanity"—a humanism that finds in the rationality of the human being some cause to celebrate the dignity of the Human in general.) In fact, Sartre claims to find the roots of this picture in Heidegger: *Being and Time* provides for him the philosophical resources to orient our thinking of the human away from some pre-determined category and instead to center human creative activity. The problem is that he builds his defense of existentialism around what he calls its basic principle that "existence precedes essence." While this is a phrase he adopts from Heidegger, Heidegger argues that he fundamentally misunderstands it, and it is this misunderstanding that points to the status of the existentialist position *as metaphysics*.

Consider, to clarify this criticism, how Sartre introduces this phrase. Using the example of a manufactured object (a book, a paper knife), he argues that the way in which the manufactured object *exists* is fundamentally different from how the human being *exists*. The former and not the latter, for example, exists in relation to some pre-determined essence, or concept, or plan. By contrast, the human being has no pre-defined purpose; she is not brought into existence in accordance with some prior concept at all. Sartre explicitly links this position to his atheism. If there is no God, he argues, then "man" cannot be "made in his image," nor can he be understood to act or behave in a way that actualizes something like a "human nature," since there is no God to conceive of that nature in the first place. For Sartre, the human being therefore *exists* before she *defines herself*.[33] He also argues that it is only through this process of self-definition or self-creation that we generate values. Something is good, on this picture—the choice to marry or not to marry, to go to war or to join the resistance, to drink coffee or tea—not in and of itself, but *because* it is chosen and so is part of a human life. Sartre reasons from this that, in choosing—and thus in generating the value of a human life—I participate in the construction of what it means to be human. If this is right, then the meaning of being human is rooted in the fact of human freedom. More precisely, it is rooted in the fact of human freedom that in turn is rooted in a way in which the human being *exists* as distinct from the existence of a stone.

To clarify Heidegger's objection, consider whom Sartre is trying to distinguish himself from in this passage. First, he is emphasizing that a human being is importantly different than other kinds of objects—there is something definitive of the human as distinct from "a table or a stone." And this is not because, following the tradition of Western metaphysics, at least since Aristotle, the human being is endowed with a *unique* essence that "elevates" it above other kinds of beings. Rather, the human being—Sartre argues—exists first without any essence at all; in this sense, the human is *nothing* until she conceives of, wills, and creates herself. Second, while Sartre is explicitly positioning himself against the idea that the human being is the creation of God the "superlative artisan,"[34] he also rejects a certain Enlightenment conception of the human that he associates with thinkers like Diderot and Voltaire.[35] In their conception of the human, he argues, the role of God is "suppressed,"[36] yet the basic theoretical apparatus remains in place, inasmuch as each individual human being is understood to instantiate something like the universal category of "man"—or of "the human," to avoid the gendered formulation—to carry within herself a universal human nature that drives her behavior and through this guides the process of self-formation. Sartre concludes, then, that the "project" of human existence is unique in the sense that the process of human self-creation, unlike the process through which, for instance, a moss or a fungus spreads, follows no set or natural plan.

Running throughout these objections, Heidegger notices, is a telling conflation. For instance, in denying any "essence" to the category of the human, Sartre retained the traditional metaphysical sense of the word "essence" (that is, where an essence is a set of properties that determine the boundaries of a concept). He likewise retained the traditional metaphysical sense of the word "existence" (that is, where "to exist" is to be present in a physical or actual way). Heidegger puts this objection by saying that Sartre flips the traditional metaphysical view (on which things exist as examples of prior, determined concepts) in order to say, more or less, that the human being *exists* before the concept of the Human is supplied with the contents that mark out its boundaries. But "a reversal of a metaphysical statement is still a metaphysical statement."[37] Recall, for instance, that on Heidegger's picture, we cannot say that a human "exists" like a stone or a rock—as, for instance, some physically present entity—with the difference that the human is a physical entity that can be creative of its own essence. We cannot do this because on Heidegger's—admittedly peculiar—formulation, only Dasein *exists*.

To guard against this existentialist misreading, Heidegger spends much of the *Letter on Humanism* modifying the language of his earlier view. He introduces the new term "ex-sistence," for instance, to better express that the "existence" of human existence is not the "existence" of the metaphysical tradition. But Heidegger's aim in doing this is precisely to make clear what is and has always been exceptional in the human way of being. As he puts it, when we fully understand the way in which the human being—or better, in which Dasein—*ek-sists*, we discover that "the highest determination of the essence of man in humanism still did not realize the proper dignity of man."[38] If we take this argument seriously, the point Heidegger ultimately lodges against the humanist tradition is not that its definitions of the human as "animal rationale, as 'person,' as spiritual-ensouled-bodily-being," should be "declared false and thrust aside"[39]—which is precisely what existentialism sought to do. Instead, the argument is that these are possible ways in which Dasein can *show* itself to different narrow perspectives. As only ever partial, however, each of these perspectives obscures other ways of being human. The problem with these perspectives for grasping the "being of the human," then, is that, for Heidegger, our openness to plurality—that is, to the interpretive possibilities of existence that are open in front of and intended throughout a human life—is what makes us human.

Heidegger on Being Human

Conclusion: The Fate of Humanism in Continental Thought

I promised in this chapter to clarify the status of humanism in Continental philosophy. I have, of course, followed only one particular path through that vast terrain: the debate on humanism between Heidegger and Sartre. The bulk of the discussion, moreover, has been centered on *Being and Time*, in order to motivate the charge that humanism entails a metaphysical perspective. So, how does this open a wider debate?

In the wake of Heidegger's *Letter*, the philosophical blow it dealt to existentialism was swiftly felt. In fact, the turn away from existentialism in the following years helped usher in the rise of structuralism and post-structuralism as emblematic of French philosophical thought. This was largely understood to signal, within French philosophy, the end of humanism. By 1955, the structuralist Claude Lévi-Strauss, perhaps expressing a kind of relief at the waning influence of existentialism (though the classism and sexism of his remark remains telling) derisively referred to Sartre's philosophy as "metaphysics for shop-girls."[40] By the 1960s, Foucault had begun to predict the "end" of "man."[41]

It is not difficult to root this turn in Heideggerian criticisms. As Heidegger underlined, for instance, throughout much of the history of humanism, the category of "the human" could be best understood as something like a "natural kind." Or, put differently, the tradition has seen the human chiefly as a kind of biologically produced category that is definable through certain essential properties, which might include the power of freedom over instinct or a capacity for rational self-reflection. In this context, we have historically been able to say of the human *sciences* (economics, anthropology, sociology, etc.) that they are scientific in much the same way that the natural or physical sciences are. That is, that they describe in objective terms the naturally occurring properties and characteristic practices that separate human beings from other living and non-living things. Since, among these properties are often assumed to be certain features (rationality, autonomy) that grant the human her essential "dignity," we have seen where this kind of naturalistic humanism often functions as a kind of "religion of humanity," to borrow a term from Comte. At least since Heidegger, much of Continental philosophy is directed against this kind of natural scientific position. This includes putatively humanist thinkers like Sartre (who singles out Comte's version of this sort of humanism as deserving of scorn). It is also the target of many explicitly anti-humanist philosophers. Much of Foucault's work, for instance, is primarily directed against humanism in this sense. Instead, Foucault emphasizes the social and historical contingency of the category of the human, and, indeed, of all categories produced through (rather than "discovered by") human inquiry. Foucault is quite explicit, then, in taking "the human" to be a "social" kind. The human is not a natural category accessible through the methods of the sciences, but a discursive category that instead must be analyzed in a way that takes seriously the shifting boundaries of the concept as shaped by dynamics of power.

There is an inherently political dimension to many critiques lodged along this line, as I have already intimated. For example, threads of decolonial and critical thought center on the historical accessibility of the category of "the human" to the poor, to women, to the colonized. The point, then, is that to reject what I have just called a "naturalistic" sort of humanism is often not merely a philosophical task, but the rejection of an historical category and attendant conceptual apparatus that has been deployed in real and materially oppressive ways. While this is not Heidegger's concern (and there would be something grotesque in seeing Heidegger as standing on the side of the historically oppressed), he nevertheless helps to show, given the metaphysical framing of naturalistic humanism, how this line of critique might arise.

But there is also, coming out of Heidegger's work, a second fault-line that concerns the philosophical resources through which we articulate the "referent" of the term "human being" in the first place. As is well known, a long-dominant conception of the human subject (as distinct both from the human being as an object and from objects of other kinds), emerges in the Cartesian "discovery" of the *cogito*, where, through reflection on the activity of thinking itself, Descartes comes to understand his status as a *thinking thing*. The resulting picture of the human being, then, is of the inherence of a mind in a physical, extended body—a conception that is discovered through isolated, rational reflection. This inherence of mind-in-body distinguishes the human subject, for instance, from other kinds of bodies that cannot think, or will, or perceive.

Descartes' is a fundamentally "substantialist" conception of the human subject. That is, the human is defined through the exercise of its essential, cognitive capacities as the stable substance, or a composite of substances, that produces them. Descartes here picks up on longstanding traditions that Heidegger explicitly critiques. The notion of the body in which action is produced by the movement of the soul; later conceptions of personhood as a function of consciousness: Each of these is a "substantialist" picture inasmuch as each component of the human being—body and mind (or soul)—is conceptualized as a kind of being that accumulates properties, that engages in or is capable of certain kinds of characteristic activities, and so on.

The threads of Heidegger's critical gesture against substantialist metaphysics are, of course, traced throughout the pages of *Being and Time*, and much of 20th and 21st century Continental philosophy continues its attempt to "overcome" Descartes. Even Sartre, for instance, who—along with Husserl—hews perhaps closest to the Cartesian picture (calling the *cogito* the "absolute truth" from which existentialism begins), re-interprets the *cogito* by centering human consciousness as a kind of originary *nothingness*. There is also a different—although not entirely incompatible—approach to "overcoming" Descartes that shapes recent Continental thought. This approach involves defining human existence through its activities alone, first by doing away with the illusion of a stable "thing" that causes or carries them out and then critiquing much of what we take to make the human "exceptional." The historical origin of this latter approach is Nietzsche. As Nietzsche argues in *Genealogy of Morals*—contrasting his view to the grammatical illusions that separate the subject, the grammatical "I," from both its action and its object—"there is no 'being' behind 'doing'"—no "doer" behind "the deed" [...] the deed is everything."[42] Picking up on this Nietzschean insight, a more recent strain of Continental thought (for instance, in Sara Ahmed, Judith Butler) continues to redefine human subjectivity in such a way that it is centered, not on the stable *thingliness* of human beings but on the event or activity of willing, of performative self-construction, and so on.

So, to what degree is *this* line of criticism resonant with Heidegger? Here, the answer is more ambiguous. On the one hand, I have tried to bring out where Heidegger's concern for the activity of Being is itself a turn away from substantializing accounts of the human subject. We have seen, for instance, that Heidegger comes to find the traditional metaphysical categories of subject and object as distorting what it means for a human being *to be*. In this sense, he shares with these strands of thought a concern with the plurality of ways of human being—ways that, perhaps, cannot be captured by the universalizing languages of humanism. But Heidegger also finds at their core a uniquely *human* way of being. While this way of being cannot, perhaps, be fully understood if we approach the human from the narrow, blinkered perspectives of traditional metaphysics and of natural or human science, this does not mean that the "dignity" or importance of human existence would have to be denied. Heidegger's later turn to thinking about the expressive possibilities of poetry and art are meant to show, in part, how these bring other ways of being human into view.

Bibliography

Aristotle. *Metaphysics*. In *Aristotle Metaphysics* Reeve, C. D. C. (trans.) with introduction and notes. Indianapolis: Hackett Publishing, 2016.

Fanon, Frantz. *The Wretched of the Earth*. New York: Grove Press, 1961.

Foucault, Michel. *The Order of Things*. New York: Penguin, 1966.

Heidegger on Being Human

Heidegger, Martin. *Being and Time*, John Macquarrie and Edward Robinson (trans.). New York: Harper & Row, 1962.

Heidegger, Martin. "Letter on Humanism". In *Basic Writings of Heidegger*, David Farrell Krell (ed.) Frank A. Capuzzi and J. Glenn Gray (trans.). San Francisco: Harper Collins, 1993.

Lévi-Strauss, Claude. *Tristes Tropique*. Paris: Plon, 1955.

Nietzsche, Friedrich. *On the Genealogy of Morals*. In *The Basic Writings of Nietzsche*, Walter Kaufmann (ed. and trans.). New York: Modern Library, 2000, p. 481.

Sartre, Jean-Paul. *Existentialism Is a Humanism*. Carol Macomber (trans). New Haven: Yale University Press, 2007.

Sellars, Wilfrid. "Philosophy and the Image of Man." In *Frontiers of Science and Philosophy*, Robert Colodny (ed.). Pittsburgh: University of Pittsburgh Press, 1962, 35–78.

Notes

1 See Martin Heidegger, "Letter on Humanism," trans. Frank A. Capuzzi and J. Glenn Gray, in *Basic Writings of Heidegger*, ed. David Farrell Krell (San Francisco: Harper Collins, 1993), 219; henceforth LH, followed by page number.

2 LH, 233–234.

3 Martin Heidegger, *Being and Time*, trans. John Macquarrie and Edward Robinson (New York: Harper & Row, 1962), p. 1; henceforth BT, followed by page number.

4 *Metaphysics*. IV.2 1003a33, trans. C. D. C. Reeve, *Aristotle Metaphysics* (Indianapolis: Hackett Publishing, 2016).

5 BT, 25.

6 BT, 24.

7 BT, 24.

8 BT, 24.

9 BT, 25.

10 BT, 25.

11 BT, 25.

12 BT, ¶2.

13 It is worth underlining at this point why, when I say that the term "Dasein" is co-extensive with human Being, this is shorthand for a *way* of being. To talk about *a* human being, Heidegger argues again and again, is to name a certain kind of being, understood in a particular way (for instance, when we call something a "human being" we are expressing that it is a member of the category "Human," when, of course there are other categories that same being is a member of). By contrast, the term "Dasein" is supposed to give Heidegger a way to zero in on a *structural feature* of human existence without specifying that the being who exists is a member of any particular category. To put this differently, we can think of "Dasein" as picking out the fact that a human being engaging in some activity (whether this is thinking about metaphysics, practicing piano, building a home, or writing an essay) is always interpretively related to her own existence, without specifying whether she interprets herself *as* a human, as a woman, as a body, or in any other *particular* way.

14 BT, 25.

15 Wilfrid Sellars, "Philosophy and the Image of Man," in *Frontiers of Science and Philosophy*, ed. Robert Colodny (Pittsburgh: University of Pittsburgh Press, 1962), 35–78.

16 LH, 219.

17 See BT, ¶7.

18 BT, 67.

19 LH, 225.

20 LH, 225.

21 LH, 224.

22 LH, 225.

23 LH, 233.

24 Jean-Paul Sartre, *Existentialism Is a Humanism* (New Haven: Yale University Press, 2007); henceforth EH, followed by page number.

25 EH, 18.

26 LH, 226.

27 LH, 226.

28 LH, 225.

29 EH, 22.
30 LH, 227.
31 See, on this point, Frantz Fanon, *The Wretched of the Earth* (New York: Grove Press, 1961).
32 LH, 227.
33 EH, 20–21.
34 EH, 21.
35 EH, 22.
36 EH, 21.
37 LH, 232.
38 LH, 233.
39 LH, 233.
40 Claude Lévi-Strauss, *Tristes Tropique* (Paris: Plon, 1955), 50.
41 Michel Foucault, *The Order of Things* (New York: Penguin, 1966).
42 Friedrich Nietzsche, *Genealogy of Morals*, Essay 1. The translation here follows that of Walter Kaufmann, *On the Genealogy of Morals*. In *The Basic Writings of Nietzsche*, ed. and trans. Walter Kaufmann (New York: Modern Library, 2000), 481.

2

Frantz Fanon

Postcoloniality and New Humanism

Deepa Jani

The field of Postcolonial Studies remains ambivalent toward the legacy of Western humanism. The field has theorized decolonization to constitute antonymous operations of interruption of humanism and inauguration of a "new humanism." Scholars and thinkers concurrently celebrated decolonization to signal the beginning of the end of humanism (and its civilizational impetus), and the beginning of the dawning of a "new humanism" for the newly minted nations. Frantz Fanon's last book *The Wretched of the Earth* (1961, hereafter *The Wretched*) remains an influential example of theorization of the antipodean impulses of decolonization.[1] While postcolonial theorists maintain that the post-eighteenth century rational, autonomous, bourgeois individual subject, the *raison d'etre* of Enlightenment humanism, who is both the Burckhardtian encyclopedic *uomo universale* and the *homo economicus* of the Robinsonade ilk, is also the normative white male imperialist subject. Gayatri Spivak succinctly notes, "There is an affinity between the imperialist subject and subject of humanism."[2] Albeit largely persuaded by postmodernism's incredulity toward metanarratives of Western humanism, few postcolonial scholars have been willing to throw the baby out with the bath water. In his last book *Humanism and Democratic Criticism* (2004), Edward Said, whose career-long struggle with the humanist tradition has attained a proverbial status in the field, offers an unequivocal defense of humanism notwithstanding its legacy of Eurocentrism and Empire:

> I believed then, and still believe, that it is possible to be critical of humanism in the name of humanism and that, schooled in its abuses by the experience of Eurocentrism and empire, one could fashion a different kind of humanism that was cosmopolitan and text-and-language bound.[3]

Said's call for a different kind of humanism for the post-9/11 era hearkens to Frantz Fanon's ethical injunction to his readers in the conclusion to *The Wretched* to imagine a "new humanism" for the new postcolonial epoch: "For Europe, for ourselves and for humanity, comrades, we must make a new start, develop a new way of thinking, and endeavor to create a new man."[4] Fanon's exhortation for a new humanism has garnered significant interest and debate among postcolonial scholars in the last 40 years over the definition and scope of the term, and over the character and nature of Fanon's humanism. A corollary to the debate on new humanism are also questions about Fanon's theorization of decolonization, its reformist agenda or revolutionary *potentia*. Some scholars agonize over Fanon's "residual humanism" that is merely a postcolonial avatar of Western humanism rehashing values and pieties of the old European form, while others celebrate Fanon's "emergent humanism" which radically breaks with the prodigious humanist theses proffered by the West.

DOI: 10.4324/9781003046004-4

In this chapter, I argue that Fanon's new humanism is neither residual nor emergent. To develop my position, I will demonstrate that Fanon theorizes decolonization as an antonymic process, which concomitantly envisions a revolutionary rupture with the Eurocentric humanist episteme and its "philosophy of man" and regime of rights, while also fashioning an emancipatory project of *Bildung* for the *Bildungsheld*, the monadic subject the postcolonial people, leading to the advancement of their consciousness from the particular to the universal, thereupon opening the possibility for the arrival of a new humanity, a decolonizing project that is paradoxically modeled on the liberal humanist narrative of the self-development of bourgeois subjectivity. Fanon conceptualizes decolonization as the total destruction of humanism as well as a beginning of a new one, what I call "a humanism without humanism," except that the former proffers a frame of reference for the latter's arrival. I contend that in Fanon's theorization of decolonization as an antithetical process lie the historical origins of the ambivalence toward the legacy of humanism in the field of Postcolonial Studies. Fanon's aporetic "humanism without humanism" postulated in *The Wretched* is without resolution, irreducible to either the residual or the emergent factions. He remains a conundrum, a profoundly revolutionary thinker and a thoroughly Europeanist one at that. For the last 40 years, the factious Fanonisms generated by the debate over the great man's humanism have been expectantly awaiting a new humanity to be delivered by their messiah, *qui n'est pas arrivé.*

Fanon's "New Humanism"

Fanon concludes his theorization of decolonization in *The Wretched* with an ethical injunction to his readers/comrades to envision a new humanism for all of humanity, not only for the newly independent nations but also for the older European nations: "For Europe, for ourselves and for humanity, comrades, we must make a new start, develop a new way of thinking, and endeavor to create a new man."[5] Anthony Alessandrini usefully reminds us that in the original French Fanon's appeal to a new humanism is a call for the growth of a new skin, rendered in the English translation by Richard Philcox as a "new start": "It seems to me that 'il faut faire peau neuve' is better rendered as 'we must grow a new skin.'"[6] A call for a new humanism is a demand for a collective ecdysis on a universal scale. This creation of new humans is the necessary corollary of decolonization, which he declares at the outset of the book,

> fundamentally alters being and transforms the spectator crushed to a nonessential state into a privileged actor [...] It infuses a new rhythm, specific to a new generation of men, with a new language and a new humanity. Decolonization is truly the creation of new men.[7]

In the process of liberation, the dehumanized colonized native wrought by the Manichaeanism of the colonial world undergoes transmutation from an object to a subject of history, from a nonbeing to a being. A process of species substitution, decolonization for Fanon materializes the scriptural injunction "The last shall be first."[8] Accordingly, decolonization is a *tabula rasa* for Fanon, a clean slate, whereby the history-making revolutionary struggle for liberation leads to a total rejection of the historical *a priori* of the European colonial episteme, culminating in a radical new beginning.

A new language and a new humanity can only emerge for Fanon from the Third World, for the European Enlightenment invention of "universal man," *uomo universale*, was cultivated in the negative space of colonial violence which provides the necessary conditions for the emergence of the Enlightenment idea of Man. In a series of statements Fanon pillories the unctuous deification of man since the Enlightenment in Western humanist discourses, which treat the human as an abstract universal: "Let us leave this Europe which never stops talking of man yet massacres him at every one of its street corners, at every corner of the world"; "Its [Europe's] only show of miserliness has been toward man, only toward man has it shown itself to be niggardly and murderously

Postcoloniality and New Humanism

carnivorous"; "When I look for man in European lifestyles and technology I see a constant denial of man, an avalanche of murders."[9] Condemning the physical and epistemic violence of European humanism that has written off the majority of humans in its invention of the abstract universal man, Fanon implores the Third World to imagine a radically new humanism that is neither a mimicry of Europe nor a civilizational race to catch up with it:

> The Third World must start a new history of man which takes account of not only the occasional prodigious theses maintained by Europe but also its crimes, the most heinous of which has been committed at the very heart of man, the pathological dismembering of his functions and the erosion of his unity.[10]

Colonialism precludes the humanity of natives in the name of humanism. Decolonization as a process of species substitution provides opportunity to the Third World to substitute the European invention of abstract universal man with "a man in full, something which Europe has been incapable of achieving."[11] A new human can only emerge in the liberation struggle, which for Fanon is necessarily violent, for "the last can be the first only after a murderous and decisive confrontation between the two protagonists."[12] Insomuch as the native is wrought in the violent, anti-dialectical Manichaeanism of the colonial geographical and epistemic configuration, a new human is fashioned in the revolutionary praxis of violence, which for Fanon provides the necessary historical preconditions for the emergence of a new humanism. From the ruins of total disorder, the primary impetus for decolonization, a new human is forged. Musing on the question of what the Algerians want to beget by means of their revolutionary praxis, Fanon responds, in the preface to his book *A Dying Colonialism* (1965), the end to the Manichean logic of colonialism:

> The new relations are not the result of one barbarism replacing another barbarism, of one crushing of man replacing another crushing of man. What we Algerians want is to discover the man behind the colonizer; this man who is both the organizer and the victim of a system that has choked him and reduced him to silence.[13]

If Eurocentric humanism created the violent, non-dialectical, Manichean world of legitimate humans and not-yet-legitimate humans, the civilized and the barbarians, then a new humanism forcefully disrupts this Manichean world invented by Europe.

The Debates Over Fanon's Humanism: Residual or Emergent?

Fanon's call to create a new history of the human has engendered compelling debate in the postcolonial field over the nature and character of his "new humanism." In particular the contention among scholars is over the relationship of Fanon's humanism with Western humanism, that is, if his humanism is merely a postcolonial avatar of Western humanism or is a true antithesis to the prodigious humanist theses postulated by the West, particularly since the Enlightenment era. Namely the quarrel is over whether Fanonian humanism rehashes the values and pieties of Eurocentric humanism, or radically departs from them. Scholars belonging to the former camp understand Fanon's humanism as "residual humanism," and the latter camp describe it as "emergent humanism."

It is important to note here that the debates over Fanonian humanism have unfolded in the last 40 years in the wake of the "postmodern turn" in theory and the inception of Postcolonial Studies in the Western academy in the late 1970s with the publication of Said's *Orientalism*.[14] Both postmodernism and postcolonialism, given their entangled legacies—which Robert Young describes when discussing the postmodern turn in theory, "European culture's awareness that it is no longer the unquestioned and dominant center of the world"—have celebrated the demise of master narratives of Europe, including the grandest metanarrative of them all, humanism.[15] Postmodern and postcolonial scholars and theorists have employed vocabulary such as "residual" or "emergent" from Raymond Williams' "epochal analysis" of the dynamic and historical variations in a cultural process when denouncing or defending someone's humanism. Williams describes "residual" elements of a cultural process in the following manner:

> The residual, by definition, has been effectively formed in the past, but it is still active in the cultural process, not only and often not at all as an element of the past, but as an effective element of the present.[16]

By "emergent," Williams means, "first, that new meanings and values, new practices, new relationships and kinds of relationships are continually being created."[17]

In the wake of High Theory, tagging so-and-so's humanism as "residual" is particularly fraught. In the introduction to his book *Humanism*, Tony Davies recounts, "I have seen two normally quite civilised and peaceable academics almost come to blows after one accused the other's latest book of 'residual humanism,' a description which was taken, and intended, as an insult of the most offensive kind."[18] Said was embroiled in one such high-profile quarrel over his "residual humanism" with James Clifford. Said, who, despite his ambivalence toward humanism throughout his intellectual history, donned the label humanist without guilt or shame, defends his "residual humanism," a charge leveled by Clifford in his influential review of *Orientalism* where he bemoans the theoretical incongruity of Said's humanist-Foucauldian frame of reference.[19] In the Afterword to *Orientalism* Said contends,

> Yet among American and British academics of a decidedly rigorous and unyielding stripe, *Orientalism*, and indeed all of my other work, has come in for disapproving attacks because of its 'residual' humanism, its theoretical inconsistencies, its insufficient, perhaps even sentimental, treatment of agency. I am glad that it has![20]

Qua Said, Fanon's humanism too has been read through this polemical frame of reference. Some scholars contend that Fanon's new humanism is a "residual humanism" largely modeled on assumptions of Western humanism, while others assert that it is an "emergent humanism" radically rupturing with the European form. The residual camp sees Fanon's theory of decolonization as merely reformative, while the emergent camp reads it as revolutionary. Fanonian Studies, for the last 40 years, has remained deeply divided over the nature and character of Fanon's humanism. Pal Ahluwalia, Homi Bhabha, Neil Lazarus, and Robert Young belong to the former faction, while Anthony Alessandrini and Malreddy Pavan Kumar belong to the latter. The polemics on Fanonian humanism revolves around questions of subjectivity, essentialism, alienation, sovereignty, dialectics, nationalism, totality, universality, and Europe. Below I elaborate on some of the central arguments within the dichotonic forms of Fanonism that have emerged in the debate.

Homi Bhabha, reminiscing about Fanon in his influential essay "Interrogating Identity: Frantz Fanon and the Postcolonial Prerogative," which was originally published as a foreword titled "Remembering Fanon" in *Black Skin, White Masks* in 1986, exalts the postmodernist *avant la lettre* Fanon for his non-dialectical thought that exorcises the governing first principles of Eurocentric liberal humanism by abandoning any understanding of the native from an abstract universalist basis, or from a liberal rights-based discourse.[21] In Bhabha's reading of Fanon, he rehearses postmodernist pronouncements on the death of the Cartesian sovereign subject of humanism, questioning individual authority by focusing on the psychoanalytic dimension of "demand and desire" when elucidating on the alienating effects of the Manichean colonial configuration. For

Postcoloniality and New Humanism

Bhabhian Fanon there is no unified autonomous colonized subject or its correlative continuous colonial history. Despite Fanon's anti-humanist precursory postmodernism, Bhabha agonizes over his "residual humanism": "It is as if Fanon is fearful of his most radical insights: that the politics of race will not be entirely contained within the humanist myth of man [...] for its psychic affects question such forms of determinism"; "Despite Fanon's insight into the dark side of man, such a deep hunger for humanism must be an overcompensation for the [...] depersonalization of colonized man."[22] For Bhabha, Fanon's "banal" and "beatific" "existentialist humanism," in his "desperate, doomed search for a dialectic of deliverance," lapses into essentialism, presuming the first principles of Eurocentric humanism, an *a priori* human essence, that is violated by colonialism.[23] Thus, Fanon's radical thought, far from being a declaration on the demise of the "philosophy of man," rehabilitates the unified autonomous colonized subject, essentially restoring the "myth of Man and Society."

Inasmuch as Bhabha is tormented by Fanon's lapses into essentialism and totality and his deep hunger for the European grand narrative of humanism, Neil Lazarus, in his article "Disavowing Decolonization," berates Bhabha, together with other postcolonial scholars, who, enamored by postmodernist critiques of totality and universality, portray Fanon as an anti-essentialist, anti-dialectical, anti-nationalist, anti-totality, and an anti-humanist postmodernist thinker: "It is clear among other things that Bhabha's Fanon would have been unrecognizable to Fanon himself."[24] Lazarus is particularly troubled by the Bhabhian Fanon's repudiation of nationalism and humanism as mere reinscriptions of totalizing bourgeois Eurocentric discourses. For Lazarus, notwithstanding Fanon's trenchant critique of bourgeois nationalism, he remains anchored in an alternative nationalism, whence he launches his radical anti-colonial humanist thought and revolutionary praxis. Lazarus contends,

> where postmodernist theory has reacted to the perceived indefensibility of bourgeois humanism and of colonial nationalism by abandoning the very idea of totality, a genuinely postcolonial strategy might be to move explicitly, as Fanon already did in concluding *The Wretched of the Earth*, to proclaim a 'new' humanism, predicated upon a formal repudiation of the degraded European form, and borne embryonically in the national liberation movement.[25]

For Bhabha the postcolonial method and strategy is necessarily anti-nationalist; conversely for Lazarus a genuine postcolonial perspective retains "the categories of 'nation' and 'universality,'" constructing a strategy that is "nationalitarian, liberationist, internationalist—from which it is possible to assume the burden of speaking for all humanity."[26] Lazarus' Fanon does not abandon the concepts of totality and universality, co-opting European metanarratives of nationalism and internationalism for the anti-colonial liberation struggle. Lazarus does not agonize over Fanon's "residual humanism," repudiating his deployment of the categories "nation" and "universality" as sheer ideals of Eurocentric derivative discourses. For Lazarus, although Fanon categorically rejects the imperialist impetus of Eurocentric humanism, his new humanism remains anchored in Europe, recuperating discourses of nationalism and internationalism, with their origins in Enlightenment and Marxist history and theory, for postcolonial strategy to restore the rights and dignity of the formerly colonized. In Lazarus' treatment, Fanon's residual new humanism is not merely a colonial hangover from the past (which afflicts Bhabha); the past effectively functions in the present affording him a *pukka* (genuinely) alternative postcolonial *modus operandi*.

Qua Lazarus and Bhabha, Pal Ahluwalia maintains that Fanon's new humanism is residual, tethered to Europe, more so because it draws on Marxism and existentialism:

> In Algeria, Fanon was forced to conceptualise a new humanism [...] Colonialism created the conditions that necessitated a new humanism. The new humanism was not a radical break

with Enlightenment humanism, because of the ways in which he drew on Marxism and existentialism.[27]

Robert Young similarly sees Fanon's new humanism as residual, moored in European thought, specifically Sartrean existentialism and Marxism. He maintains, "Marx's concept of alienation afforded a dialectical concept in which that alienation could provide the basis for a new emergence, a new state and a new humanism which would achieve a political, economic, social and cultural disalienation."[28] The experience of alienation, estrangement from the species-being, the essence of the human being, is not only the permanent condition of the European working classes, but also the colonized subjects. Thus, the creation of new humans, not alienated from their species-being, is the corollary of decolonization. Young's Fanon, a Marxist humanist, has a deep hunger for recovering human essence, that governing first principle of Western humanism, lost under colonial conditions.

Contrary to Bhabha, Lazarus, Ahluwalia, and Young, Malreddy Pavan Kumar, and Anthony Alessandrini read Fanon's humanism as emergent, one that radically ruptures European humanism. Kumar divides the postcolonial approaches to humanism into two factions—the alter-humanists and the residual humanists. Contrary to Said's residual humanism, Fanon's new humanism, he asserts, is alter-humanism, not complicit with European humanism: "there is what I would call the foundations of an alter-humanist thought—a humanism that positively enables the coloniser's ascribed *otherness*—which can be traced to the early postcolonial thinkers such as Frantz Fanon, Albert Memmi and Aimé Césaire."[29] Alessandrini similarly reads Fanon's humanism as emergent, one that engages in a struggle to radically break with European humanism:

> Fanon's struggle can be seen as the attempt to imagine and call into existence an emergent humanism that could be separated from, and indeed brought into mortal combat with, the forms of false humanism that underwrote (and continue to underwrite) massive and ongoing crimes against humanity.[30]

Criticizing Lazarus for characterizing Fanon's humanism as residual, derivative of European bourgeois humanism, he insists that Fanon's humanism is emergent and non-derivative.[31] While Alessandrini deploys Williams' keyword "emergent" to delineate Fanon's humanism, suggesting that it is not just a new phase of the dominant or derivative of it, he appears to struggle to articulate if Fanonian humanism actually succeeds in rupturing with the dominant, offering an alternative or an oppositional form of humanism. Instead he concludes that what he values in Fanon (and Said's) humanism is the agonistic struggle itself, the "working through" "with and against humanism from within."[32]

To complicate matters further, in an earlier essay "The Humanism Effect: Fanon, Foucault, and Ethics Without Subjects," Alessandrini sees congruity between Fanon's humanism and Foucault's anti-humanism. Reading against the grain, he affirms that both thinkers, often understood as being polar opposites, refuse the blackmail of the Enlightenment, interrupting the assumption of a stable, continuous, humanist subject and nostalgia for lost origins:

> I will argue that for Fanon and Foucault, this critique of the traditional humanist subject provides a way of opposing what they both see as the dangerous nostalgia for a lost moment of origin […] Fanon and Foucault both end in a moment of ethics. But it is an ethics without the sort of stable subjects assumed by humanism.[33]

In a way, although Alessandrini understands Fanon's humanism as emergent and Bhabha agonizes over its residual character, both scholars read Fanon as a postmodernist thinker *avant la lettre*, a position Lazarus forcefully protests, as discussed above. Lazarus' complaints echo Henry Louis Gates, Jr.'s objections in his well-known essay "Critical Fanonism," wherein he discusses the self-referential appropriation of Fanon by postcolonial scholars (Bhabha, Said, Spivak) who label him a precocious postmodernist:

> Fanon's current fascination for us has something to do with the convergence of the problematic of colonialism with that of subject-formation. As a psychoanalyst of culture, as a champion of the wretched of the earth, he is an almost irresistible figure for a criticism that sees itself as both oppositional and postmodern.[34]

The historical Fanon, Gates frets, is under erasure by the postmodernist frame of reference of colonial discourse theorists, appealing for a reading of Fanon that attends to his own historical particularity, rather than renders him a "global theorist."

To put it in a nutshell, the debate over Fanon's residual or emergent humanism, and the attendant question of his precocious postmodernism, hinges on key concerns, whether Fanon assumes a unified or a fragmented colonized subjectivity, whether he postulates an essential universal human subject or a subject effected by epistemic and colonial configurations, whether he presumes a homogeneity of the abstract universal or the plurality of the concrete singular, whether he champions continuity, totality, and universality or discontinuity, fragmentation, and particularity, whether his philosophy is defined by essentialism or anti-essentialism, whether his political strategy is nationalist or anti-nationalist, and whether he deploys the rights-based discourse or dismisses the liberal humanist conceptions of rights, dignity, and freedom.

Fanon's Intellectual Struggles as an *évolué*, and the Theory of Revolutionary Violence

Above I detail the main arguments and concerns in the near 40-year debate among scholars within Postcolonial Studies over Fanon's humanism, its residual or emergent character. The forms of Fanonism generated in these debates primarily revolve around the question of the place of Europe in Fanon's philosophy, that is, whether his thought is tethered or untethered to Europe. The factious Fanonisms engendered by the debate accentuates Fanon's ambivalence toward Europe. His agonistic relationship to Europe is both intellectual and internal. Although he unequivocally rejects European colonialism, Fanon's intellectual influences, such as Jean-Paul Sartre, Karl Marx, G. W. F. Hegel, and Maurice Merleau-Ponty, remain largely European. Robert Young maintains, "He [Fanon] always remained intellectually centered in Paris, and never resisted European thought as such, as much as he resisted European domination of the colonial world."[35] Young asserts that as an international activist Fanon's interest in local cultures was limited; moreover, he did not graft his European intellectual ideas to African cultures, as his knowledge and experience of said cultures was limited.[36] A product of French colonial education, Fanon was a thoroughly assimilated black man, an *évolué*, who had mastered the French language and thought, and had gained honorary citizenship in the white world:

> I can remember just over a year ago in Lyon, following a lecture where I had drawn a parallel between black and European poetry, a French comrade telling me enthusiastically: 'Basically, you're a white man.' The fact I had studied such an interesting question in the white man's language gave me my credentials.[37]

For the colonized, assimilation into the French world by virtue of French language acquisition holds the promise of species substitution, a process that eventually gets upended by decolonization in Fanon's theorization. But under colonialism, the assimilated colonized psyche is plagued by a nervous condition. For the natives the better their mastery is of the French language the closer they are to being human, but also the more their psyche begins to exhibit a "constellation of delirium." The nervous condition of the native engendered by the contrary demands of assimilation into the European world and the necessity to attain self-consciousness tormented Fanon throughout his intellectual history. Gates urges Fanon scholars to recognize the battlefield within the great man.[38] Influenced by Sartre's existentialist view of being as alienation, Fanon learned that the experience of alienation, estrangement from the species-being, was a condition of the natives. His own personal alienation as a colonized assimilated French subject trapped in an "almost the same but not quite" French mode of existence, an *évolué* black man with a white mask, is famously theorized in his first book *Black Skin, White Masks* (1952). This experience of alienation enables him to question the tenets of Eurocentric Enlightenment humanism which had promised him perks of honorary French citizenship, *liberté, égalité, fraternité*. The first book, expanding on Marxist analysis of alienation in class-based societies, propounds the thesis that alienated consciousness is correlative not only with capitalist but also colonial societies. He hopes that his book is "a mirror with a progressive infrastructure where the black man can find the path to disalienation."[39]

When the *évolué* Antillean Fanon, bedeviled by an alienated consciousness, asks the question, "What does the black man want?," his answer is disalienation, which is not only a process of liberating the self from the need for recognition from the other (demands of the Hegelian master/slave dialectic), but also the operation of liberating from oneself, from the otherness of the self: "The issue is paramount. We are aiming at nothing less than to liberate the black man from himself."[40] The alienated consciousness of the native is the outcome of a double process for Fanon, "First, economic. Then, internalization or rather epidermalization of this inferiority."[41] The colonial battlefield for Fanon was not just without but also within; the Manichean geographical configurations of compartmentalized colonial space is reproduced at the level of the psyche, wherein the native reveals a "Manichean delirium." The battlefield within Fanon—the contrary demands of assimilation and the necessity of self-consciousness, the ontological self-division of the Afro-French identity, the antipodean operations of alienation and freedom, the conundrum of the Marxist/Sartrean/psychoanalytic frames of reference and theorizing praxis of revolutionary decolonization—exhibits its own Manichean delirium. The necessity of freedom for Fanon is disalienation in the psychic and the physical realms. The corollary of decolonization is disalienation. The creation of new disalienated humans is the end goal of decolonization. A new humanism emerges when the assimilated, alienated, colonized subject finds the path to disalienation. Marx's concept of alienation afforded for Fanon, Young argues, "a dialectical concept in which the alienation could provide the basis for a new emergence, a new state and a new humanism, which would achieve a political, economic, social and cultural disalienation."[42] Fanon's philosophy sought a path to a personal and collective dialienation from coloniality.

For Fanon, decolonization as disalienation is achieved through revolutionary violence. Few of Fanon's ideas have garnered as much controversy as the thesis on violence and its relation to politics, in the chapter "On Violence" in *The Wretched*. Decolonization, according to Fanon, is a violent event resulting in unconditional substitution of the colonizer by the colonized: "Decolonization is quite simply the substitution of one 'species' of mankind by another. The substitution is unconditional, absolute, total, and seamless."[43] Given his non-dialectical understanding of the Manichean colonial space, for Fanon the colonizer and the colonized cannot co-exist, making one of them superfluous. Thus, decolonization is an agenda of total disorder.[44] The last shall be first, and the first last, only by virtue of revolutionary violence. According to Fanon, "On the logical plane, the Manichaeanism of the colonist produces a Manichaeanism of the colonized."[45] The violence of the colonized is wrought by the Manichaeanism of the compartmentalized colonial world, which is

Postcoloniality and New Humanism

its condition of possibility: The natives can liberate themselves from the ontological self-division of their psyche effectuated by the violence of colonialism only by means of counter-violence. For Fanon, there is "reciprocal homogeneity" attained when the counter-violence of the colonized balances out the violence of the colonist.[46] It is only by virtue of violent liberatory struggle that a new disalienated human is forged. Fanonian new humanism emerges from conditions of revolutionary violence, which unconditionally and absolutely supplants the colonist's humanism. For Eurocentric humanism is deeply complicit in colonial violence, in both the epistemic and physical realms. Dehumanization is the *sine qua non* for the project of humanization and civilizational upliftment of the natives. In his polemical preface to *The Wretched*, Jean-Paul Sartre notes, "Colonial violence not only aims to dehumanize them. No effort is spared to demolish their traditions, to substitute our language for theirs, and to destroy their culture without giving them ours."[47] His trenchant critique of the historical violence of European humanism continues,

> First of all we must confront [...] the striptease of our humanism. Not a pretty sight in its nakedness: nothing but a dishonest ideology, an exquisite justification for plundering; its tokens of sympathy and affectation, alibis for our acts of aggression"[48]

The universal values of Western humanism proclaiming the European as the "measure of man" produced an alienated consciousness of the colonized, who have interiorized the "epidermalization of their inferiority." For Fanon the alienated consciousness of the colonized, enlightened by violence, rebels against the "epidermalization of their inferiority." The colonized reject Enlightenment values in the liberation struggle. If the colonial world is a non-dialectical Manichean world, then decolonization unifies this heterogeneity on the basis of race and nation.[49] According to Fanon the nation and national consciousness are born in armed struggle.

One of the most prominent critics of Fanon's theory of violence is Hannah Arendt, who in the context of the turmoil of the 1960s denounces Fanon's emphasis on revolutionary violence as a means for political action, while also acknowledging in her analysis that it was Sartre's "sound and fury" preface that glorified violence:

> Sartre, who in his preface to Fanon's *The Wretched of the Earth* goes much farther in his glorification of violence than Sorel in his famous *Reflections on Violence*—farther than Fanon himself, whose argument he wishes to bring to its conclusion.[50]

What troubles Arendt most is Fanon's conclusions that revolutionary violence will lead to a new form of humanism:

> No body politic I know of was ever founded on the equality before death and its actualization in violence [...] But it is true that the strong fraternal sentiments collective violence engenders have misled many good people into the hope that a new community together with a 'new man' will arise out of it.[51]

Conversely to Fanon's vision of the birth of a new body politic through violence, Arendt concludes that Fanonian violence leads to the death of politics. In his foreword to *The Wretched*, Bhabha defends Fanon's revolutionary violence from Arendt's criticisms by reminding us that Fanon did not glorify "spontaneous violence."[52] He further asserts that Fanonian violence "is part of a struggle for psycho-affective survival and a search for human agency in the midst of the agony of oppression."[53] Fanonian revolutionary violence transforms the thing colonized to a human being, to an agent and a privileged actor: "the 'thing' colonized becomes a man through the very process of liberation."[54]

While Arendt provides a cogent argument, she does not reckon with the fact that Fanonian thesis on violence emphasizes its character as counter-violence to the original violence of colonialism, which is not merely a reactionary violence but a revolutionary one. The goal is neither mimicry of Europe nor simply species substitution, of "one barbarism replacing another barbarism, of one crushing of man replacing another crushing of man."[55] Fanon provides a prophetic and incisive critique of the nationalist bourgeoisie for precisely replacing one barbarism with another, one master with another, fundamentally betraying the revolutionary *potentia* of the liberation struggle. Fanonian revolutionary violence produces justice, not law. As the "thing" colonized cannot appeal for justice in the colonial system, they engender justice by virtue of what Walter Benjamin called "divine violence," in his influential essay "Critique of Violence." Benjamin differentiates the law-destroying divine violence from the lawmaking mythic violence:

> If mythical violence is lawmaking, divine violence is law-destroying; if the former sets boundaries, the latter boundlessly destroys them; if mythical violence brings at once guilt and retribution, divine power expiates [...] if the former is bloody, the latter is lethal without spilling blood.[56]

Benjamin understands the messianic force of divine violence as just and "pure" because it is beyond the bounds of law, neither makes or preserves laws; its principle is justice, not power. Justice for Benjamin cannot be attained through law. Divine violence, with justice as its end, is revolutionary violence, seeking the abolition of state power and breaking the cycle of lawmaking mythic violence. It, thus, founds a "new historical epoch."[57]

Qua Benjamin, Fanonian revolutionary violence is a colonial law-destroying violence, which aims to found a new humanism. It is not merely a reactionary or instrumental violence, with its end goal as mere substitution of one species by another, one state power by another. If that were the case then it would simply be a mimicry of the mythical violence of the colonial state. Fanon provides a visceral account of the lawmaking mythical violence of the colonial state, how it establishes and preserves the supremacy of the colonial law by means of absolute violence inflicted on the colonized subjects by the agents of Empire. Moreover, while Fanon does acknowledge that decolonization is also an act of lawmaking mythic violence that results in the birth of the nation-state, national identity, and national reawakening, restoring the nation to the people, his book provides a stern warning against the "pitfalls of national consciousness," squarely blaming the apathetic and the cowardly nationalist bourgeoisie for a regression to tribalism in the newly independent states:

> Instead of being the coordinated crystallization of the people's innermost aspirations, instead of being the most tangible, immediate product of popular mobilization, national consciousness is nothing but a crude, empty, fragile shell. The cracks in it explain how easy it is for young independent countries to switch back from nation to ethnic group and from state to tribe.[58]

Due to this failure of the nationalist bourgeoisie in the postcolonial nation-states, national consciousness is often substituted for ultranationalism, chauvinism, and racism.[59] In the newly minted nation-states, the colonizer is replaced by the national elite, who reinstitute the lawmaking mythic violence of the colonial state. Hence for Fanon only the peasantry is revolutionary, for "it has nothing to lose and everything to gain."[60] While the nationalist bourgeoisie, in their pursuit of power, shun the "pure" violence of the peasantry, often employing the discourse of non-violence, the rural and starving peasant knows that only through revolutionary violence can they engender justice by destroying the lawmaking mythical violence of the colonial state. Fanonian revolutionary violence is a call for justice, whose principle is the total destruction of the colonial law and state power. Fanon says at the outset of the book that he is not interested in simply recounting the lawmaking agenda of decolonization, but elucidating the justice making potential of decolonization:

> We could go on to portray the rise of a new nation, the establishment of a new state, its diplomatic relations and its economic and political orientation. But instead we have decided to describe the kind of tabula rasa which from the outset defines any decolonization.[61]

Fanon understands decolonization at the outset as a *tabula rasa*, a clean slate, an event outside and beyond law, a colonial law-destroying process, opening the possibility for justice. Fanon's ethical injunction to his readers in the conclusive sentence of *The Wretched* is to start anew, with a clean slate, a space outside and beyond the mythical violence of colonial law, a locus beyond the European episteme, which opens the possibility for justice, whence a new disalienated human can emerge and a new humanism can be founded.

Fanon's Theory of Decolonization and the Arrival of a New Humanity

Fanon theorizes decolonization as a profoundly revolutionary event, an act of total destruction of the colonial law and state power, and its attendant humanization ideology of *mission civilisatrice*, by virtue of "pure" violence. Fanon's *The Wretched*, as he announces at the outset, divulges the messianic revolutionary *potentia* of decolonization, actualized by means of colonial law-destroying "pure" violence that founds a new humanism. A new human can only emerge when the Third World "leave[s] this Europe behind," forsakes the spirit of Europe, relinquishes imitation of Europe, and abandons recreation of a third Europe. He declares that the European game is over.[62]

Despite Fanon's theorization of the revolutionary praxis of decolonization and its corollary, new humanism, intense debates have been waged in the last 40 years in the field of Postcolonial Studies over the nature and character of Fanonian new humanism, its residual or emergent character, as discussed above. This debate about Fanonian humanism is concomitantly a dispute over his theorization of decolonization. In essence, a new humanism is a consequence of decolonization. Thus, the questions that have been raised are: Is decolonization for Fanon a reformative process or genuinely a revolutionary process? Is Fanonian new humanism merely a remedial form of European humanism or truly a radical new humanism? As detailed above the debate over Fanonian humanism hinges upon his relationship with Europe, whether he is tethered or untethered to Europe. My contention is that Fanon's relationship to Europe remains deeply agonistic. Throughout his intellectual history, the *évolué* Antillean Fanon waged an internal and intellectual battle with Europe without resolution. Far from being securely on either side of the factious Fanonisms, the residual or the emergent, he remains tormented by the ontological pull between being "almost the same but not quite" French man and the black Antillean tearing off his white mask, and by the intellectual conundrum of being both a revolutionary thinker and a Europeanist one. Fanon's intellectual battle with Europe is nowhere more evident than in his theorization of decolonization in *The Wretched*. Despite the revolutionary *potentia* of decolonization that appeals for justice outside the loci of European colonial law and its humanist episteme, Fanon never fully abandons Europeanist humanist assumptions in his theorization of decolonization as a project of *Bildung* that develops and advances the national consciousness (as opposed to nationalism) of the nation-people, which is necessary for the founding of a new humanism. I demonstrate below that Fanon theorizes decolonization as constituting antipodean operations of destroying one humanism and founding another, engendering a "humanism without humanism," except that the former provides the frame of reference for the latter's emergence.

Deepa Jani

For Fanon, decolonization, on the one hand, signals the categorical rejection of European Enlightenment values by the colonized. The colonial law and state power was founded on the abstract, essentialist, and universal principles of European Enlightenment humanism that provided the moral basis and justification for the mythical violence of the colonial state. Fanon asserts that Western bourgeoisie, and their native counterparts, strategically deploy liberal humanist ideology and democratic principles to found and preserve colonial law and state power:

> When it [bourgeoisie] is strong, when it organizes the world on the basis of its power, a bourgeoisie does not hesitate to maintain a pretense of universal democratic ideas [...] Although fundamentally racist, the Western bourgeoisie generally manages to mask this racism by multiplying the nuances, thereby enabling it to maintain intact its discourse on human dignity in all its magnanimity.[63]

Here Fanon echoes his mentor Aimé Césaire who condemns the false humanism of the West that often successfully camouflages its racist world view in rights-based discourse:

> And that is the great thing I hold against pseudo-humanism: that for too long it has diminished the rights of man, that its concept of those rights has been—and still is—narrow and fragmentary, incomplete and biased and, all things considered sordidly racist.[64]

During decolonization the colonialist bourgeoisie form alliances with the native bourgeoisie to wage an ideological war with the colonized masses, sustaining the hegemony of the Eurocentric humanist episteme by warning the masses of a return to barbarism when the sun sets on Empire. The nationalist bourgeoisie engage in

> philosophic-political discourses on the subject of the rights of peoples to self-determination, the human rights of dignity [...] The nationalist political parties never insist on the need for confrontation precisely because their aim is not the radical overthrow of the system [...] They are violent in their words and reformist in their attitudes.[65]

Conversely, the colonized subject, during the struggle for decolonization, rejects the hegemony of the Eurocentric humanist discursive regime, rebuffing the discourse on the rights and dignity of man, on individuality, on rationality, on equality, and on the abstract universal. For Fanon, the liberation struggle is not a struggle for the "recognition of the inherent dignity and of the equal and inalienable rights" of the colonized, as the preamble would have it: "Challenging the colonial world is not a rational confrontation of viewpoints. It is not a discourse on the universal."[66] The colonized subject does not seek equal rights before the law with the colonizer, but a total destruction of the colonial law and its regime of rights. Justice cannot be achieved by mean of colonial law but through revolutionary violence that opens the possibility for justice beyond colonial law. Decolonization is a revolutionary process of species substitution, not an enlightened discourse on egalitarianism. Its agenda is total disorder, not replacing one master with another while maintaining the colonial law and state power. The colonized do not seek dignity, that is, an abstract universal human nature:

> For a colonized people, the most essential value, because it is the most meaningful, is first and foremost the land: the land, which must provide bread and, naturally, dignity. But this dignity has nothing to do with 'human' dignity. The colonized subject has never heard of such an ideal.[67]

For the colonized subjects, their dignity is derived not from an abstract universal value we all inherently possess and collectively participate in, for which the colonized subjects seek recognition

Postcoloniality and New Humanism

from their masters, but their dignity is acquired through their concrete hard labor of working the soil. The colonized people also have no utility for the liberal discourse on individuality and individualism, which understands the individual as a universal "free-standing self-determining person," an idea identified by Davies as a key Western invention that precipitated the revolution of modernity in Europe rather than in Asia or Africa.[68] While the colonized elite, the mimic men, seeking assimilation into the Eurocentric humanist episteme transform themselves into "petty individualists" locked in their subjectivities, the colonized subjects discover their strength and identity in the collective power of the people. During the liberation struggle

> personal interests are now the collective interest because in reality everyone will be discovered by the French legionnaires and consequently massacred or else *everyone* will be saved. In such a context, the 'every man for himself' concept, the atheist's form of salvation, is prohibited.[69]

Fanon's revolutionary praxis of decolonization takes place outside the Western humanist episteme; it seeks justice, not law, equality, rights, dignity, individuality, and recognition. Fanon rejects theorization of decolonization and the colonized subject from within the discourse of the "philosophy of man" or human rights. Decolonization for Fanon is a process of expulsion of Enlightenment values with the agenda of starting anew, with a clean slate, a tabula rasa. A new humanism emerges from this lacuna.

While, on the one hand, Fanon theorizes decolonization as an event that radically breaks with the configurations of Eurocentric humanism, his theorization of decolonization as engendering a national consciousness and a nation-people, a new humanity, by way of a process of *Bildung*, still presumes a Western humanist frame of reference. If colonialism violently produced a non-dialectical compartmentalized Manichean world, then for Fanon the liberation struggle, in its primary phase before the arrival of the nation, mobilizes the masses to a collective subjectivity, leading them toward a consciousness of themselves: "When it is achieved during a war of liberation the mobilization of the masses introduces the notion of common cause, national identity, and collective history into every consciousness."[70] In opposition to the petty individualism of the national bourgeoisie, national consciousness helps the people mature to a collective consciousness, that is, a consciousness of their freedom and realization of that freedom in the nation. When a people attain a collective self-realization, it leads to unification and detribalization of the nation.[71] Fanon asserts that when a nation is born "of the concerted action of the people, which embodies the actual aspirations of the people and transforms the state," it is dependent upon "inventive cultural manifestations for its existence."[72] Culture is the highest expression of national consciousness, facilitating the self-actualization of the people. Fanon states that national consciousness, which is not nationalism, is a necessary stage which can help the people achieve an international dimension.[73]

For Fanon, the relationship between nation, nationalism, and national consciousness is a complicated one. National consciousness that emerges during the process of decolonization before the arrival of the nation, concomitantly provides the conditions for the nation's arrival, and evolves into the nation form. Nationalism is the ideology of the nationalist bourgeoisie, derivative of European Enlightenment ideology, which often suppresses the arrival of the nation. Worse yet, when nation-states fail, nationalism transforms to chauvinism and tribalism. The political education of the masses can raise awareness leading the people to evolve, replacing "an overall undifferentiated nationalism with a social and economic consciousness."[74] Fanon contends, "If nationalism is not explained, enriched, and deepened, if it does not very quickly turn into a social and political consciousness, into humanism, then it leads to a dead end."[75] For Fanon national consciousness, born of the liberation struggle, is a necessary stage for the emergence of a new humanism; he warns that this stage cannot be circumvented, for only with the arrival of the nation can a people achieve a new humanity.

Fanon theorizes the development of national consciousness and the arrival of the nation in the context of postcoloniality as a process of *Bildung*, an evolutionary and teleological process of emancipatory self-formation and self-realization of the monadic subject, the people. The political mobilization and education of the masses, who are already embodied with the *potentia* for revolutionary violence, can raise awareness and advance their consciousness, leading to their self-actualization in the nation form. Fanon's theorization of national consciousness understands the people as a continuous and unitary subject, whose consciousness is developed in the liberation struggle. Fanon rehearses Enlightenment theories of nationalism, which Terry Eagleton reminds us understands the people "on the model of the autonomous human personality":

> The metaphysics of nationalism speak of the entry into full self-realization of a unitary subject known as the people. As will all such philosophies of the subject from Hegel to the present, this monadic subject must somehow curiously preexist its own process of materialization.[76]

He further notes that the metaphysics of nationalism assumes "a subject somehow intuitively present to itself."[77] The monadic subject, the people, progress to the nation form by attaining self-actualization by means of violence and political education. The development of national consciousness advancing to the emergence of the nation-people Fanon understands as a process of *Bildung*, a developmental, teleological, and reconciliatory process of emancipatory and ideological self-formation of the unitary subject, the people. Fanon deploys the logic of development and dialectics to characterize the historical advancement of the consciousness of the people to a higher stage of consciousness: "The insurrection proves to itself its rationality and demonstrates its maturity every time it uses a specific case to advance the consciousness of the people"; "The political education of the masses is meant to make adults out of them, not to make them infantile":

> If this act is true [building of nation], i.e., if it expresses the manifest will of the people, if it reflects the restlessness of the African peoples, then it will necessarily lead to the discovery and advancement of universalizing values [...] It is at the heart of national consciousness that international consciousness establishes itself and thrives.[78]

The Wretched is an account of the process of *Bildung* of the monadic subject, the postcolonial people, who are cast in the light of derivative Enlightenment discourse on nationalism that models the *volk* on autonomous human personality. For Fanon the decolonizing process of *Bildung* of a nation-people can bring about a new humanism. Culture plays an important role in advancing the spirit of the *volk*. Recovering radical postcolonial nationalism through his reading of Third World *Bildungsromane*, Pheng Cheah argues that novels of decolonizing nationalism staged *Bildung* of the nation-people, often represented as a "living organism," as a remedy for the suffering of colonialism, as a

> concerted effort at reaching out to the colonized masses, educating and raising their awareness so that they might rationally organize themselves into a people who can overcome the distance between itself and the colonial state and appropriate this foreign prosthesis to form a united whole.[79]

Fanon similarly understands the historical advancement of consciousness of the postcolonial people as a process of *Bildung* that leads to the unification of the nation-people, a necessary remedy to the Manichean configurations of colonialism. *The Wretched* stages the progressive and reconciliatory journey of the *Bildungsheld*, the monadic subject, the people, from the particular to the universal, starting from the individual self before merging into the collective life of the nation-people. The journey from the particular to the universal, from the individual to the nation and the world, is described by Fanon as a decolonizing process of *Bildung*: "Since individual experience is national, since it is a link in the national chain, it ceases to be individual, narrow and limited in scope, and can lead to the truth of the nation and the world."[80] Fanon's theorization of decolonization emphasizes the importance of advancing the people's consciousness from the national to the international dimension for the emergence of a new humanity.

According to Cheah, Fanon's theorization of national consciousness envisions a radical postcolonial nationalism, which like Amilcar Cabral, recognizes culture as "the most cogent example of freedom's self-actualization and our capacity to transcend finitude."[81] Here Cheah echoes Lazarus' corrective to postcolonial readings of Fanon as an anti-nationalist and anti-humanist precursive postmodernist (Bhabha). As discussed above, Lazarus asserts that Fanon never abandons grand narratives of nationalism and humanism, reading his theorization of national consciousness as a radical and an alternative form of nationalism that affords him a genuine postcolonial strategy for liberation. Cheah also reads the varied theoretical and literary conceptions of postcolonial nationalism as radical, including Fanon's, stating that postcolonial nationalism is not derivative of the European model.[82] Ironically enough, Cheah's own conceptualization of radical postcolonial nationalism as a process of *Bildung* is Hegelian, derivative of European discourse:

> My conceptualization of radical postcolonial nationalism as a process of *Bildung* echoes Hegel's characterization of the state as a spiritual individual and his extended analogy between the *Bildung* of universal spirit and the development of an individual person to maturity and meaningful membership in collective life.[83]

Borrowing from Hegel, Cheah models his conceptualization of the radical postcolonial nation on the mythological model of autonomous human personality, an assumption that remains unexamined in his work. While Cheah reads Fanon's nationalism as *not* derivative of European discourse, I contend that Fanon's theorization of national consciousness as a process of *Bildung* of the monadic subject the people *is* derivative of European Enlightenment humanist discourses, rehearsing the mythology of bourgeois individualism, autonomy, human essence, development, progress, reason, and the universal. Franco Moretti reminds us that the process of *Bildung*, staged in the classical *Bildungsroman*, that genre of bourgeois subjectivity, is the journey of the individual's socialization and normalization into the bourgeois social order.[84] The traditional project of *Bildung*, the self-development of the individual, operates within the structures and ideologies of bourgeois capitalism. Thus, in that sense, Fanon's remedy to the disease of colonial Manichaeanism is highly derivative of modern European theories of nationalism. For Fanon the decolonizing project of *Bildung*, of nation building, can open the possibility for a new humanity, that will replace the old one.

Fanon's theorization of decolonization, on the one hand, envisions a radical break with the Eurocentric humanist episteme, while, on the other hand, it imagines the advancement of the consciousness of a nation-people as a process of *Bildung*, rehearsing the European liberal humanist narrative of bourgeois individual self-development and self-realization leading to a higher stage of consciousness. Fanon theorizes decolonization as a process of the end of Western humanism and a beginning of a new humanism, a humanism without humanism, albeit the former furnishes the discursive framework for the latter's arrival. Fanon turns to European discursive models to fashion a remedy for the disease of colonialism. *The Wretched*, as I have demonstrated above, propounds decolonization as an antipodean process, a humanism without humanism. For the last 40 years postcolonial scholars have debated over the character and nature of Fanon's new humanism, its residual or emergent character. The corollary to this debate on Fanon's humanism are questions about his theory of decolonization, its revolutionary potential or reformist agenda. The factious forms of Fanonism generated by the debate see Fanon's new humanism as either residual, a postcolonial avatar of European humanism, or emergent, a radical break with the prodigious humanist theses postulated by the West. The former camp understands Fanon's theory of decolonization as reformist, while the latter camp notes its revolutionary character.

My argument is that Fanon's new humanism is neither residual nor emergent; it is irreducible to either camp. Fanon's theory of decolonization is profoundly revolutionary as well as thoroughly Europeanist. His ambivalence toward Europe is both intellectual and internal. Fanon's theoretical solution to the malady of colonialism, humanism without humanism, remains aporetic and without resolution. One can rephrase his position in a Saidean vocabulary; Fanon is *critical of humanism in the name of humanism*. Said's new humanism, propounded in his last book wherein he asks us to be critical of humanism in the name of humanism, a position that has greatly baffled scholars, is Fanonian. He is Fanon's protégé. Elsewhere I have elaborated on Said's aporetic humanism, what I have called "anti-humanistic humanism." In an essay on Chinua Achebe, I argue that Achebe's Saidean brand of text-and-language bound literary humanism engenders an impassable paradox, "anti-humanistic humanism."[85] Fanon has greatly influenced theoretical and literary conceptions of humanism within the field of Postcolonial Studies. The ambivalence that we witness toward the legacy of humanism within the field, the pronouncements of death of humanism and beginning of a new one, a humanism without humanism, especially among card-carrying humanists (Said, Achebe et al.), I contend here have their historical origins in the works of Fanon.

Fanon's theorization of the antonymous tendencies of decolonization has shaped much of the subsequent conceptualizations and discussions on the legacy of humanism in Postcolonial Studies. It has deeply divided the field over his so-called residual or emergent humanism. It is my contention that despite the differences in their respective positions, both camps harbor a deep-seated desire to see Fanon as a deliverer of a new humanity, a postcolonial messiah. The residual camp agonizes over a Fanon who could have delivered a new human (Bhabha) or is persuaded by a Fanon who can deliver a new human despite his derivative discourse (Lazarus), while the emergent camp expectantly awaits the arrival of a new human regardless of their Fanon's struggles with Europe (Alessandrini). Contemplating such expectations, the messiah, *qui n'est pas arrivé*, says:

> Why am I writing this book? Nobody asked me to. Especially not those for whom it is intended. So? So in all serenity my answer is that there are too many idiots on this earth. And now that I've said it, I have to prove it.
> Striving for a New Humanism.[86]

Bibliography

Ahluwalia, Pal. *Out of Africa: Post-Structuralism's Colonial Roots*. New York: Routledge, 2010.

Alessandrini, Anthony. *Frantz Fanon and the Future of Cultural Politics: Finding Something Different*. New York: Lexington Books, 2014.

Alessandrini, Anthony. "The Humanism Effect: Fanon, Foucault, and Ethics without Subjects," *Foucault Studies*, no. 7 (September 2009): 64–80.

Arendt, Hannah. *On Violence*. New York: Harcourt Brace Jovanovich Publishers, 1970.

Benjamin, Walter. "The Critique of Violence," in *Reflections: Essays, Aphorisms, Autobiographical Writings*, trans. Edmund Jephcott. New York: Schocken Books, 1986, 277–300.

Bhabha, Homi. Foreword to *The Wretched of the Earth*, by Frantz Fanon, trans. Richard Philcox. New York: Grove Press, 2004.

Bhabha, Homi. *The Location of Culture*. New York: Routledge, 1994.

Césaire, Aimé. *Discourse on Colonialism*, trans. Joan Pinkham. New York: Monthly Review Press, 2000.

Cheah, Pheng. *Spectral Nationality: Passages of Freedom from Kant to Postcolonial Literatures of Liberation*. New York: Columbia University Press, 2003.

Clifford, James. Review of *Orientalism*, by Edward W. Said, *History and Theory*, vol. 19, no. 2 (1980): 204–23.

Davies, Tony. *Humanism*. New York: Routledge, 1997.

Terry Eagleton, "Nationalism: Irony and Commitment," in *Nationalism, Colonialism, Literature*, ed. Terry Eagleton, Fredric Jameson, Edward Said. Minnesota: University of Minnesota Press, 1990, 23–40.

Fanon, Frantz. *A Dying Colonialism*, trans. Haakon Chevalier. New York: Grove Press, 1994.

Fanon, Frantz. *Black Skin, White Masks*, trans. Richard Philcox. New York: Grove Press, 2008.

Fanon, Frantz. *The Wretched of the Earth*, trans. Richard Philcox. New York: Grove Press, 2004.

Gates, Jr., Henry Louis. "Critical Fanonism," *Critical Inquiry*, vol. 17, no. 3 (Spring 1991): 457–70.

Jani, Deepa. "Chinua Achebe's *Things Fall Apart*: Literary Humanism and the Question of Human Dignity," *Research in African Literatures*, vol. 52 no. 2, forthcoming.

Kumar, Malreddy Pavan. "(An)other Way of Being Human: 'indigenous' alternative(s) to postcolonial humanism," *Third World Quarterly*, vol. 32, no. 9 (2011): 1557–72.

Lazarus, Neil. "Disavowing Decolonization: Fanon, Nationalism, and the Problematic of Representation in Current Theories of Colonial Discourse," *Research in African Literatures*, vol. 24, no. 4 (1993): 69–98.

Moretti, Franco. *The Way of the World: The Bildungsroman in European Culture*. New York: Verso, 2000.

Said, Edward. *Humanism and Democratic Criticism*. New York: Columbia University Press, 2004.

Said, Edward. *Orientalism*. New York: Vintage Books, 1979.

Sartre, Jean-Paul. Preface to *The Wretched of the Earth*, by Frantz Fanon, trans. Richard Philcox. New York: Grove Press, 2004.

Spivak, Gayatri. *In Other Worlds: Essays in Cultural Politics*. New York: Routledge, 2006.

Williams, Raymond. *Marxism and Literature*. Oxford: Oxford University Press, 1977.

Young, Robert J. C. *Postcolonialism: An Historical Introduction*. Oxford: Wiley-Blackwell, 2001.

Young, Robert J. C. *White Mythologies: Writing History and the West*. New York: Routledge, 1990.

Notes

1 Frantz Fanon, *The Wretched of the Earth*, trans. Richard Philcox (New York: Grove Press, 2004).

2 Gayatri Spivak, *In Other Worlds: Essays in Cultural Politics* (New York: Routledge, 2006), 277.

3 Edward Said, *Humanism and Democratic Criticism* (New York: Columbia University Press, 2004), 10–11.

4 Fanon, *The Wretched of the Earth*, 239.

5 Ibid., 239.

6 Anthony Alessandrini, "The Humanism Effect: Fanon, Foucault, and Ethics without Subjects," *Foucault Studies*, no. 7 (September 2009): 72.

7 Fanon, *The Wretched of the Earth*, 2.

8 Ibid., 2

9 Ibid., 235–6.

10 Ibid., 238.

11 Ibid., 236.

12 Ibid., 3.

13 Frantz Fanon, *A Dying Colonialism*, trans. Haakon Chevalier (New York: Grove Press, 1994), 32.

14 Edward Said, *Orientalism* (New York: Vintage Books, 1979).

15 Robert J. C. Young, *White Mythologies: Writing History and the West* (New York: Routledge, 1990), 19.

16 Raymond Williams, *Marxism and Literature* (Oxford: Oxford University Press, 1977), 122.

17 Ibid., 123.

18 Tony Davies, *Humanism* (New York: Routledge, 1997), 3.

19 James Clifford, review of *Orientalism*, by Edward W. Said, *History and Theory*, vol. 19, no. 2 (1980): 204–23.

20 Said, *Orientalism*, 339.

21 Homi Bhabha, *The Location of Culture* (New York: Routledge, 1994).

22 Ibid., 61.

23 Ibid., 61, 41.

24 Neil Lazarus, "Disavowing Decolonization: Fanon, Nationalism, and the Problematic of Representation in Current Theories of Colonial Discourse," *Research in African Literatures*, vol. 24, no. 4 (1993): 89.

25 Ibid., 93.

26 Ibid., 93.

27 Pal Ahluwalia, *Out of Africa: Post-Structuralism's Colonial Roots* (New York: Routledge, 2010), 62.

28 Robert J. C. Young, *Postcolonialism: An Historical Introduction* (Oxford: Wiley-Blackwell, 2001) 271.

29 Malreddy Pavan Kumar, "(An)other Way of Being Human: 'indigenous' alternative(s) to postcolonial humanism," *Third World Quarterly*, vol. 32, no. 9 (2011): 1559.

30 Anthony Alessandrini, *Frantz Fanon and the Future of Cultural Politics: Finding Something Different* (New York: Lexington Books, 2014) 57.

31 Ibid., 63.

32 Ibid., 73.

33 Alessandrini, "The Humanism Effect," 66.

34 Henry Louis Gates, Jr., "Critical Fanonism," *Critical Inquiry*, vol. 17, no. 3 (Spring 1991): 458.

35 Young, *Postcolonialism*, 276.

36 Ibid., 276.

37 Frantz Fanon, *Black Skin, White Masks*, trans. Richard Philcox (New York: Grove Press, 2008), 21.

38 Gates, "Critical Fanonism," 470.

39 Fanon, *Black Skin, White Masks*, 161.

40 Ibid., xii.

41 Ibid., xv.

42 Young, *Postcolonialism*, 271.

43 Fanon, *The Wretched of the Earth*, 1.

44 Ibid., 2.

45 Ibid., 50.

46 Ibid., 46.

47 Jean-Paul Sartre, preface to *The Wretched of the Earth*, by Frantz Fanon, trans. Richard Philcox (New York: Grove Press, 2004), l.

48 Ibid., lviii.

49 Fanon, *The Wretched of the Earth*, 10.

50 Hannah Arendt, *On Violence* (New York: Harcourt Brace Jovanovich Publishers, 1970), 12.

51 Ibid., 69.

52 Homi Bhabha, foreword to *The Wretched of the Earth*, by Frantz Fanon, trans. Richard Philcox (New York: Grove Press, 2004), xxxv.

53 Ibid., xxxvi.

54 Fanon, *The Wretched of the Earth*, 2.

55 Fanon, *A Dying Colonialism*, 32.

56 Walter Benjamin, "The Critique of Violence," in *Reflections: Essays, Aphorisms, Autobiographical Writings*, trans. Edmund Jephcott (New York: Schocken Books, 1986), 297.

57 Ibid., 300.

58 Fanon, *The Wretched of the Earth*, 97.

59 Ibid., 103.

60 Ibid., 23.

61 Ibid., 1.

62 Ibid., 235–9.

63 Ibid., 109.

64 Aimé Césaire, *Discourse on Colonialism*, trans. Joan Pinkham (New York: Monthly Review Press, 2000), 37.

65 Fanon, *The Wretched of the Earth*, 21–2.

66 Ibid., 6.

67 Ibid., 9.

68 Davies, *Humanism*, 15–17.

69 Fanon, *The Wretched of the Earth*, 11–2.

70 Ibid., 51.

71 Ibid., 141.

72 Ibid., 179.

73 Ibid., 179.

74 Ibid., 93.

75 Ibid., 144.

76 Terry Eagleton, "Nationalism: Irony and Commitment," in *Nationalism, Colonialism, Literature*, ed. Terry Eagleton, Fredric Jameson, Edward Said (Minnesota: University of Minnesota Press, 1990), 28.

77 Ibid., 29.

78 Fanon, *The Wretched of the Earth*, 95, 124, 180.

Postcoloniality and New Humanism

79 Pheng Cheah, *Spectral Nationality: Passages of Freedom from Kant to Postcolonial Literatures of Liberation* (New York: Columbia University Press, 2003), 239.

80 Fanon, *The Wretched of the Earth*, 140–1.

81 Cheah, *Spectral Nationality*, 237.

82 Ibid., 6.

83 Ibid., 237.

84 Franco Moretti, *The Way of the World: The Bildungsroman in European Culture* (New York: Verso, 2000), viii–ix.

85 Deepa Jani, "Chinua Achebe's *Things Fall Apart*: Literary Humanism and the Question of Human Dignity," *Research in African Literatures*, vol. 52 no. 2, forthcoming.

86 Fanon, *Black Skin, White Masks*, xi.

3

Edward Said and Humanism

Masoud Farahmandfar

Edward Wadie Said had a global impact in many fields of the humanities. The book he is best remembered by is doubtless the 1978 volume *Orientalism*, which influenced the fields of anthropology, sociology, and literary studies. Edward Said, a Palestinian-American, was a professor at Columbia University's School of Comparative Literature in New York before his death. He was a pro-Palestinian scholar, critic, intellectual, and political activist who was born in British-ruled Jerusalem on November 1, 1935, and died of leukemia on September 25, 2003, in the United States.

Said laid the foundations of postcolonial theory by writing the trail-blazing *Orientalism*, which was a deconstruction of Orientalist discursive knowledge; the theory was later developed by thinkers such as Homi Bhabha (1949–) and Gayatri Spivak (1942–). The hybrid position of Said, as a Christian Arab Palestinian living in the United States, placed him in a liminal and in-between position, which, as Homi Bhabha's later described it, was a position of power for him because it enabled a re-evaluation of the presuppositions of colonial identity, and this re-evaluation led to the dismantling and displacement of all bases of domination and discrimination. That is perhaps why Said's work engages with writers like Joseph Conrad and Jonathan Swift, and thinkers such as Adorno and Auerbach, because they too have been in exile, and lived in-between cultures and nations. Swift and Conrad's writings also reveal a sense of being "out of place." In fact, it is this awareness of the "unhomeliness" that causes the likes of Conrad, Swift, Auerbach, Adorno, and Said to turn to literature and, in general, to writing, because it becomes "a place for living." Edward Said was the embodiment of a humanist thinker who believed in the tradition of humanist literary criticism of Matthew Arnold and Frank Raymond Leavis, and at the same time sought to complement them and update them to answer the world's questions.

None of Said's works have been as admired by both the academic world and the public sphere as *Orientalism*. Here Said states that a set of misconceptions underlies the West's view of the East, and that there has been a persistent intellectual bias among Europeans and Americans against Arab Muslim peoples and other non-western cultures. Said argues that Orientalism has served as a tool for the continued dominance of imperialism. Said's most important argument in his theory of Orientalism is that Orientalist "texts" not only create "knowledge" of "reality," but also create the very reality they seem to describe. Over time, such knowledge and reality produce a tradition that then shapes all subsequent knowledge about the East. And this epistemological, invented tradition is tied to the structures of economic and political power.

DOI: 10.4324/9781003046004-5

Three years before the publication of *Orientalism*, Said published *The Beginnings: Intention and Method*, in which he outlined his line of work and thought. When Said entered academia in the 1960s and 1970s, new criticism, structuralism, and deconstruction, which are "textualist" approaches, dominated American literary criticism and theory, but Said opposed these merely textualist methods because he believed that "form" is always "contextual." That is, the cultural, political, and social context of the text should not be considered in isolation from the form. Said was in favor of the spatial turn in literary theory and warned against the disregard of history in literary studies. In *Humanism and Democratic Criticism*, he voiced his concern:

> This has effectively detoured the humanities from its rightful concern with the critical investigation of values, history, and freedom, turning it, it would seem, into a whole factory of word-spinning and insouciant specialties, many of them identity-based, that in their jargon and special pleading address only like-minded people, acolytes, and other academics [...] The humanities have become harmless as well as powerless to affect anyone or anything.[1]

Following Vico, Said sought to discover the text's affiliations with history and the world around him. He was opposed to mere textualism. Said aimed at exploring the interactions of space, representation, and cultural forms. Accordingly, a humanist is devoted to secular criticism, which is informed by the idea of what Said calls "worldliness."

Said believes that every intellectual should be equipped with the weapon of critical consciousness. Critical consciousness, for Said, is associated with the concept of "being-in-the-world" or "worldliness." In his view, every text happens in the world. He argues against purely formalist literary criticism and movements such as "art for art's sake," which argues that a literary text is important in itself, regardless of its historical, cultural, and political contexts. For Said, a literary critic who staunchly believes that a work is valid only by its own existence and must be separated from other aspects is a critic who does not have social awareness and therefore cannot have a significant impact on his society, because s/he will most likely unquestioningly follow the dominant discourse of power.

Said objects to "cloistral" scholarship, which has cut itself off from the world and its "affiliative relationships," simply because "new cultures, new societies, and emerging visions of social, political, and aesthetic order now lay claim to the humanist's attention."[2] A text is thus "a network of often colliding forces" and "in its actually *being* a text is a being in the *world*."[3] This idea of "worldliness" is expounded in Said's *The World, the Text, and the Critic*, which is a collection of essays. Similar to Lukács, who believed in the "essay" form as the poetry of the world of prose,[4] Said held the essay in high esteem for its bold power of intervention. In the aforementioned collection of essays, Said voiced his concern about the increasing textualism of literary theory that followed the principle of non-intervention which, for one thing, ignores history and "the historical process," which is the "central core of humanist" thinking:

> [e]ach essay in this book affirms the connection between texts and the existential actualities of human life, politics, societies, and events. The realities of power and authority—as well as the resistances offered by men, women, and social movements to institutions, authorities, and orthodoxies—are the realities that make texts possible, that deliver them to their readers, that solicit the attention of critics.[5]

What he thus calls secular criticism in this book is not synonymous with a retreat from the sociopolitical facts of the time. Instead, "most of the political and social world becomes available for critical and secular scrutiny."[6] This secular critical consciousness is characteristic of a humanist.

Humanism

The root of the word *humanism* is *humanitas*, a Latin term that itself has roots in the Greek terms φιλανθρωπία (*philanthropia*) and φιλάνθρωπος, each of which revolves around the notion of love for/of human beings. In classical Athens, teachings based on human values (e.g., philosophy, art, science, etc.) formed the core concepts of governance and civic engagement that were held in high esteem. Protagoras and other philosophers advocated the idea that the human being was the measure of all things,[7] and Sophocles wrote that "Many things are wonderful, but nothing more wonderful and awesome than man" [πολλὰ τὰ δεινὰ κοὐδὲν ἀνθρώπου δεινότερον πέλει].[8] However, after Greece lost its independence and power was transferred to Rome, humanism, that is, humanist teachings (it was not yet a term; those teachings that relied on man were then called *paideia* [παιδεία] in Greece), resurfaced in Rome. However, there was rather less emphasis on freedom and democracy in the newly established Roman Empire of Augustus than there had once been in Periclean Athens[9]—and in the even less democratic decades following the end of Augustus' reign, Christianity emerged.

With the advent of Christianity, every definition of man and the world was tied to God and the Divine, all came into the realm of Christianity, and little by little Christianity became the dominant discourse, both in the domains of belief, and in the realms of science. The Church claimed to be the sole preserver of divine truth on earth while insisting that science and philosophy were in the service of Christian theology, and so education was monopolized by the monastery.[10] As a result, individual independence in both material life and non-material life (education, thought and research) was denied the priority of place it had once possessed. Man became imperfect, weak, and sinful by nature, and doomed to the eternal humiliation he inherited from his father, Adam.[11]

In the post-Augustine Middle Ages, Man found himself caught in a struggle between the two cities of Satan and God,[12] and this polar conflict sometimes manifested itself as a struggle between the two schools of morality, natural and divine, sometimes as a conflict between reason and heaven, between physical and mental beauty, the mortal and the eternal, and finally in the conflict between worldly and ecclesiastical organizations, and believed that there was an inherent difference between the two sides of the conflict. The excessive pressure of the Church, and the forceful approach of its agents who considered themselves the guardians of the world order (condemning scientists and thinkers in the courts of inquisition while regarding scientific work as evil interference in the affairs of the world), among other factors, paved the way for the Renaissance, which was, in part, a cry of protest against some extreme currents of the Middle Ages.[13]

Desiderius Erasmus (1466–1536) was one of the pioneers of humanism who, in the face of the Church's monopoly, sought to reform religion even as the more radical Martin Luther (1483–1546) sought to deny the power of the Church as a mediator between man and God.[14] Man in the Middle Ages had become a passive being before the Church, but the Renaissance was the birth of a movement that sought to restore a sense of freedom and agency: Humanism.

Humanism, in its most-familiar historical sense, was a philosophical and literary movement that emerged in Italy in the second half of the fourteenth century and spread to other European countries. The aim of this cultural movement was to liberate the inner forces of man, according to the classical texts of ancient Greek and Roman culture, such as those written by Virgil and Homer. During and after the Renaissance, humanism was influenced by the ancient Greek (Hellenistic) view of man. In this view, human individuality is a spiritual position that carries an infinite value and dignity. Such views are recognizably part of the philosophical foundation of the Enlightenment. So when Kant advises, "human nature is capable of [...] an elevation above every motive that nature can oppose to it,"[15] he is contributing to a humanist ethics that has its roots in Renaissance (and earlier Greek) thought. It is called "humanist ethics" because for Kant, "it is not the case that we are first free and then, later, deign to adorn our freedom with moral obligations but, on the contrary, it is our moral commitments that make us free". Even in the ideas of Nietzsche, who is often considered an anti-humanist, the Übermensch is a person who is aware of the plight of man and is the builder of his own values. Nietzsche's objection is to "scandalously overmoralistic language with which practically all modern judgments about men and things are smeared."[16] To confuse humanism with ideology is an example of "the will turning against life."[17] Nietzsche then believes that man should start from the beginning and decide about good and evil. Overall, apart from the focus on human beings that forms the core of humanist thought, there are other components to this way of thinking, some of which are as follows:

1 Belief in reason, skepticism, and practical method as a means of discovering the truth and building a human society
2 Emphasis on reason and authority as the basic dimensions of human existence
3 Building a society based on autonomy and moral equality
4 Belief in an open and pluralistic society
5 Emphasis on democracy
6 Commitment to the principle of separation of religious institutions from the government.

Edward Said's Take on Humanism

In Iranian academia, Edward Said is considered a very respectable critic and a much-quoted intellectual. This is mostly because of his unwavering support for the Palestinian cause, his rejection of colonial and neo-colonial policies, and his occasional references to Iran and the importance of native culture in anti-imperialist decolonization in both *Orientalism* and *Culture and Imperialism*. Most of his works have been translated into Persian and have been the subject of academic research. However, his work on humanism has not received the attention it deserves in Iran. Perhaps this is because of misinterpretations of his main argument, or simply because of the fact that secular thinking is not very much welcome in the Islamic Republic.

In popular perception in Iran, *humanism* means giving the place of God to the human being, and it is thought that the concept drives religion out of formal public life. It is also said that humanists do not even accept personal religious beliefs. However, the multiple and varied meanings of the concept of humanism show that this is a common misconception and refers only to one reading of the concept. There are other readings as well—ones that do not necessarily take God out of the picture. And nowhere does Edward Said equate humanism with the denial of religion.

The first manifesto of humanism in the United States was presented in 1933, which, of course, was a form of religious humanism. The proclamation was written by the American Unitarian clergyman Raymond Bragg (1902–1979) and the Canadian philosopher Roy Sellers (1880–1973). Many American philosophers, thinkers, and intellectuals, such as John Dewey and some American monotheistic clerics, signed the manifesto. Therefore, humanism does not necessarily mean the denial of religion.[18]

Furthermore, if we think of humanism as a system of thought that inwardly rejects or reconstructs or reinterprets traditional religious teachings in such a way that they can be reconciled with reason, then in a sense it can be said that the classical tradition of Islamic philosophy (e.g., Avicenna) is humanistic. The word "humanism" has its roots in the Greek word *paideia* [παιδεία], which translates into German as *Bildung*, meaning upbringing, instruction, and education. And this is something that is approved in all religions, including Islam. Pope Francis, the spiritual leader of the world's Catholics, traveled to South America and the city of Rio de Janeiro in 2013 to speak in favor of "integral humanism" and "the culture of encounter and relationship."[19] This is what Edward Said is looking for in *Humanism and Democratic Criticism*:

not a "one-way interrogation" but "a sympathetic dialogue of two spirits across ages and cultures who are able to communicate with each other as friendly, respectful intelligences trying to understand each other from the other's perspective."[20] This is therefore the "crucial element of *human* intellectual power and will."[21]

In *Representations of the Intellectual*, Said enumerates certain characteristics for intellectuals, the most important of which is

> to confront orthodoxy and dogma (rather than to produce them), to be someone who cannot easily be co-opted by governments or corporations, and whose *raison d'etre* is to represent all those people and issues that are routinely forgotten or swept under the rug.[22]

The intellectual endorsed by Said is a person who can neither be easily predicted nor made to accept an unchangeable slogan, party policy, or dogma. In his view, the intellectual must be one who questions the privilege of patriotic nationalism, collective thinking, and class, racial, or sexual discrimination. In the world of literature, Said refers to "certain unusual nineteenth- and early-twentieth-century novels: Turgenev's *Fathers and Sons*, Flaubert's *Sentimental Education*, Joyce's *A Portrait of the Artist as a Young Man*."[23] In Turgenev's novel, Bazarov is a young nonconformist intellectual who acts what he believes and "What we remember of Bazarov is the sheer unremitting force of his quest and deeply confrontational intellect."[24] And in Joyce's *Portrait*, again a young thinking man, Stephen Dedalus, resists being forced into a clichéd role or routine:

> I will tell you what I will do and what I will not do. I will not serve that in which I no longer believe whether it call itself my home, my fatherland or my church: and I will try to express myself in some mode of life or art as freely as I can and as wholly as I can, using for my defence the only arms I allow myself to use—silence, exile, and cunning.[25]

Said believes that intellectuals should be amateurs (in the sense of the Latin *amator*, or lover of an object, action, or idea), just like Bazarov or Stephen Dedalus. This means their acts should be motivated by emotion and sorrow, not short-sighted profiteering and selfishness. The intellectual soul, as an amateur, can intervene in the monotony of the pure profession in which most of us are involved and transform it into something more vivid and fundamental. In this sense, a Saidian intellectual is a humanist. He puts man at the center of values, and firmly believes that everything starts from man and ends in man, and there is no truth higher than man.

For Edward Said, what is meant by humanism is two things: that man is a maker of his own history and he is able to expand this production and open it to renewed horizons, and that man's capabilities are much the same, without considering races, religions, and cultures, despite different contexts that support the goals of man in a specific environment. This perception prompted Said to reject Eurocentrism, and led him to defend human cultural pluralism.

The development of humanism could well benefit from a sense of connection with other cultures and societies. Humanism is inseparable from the world. Every field of human knowledge is connected with other fields, and nothing happens in this world that can remain separate and apart from foreign connections. And in fact, solutions to human oppression and suffering can only be found in a context that is more broadly embedded in history, culture, and socio-economic realities. An intellectual's role is to expand these areas of discussion. A more dangerous issue is that education today is threatened by the many nationalist and religious fundamentalisms that are spreading in the media. Media images can easily direct public opinion in times of crisis and insecurity, and if they fail to do their job impartially and with fairness (which often seems to be the case), the whole world will suffer. Said's *Covering Islam: How the*

Media and the Experts Determine How We See the Rest of the World offers good examples of such cultural stereotyping, and concludes:

> By using the skills of a good critical reader to disentangle sense from nonsense, by asking the right questions and expecting pertinent answers, anyone can learn about either "Islam" or the world of Islam and about the men, women, and cultures that live within it, speak its languages, breathe its air, produce its histories and societies. At that point, humanistic knowledge begins and communal responsibility for that knowledge begins to be shouldered. I wrote this book to advance that goal.[26]

Now we understand why Said looks for amateurs, because the so-called experts, instead of contemplation, critique, and rational thought (the principles based on the theory of secularism on which man has built history), "have tended to use their standing as experts to deny—and sometimes even to cover—their deep-seated [ideological] feelings."[27] And these ideological feelings are not exclusive to the Western domain of knowledge; the situation in some Arab countries is not better: As their governments are incapable of standing against the hegemonic prevalence of the West (and the United States in particular), they devote all their energy to suppressing and dominating their nations. Hence, anger and resentment are formed that do not allow these societies to open up. In these societies the theory of secular humanism is sometimes reduced to a superficial understanding due to failures of analysis and understanding, or the emergence of religious motives based on a kind of blind indoctrination and the disappearance of all modern and rival teachings. The idea behind the horrific conflicts and wars that have taken place has been to unite all nations under one flag and bring them to a false unity and a group identity for people who are very different from each other. This is not at all a goal of humanism. Moving away from the hypothetical clash of civilizations, we must focus on intertwined civilizations. Throughout history, civilizations have taken many things from each other and have coexisted long before our theories and hypotheses come into being. For Said, humanism, if not the last, is one of our most practical strongholds to confront the inhumane policies and oppressions that have corrupted the history of humanity.

It is important here to return to Said's notion of *worldliness*. For him, a text is not created in a vacuum but is woven into a time and place, a circumstance and a context. So, texts are always in the world, and hence worldly. And by virtue of that "worldliness itself the intellectual's social identity should involve something more than strengthening those aspects of the culture that require mere affirmation and orthodox compliancy from its members."[28] For Said, the humanist intellectual has the will and passion to speak truth to power and to resist ideological tampering.

Said equates humanism with criticism of the status quo. He says the essence of humanism, that is, its existential essence, consists only of human self-knowledge, in its broadest sense, derived from the totality of human races and ethnicities, and is merely a step toward the "self-flourishing" of all human beings.

Of course, Said avers that humanism has not always been humane, because at different points in time it signified only to European people. Some of the great thinkers of the Enlightenment, such as the English philosopher David Hume, distinguished between civilized Europeans, who are entitled to prosperity and happiness, and "those barbarians" who should be tamed. Said accepts that "humanism as an attitude or practice is often associated with very selective elites, be they religious, aristocratic, or educational";[29] therefore, he tries to redefine humanism in such a way as to take into account what it has suppressed or ignored throughout history.

In his "Introduction" to *Orientalism*, Said lucidly draws a line between pure and political knowledge, and accordingly between pure (secular, amateur) humanism and political humanism.

The latter, for example, has been helpful to the construction of Orientalist stereotypes which led to the binary opposition of us versus them: "This opposition was reinforced not only by anthropology, linguistics, and history but also, of course, by the Darwinian theses on survival and natural selection, and—no less decisive—by the rhetoric of high cultural humanism."[30] So if Said sets out to redefine humanism on the basis of secular resistance, it is because of the fact that even "in the best Orientalist work done—represented in the impressive careers of Massignon and Gibb himself—we will find elements in common with the best humanistic scholarship of the period."[31] Their starting point was a conscious or unconscious belief (backed by the Enlightenment doctrines) that there is an essential difference between the West and the East. On this account, Said's *Orientalism* or *Culture and Imperialism* were attempts to practice secular humanist criticism as he knew it; he clarified his idea when he talked about the revival of oppressed cultures, especially in the colonial framework.

Said then argues that in the act of redefining humanism, we cannot continue to only rely ourselves on Greek, Roman, and Hebrew cultures, but we need to include all cultures from all different races and ethnic groups. For example, in understanding Islam, one cannot employ a "Greek humanistic tradition";[32] otherwise, misconceptions will ensue. Also, for Said, it is absolutely absurd for an advocate of humanism today to unthinkingly accept the ideas of the classical European Enlightenment without criticism: in that way, these ideas would simply calcify into a "tradition" among other rejected traditions. Said's position in this regard is completely clear: He condemns any blind imitation and following of traditions.

Although preserving traditions is part of any national culture, rendering such traditions rigid and mummified is an expression of an "inhuman" tendency or an indication of unethical utilitarian perceptions, or a blatant crisis that pushes toward the "invention of traditions," which has become a common tendency. Humanism, however, should be a continuous path of self-knowledge and self-realization, in which all peoples participate, and human minds are shaped by human minds, not the "European mind" alone. That is why Said repudiates the professional humanism of Harold Bloom and his *Western Canon*, along with others who in Said's view hijacked the concept and colonized it in the West. Nonetheless, in his denial of this monolithic humanism, Said does not turn a blind eye to the genius and influence of much of Western literature. He argues that "Harold Bloom has become the popular spokesman of the most extreme kind of dismissive aestheticism calling itself canonical humanism."[33] Said goes on to say:

> In his incessant, grab-bag evocations of what he dismissively calls the school of resentment, Bloom includes everything said or written by the non-European, non-male; non-Anglo educated upstarts who don't happen to agree with his tiresome vatic trumpetings. Certainly one can accept, as I do, the existence of greater as well as lesser achievements in the arts, and even achievements that are entirely uninteresting (no one can like everything, after all): but I would never admit that something was humanistically, intrinsically uninteresting just because it was not one of ours or because it belonged to a different tradition or came from a different perspective and experience and was the result of different processes of work, as in Saul Bellow's appallingly condescending phrase, "show me the Zulu Proust." Bloom's opinions about the humanistic canon show an absence rather than an invigorating presence of mind.[34]

Said argues that Bloom's canonization of Western literature leads not to a dialogue of cultures but to a clash and conflict of cultures. He believes that ideology in any form could threaten the new order of humanism because it is contrary to the liberal spirit of humanity. Thus, a humanist cannot be an ideologist.

A humanist cannot take a definite position except in defense of humanity. He must feel close to all ideas and consider only human beings in acknowledging or rejecting opinions. Based on this perspective, Edward Said criticized American neo-conservative humanism of his time:

humanism is not a way of consolidating and affirming what 'we' have always known and felt, but rather a means of questioning, upsetting, and reformulating so much of what is presented to us as commodified, packaged, uncontroversial, and uncritically codified certainties.

This included, for example, the Western canon.[35] Humanism is to a large extent a movement to resist preconceptions, and it opposes all kinds of ready-made clichés. Far from being governed by, or predetermined by, economic and social conditions, humanism's deeper concern here is neither symmetry nor identification, but rather the dialectic of contradictions.

The opposition between inequitable humanism, which is exclusive and the secular, amateur humanism, which is inclusive is an "opposition [that] implies two different perspectives, two historiographies, one linear and subsuming, the other contrapuntal and often nomadic,"[36] and the latter is more relatable to historical reality. In *Culture and Imperialism*, Said rightfully reminds us that "all cultures are involved in one another; none is single and pure, all are hybrid, heterogenous, extraordinarily differentiated, and unmonolithic,"[37] and thus a humanist should be attentive to the hybridity of cultures and cultural products. Said argues in favor of self-criticism that may repair some of the deficiencies of exclusive, canonical humanism; Said calls for an openness to other cultures, as it is a source for better self-understanding.

Overall, the basis of knowledge is allowing the other within the self and opening up a dialogue; then, the other merges and disappears in the self. The continuity of relationships between individuals and cultures, in an environment that is constantly changing, requires constant *negotiation* of boundaries and perceptions of self and other.

Conclusion

Edward Said lived a lifetime of attachment to humanism, and even in the 1960s and 1970s, when critical theory and cultural studies were at their height and traditional humanism was under attack, he still believed that humanism offered valuable ideas for life. Self-awareness was its highest achievement, though he believed that self-awareness without self-criticism and trying to be open to other thoughts would be futile.

Said never really believed in the crisis of humanism, and he argued that the problems of humanism stemmed from a misunderstanding of its nature; some people mistakenly think that there is a constant opposition between tradition and the complexities of today's advanced world, and that humanism cannot offer solutions.

Said affirms that it is possible to criticize humanism in the name of the humanist idea, so he learns from the transgressions committed in the name of Eurocentrism and is able to formulate another type of humanism that is not exclusive. Saidian humanism follows the secular idea that the historical world is made by *all* men and women, not merely by white European men. This humanism is freed from any centralization, and is not an extension of neo-colonialism, its perspective, and its hierarchy. Said's insistence on *contrapuntal* reading underscores the multiplicity of voices and their interaction, without reducing them to a dominant voice; he was against cultural homogenization.

Accordingly, Said proposes "democratic criticism" as an alternative to the rigid criticism that is based on preconceived standards that are inseparable from both the old and the contemporary forms of Western supremacist thought. Democratic criticism introduces new standards and elements, and keeps the door open to new developments in the realm of literature and criticism. It mainly means placing criticism at the core of human thought, since criticism is a form of democratic freedom and is an ongoing exercise of accountability and the accumulation of knowledge that is open, not closed, on the historical facts. Said rejects the idea of exclusive walls. When Western standards line up alongside other standards presented by non-Western literary and cultural sites, we are truly heading toward democratic humanism, which produces fertile pluralism that is open to all points of view.

It is truer than ever to say that the new generation of humanist researchers is more in tune than all their predecessors with the decentralized, non-European, feminist, and postcolonial energies and currents, and the work of Edward Said remains at the forefront of these new developments in the ongoing story of humanism.

Bibliography

Davies, Tony. 1997. *Humanism*. New York: Routledge.

Dierksmeier, Claus et al. (Eds.) 2011. *Humanistic Ethics in the Age of Globality*. New York: Palgrave.

James, William. 1905. "The Essence of Humanism," *The Journal of Philosophy, Psychology and Scientific Methods* 2 (5): 113–118.

Jarrahi, Saeed. 2011. *Umanism dar Falsafe* [Humanism in Philosophy]. Tehran: Mafākher Publishers.

Joyce, James. 2000. *A Portrait of the Artist as a Young Man*. Ed. Jeri Johnson. Oxford: Oxford University Press.

Lukács, Georg. "On the Nature and Form of the Essay," in *Soul and Form*. Trans. Anna Bostock. Cambridge, MA: The MIT Press, 1974.

McGuire, Martin R. P. 1953. "Mediaeval Humanism," *The Catholic Historical Review* 38 (4): 397–409.

Nietzsche, Friedrich. 2007. *On the Genealogy of Morality*. Trans. Carol Diethe. Cambridge: Cambridge University Press.

Said, Edward W. 1979. *Orientalism*. New York: Vintage Books.

Said, Edward W. 1981. *Covering Islam: How the Media and the Experts Determine How We See the Rest of the World*. New York: Vintage Books.

Said, Edward W. 1983. *The World, the Text, and the Critic*. Cambridge, Massachusetts: Harvard University Press.

Said, Edward W. 1994. *Culture and Imperialism*. New York: Vintage Books.

Said, Edward W. 1996. *Representations of the Intellectual*. New York: Vintage Books.

Said, Edward W. 2004. *Humanism and Democratic Criticism*. New York: Columbia University Press.

Sophocles. 1912. *Sophocles. Vol 1: Oedipus the King. Oedipus at Colonus. Antigone*. The Loeb Classical Library, 20. Ed. Francis Storr. London; New York: William Heinemann Ltd.; The Macmillan Company.

Sophocles. 2009. *The Theban Plays: Oedipus the King, Oedipus at Colonus*, and *Antigone*. Trans. Ruth Fainlight and Robert J. Littman. Baltimore: The Johns Hopkins University Press.

Wetzel, James, ed. 2012. *Augustine's City of God: A Critical Guide*. Cambridge: Cambridge University Press.

Notes

1 Edward W. Said, *Humanism and Democratic Criticism* (New York: Columbia University Press, 2004), 14.

2 Edward W. Said. *The World, the Text, and the Critic* (Cambridge, MA: Harvard University Press, 1983), 21.

3 Ibid., 33.

4 Georg Lukács, "On the Nature and Form of the Essay," in *Soul and Form*. Trans. Anna Bostock (Cambridge, MA: The MIT Press, 1974).

5 Ibid., 5.

6 Ibid., 24.

7 Tony Davies. *Humanism* (New York: Routledge, 1997), 107.

8 Sophocles, *Antigone*, line 332. In Sophocles. *Sophocles. Vol 1: Oedipus the King. Oedipus at Colonus. Antigone*. The Loeb Classical Library, 20. Ed. Francis Storr (London; New York: William Heinemann Ltd.; The Macmillan Company, 1912).

9 See, for example, Augustus' attempts to regulate Roman morality and private relationships. The *Lex Iulia de Maritandis Ordinibus* of 18 BCE restricted marriage between the social classes, and the *Lex Iulia de Adulteriis Coercendis* of the same year made adultery punishable by banishment.

10 That is why the "early Humanists created the derogatory term, mediaeval, to designate the period from the close of antiquity to their own times as a dark and culturally inferior age" (Martin R. P. McGuire, "Mediaeval Humanism," *The Catholic Historical Review* 38 (4), 1953: 397).

11 See Saeed Jarrahi. *Umanism dar Falsafe* [Humanism in Philosophy]. Tehran: Mafākher Publishers, 2011; Martin R. P. McGuire, "Mediaeval Humanism," *The Catholic Historical Review* 38 (4), 1953: 397–409.

12 James Wetzel in *Augustine's City of God: A Critical Guide* (2012: 1) expands this idea as follows: "The more damning designations are reminders that the earthly city has its roots in hell, where fallen angels, having become demons, are doomed to reside. Members of the earthly city bind themselves through sin to a demonic love—a profound, soul-defining love, but a love so thoroughly perverted that it has become both impossible to satisfy and an endless source of suffering. Meanwhile, members of the heavenly city on earth, who through grace are being made fit company for angels, endure the purgation that rids their love of its demonic propensities."

13 Jarrahi, 2011.

14 Erasmus and Sir Thomas More (1478–1535) tried to reconcile the lore of the (pagan) past with Christian thought; in fact, "[h]umanism was founded on [this] ambition to recapture the legacy of classical literature." dreamed of the victory of humanism and in this way, he spared no effort and sometimes even criticized some prominent religious figures. In 1501, in a lecture on St. Augustine's *City of God*, More "takes the opportunity to criticize the saint's view on the corporeality of demons [...] Such an approach to religious authority is evidence of More's adherence to the critical standards of humanism" (Baker-Smith, Dominic, "Thomas More." *The Stanford Encyclopedia of Philosophy* [Winter 2019 Edition], Edward N. Zalta, ed.). https://plato.stanford.edu/archives/win2019/entries/thomas-more.

15 Dierksmeier et al., 85.

16 Friedrich Nietzsche. *On the Genealogy of Morality.* Trans. Carol Diethe (Cambridge: Cambridge University Press, 2007), 101.

17 Ibid., 17.

18 In "The Essence of Humanism" (1905), William James cogently says: "I myself read humanism theistically and pluralistically [...] Read thus, humanism is for me a religion susceptible of reasoned defense, though I am well aware how many minds there are to whom it can appeal religiously only when it has been monistically translated. Ethically the pluralistic form of it takes for me a stronger hold on reality than any other philosophy I know of" (114).

19 http://www.vatican.va/content/francesco/en/speeches/2013/july/documents/papa-francesco_20130727_gmg-classe-dirigente-rio.html; accessed on April 10, 2021.

20 Said. *Humanism and Democratic Criticism*, 92.

21 Ibid., 103.

22 Edward W. Said. *Representations of the Intellectual* (New York: Vintage Books, 1996), 11.

23 Ibid., 14.

24 Ibid., 15.

25 James Joyce. *A Portrait of the Artist as a Young Man.* Ed. Jeri Johnson (Oxford: Oxford University Press, 2000), 208.

26 Edward W. Said. 1981. *Covering Islam: How the Media and the Experts Determine How We See the Rest of the World* (New York: Vintage Books, 1981), 36.

27 Ibid., 57.

28 Said, *The World, the Text, and the Critic*, 24.

29 Said., *Humanism and Democratic Criticism*, 16.

30 Edward W. Said. *Orientalism* (New York: Vintage Books, 1979), 227.

31 Ibid., 258.

32 Ibid., 104.

33 Said, *Humanism and Democratic Criticism*, 27.

34 Ibid.

35 Ibid., 28.

36 Edward W. Said. *Culture and Imperialism* (New York: Vintage Books, 1994), xxv.

37 Ibid.

4

"A Different Kind of Humanism"

Edward Said's Césairian Critical Humanism

Sauleha Kamal

Perhaps the most divisive aspect of Edward Said's scholarship in postcolonial circles is his unshakable adherence to humanism. In the final years of his life, Edward Said dedicated his energies toward defending humanism, a system that had at the time of post-humanism, and, in the wake of the anti-humanism of the 1960s and 1970s, become a largely dormant issue.[1] As he underwent intense chemotherapy, he delivered a series of lectures on humanism at Cambridge and Columbia[2] and later developed these lectures into his final book, *Humanism and Democratic Criticism*, published posthumously in 2004. While Said had viewed himself as a humanist throughout his academic career, what is known as his late style was marked by a renewed insistence on academic humanism in the philological vein of Auerbach and Spitzer[3]—the tradition in which Said was originally trained. In this return, critics such as James Clifford read a contradiction owing to the dependence of his arguments on Foucauldian and other (anti-humanist) French theory.[4] But Said, who insisted that this engagement did not affect his own affiliation to the humanist tradition, explains to his readers that, at its core, his humanism is based on the premise that "attacking the abuses of something is not the same thing as dismissing or entirely destroying that thing,"[5] a premise that is very Césairian at heart. The relationship between Aimé Césaire's biting critique of humanism in *Discourse on Colonialism* (1950) and Said's humanism is one that has been sorely overlooked in assessments of Said's humanism. This relationship, however, is infinitely useful in understanding Said's loyalty to humanism.

This chapter will explore Said's critical humanism as developing from Césaire's critique of a certain kind of humanism before moving on to establish the difference between Said's Césairian humanism and later modes, including Fanon's ethical anti-humanism and the anti-humanism that gained popularity thereafter. It will use this exploration to examine the "different humanism" that Said creates out of Césaire's work to finally confront the question of why Said chooses to adhere to humanism at all. For the purposes of this chapter, humanism is primarily defined in two distinct Saidian ways:

1. Traditional, Eurocentric humanism, which Said argues is a distortion of humanism;
2. Critical humanism, for which he advocates and under which he constellates criticism and humanism.[6]

I argue that Said develops his critical humanism out of Césaire's fledgling "alter-humanism"[7] because of its positioning as an alternative to traditional, Eurocentric humanism. Said's ambitious rehabilitation of humanism is, then, a "two-pronged" project[8] which must reclaim humanism

60   DOI: 10.4324/9781003046004-6

from both "French theory tout court anti-humanism" and traditional, Eurocentric humanism[9]. To begin, it inherits and incorporates Césaire's criticism of traditional humanism—Said, after all, as Timothy Brennan observes, saw himself as building on a postcolonial tradition, the direction of which he saw as having "come ultimately from earlier generations."[10]

Césaire's polemical *Discourse on Colonialism* features a biting critique of humanism and its complicity in the colonial project in a memorably poetic rhythm. Here, Césaire focuses on exposing the hypocrisy of Western humanists, such as Renan, Gobineau, and Caillois, who appeal to Enlightenment universal humanism[11] even as they employ its logic to sanction the violence of colonialism. As Mara De Gennaro notes, what most disgusts Césaire about the humanists is "their failure to universalize the humanism they claim for their 'race' alone."[12] This racial exclusivity cements the argument that theirs is not a universal humanism at all but a racialism that simply masquerades as humanism.[13] That they have called this racialism "humanism" is evidence of the narrow, racialized definition of "human" to which so-called traditional humanists subscribe. Césaire considers the reaction of horror to Hitler's crimes, which, he notes, stands in direct contradiction to the perpetration of crimes in the colonies:

The very distinguished, very humanistic, very Christian bourgeois of the twentieth century ... has a Hitler inside him ... that if he rails against him, he is being inconsistent and that, at bottom, what he cannot forgive Hitler for is not a *crime* in itself, *the crime against man*, it is not *the humiliation of man as such*, it is a crime against the white man, the humiliation of the white man.[14]

The strategic juxtaposition of the "humiliation of man" and "humiliation of the white man" drives home the inconsistencies in Western humanism. Russell West-Pavlov reads Césaire as explicating Europe's "shocked reaction to colonial practices on its own continent that would hitherto only be found elsewhere."[15] This exclusive humanism is flawed, then, precisely because it is premised on a very narrow definition of human. Césaire, notably, does not reject humanism tout court on the basis of this narrow definition; instead, he overturns it in "the name of something truly universal"[16] and imagines its potential power to "effect political and moral good" once it is rid of its corruptions.[17]

What, then, is this other, truly universal humanism? Malreddy Kumar calls it "alter-humanism"[18]: "a humanism that positively enables the colonizer's ascribed *other*ness"[19] and Bashir Abu-Manneh dubs it "political humanism,"[20] a term that captures Said's commitment to humanism and "his preoccupation with uncovering culture's complicities in injustice and power and exposing its role in historical injury."[21] It is this humanism that Said extends into his critical humanism when he inherits the task of curing humanism of these corruptions. When Said writes against the idea that "we [the global West] represent a humane culture; they [the rest of the world], violence and hatred. We are civilized, they are barbarians,"[22] he explicitly defines the kind of "us and them" humanisms in which he is not interested; ones that purport Western culture ("we") as the defender of humanism against Othered cultures ("they"). Humanism, instead, does not belong to any particular race or nation in its Césairian and Saidian inception. Hence, Said strategically stresses Spitzer's emphasis on the *human*, not *European*, mind.[23] When humanism is defined as a system reliant on the *human*, not European, mind's capacity for critique, then, pseudo-humanism can no longer be treated as humanism.

Something must change now that the colonial discourse that "canonized European humanism" is a device with the potential to "transform the 'raw man' (native) into a 'real man'"[24] no longer holds. Postcolonial theory, with its insistence that the native had "always already been 'human,' but had simply been disfigured as the 'not-yet-human' in the discourses of European humanism,"[25] imagines another humanism. This humanism is both beyond the "narrow and fragmentary, incomplete and biased,"[26] "de-humanizing"[27] elitist humanism espoused by the new humanists, and conservatives, such as Allan Bloom,[28] that "[aimed] to protect a traditional European canon and so-called 'European values.'"[29] To separate his universal humanism from these humanisms, Said uses the example of Northrop Frye's "The Anatomy of Criticism,"[30] which, though it "claimed to be talking about literature, humanistically" was "almost entirely Eurocentric," divorced from historical and political contexts and devoid of any reference to women's or minority genres and notions of "the humanistic world of agency and work." Said calls this type of "humanism" outdated and narrow and, in fact, not humanistic at all,[31] despite its claims to the contrary, much as Césaire previously censured pseudo-humanism as de-humanizing. It is easy to hear echoes of Césaire's indictment of Renan when Said points to the basic hypocrisy of traditional humanists: Petrarch and Boccaccio raised no objections to colonialism, writes Said, even as they lauded "the human" and the American founding fathers' insisted on the "rights of men" even as they stood for inhumane offenses such as slave trade and Native American genocide.[32] Again, we come to the problem of differing definitions of human.

Said's solution is to re-define human as a universal term. He does this by stressing a universal, cosmopolitan humanism[33] and focusing on cultural exchange, true to the Césairian belief that "exchange is oxygen."[34] Consider Said's reading of Césaire:

> If I may quote some lines by the great Martiniqueian poet, Aime Cesaire that I used in my book *On Culture and Imperialism*, and I never tire of quoting these lines, and he speaks here for man, l'homme in French, but 'the work of man is only just beginning and it remains to conquer all the violence entrenched in the recesses of our passion and no race possesses the monopoly of beauty, of intelligence, of force, and there's a place for all at the rendezvous of victory' and what they imply, these sentiments prepare the way for dissolution of cultural barriers as a kind of blockage between cultures as well as of the pride that prevents ... benign globalism.[35]

Said chooses to quote Césaire at a moment where he underlines the importance of the work of man "which is just beginning," work that Said continues in his defense of humanism. This much is clear in his reading of this passage and Césaire's l'homme, or man,[36] as "[preparing] the way for [the] dissolution of cultural barriers" in order to move toward a more globalized world. When Said argues that Samuel Huntington and Harold Bloom both "radically misinterpreted what it is about cultures and civilizations that makes them interesting," he does so on the basis of them ignoring the "combinations and diversity, [and] countercurrents [of civilizations], the way they [conduct] compelling dialogue with other civilizations."[37] Like Césaire, Said understands the value of cultural exchange and is afraid that, in our haste to dissociate ourselves from the evils of colonialism carried out in the name of humanism, we would also lose a system that can be effectively engaged in the service of human unity and intercultural coexistence.[38] That Said imagines a real or universal humanism, then, is not unfounded, but to realize it Said must disabuse his readers of the notion that humanistic inclinations are exclusive to the Western world and shatter the myth of the "Western miracle."[39] Quoting George Makdisi's studies on Islamic contributions to the rise of humanism that trace humanistic practice to twelfth-century Muslim madaris, college, and universities,[40] Said notes that, while he primarily cites evidence of an Islamic humanistic tradition, this is only because of his own familiarity with it and not for any shortage of humanistic practice in Indian, Chinese, African, or Japanese traditions.[41] Said makes a point to define his humanism as transhistorical and global, displacing humanism from the West rather than succumbing to the erasure of non-Western traditions from humanism or, conversely, to reject humanism altogether. This move allows Said to both drive home Césaire's belief that Europe succeeded because of exchange, not exceptionalism, and preserve humanism in the postcolonial world.

Instead of simply abandoning humanism altogether, a tempting proposition,[42] Said intends to separate *his* critical, "real"[43] humanism from the abhorrent traditional humanism and its abuses. To use his term from the inaugural chapter of *Humanism and Democratic Criticism*, "Humanism's Sphere,"[44] Said is interested in re-defining what deserves to be included within humanism's sphere. If humanism is a pre-existing sphere, then, its bounds are set by its values, not any particular culture. If all humans are human and no culture is privileged, then certain outdated modes that masquerade as humanism must be expelled from this sphere. The humanism of this sphere is, then, a humanism that "prompts an activist return to the 'great works' of humanism, with the understanding that humanism itself be rezoned to avoid misleading cartographic divisions between European and non-European cultures."[45] Like Césaire's humanism, with its "reconfiguration of geographical space, which, far from simply returning the black man to Africa, brings him into contact with territories across the world,"[46] Said's rezoning embraces Césaire's rejection of European humanism as corrupt racialism[47] without dismissing humanism. Where Césaire merely refuses to dismiss "a universalism that is removed from its abuses,"[48] however, Said sets out to find this universal humanism, which for him, is real humanism, since Europe was never essential to humanism.

In an earlier work, *The World, Text and Critic*, Said's discomfort with the role of critics and theorists, as well as with the limited definition of humanism, is apparent. He writes,

> we are humanists because there is something called humanism, legitimated by the culture, given a positive value by it … the formal, restricted analysis of literary-aesthetic works validates the culture, the culture validates the humanist, the humanist the critic, and the whole enterprise the state. Thus authority is maintained by virtue of the cultural process, and anything more than refining power is denied the refining critic.[49]

Chafing against the idea of humanism as an ideology that ends up upholding existing power structures, Said attempts to insert political action into humanism. Here, he specifically takes issue with "the harmless rhetoric of self-delighting humanism"[50] and calls on critics to instead "read and write with a sense of the greater stake in historical and political effectiveness."[51] As Pannian observes, Said emphasizes "the oppositional potential of Western humanism"[52] and endeavors to deploy "the very strengths of the West in the struggle against the West [believing that] the values of humanism can be used against imperialist notions of culture."[53] This is, doubtless, incompatible with Foucauldian understandings of humanism which consistently tie humanism to subjective European judgment. Given Said's reliance on Foucault and his structuralism, underpinned as it was by anti-humanistic assumptions, it makes sense that questions arise about Said's humanism, but before addressing more of these questions, it is useful to point out that while Said's *Orientalism* was grounded in Foucault, he nevertheless evokes Vico in the introduction to *Orientalism*. This small instance of coexistence between the humanist Vico and the anti-humanist Foucault suggests that for Said, the two thoughts need not be contradictory. Indeed, Pannian[54] and Ashcroft[55] agree that Said ultimately saw *his* humanism as simultaneously traditional *and* oppositional.

For Said, humanism becomes the very system that questions and criticizes pseudo-humanism[56] and, in "questioning, upsetting, and reformulating,"[57] becomes the very force that prevents "mummification" into tradition[58] or, what Césaire calls the atrophying of civilization.[59] Yumna Siddiqi understands this about Said's humanism, which she says, "properly understood, has an unsettling rather than a stabilizing effect."[60] Said's humanism must, therefore, be looked at primarily as a critical practice, distinct from the larger historical body of humanism. Said's definition of humanism in his 1999 MLA address is useful here,

> Humanism is disclosure; it is agency; it is immersing oneself in the element of history; it is recovering what Vico calls the topics of mind from the turbulent actualities of human life … and then submitting them painstakingly to the rational processes of judgment and criticism.[61]

This humanism involves a Vichian commitment to submitting to "rational processes of judgment and criticism." The distinction that the abuses of a thing are not the thing itself[62] is an important one for Said and understanding this distinction helps in answering the larger question of why the author of *Orientalism* should align himself with a belief system that endorsed its offenses. Evidently, Said is looking to point to a different kind of humanism[63] altogether, one that, as the next section will discuss, is, for Said, the "real" humanism.

Defining Real Humanism

In his essay "On Late Style: Edward Said's Humanism," Pal Ahluwalia contends that Saidian humanism is a Fanonian project[64], but as I have argued, Said's humanism is more akin to Césaire's. Notably, Said re-defines humanism after proving that traditional humanism is not humanism at all and introducing his own universal version, while Fanon proposes a "strategic anti-humanism knowledgeable of the history of humanism."[65] Even when he turns to Fanon, it is with Césaire that Said associates him[66]: "Like Césaire before him," writes Said, "Fanon impugns imperialism for what it has created by acts of powerful rhetoric and structured summary."[67] This suggests that he sees Fanon as participating in a Césairian project, much like himself, albeit in different ways. Though Said recognizes the need for an "epistemological revolution" for Fanon and understands his use of violence as "a cleansing force" in the anti-colonial struggle[68] he does not adopt his model into his own work, nor does he rely on life to "spring up again [only] out of the rotting corpse of the settler."[69]

A memorable moment, here, is when Said praises Fanon for his use of the word "humanism" in a context free from "the narcissistic individualism, divisiveness, and colonialist egoism."[70] It is this freeing of humanism that Said attempts in creating another sphere for humanism in *Humanism and Democratic Criticism*. It is worth examining how Said reads Fanon. Of Fanon's "Pitfalls of Nationalism," Said writes,

> National consciousness, he says, "must now be enriched and deepened by a very rapid transformation into a consciousness of social and political needs, in other words into [real] humanism."[71]

Said's addition of the word "real" in the square brackets is telling. With it, Said alludes to both the distinction between critical humanism and traditional humanism and the idea that there is a "real," universal humanism somewhere that can and must be recuperated.[72] That Said is invested in recuperating humanism, rather than creating it anew, is precisely why, for all his praise of—and respect for—Fanon, it is not surprising that he comes to fault Fanon in *Freud & the Non-European*.[73] Fanon, writes Said, indicts Europe and its ways but fails to provide his readers with "anything like a blueprint for the new ways he has in mind."[74] This omission is especially frustrating for the pragmatist in Said, who is thoroughly committed to usable, worldly critique.[75] Rajagopalan Radhakrishnan criticizes Said for expecting Fanon, who was "writing in and during and through colonialism," to provide such a blueprint when Said himself cannot articulate a complete solution "fifty years after the momentous decades of decolonization."[76] While Said's purpose in pointing out this deficiency in Fanon's work appears to be rooted in a desire to create a space to provide a blueprint himself, a practical next step, this is nevertheless a blind spot for Said. However, it is fair to say that what Said resists is not Fanon's work, or his own work in *Orientalism*, but the lack of direction for a way forward after acknowledging Walter Benjamin's observation that "every document of civilization is also a document of barbarism."[77] Remarking that "humanists should especially be able to see exactly what [this observation] means,"[78] Said completes the transformation of humanism from traditional humanism to critical, Saidian, or "real," humanism.

Whether this transformation is wholly convincing or not is another matter and one that anti-humanists and scholars continue to debate. Chief among these complaints is that Said's work is immersed in secular criticism—a relevant concern in a post-Talal Asad world in which scholars question whether there can even be such a thing as secularism. For Said, however, secular criticism does not "imply the rejection of universalism"[79] but the exact opposite. As is apparent from the above, Said is aware that knowledge is not innocent, and he makes no attempts to argue otherwise. Even Said's secularism is very much a secularism articulated from what Mufti has called a minority position.[80] Abu-Manneh views Said's propensity toward secular criticism as a way to "re-engage with the world, actively interfere in it, and undermine the unjust status quo."[81] Indeed, Radhakrishnan also notes that Said's criticism of high theory is connected to his humanism and Said finds in humanism, the tools to resist "the elitism of an exclusively academic-specialist paradigm of knowledge [in favor of] a possibility for alternatives and the perennial widening of human possibilities."[82] Even on its own, this changes how we approach Said's arguments, but additionally it is also apparent that while Saidian humanism may be modeled on Auerbach and Spitzer's philological humanism, it is, as Pannian observes, also filtered through "the anti-humanist period of the 1960s."[83] Viewed in this manner, Said's humanism and secular criticism take on qualities that make them very different from their traditional understandings.

"A Usable Praxis": Why Humanism?

> What concerns me is humanism as a usable praxis for intellectuals and academics who want to know what they are doing, what they are committed to as scholars, and who want also to connect these principles to the world in which they live as citizens.[84]

Having discussed Said's use of Césairian critique to formulate his critical humanism, it is worth asking why Said undertakes this project in the first place. As Radhakrishnan puts it, why does Said choose to "locate critical activity within the body proper of humanism, rather than situate it without?"[85] For Said, the value of humanism as a system of criticism is too great to throw out with the "bathwater of discredited colonial or racist projects."[86] Radhakrishnan attributes this to humanism's "usable past,"[87] which provides Said with the opportunity to engage with "a continuous macropolitical horizon that will enable certain progressive connections, which eventually will result in the formation of a canon, i.e., a good and inclusive canon."[88] Viewed as such, Said's yearning for a pragmatic solution, "a usable praxis" already allows him to separate the humanism he favors from traditional humanism. However, it is also important to keep in view other reasons for Said's commitment to humanism. Jane Hiddleston has attributed the enduring allure of this "grand yet curiously empty"[89] term over postcolonial criticism to the simple fact that it "requires an understanding at once of collectivity and of irreducible otherness"[90] and while this consideration, may not be foremost in Said's thought, it is certainly worth mentioning especially in light of Said's Césairian commitment to cultural coexistence[91] with an acknowledgment of difference or heterogeneity.[92] As Apter notes, Said's insistence on fashioning a different humanism does not simply emerge from his admiration of the literary merit of "great books" but from his belief that humanism is the key to "futural parameters for defining secular criticism in a world increasingly governed by a sense of identitarian ethnic destiny."[93] Finally, another point to consider is the relatively minor matter of Said's propensity toward reclamation. Just as Said previously plucked out the term "Orientalism," "which lay dormant in Western philology"[94] and reanimated it as "a critical episteme ... for an anti-imperialist understanding of world culture,"[95] so he mobilizes the term "humanism" to his own ends so that it comes to denote the universalist understanding of "human," an understanding he posits it should have always had, but for the corruption that came to permeate it.

Despite Said's attempts to *reclaim* this term and promote "a different kind of humanism," objections continue to be leveled against him for having used it at all. Robert Young and James Clifford[96] find it problematic that Said appropriates the idea of the human from Western humanist tradition to critique the "anti-humanist nature of Orientalism."[97] Said responds that "it is possible to be critical of humanism in the name of humanism."[98] This is a rewriting of the Calibanian moment:[99] *you taught me the tools of critique, now my profit is to apply them back onto you.* Said chooses to, in the words of De Gennaro's title, "fight humanism with humanism."[100] Radhakrishnan casts doubt over the possibility of such an endeavor. He argues that "contrary to Said,"[101] the abuses committed in the name of humanism were "very much in the spirit of humanism."[102] This is the crux of the main debate over Said's attempt to rescue humanism. That humanism has a history of abuse is an established fact for Said; Said's distinction is that humanism is also the only cure for the abuses practiced in its name.[103] For Said, humanism is explicitly not the humanism of the "Cartesian sovereign consciousness or autonomous subject celebrated by Western Enlightenment thought,"[104] but a deliberately re-defined humanism that has separated itself from the essentializing and totalizing[105] humanism "in the spirit" of which those abuses were committed. Said uses the term "humanism," then, to his own pragmatic political ends in his creation of the sphere of critical humanism, which simultaneously stands in defiance to both traditional tout court humanism and anti-humanism.

The possibility of such a new, untainted humanism continues to be a source of debate, however, and most anti-humanist scholars have read a contradiction between the Said of *Orientalism* and the humanist. Terry Eagleton reads Said's late style overtures into humanism as a moment that sees merging of the two *Saids*: "Said the cultivated middle-class academic converg[ing] with Said the courageous champion of the oppressed." However, he does chide Said for "never really tak[ing] issue with the suspiciously sanguine aspects of humanism."[106] Similarly, like Radhakrishnan, who argues that it is not possible to exorcise humanism from the abuses committed in its name, Wael Hallaq also contends that such a return to humanism is untenable considering the racism embedded within Auerbach's original work. However, rather than imagining two different Saids converging or existing in opposition to one another, Hallaq posits that Said's humanism does not so much contradict *Orientalism* as form a key part of it. In his introduction to *Restating Orientalism* (2018), Hallaq argues that a "true political critique of Orientalism"[107] would have to go beyond Said and start with the "foundations that gave rise to a particular conception of nature, liberalism, secularism, secular humanism, anthropocentrism, capitalism, the modern state, and much else that modernity developed as central to its project."[108] For Hallaq, Said leaves these foundations largely intact[109] such that *Orientalism* is "defined by a series of premises and assumptions that reinforce the very modernist and liberal positions that gave rise to Orientalism in the first place."[110]

While this critique opens too many larger questions for one chapter to adequately address, I will focus on the aspects of it that pertain to humanism. For Hallaq, there is no conflict between the two Saids because he observes, "Said's narrative, reflecting a particular and narrowly defined conception of power and knowledge claimed to hail from Foucault, remained faithful to the Enlightenment notions of secular humanism."[111] I would like to offer, here, that Said never purported to be completely aligned with Foucault, even though some of his most well-known theories build on Foucault and French theory. Said, who is concerned with humanism as critical practice, recounts how at the time that he is writing, French theory has long since brought about "a severe if not crippling defeat of what was considered traditional humanism by the forces of structuralism and post-structuralism"[112] and moved academic practice toward anti-humanism instead. Said insists that despite this, he continues to adhere to humanism largely because he "[does not] see in humanism only … totalizing essentializing trends."[113] By saying this, Said returns to his insistence that there is a *humanism* beyond the traditional, Eurocentric humanism that is complicit in colonialism. That other traditional humanism is what anti-humanism and Said's humanism—inclusive and universal in its scope and character—both stand against. That this humanism exists is unquestionable for Said, who points toward examples of what he sees as humanistic endeavors outside the West, for instance, in the South African liberation struggle.[114]

Said's humanist scholarship ultimately emerges out of his commitment to secular criticism that "must think of itself as life-enhancing and constitutively opposed to every form of tyranny, domination, and abuse; its social goals are noncoercive knowledge produced in the interests of human freedom."[115] A humanism that is unequivocally "opposed to every form of tyranny, domination, and abuse" certainly cannot be the traditional humanism which was used, in many instances, to justify "tyranny, domination, and abuse" with its rigid definitions of the word human itself. It is telling that Said's break with Foucault is grounded not in his radicalism but in what Said criticized as a "false universalism, making broad generalizations on the basis of French evidence"[116] as well as the fact that Foucault "showed no real *interest in the relationships his work had with feminist or postcolonial writers facing problems of exclusion, confinement, and domination.*"[117] This is apparent in the way in which, as Siddiqi, who calls Said "an anti-humanist humanist to the last,"[118] notes, Said rejects the dominant humanism of conservative intellectuals such as Allan Bloom who attempt to emphasize what they call European values and who try to protect the traditional canon through their humanism.[119] Ultimately, Said's attempt to preserve humanism, then, is an attempt to unsettle it and expand or even collapse its borders. The question of whether such an attempt is possible has, of course, drawn its share of skeptical looks.

Perhaps it is in anticipation of such skepticism that Said turns to Césaire and Fanon in his attempts, and perhaps this is also why a "usable praxis"[120] is crucial to Said owing to the intertwined history of humanism and criticism.[121] As such, he could hardly be persuaded to give up humanism for anti-humanism, a system that, for him, is highly impractical.[122] Pannian concentrates on Said's use of the word "usable" here. He points out that the word differentiates Said's intended project from one that would merely be "instrumental," before going on to note that "while the instrumental scope presupposes possession, the usable scope involves practice."[123] If, for Said, humanism and criticism are "invariably associated," then as Hole notes, anti-humanist theory's dismissal of humanism altogether indicates a dangerous fate for criticism as well.[124] With the methods of critique, he articulates under the umbrella of humanism in *Humanism and Democratic Criticism*, Said hopes to preserve anti-humanist theory's powerful critique of humanism's abuses while retaining humanism as a system.

The strategies that allow Said to accomplish this are a contrapuntal reading and a return to philology. Derived from music, contrapuntal reading is a Saidian method of reading texts in light of their structural dependency on historically disadvantaged groups, in order to recover the forgotten other back into the text.[125] It is this method that makes it possible for Said to read Joseph Conrad and Jane Austen[126] on their own merits without losing sight of their historical contexts and complicity in the colonial project. For Said, it is imperative that readers, in the time of post- and anti-colonialism, realize that novels cannot be reduced to the historical, socio-political forces that shaped them as they are in what he calls "an unresolved dialectical relationship with them."[127] When viewed from this perspective, it is possible to understand the urgency with which Said sought to save humanism from anti-humanist forces. Introducing this contrapuntal reading into humanism, allows Said to incorporate criticism of humanism into the humanist project itself.

Furthermore, the return to philology,[128] that Timothy Brennan associates with Said's inquisitive voice,[129] lies at the heart of the humanistic tradition for Said. It is not surprising that he finds a solution to the problems that plague humanism in the long-neglected practice of philology: "literally, the love of words."[130] Said turns to philology as a discipline to reinvigorate the act of reading. Even Hallaq's critique of *Orientalism* retains a belief in the value of philology to the extent that the new path that Hallaq charts for the future of Orientalism involves improving upon philology to create

> a new philology centered on what may be called *heuristic historicism*; the Oriental traditions will cease to be the locus of revaluation and reengineering, and will instead stand as the repertoire of thought that will instruct in refashioning a new Orientalist self.[131]

The enduring value of philology is as evident here as it is for Said.

It is through philology that Said articulates a thorough method of reading that involves engaging with a text deeply and on multiple levels.[132] For this, Said couples Spitzerian philology that encourages the "scholar-humanist-reader" to read from "the surface to the inward life-center"[133] with *Ijtihad*, a technique he borrows from the Islamic tradition. *Ijtihad*, which Said defines as "a component of personal commitment and extraordinary effort," is indispensable to his philological reading. He recalls, here, the way the Quran is meant to be read by Muslims: repeatedly and with rapt attention, revered as it is as the Word of God that can never be fully understood. While Said's purpose is not to suggest that all readers imitate Spitzerian or Auerbachian levels of close reading,[134] he does insist that readers make the best attempt to engage with texts in the humanistic vein. This is crucial precisely because, for him, humanism is not an elitist engagement for the select few that holds no bearing on the so-called real world. As Ahluwalia notes, Said "reminds us about the centrality of the worldliness of theory" and the need to recognize the "connection between texts and the existential actualities of human, life, politics, societies, and events."[135] Engagement with theory is important, then, precisely because it is not divorced from the socio-political realities of life at all.

In conclusion, Said realizes the universal humanism that lingers in the margins of Césaire's *Discourse on Colonialism* by demarcating a new sphere for humanism, one that is both separate from the various discredited humanisms, and critical and inclusive at its very core. This humanism, for Said, is the first step in achieving the true potential of humanistic culture as "coexistence and sharing." Despite questions presented to him about adherence to Foucauldian paradigms, Said's strategy remains to leverage the "values of humanism … against imperialist notions of culture."[136] Thus, Said continues to operate in an Enlightenment paradigm even though his ends are not the original ends of the Enlightenment. Said's turn to humanism is a call to recover it from "the abuses of humanism."[137] Even as questions arise around the rehabilitation of humanism, Said accomplishes what he set out to do in his volume on humanism: issuing the positive reminder that "far more than they fight, cultures coexist and interact fruitfully with each other."[138]

Bibliography

Primary Sources

Césaire, Aimé, *Discourse on Colonialism*, translated by Joan Pinkham. "A Poetics of Anticolonialism," New Introduction, Robin D.G. Kelley (New York: Monthly Review Press, 2000).
Said, Edward W., *Culture and Imperialism*, 1st ed. (New York: Knopf, 1993).
Said, Edward W., *Humanism and Democratic Criticism* (Basingstoke: Palgrave Macmillan, 2004).
Said, Edward W., "Michel Foucault, 1926–1984," in *After Foucault: Humanistic Knowledge, Postmodern Challenges*, ed. by Jonathan Arac and the University of Illinois at Chicago (New Brunswick: Rutgers University Press, 1988).
Said, Edward W., "The Myth of the Clash of Civilizations," *Media Education Foundation*, 1998. http://www.mediaed.org/transcripts/Edward-Said-The-Myth-of-Clash-Civilizations-Transcript.pdf [accessed December 14, 2016].
Said, Edward W., "Presidential Address 1999: Humanism and Heroism," *PMLA*, 115 (2000), 285–291, doi: 10.2307/463449
Said, Edward W., *The World, the Text, and the Critic* (Cambridge: Harvard University Press, 1983).
Said, Edward W. and Rose, Jacqueline, *Freud and The Non-European*, 1st ed. (London: Verso, 2003), pp. 13–55.
Shakespeare, William, *The Tempest*, ed. by Frank Kermode (London: Methuen, 1964).

Secondary Sources

Abu-Manneh, Bashir, "Said's Political Humanism: An Introduction," in *After Said: Postcolonial Literary Studies in the Twenty-First Century*, ed. by Bashir Abu-Manneh, After Series (Cambridge: Cambridge University Press, 2018), pp. 1–19. doi: 10.1017/9781108554251.001

Ahluwalia, Pal, "On Late Style: Edward Said's Humanism," in *Edward Said and The Literary, Social, And Political World*, 1st ed. (New York: Routledge, 2009), 150–164.

Apter, Emily, "Saidian Humanism," *Boundary* 2, 31 (2004), 35–53. doi: 10.1215/01903659-31-2-35

Brennan, Timothy, "Edward—Timothy Brennan," politicsandculture.org, 2004. https://politicsandculture. org/2010/08/10/edward-timothy-brennan-2 [accessed December 12, 2016]

Clifford, James, "On *Orientalism*." *The Predicament of Culture: Twentieth-Century Ethnography, Literature, and Art* (Cambridge: Harvard University Press, 1988), 225–276.

"Contrapuntal Reading—Oxford Reference," oxfordreference.com, 2016. http://www.oxfordreference. com/view/10.1093/oi/authority.20110803095635664 [accessed December 12, 2016]

Dayal, Samir, "Ethical Antihumanism" in *Edward Said and Jacques Derrida*, 1st ed. (Newcastle: Cambridge Scholars Publishing, 2008), 220–250.

De Gennaro, M., "Fighting 'Humanism' On Its Own Terms," *Differences* 14 (2003), 53–73. doi: 10.1215/10407391-14-1-53.

Eagleton, Terry, "Human, All Too Human," April 22, 2004. https://www.thenation.com/article/archive/ human-all-too-human/

Gopal, Priyamvada, "Humanism for a Globalised World," newhumanist.org.uk, 2013. https://newhumanist. org.uk/articles/4458/humanism-for-a-globalised-world [accessed December 12, 2016]

Hallaq, Wael B., *Restating Orientalism: A Critique of Modern Knowledge*. New York: Columbia University Press, 2018.

Hiddleston, Jane, "Aimé Césaire and Postcolonial Humanism," *The Modern Language Review* 105 (2010), 87–102.

Hole, Jeffrey, "Said, Humanism and the Neoliberal University" in *The Geocritical Legacies of Edward W. Said*, 1st ed. (New York: Palgrave Macmillan, 2015), 63–83.

Kumar, Malreddy, "(An)other Way of Being Human: 'Indigenous' Alternative(s) to Postcolonial Humanism," *Third World Quarterly* 32, 9, tandfonline.com, 2016. http://www.tandfonline.com/doi/ abs/10.1080/01436597.2011.618624?src=recsys&journalCode=ctwq20 [accessed December 12, 2016]

Li, Victor, "Edward Said's Untidiness," postcolonial.org, 2016. http://postcolonial.org/index.php/pct/ article/view/309/106 [accessed December 14, 2016]

Mitchell, W. J. T., "Secular Divination: Edward Said's Humanism," *Critical Inquiry* 31 (2005), 462–471. doi: 10.1086/430975.

Mufti, Aamir, "Auerbach in Istanbul: Edward Said, Secular Criticism, and the Question of Minority Culture," *Critical Inquiry* 25 (Autumn 1998), 95–125.

Pannian, Prasad, "Intellectuals as Subjects of Action in the Age of New Humanism." In *Edward Said and the Question of Subjectivity*, by Prasad Pannian, 93–125 (New York: Palgrave Macmillan US, 2016). doi: 10.1057/9781137543592_5.

Radhakrishnan, Rajagopalan, "Edward Said's Literary Humanism," *Cultural Critique*, 67, 1 (2007), 13–42. doi: 10.1353/cul.2007.0032.

Siddiqi, Yumna, "Edward Said, Humanism, and Secular Criticism," *Alif: Journal of Comparative Poetics* 25 (2005), 65–88. www.jstor.org/stable/4047452.

Walker, Keith L., "The Transformational and Enduring Vision of Aimé Césaire," *PMLA*, 125 (2010), 756–763. doi: 10.1632/pmla.2010.125.3.756.

Young, Robert, *White Mythologies: Writing History and the West* (London: Routledge, 1990).

Notes

1   W. J. T. Mitchell, "Secular Divination: Edward Said's Humanism," *Critical Inquiry*, 31, 2 (2005), 462.
2   Edward W. Said, *Humanism and Democratic Criticism*, 1st ed. (New York: Columbia University Press, 2004), xvi.
3   W. J. T. Mitchell, 462.
4   Edward W. Said, *Humanism and Democratic Criticism*, 8–9.
5   Ibid., 13.
6   Ibid., 7.
7   Malreddy Kumar "(An)other Way of Being Human: 'Indigenous' Alternative(s) to Postcolonial Humanism." *Third World Quarterly* 32, 9 (2016), 1561.
8   Rajagopalan Radhakrishnan, "Edward Said's Literary Humanism," *Cultural Critique*, 67, 1 (2007), 13.
9   Ibid.
10   Timothy Brennan, "Edward—Timothy Brennan," politicsandculture.org, 2004, n.p.

11 Aimé Césaire and Robin D. G. Kelley, *Discourse On Colonialism*, 1st ed. (New York: Monthly Review Press, 2000), 37

12 M. De Gennaro, "Fighting 'Humanism' On Its Own Terms," *Differences*, 14, 1 (2003), 57–58.

13 Ibid.

14 Aimé Césaire and Robin D. G. Kelley, *Discourse On Colonialism*, 3.

15 Russell West-Pavlov, "Said, Space and Biopolitics: Giorgio Agamben's and D. H. Lawrence's States of Exception" in *The Geocritical Legacies of Edward W. Said*, 1st ed. (New York: Palgrave Macmillan, 2015), 17–41.

16 De Gennaro, M., "Fighting 'Humanism' On Its Own Terms," *Differences*, 14, 1 (2003), 58.

17 Ibid., 58.

18 Malreddy Kumar, 1561.

19 Ibid.

20 Bashir Abu Manneh, "Said's Political Humanism: An Introduction," 1–19.

21 Ibid., 3.

22 Edward W. Said, *Humanism and Democratic Criticism*, 8.

23 Ibid., 26.

24 Malreddy Kumar, 1560.

25 Ibid.

26 Aimé Césaire and Robin D. G. Kelley, *Discourse On Colonialism*, 3.

27 Ibid.

28 Edward W. Said, *Humanism and Democratic Criticism*, 17–20.

29 Yumna Siddiqi, "Edward Said, Humanism, and Secular Criticism," *Alif: Journal of Comparative Poetics* 25 (2005), 81.

30 Edward W. Said, *Humanism and Democratic Criticism*, 39–40.

31 Ibid., 27.

32 Ibid., 46.

33 Rajagopalan Radhakrishnan, "Edward Said's Literary Humanism," *Cultural Critique*, 67, 1 (2007), 19.

34 Aimé Césaire and Robin D. G. Kelley, *Discourse On Colonialism*, 2.

35 Edward W. Said, "The Myth of the Clash of Civilizations," *Media Education Foundation*, 1998.

36 Note that, here, Said takes issue with the gendered "l'homme," or "man" and treats Cesaire's l'homme, thereafter, as meaning "human" rather than just man alone.

37 Edward W. Said, *Humanism and Democratic Criticism*, 27–28.

38 Ibid., xvi.

39 Ibid., 53–54.

40 Ibid., 54.

41 Ibid.

42 Ibid., 33.

43 The idea of a real humanism will be explained shortly.

44 Ibid., 1.

45 Emily Apter, "Saidian Humanism," *Boundary* 2, 31.2 (2004), 52.

46 Jane Hiddleston, "Aimé Césaire and Postcolonial Humanism," *The Modern Language Review* 105, 1 (2010), 90.

47 Ibid., 95–100.

48 M. De Gennaro, 58.

49 Edward W. Said. *The World, the Text, and the Critic* (Cambridge: Harvard University Press, 1983), 175.

50 Ibid., 225.

51 Ibid.

52 Pannian, 118.

53 Ibid.

54 Ibid., 119.

55 Ashcroft, "Edward Said's Humanism," 4–5.

56 Edward W. Said, *Humanism and Democratic Criticism*, 21–22.

57 Ibid., 28.

58 Ibid., 32.

59 Aimé Césaire and Robin D. G. Kelley, *Discourse On Colonialism*, 2.

60 Yumna Siddiqi, 81.

61 Said, Edward W., "Presidential Address 1999: Humanism and Heroism," *PMLA* 115 (2000), 290.

62 Edward W. Said, *Humanism and Democratic Criticism*, 13.

Edward Said's Césairian Critical Humanism

63   Ibid., 11.
64   Pal Ahluwalia, "On Late Style: Edward Said's Humanism," in *Edward Said and the Literary, Social, and Political World*, 1st ed. (New York: Routledge, 2009), 152.
65   Samir Dayal, "Ethical Antihumanism" in *Edward Said and Jacques Derrida*, 1st ed. (Newcastle: Cambridge Scholars Publishing, 2008), 220.
66   Edward W. Said, *Culture and Imperialism*, 1st ed. (New York: Knopf, 1993), 324–325.
67   Ibid., 325.
68   Ibid., 327.
69   Ibid., 328.
70   Ibid., 325.
71   Ibid., 325.
72   Rajagopalan Radhakrishnan, 16.
73   Edward W. Said and Jacqueline Rose, *Freud and The Non-European*, 1st ed. (London: Verso, 2003), 20–21.
74   Ibid.
75   Pal Ahluwalia, 151–152.
76   Ibid.
77   Ibid.
78   Ibid.
79   Siddiqi, 73.
80   Mufti, 112.
81   Bashir Abu-Manneh, 4.
82   Radhakrishnan, 27.
83   Pannian, 118.
84   Edward W. Said, *Humanism and Democratic Criticism*, 6.
85   Radhakrishnan, 18.
86   Priyamvada Gopal, "Humanism for a Globalised World," newhumanist.org.uk, 2013.
87   Rajagopalan Radhakrishnan, 19.
88   Ibid.
89   Jane Hiddleston, "Aimé Césaire and Postcolonial Humanism," *The Modern Language Review*, 105, 1 (2010), 101.
90   Ibid.
91   Edward W. Said, *Humanism and Democratic Criticism*, xvi.
92   Ibid., 21.
93   Emily Apter, 43.
94   Ibid., 52.
95   Ibid.
96   James Clifford, *"On Orientalism." The Predicament of Culture: Twentieth-Century Ethnography, Literature, and Art* (Cambridge: Harvard University Press, 1988), 225–276.
97   Robert Young, *White Mythologies: Writing History and the West* (London: Routledge, 1990), 131.
98   Edward W. Said, *Humanism and Democratic Criticism*, 11.
99   William Shakespeare, *The Tempest*, ed. by Frank Kermode (London: Methuen, 1964), I. 2.
100   M. De Gennaro, 57.
101   Rajahopalan Radhakrishnan, 17.
102   Ibid.
103   Yumna Siddiqi, 80.
104   Victor Li, "Edward Said's Untidiness," postcolonial.org, 2016.
105   Edward W. Said, *Humanism and Democratic Criticism*, 10.
106   Terry Eagleton, "Human, All Too Human," April 22, 2004, n.p.
107   Wael Hallaq. *Restating Orientalism: A Critique of Modern Knowledge* (New York: Columbia University Press, 2018), 4
108   Ibid.
109   Ibid.
110   Ibid., 242.
111   Ibid., 232.
112   Ibid., 9.
113   Ibid.
114   Ibid.

115 Said, "World, Text and Critic," 29.
116 Yumna Siddiqi, 79.
117 Edward W. Said, "Michel Foucault, 1926–1984," in *After Foucault: Humanistic Knowledge, Postmodern Challenges*, ed. by Jonathan Arac and University of Illinois at Chicago (New Brunswick: Rutgers University Press, 1988), 9.
118 Siddiqi, 85.
119 Ibid., 81.
120 Ibid., 6.
121 Ibid., 23.
122 Ibid., 33.
123 Pannian, Prasad. "Intellectuals as Subjects of Action in the Age of New Humanism." In *Edward Said and the Question of Subjectivity*, by Prasad Pannian, 93–125 (New York: Palgrave Macmillan US, 2016), 118.
124 Jeffrey Hole, "Said, Humanism and the Neoliberal University" in *The Geocritical Legacies of Edward W. Said*, 1st ed. (New York: Palgrave Macmillan, 2015), 71.
125 "Contrapuntal Reading—Oxford Reference," oxfordreference.com, 2016.
126 Edward W. Said, *Humanism and Democratic Criticism*, 64.
127 Ibid.
128 Ibid., 57–83.
129 Timothy Brennan, "Edward—Timothy Brennan," politicsandculture.org, 2004.
130 Ibid., 58.
131 Hallaq, 257.
132 Brennan, 59.
133 Ibid., 64.
134 67.
135 Pal Ahluwalia, 151–152.
136 Pannian, 118.
137 Edward W. Said, *Humanism and Democratic Criticism*, 13.
138 Ibid., xvi.

5

Sloterdijk's Love Letter on Humanism

Daniel Adleman

In 1999, media philosopher Peter Sloterdijk delivered a lecture titled "Rules for the Human Zoo: A Response to the Letter on Humanism" at a conference in Elmau, Bavaria, on the topic of the troubled legacy of German philosopher Martin Heidegger. Sloterdijk's lecture, which was later published in essay form, exhumes the genesis of humanism in the literary practices of classical antiquity. He then argues, both with and against Heidegger, that humanism has always existed within a continually metamorphosing, simultaneously biological and technological, milieu that harbors a bewildering array of potentials for the intertwined trajectories of humankind and the humanities.

According to Sloterdijk's genealogy, humanism emerged out of the reading and writing culture of the ancient Greco-Roman humanities, a media regime organized around the cultivation of a "circle of friends" dedicated to unfolding a "continuing process of justice and self-discovery."[1] Drawing on the work of Martin Heidegger, Friedrich Nietzsche, Cicero, and Plato, he articulates our profound indebtedness to humanism as a media-rhetorical strategy for self-cultivation and constraining our bestial impulses. "It is part of the credo of humanism," writes Sloterdijk, "that human beings are 'creatures capable of suggestion,' and that it is therefore extremely important to expose them to the right kinds of influences."[2] Humanism, according to this view, is one of many medial processes that empower humanity to constitute and transform itself. The paramount question for Sloterdijk is not, then, whether humanistic values should still play a role in influencing the trajectory of history but whether they are capable of doing so amidst the clamor of more influential discourses and technologies.

This behooves what he refers to as thoughtful "archivists" of the humanistic scene to reflect on the disciplinary, technological, and eco-biological pathways that modernity is opening up for humanity's self-overcoming since many of them fly in the face of humanistic notions of technology, progress, civility, and hope. In this vein, my chapter will track and take up Sloterdijk's nuanced argument about the importance of the humanistic tradition as a succession of philosophical "love letters" between prospective friends dedicated to the endlessly elusive task of shepherding "the political animal" into a better world. I will then track the itinerary of Sloterdijk's essay as it was taken up in an incendiary media environment in a manner that seems to demonstrate the eclipse of epistolary culture that his essay bemoans.

Calming the Inner Beast

Sloterdijk's essay begins with a backward glance at the itinerary of humanism, from the Athenians to the Romans to the rest of the world. He observes that when Cicero first popularized the term

DOI: 10.4324/9781003046004-7

humanitas to describe Rome's inheritance and remediation of Athenian culture, he did so with a view to activating an unfolding social network predicated on a culture of writing:

> That which has been known since the days of Cicero as humanism is in the narrowest and widest senses a consequence of literacy. Ever since philosophy began as a literary genre, it has recruited adherents (followers) by writing in an infectious way about love and friendship. Not only is it about love of wisdom; it is also an attempt to move others to this love. That written philosophy has managed from its beginning more than 2500 years ago until the present day to remain virulent (contagious) is a result of its capacity to make friends through its texts. It has been reinscribed like a chain-letter through the generations.[3]

As per its etymology, *philosophia* (the love of wisdom and critical thinking) is bound up with the friend-making love of kindred philosophical spirits. By excavating the largely overlooked philosophical and rhetorical curriculum of ideas from the dusty archive of Athenian writing, Cicero went against the grain of a chauvinistic Roman culture that dismissed its Greek predecessor as moribund and effete. In so doing, he announced himself as an amicable recipient of the Athenian "chain letter," thereby facilitating its elaboration and further transmission.

Cicero's popular writings, according to Sloterdijk, set the stage for "Roman readers to be seduced by the missives of the Greeks."[4] If Cicero had not rendered his countrymen into "recipients of the Greek messages [...] there would have been no recipients."[5] Fast-forwarding to the dissemination of humanism across the continent, he speculates: "Had the Romans with their extraordinary receptivity not come into play, the Greek message would never have reached western Europe, which retains to this day an interest in humanism."[6] He therefore frames the history of humanism as intergenerational, international, friendship-founding telecommunication in the medium of writing. This epistolary network culminated in the flourishing of humanism across Europe and much of the world until the mid-twentieth century.[7]

Sloterdijk's account of the trajectory of the humanist tradition hinges on a media-archeological analysis of the humanist paradigm. In a classicist vein, he points to the longstanding connection between an education in the *humanities* with the Ciceronian ideal of *humanitas*, which he frames as "taming" humanity through reading rather than "bestializing" it through competing media:

> Anyone who is asking today about the future of humanity and methods of humanization wants to know if there is any hope of mastering the contemporary tendency to the bestialization of humanity. It is disturbing that bestialization, now as ever, tends to accompany displays of great power, whether as open warfare or raw imperial power, or in the daily degradation of human beings in entertainments offered on the media. The Romans influenced Europe by providing archetypes for both—on the one hand, their overweaning militarism, on the other, their precedent-setting entertainment industry of bloody games. The latent message of humanism, then, is the taming of men; and its hidden thesis is: reading the right books calms the inner beast.[8]

The erotic "telecommunicative bridge" engendered by the amiable, humanizing media of the literary humanities, claims Sloterdijk, long operated as a fragile bulwark against the seductive bestializing media of different technological eras, from classical antiquity until the mid-twentieth century. But in the wake of the barbaric tragedies of the twentieth century and at the dawn of the age of a new media era, he pauses to reflect on the viability of humanism as a humanizing system of techniques.

Sloterdijk's rear-view-mirror account of the rise and fall of humanism is not merely a nostalgic conservative panegyric. His claim that humanism "calms the inner beast" is a much more ambivalent assertion that sets the stage for an ethically charged philosophical investigation into literate culture's role as a multivalent form of anthropotechnics, the technological constitution of the "political animal" within an ever-ramifying media environment. "The phenomenon of humanism," he writes, "deserves attention today primarily because it reminds us (however indirectly and embarrassingly) that human beings [...] are constantly subjected simultaneously to two pressures,"[9] the disinhibiting, bestializing pressures and the constraining, humanizing ones. Because human beings are bombarded with a groundswell of cultural, technological, and eco-biological stimuli, a humanistic outlook dictates that it is "extremely important to expose them to the right kinds of influences."[10] This leads him to conclude that

> the question of how a person can become a true or real human being becomes unavoidably a media question, if we understand by media the means of communion and communication by which human beings attain to that which they can and will become.[11]

The Purveyor of Being

Sloterdijk begins his contribution to the telecommunicative chain letter with a response to a 1946 Martin Heidegger text, "Letter on Humanism." Heidegger's essay is itself a reproduced letter responding to a question about humanism from the young French philosopher Jean Beaufret. After reading Jean-Paul Sartre's famous domestication of Heidegger's philosophy in *Existentialism is a Humanism*, Beaufret asked Heidegger if the term *humanism* could not be rehabilitated and integrated into existential philosophy, as Sartre seemed to believe it should be.[12] Heidegger responded to Beaufret's query by letter, which was later published in essay form.

Identifying his philosophical orientation with neither Sartre's existential philosophy nor his particular brand of humanism,[13] Heidegger, according to Sloterdijk's reading, "analyzed and criticized the characteristics of European humanism; and, in so doing, he opened up a transhumanistic or post-humanistic era [...] one in which a considerable portion of the philosophical consideration on man has taken place ever since."[14] Much of Heidegger's response dwells on the extent to which "every humanism remains metaphysical" in that it "presupposes an interpretation of beings without asking about the truth of being."[15] Cycling through Marxism, Christianity, and Platonism, which he characterizes as resolutely humanistic worldviews, Heidegger argues that "[m]etaphysics does not ask about the truth of Being itself. Nor does it therefore ask in what way the essence of the human being belongs to the truth of Being."[16]

While the metaphysical tradition has been content to characterize the human as "the rational animal" or "the political animal," Heidegger dismisses the "biologism" of characterizing the human essence as bound up with its animality. Avoiding the temptation to align his brand of philosophical inquiry with recent scientific discoveries about the inner workings of nature, he insists, "The fact that physiology and physiological chemistry can scientifically investigate the human being as an organism is no proof that in this 'organic' thing, that is, in the body scientifically explained, the essence of the human being consists."[17] In the case of the discovery and manipulation of atomic energy, he adds, "It could even be that nature, in the face of it, turn[ed] toward the human being's technical mastery, is simply concealing its essence."[18] This concern about the drowning out of more primordial philosophical conceptions of human activity by technological and economic frameworks also reverberates through his 1949 essay "The Question Concerning Technology," in which Heidegger famously insists that "the essence of technology is by no means anything technological."[19]

Characterizing both humanist and scientific approaches to the question concerning the essence of the human as insufficiently humane,[20] Heidegger claims that these anthropocentric frames "do not set the *humanitas* of the human being high enough."[21] In contrast to these excessively metaphysical approaches, he insists that

[t]he human being is rather "thrown" by being itself in to the truth of being, so that ek-sisting in this fashion he might guard the truth of being, in order that beings might appear in the light of being as the beings they are [...] The human being is the shepherd of being.[22]

There is an intractable problem, claims Heidegger, with entrenched humanistic characterizations of the human being as the rational, language-using animal:

the human being is not only a living creature who possesses language along with other capacities. Rather, language is the house of being in which the human ek-sists by dwelling, in that he belongs to the truth of being, guarding it.[23]

Inasmuch as human beings can be understood to possess and wield language, they must also be understood as operating within it and "ek-statically" (i.e., kinetically thrown out of the past and projecting into the future) under its sway. As anointed shepherds of Being, humans are, Heidegger contends, nonetheless itinerant tenants on its property and obligated to pay a form of ontological rent by submitting themselves to its ascetic dictates.

Sloterdijk summarizes Heidegger's strategy as a sort of deeper fidelity to the spirit of humanism that nonetheless relinquishes the term:

The word "humanism" must be abandoned if the real task of thinking, which has shown itself to have been exhausted in the humanistic or metaphysical tradition, is to be furthered in its original unity and irresistibility [...] Heidegger offered to prepare the way for an end to the most radical omission of European thought, namely, the refusal to pose the question of the Being of Man in the only appropriate (that is, the existential-ontological) way.[24]

According to this reading, Heidegger believed that his project had "transcended and surpassed humanism" by taking up the human "as a clearing for Being."[25] His deracinated, "ek-static" man is called to a pastoral regimen of "taming and befriending" that is much more demanding and comprehensive than "any humanistic debestializing" or "any love for texts that speak of love."[26] In so doing, he "indirectly retains the most important function of classical humanism—namely, the befriending of man through the word of the other—indeed, he radicalizes this drive to befriend and transfers it from mere pedagogy to the center of ontological consciousness."[27]

Sloterdijk avers that Heidegger "elevated Being to the sole author of all important letters and placed himself as their current scribe [...] More precisely, [Being] addresses them to spiritually advanced friends, to receptive neighbors, to groups of silent herdsmen."[28] However, because Heidegger's pastoral system "reveals no way in which a society can be constructed out of neighbors of Being,"[29] it is incommensurable with the humanistic logic that dominates Western schools and nation-states. This leads Sloterdijk to dwell on Heidegger's proposal that, in the mid-twentieth century, there were "three candidates for a humanistically bedecked form of world domination"[30]: bolshevism, fascism, and Americanism. At this point in the essay, Sloterdijk pauses to reflect on Heidegger's stern critique of fascism, in particular. In the wake of the Second World War, Heidegger critiqued fascism as an aberrant "synthesis of humanism and bestiali[zation], that is as a paradoxical coincidence of restraint and license."[31] Heidegger insisted that, even more than bolshevism and Americanism, fascism is caught up in a decadent anthropocentrism that fetishizes the central role of the strong man in the affairs of the state. Still, his earlier complicity with the Nazi regime while he served as rector at the University of Freiburg justifiably gives some observers pause about Heidegger's ethical compass and the sincerity of his analyses.[32]

Despite the fact that Heidegger's "ontological shepherd's game [...] seems totally anachronistic"[33] to contemporary European thought, Sloterdijk exhumes it to reflect on the fate of humanism, as a taming anthropotechnology, in the wake of the maelstrom of fascist disinhibition and the false promises of American-style liberal democracy. What regimen can tame and civilize humanity, asks Sloterdijk, "when the role of humanism as the school for humanity has collapsed?"[34] Summoning the short-circuited legacy of the Enlightenment, he asks what hope there might be for humanity when "after all experiments to grow the species up, it remains unclear what it is to be a grown-up."[35]

Sloterdijk views Heidegger's letter as an announcement of the death of humanism insofar as "there is no path from humanism to this acute ontological exercise in humility"[36] for dispossessed aspiring shepherds of Being. Heidegger's critique of humanism, writes Sloterdijk, prescribes an "asceticism that goes far deeper than that achievable through any humanistic education."[37] Only through such a discipline could "a society of knowers beyond the humanistic literary society" take root. Heidegger's post-humanistic society would "no longer place [...] humans at the centre"[38] out of a realization that people "exist only as neighbors of being, and not as independent homeowners or as tenants in landlordless apartments."[39] Intriguingly, he seizes on this forward-looking deliberation about the post-humanistic future of humanity as an opportunity to follow Heidegger's "zoopolitical" hyperlink to the past, first to the work of Heidegger's pre-eminent forebear Friedrich Nietzsche and then further back to the dawn of Western philosophy in the writings of Plato.

Nietzsche's Epistle

In *Thus Spoke Zarathustra: A Book for All and None*, Nietzsche's "rhapsodic poetry"[40] tracks the Persian prophet Zarathustra's fictional philosophical odyssey to preach about the overcoming of humankind's most moribund dispositions. In this pioneering philosophical narrative, Zarathustra wanders through mountains and valleys, extolling the virtues of the *Ubermenschen* to come. In a chapter called "Of the Virtues that Make Small," Zarathustra arrives at a town full of inordinately tame, shrunken people:

> They are uniform, decent and kind among themselves, as grains of sand are uniform, conforming and decent with each other. Modestly accept a kindness—that means, submit! Basically they want only one thing: that no one harm them. Virtue is that which makes them modest and tame: it is that that turns the wolf to the dog, and men themselves to mankind's favourite pet.[41]

Sloterdijk characterizes Nietzsche's narrative as a "theoretical discourse about man as a taming and nurturing power."[42] According to Sloterdijk, Nietzsche frames turn-of-the-century European humanity as a confused assortment of "profitable breeders who have made out of wild men the last men."[43] "It is clear," writes Sloterdijk,

> that this could not be done with humanistic education alone [...] [T]he humanistic horizons have been pried apart, so that the humanist can no longer only think, but can move on to questions of taming and nurture: The humanist directs himself to the human, and applies to him his taming, training, educational tools.[44]

Sloterdijk asserts that if taming has taken on an undead life of its own and has firmly established itself as its own unsettling *raison d'être*, then his own favored humanistic distinction between taming and bestializing techniques is further complicated in a manner that requires closer scrutiny.

Heidegger's account of the human as a potential shepherd of Being, it turns out, is still too parochial to account for the ambiguous role of the human organism in the mess of modernity.

Insofar as humanity figures as shepherd, it also plays the role of sheep. One insidious aspect of this dual role, according to Nietzsche, is a feedback loop whereby humanity qua shepherd tames itself qua sheep and then derives self-esteem from its own docility, which it mistakes for virtue and agency. "Nietzsche, who read Darwin and Paul equally carefully," alleges Sloterdijk, "thought to see behind the horizon of scholarly man-taming a second, darker horizon. He perceived a space in which the unavoidable battle over the direction of man-breeding would begin."[45] Anodyne narratives about the ineluctable momentum of the Enlightenment will therefore have to contend with humanity's manifold self-breeding subroutines, some of which have flown off the rails of competent, benevolent shepherding procedures.

The villagers' self-domesticating imbecility bespeaks of the fact that certain forms of taming are much more deleterious and perverse than Heidegger's dichotomous account would seem to accommodate. Underlying Sloterdijk's critique is the recognition that humanism is one of a number of anthropotechnic strategies for constituting and reconstituting the human. "At no time," writes Sloterdijk, "was it, or will it be, possible to accomplish the taming and befriending of men with letters alone. Certainly, reading was a great power for the upbringing and improvement of men. It still is today, to some extent."[46] Nevertheless,

> breeding, whatever form it may have taken, was always present as the power behind the mirror. Reading and breeding have more to do with each other than culture historians are able or willing to admit [...] If, despite Heidegger's prohibition, one wanted to speak anthropologically, one could define humans of the historical period as animals, some of whom could read or write. By taking a single step further, one could define them as animals that reproduce or breed themselves, while other animals are bred [...] This is similar to Nietzsche's claim in *Zarathustra* that few of the people in small houses will to live there. Most are willed into them. They are objects, not agents, of selection.[47]

Sloterdijk purports that Nietzsche's account is, in a sense, more contemporary than Heidegger's in that it considers the anthropotechnological dimension of an entire form of life, of which language is merely one charged component. When speaking beings "gather into larger groups and connect themselves not only to linguistic houses but also build physical houses, they enter the arena of domestication. They are now not only sheltered by their language, but also tamed by their accommodations."[48] Although language may be the house of Being, it is not the only structure that houses and shapes human spheres of activity. Humanity may still be a shepherding species, yet it all-too-frequently misevaluates its own governmental prowess to the extent that it turns its domesticating techniques on itself while rationalizing its self-subordination as virtue. There is no good reason, avers Sloterdijk, for philosophers to assume that any Invisible Hand will steady this process in a philanthropic direction.

Plato's Postcard

Nietzsche's derogation of humanity's propensity to mistake passive conformity for virtue and innocuousness for the good life leads Sloterdijk to reflect on the genesis of zoopolitical thought in the Western philosophical tradition. He locates this primal scene in Plato's *Politikos* (*The Statesman*). *Politikos* stages a conversation between Plato's teacher Socrates, the Stranger, and a young boy also named Socrates. The Stranger proposes two analogs for the simultaneously practical and theoretical task of governing human populations. The first is shepherding and the second is weaving. The statesman must be like a wise, benevolent shepherd that leads their flock in the most adroit fashion. They must also be like a weaver that is able to combine and bring out the best attributes in the citizenry.

Sloterdijk is especially interested in the conceptual role of shepherding in the dialogue:

> With this project Plato prompted an intellectual discomfort in the Human Zoo that could never again be completely quieted. Since *The Statesman* and *The Republic* there have been discourses which speak of human society as if it were a zoo which is at the same time a theme-park: the behavior of men in parks or stadiums seems from now on a zoo-political task. What is presented as reflections on politics are actually foundational reflections on rules for the maintenance of the human zoo. If there is one virtue of human beings which deserves to be spoken about in a philosophical way, it is above all this: that people are not forced into political theme-parks, but rather put themselves there. Humans are self-fencing, self-shepherding creatures. Wherever they live, they create parks around themselves. In city parks, national parks, provincial or state parks, eco-parks—everywhere people must create for themselves rules according to which their comportment is to be governed.[49]

At the dawn of the Western philosophical tradition, Plato set in motion a narrative tropology whereby human society must be understood as "self-fencing" and "self-shepherding" in auto-erected parks. Far from Heidegger's dignified shepherd of Being, the figure of the human being conjured by Plato and Nietzsche is a much more unsettled and unsettling creature that can play a wide variety of roles in the arc of its self-exploration and self-development. In spite of popular dismissals of humanism, Sloterdijk maintains that the humanistic tradition still offers a groundswell of philanthropic guidance for those concerned about the unfurling of civilization at the turn of the millennium.

After reflecting on the trope of the good shepherd, Sloterdijk observes, Plato "switches to another metaphor,"[50] that of the weaver. The most important aspect of shepherding is breeding the ideal citizenry by weaving together optimal attributes:

> The true, the real basis for the art of the king lies not in the vote of the public, which gives or withholds trust from their rulers as it will. Nor does it lie in inherited privilege or recent accumulation of power. The Platonic master finds the reason for his mastery only in the expertise he has in the odd and peculiar art of breeding. Here we see the re-emergence of the expert-king, whose justification is the insight about how, without doing damage to their free will, human beings can best sort themselves out and make connections.[51]

The rhetorically astute Platonic statesman knows "how to bring together free but suggestible people in order to bring out the characteristics that are most advantageous to the whole."[52] Under his direction, "the human zoo can achieve the optimum homeostasis. This comes about when the two relative optima of human character—warlike courage and philosophical-humanistic contemplation—are woven together in the tapestry of the species."[53]

The question of breeding, which Sloterdijk insists impregnated the Athenian humanistic tradition at the outset, leads him to return to the question of biotechnology. Those who are acquainted with both the arc of the liberal humanist tradition and the disaster of "fascist eugenics" will be taken aback at the "explosiveness of these considerations,"[54] claims Sloterdijk. Plato "puts in the mouth of the Stranger" a program of humanistic society that seems to anticipate the contemporary biotechnological era.[55] But there is a snag: Plato's optimal patriarchal shepherd is modeled on the divine shepherd, the deity function. If modern technocratic society has, for the most part, abandoned the pretense of divine guidance, then we must entertain the possibility that the cybernetic shepherding principle has been absorbed into a deracinated zoopolitical scene. Such a matrix is not fit to house Being. It is, rather, a nexus of "breeding without breeder, an agentless biocultural drift."[56]

Daniel Adleman

Though Slotedijk has resigned himself to the deflation of humanism as an anthropotechnological force in the twenty-first century, he nonetheless remains invested in its continuing participation in the social fabric. For Sloterdijk, the explosion of biotechnology and new media should ignite renewed interest in the humanistic tradition's archive of conversations about the constitution of humanity, the place of technology, and the most erudite understandings of political life.

He concludes with a modest assessment of the continuing relevance of the humanist tradition:

> Two thousand years after Plato wrote it seems as if not only the gods but the wise have abandoned us, and left us alone with our partial knowledge and our ignorance. What is left to us in the place of the wise is their writings, in their glinting brilliance and their increasing obscurity.[57]

The few fellow travelers who are still interested in plumbing the archives will perhaps unearth some illuminating letters from friends. "Everything suggests that archivists have become the successors of the humanists," writes Sloterdijk. "For the few who still peer around in those archives, the realization is dawning that our lives are the confused answer to questions which were asked in places we have forgotten."[58]

Getting the Drift

Two decades after Sloterdijk inked "Rules for the Human Zoo," the internet dominates cultural production, mRNA and CRISPR are household terms, and the world has been engulfed by a virus that may well have been genetically modified in a biomedical laboratory. In the wake of all these techno-ecological ruptures, many of Sloterdijk's assessments about the technological and genetic arc of humanity register as almost common-sensical footnotes. Yet his essay was at the heart of a scandal that rocked the German philosophical and media establishments. The ripples that this perturbation sent out speak to the trenchancy of his chain letter and the import of its current itinerary.

After Sloterdijk presented his lecture at Elmau in 1999, the eminent German political philosopher Jürgen Habermas went to the trouble of surreptitiously procuring a bootleg copy of the script. Habermas, who had not been present at the conference, then "sent a letter to various journalists—of which, despite his initial denying its existence, a facsimile was later published in the *Frankfurter Allgemeine Zeitung* (16/09)—with instructions for publishing a number of rather sensational critiques of Sloterdijk's text."[59] In the letter, Habermas refers to Sloterdijk's text as "genuinely fascistic."[60] "In the ensuing scandal," writes Sjord van Tuinen, "Sloterdijk was branded a philosophical parvenu, a popstar of thought, a fascistoid breeder of the Übermensch, a cynical ideologist of Grand Politics, but also simply the new Nietzsche."[61] In one of the most bizarre of these accusations, Habermas acolyte Thomas Assheuer, editor of *Die Zeit*'s cultural pages, wrote a hyperbolic article titled "The Zarathustra Project" in which he accuses Sloterdijk of engaging in "quasi-totalitarian" philosophy and, in supposedly Nietzschean fashion, "coldly envision[ing] the diabolical potentials of genetic research."[62]

Over 600 articles were written about the scandal. The resulting powder keg, writes van Tuinen, "was a telling display of what it means to do journalism and philosophical or literary critique in a public sphere dominated by increasingly indifference-producing, non-friendship-constituting and therefore post-humanist mass media."[63] Slovenian philosopher Slavoj Žižek, one of the first prominent European figures to rise to Sloterdijk's defense, insists that Habermas perpetrated a "ridiculous over-reaction to Sloterdijk's Elmau speech" by bending over backward to detect "the echoes of Nazi eugenics in the (quite reasonable) proposal that biogenetics compels us to formulate new rules of ethics." Žižek characterizes Habermas' onslaught as "a rather sad spectacle" meant "to control the explosive results of biogenetics, to curtail the philosophical consequences of biogenetics."[64] He concludes that Habermas' efforts to reroute the narrative are symptomatic of the perhaps understandable but naïve "fear that something would effectively happen, that a new dimension of the 'human' would emerge, that the old image of human dignity and autonomy would [not] survive unscathed."[65]

In September 1999, Sloterdijk penned an open letter to both Assheuer and Habermas in *Die Zeit*. In response to "The Zarathustra Project," he chides Assheuer for his convenient misreading of "Rules for the Human Zoo" and accuses him of passively relaying his mentor's flight of fancy, which borders on "science fiction" when compared with the words found in the original text. He then moves on to Habermas, whom he accuses of initiating a malicious "whisper chain" with a view to excommunicating Sloterdijk from the liberal humanistic fold.[66]

Habermas' sovereign orchestration of the media's response behind closed doors is especially ironic, notes Sloterdijk, since he is revered in Germany as a "theorist of democratic dialogue" and standard-bearer of the Enlightenment tradition of free speech. While Habermas purported to advocate for openness and freedom of speech as vehicles of democratic rationality, he appears to have orchestrated an entire nexus of disinformation meant to preclude open dialogue about a timely philosophical question:

> You finally wanted to reveal what your extended concept of communicative action looks like [...] In any case, we now know better, through you and your docile students, what you mean by discussing, by thinking, by approaching problems, by the public and by openness. You have exemplified how poor reading can be used as a weapon, and you arranged a scene that helped us understand how dyslexia makes interesting connections with opportunism in overly loyal students.[67]

Willem Schinkel and Liesbeth Noordegraaf-Eelens write that Sloterdijk's letter "unmasks Habermas's liberalism of communication and discourse ethics as manipulati[on] behind the scenes," and they take him to task for endeavoring to scapegoat Sloterdijk for the legacy of German fascism "without so much as starting a dialogue with Sloterdijk himself."[68] By refusing to debate his rival while coordinating this media campaign, Habermas seemed to demonstrate Sloterdijk's diagnosis of the demise of epistolary philosophical friendship with the advent of a volatile digital media arena. When the dust settled, Sloterdijk "at once secured his place in the upper echelons of the German public and intellectual scene."[69]

Habermas' evasion of public debate is especially lamentable since he does elsewhere voice cogent, measured concerns about the seductions of Heidegger's pastoral rhetoric, his uptake of Nietzsche, and connections between some of Heidegger's seemingly apolitical ideas and the tenets of National Socialism. A decade before Sloterdijk first delivered "Rules for the Human Zoo," Habermas authored a powerful critique of Heidegger in "Work and Weltanschauung: The Heidegger Controversy from a German Perspective," wherein he argues that Heidegger's "Letter on Humanism" must be read from the perspective of his complicity with the Nazi regime. After exploring Heidegger's chauvinist account of the German language's singular authentic umbilical cord to the classical Greek tradition, he launches into a scathing historicization of Heidegger's philosophical obfuscation of the horrors of Nazism:

> Heidegger dealt with the theme of humanism at a time when the images of the horror that the arriving Allies encountered in Auschwitz and elsewhere had made their way into the smallest German village. If his talk of an "essential happening" had any meaning at all, the singular event of the attempted annihilation of the Jews would have drawn the philosopher's attention (if not already that of the concerned contemporary). But Heidegger dwells, as always, in the Universal. His concern is to show that man is the "neighbor of Being"—not the neighbor of man.[70]

Habermas writes that Heidegger's discourse on humanism did more than ignore the horrors of Nazism. He makes the compelling case that, well into the 1930s, Heidegger believed that National Socialism was the most humanistic political creed because only a philosophically informed fascism could protect Europe from a dystopian technological deluge that threatened to unhinge humanity from its pastoral destiny.[71] According to Habermas, there are radioactive traces of Heidegger's inhumane investment in Nazism across his writings on humanism and the history of Being. This is certainly a matter that he could have brought to Sloterdijk's attention with a view to bringing out the best in his colleague's encomium to the humanist tradition.

The missed encounter between Sloterdijk and Habermas is all the more unfortunate since, in spite of their disparate philosophical styles and enthusiasms, they would likely have discovered vibratory common ground on the topics of the corrosive potentials of biotechnology and the perennial lures of fascism.[72] Unfortunately, an open debate between two of the titans of the German humanistic tradition would never take place, and the German public was deprived of what should have been a philosophical exchange between friends, or at least well-humored acquaintances.

Habitat for Inhumanity

Perhaps "Rules for the Human Zoo" is best understood as a telecommunicative love letter that was routed through a whisper chain and submitted to the telephone game before resurfacing as a warning about the entangled coextensive arcs of humanism, technology, and politics in the digital twenty-first century. Against the tide of efforts to police the influx of technomodernity into philosophical dialogues, Sloterdijk's own purloined letter advocates for a very different orientation. Having emerged relatively intact from machinations to stigmatize its speculations, "Rules for the Human Zoo" argues for a more malleable approach to philosophy that, even as it navigates the archives for clues about our symbolic constitution, opens itself to the vicissitudes of a world that will never cease to bombard humanity with new exigencies and unexpected mysteries.

Humanism has always brandished an admixture of inherited and newly invented concepts, tropes, and technologies with a view to carving out a position in the world. If philosophy is to survive the maelstroms of modernity (some of which harbor genuinely fascistic potentials), philosophers will need to demonstrate their ability to wield an amalgam of old and new frameworks to apply them to a volatile, protean world that never stops disrupting the experience of what it means to be a person. Within a mediatic arena that forces book culture to compete with more alluring and mesmeric technologies, many would-be recipients of Plato's chain letter will turn away from what seems like a parochial atavism, the practice of sending and receiving letters that interrogate the question of what it means to be a human being. Even as some of humanism's standard-bearers abscond from its principles, Sloterdijk's letter demonstrates that the humanizing intergenerational love letter will never altogether vanish from a world in which "our lives are the confused answer to questions which were asked in places we have forgotten." It remains to be seen how many of us will continue to attune ourselves to the echoes of these queries amidst the roar of the arena.[73]

Bibliography

Assheuer, T. "*Das Zarathustra-Projekt*." *Die Zeit*. September 2, 1999. https://www.zeit.de/1999/36/199936. sloterdijk1_.xml.

Cumming, Robert Denoon. *Phenomenology and Deconstruction, Volume 1: The Dream is Over*. Chicago: University of Chicago Press, 1991.

Habermas, Jürgen. "Work and Weltanschauung: The Heidegger Controversy from a German Perspective." Translated by Steve McCumber. *Critical Inquiry* 15, No. 2 (1989): 431–456.

Heidegger, Martin. "Letter on Humanism." Translated by Frank Capuzzi. *Pathmarks*, 239–276. Edited by William McNeill. Cambridge: Cambridge University Press, 1998.

Sloterdijk's Love Letter on Humanism

Heidegger, Martin. "The Question Concerning Technology." Translated by William Lovitt. In *Basic Writings: From Being and Time (1927) to The Task of Thinking (1964)*, 307–342. Edited by David Farrell Krell. San Francisco: Harper and Row, 1993.

Nybakken, Oscar E. "*Humanitas Romana*." *Transactions and Proceedings of the American Philological Association* 70 (1939): 396–413. doi: 10.2307/283098.

Rabinbach, Anson. "Heidegger's Letter on Humanism as Text and Event." *New German Critique*, No. 62 (1994): 3–38. doi: 10.2307/488507.

Sartre, Jean-Paul. *Existentialism Is a Humanism*. Translated by Carol Macomber. New Haven: Yale University Press, 2007.

Schinkel, Willem and Noordegraaf-Eelens, Liesbeth. "Peter Sloterdijk's Spherological Acrobatics: An Exercise in Introduction." In *In Media Res: Peter Sloterdijk's Spherological Poetics of Being*, 7–28. Edited by Willem Schinkel and Liesbeth Noordegraaf-Eelens. Amsterdam: Amsterdam University Press, 2011.

Schultz, Norman. "The Controversy About Sloterdijk's 'Rules for the Human Zoo': Between Continental-Analytic Philosophy and Tropological Thinking." *Philosophy Today* 64, No. 1 (2020): 221–238.

Sloterdijk, Peter. "The Human-Park Speech and its Aftermath." Translated by Steve Corcoran. In *Neither Sun Nor Death*, 45–136. With Hans-Jürgen Heinrichs. Los Angeles: Semiotext(e), 2011.

Sloterdijk, Peter. "*Die Kritische Theorie ist Tot. Peter Sloterdijk Schreibt an Assheuer und Habermas*." *Die Zeit*. September 9, 1999. https://www.zeit.de/1999/37/199937.sloterdijk_.xml (accessed May 1, 2021).

Sloterdijk, Peter. "Rules for the Human Zoo: A Response to the Letter on Humanism." Translated by Mary Varney Rorty. *Environment and Planning D* 27, No. 1 (2009): 12–28.

Van Tuinen, Sjord. "'Transgenous Philosophy': Post-humanism, Anthropotechnics and the Poetics of Natal Difference." In *In Media Res: Peter Sloterdijk's Spherological Poetics of Being*, 43–66. Edited by Willem Schinkel and Liesbeth Noordegraaf-Eelens. Amsterdam: Amsterdam University Press, 2011.

Žižek, Slavoj. *The Parallax View*. Cambridge: MIT University Press, 2006.

Notes

1 Peter Sloterdijk, "Rules for the Human Zoo: A Response to the Letter on Humanism," trans. Mary Varney Rorty, *Environment and Planning D* 27, No. 1 (2009/1999): 13.

2 Ibid., 15.

3 Ibid., 12.

4 Ibid.

5 Ibid., 12–13.

6 Ibid., 13.

7 See Oscar E. Nybakken, "Humanitas Romana," in *Transactions and Proceedings of the American Philological Association* 70 (1939): 396–413. Sloterdjijk's account of the history of Cicero's telecommunicative network actually draws on conventional classicist accounts. Nybakken adds that Roman culture slowly abandoned the concept of *humanitas* in the years after Cicero's death. It would appear that after Quintilian's lifetime (25–100 AD), it remained more or less dormant until humanism, as preserved in Cicero's books and letters, was revived in the Italian Renaissance in the form of *studia humanitatis* ("studies of humanity"). This curriculum included canonistic studies in philosophy, rhetoric, grammar, history, literature, Greek, and Latin.

8 Sloterdijk, "Rules," 15.

9 Ibid.

10 Ibid.

11 Ibid.

12 See Jean-Paul Sartre, *Existentialism Is a Humanism*, trans. Carol Macomber (New Haven: Yale University Press, 2007), 22–23. Citing Heidegger as a significant influence, Sartre counterpoises his idiosyncratic existentialist definition of humanism against what he views as retrograde received notions. Sartre's existentialist humanism radically responsibilizes every individual, tasking subjects with both defining their own purpose in life and attending to the well-being of all of humanity. In this regard, Sloterdjik's conclusions may bring him closer to Sartre's prescriptions than to Heidegger's.

13 See Robert Denoon Cumming, *Phenomenology and Deconstruction, Volume 1: The Dream is Over* (Chicago: University of Chicago Press, 1991), 74–76. According to Cumming's account of their primarily epistolary relationship, Heidegger did not see much of value in Sartre's text. After Sartre sent Heidegger a signed copy of his book, Heidegger took fleeting interest in his French counterpart as a potential

advocate. After Germany's defeat, Heidegger was badly in need of such endorsements because a stigma had accrued to his body of work on account of his previous association with the Nazi party.

14 Sloterdijk, "Rules," 17.

15 Martin Heidegger, "Letter on Humanism," trans. Frank Capuzzi, in *Pathmarks*, ed. William McNeill (Cambridge: Cambridge University Press, 1998), 245.

16 Ibid., 246.

17 Ibid., 247.

18 Ibid.

19 Martin Heidegger, "The Question Concerning Technology," trans. William Lovitt, in *Basic Writings: From Being and Time (1927) to The Task of Thinking (1964)*, ed. David Farrell Krell (San Francisco: Harper and Row, 1993), 311. Sloterdijk's reading of this essay constitutes a big part of the subtext of "Rules for the Human Zoo." As in his "Letter on Humanism," "The Question Concerning Technology" dwells on what Heidegger views as the folly of popular conceptualizations of technology that emphasize human mastery over putatively neutral technological apparatuses that actually dwarf the humanistic tradition's capacity to influence the destiny of life on this planet.

20 See Nybakken, "Humanitas," 412–413. Erasmus' conception of *humanitas* integrates the Roman ideal of philanthropic participation in the body politic. For Vittorino, *humanitas* represents "Cicero's and Quintilian's ideals of a man who is not only a self-contained scholar but also an active participant in the affairs of men."

21 Heidegger, "Letter," 251.

22 Ibid., 252.

23 Ibid., 254.

24 Sloterdijk, "Rules," 17.

25 Ibid., 18.

26 Ibid.

27 Ibid.

28 Ibid., 19.

29 Ibid.

30 Ibid.

31 Ibid., 20.

32 See Anson Rabinbach, "Heidegger's Letter on Humanism as Text and Event," *New German Critique*, No. 62 (1994): 5–6. A wide variety of critics, from Adorno to Habermas, have justifiably taken issue with Heidegger's seeming complicity with the Nazi regime and view his philosophy as irremediably tainted as obscurantist Nazi propaganda. Sloterdijk certainly does not skirt the issue of Heidegger's political history and ethical compass. Nonetheless, a number of German philosophers still equate the excavation of Heidegger's body of work with the erasure of Nazi barbarism. This painful association has undoubtedly contributed to the "Rules for the Human Zoo" scandal.

33 Sloterdijk, "Rules," 20.

34 Ibid.

35 Ibid.

36 Ibid., 19.

37 Ibid.

38 Ibid.

39 Ibid.

40 Ibid., 22.

41 Qtd. in Sloterdijk, "Rules," 22.

42 Sloterdijk, "Rules," 22.

43 Ibid.

44 Ibid.

45 Ibid.

46 Ibid.

47 Ibid., 23.

48 Ibid., 21.

49 Ibid., 25.

50 Ibid., 26.

51 Ibid.

52 Ibid.

53 Ibid.

54 Ibid.
55 Ibid.
56 Ibid., 23.
57 Ibid., 27.
58 Ibid.
59 Sjord van Tuinen, "'Transgenous Philosophy': Post-humanism, Anthropotechnics and the Poetics of Natal Difference," in *In Media Res: Peter Sloterdijk's Spherological Poetics of Being*, eds. Willem Schinkel and Liesbeth Noordegraaf-Eelens (Amsterdam: Amsterdam University Press, 2011), 45.
60 Stephan Müller-Doohm, *Habermas: A Biography* (Cambridge: Polity, 2016), 1071. Müller-Doohm also entertains the theory that Sloterdijk deliberately deployed provocative language in "Rules for the Human Zoo" in order to goad his rivals into the philosophical battle that ensued. Nevertheless, it is hard to believe that he could have predicted that Habermas would go to the trouble of procuring a transcript of his lecture from the philosophy conference and then circulate it among journalists who would uniformly defer to his tendentious interpretation of the text. Müller-Doohm also explores Habermas' much more understandable longstanding reservations about both Nietzsche and Heidegger, both of whose views he regards as antithetical to his liberal democratic project, but nonetheless faults him for attributing these views to Sloterdijk.
61 Van Tuinen, "Transgenous," 45.
62 Thomas Assheuer, "Das Zarathustra-Projekt," *Die Zeit* (Berlin, Germany). September 2, 1999. In the aftermath of journalist Steven Geyer's disclosure that Assheuer had written the article at Habermas' behest, Assheuer's "quasi-totalitarian" remark was quietly removed from the archived version of the article.
63 Van Tuinen, "Transgenous," 45.
64 Slavoj Žižek, *The Parallax View* (Cambridge: MIT University Press, 2006), 179.
65 Ibid.
66 Peter Sloterdijk, *"Die Kritische Theorie ist Tot. Peter Sloterdijk Schreibt an Assheuer und Habermas," Die Zeit* (Berlin, Germany). September 9, 1999.
67 Ibid.
68 Willem Schinkel and Liesbeth Noordegraaf-Eelens, "Peter Sloterdijk's Spherological Acrobatics: An Exercise" in introduction to *In Media Res: Peter Sloterdijk's Spherological Poetics of Being*, eds. Willem Schinkel and Liesbeth Noordegraaf-Eelens (Amsterdam: Amsterdam University Press, 2011), 17.
69 Ibid.
70 Jürgen Habermas, "Work and Weltanschauung: The Heidegger Controversy from a German Perspective," trans. John McCumber, *Critical Inquiry* 15, No. 2 (1989): 449.
71 Ibid., 447.
72 See Norman Schultz "The Controversy About Sloterdijk's 'Rules for the Human Zoo': Between Continental-Analytic Philosophy and Tropological Thinking," *Philosophy Today* 64, No. 1 (2020): 221–238. Schultz claims that the most significant rift between the Habermas and Sloterdijk camps is ultimately more stylistic than substantive. As a paragon of German democratic philosophy, Habermas values lucidity and ratiocination. Sloterdijk's approach, on the other hand, is poetic and tropologically dense, to the point of antagonizing prevalent German analytic philosophical conventions. In this regard, his style is much closer to the German media theory tradition exemplified by the work of Friedrich Kittler and Bernhard Siegert.
73 See Peter Sloterdijk, interview with Hans-Jürgen Heinrichs, "The Human-Park Speech and its Aftermath," trans Steve Corcoran, in *Neither Sun Nor Death* (Los Angeles: Semiotext(e), 2011), 45–136. Over the course of this interview, Sloterdijk looks back on the scandal and elaborates on the trope of the inhumane digital media arena, which he characterizes as operating in accordance with a thanatotic cybernetic logic.

6

The Animal Turn as a Challenge to Humanism

Krzysztof Skonieczny

Introduction

In this volume, humanism is understood primarily as putting the human in the center of the world and the liberation from tyranny, be it divine or human. This understanding makes it a double-edged weapon. First, it is situated against the idea that the values by which men and women direct their lives need to have a non-human origin—to put it simply, that they need to come from a God or from gods. Second, and more importantly for the present chapter, it is based on the premise that it is the simple fact of being human, and not belonging to a specific *variety* or *kind* of human being, that is important for our stature in the ontological and ethical sense.

From this simple definition, it seems clear that any humanism needs to be—to use Richard Ryder's term popularized by Peter Singer—*speciesist*, i.e., that it values one *biological species* higher than any other, with the only criterion taken into consideration being the simple fact that one belongs to this species.[1] For that reason, humanism has been the target of attacks from scholars and activists arguing for the inclusion of animals both into the theoretical project usually associated with humanism (i.e., the "humanities" widely construed) and our ethical considerations. Conversely, the so-called *animal turn*—an increased interest in the human–animal relationship in the humanities and social sciences that can be traced back to the 1970s—has been seen by some as a danger to the humanist project, as it is believed that this manner of widening the theoretical and ethical scope can be detrimental to the notion of human uniqueness that has been central to humanism.

In this chapter, I try to show that rather than being a danger to the humanist project, the philosophers and scientists who have been part of this turn—regardless of if they are Darwinists, anti-humanists or posthumanists—can actually be seen as drawing radical consequences from humanism. In other words, recognizing the human closeness to animals does not outright negate humanism, but rather fits the logic of the humanist project, even if it does so in a challenging way.

I am not speaking of the "humanist project" by accident. The idea of humanism was, in this or other form, present in the Western world at least since Protagoras and his famous dictum that "Man is the measure of all things." Regardless of how we interpret his words, it is clear that Ancient Greek humanism was quite far from our current belief that to call oneself a "humanist" one must work toward a community that equally includes all humans, regardless of gender, creed, ethnicity, sexual orientation, etc. Indeed, not many (if any at all) great "humanists" before the late 19th century can live up to those standards. Ancient Greeks almost universally condoned slavery and the subjugation of women, and many of the greatest Enlightenment thinkers—Hume and Kant notwithstanding—were (at least according to our current standards) outright racist. In other

86   DOI: 10.4324/9781003046004-8

words, the idea that humanism includes everyone that is—in the biological sense—human is a historical development. This shows that humanism has not sprung from the ground as a ready set of principles, but rather needs to be understood as a *project* that has been painstakingly developing through centuries.

Traced in this way, the development of the humanist project shows that the equation of the subject of humanism with the human as a member of a biological species is problematic. For centuries, many if not most members of our species have not been thought of as subjects of humanism. This observation has two consequences. First, it renders problematic the idea that humanism can be straightforwardly called *speciesist*—if it has ever been true, it was only, at best, for the last few hundred years. In fact, from this point of view, *speciesism* is as much a possible flaw of humanism as it is an important, "progressive" development. Second—and conversely—it complicates the notion that humanism cannot profit from its widening so as to include something *other than the human*. While this conclusion may seem counterintuitive at best, I believe it can be shown that the animal turn offers such a widening and, even though it certainly proposes a challenge to the humanist viewpoint, it should also be seen as a continuation of some of the most valuable tendencies of humanism.

The Animal Turn

Throughout this chapter, I am using a rather wide understanding of the term "animal turn" as a process that began around the 1970s; Peter Singer's *Animal Liberation* is often mentioned in this context as a foundation for the increased interest in human–animal relationships. In the tradition of analytic philosophy, a number of works soon followed, with, for example, Mary Midgley's *Beast and Man* or Tom Regan's *The Case for Animal Rights* being often cited as crucial.[2] It is from these works (and authors) that some of the key developments in human–animal studies stem, with the 1994 Great Ape Project—a proposal to grant basic rights to some non-human primates, which later turned into an organization with the same name—initiated by Singer and Paola Cavalieri, being perhaps the most known.[3]

In the tradition of continental philosophy, the period from the 1970s also saw an interest in what was dubbed the "animal question," particularly from the anti-humanistically inclined thinkers, who saw in the (reprehensible) approach to animals one of the key tenets of the modern ontology of the subject, which they were intent on criticizing. Some crucial works include texts by Gilles Deleuze and Felix Guattari,[4] much of Jacques Derrida's later work,[5] and occasional forays into the field by Giorgio Agamben and others. In the 2000s and 2010s, the reinterpretations of these authors' texts have become the cornerstone of what Kenneth Shapiro calls the "Third Wave"[6] of human–animal studies, which focused on the theoretical problems surrounding the division between the human and the animal.

Aside from philosophical works, the increasing interest in human–animal relationships was also visible in other disciplines in the humanities and social sciences. The Anglican theologian Andrew Linzey introduced the question to theology in numerous texts, notably *Animal Rights: A Christian Assessment of Man's Treatment of Animals* and *Animal Theology*. The field of history also saw an increase of interest in the animal question, accompanied by a shift of perspective, described thusly by Erica Fudge:

> while [...] agricultural history tends to focus on animals only insofar as they offer a way of understanding particular farming practices, or changes in patterns of consumption, an animal history of agriculture—that is, a history that presents animals as being more than backdrops to, and props in, human affairs—can enable us to think about how livestock animals

changed the environments and the cultures they lived within; or how humans and animals lived together in emotional as well as economic relationships […] [S]uch work recognizes animals as actors.[7]

Some examples of books taking this perspective, aside from Fudge's own work,[8] include the works of the French historian Eric Baratay;[9] comprehensive lists of pertinent sources can be found in Fudge,[10] Ritvo,[11] and Roscher et al.[12]

In the realm of art history and art theory, a similar move from regarding animals as objects of art to seeing them as actual subjects; this of course follows an increased interest in the human–animal relationship (and generally environmental questions) in contemporary art. Some critics are predominately preoccupied with ethical questions, asking whether the use of animals by particular artists is moral or not.[13] Others—while not losing the ethical perspective—are less inclined to judge artists and more to ask about "contemporary art's distinctive contribution to understandings of human–animal relations."[14] A list of sources can be found in Zammit-Lucia.[15]

The animal turn has also had a profound impact on the study of literature; this is somewhat also an effect of the heightened interest that writers show in tackling the animal question. Even a modest summary of the existing literature would be far beyond the scope of this chapter, with, for example, the Palgrave Studies in Animals and Literature series alone already including 27 books on themes as varied as zoopoetics,[16] animals in Victorian literature[17] or in 21st-century fiction;[18] useful introductory texts are provided by McHugh et al.[19] and Borgards.[20]

History

As said before, one of the key aspects of the animal turn is the opposition to how animals were depicted and understood in Western thought, especially in the Modern period. This section presents a short overview of the key points of this modern paradigm; for the sake of clarity I am generally presenting this paradigm in the way that it is described in the human–animal studies literature, which is built on an opposition to it. This means that I am not taking into account works that seek to reinterpret the mentioned thinkers or parts of their work in order to show possible "pro-animal" stances, as is done, for example, by Christine Korsgaard,[21] who shows that there can be a place for animals in Kantian ethics.

I also do not analyze in detail the possible affinities between the various thinkers involved in the animal turn—which is a term usually used in reference to Western academic discourse aiming to counter a specifically Western (or even European) approach to animals—and other philosophical and religious traditions, especially those that espouse the generalized rule of nonviolence (*ahimsa*), i.e., Hinduism, Buddhism, or Jainism. These affinities have been explored in numerous texts, for example, in Regan;[22] useful introductions to various traditions of understanding the relationships between humans and animals (or the environment broadly construed) can be found in Jamieson.[23]

The paradigm of the modern Western attitude to animals is usually described as having been introduced by Rene Descartes, most famously in the *Discourse on the Method*. Descartes begins by saying that his analysis of the human body revealed that none of the functions require thinking, and that all these functions are those which we can be said to share with "animals without reason."[24] In fact, the human body, when analyzed on its own, can be regarded as "a machine which, having been made by the hands of God, is incomparably better ordered than any machine that can be devised by man."[25] Crucially, he adds: "if any such machines had the organs and outward shape of a monkey or of some other animal that lacks reason, we should have no means of knowing that they did not possess entirely the same nature as these animals."[26] In other words, the bodies of humans and animals are to be included in the same metaphysical order as machines—that of pure materiality, or, in Descartes' parlance, extensiveness. The key difference between humans and animals is that while the former have a rational soul, the latter do not.

This division has two important consequences, which are also ways in which the animal can be easily differentiated from the human. First, lacking a rational soul, animals cannot speak. This does not mean that they cannot utter human-like words—Descartes notes this ability among monkeys and parrots—or that they are mute and do not communicate their desires or their pain, immediately connected with the current state of their body. It does, however, mean that they cannot communicate their thoughts, clearly, because they do not have any.

The second consequence is that the purely bodily/mechanical nature of animals allows them— perhaps paradoxically—to be more perfect in certain tasks than we are. As Descartes points out:

> although many animals show more skill than we do in some of their actions, yet the same animals show none at all in many others; so what they do better does not prove that they have any intelligence, for if it did then they would have more intelligence than any of us and would excel us in everything. It proves rather that they have no intelligence at all, and that it is nature which acts in them according to the disposition of their organs.[27]

In other words, reason or intelligence is always a general skill, whose nature—especially its capability to exercise *free* decisions that are not bound to the mechanistic laws of nature—invites imperfection. If some animals are faster, stronger, more agile, or perceptive than us, it is only because they have been designed (programmed, we would say in today's parlance) to be so.

Regardless of how one decides to frame it—freedom vs mechanism, response vs reaction (pace Derrida), *res cogitans* vs *res extensa*, body vs soul—the difference between man and animal is, for Descartes, absolute. There is no in-between, there are no animals that have *some* intelligence, nor are there ontological differences between different species of animals—a monkey is as much an animal as a parrot or a sponge. Perhaps even more importantly, this difference is highly consequential in the realm of practice, i.e., the ethical situation of animals.

If animals are—for all intents and purposes—machines, then all their reactions are purely mechanical. They shy away from things that hurt them because they are programmed to keep their bodily integrity; they scream when hurt because it is their reaction, not because they "feel" pain in the human sense of the term, one that would require an immortal soul. Nicolas Malebranche, a 17th-century priest and post-Cartesianist, occasionalist philosopher, sums this up in a particularly poignant—perhaps even grotesque—way:

> they eat without pleasure, cry without pain [...] desire nothing, fear nothing, know nothing; and if they act in a manner that demonstrates intelligence, it is because God, having made them in order to preserve them, made their bodies in such a way that they mechanically avoid what is capable of destroying them.[28]

Malebranche reinforces this thesis with a theological argument that Gilbert Simondon ironically calls "touching":[29] "if they were capable of feeling, this would mean that under an infinitely just and omnipotent God, an innocent creature would suffer pain, which is a penalty and a punishment for some sin."[30] In other words, animal suffering would be so ethically unjust that it cannot be said to exist. Any pain that they seem to feel can be safely removed from our ethical consideration of animals themselves.

While Malebranche's absolute disavowal of animal pain might be an extreme case, even among philosophers that would admit its existence, the refusal to take this pain directly into account in ethical frameworks is rather typical. In one of the most influential Western ethical theories, Immanuel Kant argues that the only beings that are to be directly taken into account in our ethical considerations are humans (or other rational beings), as through their rationality they are able to formulate moral laws and act in accordance with them.

> So far as animals are concerned—Kant says—we have no direct duties. Animals are not self-conscious and are there merely as a means to an end. That end is man [...] Our duties toward animals are merely indirect duties toward humanity. Animal nature has analogies to human nature, and by doing our duties to animals in respect of manifestations of human nature, we indirectly do our duty toward humanity.[31]

This manner of thinking—which can be traced back at least to Thomas Aquinas, who gave it a theological justification—does not, of course, mean that Kant (or Aquinas for that matter) would condone wanton cruelty against animals. Indeed, we should, for example, reward our dogs for their service to us, and we should not kill them once they have stopped being useful. But this is not because—as Kant says—we would harm the dog directly. Instead, somebody who harms animals

> thereby damages the kindly and humane qualities in himself, which he ought to exercise in virtue of his duties to mankind. Lest he extinguish such qualities, he must already practice a similar kindliness towards animals; for a person who already displays such cruelty to animals is also no less hardened towards men.[32]

What this amounts to is that in our ethical considerations deeds towards animals only figure as analogies to our deeds towards humans and do not count in themselves. Conversely, of course, since animals have no reason, they cannot also be held accountable for their misdoings—they cannot be what is sometimes called "moral agents"; they do not belong to the class of beings whose behavior can be judged in moral terms. Once again, they are—albeit in a non-theological sense of the term—innocent.

Summing up this very cursory sketch of the Western attitude to animals, one can see a very particular set of traits. Animals are not rational; indeed, they are machines that perfectly follow the laws of Nature. They cannot speak; if by "speak," we mean the human way of using language. Not belonging to the realm of morality (either because they have not committed the original sin or because of their lack of rationality), they are innocent and their actions cannot be judged in the moral sense of the term. They are not direct objects of ethics, which means that any harm that befalls them is only ethical harm if it also somehow harms humans; in radical versions of this paradigm, they cannot be harmed at all, since any pain they might feel is not *actual* pain. Their lack of speech and ethics also means that they cannot form political communities in the human sense of the term.

As I show in the next part of this chapter, thinkers and researchers engaged in the "animal turn" have put each of these theses in question. And, much as the attitude described above had been dominating for much of the Modern period, it has also been challenged before the second part of the 20th century. Interestingly and contrary to the sometimes voiced belief that engagement in animal advocacy is somehow irreconcilable with the care about humanitarian causes—the people engaged in various pro-animal movements or otherwise (practically or theoretically) calling for the reassessment of our approach to animals have often been the same people who were engaged (for humanist reasons) in the reappraisal of the Western culture's attitude towards its other "others"—be it women, non-whites or non-Christians.[33]

Judging from the attention it has received, the most piercing call for the ethical consideration of animals came from Jeremy Bentham. It is interesting to note that while it was only given as a footnote in the *Introduction to the Principles of Morals and Legislation*, it put animals in the same logic as ethnic or racial minorities; their suffering, being the same in kind, should be equally important for our moral considerations as that of those whom we call "human." This logic of inclusion is characteristic of humanism:

> The day has been, I grieve to say in many places it is not yet past, in which the greater part of the species, under the denomination of slaves, have been treated by the law exactly upon the same footing, as, in England for example, the inferior races of animals are still. The day may come when the rest of the animal creation may acquire those rights which never could have been withholden from them but by the hand of tyranny. The French have already discovered that the blackness of the skin is no reason why a human being should be abandoned without redress to the caprice of a tormentor. It may come one day to be recognized, that the number of the legs, the villosity of the skin, or the termination of the os sacrum, are reasons equally insufficient for abandoning a sensitive being to the same fate? What else is it that should trace the insuperable line? Is it the faculty of reason, or, perhaps, the faculty of discourse? But a full-grown horse or dog, is beyond comparison a more rational, as well as a more conversible animal, than an infant of a day, or a week, or even a month, old. But suppose the case were otherwise, what would it avail? the question is not, Can they reason? Nor, Can they talk? But, Can they suffer?[34]

The Darwinian Approach

The same logic of inclusion is invoked in the first pages of Peter Singer's *Animal Liberation*, a book that was instrumental for the inception of the contemporary pro-animal movement. Singer starts his book by invoking an early anti-feminist text, Thomas Taylor's *A Vindication of the Rights of Brutes*, a satirical answer to Mary Wollstonecraft's *A Vindication of the Rights of Woman*, in which the author uses a "slippery slope" logic to show that Wollstonecraft's arguments can also be used to fight for the rights of animals, which, in his view, was of course preposterous.[35] Singer, however, believes that Taylor might have inadvertently been on to something—indeed, in the first few pages, he argues that if the utilitarian principle of equal consideration of interests (on which, he says, we all generally agree) is to be treated seriously, then it must be applied to all beings that have interests, regardless of gender, ethnicity, nationality, *and* species membership. This, of course, does not mean that Singer claims that animals should be treated *the same* as humans. His principle of equality only covers the equal consideration of (often different) interests, and not equality of treatment of all beings.[36]

The baseline for having or not having interests is the ability to feel pain; as the argument goes, any being who feels pain has an interest in avoiding it. The higher up the evolutionary ladder we go, the more interests a being has—it is clear that, say, an ape cares about more things and in a deeper manner than does a lizard, because thanks to its more complex brain it relates to the world in a much more complex manner. It is this kind of reasoning that makes Singer's utilitarianism compatible with endeavors such as the Great Ape Project, seeking the extension of basic rights to great apes.

Explicitly or implicitly, any argumentation such as Singer's must be based on the rejection of human exceptionalism, at least in the strong, metaphysical sense that was present in the Cartesian or Kantian reasonings described above. The foundation for such a rejection—aside from simply trusting the commonsense observation that a hurt animal feels pain in a similar manner a human does—is usually Darwinian in nature. The core insight is, of course, that since all animals (in fact all living beings) have come to existence by means of a unitary process of evolution by natural selection, all changes between individuals and species are ultimately of a quantitative and not qualitative nature. Since no metaphysical particle has been added to humans in the course of their evolution, the same goes for the difference between animals and humans. This is why Matthew

Calarco calls Singer's approach—as well as all the others analyzed in this subchapter—"identity" approaches, as they are based on the observation that in the ways that matter (ethically, ontologically, politically) there is an underlying identity connecting humans and animals.[37]

One might argue that Singer's particular version of the identity approach is not at odds with humanist exceptionalism—admitting that animals have interests or simply that they feel pain does little to upend the idea that, for example, the cognitive faculties of humans, especially their use of language, makes them qualitatively different (and superior) than other animals. This, however, would be a very different understanding of what constitutes a "qualitative difference" between humans and animals—if one accepts even the simple Darwinian argument offered here, one needs to acknowledge that this qualitative difference nonetheless comes into being thanks to a qualitative change brought about by evolution.

Regardless of this, the Darwinian approach offers more forceful challenges to humanist exceptionalism. On the one hand, a growing body of scientific studies have shown that numerous animals—most famously great apes, crows, dolphins, or octopi—have been shown to possess cognitive abilities that have heretofore been associated only with humans, from high-level intelligence to the ability to learn human language and creatively use it.[38] They have also been shown to possess empathy and other high-level emotional traits, as well as forming complicated political communities.[39] All that makes any human exceptionalism that is based on traits such as reason, language, politics or ethics highly problematic.

On the other hand, there have been attempts to extend ethical frameworks other than utilitarianism—more "exceptional" than utilitarianism—to non-human animals. In a series of influential books—most famously, *The Case for Animal Rights*—Tom Regan sought to expand rights theory to non-human animals. Regan claims that no other theory—not utilitarianism, not contractarianism, not any view based on promoting kindness and discouraging cruelty—can grasp that we should have direct duties to individual animals in the same way that we have direct duties to individual humans (embodied in our idea of *human rights*). To reinforce this view, Regan points to another key similarity between animals and humans:

> the really crucial, the basic similarity is simply this: we are each of us the experiencing subject of a life, a conscious creature having an individual welfare that has importance to us whatever our usefulness to others. We want and prefer things, believe and feel things, recall and expect things. And all these dimensions of our life, including our pleasure and pain, our enjoyment and suffering, our satisfaction and frustration, our continued existence or our untimely death—all make a difference to the quality of our life as lived, as experienced, by us as individuals. As the same is true of those animals that concern us (the ones that are eaten and trapped, for example), they too must be viewed as the experiencing subjects of a life, with inherent value of their own.[40]

The expansion of rights theory to animals is, of course, a much more radical move than doing the same with utilitarianism. The claim that (some) animals experience their lives in a way that is much like ours is much more poignant than simply saying that they have "interests" or feel pain. More interestingly, the rights view has one of its key sources in Kantian deontology, which, as I described above, is an example of radical human exceptionalism. By expanding this theory to animals, Regan is—in a way—expanding humanism to animals.

What Regan does with ethics, Sue Donaldson and Will Kymlicka do with politics. In *Zoopolis. A Political Theory of Animal Rights*,[41] they expand not just basic rights, but also a whole framework of international relations to the relations of humans with non-human animals. In their view, the model for our relationships with domesticated animals should be the one we use for the citizens of our countries; synanthropic or liminal animals—those who live alongside humans, for example, in cities, but are not domesticated, such as rats, racoons, or pigeons—should be given a status similar to denizens; and wild animals should be treated as inhabiting their own, sovereign countries.

A similarly wide-ranging theory was proposed by Martha Nussbaum, who sees her own *capabilities approach*—an alternative to rights theory—as a valid framework for understanding justice not only between humans, but also between humans and non-human animals (see Nussbaum 2007).

As said, all these theorists propose that since (some) animals possess the kinds of traits that humans see as worthy of taking into account in our ethical and political frameworks, these animals should also be included in those frameworks. In other words, whatever we deem worthy of protection and care in humans also exists in non-human animals—and this is why those non-human animals deserve protection and care. The Darwinian (or "identity", or "expansionist") approach can be summed up in a claim that, at least in some ways, at least some animals, are human in an ontologically, ethically, and politically important sense of the term.

The Anti- and Posthumanist Approaches

While the Darwinian approaches such as those described above are certainly the most known and widely discussed, especially within the public sphere at large, they have come under some scrutiny not only because they are said to undermine the human exceptionalism that is understood by many as a cornerstone for humanism, but also for the exact opposite reason—that they are, in fact, *too humanist*. They have largely come from thinkers critical of humanism in general. In this part I will show that even these approaches have a much more complicated relationship to humanism than what the simple monikers of anti- or posthumanism seem to suggest.

One such critique is waged by Rosi Braidotti, a posthumanist who recognizes her antihumanist inspirations. She calls Singer, Nussbaum, and other "identity" theorists "compensatory humanists." By this, she means that through their expansionism, these thinkers try to "make up" for the flaws of original, anthropocentric humanism, and proceed to do so through the

> reassess[ment of] the validity of a number of humanist values. These concern anthropomorphic selves, who are assumed to hold unitary identity, self-reflexive consciousness, moral rationality and the capacity to share emotions like empathy and solidarity. The same virtues and capabilities are also attributed to nonanthropomorphic others. The epistemological and moral assumptions that underscore this position have been in place since the Enlightenment, but were previously reserved for humans only, to the detriment of all non-human agents such as animals and plants. Animal rights people, whom I define as post-anthropocentric neo-humanists, converge on the need to uphold and expand on these values across all species.[42]

In other words, what is wrong with humanism is not the fact that we have failed to recognize aspects of humanity in non-human animals, but the concept of humanity and humanism itself.

For the purposes of this short exposition, Braidotti's understanding of humanism can be summarized as the universalization of a certain way of being human (i.e. white, male, European, able-bodied, etc.), which leads to the exclusion of a vast number of beings, both human and non-human. And while the answer to that conundrum for Braidotti (and other thinkers making similar arguments) is what is needed is a wholesale rejection of humanism (antihumanism) or its transcendence (posthumanism), I would like to argue that the motivations that move those thinkers to reject humanism in the face of the challenge posed by the animal are actually humanist in spirit (if not in name). In particular, I would like to argue that they pick up two of the key themes crucial to humanism, namely the liberation from all forms of oppression—with a special focus on theological oppression—and the building of a more equal community.

As said before, Braidotti's criticism is heavily inspired by (although also critical of) earlier anti-humanist tendencies present, especially in the 20th-century French poststructuralist philosophies, for example, in the works of Deleuze, Derrida or Foucault. As I indicated before, especially those first two thinkers have been influential for the animal turn (if not an outright part of it). Derrida's critique of the humanist understanding of animals—for example, through the deconstruction of the human/animal and response/reaction oppositions,[43] or by coining the concept "carnophallogocentrism"[44] to show how meat-eating is intimately linked with other aspects of Western subjectivity—is perhaps more widely discussed in the literature, but I believe that the analysis of Deleuze and Guattari's notion of *becoming-animal* is more instructive for those who want to understand the stakes of the anti-humanist critique of humanism and the way animals fit into this picture.

Deleuze and Guattari see becoming-animal not as an end, but as a part of a wider process of liberation from "the organism, signifiance and subjectification."[45] Put simply, they see all these—the fact that the human body is structured like an organism, the fact that we are using language in a particular signifying regime, and that we are ontologically structured as subjects—as not only the effects of social structures, but malicious effects. Our subjectivity—as they claim in *Anti-Oedipus*—was rightly described by Freud and psychoanalysis as oedipal, but Freud got a crucial thing wrong. For Freud, the chain of causality went from the individual and his family to society; society is, in a way, modeled after the individual, oedipal psyche. Deleuze and Guattari claim that, on the contrary, the individual psyche—or, in fact, our whole subjectivity—is shaped by social forces, which are defined by the interplay of the capital and the state. The role of psychoanalysts in this system is not to "discover" the unconscious drives or desires that shape their patients' subjectivity, but rather to impose, via psychoanalytic therapy, a certain model of subjectivity that best fits the capitalist mode of production. Put simply, Deleuze and Guattari see human subjectivity not as an objective state of affairs but as an effect of outside forces.

Becoming-animal is one of the strategies that Deleuze and Guattari propose to liberate oneself from this externally imposed subjectivity. The kind of animals that Deleuze and Guattari have in mind is neither the household pets (who for them is equally oedipalized as a human subject), nor symbolic, archetypal animals of the kind that Jungian psychoanalysts are adept at understanding, but rather "more demonic animals, pack or affect animals that form a multiplicity, a becoming, a population, a tale."[46] Rats, wolves, or lice are some of their favorite examples, but in essence any animal can be appropriate for the task if it is understood in a proper manner. What is important is that not only is the animal a member of a pack or band, but also that the animal is itself thought of as multiple and not a single, autonomous subject. On the political level, becomings-animal are proper to societies or groups that oppose the political apparatus of the state, for example, "hunting societies, war societies, secret societies, crime societies."[47]

Within such multiplicities, Deleuze and Guattari see special individuals—whom they call "anomalous" individuals, who are not simply opposed to, for example, state powers, but operate according to a wholly different logic—who they sometimes dub "sorcerers." It is those individuals on whom they focus their more detailed analyses, which include Gregor Samsa's becoming-cockroach or Captain Ahab's becoming-whale. Each of them opposes a system of state or capitalist power (embodied by the company for which Samsa works or Nantucket's usual "business" of whaling) by forming a special bond with an animal.

This vision is also staunchly anti-theological—Deleuze and Guattari often juxtapose the "revolutionary" sorcerer and the "reactionary" priest. Becoming-animal operates in the realm of pure immanence, with no place for transcendence or any other vertical or hierarchical relations. This "flat" ontology, heavily inspired by Spinoza, is an approach that is shared by posthumanist thinkers such as Donna Haraway, who also cites Alfred North Whitehead and the evolutionary biologist Lynn Margulis as her most important inspirations.

The Animal Turn as a Challenge to Humanism

Margulis is most famous for her symbiogenesis theory, which claims that the animal and plant cells have come into being through a process of endosymbiosis, that is the merger of simpler, procaryotic organisms into more complex cells with organelles such as mitochondria or plastids. While this part of her theory is widely accepted in contemporary biology, Margulis went on to propose that symbiosis—and not competition, as commonly believed in Neo-Darwinism—is the most important driver of evolution.[48]

Posthumanists such as Braidotti, Haraway or Myra Hird believe that ideas like this, even though seemingly confined to biology, should also inform our understanding of human societies and the relationships between humans and other species. Criticizing Deleuze and Guattari for the fact that their notion of becoming-animal, while political in nature, uses animals only as a means to an end—that is that "actual" animals don't even get in the picture—Haraway proposes a more complicated idea of a human–animal community. For her *Companion Species Manifesto*, dogs are pivotally important and since these animals have lived beside humans for as much as 20,000 years, they are biologically and culturally linked with us to a degree that makes the distinction between human and animal (or nature and culture) highly problematic.

Haraway is clear that her goal is to create a new ethics and politics of "significant otherness,"[49] which would make life in the current times (which she recognizes are highly troubled, also because of the complicated nature of the relationships between what we call nature, culture and technology in modern societies) more "livable."[50] She bases these ethics and politics on the notion that only through the recognition of the vast networks of relationships that create us can we strive for making sense of our current predicament. On the level of ontology, this of course means putting relations before subjects (it is relations that create subjects, and not vice-versa), which is of course contrary to the humanist ideal of the autonomous, rational individual human being.

Conclusions

The thinkers and researchers involved in the animal turn certainly challenge an important tenet of humanism—human exceptionalism. According to their view, any understanding of the human that places him or her above the animal realm in a qualitative manner is untenable on the theoretical level and noxious on the practical level. Neither Singer and Regan, nor Deleuze and Guattari, nor Haraway and Braidotti would subscribe to, for example, the Kantian version of Enlightenment humanism.

However, even if they sometimes vehemently criticize humanism and would deny any subscription to its ideals and values, if we treat humanism as a project rather than a set of rules that have been cast in stone at a given historical moment—for example, in the Enlightenment or 15th-century Italy—we can see that to a large extent these theories can be treated as an extension of this project.

It is especially visible in the case of the Darwinian approach, which in many cases simply expands ethical and political frameworks that were built around humanist values to other beings. What those theorists seem to be saying is that humanism is a valid project, but it is perhaps a misnomer, because the traits which we value ethically in humans are also present outside our species.

Anti- and posthumanist theorists propose a much more fundamental reappraisal of humanism, but it can also be argued that their approaches share some motivations with the humanist project. Deleuze and Guattari, in their notion of becoming-animal, seek to liberate the subject from a form of oppression that they find in subjectivity itself. Haraway engages with companion species because she believes that only through such an engagement can we form a truly just (or, in her words, livable) community.

Regardless of whether or not we find the idea of including non-human animals in the humanist project tempting, dangerous, much needed, or outright absurd, given the recent advances of not only biology and ethology, but also philosophy and theory in general, it seems impossible for any future humanism—if there is to be one—to do without some form of serious engagement with non-human animals.

Bibliography

Adams, Carol J. *The Sexual Politics of Meat: A Feminist-Vegetarian Critical Theory.* London: Bloomsbury Academic, 2015.

Baker, Steve. *Artist Animal.* Minneapolis: University of Minnesota Press, 2013.

Baratay, Eric. *Le Point de Vue Animal. Une Autre Version de Histoire.* Paris: Seuil, 2012.

Baratay, Eric, and Elisabeth Hardouin-Fugier. *Zoo: A History of Zoological Gardens in the West.* London: Reaktion Books, 2002.

Bentham, Jeremy. *An Introduction to the Principles of Morals and Legislation*, Volume 2. London: W. Pickering, 1823.

Borgards, Roland. "Introduction: Cultural and Literary Animal Studies." *Journal of Literary Theory* 9, No. 2 (2015): 155–160. doi: 10.1515/jlt-2015-0008.

Braidotti, Rosi. *The Posthuman.* Cambridge: Polity Press, 2013.

Calarco, Matthew. *Thinking Through Animals: Identity, Difference, Indistinction.* Stanford: Stanford Briefs, 2015.

Cavalieri, Paola and Peter Singer. *The Great Ape Project. Equality Beyond Humanity.* New York: St. Martin's Press, 1994.

Deleuze, Gilles and Felix Guattari. *Kafka. Toward a Minor Literature.* Translated by Dana Polan. Minneapolis: University of Minnesota Press, 1986.

Deleuze, Gilles and Felix Guattari. *A Thousand Plateaus.* Translated by Brian Massumi. Minneapolis: University of Minnesota Press, 2005.

Derrida, Jacques. *The Animal that Therefore I Am.* Translated by David Wills. New York: Fordham University Press, 2008.

Derrida, Jacques. *The Beast and the Sovereign. Volume I.* Translated by Geoffrey Bennington. Chicago: University of Chicago Press, 2009.

Derrida, Jacques and Jean-Luc Nancy. "Eating Well." In *What Comes After the Subject?*, edited by Eduardo Cadava, Peter Connor and Jean-Luc Nancy. London and New York: Routledge, 1991, 96–119.

Descartes, Rene. *The Philosophical Writings of Descartes. Volume I.* Translated by John Cottingham et al. Cambridge: Cambridge University Press, 1985.

Driscoll, Kári, and Eva Hoffmann, eds. *What Is Zoopoetics? Texts, Bodies, Entanglement.* Cham: Palgrave Macmillan, 2018.

Donaldson, Sue and Will Kymlicka. *Zoopolis. A Political Theory of Animal Rights.* Oxford: Oxford University Press, 2001.

Fudge, Erica, ed. *Renaissance Beasts: Of Animals, Humans, and Other Wonderful Creatures.* Urbana and Chicago: University of Illinois Press, 2004.

Fudge, Erica, ed. "What Was It Like to Be a Cow?: History and Animal Studies." In *The Oxford Handbook of Animal Studies*, edited by Linda Kalof. Oxford: Oxford University Press, 2017, 258–278.

Haraway, Donna. "The Companion Species Manifesto. Dogs, People and Significant Otherness." In *Manifestly Haraway.* Minneapolis and London: University of Minnesota Press, 2016, 91–198.

Jamieson, Dale, ed. *A Companion to Environmental Philosophy.* Malden and Oxford: Blackwell Publishers, 2001.

Kant, Immanuel. *Lectures on Ethics.* Translated by Peter Heath. Cambridge: Cambridge University Press, 1997.

Korsgaard, Christine. "Fellow Creatures: Kantian Ethics and Our Duties to Animals." Tanner Lecture on Human Values delivered on February 6, 2004. https://tannerlectures.utah.edu/_documents/a-to-z/k/korsgaard_2005.pdf (Accessed June 23, 2021)

Linzey, Andrew. *Animal Rights: A Christian Assessment of Man's Treatment of Animals.* London: SCM Press, 1976.

Linzey, Andrew. *Animal Theology.* Chicago: University of Illinois Press, 1994.

Malamud, Randy. "Americans Do Weird Things with Animals, or, Why Did the Chicken Cross the Road?" In *Animal Encounters*, edited by Tom Tyler and Manuela Rossini. Leiden: Brill, 2009, 73–96.

Malebranche, Nicolas. *The Search After Truth: With Elucidations of The Search After Truth.* Translated and edited by Thomas M. Lennon, Paul J. Olscamp. Cambridge: Cambridge University Press, 2007.

Margulis, Lynn. *Symbiotic Planet. A New Look at Evolution.* New York: Basic Books, 1988.

Mazzeno, Laurence W., and Ronald D. Morrison, eds. *Animals in Victorian Literature and Culture. Contexts for Criticism*. Cham: Palgrave Macmillan 2017.

McHugh, Susan, Robert McKay and John Miller, eds. *The Palgrave Handbook of Animals and Literature*. Cham: Palgrave Macmillan, 2021.

Midgley, Mary. *Beast and Man. The Roots of Human Nature*. New York: Routledge, 2003 [1978].

Nussbaum, Martha. *Frontiers of Justice. Disability, Nationality, Species Membership*. Cambridge: The Belknap Press, 2007.

Parry, Catherine. *Other Animals in Twenty-First Century Fiction*. Cham: Palgrave Macmillan, 2017.

Regan, Tom. "The Case for Animal Rights." In *In Defense of Animals*. Edited by Peter Singer. New York: Basil Blackwell, 1985, 13–26.

Regan, Tom, ed. *Animal Sacrifices. Religious Perspectives on the Use of Animals in Science*. Philadelphia: Temple University Press, 1986.

Regan, Tom. *The Case for Animal Rights*. Berkeley and Los Angeles: University of California Press, 2004 [1983].

Ritvo, Harriet. "History and Animal Studies." *Society & Animals* 10, 4 (2002): 403–406.

Roscher, Mieke, André Krebber and Brett Mizelle, eds. *Handbook of Historical Animal Studies*. Oldenburg: De Gruyter, 2021.

Shapiro, Kenneth. "Human-Animal Studies: Remembering the Past, Celebrating the Present, Troubling the Future." *Society & Animals* 28, 7 (2020): 797–833, doi: 10.1163/15685306-BJA10029

Simondon, Gilbert. *Two Lessons on Animal and Man*. Translated by Drew S. Burk. Minneapolis: Univocal, 2011.

Singer, Peter. *Animal Liberation*. New York: Ecco, 2002 [1973].

Waal, Frans de. *Are We Smart Enough to Know How Smart Animals Are?* New York: W. W. Norton & Company, 2016.

Waal, Frans de. *Mama's Last Hug. Animal Emotions and What They Tell Us About Ourselves*. New York: W.W. Norton & Company, 2018.

Zammit-Lucia, Joe. "Practice and Ethics of the Use of Animals in Contemporary Art." In *The Oxford Handbook of Animal Studies*, edited by Linda Kalof. Oxford: Oxford University Press, 2017, 433–455.

Notes

1 See Peter Singer, *Animal Liberation* (New York: Ecco, 2002 [1973]).

2 For example, in Kenneth Shapiro, "Human-Animal Studies: Remembering the Past, Celebrating the Present, Troubling the Future." *Society & Animals* 28, 7 (2020): 797–833.

3 See Paola Cavalieri and Peter Singer. *The Great Ape Project. Equality Beyond Humanity* (New York: St. Martin's Press.1994).

4 See *Kafka. Toward a Minor Literature*. Translated by Dana Polan (Minneapolis: University of Minnesota Press, 1986). See also *A Thousand Plateaus*. Translated by Brian Massumi (Minneapolis: University of Minnesota Press, 2005).

5 See *The Animal that Therefore I Am*. Translated by David Wills (New York: Fordham University Press, 2008). See also *The Beast and the Sovereign*. Volume I. Translated by Geoffrey Bennington (Chicago: University of Chicago Press, 2009).

6 Shapiro, 2020.

7 Erica Fudge. "What Was It Like to Be a Cow?: History and Animal Studies." In *The Oxford Handbook of Animal Studies*, edited by Linda Kalof (Oxford: Oxford University Press, 2017), 261.

8 Erica Fudge, ed. *Renaissance Beasts: Of Animals, Humans, and Other Wonderful Creatures* (Urbana and Chicago: University of Illinois Press, 2004).

9 See Eric Baratay and Elisabeth Hardouin-Fugier. *Zoo: A History of Zoological Gardens in the West* (London: Reaktion Books, 2002). See especially Eric Baratay. *Le Point de Vue Animal. Une Autre Version de Histoire* (Paris: Seuil, 2012).

10 "What Was It Like to Be a Cow?: History and Animal Studies." In *The Oxford Handbook of Animal Studies*, edited by Linda Kalof (Oxford: Oxford University Press, 2017), 258–278.

11 Harriet Ritvo. "History and Animal Studies." *Society & Animals* 10, 4 (2002): 403–406.

12 Mieke Roscher, André Krebber and Brett Mizelle, eds. *Handbook of Historical Animal Studies* (Oldenburg: De Gruyter, 2021).

13 See Randy Malamud. "Americans Do Weird Things with Animals, or, Why Did the Chicken Cross the Road?" In *Animal Encounters*, edited by Tom Tyler and Manuela Rossini (Leiden: Brill, 2009), 73–96.

14 Steve Baker. *Artist Animal* (Minneapolis: University of Minnesota Press, 2013), 3.

15 Joe Zammit-Lucia. "Practice and Ethics of the Use of Animals in Contemporary Art." In *The Oxford Handbook of Animal Studies*, edited by Linda Kalof (Oxford: Oxford University Press, 2017), 433–455.

16 Kári Driscoll and Eva Hoffmann, eds. *What Is Zoopoetics? Texts, Bodies, Entanglement* (Cham: Palgrave Macmillan, 2018).

17 Laurence W. Mazzeno and Ronald D. Morrison, eds. *Animals in Victorian Literature and Culture. Contexts for Criticism* (Cham: Palgrave Macmillan 2017).

18 Catherine Parry. *Other Animals in Twenty-First Century Fiction* (Cham: Palgrave Macmillan, 2017).

19 Susan McHugh, Robert McKay, and John Miller, eds. *The Palgrave Handbook of Animals and Literature* (Cham: Palgrave Macmillan, 2021).

20 Roland Borgards. "Introduction: Cultural and Literary Animal Studies." *Journal of Literary Theory* 9, No. 2 (2015): 155–160.

21 Christine Korsgaard. "Fellow Creatures: Kantian Ethics and Our Duties to Animals." Tanner Lecture on Human Values delivered on February 6, 2004. https://tannerlectures.utah.edu/_documents/a-to-z/k/korsgaard_2005.pdf (accessed June 23, 2021).

22 Tom Regan, ed. *Animal Sacrifices. Religious Perspectives on the Use of Animals in Science* (Philadelphia: Temple University Press, 1986).

23 Dale Jamieson, ed. *A Companion to Environmental Philosophy* (Malden and Oxford: Blackwell Publishers, 2001).

24 Rene Descartes. *The Philosophical Writings of Descartes.* Volume I. Translated by John Cottingham et al. (Cambridge: Cambridge University Press, 1985), 134.

25 Ibid., 139.

26 Ibid.

27 Ibid., 141.

28 Nicolas Malebranche. *The Search After Truth: With Elucidations of The Search After Truth.* Translated and edited by Thomas M. Lennon, Paul J. Olscamp (Cambridge: Cambridge University Press, 2007), 494–495.

29 Gilbert Simondon. *Two Lessons on Animal and Man.* Translated by Drew S. Burk (Minneapolis: Univocal, 2011), 75.

30 Malebranche, 323.

31 Immanuel Kant. *Lectures on Ethics.* Translated by Peter Heath (Cambridge: Cambridge University Press, 1997), 212.

32 Ibid.

33 For examples, see Carol J. Adams. *The Sexual Politics of Meat: A Feminist-Vegetarian Critical Theory* (London: Bloomsbury Academic, 2015).

34 Jeremy Bentham. *An Introduction to the Principles of Morals and Legislation*, Volume 2. (London: W. Pickering, 1823), 235–236.

35 Singer, 3

36 Ibid., 5.

37 Matthew Calarco. *Thinking Through Animals: Identity, Difference, Indistinction* (Stanford: Stanford Briefs, 2015).

38 See Frans de Waal. *Are We Smart Enough to Know How Smart Animals Are?* (New York: W. W. Norton & Company, 2016).

39 See Frans de Waal. *Mama's Last Hug. Animal Emotions and What They Tell Us About Ourselves* (New York: W.W. Norton & Company, 2018).

40 Tom Regan, ed. *Animal Sacrifices. Religious Perspectives on the Use of Animals in Science* (Philadelphia: Temple University Press, 1986), 186.

41 Sue Donaldson and Will Kymlicka. *Zoopolis. A Political Theory of Animal Rights* (Oxford: Oxford University Press, 2001).

42 Rosi Braidotti. *The Posthuman* (Cambridge: Polity Press, 2013), 76.

43 See Jacques Derrida. *The Animal that Therefore I Am.* Translated by David Wills (New York: Fordham University Press, 2008).

44 See Jacques Derrida and Jean-Luc Nancy. "Eating Well." In *What Comes After the Subject?*, edited by Eduardo Cadava, Peter Connor and Jean-Luc Nancy (London and New York: Routledge, 1991), 96–119.

45 Gilles Deleuze and Felix Guattari. *A Thousand Plateaus*, 159.

46 Ibid., 241.

47 Ibid., 242.

48 See Lynn Margulis. *Symbiotic Planet. A New Look at Evolution* (New York: Basic Books, 1988).

49 Donna Haraway. "The Companion Species Manifesto. Dogs, People and Significant Otherness." In *Manifestly Haraway* (Minneapolis and London: University of Minessota Press, 2016), 95.

50 Ibid., 96.

PART II

Literary Perspectives on Humanism, East and West

7
Mapping Indic Humanism(s) in Vedic Medical and Post-Vedic Tāntric Epistemologies

Abhisek Ghosal

Introduction

The term humanism consists of both "human" meaning us and "ism" referring to a form of ideology. The conflation of two terms is reflective of how society is often understood both in terms of humancentric thoughts and how human beings are ideologically held superior to non-human beings in the world. Put into other words, humanism generally connotes the celebration of human potentials over the potentials of other living (and non-living) beings in the world in terms of rationality and ratiocination, and insists that human beings need to be regarded as the parameters for both understanding and taking the measure of the progress and development of the world. According to Humanist International, a humanist organization of international repute, humanism celebrates:

> a democratic and ethical life stance that affirms that human beings have the right and responsibility to give meaning and shape to their own lives. Humanism stands for the building of a more humane society through an ethics based on human and other natural values in a spirit of reason and free inquiry through human capabilities. Humanism is not theistic, and it does not accept supernatural views of reality.[1]

This line of thought implies that humanism is at bottom, both a celebration of humanness and an ideological position that upholds all the rights and capacities of human beings. A humanist is someone who proposes that human beings are the best "curators" of different epistemes and can understand the world around them better than any other living being, since human beings are blessed with the power of ratiocination and potential. Andrew Copson is one important scholar who has claimed that "Humanism begins with the human being and asserts straight away that the active deployment of his or her senses is the way to gain knowledge."[2] What is even more interesting is that humanism is not an unalterable standpoint and thus is frequently dragged into several interdisciplinary interpretations. In fact, one might more accurately refer to humanism in the plural, as humanisms. It is usually believed that being the dominant species in the world, human beings can rule the roost and challenge the throne of God. In a way, the world is in the hands of human beings who are free subjects and have the freedom of choice. Human beings create knowledge systems to comprehend the functioning of the world and have unflinching faith in autonomy. For Peter Berry, liberal humanists are those who "believe in 'human nature' as something fixed and constant."[3] In Berry's view, this means that liberal humanists set up epistemic frameworks which uphold the unwavering and constant nature of human beings across time and space.

DOI: 10.4324/9781003046004-10

This implies, for instance, that human attitudes to worldly affairs remain constant and can exceed contextual limitations. This further implies that the characteristic features of human attitudes are unchanging and not subject to spatio-temporal alterations.

At this point, one may stop and ponder a few questions: Is Western liberal humanism to be regarded as the whole of the humanist tradition? Are there no alternative humanist discourses? Does Western liberal humanism (especially when considered as a phenomenon that emerged as a distinct philosophical school of thought in the second half of the preceding century) have semantic and syntactic proximity to, for example, Indic humanism(s)? Is Indic humanism a derivative of a general conception of humanism? What is the crux of the Indic brand of humanism? Do Indic humanism(s) have distinctive epistemological structures and strictures? These simple yet unsettling questions lead one to delve deeper into the ways through which Indic humanism(s), as a philosophical standpoint, began to grow up in Vedic medical and post-Vedic tāntric traditions.

Indic Humanism(s): A Critical Overview

Unlike classical humanism, which originated in Greece and Rome and is commonly held to be the source for Western conceptualizations of humanism, Indic humanism(s) began to appear in varied manifestations along with the progression of Vedic and post-Vedic cultural and epistemological traditions. At this point, it needs to be mentioned that Indic humanism has to be comprehended in plural terms (thus, as Indic *humanisms*) not only because it manifests in diverse forms in different political and cultural narratives, but also because it is charged up with layers of significance and connotation. Nuanced understanding of the term "Indic humanism(s)" can help one comprehend its polyvalence and multidimensionality.

One of the significant traits of Indic humanism(s) can be found in an emphasis on plurality. Whereas Renaissance humanism celebrated the power of "man" over other living beings and upheld the rational faculties of "man" to interrogate the existence and the role of the God behind the creation of this universe, Indic humanism(s) originating in Vedic and post-Vedic periods emphasized the coexistence of all living beings in the world (thus anticipating the contemporary animal studies movement, for example).[4] Indic humanism(s) have had distinct connections with spirituality and the non-human world. It reflects how the virtues and values of human beings gave due and equal importance to the spiritual aspects of life. Humanisms developed in ancient India were mostly grounded on human reasoning and subjectivity, and more importantly allowed people to think freely. Therefore, contemporary humanism(s) were not divested of the spiritual aspects which played important roles in the lives of human beings.

Unlike Western conceptions of humanism, Indic humanism(s) upheld both human reasoning potentials and the coexistence of all living beings, along with human interventions into spiritual affairs, scientific advancements, cosmological explorations, and plurality in terms of thinking and practice, to name only a few among many elements. The forms and manifestations of Indic humanism(s) are manifold. One may find traces of humanism in many different Vedic and post-Vedic epistemic traditions. For instance, in the field of Vedic religious practices, one may find how humanistic thoughts are entwined therein. As Pratap Chandra pertinently observes:

> The basis of karma-kanda or Vedic ritualism was the belief that the mantras were more powerful than these anthropomorphic gods. If the rituals were carried out correctly the gods had no option but to grant whatever boon was sought by whatever kind of man or demon.[5]

Vedic ritualistic practices carried out by human beings were too powerful to be denied by gods. Chandra continues to comment on the "radical plurality" exhibited by means of free-thinking and reasoning in ancient India:

Mapping Indic Humanism(s)

[the] kind of free and utterly unfettered thinking we notice in them is perhaps not imaginable even in modern times. That society or a particular group in it could exercise some sort of thought-control over the masses was clearly unthinkable in those days. Both exhibit radical plurality, of both ideas and customs.[6]

Chandra is right in arguing that in ancient Indian society, pluralism, coexistence, rationality, and freedom of thought used to work hand in hand, resulting in remarkable human progress and development. The advancements of ancient Indian society in terms of science and technology, cosmology and astrology attest to the dissemination of humanistic thoughts in different disciplines. Although the concept of "humanism" is relatively newer than Vedic and post-Vedic cultural practices, humanistic ideas found in different epistemic traditions reveal that humanism(s) originating in Vedic and post-Vedic periods were in a nascent state and left profound impacts on the subsequent emergence of different schools of thought supported by anthropocentrism.

The Indic brand of humanism has been, to a large extent, shaped by Vedic and post-Vedic epistemic traditions. The word *Veda* means a storehouse of knowledge and is comprised of *Samhitā*, *Brāhmaṇa*, *Āraṇyaka*, and *Upaṇṣad*. Etymologically speaking, the word *Veda* is derived from the root word "Vid" and refers to a kind of knowledge that can neither be verified by human sensory organs nor contested by means of human ratiocination. Knowledge of Veda is thus supposed to be an incontestable epistemic repository and has been instrumental in mapping the contours of Indic humanism. Whereas *Ṛgveda*, the oldest and possibly the richest literary repository, mainly deals with the formative and evolutionary decades of humanism, *Sāmveda* incorporates the enormous role of music in the construction of humanism, *Atharbaveda* focuses on human explorations in the field of medical humanities and *Yayurveda* consists of mantras for yajñas.[7] The *Vedas* led humanity in varied directions and have been a reference point for human progress. If one studies different branches of *Veda*, one can understand that in the Vedic period different dimensions of humanism were celebrated and put into practice. Such concepts as freedom, family, logic, culture, social stratification, technological innovation, and scientific discovery have been elaborated at length in the *Vedas*. For instance, during Vedic times, women used to enjoy the freedom to utter Vedic mantras like men; they used to take a public part in worshiping; they used to teach young children:

> purākalpekumārīnāṁmauñjībandhanamiṣyate /
> adhāpanaṃca vedānāṁsābitrībacanaṁtathā //[8]
> [During ancient times, young and unmarried girls used to wear sacred threads; used to read Vedas; used to utter sābitrī mantras.][9]

Additionally, women used to engage in embroidery, domestic works, dyeing, woodworks, craftwork, and so on. Along with men, women were authorized to take on enemies in war. In *Ṛgveda*, it is found that an Aryan warrior said: *"striyo hi dāsaāyudhānicakrekiṁ me karannabalāasyasenā?"* [Dāsjāti (possibly referring to the *sudra* community) engages their women in warfare as weapons; what damage would their naïve women troops cause to me?].[10] Besides this, there are references to polygamous relationships. Women used to walk ahead of their spouses. They were held as the better "half" of their husbands. In *Sāmveda*, there are plenty of references that suggest that women learned music, dances, and musical instruments. In fact, Sukumari Bhattacharyya maintains that courtesans used to work as spies on behalf of the government.[11]

Common folks were clearly concerned about Nature and its various dimensions. Yogiraj Basu argues that common folks used to join different professions to earn their livings:

> Akṣairmādivyahkṛṣimitkṛṣaswabittaramasvabahumanyamānah /
> Tatra gabahkitabatatrajayatanmevicaṣtesabitāyamaryah //[12]

[Do not play pāśā, do cultivation. Agricultural works can bring in fame and wealth. Through cultivation your cow shall find [...] —Sabitādeva speaks this to me.][13]

Apart from this, people used to build up roads and carriages, join the gold-mining industry, the leather industry, the linen industry, the iron industry, public works, the port industry, the weapons-making industry, astrology, etc.

In the post-Vedic period, different human values were reconsidered and re-explored. For instance, during the period of *Rāmāyaṇa* and *Mahābhārata*, humanism took on different manifestations. With the developments of language and culture, human society was gradually unfolding. In *Rāmāyaṇa*, one may find vivid descriptions of land, oceans, mountains, forests, cultural organization, as well as the development of urbanity, warfare, migration, and so on. In *Mahābhārata*, one may trace practices of domesticity, familial dispute, exile, warfare, politics, ethics, economics, and heroism, to name only a few. *Gītā* focuses on different *yogās*[14] for human life, including *karmayoga*, *gñānyoga*, *bhaktiyoga*, *biṣādayoga*, *rājayoga*, and so on. In a gesture toward the "universality" of Indic humanism(s), Professor Suresh Chandra Bandhapadhyay argues (in *History of Sanskrit Literature: Veda, Epic, Purāṇa, Philosophy, Alaṁkāra, and Tantra*) that *Gītā* does not belong to any religion, but is the essence of all religious consciousnesses. The significance of *Gītā* is timeless and has been the source of different branches of humanism. Later, Manu in his *Dharmaśāstra* codified various aspects of life, human rights, and laws concerning humanity at large. In this book, Manu analyzed different offshoots of criminology, including penology and victimology, and suggested legal procedures to follow when dealing with various types of crime and criminal behavior. As P. V. Kane observes, *Dharmaśāstra* deals with:

> several *varṇas* (classes), *āśramas* (stages of life), their privileges, obligations and responsibilities; the *saṁskāras* performed on an individual (from *garbhādhāna* to *antyeṣṭi*); the duties of the *brahmacārin* (the first *āśrama*); *anadhyāyas* (holidays on which Vedic Study was stopped); the duties of a *snātaka* (one who has finished the first stage of life); *vivāha* (marriage) and all matters connected therewith; the duties of the *gṛhastha* (house-holder's stage); *śauca* (daily purification of body); the five daily *yajñas*; *dāna* (gifts); *bhakṣyābhakṣya* (what food should one partake of and what not); *śuddhi* (purification of persons, vessels, clothes, etc.); *āśauca* (impurity on birth and death); *antyeṣṭi* (rites on death); Śrāddha (rites performed for the deceased ancestors and relatives); *strīdharma* (special duties of women) and *strīpuṁdharma* (duties of husband and wife) [...] *vyavahāra* (judicial procedure and the sphere of substantive law such as crime and punishments, contracts, partition and inheritance, adoption, gambling, etc.) [...] *śānti* (rites on the happening of portents of for propitiating the planets, etc).[15]

The wide corpus of *Dharmaśāstra* had undoubtedly contributed to the developments of humanism. While explaining the semantic connotations of *Dharmaśāstra*, Kane maintains that *Dharmaśāstra* does not necessarily speak of religious codes of life but

> a mode of life or a code of conduct, which regulated a man's work and activities as a member of society and as an individual and was intended to bring about the gradual development of a man and to enable him to reach what was deemed to be the goal of human existence.[16]

The preaching and teaching of this great work enriched post-Vedic epistemic traditions on the one hand, and brought some unexplored dimensions of humanism to the notice of common folks and posterity, on the other. One of those dimensions is the relation between medicine and specifically human concerns, akin to what we often refer to now as the medical humanities.

Mapping Indic Humanism(s)

Critical Deliberations on Indic Humanisms in Vedic Medical Humanities

What are the medical humanities? How do they bear the traces of humanism? David Greaves and Martyn Evans note that there are some critics who have attempted to define this domain of research as "complementing medical science and technology through the contrasting perspective of the arts and humanities"[17] and there are some other critics who map it as an attempt to "refocus the whole of medicine in relation to an understanding of what it is to be fully human," while further noting that "the reuniting of technical and humanistic knowledge and practice is central to this enterprise."[18] Following these perspectives, one may argue that the medical humanities represent an integration of medical sciences and humanities for the sake of greater knowledge of the human body. What is important here to note is that the integration of different disciplines is intended not merely to examine intra-subjective and inter-subjective movements within the human body but also to foreground the problems of human bodies. Des Fitzgerald and Felicity Callard work out the nexus between the figure of the human and the medical humanities:

> We are in search of a different set of dynamics for the medical humanities—one in which both the generative and the inert are properties of an entangled field of bio/social/cultural life: one that would not establish at its heart those wearyingly familiar encomia—an "ethical life" and a "good death."[19]

On the other hand, while commenting on the relevance of medical humanities, Mary Terrell White thinks that the integration of medicine and humanity can bring out some interesting insights for closer clinical examination of illness, while noting that she is "a fervent believer in the value of medical humanities as a source of insight into the social and institutional practices of medicine."[20] Unlike White, Therese Jones and Delese Wear understand medical humanities "as a series of competing texts, each reflecting different—and sometimes competing—discourses: medical humanities as historical text, as race/ gender/class text, as hermeneutical text, as postmodern text, as autobiographical/biographical text, as aesthetic text, and as ethical text."[21] Jones and Wear portray the medical humanities as consisting of competing discourses that offer various hermeneutical models to explore interdisciplinary problems.

During ancient times, though people did not use anything like the term "medical humanities," they nonetheless engaged in practices we now identify as congruent with what we refer to by that term. The nascent stage of what we now think of as the medical humanities can be traced back to the Vedic period, and particularly in *Āyurveda*, *Artharvaveda*, and *Carakasṁahitā*. For instance, in Āyurvedic narratives, one may find the names of medicines, their applications, and healing strategies. Michael Cheng-Tek Tai cogently argues that:

> The Atharvaveda, also known as the fourth Veda in Hinduism, is a collection of poems by a popular medicine man who aided individuals in their homes with rituals to alleviate personal and family crises. The rituals were usually intended for times of illness.[22]

Tai is right in pointing out that Atharvaveda provides key medical insights which, written in poetic form, help people deal with illness at home. Tai has also commented on the wider significance of Āyurveda as a system of medicine that is instrumental in treating corporeal disorders. Tai further argues that:

> Ayurveda sees the person as grounded in nature, a microcosm within the macrocosm. Diet, soil, season, time and place are all factors that affect a person's being. Since a person is a composition of physical, mental, social and spiritual elements, keeping balance of all these

is important. Ayurveda views the person as an integrated whole and not just an aggregate of several body parts.[23]

What is interesting about Āyurveda is that it teaches medics to consider a human body as a microcosm within a macrocosm and to view a human body as an "integrated whole" instead of an "aggregate" of different body organs. Due to this approach, and unlike other domains of medicine, Āyurvedic medicine does not induce the side effects all-too-common to more fragmented approaches to medicine. As S. N. Tripathi and Andree Hegy pertinently observe:

> Āyurvedic medicine has advantages in comparison to all other medical sciences. It has no systematic and side effects of any kind during and after treatment [...] Besides this, it [Āyurvedic medicine] also gives the following:

> 1. It maintains original components of the body
> 2. It increases self-body resistance
> 3. It keeps away all psychosomatic disorders
> 4. It maintains aging factors
> 5. It treats only root causes and gives long term cure
> 6. It keeps away from the cortisone
> 7. It combines other help if there is no harm to the body[24]

What is significant is that all these healing tips are provided to improve human wellbeing. Besides this, in *Āyurveda*, human embryological insights can be traced. Whereas in *Yayurveda*, it is put forward that the physical and psychological maturity of women is of profound import where good progeny is concerned, in *Atharvaveda*, it is prescriptively suggested that only physically and psychologically fit men and women should indulge in coitus. Abhimanyu Kumar refers to *Manusmṛti*, where the process of archiving progeny of long life, intellect and healthy body is laid down, contending that: "[t]he use of garbha-mantra for purification of garbha, homa-mantra at the beginning of coitus, baijika-mantra to eradicate the abnormalities likely to come in fetus due to impurities of mother was advised."[25] This suggests that the medical humanities were in their nascent stage during the Vedic period. In *Carakasaṁhitā*, one may find references to surgical instruments and methods of surgery, which indicates that different clinical treatments were used on human beings. Most importantly, human health was one of their primary concerns, which explains why the Vedic period excelled in medical humanities. In other words, humanism informs the field of medicine, not merely to protect human lives from different corporeal malfunctions, disorders, and diseases, but also to celebrate human prowess in inventing ways of catering to human health needs.

One may find references to surgical methods and instruments in *Caracasamhitā*, where it is suggested how physicians are supposed to treat a disordered body. In a way, human potential and individuality was privileged and foregrounded in giving clinical treatments to patients. Different innovative surgical methods reveal that medics at that time used to engage themselves in complex operations to specifically tailor clinical service to individual patients. Reflecting this practice, one of the most important aspects of Āyurvedic medicine is its emphasis on plurality and coexistence. It is believed in Āyurvedic medicine that the human body is made up of a multiplicity of functions, and the ordered coordination between these functions is ensured through considering the multiple purposes served by specific bodily organs. Āyurvedic diagnostic methods are grounded in this view of plurality and multiplicity. As M. S. Valiathan observes: "[Diagnosis] was given great importance. It was based on interrogation, inspection, palpation and listening to bowel sounds, etc. In fact all senses, excluding taste, were employed in the diagnostic process."[26] This refers to the fact that diagnostic processes were not monolithic, but assumed the need to take into account

Mapping Indic Humanism(s)

both the multiplicity and wholeness of each individual patient. In this light, Āyurveda insists that physicians need to interrogate, inspect, and investigate illness by means of clinically examining the patient in front of them, treating him or her as unique, rather than merely making assumptions based on past experience with previous patients.

Valiathan elsewhere argues that the Āyurvedic medical system is steeped in Indian philosophy and thus provides an ideal platform for physicians to showcase their clinical talents. Valiathan goes on to contend that the

> influence of *Samkhya* and of *Nyaya-Vaiseshika* systems, in particular, on the developmental of the philosophical basis of *Ayurveda* was considerable. Examples of this influence may be seen in the Ayurvedic belief in the utility of analysis and the reliability of reason and the acceptance of the reality of the external world.[27]

Valiathan subtly brings out how Āyurveda recognizes human cognitive potentials and logical power.

One may refer to advanced medical systems prevalent in ancient Indian society, which gets reflected in *Atharvaveda*. The mantras and sūktas found in *Atharvaveda* prepare the ground for the emergence of Āyurveda as an Indic medical practice. If one closely looks at *Atharvaveda*, one shall find how a priest-cum-physician used to engage in treating corporeal disorders. For instance, in *Atharvavede Bharatiya Samskriti*, Narayan Chandra Bhattacharyya[28] observes that priests used to rely on clinical formulations embedded in mantras to cure illness; used to put enormous emphasis on the medicinal value of water and plants; and used to take recourse to homemade clinical measures to ameliorate illness. It was believed that priests' philosophical insights and medicinal plants charmed by mantras could eradicate illness. For instance, in order to treat hemorrhages, priests used to insist that a particular type of grass called "muñjāghās" charmed by mantras could be used. In order to reset the broken limbs, priests used to prescribe the use of "arūṇdhuti latā" (a particular type of vine). These clinical measures are striking even today, not only because these clinical measures are mixed up with mantras, but also because these are grounded in advanced medical insights.

Elucidating Indic Humanisms in Post-Vedic Tāntric Traditions: Critical Reflections

Moving from Vedic to post-Vedic forms of humanism, we come to the various manifestations of tantra. Jeffrey S. Lidke has attempted to formulate a theory of tantra-ecology by means of considering Rita Dasgupta Sherma's article "Sacred Immanence: Reflections of Ecofeminism in Hindu Tantra" where she teases out some onto-epistemic affinities between tantra and ecology:

> (1) celebration of all aspects of life (2) elevation to ultimacy of a feminine principle linked to materiality; (3) possibility for liberation of female gender from constraints of "fertility and nurturance alone"; (4) affirmation of phenomena as Goddess; (5) articulation of a discourse of empowerment for the marginalized; (6) veneration of the body and its sensations; (7) absence of a spirit/matter dichotomy.[29]

The purposing of drawing this critical excerpt is to underscore how the human body is given due importance in tāntric traditions. It is believed in tāntric traditions that even after the death of a human body, it does not get separated from Nature; rather, it gets tied up with Nature in "discriminative integration." In tāntric traditions, humanism is celebrated in terms of upholding the enormous significance of self in relation to other, while the union of the human body with Nature is accomplished by the power of mantras and tāntric *sādhakas* (religious worshippers) who visualize the world beyond merely physical realities. Bruce M. Knauft emphasizes concepts like "self-possessed" and "self-governed" while elucidating how tāntric *sādhakas* slip into the world of immanence by first understanding the "self" and then the "outside" world: "Tantric adepts aspire through meditation, visualisation, and mind-training to dissolve normal selfhood and simultaneously embrace both 'conventional' and 'ultimate' reality." [30] One may here note that in tāntric traditions, *sādhakas* first delve deeper into the "self" so as to go beyond the boundary of "self" in an attempt to connect the "self" with the "outside" world. Along related lines, the subversive potentials of tantra are explored by Farah Godrej, who contends that "Tantra, a dissident tradition of thought and practice, contains a progressive potential for critiquing and subverting the hierarchical, masculinist politics of gender, sexuality, and caste in contemporary India."[31] Godrej implies that tāntric traditions deal with human knowledge and are capable of subverting human epistemic formulations. In other words, tāntric politics can bring about definitive changes in a human pursuit of knowledge.

Here, one may pause and ponder the following questions: What is tantra? How is tantra different from other epistemological traditions? It is generally believed that tantra originated out of the dialogic interactions between Śiva and Śakti. Whereas other epistemic traditions seem to offer longer ways to reach desired things, tāntric traditions offer the shortest and finest way to sort out different issues. As Geshe Ngawang Dhargyey et al. argue: "The path to Enlightenment outlined by the non-tantric systems of the Mahâyāna is very long [...] The tantric path, on the other hand, is short; indeed, the desired goal may be, and has been, reached within one lifetime."[32] Dhargyey et al. argue that tāntric tradition is a powerfully deviant school of thought that at once expands the horizon of "human" knowledge and at times broadens "human" understanding of "self" and its intrinsic connections with Nature.

In the landmark book, *The Self Possessed: Deity and Spirit Possession in South Asian Literature and Civilization*, Frederic M. Smith outlines the arguments of Bhāskarācārya, who contends that "a liberated person may assume many constructed bodies (nirmāṇaśarīrāṇibahūni) at will."[33] As Smith explains, "Bhāskarācārya then wonders whether these bodies possess their own independent consciousness and mind."[34] What is important here to note is that "body" occupies a central position in tāntric traditions and has been exploited for many reasons. While commenting on the functionality of tāntric systems, Smith observes:

> In *svasthāveśa*, a medium causes a spirit or deity to descend into any one of several reflective objects or into the body of a young boy or girl, after which the medium or youth answers questions from a client regarding events of the past, present, or future.[35]

With this idea in mind, one may stop and ask: How is humanism linked to such tāntric systems? Do tāntric traditions reflect humanism in practice? To respond to these pertinent questions, one may straightaway refer to Suresh Chandra Bandhopadhyay's intervention into tāntric tradition. Bandhopadhyay argues that as the word "tantra" is supposed to have come from the root word "tan," which refers to a means through which the domain of knowledge can be enlarged, expanded, and extended.[36] Along similar lines, Arthar Avalon makes a significant observation: "It is by virtue of the direct knowledge of Brahman in the form of Śhiva and Śakti that tāntric *Sādhakas* ever conquer the world. Strengthened by it, the *Sādhaka* does not deign even to cast a look at other Śāstras."[37] This points to the fact that a tāntric *sādhaka* attempts to attain a greater knowledge of the world by means of worshiping Śiva and Śakti.

Tāntra is generally classified into three broad types—"āgama," which is indicative of Śaivic tradition,[38] "saṁhitā," which refers to the vaiṣnavtāntric standpoint,[39] and "tantra," which is associated with Śakta views.[40] Taking a cue from Bandhopadhyay's interventions into tantra, it can be tenably posited that the role of the body is instrumental in putting tāntric traditions into

Mapping Indic Humanism(s)

practice. In tāntric traditions, *sādhakas* insist that by means of hard tāntric practices, it is possible to go beyond the confinements of the human body. What is interesting is that the figuration of a goddess (for instance, Kāli) or the presence of a human body part is of profound importance to get hold of the greater knowledge of the non-dualistic discourses of the universe. Elaborating on this view, Thomas B. Ellis maintains that "Tantra is the denouement of the universal, religio-martial campaign against the biological body."[41] However, Ellis goes on to argue that even in such tāntric traditions, bodily activities are held to be very important, for a seasoned tāntric *sādhaka* attempts to connect to the outer world through them. In other words, possession over any body is *energetically actualized* in such a way that it empowers a *sādhaka* to establish links between human discourses of a physical body and its spiritual counterparts. It is by the help of tāntric mantras that *Sādhakas* attempt to take control of a body. By exploiting the esoteric power of mantras, *Sādhakas* delve deeper into the connections between "body" and its surrounding Nature. Associating the body with the religio-spiritual world conditioned by the spell of possession identifies tāntric epistemic traditions as a humanist endeavor, because in such in tāntric epistemic traditions, human *sādhakas* make religio-spiritual attempts to articulate the interconnections between the "human" world and the "outside" world. In so doing, sādhakas attempt to solve various human problems: mental, social and religious.

To showcase the effects of tantra on humanism (and vice versa), one may straightaway refer to the fact that the function of tantra is understood from different angles. Sometimes, it is understood to be a "continuum or continuity" in so far as the quest of *Sādhakas* for the greater paradigm of knowledge is concerned. It is undeniably true that humanity at large, since its infancy, has been continuously searching for greater understanding, and thus continuity turns out to be a leitmotif in humanity's quest for such epistemic enrichment. In this vein, Steven Neal Weinberger makes an important argument: although there are different sub-strata within tantra, the idea of a "continuum or continuation" is an integral part of tantra and is also reflective of one of the significant dimensions of humanism. Following the work of Butön, Weinberger pertinently observes:

> As for tantras that are the expressive words (that is, the texts themselves), Butön explains that because the collections of words that teach the meanings expressed are "connected and continuous." They are tantras ... in this explication of "tantra" the emphasis [is] on the sense of continuity and/ or continuum.[42]

One may also argue how tantra, like the fluidity of humanism, cannot be restricted within a single historical period. Just as humanism found varied epistemic manifestations in Vedic and post-Vedic periods, tantra, in the words of Hugh B. Urban, re-emerges as a

> conflicted, contested, and contradictory category, passed back and forth between Indian and Western imaginations, undergoing new transformations in each new historical encounter […] As a dialectical category, Tantra is not singular or stable; it is something that is "non-homogeneous" and "fragmented," "which on account of its awkwardness of fit, cracks, and violent juxtapositionings can actively embody both a presentation and counter-presentation of historical time."[43]

This view maintains that tantra is an open-ended discursive field where different contrary discourses jostle with each other. Tantra helps one *Sādhaka* connect "body" with the "outside" world, while tāntric epistemic traditions empower *Sādhakas* to question the superiority of one human knowledge system over another. In this context, it can be argued that tāntric traditions are humanist traditions, an insight that makes room for post-Vedic humanistic thought in a contemporary world.

Abhisek Ghosal

Indic Humanism(s): Oneness In Diversity

Indic humanism(s) have been unfolding since the Vedic period and have been adapting ceaselessly in accord with socio-cultural and political changes across time. Reflections of humanism(s), particularly in Vedic medical and post-Vedic tāntric traditions point to the fact that if one wishes to trace out the nascent developments of Indic humanism(s), one has to grapple with the above mentioned epistemic traditions. Traces of Indic humanism(s) in these epistemic traditions reflect how, since a nascent stage, Indic humanism(s) have been branching off into varied directions and are in dialogue with both medical and tāntric traditions. Unlike Western humanism(s), Indic humanism(s) have long been celebrating the "oneness" or unity existing in various seemingly separate singularities. Renowned Indic Studies scholar Kapila Vatsyayan, while repositioning Man's position in Nature, propounds: "the more fundamental and universal the concept, the greater the probability and possibility of diverse interpretations at multiple levels."[44] In their fundamentality and universality, Indic humanism(s), including Vedic medical and post-Vedic tāntric traditions, corroborate the veracity of Vatsyayan's insight.

Bibliography

Avalon, Arthar. *Principles of Tantra: The Tantratattva of* Ṣhrīyukta Śhiva *Chandra Vidyārṇava Bhattāchāryya Mahodaya*. Madras: Ganesh and Co. Madras Ltd., 1952.

Bandhopadhyay, Suresh Chandra. *SanskritaSāhityerItihās: Veda, Epic, Purāṇa, Dharśaṇa, Alaṁkāra O Śāstra* [*History of Sanskrit Literature: Veda, Epic, Purana, Philosophy, Alamkara, and Tantra*]. Kolkata: A. Mukherjee and Company Private Ltd., 1982.

Basu, Yogiraj. *Veder Parichoy* [*The Identity of Veda*]. Calcutta: Pharma K.L.M. Private Ltd., 1980.

Berry, Peter. *Beginning Theory: An Introduction to Literary and Cultural Theory*. New Delhi: Viva Books, 2013.

Bhattacharyya, Narayan Chandra. *Atharvavede Bharatiya Samskriti* [*Indian Culture in Atharvaveda*]. Kolkata: Sanskrit Pushtaka Bhandar, 1963.

Bhattacharyya, Sukumari. *Prachin Bharat Samaj O Sahitya* [*Ancient Indian Society and Literature*]. Kolkata: Ananda Publishers, 1987.

Chandra, Pratap. "Ascent to Humanism." *India International Centre Quarterly* 15, No. 4 (1989). 63–68. http://www.jstor.com/stable/23002028.

Copson, Andrew. "What Is Humanism?" In *The Wiley Blackwell Handbook of Humanism*, edited by Andrew Copson and A. C. Grayling. Sussex: John Wiley & Sons, Ltd., 2015, 1–33.

Dhargyey, Geshe Ngawang, Sherpa Tulku and Jonathan Landaw. "What is Tantra?" *The Tibet Journal* 4, No. 2 (1979), 58–60. http://www.jstor.com/stable/43299945.

Ellis, Thomas B. "Disgusting Bodies, Disgusting Religion: The Biology of Tantra." *Journal of the American Academy of Religion* 79, No. 4 (2011), 879–927. http://www.jstor.com/stable/41348744.

Fitzgerald, Des, and Felicity Callard. "Entangling the Medical Humanities." In *The Edinburgh Companion to the Critical Medical Humanities*, edited by Anne Whitehead and Angela Woods. London: Edinburgh University Press, 2016, 35–49.

Godrej, Farah. "Orthodoxy and Dissent in Hinduism's Meditative Traditions: A Critical Tantric Politics?" *New Political Science* 38, No. 2 (2016), 256–271. doi: 10.1080/07393148.2016.1153194.

Greaves, David, and Martyn Evans. "Medical humanities." *Medical Humanities* 26, (2000), 1–2. https://mh.bmj.com/content/medhum/26/1/1.full.pdf.

Humanist International. "What is humanism?" Accessed on July 11, 2020, https://humanists.international/what-is-humanism. (n.p.)

Jones, Therese and Delese Wear. "The Medical Humanities." *Perspectives in Biology and Medicine* 50, No. 3 (2007), 317–320. https://muse.jhu.edu/article/218324/pdf.

Kane, P.V. *History of Dharmaśāstra (Ancient and Medieval Religious and Civil Law)*. Poona: Bhandarkar Oriental Research Institute, 1941.

Knauft, Bruce M. "Self-possessed and Self-governed: Transcendent Spirituality in Tibetan Tantric Buddhism." *Ethnos* 84, No. 4 (2019), 557–587. doi: 10.1080/00141844.2017.1313289.

Kumar, Abhimanyu. *Ayurvedic Concepts of Human Embryology*. Delhi: Chaukhamba Sanskrit Pratishthan, 2017.

Lidke, Jeffrey S. "Towards a Theory of Tantra-Ecology." *Sutra Journal: A Curated Journal On Art, Culture and Dharma* (2016), n.p.

Smith, Frederic M. *The Self Possessed: Deity and Spirit Possession in South Asian Literature and Civilization.* New York: Columbia University Press, 2006.

Tai, Michael Cheng-Tek. "The Way of Asian Bioethics." *Asian Bioethics Review* (2008), 15–23. https://muse.jhu.edu/article/416270/pdf.

Tripathi, S. N., and Andree Hegy. *Ayurvedic Medicine, Human Life and Vedas.* Varanasi: Chowkhamba Krishnadas Academy, 2019.

Urban, Hugh B. "Conclusion: Reimagining Tantra in Contemporary Discourse." In *Tantra: Sex, Secrecy, Politics, and Power in the Study of Religion.* New York: California University Press, 2003, 264–282.

Valiathan, M. S. "An Ayurvedic view of life." *Current Science* 96, No. 9 (2009), 1186–1192. http://www.jstor.com/stable/24105407.

Valiathan, M. S. "Glimpses of ancient Indian medicine." *Current Science* 59, No. 10 (1990), 531–533. https://www.jstor.org/stable/24093578.

Vatsyayan, Kapila. *Foreword* to *Man in Nature.* 3–5. Edited by Baidyanath Saraswati. New Delhi: D. K. Printworld Pvt. Ltd. 1995.

Weinberger, Steven Neal. *The Significance of Yoga Tantra and the Compendium of Principles (Tattvasaṃgraha Tantra) within Tantric Buddhism in India and Tibet.* 2003. University of Virginia, Ph.D. dissertation. http://citeseerx.ist.psu.edu/viewdoc/summary?doi=10.1.1.175.3313.

White, Mary Terrell. "Why Not Medical Humanities?" *The American Journal of Bioethics* 2, No. 4 (2010), 34. https://muse.jhu.edu/article/37947.

Notes

1 Humanist International. "What is Humanism?," n.p. https://humanists.international/what-is-humanism (Accessed July 11, 2020)

2 Andrew Copson. "What Is Humanism?" In *The Wiley Blackwell Handbook of Humanism*, edited by Andrew Copson and A. C. Grayling (Sussex: John Wiley & Sons, Ltd., 2015), 6.

3 Peter Berry. *Beginning Theory: An Introduction to Literary and Cultural Theory* (New Delhi: Viva Books, 2013), 3.

4 See, for example, the *Yogasūtra* of Pantanjali (2.30–2.31), where the principles, duties, and benefits of *ahiṃsā* (non-violence) and *satyā* (truthfulness), among others, are not limited to interactions between human beings, but extended to all living creatures.

5 Pratap Chandra. "Ascent to humanism." *India International Centre Quarterly* 15, No. 4 (1989), 64.

6 Ibid., 65.

7 The term "yajña" refers to a ritualistic practice where priests perform prayers to the God. The tradition of "yajña" is integral to the Indic religio-cultural traditions. "Yajña" was used to be performed in a sacred place where different religious customs are carried out. In a "yajña," various mantras were used to be piously articulated to help human beings get rid of miseries and problems. People used to believe that it is by performing a "yajña," the anger of a God or Goddess can be mitigated. Sometimes, various domestic animals were used to be butchered during the time of "yajña" so as to satisfy different Gods and Goddesses.

8 Quoted in Yogiraj Basu. *Veder Parichoy [The Identity of Veda]* (Calcutta: Pharma K.L.M. Private Ltd., 1980), 197.

9 This quotation is drawn to underscore women's involvements in intellectual practices. All the translations in this chapter are my own.

10 Basu, 206.

11 Sukumari Bhattacharyya. *Prachin Bharat Samaj O Sieahitya [Ancient Indian Society and Literature]* (Kolkata: Ananda Publishers, 1987), 62.

12 Quoted in Basu, 208.

13 Among the different professions prevailing in society, agriculture was one of the more lucrative professions common at that point in time. Agricultural works were held in high esteem, for people engaged in this sort of profession used to earn both name and fame.

14 The term "yoga" has different meanings in Indic epistemic traditions. For instance, in *Gītā*, yoga means intellectual way of doing. In Indic philosophical traditions, yoga is understood to be a factor that is responsible for uninterrupted intellectual thinking. Different yogic sūtras are systematically narrativized in Patanjalī's *Yogasūtra*. The idea of yoga can be found in *Ṛgveda*. Different dimensions of yoga can also be located in Kathoupanisad where it is said that at the extreme point of yoga, different psychological

activities including thinking power, expansion of thought, ability to sense something around, etc., slip into a sort of inertia for the time being. This state of mind does not prove that one has become inactive; rather, it hints at one's proximity to *moksha*. Yogic practices are primarily meant for enhancement of one's ratiocinative power, the eradication of psychological anxieties, relief from physiological ailments, the enrichment of one's workability, and so on.

15 Kane, P. V. *History of Dharmaśāstra (Ancient and Medieval Religious and Civil Law)* (Poona: Bhandarkar Oriental Research Institute, 1941), 1.

16 Ibid., 2.

17 David Greaves and Martyn Evans. "Medical humanities." *Medical Humanities* 26 (2000), 1.

18 Ibid.

19 Fitzgerald, Des, and Felicity Callard. "Entangling the Medical Humanities." In *The Edinburgh Companion to the Critical Medical Humanities*, edited by Anne Whitehead and Angela Woods (London: Edinburgh University Press, 2016), 43–44.

20 Mary Terrell White. "Why Not Medical Humanities?" *The American Journal of Bioethics* 2, No. 4 (2010), 34.

21 Therese Jones and Delese Wear. "The Medical Humanities—Introduction." *Perspectives in Biology and Medicine* 50, No. 3, 318.

22 Michael Cheng-Tek Tai. "The Way of Asian Bioethics." *Asian Bioethics Review* (2008), 17–18.

23 Ibid., 19.

24 S. N. Tripathi, and Andree Hegy. *Ayurvedic Medicine, Human Life and Vedas* (Varanasi: Chowkhamba Krishnadas Academy, 2019), 2.

25 Abhimanyu Kumar. *Ayurvedic Concepts of Human Embryology* (Delhi: Chaukhamba Sanskrit Pratishthan, 2017), 3.

26 M. S. Valiathan. "An Ayurvedic view of life." *Current Science* 96, No. 9 (2009), 1190.

27 M. S. Valiathan. "Glimpses of ancient Indian medicine." *Current Science* 59, No. 10 (1990), 484.

28 Narayan Chandra Bhattacharyya. *Atharvavede Bharatiya Samskriti* [*Indian Culture in Atharvaveda*] (Kolkata: Sanskrit Pushtaka Bhandar, 1963), 112–115.

29 Jeffrey S. Lidke. "Towards a Theory of Tantra-Ecology." *Sutra Journal: A Curated Journal On Art, Culture and Dharma* (2016), n.p.

30 Bruce M. Knauft. "Self-possessed and Self-governed: Transcendent Spirituality in Tibetan Tantric Buddhism." *Ethnos* 84, No. 4 (2019), 557.

31 Farah Godrej. "Orthodoxy and Dissent in Hinduism's Meditative Traditions: A Critical Tantric Politics?" *New Political Science* 38, No. 2 (2016), 256.

32 Geshe Ngawang Dhargyey, Sherpa Tulku and Jonathan Landaw. "What is Tantra?" *The Tibet Journal* 4, No. 2 (1979), 58.

33 Frederic M. Smith. *The Self Possessed: Deity and Spirit Possession in South Asian Literature and Civilization* (New York: Columbia University Press, 2006), 297.

34 Ibid.

35 Ibid., 417.

36 "Tanyatevistāryategñāmanena" (*SanskritaSāhityerItihās: Veda, Epic, Purāṇa, Dharśaṇa, Alaṁkāra O Śāstra* [*History of Sanskrit Literature: Veda, Epic, Purana, Philosophy, Alamkara, and Tantra*] [Kolkata: A. Mukherjee and Company Private Ltd., 1982], 268). This reflects tantra's ability to expand one's horizon of knowledge. In other words, tāntric thoughts stretch the limit of one's knowledge and sometimes help him/her step into the world of immanence.

37 Arthar Avalon. *Principles of Tantra: The Tantratattva of Ṣhrīyukta Śhiva Chandra Vidyārṇava Bhattāchāryya Mahodaya* (Madras: Ganesh and Co. Madras Ltd., 1952), 209.

38 Śaivic tradition suggests that tantra originated out of the dialogic interactions between Śiva and Pārvatī, where Śiva like a teacher, responds to all the questions of Pārvatī who like an obedient disciple, asks questions to Śiva. In this tradition, Śiva occupies central position and Pārvatī stands as an Other to Him.

39 In this tradition, God Viṣṇu is held to be at the centre of all dialogic interactions and is venerated in different incarnations. Vaishnavism consists of Vedic and non-Vedic religious traditions. In a way, Vaishnava tantra is grounded on an amalgamation of different trans-regional religious traditions. Thus, *Saṃhitā* traditions celebrate pluralistic views within tāntric system of thought.

40 Śākta tantra conceives Śakti to be the supreme of all earthly existences. In this tradition, it is believed that Śakti has the power of creation and is the figuration of energy. All beings come from Śakti and finally end up returning to Śakti. Śākta tāntric traditions are heavily grounded on the female Divine which controls the cosmos. At this point, it needs to be mentioned that Śākta tantra does not promote enormity of feminine power but recognizes the authoritative voice of the female Divine in the universe. Disciples of Śākta tantra offer prayers to different incarnation of Devi.

Mapping Indic Humanism(s)

41 Ellis, Thomas B. "Disgusting Bodies, Disgusting Religion: The Biology of Tantra." *Journal of the American Academy of Religion* 79, No. 4 (2011), 910.

42 Steven Neal Weinberger. *The Significance of Yoga Tantra and the Compendium of Principles (Tattvasaṃgraha Tantra) Within Tantric Buddhism in India and Tibet* (University of Virginia, Ph.D. dissertation, 2003), 14–15.

43 Hugh B. Urban. "Conclusion: Reimagining Tantra in Contemporary Discourse." In *Tantra: Sex, Secrecy, Politics, and Power in the Study of Religion* (New York: California University Press, 2003), 265.

44 Vatsyayan, Kapila. "Foreword to *Man in Nature*." 3–5, edited by Baidyanath Saraswati (New Delhi: D. K. Printworld Pvt. Ltd. 1995), 3.

8

Reformative Aspect of *Bhasha* Literatures and Aging in India

Old Age, Body and Locale in Hindi Short Stories

Saurav Kumar

One important element in any comprehensive discussion of humanism (and human issues) in literature is the representation of aging and its social effects and consequences. The present chapter aims to explore this question through the reformative aspect of *Bhasha*[1] literatures, drawing on the work done by U. R. Ananthamurthy and G. N. Devy on Indian literary tradition. The chapter will concentrate on Premchand's "Boodhi Kaaki," Gyanranjan's "Pitaa," and Priyamvad's "Palang"[2] to explore how these literary experiences of aging, along with the locales in which they are based, can be pivotal in understanding the marginalization of aging bodies in India.

U. R. Ananthamurthy divides Indian literary tradition into two categories – *Marga* and *Desi*. While *Marga* stands for the classics in Sanskrit, *Desi* refers to the narratives in *Bhasha* literatures. The critic also redefines *Marga* and *Desi* by calling them front yard literatures and backyard literatures, respectively. He assesses the importance of *Desi* or literatures in the *Bhashas* in two ways. First, *Desi* provides "a local habitation and name" to the values inherent in Sanskrit narratives and thus allows those values to interact with "folk imagination."[3] Second, *Desi* covers "the world of women, shudras and therapeutic herbs"[4] (therefore, backyard) and serves as an inexhaustible source of themes for narratives.

Desi or backyard literatures revitalize the frontyard in a situation in which the literatures in a higher position in a social hierarchy become "too pompous, loud and artificially rhetorical" and lose "the flexibility, truthfulness and earthiness of common speech."[5] While Ananthamurthy relies on this "revitalizing" potential in *Bhasha* literatures for saying that they deserve a prominent place among different literary traditions, the "reformative" aspect of backyard literatures deserves equal attention and needs to be taken seriously. Literatures in the *Bhashas* contain a long tradition of narratives dealing with repressed and socially deprived voices (those of women, untouchables, children, older people, etc.) and the politics inherent in their socio-cultural exclusion. This reformative aspect of *Bhasha* literatures has much to do with the inexhaustible richness of the "backyards" or locales in which they take birth. Ananthamurthy identifies this richness when he states: "Sanskrit, as a language, has no backyard of its own; it has to yield its place to the *Bhashas* in the backyards for the continuity of its spiritual substance."[6]

G. N. Devy looks at the distinction between *Marga* (mainstream) and *Desi* (regional) in terms of mainstream literature and para-literature.[7] Devy conceptualizes "the other, suppressed or subcultural literary phenomena"[8] using the epithet "para," which means "by the side of, beside, alongside of, past and beyond."[9] Para-literature stands for all those literatures which are "socially parallel, linguistically parasitical, psychologically paranoid and historically parenthetical."[10] When new literary traditions emerge from an established literary tradition, the new literatures are initially

114   DOI: 10.4324/9781003046004-11

considered taboo/para-literatures. According to Devy, this is particularly true for literatures of modern Indian languages: "in the initial period of development of these new traditions, the period of transition from Sanskrit to these new languages was seen as a gradual vulgarization."[11]

Devy also recognizes the "reformative" aspect of *Bhasha* literatures when he says that para-literature "accurately reflects the patterns of social repression."[12] Para-literature covers literatures produced by and for women and children, "two major repressed segments of most communities."[13] The literary criticism and history "controlled by males and adults" have often attached "a lower aesthetic value" to literatures produced by and for women and children. In a way, para-literature represents the literatures of all those "others" whose "literary requirements and aesthetic sensibilities are taken less seriously than they deserve."[14]

In Hindi literature, there are a handful of short stories that center around old age and its problems. Among them, the important ones are Premchand's "Boodhi Kaaki," Bhishm Sahni's "Chief ki Daawat," Usha Priyamvada's "Waapasi," Kashinath Singh's "Apna Raastaa Lo Baba," Akhilesh's "Jal Damru Madhya," Gyanranjan's "Pitaa," and Priyamvad's "Palang." While most of the mentioned stories focus on socio-cultural dynamics associated with dependency and frailty in old age, only a few (Premchand's "Boodhi Kaaki," Gyanranjan's "Pitaa" and Priyamvad's "Palang") explicitly unfold different meanings assigned to the bodies of older people in Indian society.

Premchand's "Boodhi Kaaki"

Premchand's "Boodhi Kaaki" is set in a pre-independence agrarian scenario. It is about an old woman who lives with the family of her nephew. Boodhi Kaaki is a widow and does not have any relatives except her nephew and his family. Her nephew's name is Buddhiram. Buddhiram and his wife, Rupa, have two sons and a daughter (Ladli). Food is one of the basic necessities of life. Boodhi Kaaki often faces humiliation for asking for food despite the fact that she has handed over all her wealth to her nephew. "She would be lying uncared for." The members of the family often "did not give her food on time or in sufficient quantity." "The old aunt [Boodhi Kaaki] had lost all senses except that of taste." She is almost blind and crawls instead of walking: "[a]ll her limbs – eyes, hands and legs – had given way." She is emotionally vulnerable. She wails a lot. "[S]he cried and sobbed at the top of her voice, not in a subdued tone." Boodhi Kaaki suffers from the denial of language. She doesn't talk. She does not have the agency to express her opinions – "She had no other means to draw the attention to herself except by crying."[15]

The story is centered around a single incident – the tilak ceremony of Buddhiram's elder son, Sakharam. People gather in the house of Budhiram in order to celebrate the occasion. Delicious food is being prepared. Boodhi Kaaki is excluded from the ceremony. She is "dejected," for she is forced to be confined to her room. "The spicy aroma was making her restless." She wonders: *"They won't give me any puries. I guess. It's so late, but no one has brought me any food. It seems everyone has eaten. Nothing has been left for me."* She wants to cry, but then stops thinking that her crying would be treated as an ill omen. "Kaaki's imagination took wing as she thought of the puris dancing before her." She decides to go to the place where food is being prepared. "Having decided, Kaaki sat on all fours and, leaning on her hands, got across the threshold with difficulty and slowly crawled to the pan" in which the puris are being prepared. When Rupa spots Boodhi Kaaki sitting near pan, she starts yelling at the poor old woman. "Just as the frog pounces upon snail, she pounced on Kaaki." Here, what Rupa says is not only humiliating Kaaki, but also consists of ageist tones: "Is your belly on fire already? Is it a stomach or a warehouse? Couldn't you sit still in the room? ... May God burn your tongue."[16] Ageism is the discrimination meted out to elders at different levels – social, cultural, economic, and linguistic. Kaaki does not react to Rupa's derogatory remarks. She crawls back to her room.

Boodhi Kaaki starts waiting for her turn to eat. She regrets "her adventure that had brought so much humiliation." After waiting for some time, she again comes to the courtyard. The old woman slowly drags herself to the place where the guests are feasting. "Several men stood up, startled. They exclaimed, 'Who is the crone? Where has she come from? Take care she doesn't touch you.'" This time, Buddhiram becomes furious at the appearance of the old woman before the eating guests. He holds the body of Kaaki with both hands and literally throws her into her room. "Kaaki's imaginary scene was destroyed in a moment by the blow of a whirlwind."[17]

Everyone except Kaaki finishes eating. Nobody cares to take food to the old woman. "No one took mercy on her old age, her destitution and her helplessness, except Ladli, who felt an ache for her grandmother." Ladli is very close to Kaaki. She is an "innocent and simple-hearted" girl. Ladli's heart had melted for Boodhi Kaaki when she saw her parents maltreating the old woman before guests. The little girl takes her own portion of puris to Kaaki. Boodhi Kaaki immediately finishes the meager portion of puris and then craves for more puris. "When the bridge of contentment breaks, then one's cravings cross all limits. If drunkards are reminded of alcohol, they are blinded by their desire for it. Kaaki's impatient mind was carried away by the strong current of her desire." The old woman ultimately asks Ladli to take her to the place where guests were eating. Ladli holds her hand and accompanies her to the dining place "which was now strewn with leaf plates in which people had taken their food."[18] Out of irresistible hunger, the poor Kaaki begins picking the leftovers from the leaf plates and eating them.

The text shows how the discrimination meted out to aging bodies can be so extreme that it can even lead to their animalization. The entire story covers a circle of animalization. The circle begins when we come to know that Boodhi Kaaki crawls and cannot walk. Crawling is associated with four-legged beings. Only animals walk on four legs. The circle gets completed at the end of the story when she transgresses all human boundaries and begins eating the leftovers from leaf plates.

In the story, ageism or discrimination against elders can be perceived on two levels – first, at the level of characters and incidents, and second at the level of narration and text. Boodhi Kaaki is consistently maltreated by Buddhiram and his wife, Rupa. The children of Buddhiram (except Ladli) often tease the old woman. Rupa hurls abuses at Kaaki during the tilak ceremony of Sakharam. The old woman is physically manhandled by Buddhiram. The incident is a result of Kaaki's determination to enter mainstream humanity. She is consistently trying to push boundaries of the limited acceptance inside which she is caged, but Buddhiram forces her back to the fringes of humanity. The sudden appearance of the hungry old woman in the dining room creates chaos among the guests, and they start chiding Kaaki. This situation shows that the physical ugliness of old age is often hated with a kind of moral ugliness by those who are young. As a result, Kaaki is treated as an untouchable.

The story was written in pre-independence India, from a liberal humanist perspective. It is based on certain fixed "universal" ideas about old age. The very first line of the story repeats a stereotypical association between an old person and a child – "buḍhāpā bahudā bacapana kā punarāgamana huā karatā hai."[19] [How often old age returns to the state of childhood.] An old person is equated to a child. One important factor behind such a comparison is their dependency on young/younger people. One upshot of conforming to this idea can be seen in the latter part of the story, when the narrator uses the qualifier "buddhihīna" (dim-witted) for Kaaki. "kākī buddhihīna hote hue bhī itanā jānatī thī ki maiṃ vaha kāma kara rahī hūṃ, jo mujhe kadāpi nahīṃ karanā cāhie."[20] "However dim-witted, Kaaki knew very well that she was doing something she shouldn't do."[21] The way the old woman interprets different odd situations she faces proves that she is not "buddhihīna" at all.

Reformative Aspect of Bhasha *Literatures*

When Rupa sees her mother-in-law eating the remains of food picked over by the guests, she thinks a *brahmani* (Boodhi Kaaki) is doing something which is very unholy. The way she interprets the old woman eating the leftovers is linguistically very ageist:

> Her state at that moment was akin to the feeling of a cow that sees its own throat being slit. What can be a more pitiful sight than a Brahmin woman looking for food in the left-overs? For some morsels of puris her mother-in-law was taking recourse to such a lowly and reprehensible act![22]

Being a God-fearing woman, she feels guilty observing a *brahmani* forced to do such an "unholy" business. The entire incident actually has a religio-cultural angle – "Who is responsible for this *adharma*?" She raised her hands toward the heavens and said with a pure heart, "My God. Have pity on my children. Do not punish me for this *adharma*. I'll be ruined."[23] Such an angle has long-term repercussions in aging in the Indian context. Premchand uses the metaphor of a dog sitting before guests for hungry Boodhi Kaaki sitting before the hearth. In Premchand, animal metaphors have a continual presence. At the authorial level, no problem can be seen in such a comparison. At the level of the text, the use of the animal metaphor stands for the dehumanization or animalization of Kaaki.

The only respite in the life of Boodhi Kaaki is a small girl, Ladli. Ladli often feels sad about the precarious situation of Boodhi Kaaki. Child–elder relationships are a major motif in the literary narratives on old age, where children understand aging people very well. In narratives, there are some normative characters (in most cases, mother and father). Others in families (children, elders, and pet animals) operate around them. All these "others" feel a sort of oneness with one-another, for all of them lack agency. So, they often form attachments among themselves.

Gyanranjan's "Pitaa"

Gyanranjan's "Pitaa" is about a middle-class Indian joint family impacted by modernization. It is the story of an aging father who adheres to a traditional lifestyle and is disliked by his grown-up and married children for criticizing their modern way of living. The story is set in the times when post-independence India is in the full grip of a tussle between the traditional Indian values represented by older people and the modernization of Indian society advocated by a younger generation. The narrator of the story is the old man's married son. Throughout the story, the narrator addresses the old man as "pitaa."

At the beginning of the story, the narrator reaches his house on one summer night. He enters his room, and switches on the light for a moment. He finds his wife and child sleeping on the bed placed on the floor. It is one of those summer nights on which people feel uneasy and sweat intensely: "āja behada garmī hai. rāste bhara mem jitane loga mile, una sabane usase garma aura becaina kara dene vāle mausama kī bāta kī. kapaRom kī phajīhata ho gaī."[24] [Today, the weather is extremely hot. On the way, people I came across talked about the weather that was making everyone restless. Clothes were in pathetic condition (because of intense perspiration)]. The married son then takes note of his father sleeping in the open. The father has just got up because of some noise. He scolds the cat who has begun crying. After some moments, the cat again starts crying. This time, the father picks up a cudgel and hurls it in the direction from which the cat's noise is coming. In India, traditionally, people consider the crying of a cat at night to be a bad omen. Here, the father's reaction to the crying of the cat has multiple implications. On the one hand, the old father may be considered superstitious. On the other hand, he is the representative of the elders who still conforms to the traditional knowledge system in order to make sense of actions and events. That knowledge system, which is purely based on commonsense understanding, is fast decaying after modernization has drawn the attention of younger people. The father's determination to make the cat stop crying also shows he is highly concerned about protecting his loved ones from any danger.

When the son was entering the home, he had spotted the father standing beside his charpoy. The old man was scratching the sweat on his back with his vest. The narrator understood that his father was unable to sleep because of extremely hot weather. Simultaneously, he was angry at this situation. The family members often asked the father to sleep under the fan, but the latter never listened to them.

The narrator is concerned about his father. He feels bad for him. While other family members are taking sound sleep under fans, his father likes to keep himself restless for the whole night. "gajaba to pitā kī jida hai, vaha dūsare kā āgraha anurodha māne taba nā! patā nahīṃ kyūṃ, pitā jīvana kī anivārya suvidhāoṃ se bhī ciḍhate haiṃ."[25] [The father is extremely stubborn. He never cares about the requests of others! I am unable to understand why my father is critical of even the basic necessities of life.] The father stands for hours on *chowk* (a cross on which four paths mingle) before hiring a rickshaw after bargaining for a cheap fare. In the beginning, people used to tease him for his way of life. With the passage, they understood that he would not listen to anyone. No one has ever seen the father brushing his teeth before the wash basin. Nor has he ever used the bathroom having the shower. He is fond of doing *daatun-kulla* [brushing his teeth with a twig] near the tap in the garden. Before taking a bath outside the house, he applies oil to his body. He likes to bathe in the open and clean the dirt on his back and chest with his sacred thread. The father seldom tastes the biscuits and costly fruits that his children bring from the market. He is fond of taking simple food and never gets influenced by the value of other food items. This son, who liked to buy apples from Kullu and *dhotis* (*dhoti* is a traditional Indian attire) from the Delhi Emporium for his father, has now turned critical of his father.

As the night lingers, the son comes to think that the father has perhaps slept: "isa vicāra se ki pitā so gae homge, use parama śāṃti milī aura lagā ki vaha bhī aba so sakegā."[26] [Wondering that his father had slept, the son took a sigh of relief and started thinking of sleeping.] The son drinks water and peeps outside the window in order to check if the father is asleep. The father is still awake. The sight of the still-awake father momentarily overcomes the narrator's desire to sleep. The father has wrapped up the bedding and places it at one side of the charpoy. Taking water from the *suraahi* (earthen pitcher) nearby, he sprinkles it on the ropes of the charpoy. Then he drinks water and soon falls asleep. The night is about to end. The narrator stops peeping outside the window and returns to his room. The air inside the room is as hot as the loo wind. He wonders the air outside the house must also be very hot. But he is relaxed now, for the father has now slept.

Gyanranjan's "Pitaa" deals with the intergenerational conflict on account of the clash of values – in Indian families under the influence of modernization, the traditional values of the older people directly confront the modern way of life the younger people strongly relate to. The younger family members firmly believe in modernizing their lives. They want the elders of the family to adopt the modern way of life. In the story, the father is adamant not to give up his traditional Indian life. It is this attitude of the father that leads to his marginalization within his own family. The father in "Pitaa" can be likened to Gajaadhar Babu of Usha Priyamvada's "Waapasi," and the Gandhian sweet vendor of R. K. Narayan's *The Vendor of Sweets*. In Usha Priyamvada's "Waapasi," Gajaadhar Babu retires from government service and shifts from his workplace to his home. He struggles hard to cope with the modern lifestyle of his grown-up children. Unlike him, his wife has always lived with the children and has no problem with their lifestyle. As time passes, he comes to realize that he has brought imbalance into the daily routine of other family members and that he is "unwanted" by his own children and his wife.

The dejected old man returns to his workplace and begins doing a private job there. In a similar vein, R. K. Narayan's *The Vendor of Sweets* portrays an aged sweet vendor from Malgudi who believes in the Gandhian way of life. He sends his grown-up son to the US for higher study. The son returns to Malgudi with an American girlfriend. He boasts of the lifestyle that he has enjoyed in the US and continuously "accuses" his father of being an old man with an outdated way of living.

Priyamvad's "Palang"

Priyamvad's "Palang" is about an aging mother and her grown-up son. They reside in a room that is mostly occupied by a large bed or *palang*. The narrator of the story is the son himself. The very first sentence of the story brings together its beginning and end:

> usa sāla jaba palāśa kī naṃgī chitarī śākhoṃ kā pahalā phūla khilā taba māṃ svastha thī … jaba pūrā peR dahakatā jaṃgala bana gayā taba taka māṃ bīmāra paR cukī thī aur jis rāt akasamāt bhayānaka bāriśa se sāre phūla ṭūṭa kara gira gae the aura peḍa ke nīce kucale surkha phūloṃ kā daladala bana gayā thā, māṃ mara gaī thī.[27]
>
> [That year, when the first flower appeared on naked and well-spread branches of *palash* [a kind of tree], my mother was healthy. When the entire tree transformed into the forest fire, my mother was ailing. On the night when the heavy rain made all the flowers of the tree fall on the ground, my mother had passed away.]

The room in which the mother and the son live is small and is in pathetic condition. It has three corners. In one of the corners, there is the *palang* (a large bed) on which they sleep. Out of the two other corners, one belongs to the mother and another to the son. In the entire room, it is only the large bed that possesses some sort of grandeur. The mother feels proud of it, having gotten it on the occasion of her marriage. In the past, the mother used to sleep with her husband on the same bed, and now the narrator feels that she loves her bed more than him. Often, after completing her daily chores, the mother stares at the bed for a long time.

The mother often tries not to disturb her sleeping son while doing her daily chores. Her activities are so organized and controlled that the narrator anticipates each of her activities without opening his eyes. After waking up in the morning, she washes everything, including her body, very properly. Sometimes, she appears in scanty clothing. At that time, her hanging wrinkles and bent back seem to be caught in a sort of eternal uncertainty. Often, she appears in this way as if unaware of her near-nudity. Seeing her in this state, the son closes his eyes and turns away from her.

This state of the mother gives birth to a bizarre kind of hate inside the son. He wants her to behave herself, but then fears that this interference in her daily routine may embarrass her to the extent of ruining the balance of her organized life. Despite this fear, he fails to hide his hate for her for the same reason. After leaving the bed, he does not speak to her. She, out of fear and sadness, stares at his angry face. Sometimes, gathering some courage, she asks him if he is unwell. The narrator fails to understand how his mother comes to know the reason behind his anger. Next time when she washes herself, she either avoids appearing before him with her almost nude body or assures herself that he is sleeping before passing by him.

One day, the narrator drinks a lot of wine. He has had a fight with his beloved. His beloved wants to get married to him as soon as possible. She thinks he is not marrying her since his room does not have the fourth corner. She wants him to remove the bed so that they may spend their married life in the corner it currently occupies. However, the son knows that it is impossible for his mother to get away from her *palang*:

Saurav Kumar

rāta ko jaba māṃ mere sāth usa palaṃga para leṭatī thī tabhī vaha apanī dinabhara kī cuppī … mere sannāṭe … apanī āāṃkhoṃ kī saphedī … jhurriyoṃ se bāhar ā pātī. mere hāthoṃ ko chutī yā sira para hātha pherā detī.[28]

[In nights, when my mother laid herself with me on the large bed … she came out of her silence of entire day … my blankness … the whiteness of her eyes … wrinkles. She touched my hands or pampered my head with her hand.]

Sometimes the son smiles and this prompts her to speak about the legacy of the bed – the memories associated with the bed. The large bed is in a way the expression of her existence. On this bed only, she can feel her intimacy with him, the sole respite of her last years.

The mnemonic devices known as *memory palace* and *memory mirror* are two strategies of associative memory, which older people use for identifying themselves with their homes. In the memory palace, a yoking of vision and movement takes place:

mental images linked to actually seen objects can be recalled by moving through, or imagining oneself moving through, the remembered spaces of the house … Implicit in this approach is the belief that orderly surroundings make memory possible allowing us to find stored memories as easily as we can find the solid and definable features of the building."[29] In mirror palace, "[t]he physical representation of home thus becomes a representation not only of the owner's identity but also of his or her life story.[30]

While memory palace is concerned with the navigation of remembered spaces, memory mirror is related to the identification with possessions. Robert Rubinstein, Janet Kilbride, and Sharon Nagy express that, for aging homeowners, their "personal possessions and objects" are "more than just shrines to the past, since their efficacy is often in the present, in that they help to bring the past into the present when the past may have been forgotten or overwhelmed."[31] Each of these devices can be seen in the way "Palang" reaches its conclusion.

The mother knows her son's beloved. Whenever the younger woman comes to the room along with the narrator, the mother makes her sit in her corner and talks with her a lot. Whenever the old woman interacts with the son's beloved, the narrator feels that his mother is burdened with a guilty conscience: "sambhavataḥ māṃ ke aṃdara hamāre sambandhoṃ ke kāraṇ svayam ko lekara koī aparādhabodha thā jise vaha usa aurata se adhika bāteṃ karake, adhika svāgata karake dabāe rahatī thī."[32] [Perhaps, inside the mother, there was a sense of guilt because of our relations [the relation between the mother and the son, and that between the son and his beloved]]. With her welcoming gesture and company that she accorded to her son's beloved, she used to try her best to hide her sense of guilt. Here, the guilty conscience of the mother can be related to the kind of intimacy that she shares with her son. The quoted sentence arguably stands for the repression of the sexuality of the old woman on account of the stereotypical negative associations between sexuality and aging bodies. The old woman often leaves the narrator and his beloved alone in the room. She goes to the neighborhood and returns to the room after hours.

The narrator then comes back to what happened on that night when he drank a lot of wine. The night is cold. He yearns for sex with his beloved. When he goes to his beloved lying on her bed, she humiliates him. She says unless he replaces the *palang* with her, she would never go to his room. The narrator reacts angrily to the harsh words of his beloved and physically assaults her. When he returns home, the mother cautions him about excessive drinking. In reply to her caution, the son hisses in his sleep: "vaha nīca hai"[33] [she [his beloved] is of an inferior kind]. The next morning, the old woman comes out of the bathroom in order to do something. She is completely naked. The narrator becomes shocked seeing her in this state. He immediately leaves the *palang* and banishes the naked mother from the room. The mother looks at his face. Encountering his

Reformative Aspect of Bhasha *Literatures*

hate for her on his face, she freezes in place. She feels guilty for what she has done. In Priyamvad's "Palang," the relation between the mother and the son definitely has a psychoanalytic angle – the intimacy they both share contains traces of the Jocasta complex. Jocasta complex is a term proposed by Raymond de Saussure. In psychology, it generally refers to the incestuous sexual desire of a mother toward her son. However, it "has various degrees of intensity – from the maternal instinct, slightly deformed, to a frank sexual attachment in which both physical and psychic satisfaction is found."[34]

On a later night, the narrator announces that he is going to marry his beloved. He also tells his mother that he will remove the *palang* from the room to create space for his married life. The old woman dies that same night. The story thus demonstrates how objects associated with older people (a large bed in the case of "Palang") can serve as the store-houses of their past memories and how the replacement of these objects with new ones can deeply affect the existence of elders. Dena Shenk, Kazumi Kuwahara, and Diane Zablotsky have worked on the issue of the attachments elderly widows feel to their homes. In their shared analysis, they use "life-course perspective," which says, "[e]ach person's journey through life can be viewed as a road map, offering many alternative routes to many alternative destinations," in order to address memory palace from the perspective of elderly widows. Applying this topographical model for life on homes, they say: "[t]hese assumptions led us to believe that the home, and its contents, would represent anchors to the woman's past role as wife (and mother) and provide representations and guideposts to her future life as a widow."[35]

Historically, the presence of reformative potential in *Bhasha* literatures can be traced back to their evolution from Middle Indo-Aryan and Tamil. "At the time the *bhasas* emerged from Middle Indo-Aryan and Tamil, the concepts related to time, language and self underwent fundamental changes. In a cultural movement of turning away from classical formalism, the *Bhashas* humanized these concepts."[36] The humanization of *Bhashas* as they moved away from classical formalism "brought about a conflict between the cosmic and the human, the metaphysical and the aesthetic, the metropolitan and the vulgar. It was a conflict that involved a clash between idealistic worldview and a pragmatic world-view."[37] The development of *Bhakti* poetry, "a natural consequence of the emergence of the *bhasa* literatures,"[38] can be perceived as the democratization/regionalization of the same process. The *Bhakti* movement was subversive of *Marga* traditions in two ways. First, the *Bhakti* poets were opposed to the rigorous pedagogical methods of *Marga* traditions. They "thought of formal scholarly training as a stumbling block in the way of perceiving the truth of life, and as a rigid outmoded form that was unwilling to assimilate the new perception of life."[39] Second, "[s]ociologically, [the] devotional poetry [of the *Bhakti* period] was a challenge posed by the oppressed classes to the brahminical monopoly of cultural and scriptural knowledge."[40]

Bhakti traditions were indifferent to formulating new theories based on the new aesthetic of life and the new kind of poetics that they believed in because "the sole aim of bhakti poetry was to challenge *Marga* traditions, traditions of logically rigorous philosophical systems."[41] Also, in the *Bhakti* period, the political order was feudalistic, and the rise of *Bhakti* as "dissent at popular level was dreaded by all rulers."[42] The ruling classes did not welcome the upsurge of *Bhakti* traditions. They "continued to provide uninterrupted patronage to Sanskrit-based formal education all through middle centuries."[43] As a result, "formal education belonged to *Marga*, while the experiences of life [were] perceived and articulated through *Desi* ideolects."[44] Finally, the "gap between lived experience and formalized knowledge" and the feud between *Marga* and *Desi* were not only "at the root of the non-emergence of critical discourse relevant to *Bhakti* literature,"[45] but were also responsible for the beginning of a long historical period (from the 12th century to the 18th century) that, according to Devy, fell prey to cultural amnesia in Indian literary criticism. When Devy says that the period has fallen prey to cultural amnesia, he means to say there is no significant literary criticism on the *Desi* literatures written in the same period, and the period thus is till now "the phase of forgetfulness."

Saurav Kumar

Conclusion

Premchand's "Boodhi Kaaki," Gyanranjan's "Pitaa," and Priyamvad's "Palang" represent three different narratives of old age. The stories are set in three different locales and interrogate in detail various kinds of exclusion that older people face in Indian society. These exclusions differ from one-another in terms of the locale they are set in. The present study shows that the experiences of old age and the process of aging vary across time and space. *Bhasha* literatures are full of a thematic richness that has successfully translated into words the concerns and voices of those who are culturally marginalized and forced to survive at the fringes of society (untouchables, the disabled, elders etc.). The reformative aspect of *Bhasha* literatures is deeply rooted in their origin from the "backyard" of the society (from the stories and songs of the common people).

The reformative aspect of *Bhasha* literatures can play an important role in the large project of alleviating cultural amnesia in Indian literary criticism – a project that basically stands for creating substantial literary criticism on *Desi* literatures that were produced right from the *Bhakti* period to the colonial era. This reformative aspect, on account of being present in *Desi* traditions from the time of emergence of *Bhashas*, can be a common feature among different *Bhasha* literatures and thus can help "formulate a pragmatic literary historiography for *Bhasha* literatures,"[46] one which can help illuminate the all-too-human problems of physical aging and social marginalization.

Bibliography

Ananthamurthy, U. R. "Literature in the Indian *Bhashas*: Front Yards and Backyards." In *Indian English and 'Vernacular' India*, edited by Makarand Paranjape and G. J. V. Prasad, 149–152. Delhi: Pearson, 2010.

Campbell, Robert Jean. "Jocasta Complex." *Campbell's Psychiatric Dictionary*. 8th ed. New York: Oxford University Press, 2004.

Devy, G. N. *After Amnesia: Tradition and Change in Indian Literary Criticism*. Bombay: Orient Longman, 1995.

Devy, G. N. "Literary History and Translation: An Indian View." *Meta* Vol. 42, No. 2 (1997): 395–406. doi: 10.7202/002560ar.

Gyanranjan. "Pitaa." In *Pratinidhi Kahaniyan*, New Delhi: Rajkamal Paperbacks, 2015, 14–22.

Krasner, James. "Accumulated Lives: Metaphor, Materiality, and the Homes of the Elderly." *Literature and Medicine* Vol. 24, No. 2 (Fall 2005): 209–230. doi: 10.1353/lm.2006.0008.

Kumar, S. (Translator). "The Bed" by Priyamvad. *Indian Literature* Vol. 65, No. 1 (2021): 127–132.

Premchand. "Boodhi Kaaki." In *Manjusha: Premchand ki Sarwashreshtha Kahaniyaan*, edited by Amritrai, 33–42. Allahabad: Hans Prakashan, 2010.

Premchand. "The Old Aunt." Translated by M. Asaduddin. *Berfrois: Literature Ideas Tea* (2015): n.p. https://www.berfrois.com/2015/07/the-old-aunt-premchand (Accessed 10 February, 2019).

Priyamvad. "Palang." *Sahitya Varshiki India Today* (1993–1994): 78–80.

Rubinstein, Robert L., Janet C. Kilbride, and Sharon Nagy. *Elders Living Alone: Frailty and the Perception of Choice*. New York: Aldine de Gruyter, 1992.

Shenk, Dena, Kazumi Kuwahara, and Diane Zablotsky. "Older Women's Attachments to Their Home and Possessions." *Journal of Aging Studies* Vol. 18, No. 2 (2004): 157–169. doi: 10.1016/j.jaging.2004.01.006.

Notes

1 This is commonly described as a western dialect of Hindi, and is spoken by nearly 600,000 people in India.

2 Gyanranjan's "Pitaa" and Priyamvad's "Palang" have been translated into English by the author of this chapter. "The Bed" (the chapter author's English translation of Priyamvad's "Palang" appeared in the January–February 2021 issue of *Indian Literature*, a journal published by Sahitya Akademi (Kumar, S. (Translator). "The Bed" by Priyamvad. *Indian Literature* Vol. 65, No. 1 (2021): 127–132).

3 U. R. Ananthamurthy. "Literature in the Indian *Bhashas*: Front Yards and Backyards." In *Indian English and 'Vernacular' India*, edited by Makarand Paranjape and G. J. V. Prasad, 149–152 (Delhi: Pearson, 2010), 150–151.

4 Ibid., 151.

Reformative Aspect of Bhasha *Literatures*

5 Ibid.
6 Ibid.
7 G. N Devy. 1997. "Literary History and Translation: An Indian View." *Meta* Vol. 42, No. 2 (1997): 397.
8 Ibid., 395.
9 Ibid., 396.
10 Ibid.
11 Ibid.
12 Ibid.
13 Ibid.
14 Ibid.
15 Premchand. "Boodhi Kaaki." In *Manjusha: Premchand ki Sarwashreshtha Kahaniyaan.* Edited by Amritrai (Allahabad: Hans Prakashan, 2010) n.p. Unless otherwise noted, all translations are my own.
16 Ibid.
17 Premchand. "The Old Aunt." Translated by M. Asaduddin. *Berfrois: Literature Ideas Tea,* n.p. https://www.berfrois.com/2015/07/the-old-aunt-premchand, 2015.
18 Ibid.
19 Premchand, 2010, 33.
20 Ibid., 41.
21 Premchand, 2015, n.p.
22 Ibid.
23 Ibid.
24 Gyanranjan. "Pitaa." In *Pratinidhi Kahaniyan* (New Delhi: Rajkamal Paperbacks, 2015), 15.
25 Ibid., 16.
26 Ibid., 21.
27 Priyamvad. "Palang." *Sahitya Varshiki* [India Today], 1993–1994, 78.
28 Ibid., 79.
29 James Krasner. "Accumulated Lives: Metaphor, Materiality, and the Homes of the Elderly." *Literature and Medicine* Vol. 24, No. 2 (Fall 2005): 213.
30 Ibid.
31 Robert L. Rubinstein, Janet C. Kilbride, and Sharon Nagy. *Elders Living Alone: Frailty and the Perception of Choice.* (New York: Aldine de Gruyter, 1992), 83.
32 Priyamvad, 79.
33 Ibid.
34 Robert Jean Campbell. "Jocasta Complex." *Campbell's Psychiatric Dictionary.* 8th ed. (New York: Oxford University Press, 2004), 355.
35 Dena Shenk, Kazumi Kuwahara, and Diane Zablotsky. "Older Women's Attachments to Their Home and Possessions." *Journal of Aging Studies* Vol. 18, No. 2 (2004): 158.
36 G. N. Devy. *After Amnesia: Tradition and Change in Indian Literary Criticism* (Bombay: Orient, 1995), 18.
37 Ibid.
38 Ibid., 87.
39 Ibid., 90.
40 Ibid.
41 Ibid., 88.
42 Ibid., 90.
43 Ibid, 91.
44 Ibid.
45 Ibid.
46 Ibid., 56.

9

Humanistic Approaches in Hindi Literature

From Medieval to Modern Times

Prachi Priyanka

Introduction

In the Western world, the Renaissance holds a significant place as it initiated a major shift in European thought and worldview. It questioned long-held beliefs on religious dogmas and created an environment that encouraged curiosity to know the self and the world. Renaissance humanism was the study of ancient Greek and Roman texts with the goal of promoting new norms and values in society. It was a paradigm shift in the approach toward learning, as until then a religious worldview dominated human understanding. Through a study of various disciplines like grammar, history, poetry, and philosophy, Renaissance humanists promoted the idea that people should be educated in a variety of disciplines to participate in social and political life with greater effect. To put it in simpler terms, humanism applied to the overreaching social and intellectual philosophies of man, and thereby the celebration of individual spirit.

The word humanism comes from the Latin word *humanitas*, which implies a search for perfection of the human soul and the development of the full potential of each individual. Humanism signifies that in each human soul there is a great power that can be awakened and inspired to reach the ideal of perfection. It was based on a firm belief in the beauty, worth, and dignity of man—thereby liberating man from the pre-conceived notion that we humans are something sinful and hence to be controlled by the Church. With the decline in dominance of the Church, humanism gained popularity. The interest in God, saints, and the afterlife gave way to a curiosity to know the natural world and the workings of the universe. Man became the subject of study—the "measure of all things."[1]

Historians believe that there were two main reasons for the decline of the Church—first, the bubonic plague that devastated half the population of the Western world led to disenchantment with the Church and a natural urge to seek explanations for their suffering. The second reason could be the impact of the rise of the market economy, which made people break free from the stuffy, impractical, and rigid norms of the Church. Man became keen to explore the human capacity to learn, create, and enjoy life in a more secular manner. This is particularly seen in the writings of Petrarch, often considered to be the Father of Humanism. In one instance, he states "Sameness is the mother of disgust, variety the cure!"[2] These ideals were further expressed in the famous speech, *The Dignity of Man*, in which the renowned orator Mirandola states, "You with no limit or no bound, may choose for yourself!"[3] All these were new norms established to fill man with boundless energy and dreams to achieve his truest potential.

124

DOI: 10.4324/9781003046004-12

Humanism is defined by The International Humanist and Ethical Union as:

> a democratic and ethical life stance which affirms that human beings have the right and responsibility to give meaning and shape to their own lives. It stands for the building of a more humane society through an ethics based on human and other natural values in a spirit of reason and free inquiry through human capabilities. It is not theistic, and it does not accept supernatural views of reality.[4]

Thus, humanism lays emphasis on man, his strong will-power, his duties and accomplishments. It believes in the power of man and glorifies him by saying that man is the measure of all things and that he determines his own destiny:

> The main tenets of humanism are, faith in man and bright future, rejection of life other than the one on this earth, religion, divine power and celestial joy, declaration of man's freedom rejecting fatalist views and establishment of a free and just society wherein man can develop his personality fully.[5]

Indian Humanism: A Different Perspective

In our own time, a typical humanist from the Western perspective is essentially an atheist who believes in the dignity of man and denies his dependence on God for any worldly gains or spiritual uplift. And therein lies the major difference in how Indian humanism approaches the concept. The essence of Indian humanism is the proclamation of *Ayam atma Brahman*,[6] which means that the human self is great and cosmic. It does not deny the existence of God. Instead, Indian humanism is the perfect blend of materialism and spiritualism—a phenomenon of nature called integral humanism. Man, according to Indian humanism, is not a mere biological entity, but also a spiritual entity that aims to cultivate sublime goals. According to integral humanism, society is self-manifested and self-sufficient. The individual is a tangible expression of society. And equally true is the fact that any society is a collective expression of the individuals taken together. Hence the development of social good and individual good are understood to be aligned. While there is a lack of spirituality in Western humanism; the integral humanism of Swami Vivekananda, Shree Aurobindo, Rabindranath Tagore, and Pandit Deen Dayal Upadhyaya incorporates spiritualism in humanism. According to the Divine Principle, the supreme soul (*Parmatman*) exists in every phenomenon of nature in the form of *Atman* (soul), and the unique combination of *karma* yoga, *Bhakti* yoga, and *gyana* (or *jnana*) yoga is there to serve the purpose of Man's spiritual and material elevation.

Chaturvidha Purushartha,[7] which is the ultimate objective of Indian humanism, is propounded by Saint Manu. It is based on four-fold eternal values: *dharma* (moral values), *artha* (financial prosperity), *kama* (physical pleasure), and *mokshya* (self-realization). *Dharma* defines rules and regulations to be followed by an individual or society for progress and harmony. *Artha* allows for materialistic wealth and prosperity. *Kama* is an indulgence in natural desires, while *mokshya* is attained by proper adherence to *dharma*. *Artha* and *kama* are born out of worldly desires, and hence they need to be monitored by *dharma*. In addition, the significance of *chiti* is prime in integral humanism. *Chiti* is akin to the spirit of Hegel or the *elan vital* of Bergson and can be understood as the supreme consciousness in which the material and spiritual prosperity of a nation is augmented. According to Pandit Deen Dayal Upadhyaya:[8]

> Chiti is the touchstone on which each action, each attitude is tested, and determined to be acceptable or otherwise. "Chitti" is the soul of the nation. On the strength of this "Chiti," a

nation arises, strong and virile if it is this "Chiti" that is demonstrated in the actions of every great man of a nation.

Thus, an individual becomes instrumental in bringing forth the soul of the nation, *chiti*. It is evident from this explanation how nationalism is invariably interrelated with an individual. *Chiti* acts as the integrating chord, balancing the wheel of all of humanity. As we navigate through Indian history, we will observe the humanistic tendencies observed in the poetry and prose of Hindi literature—examining various facets of socio-cultural influences in the process.

Love, Devotion, and Communal Harmony in *Bhakti* Poetry

Bhakti poetry[9] has its roots in some significant social changes in the eleventh and twelfth centuries and was in fact a pan-Indian uprising of the people's culture against feudalism. It was a rebellion of the common masses against upper-caste zamindars and priests who oppressed the poor through religious hypocrisy and did not allow the lower castes to read religious texts or enter temples. All these created dissatisfaction in people, and they found escape in direct communion with God through *Bhakti* culture. Some of the classic medieval literature in Hindi literature was composed under the influence of the *Bhakti* movement. Works like *Padmavat*[10] by Malik Muhammad Jayasi, *Ramcharitmanas*[11] by Tulsidas, and *Sur Sagar*[12] by Surdas were written in Awadhi and Braj bhasha—dialects which later developed into the khadi boli Hindi language. This was also the age of tremendous integration between Hindu and Islamic elements in arts. With the emergence of Muslim *Bhakti* poets like Abdul Rahim-I-Khana,[13] a great devotee of Krishna, the communal divide between the two religions was bridged. Secular love was also propounded by Kabir through his universally acclaimed *dohas* (couplets).

During the medieval era, Hindi literature was popular in the Avadhi dialect and was dominated by religion—encouraging an emphasis on faith in the power of supernatural agencies and unquestioned surrender to the will of the gods and goddesses supposed to reside in heaven. Thus, other-worldliness was an important aspect of this literature. However, the focus gradually shifted to the mundane affairs of ordinary people and expression of their sorrows and sufferings. A new tone of humanism could be witnessed in the *Bhakti* poets who would lament the situation of a man mired in the experience of daily drudgery or the recurring cycle of sorrows and privations. The Sufi and saint poets preached equality and denounced casteism and communalism. They were inspired by and devoted to a feeling of the common good. Their anti-feudalist consciousness found expression even in the forms of human relations and sentiments expressed in their poetry.

One of the greatest poets of medieval India was Kabir—widely considered to be a perfect living saint, accepted and revered by both Hindus and Muslims as the direct incarnation of the Supreme Being. His utterances were so powerful that people took him to be a prophet of a new path and followed him on *Kabir Panth* (the path of Kabir). He promoted the importance of careful and clean living among neighbors and members of society, as well as observance of simple rules of good conduct such as non-covetousness, self-restraint, honesty, and mercifulness. The emergence of Kabir was due to the conditions of the age and also the needs of the age. What he expressed was already there in the Vedas, Vedanta, and Upanishads. It was the humanitarian dimension that he added to the insights of those works that made him immensely popular. Kabir's *dohas* are pithy poetic statements, and they illustrate the poet's personality and attitudes. Through couplets like "Boye pera babool ka, aam kahaan te hoi";[14] Kabir suggests that those who plant thorny acacia will not get sweet and juicy mangoes to eat. Similarly, in another couplet, "Aisi vaani boliye, man ka apa khoi"[15] he advises one to talk sweetly without the rage of jealousy—so that your own self cools down and others are pacified. Kabir's *dohas* have a particularly multi-faceted structure. They have wit and intelligence, and a tendency to project multiple meanings through apt use of imagery.

But what is most remarkable is that they are full of worldly wisdom, which steadily elevates into a philosophic understanding of life.[16] In the couplet "Says Kabir, I weep on seeing / The grindstone at work // For not a grain comes out whole / From the grinding trap,"[17] the simile is used to express in graphic terms how a man is reduced to nothingness by the forces of evil operating in the world and in himself. Recited in a simplistic manner to make ignorant, illiterate people understand the philosophy of love and life, Kabir's *dohas* strived to bring people to live together in harmony and embrace compassion. His poetry is relevant to date as we see around us a world torn apart by prejudices and intolerance. His couplets resonate with a humanistic ring:

> Is East the abode of Hari / And west that of Allah?
> Search your heart for both of them / there live both Karim and Ram
> They are one and the same / Creator of the Universe[18]

In the history of Hindi literature, *Bhakti* poetry played a crucial role in the evolution of literary perspectives, poetic sensibilities, and critical vision through the popularity of art and literature. The new kind of cultural awareness during this period made literature more people-oriented— freeing it from the shackles of classicist literatures of the Sanskrit, Pali, Prakrit, and Apbhrasha[19] traditions. The *Riti-kaavy Kaal*[20] that followed the *Bhakti* era was mainly about court poetry, which took literature further from the grim realities of life. As well as emphasizing poetic devices and the development of theories on poetry, love, sensuousness, and layered eroticism began to dominate the realm of poetry. The emotional content of *Bhakti* was taken over by emphasis on poetic devices and the development of theories on poetry. The *Sagun*[21] form of *Bhakti* poetry further split into two schools—*Ram Bhakti* and *Krishna Bhakti*.[22] Most of the poems written during this period were filled with praise for love and the charms of Lord Krishna and his consort, Radha. The personification of gods was a humanistic approach to see the divine embodying human attributes. In Surdas's poetry, Krishna's love for Radha and other Gopikas[23] is free from feudalist moral conventions. This concept of unrestrained love and the portrayal of its evolution in the form of human relations is in opposition to the feudalist perspective on love and marriage. The variety, depth, and comprehensiveness of generous forms of simplistic human love as portrayed in Surdas's poetry are seldom found elsewhere. No love-poet in Hindi is as great as Surdas. His description of profound affection has the power to evoke and preserve humanity even in inhuman situations.

The humanistic aspects of *Bhakti* poets are also exemplified in the way they narrate stories of Krishna and Rama to celebrate heroism against injustice and exploitative forces. Though these are stories of Hindu gods, they stand for rebellion against the despotism of the feudal system and allow common people to aspire to realize their ideals and struggle against the adversities of life. The all-pervasive tales by Tulsidas and Surdas talk about establishing a benevolent socio-political order by killing inequitable, oppressive, and tyrannical rulers. This anti-feudal approach expresses concern for public welfare and the value of human relationships and sentiments in any age. If *Ramrajya*[24] in Tulsidas is a public desire for a justice-loving political order, Krishna's love for Radha in Surdas's poetry is based on a concept of unrestrained love and devotion. We may find different forms of love in Kabir, Jayasi,[25] Surdas, and Meera[26]—but despite the variations, the underlying emotion is constant. The *Bhakti* poets consider nothing above humanity—caste, class, race, gender, creed, or an illusionist view of the world. These poets aimed to replace the existing social order based on all kinds of discrimination with a more humanistic approach based on equality and freedom for all.

The High Ideals of Early Hindi Literature

Humanism and humanitarianism have often been confused or used interchangeably; however, the two words are different. While humanism emphasizes intellect, is centered on individuality, is scientific and more realistic in approach, humanitarianism is idealistic about advocating traditional moral and cultural values, is more comprehensive, and addresses society as a collective whole. Until the Bhartendu era, Hindi writers were more humanitarian than humanistic in their approach. It was only after the Renaissance in the West that Indian writers began to be influenced by humanism and pursued a shift in their interpretation of society, religion, morality, and man in this new light. Raja Ram Mohan Roy, Dayanand Saraswati, Ramkrishna Paramhansa, and Swami Vivekanada were the precursors of this new enlightenment. Balkrishna Bhatt referred to literature of this era as marked by the evolution of people's sensibilities which was in continuation of the fundamental characteristic of the *Bhakti* movement.[27] Though *Bhakti* poetry was neglected by the aristocracy in the age of formalist court poets and feudalist poetic interests, it undoubtedly remained the main source of fulfilling cultural aspirations of the common masses. It became possible to recognize the significance of the democratic aspects of the *Bhakti* movement and literature when an awareness of nationalism and democratic culture came into being with the rise of the Renaissance and the freedom movement in the modern period.

In Hindi literature, Bhartendu brought new progressive ideas—spirituality giving way to worldly problems and seeking their resolution. The development of khari boli Hindi is significant in the Bhartendu era. New forms of writing developed in Hindi—to propagate a new consciousness of the modern era along with an understanding of social contradictions that existed in the period. The writers acknowledged the need for a national renaissance, and connected literature with public life. In the era of Bhartendu, women suffered under a rigid caste system and orthodox rituals. Treated as subordinates in society, they remained illiterate, vulnerable victims of child marriage, the *purdah* system,[28] and *sati pratha*.[29] Bhartendu exposed the follies of orthodox thinking and social issues that recur in his writings. A great focus was given to the nationalist thinking of modern India—a unifying feeling that was new to the nation and can be considered as an essential concomitant to humanism in literature. Hailed as the national poet of India, Maithili Sharan Gupt made significant contributions in establishing khari boli Hindi on firmer grounds. His poems (such as: "That which is not filled with emotions and where juices do not flow / That heart is a stone in which there is no love for home.")[30] were full of high idealism, sensitive toward the sufferings of women, and infuse patriotism in citizens.

Bhartendu yug was followed by *Dwivedi* yug—named after Mahavir Prasad Dwivedi, who played a crucial role in establishing modern Hindi by broadening its subjects to nationalism and social reform. He was the editor of the first magazine in Hindi, and through this venture he encouraged writings concerned with social issues and moral values. As a literary critic, Dwivedi made two significant contributions to Hindi literature. First, he helped to improve the taste of his readers by working toward refining contemporary writing and producing good quality literature. Second, he advocated a humanistic approach to literature. "He emphasized seriousness of purpose, utility, concern for human welfare, flawlessness and novelty of style as the norms of literature as against the formalist's concern for nuances of style or the hedonist's concern for pleasure in literature evaluation."[31]

Celebration of Individualism

Chhayavad or neo-romanticism was a movement that can be defined by the creative energy of three pillars of Hindi poetry: Jai Shankar Prasad, Suryakant Tripathi Nirala, and Sumitranandan Pant. It refers to an era marked by an upsurge of romantic and humanist content. Self and personal expression with an inclination toward themes of love, nature, and mysticism were visible characteristics of the writing of the time. In her popular poem "Main Neer Bhari Dukh ki Badli,"[32]

Humanistic Approaches in Hindi Literature

Mahadevi Varma laments the state of the girl child. Using the first-person narrative, she keeps human experiences and emotions at the center of existence as she describes the sorrowful journey of a girl who is fragile and vulnerable like a clay doll.

Nirala was a *Chhayavadi* poet whose works are critically acclaimed for the wide range of human emotions they express. Many of them express rebellion against didactic, superficial, and shallow or conventional poetry. Through the expression of their vulnerable selves, these writers and poets connected with the masses, and the relatability of the emotions evoked allowed people to share and celebrate the experiences described in the poetry. The mystic tone of Nirala and other *Chhayavadi* poets was profound in thought, music, and exquisite metaphors. In "Juhi ki Kali,"[33] he presented a picture of love that was at once earthy and ethereal. In poems like "The Beggar"[34] and "Breaking Stones,"[35] we witness the harsh realities of life and the plight of the oppressed sections of society. Sometimes, the cruel injustice of society makes the poet suffer in pain. However, though sadness flashes intermittently, it does not let the indomitable spirit of the poet recede into self-pity. Not only through poetry, but also through the medium of prose, Nirala expressed his thoughts about man and the universe. His autobiography "A Life Misspent" asserts the poet's humanistic ideology by laying bare his soul to readers.

One of the important elements of humanism is to give prominence to individualism. Autobiography as a genre predominantly takes a retrospective approach to narrate the sequence of events in the author's life—allowing them to reconstruct their personal growth within a given historical, social, and cultural framework. In his autobiography, Nirala talks about his wife's memories as a pillar of strength, his devotion to Saraswati, the Goddess of knowledge, and his allegiance to Hindi—all fused into one. Thus, the humanistic approach of the writer is evident in the choice of his subject, exposition of his vulnerability, and the celebration of indomitable spirit in the face of fate. In "Saroj-Smriti," one of the most poignant poems written in Hindi, he writes an elegy in memory of his daughter, who also died young:

> In you I saw the courage
> The first singing of my own spring
> That love without embodied form
> The feeling I'd poured out
> In my poems and once had sung
> With my lost darling,
> Filling my senses now
> With passionate joy.[36]

Nirala, like other *Chhayavadi* poets, shared a strong communion with living spirits of Nature, making us aware of the wisdom of *advait* philosophy.[37] Some of the poems of Nirala are mystical in nature and bask in the rich humanity of the medieval poetry of the *Bhakti* movement. In his last poem, he writes:

> The poison of a life infected with literature
> has been exhausted.
> In my inmost heart the lamp
> of the divine command is lit
> Another dawning
> another burning
> and returning
> of the heart[38]

Nagarjun gave to Hindi poetry something that could only have been written after Nirala. Just like Nirala, with his poems such as "Kukkurmutta"[39] he had freed poetry from the constraints of writing on "suitable" subjects for poetry; similarly, Nagarjun in his poems "Paine Daanton wali," "Kar do Vaman," and "Mann Karta hai" breaks down all shackles of conventional content and poetic form. His poems exhibit such authenticity of consistent experiences that at one time Nagarjun remarked, "Put all my poems together, and that will become my autobiography."[40] His poems are stories of ordinary people who struggle to make their living. His poem "akaal aur uske baad"[41] is a heart-wrenching work on famine where people starved for days. "A poet later / I am a human being first" so said he, in another poem, "Manushya Hoon."[42] Nagarjun was forthright and direct like Kabir in his ability to confront reality with a rare ruthlessness.

One of the stalwart figures of Hindi literature who is known for extensive research on medieval religious movements in India and highlighted the genius of Kabir through his criticism is Acharya Hazari Prasad Dwivedi. Inspired by great personalities like Shri Madan Mohan Malviya, Nandalal Bose, and Rabindranath Tagore, Acharya Dwivedi upheld Indian culture with absorbing passion. According to him, only "by cultivation of the virtues of truthfulness, non-violence, self-restraint, devotion and universal love with the aid of constant practice and dispassion"[43] can man lead himself toward the path of the highest life. Dr Dwivedi's views on literature revolve around "the general good of man." At the very beginning of his essay, "Man Alone is the Subject of Literature," he states:

> I am inclined to view literature from the point of view of man. I have hesitation to call that wordy piece of work as literature which cannot rescue man from misfortunes, inferiority and parasitism, which cannot illumine his soul or make his heart sympathetic and sensitive to the distress of his fellow-beings.[44]

We need to understand here that Dr. Dwivedi's humanism was as much different from the spiritual humanism of the saint poets of the Nirguna school[45] as it was from the communistic humanism of Marxism. While the poets of the Nirguna school sing "zealously of the fundamental unity of man, tend to make him more of an escapist seeking refuge from the struggle in the present in life musings of the world to come,"[46] Dr. Dwivedi rejects this approach for it will make man indifferent to the realities of life and he would not make the necessary effort to bring about any change in the system. Similarly, he disagreed with the Marxist approach grounded in the theory of dialectical materialism, which emphasized the materialistic aspects of real-world conditions such as class, labor, and socio-economic conditions. Numerous examples can be cited from his writings to support his theistic or spiritual approach to life.[47]

Compassion for the Downtrodden

The writer who was crucial in bringing realism to Hindi prose literature was Munshi Premchand. Before him, literature revolved around magical stories that were based on religious themes distant from the realistic concerns faced by the masses.

> In its basic thrust Premchand's literature focuses on an almost total collapse of reciprocity and the intense exploitation of peasantry by various forces. The landlords and their agents, the colonial state and its officials, the moneylenders, and the priests all suck the peasants dry and force them to lead a sub-human existence.[48]

Premchand visualized a period when there existed a reciprocal relationship between landlords and peasants. It was not a harmonious or ideal relationship, but there were certain norms that were followed for generations. This reciprocal relationship between peasants and landlords during the pre-colonial period was not a system of welfare but a system of locally negotiated mutual understandings in a time when land was in abundance, labor was scarce, and politics did not affect the common people so adversely. However, things started to change with colonial intervention, which destabilized the customary system of rights and introduced exploitative mechanisms like private property, high revenue demands, and the promotion of cash crops. All these added to the woes of poor farmers and made them vulnerable to the manipulations of zamindars and privileged masters, who had become more powerful under the British regime.

Premchand believed that as a writer he had a moral commitment to direct his literary efforts toward depictions of peasant society. In the early years of his career, though he would talk of the need to "awaken and embrace the villagers,"[49] his writing did not demonstrate a connection with rural people and their sensibilities. Also, his efforts to include peasants into national mainstream literature showed a condescending attitude where the rustic poor needed to be reformed, beautified, and treated lovingly. The villagers, thus, remain as passive outsiders in his stories, until the First World War, after which his involvement with the peasantry became significant and noticeable. The dual influences of Leo Tolstoy and the Russian Revolution of 1917, as well as Gandhian anti-modern principles and strategies to involve peasants in the freedom struggle, all deepened Premchand's interest in peasant lives and their issues. He became the first writer in the Hindi-Urdu streams of Indian literature to comprehensively take up the theme of peasants' lives and struggles. The oppression narratives of the peasantry in "Balidaan" (Sacrifice) and "Vidhwans" (Catastrophe) show the anguished lives of the poor rural masses. However, what is remarkable is that the peasants he portrays are initially defiant and unbending in the face of the torments inflicted by the landlords, until they finally succumb. In addition, poetic justice is met in these stories by making the tormentors also suffer in the process. In "Balidaan," after the death of the tenant, the landlord increases the rent, and when the tenant's son is unable to pay the huge amount, the land is transferred to another person. To save himself from disgrace, the son commits suicide, but the landlord's mission remains unaccomplished as the ghost of the tenant now guards the land. Similarly, in the story "Vidhwans," an old Gond woman, Bhungi, silently suffers the torment of the landlord till he orders his men to burn her house. In utter despair, she ends her life by jumping into the same fire. However, Premchand brings the element of poetic justice to the story by punishing the landlord for his misdeed:

> As the fate would have it, this conflagration engulfs, besides some peasants' huts, the landlord's entire barn and his splendid mansion, and while he watched, it tossed like a ship amid wild waves and disappeared in the sea of fire. The sound of lamentation that broke out amidst the ashes was even more pitiful than Bhungi's grievous cries.[50]

This idealist vision of Premchand is also seen in his story "Premashram" (Abode of Love), where scientific reforms and improvised mechanisms of agriculture bring happiness and prosperity to the lives of peasants. Thus, Premchand builds a Utopian vision where his humanist, equalitarian, and socialist ideas promise a more congenial world for the rural masses. One of the most remarkable stories of Premchand, "Kafan" (The Shroud) highlights the basic need of existence—freedom from hunger. Through the characters of Ghisu and Madhav, Premchand depicts the lives of a father and son, who live in utter poverty. They raise money for the last rites of Madhav's wife, but spend it on satiating their hunger and desire to drink. The story seems to comment on the state of abject poverty of lower-caste people for whom hunger forms the core of life, and mourning becomes a luxury.

Besides giving a glimpse into the woes of peasants' lives, Premchand also emphasized the uplifting of women and their role in society. In 1936, he announced at the Conference of All India Progressive Writers' Front that it is the duty of a writer to protect and argue in favor of those who are oppressed, suffering, or deprived—whether an individual or a group.[51] And the oppression faced by women in Indian society deeply concerned him. In his stories, we meet women from different strata of society, class, caste, educational background, and familial responsibilities. In the story "Kusum," we encounter an abandoned wife who is self-righteous when she revolts against the system of dowry and instead focuses on becoming independent in life. "Veshya" (1933) and "Do Kabrein" (1930) examine in different ways the attitude of society toward prostitutes.[52] When Madhuri, a prostitute and the main protagonist of the story "Veshya," desires to live the simple life of a housewife away from the glitter of her courtesan existence, it raises doubts about the question of loyalty—to which she defiantly says: "If I am corrupt, so are the men who visit this place."[53] By giving her a voice, Premchand probes taboo subjects and stimulates readers to question their own integrity before judging others. In "Do Kabrein" too, Premchand protests social injustice toward prostitutes through the character of Sulochana, who struggles for an identity caught between the role of a housewife and a prostitute's daughter. Though most of the women in Premchand's stories come from the affluent class, it is the women from the middle and lower classes that actually show virtues of inner strength and probe deeply into readers' minds. Prostitution was a complex social problem, prevalent in society, and Premchand raised humanistic concerns through his stories. In a note titled "On the Treatment of Prostitutes," Shri Jawaharlal Nehru, then chairman of the Allahabad Municipality, raised his concerns about the issue of prostitution: "If we could raise the status of women and afford them honorable careers we would do more toward the lessening of the evil than by any number of laws."[54]

Peasant Narratives and Migratory Labor

The situation did not improve for peasants even after independence from the British was achieved. Research studies claim that in the second five-year plan (commenced in 1956), the bulk of the state development fund focused on heavy industry, despite the fact that 75% of the population was engaged in agriculture and only 11% of the population were employed in industry. The literature of the period understood and reflected these loopholes in government initiatives and approaches—the huge neglect toward rural society that served to deepen the gap between social classes. The stories and novels from this period, therefore, were often meant to highlight how the state failed to implement meaningfully appropriate agrarian policy, education policy, or empowerment policy for agrarian society, a failure that perpetuated immense chaos, ignorance, and confusion leading to frustration in rural men and women who depended on subsistence. In postcolonial narratives, the peasant is surrounded by invisible agencies of control that he finds himself stuck in amidst government policies, wealthy landowners, and middlemen, and a dizzyingly complicated political economy. These peasant narratives recognize the hardships and turmoil of poor farmers, and their resilience in suffering the vagaries of weather and other hardships, but they also celebrate the heroic efforts such farmers put forth amidst the uncertainty created by the absence of any social security. Damodar Dutta Dixit, Markendeya, and Shailendra Mohan, through their peasant stories, bring forth struggles such as "unequal education and illiteracy, lack of employment, indebtedness, precarious monsoon, daughters and dowry and mass migration of the rural poor."[55] These peasant narratives invoke the period from the 1960s to 1990s that shares a deeper understanding of the impact of economic and cultural arrangements that gradually reduced the personal autonomy of peasants.

According to Ashis Nandy, violence against the poor, rural population of the country is most prominent in such welfare projects as land ceiling, green revolution, and even the various loan schemes run by the government.[56] Damoder Dutta Dixit's story "Darvaje vala Khet" (Farm at the Door) probes the damage done to small peasants through state development programs like Chakbandi (Land Consolidating Act). While the intent of the program was to assemble the scattered small lands of peasants in close vicinity to provide irrigation benefits, local officials and village chiefs manipulated the agenda to suit their own interests. Hence, the rich, powerful landowners and village functionaries joined hands to snatch the fertile lands of small landholders—thereby leaving them to work in useless plots, either barren or water-logged pieces threatened by flood.

Humanistic Approaches in Hindi Literature

Through the tale of the principal characters, Deenanath and Ramesh, the story brings out the greed of the upper-class and prevailing caste politics working in alliance to consolidate power over the poor peasants.

In another story, "Underweighment" (Underweighing), Damoder Dixit laments the difficult lives of sugar cane growers in India who are tormented by the state agencies through blatant cheating in measurements, inordinate delays in payment from the sugar mills, and the amount of harassment the peasants have to bear in the scheme of things. Maiku, the principal character in the story reminds us of Halku in Premchand's "Winter's Night", both stories being a comment on how tough the harsh winters could be for the laboring community. In the village of Karmaha, Maiku sets out on a bullock cart borrowed from his neighbor, Shivacharan, after a lot of pleading in order to carry bundles of sugar cane to the Cane Purchase Centre, and then returns the cart the following evening. However, not only does the weighing man cheat Maiku and make him wait at the corner for complaining about it, he is bullied, heckled, and humiliated despite constant pleading. Finally, when Maiku leaves for home, he is exhausted, hungry, and in utter despair:

> What kind of bargaining is this? When a shopkeeper sells a thing he keeps the money first. Buy wheat—first give the money. The sale of cane however is outrageous. Only a year ago, the factory paid the cost of cane after 8 months. He feels cold and sleepy.[57]

When Maiku's wife checks on him in the morning, he is dead. Through the tragic end of Maiku, the story strives to highlight how state machinery facilitates the control and authority of Maiku's tormentors, depriving him of all agency and basic human rights.

Markandaya's story "Bhudan" (Gift of Land) is built on the context of the *Bhudan* movement, which was initiated by the government in order to secure voluntary donations of land and distribute it to the landless, but soon the agenda of the movement became coercive, insisting that one-sixth of land from all landowners must be given up. The narrative in "Bhudan" examines, through the journey of Ramjatan, how the campaign for distributing land to the landless was fraught with calculations designed to serve the interest of the privileged. Ramjatan is coaxed by the influential Thakur of the village to give up a piece of land to gain five times more land in exchange. However, by the time he realizes his mistake, it is too late. The land that he had received in return existed only in the papers of the village accountant—for, in reality, it was in the riverbed of Gomti. Reduced to being a meager laborer, Ramjatan succumbs to asthma and dies a tragic death. The writer brings out the harsh realities of illiterate sections of society who are vulnerable to being manipulated into entering a kind of Faustian bargain whereby they trade away their agency in search of greater livelihood and security.

Shailendra Mohan's story "Uttha Puttar" (Wake up Son) touches on issues concerning the gritty truths about farming life and the migration of laborers to the cities. Migrant labors live on the margins of subsistence and suffer constant exposure to the twin threats of disease and death. The storyteller, Muktesar Kamat, is in debt, and because of this, his son Ramsaran leaves for Punjab to work as a laborer. Ramsaran would occasionally send money home to pay off the debts, but one day he goes missing. The anguish of the father is described in a heart-rendering manner when he learns how the wealthy owner had accused Ramsaran of theft, and how that accusation had led to him fleeing. "Mukteswar looked at the sky unblinking; his eyes pleading: come back Ram Saran, the loan of the moneylender has been paid. Now never go to Punjab. Upon the banyan tree, the dove was repeatedly singing 'Wake up son, it's over.'"[58] The story conveys the desolation and grief of poor rural dwellers, and the effects on the family when the sole income earner suffers in isolation and dies in anonymity.

Dominick La Capra reads Freud's notion of melancholia as characteristic of an arrested process in which the depressed, self-berating, and traumatized are self-locked in compulsive repetition, possessed by the past, facing a future of impasses, while remaining narcissistically identified with the lost object.[59] While mourning brings the possibility of engaging trauma and reinvestment in life that allows one to begin again, trauma is a state of loss that brings about interminable grieving. In the world of peasant characters like Deenanath, Maiku, and Muktesar, there is pain, despair, and constant struggle to survive against the brutal system that puts them in the throes of humiliation, uncertainty, and oppression. James C. Scott, who closely examines the relationship between state and agrarian life, concludes that "if development is about anything it is about peasant livelihoods and the improvement of peasant lives more generally."[60] The narratives of the peasantry in Hindi literature from Premchand to the postmodern period

> draw us impulsively to participate in their lives as a repository of ethnographic experiences— localized truths, carrying orally transmitted cultures—the pathos, exuberance and resilience driving them to go on and on and struggle for subsistence until it is beyond endurance.[61]

Turmoils of Modern Man

Modernist ideas were influential in shaping the literature of the twentieth century. The impact of the two world wars in India (and elsewhere) was evident in a certain helplessness and loss of faith in human endeavors. Hindi writers turned inwards to deal with the angst-ridden world outside that seemed meaningless and barren. On India's literary horizons, writers were to face a sense of alienation in changing circumstances post-Independence. The modernist writers of the West were a source of inspiration for Hindi writers, and they tried to catch up with the changing trends in form, experimenting with poetry, prose and drama. These literary enthusiasts in Hindi were termed experimentalists or Prayogvadi. Most Indian writers turned toward the West to appropriate the ethos and style of modernism, thereby distancing themselves from locally-inflected depictions of ground reality and daunting social concerns that called for attention. Hindi literature in India during the 1950s saw a juxtaposition of realism and modernism similar to Georg Lukacs's observation in "The Meaning of Contemporary Realism." The two schools of thought, Pragativad[62] (Progressivism) and Prayogvad[63] (Experimentalism), represented the trends of realism and modernism in Hindi literature, respectively, and the clash generated a great deal of debate as a consequence.

The social milieu in India was full of contradictions. While on the one hand, there was the disintegration of family structures, leading to new situations and unfamiliar personal issues; on the other hand, there were constricting circumstances brought by capitalist culture giving way to growing opportunism in the middle-class. Experimental poets like Agyeya stressed the isolation of the individual from concrete social and humanistic processes; while poets associated with real tensions and conflicts tried to understand the working of people's minds and empathize with the oppressed victims in life. Kedarnath Singh's poetry echoes hope and faith in mankind when he writes about how all lives are connected:

All the bloods on earth are one
Making the same journey
Running up and down
One earth-length body
No, rest they do not want
The drop that drips in Syria
Is heard by the child's heartbeat in my village
Hundreds of crores of hearts

Beating in the same rhythm
Making the world turn
All these bloods
Chatting with other bloods.[64]

The pain and compassion that Kedarnath felt for all mankind is voiced in these powerful lines:

How long does it take for a hand of my country
to reach a gaping, hungry mouth
How many years?[65]

Another significant poet who tried to bring about change in society with his modernist writings was Gajanan Madhav Muktibodh, who worked with the progressive movement at the grassroots level. He argues that "the social condition of colonisation and exploitation strangulate the individual" who is further pulled down by orthodoxy and class hierarchy. The individual, oppressed under the rigidity of the caste system and the resulting dissatisfaction due to social status, finally cries in protest, which leads to an "explosion of emotion."[66] The individual thus becomes the subject of modernist writing. The division between modernists and progressives widened with time and gave rise to a clear-cut diversion in their purposes, styles, and approaches toward writing. In Hindi literature, the writers divided themselves between those who used writing as a tool to focus on collective social injustice, and others who focused on the predicament of individuals in a fragmented society. According to Muktibodh, it is the business of every writer with a scientific attitude "to observe, understand, analyse and systematise facts and evaluate them and also to evolve appropriate methods and a suitable approach to uproot evil aspects and promote healthier features" in life.[67]

Scientific advancement had influenced the perception of man's role in society. Gopal Das Saxena Neeraj believed it was important for poets to stand for humanity. He remarked: "Poetry stands for humanism. There is no bigger truth in the world than the human himself. I don't believe in God or reincarnation or the soul. This is the age of science." In another instance, he also commented on the relationship between art and society:

Art cannot run away from the exploitation and injustice that pervades society today. If art would not walk hand in hand with social/humanitarian concerns; it would become "self-centred, deficient in reality" and "would eventually commit suicide."[68]

Human Rights in Janvadi Sahitya

Postmodern Hindi literature reflects a combative mood on the question of human rights and concern for oppressed sections of society. The writers rejected the "ideology-free" modernistic approach of the 1950s and early 1960s and emphasized experiential realism through their writings. The subject matter shifted from peasant narratives to the anguish of the middle classes struggling in urban settings. These writers stressed that stories should strive for social realism, and returned to the tradition of story writing established by Premchand. Some of the noteworthy Hindi short story writers who depicted the oppressed and disadvantaged sections of society in their works include Abdul Bismillah, Uday Prakash, Sanjiv, Mithileshwar, Ramesh Upadhyay, and many others. Two important external developments that triggered the interest of literary artists on wider concerns of the society were the Naxalbari peasant revolt of 1967 in Northern Bengal and the emergency imposed on the country by Mrs. Gandhi in 1975. While the Naxalbari revolt drew attention to issues of human and democratic rights, the latter highlighted issues of human and democratic rights at the pan-India level and gave an anti-establishment tone to Hindi texts. The effect of Naxalbari was not only on national politics, but also on the literary scene where writers and poets depicted the aggressive struggle of affected people. In Hindi literature, *Janvadi* or democratic poetry evolved:

> Under the same constitution
> A whining palm stretched out
> In hunger is called
> a "pity."
> And a fist clenched
> in hunger
> is called
> Naxalbari.[69]

One striking influence of the Naxalbari revolt was that it "destroyed the myth about the passivity of the Indian peasantry, incapable of fighting against injustice."[70] Moreover, the Naxalbari uprising changed the thematic concern of Hindi short stories that used to revolve around the lives of middle-class people in urban settings. The struggles of the rural masses once again began to demand the attention of Hindi writers. From the late 1970s and early 1980s onwards, *Janvadi kahani* claimed that the urban-life stories of interpersonal relationships marked a corrupting influence of Western modernism. Instead, they emphasized characters invested with class consciousness and depicted their struggles to provide the underpinning for an anti-modernist stance.

"Asharh ka Ek Din" by Jawahar Sinh is set during the monsoon months where it describes the hopes and despairs of a Harijan couple stuck in a flooded straw-hut house in a village. The husband is infuriated at the injustice they have to suffer at the hands of their upper-class masters and complains: "What kind of justice is this that some people don't have a hand's breath of land, others own thousands of bigha … This won't do anymore. You stand ready, united, these big people will have to give up their land."[71] The sentiment of class struggle expressed here echoes the Naxalbari experience through Bhagelu's newly acquired faith in "organized struggle" as a means of acquiring land for the downtrodden. Bhagelu's wife, however, dampens his spirit and has a more realistic appraisal of the situation when she laments: "The poor will remain poor and the rich will remain rich."[72] It is the inhuman treatment of Harijans that pains her: "The masters hardly think of us poor hairjans as human."[73] The story ends on a tragic note when Bhagelu rejects working for his masters and reaches a starvation point where he is forced to send his wife to sleep with Bisesar Tivari, before he later stops her halfway. Instead, he goes to steal sweet potatoes from the field of his masters, where he is shot dead. The writer ends the story with a final line filled with gloom and despair: "The sun rose next morning spreading a very clean light. Wrapped up in a shroud cleaner than the light Bhagelu's corpse lay in his courtyard."[74]

Madhukar Singh, another leading writer in the realm of Hindi literature set his stories primarily among the rural and underprivileged to highlight existing class conflict, insensitivity, and hypocrisy in society. In the story "Harijan Sevak" (Servant of the Harijans) we meet Munsi Ramsaranlal, a follower of Gandhian principles and one who is committed to educating Harijan children. However, the disparity between his beliefs and his practice is revealed when he insists on maintaining distance with the Harijan students because any proximity with them could pollute his religion. The writer describes the lives of these lower-caste people who were treated as untouchables. "The whole of the Harijan district works for them twelve months a year like animals and is still half-clad and half-starved. The honour of our women is also in their hands."[75] The Harijans in the story revolt because of the low wages they receive, despite all their hard work, but are defeated in their struggle against powerful upper-caste moneylenders and landlords. There is a bomb explosion in the Harijan district and many houses are burned down, while those who survive are put in jail with the accusation of a probable Naxalite connection. In another story, "Lahu Pukaare Aadmi"[76] (Blood says Human Beings), Madhukar Singh insists how basic human rights are also not allowed in lower-caste communities like Nagina, which is a victim of social prejudice and deprivation. In one instance in the story, the Mushar community is even compared to pigs—stating none of them deserve pity.[77]

Resistance, Rage, and Revolt Against Oppression

The presence of social divisions in Indian society is a harsh reality in terms of caste, class, and gender. Such divisions have also been detrimental to the harmonious growth of the nation as a whole. *Dalits*, *adivasis*, and women have been continually pushed to the periphery by the patriarchal system and the class hierarchy established by a traditional Brahmanical structure of oppression. Dalits are people from the lowest castes in India (given so little regard that they are technically beneath or outside the caste system), and despite anti-discrimination legislation, they have been abused, exploited, manipulated, and treated in the most inhuman ways possible. Bereft of land and dignity, they live on the outskirts of villages and remain in servitude to the higher castes. Forced to work as manual labors like scavengers or in bonded-labor on their own land, they have lived starved, illiterate, and homeless. Having lost their faith in government policies and state laws, these Harijans know that organized struggle is the only means of their deliverance. Dr. B. R. Ambedkar, a Dalit from a poor family who armored himself with education, was one of the first political thinkers to describe the Indian caste system as a form of graded inequality, and he argued for its annihilation in order to build a democratic society. The concepts of human dignity, equality and freedom that are integral to the *Dalit* movement were central tenets of Ambedkarite politics.

While the writings of Premchand describe the abject poverty of down-trodden characters like Ghisu, Hori, Dhaniya, and Halku to raise them onto pedestals as heroes and heroines, it took many years for Dalits to come forward to write about their own horrifying experiences as individuals and communities. Though Dalit writing as a genre had a strong presence in regional languages like Marathi and Gujarati in the 1970s, it emerged as a significant stream of expression in Hindi literature only in the 1990s, giving powerful and widespread expression to sentiments like those seen below:

> While Brahmins and Kshatriyas are allowed to rise and rise
> "Wear your old clothes," for us is the advice.
> No wealth can we earn, what we save is not secure,
> Sheer depression is our lot, since we are always dubbed impure.
> Lower in stature than dogs or cats or flies,
> Provided no habitation under the village skies,
> We labour like bullocks, with no returns to await,
> Just abuses and thrashings are our fate.
> Our toils are enforced, not even food as recompense,
> Our children wail with hunger,
> their torture makes no sense.
> O listen, o Hindus, on you only misfortunes will descend
> For shedding the tears of innocents, and for their suffering without end![78]

The earliest record of Dalit writing is this composition from the late nineteenth or early twentieth century. The poem is a sharp critique of the oppression of Dalits. Achhutanand's writings refer to the under-castes as a collective entity and describes their plight through stirring narratives of resistance. Dalit stories about the past, as Sarah Beth Hunt has pointed out in her book *Hindi Dalit Literature and the Politics of Representation*, were in circulation for a long time through printed material that Dalit presses produced.[79] Pamphlets were a popular medium through which Dalits expressed their new literary culture to create consciousness in the community.

Autobiography as a genre gave dynamic assertion to the "lived reality" of several Dalit writers. "Apne Apne Pinjre"[80] by Mohandas Nimishray and "Mera Bachpan Mere Kandhon Par"[81] by Sheoraj Singh Bechain were written by members of the *Chamar* Dalit community. The most prominent among these personal narratives is Omprakash Valmiki's powerful work "Joothan"[82] that meticulously provides painful details of the rotten lives of Dalits. Set in a village in western Uttar Pradesh, which was dominated by upper-class local representatives, Valmiki creates a heart-wrenching description of his parents' work of cleaning people's toilets. Keen to learn, he finds a space inside the local school, but his teacher would embarrass him by asking him to clean school toilets. Not only does the text highlight the way Dalits were subjected to inhuman treatment, it also interrogates how the "dirty labor" of their class was the only means of livelihood for Dalit communities, and how they had to live with the tags dirty and polluted while sustaining themselves on the leftovers of upper-caste households. In a poem titled "My Ancestors," Valmiki describes the humane virtues of his simplistic and exploited forefathers who lived their lives in utter distress:

> They did not know
> how to loot
> the weak and the innocent!
> Did not know
> that murder
> is the badge of courage
> that robbery is not a crime
> it is but culture
> how innocent they were
> my ancestors
> humane
> yet untouchable.[83]

Rajendra Yadav was among the first literary figures to give an organized space to Dalit voices in Hindi, with writers like Shyoraj Singh Bechain, MohanDas Naimishrai, Surajpal Singh Chauhan, and Omprakash Valmiki. The equally powerful voice of Maitrayee Pushpa not only found space to express herself in "Hans" but formed a new breed of feminist writers such as Prabha Khetan and Archana Verma to facilitate women writers to enter unchartered territories.

Dalitist humanism stresses the debrahmanization of Indian civil society. The worldview Dalit humanism contests is one equated with a divine experience in the past, and not in the future, reserving others to the condition of marginality, especially that expressed through the system of caste. To this end, Hazari Prasad Dwivedi's book *Kabir* not only transformed the understanding of Kabir as a medieval poet of Dalit origin, it also accommodated Dalits within the mainstream literature.

Conclusion

Dr. S. Radhakrishnan emphasizes the importance of humanism in a man's life. He says:

> In recognising the central importance of man in the scheme of things—and emphasizing his freedom and individuality, and creative power—his role in shaping and moulding his environment with a view of making a better and happier world, humanism preached the gospel of activism, full of hope and promise for the future of mankind—a philosophy likely to rescue man from the slough of despondency and vivify him with self-confidence and faith in his own power as the shaper, not only of his own destiny, but as one who is also destined to play an effective part in the larger field of human welfare and progress.[84]

In summary, this chapter highlights how humanism pervades the entire history of Hindi literature from medieval to modern times, manifesting in a range of human emotions. Indian humanism enables a man to lead an integral life along with his duties toward society, the state, the nation, and the natural world. Humanists like Raja Ram Mohan Roy were essentially driven toward fighting social ills and contemplated a universal religion embraced by all mankind. Tagore and Gandhi as humanists proclaimed that the devotion to God lay in service of fellow human beings. The Indian humanist philosopher Dr. M. N. Roy expounded a radical humanism that insisted man was essentially a moral and rational being with an inherent potential to build just social order. While Roy's philosophy glorified the individual against the nation, Mulk Raj Anand evolved an eclectic philosophy termed "comprehensive historical humanism." While he takes cognizance of man's greed, lust and cruelty, he believes that man is potentially capable of rising from these lower passions to noble and magnificent heights of love, compassion and sacrifice.[85]

Different facets of humanism are expressed in a wide-ranging Hindi literature that celebrates devotion and communal harmony during times of sectarian divide. It inculcates nationalistic fervor and high ideals during the Bhartendu era, and joins in compassion with the underprivileged, marginalized, and downtrodden in society. Indian humanism pays attention to the emancipation of women, Dalits, and laborers from the grip of exploitation and oppression suffered in silence. Premchand's stories and peasant narratives show concern for the migrant workers and the landless laborers toiling hard in the fields of feudal lords. Through their writings in various genres, Hindi scholars have asserted their faith in man's willingness to fight back and not succumb to despair in the face of hardships. The concept of humanism in India is closer to the kinds of reform in a culture where human values and needs are more important than religious or supernatural beliefs. This chapter examines various ways in which humanism combines with politics in the literature of the colonial period to incite love for the nation, instill love and compassion to bring about social change, and offer a release to express the self and become a powerful voice of resistance against all kinds of oppression. Indian humanism brings forth the idea that social welfare not only depends on the material prosperity of society but also depends on the spiritual prosperity of individuals. The material and spiritual combination of integral humanism in India is conducive to the healthy growth of both individual and society. In this context, Gurudev Ravindra Nath Tagore's statement expresses the essence of humanism:

When a man does not realize his kinship with the world, he lives in a prison whose walls are alien to him, when he meets the external spirit in all objects, then he is emancipated for then he discovers the fullest significance of the world into which he is born; then he finds himself in perfect truth, and his harmony with the all is established.[86]

The fundamental difference between Indian humanism and Western humanism is that Westerners often emphasize the human body and the satisfaction of its desires as the ultimate objective of life. But the Indian concept regards the body as an instrument for sublime aims with a balance of the four facets of wholesome living[87]. Thus, the essence of integral Indian humanism lies in the spiritual aspect of Man that renders him Divine.

Bibliography

Anand, Mulk Raj. *Apology for Heroism*. Arnold-Heinemann, 1975.

Basu, Tapan. "The Dalit Personal Narrative in Hindi Reflections on a Long Literary Lineage". *Biography* 40, No. 1 (2017): 44–63. doi: 1353/bio.2017.0002.

Bhanot, S.D. "Lofty Humanism of Hazari Prasad Dwivedi." *Indian Literature* 11, No. 3 (1968): 53–61. http://www.jstor.org/stable/23329592 (Accessed August 31, 2021)

Copson, Andrew. *The Wiley Blackwell Handbook of Humanism*. Chichester, West Sussex: Wiley Blackwell, 2015.

Cybil, K. V. "Dalit Humanism, Literature and 'Technologies of Deification': Understanding the Politics of Matang Samaj." *Economic and Political Weekly* 48, No. 51 (2013): 60–67.

Dixit, Damoder Dutta. "Darvaje vala Khet" ("The Farm at the Door"). *Amrit Prabhat, Masik Patrika* (Monthly Magazine), Lucknow, December 9, 1984.

Encyclopaedia of Indian Literature/Devraj to Jyoti. Eastbourne: Gardners Books, 1995.

Gupta, Charu. "Portrayal of Women in Premchand's Stories: A Critique." *Social Scientist* 19, No. 5/6 (1991): 880113. doi: 10.2307/3517875 (Accessed August 31, 2021)

Hourani, Fayek S. 2012. *Daily Bread for Your Mind and Soul: A Handbook of Transcultural Proverbs and Sayings*. Bloomington: Xlibris Corporation.

Kabir. *Couplets from Kabīr*. Edited, translated, and compiled by G.N. Das. Foreword by Ranganath Mishra. Introduction by J.M. Mohanty. 1st ed. Delhi: Motilal Banarsidass Publishers, 1991.

Kalsi, A. S., and ‫س‬ .‫أ‬ ‫كلسي‬. "Human Rights in the Contemporary Hindi Short Story/‫القصة‬ ‫في‬ ‫الإنسان‬ ‫حقوق‬ ‫الهندية‬ ‫باللغة‬ ‫المكتوبة‬ ‫المعاصرة‬ ‫القصيرة‬." *Alif: Journal of Comparative Poetics* 13 (1993): 144–169. www.jstor.org/stable/521796.

Lukâcs, Georg. "The Ideology of Modernism," in *The Meaning of Contemporary Realism*, translated by John and Necke Mander, London: Merlin, 1963, 17–46.

Madhukarsinh. "Lahu pukare adml,§§," in *Pahla Path*. Allahabad: Anamika Prakashan, 1982, 77–91.

Mansarovar (Selected Stories of Premchand), 8 volumes, MS 1 to 8, New Delhi: Prakashan Sansth, 1997.

Markandeya. "Bhudan" ("Gift of Land"), in *Markandeya, ki Kahaniyan*. Allahabad: Lokbharti Prakashan, 2002.

Mehta, Mahesh. *Upadhyaya's Integral Humanism: The Concept and Applications*. Edison, NJ: Deendayal Upadhyaya Committee of America, 1980.

Mohan, Shailendra. "Uttha Puttar" ("Wake up Son"), in *Kosi Ke Us Paar* (Across the River Kosi), ed. by Neel Ramesh Kamal. Patna: Sanjay Prakashan, 1991.

Muktibodh. "Pragativad: Ek Drishti" in *Rachanavali*, Vol. 5. Delhi: Rajkamal Prakashan, 1980.

Narendrasinh. *Sathottari Hindi Kavita Mein Janvadi Chetna* (*Janvadi Consciousness in post-1960s Poetry*). New Delhi: Vani Prakashan, 2012.

Naik, Madhukar K. *Perspectives on Indian Poetry in English*. New Delhi: Abhinav, 1984.

Nandy, Ashis. *The Romance of the State: And the Fate of Dissent in the Tropic*. London: Oxford University Press, 2003.

Nehru, Jawaharlal, and Jagat S. Bright. *Selected Writings of Jawaharlal Nehru: Selected Statements and Pick-of-the-Basket Quotations from the Writings of Jawaharlal Nehru, 1916–1950: Dealing with the Shape of Things to Come in India and the World*. Indian Printing Works, 1951.

Pandey, Manager, and Alka Tyagi. "Bhakti Poetry: Its Relevance and Significance." *Indian Literature* 45, No. 6 (206) (2001), 129–138. www.jstor.org/stable/23345761 (Accessed June 30, 2021)

Pico Della Mirandola, Giovanni. *Oration on the Dignity of Man*, ed. by Sebastian Michael, trans. by Charles Glenn Wallis. Optimist Books by Optimist Creations, 2018.

Radhakrishnan, S. *History of Philosophy—Eastern and Western*, Vol. II. London: George Allen & Unwin, 1953.

Satchidanandan, K. *Indian Poetry: Modernism and After*. New Delhi: Sahitya Akademi New Delhi, 2001.

Scott, James C. *The Moral Economy of the Peasant: Rebellion and Subsistence in South East Asia*. New Haven and London: Yale University Press, 1976.

Singh, Javahar. "Asarh ka ek din," in *Dalit Jivan ki Kahaniyaan* (The Stories of Oppressed Life), ed. Girirajsarn. Delhi: Prabhat Prakashan, 1986, 52–66.

Upadhyay, Shashi Bhushan. "Premchand and the Moral Economy of Peasantry in Colonial North India." *Modern Asian Studies* 45, No. 5 (2011): 1227–1259. http://www.jstor.org/stable/25835717 (Accessed August 31, 2021)

Vālmīki, Omaprakāśa. *Joothan: An Untouchable's Life*. Translated by Arun Prabha Mukherjee. New York: Columbia University Press, 2008.

Vanashree. "Struggling Peasantry in Literary Narratives." *Indian Literature* 59, No. 4 (288) (2015): 182–200. Accessed August 31, 2021. http://www.jstor.org/stable/44479387.

Vaughn, Lewis, and Austin Dacey. *The Case for Humanism: An Introduction*. Lanham, MD: Rowman & Littlefield, 2003.

Wilkerson, Sarah Beth. *Hindi Dalit Literature and the Politics of Representation*. Cambridge: University of Cambridge, 2006.

Notes

1 The Ancient Greek philosopher Protagoras (490–420 BCE) is said to have made this statement which is interpreted by Plato to mean that there is no objective truth because the individual being and not God, or any moral law is the ultimate source of value.

Humanistic Approaches in Hindi Literature

2 The saying is attributed to Francesco Petrarch. He was a scholar and poet of early Renaissance Italy, and one of the earliest humanists.

3 The fifteenth-century Italian Renaissance writer Giovanni Pico della Mirandola believed that the moral worth of a human being is closely associated with his ability to choose his own destiny. Pico declared that God made man with the power of free judgement and hence man was not confined or restricted by any bounds.

4 Lewis Vaughn and Austin Dacey. *The Case for Humanism: An Introduction* (Lanham: Rowman & Littlefield, 2003), 7.

5 *Encyclopaedia of Indian Literature/Devraj to Jyoti* (Eastbourne: Gardners Books, 1995), 1588.

6 The Sanskrit term *Ayam* means "this." "*Atma*" refers to self or the soul. *Brahma* is Brahman, the Supreme Entity. Hence *Ayam Atma Brahma* means "Atman is Brahman." This Atman is Brahma. And Brahma is the Supreme Entity which alone is real.

7 Purushartha is a Sanskrit word. Purusha meaning man, *arth* means an object of desire. Purushartha means objective of human life. Chaturvidha means the four groups. Hindu scriptures enlist four objects of desire: dharma, artha, kama and moksha. These represent the choice of how to live a good and pleasurable life as a selection between one's competing desires.

8 Pandit Deen Dayal Upadhyaya was an Indian politician and a firm believer in right-wing Hindutva ideology. He came up with the concept of integral humanism. In a series of lectures he delivered in Bombay between April 22–April 25, 1965 he addressed the workers of a political organization. The lectures carry immense academic value which make him a philosopher, thinker, and a visionary.

9 The *Bhakti* movement emerged in medieval India—originating in the seventh-century Tamil south India, and spreading northwards. It was a devotional movement in Hinduism that regionally developed around different gods and goddesses, such as Vishnu, Shiva. The movement has traditionally been considered as an influential social reformation in Hinduism, and provided an individual-focused alternative path to spirituality regardless of one's caste of birth or gender.

10 Padmavat (1540–1541) is an epic poem describing the historic siege of Chittor by Alauddin Khilji in 1303, India. It was written by Sufi poet Malik Muhammad Jayasi in the Hindustani language of Awadhi. It is the oldest extant text among the important works in Awadhi.

11 Ramcharitmanas is an epic poem in the Awadhi language composed by the sixteenth-century Indian *Bhakti* poet Tulsidas. It narrates the life and deeds of Lord Rama and is considered to be one of the greatest works of Hindu literature.

12 Sursagar is a collection of poems by the sixteenth-century poet, Surdas. The poems are based on the stories of the childhood of Krishna found in the Bhagavata-purana. The poems are some of the finest expressions of Braj-bhasha, a literary dialect of the Hindi language.

13 Abdur Rahim Khan-e-Khanan was a linguist who wrote extensively in Braj, Sanskrit, Arabic, and Persian. He was one of the nine gems in the emperor Akbar's court and a strong proponent of an all-encompassing culture of inclusiveness. Popular in Hindi textbooks as a medieval *Bhakti* poet, his dohas are a significant contribution to establishing love and harmony in the lives of people from various communities. The mystical element also adds depth to his poetry. In one of his dohas he says: हमिन गली हैं सांकरी, दूजो नहीं ठहराई / अपु अहइ तो हरिनहीं, हरि तो आपुन नहीं , which means in translation: The alley is narrow, Rahim, it won't take both of us // If I go, the lord can't; and if the lord does I can not.

14 करता था सो क्यों किया, अब कर क्यों पछितिाय ।बोया पेड़ बबूल का, आम कहाँ से खाय ॥ 168 ॥ The doha implies that you feel remorse for the wrong deed you have done. You will have to bear the consequences of it just as if you sow thorny acacia, you cannot be rewarded with juicy mangoes from it. All original-language quotations from Kabir are from *Couplets from Kabīr*. Edited, translated, and compiled by G.N. Das. Foreword by Ranganath Mishra. Introduction by J.M. Mohanty. 1st ed. (Delhi: Motilal Banarsidass Publishers), 1991.

15 ऐसी बानी बोलिए, मन का आपा खोय ।औरन को शीतल करै, आपहु शीतल होय ॥ The doha implies that one should speak in a voice that is gentle and compassionate—for it will not only soothe and win the heart of the listener but also calm the speaker's heart.

16 Jatindra Mohan Mahanty. *Introduction to Couplets from Kabīr*. Edited, translated, and compiled by G.N. Das. Foreword by Ranganath Mishra. Introduction by J.M. Mohanty. 1st ed. Delhi: Motilal Banarsidass Publishers, 1991, xi.

17 चलती चक्की देख के दिया कबीरा रोए। दूई पाटन के बीच में साबुत बचा न कोई॥

18 यदि ईश्वर मस्जिद के भीतर है, तो यह दुनिया किससे संबंधित है?
यदि राम उस छवि के भीतर हैं जो आपको तीर्थ यात्रा पर मिलती है,
फिर यह जानने के लिए कौन हैं कि इसके बिना क्या होता है?
हरि पूर्व में हैं, अल्लाह पश्चिम में हैं।

Prachi Priyanka

अपने दिल के भीतर देखो, वहाँ आप करीम और राम दोनों को पाएंगे;
दुनिया के सभी पुरुष और महिलाएं उसके जीवंत रूप हैं।
कबीर अल्लाह के बच्चे हैं और राम के: वह मेरे गुरु हैं, वे मेरे पीर हैं (*कबीर, III.2, द्वारा अनुवादित रविंद्रनाथ टैगोर*)

19 Apbhrasha is a term used to refer to languages spoken in North India before the rise of modern languages.

20 The period between 1650–1850 AD in North Indian literature has been called Reeti Kaal or the Shringar period. The rise of the Reeti Kaal was driven not by the interest of the public; instead it was characterized by the interest and taste of the patrons. According to Hazari Prasad Dwivedi, if the poets of the *Bhakti* period took inspiration from ancient literature; the poets of Reeti Kaal were influenced by Sanskrit literature of much later times.

21 Saguna *Bhakti* is the practice of recognizing and honoring God as it is manifested in all forms. The saguna aspect of God cannot be realized without realizing the eternal divine consciousness of God, known as Nirguna, which is absolute and omnipresent. Saguna and Nirguna are two branches of *Bhakti* or devotion.

22 In Hinduism, Krishna and Rama were incorporated into Vaishnavism as incarnations of Lord Vishnu. Whereas Krishna is adored for his mischievous pranks and amorous dalliances, Rama is conceived as a model of reason, right action, and desirable virtues.

23 Gopikas were wives or children of Gopas of Vrindavan. *Gopi* is a Sanskrit word that means "female cowherd," "wife of a cowherd," "milkmaid," or "female guardian." In Hinduism, it typically refers to the cow-herding girls and women who were devoted to Krishna. Lord Krishna, a major deity and sometimes worshiped as the supreme deity, was himself a cowherder, because he was secretly shifted from Mathura to Vrindavan as a means to save his life from the evil Uncle, King Kansa. It was among the cowherds that the young Krishna gained a reputation as a prankster and a lover. According to Hindu mythology, Krishna would play his flute and the gopis would come to him and dance around. Some literature says he multiplied himself so he could dance with each. The gopis became a symbol of *suddha Bhakti*, the highest unconditional love for God.

24 The concept of Ramrajya means a kingdom that is administered in an impartial, smooth and divine manner based on pure moral authority. This term comes from the peaceful and just regime of Lord Rama who loved and cared for all his subjects.

25 The Sufi work Kanhāvat "The story of Krishna" (1540) is attributed to the Avadhi Sufi author Malik Muhammad Jāyasi. He was an Indian Sufi poet and pir and most famous for his epic Padmaavat.

26 Meerabai was a sixteenth-century princess who faced lot of criticism for the manner in which she completely surrendered herself to the worship of Lord Krishna. A Hindu mystic poet and an ardent devotee of Krishna, she is celebrated as a *Bhakti* saint, particularly in the North Indian Hindu tradition.

27 Balkrishna Bhatt was one of the most important essayists of his age. With a great variety of subjects and richness of style, he wrote articles that were thought-provoking and reflected his mature thinking. He also ran a magazine, "Hindi Pradip," for 32 years. Balkrishna Bhatt, "Charitra-palan," in *Balkrishna Bhatt ke Shreshtha Nibandh*, ed. by Satya Prakash Mishra (Allahabad: Lokbharati Prakashan, 1998), 114–116.

28 Purdah in Urdu means curtain or veil. This practice was prevalent and very common in India among the Muslim and Hindu communities. It not only meant covering the head and body physically but also led to the segregation of women in all aspects of life.

29 *Sati pratha* was a historical Hindu practice in which a widow sacrificed herself by sitting atop her deceased husband's funeral pyre. The life of a woman after the death of her husband was considered to be meaningless and burdensome. Often to show their commitment towards their men, women either chose to end their lives on the pyre of their husbands or were pushed by society to do so. The Bengal Sati Regulation which banned the Sati practice in all jurisdictions of British India was passed on December 4, 1829, by the then Governor-General Lord William Bentinck.

30 Quoted in *Sadhana Path*, No. 8, February 2018. Diamond Publications, 55. जो भरा नहीं है भावों से, जिसमें बहती रसधार नहीं, वह हृदय नहीं पत्थर है, जिसमें स्वदेश का प्यार नहीं

31 *Encyclopaedia of Indian Literature/Devraj to Jyoti* (Eastbourne: Gardners Books, 1995), 1129.

32 The poem title means "I am a cloud filled with tears of grief." It is a short poem that can be found in its original form at http://kavitakosh.org // मैं_नीर_भरी_दुख_की_बदली/_महादेवी_वर्मा

33 The poem "Juhi Ki Kali" is a poem composed by Suryakant Tripathi Nirala, in which Juhi's *kali* (bud/flower) and the *pawan* (wind) have been anthromorphized. The bud is in love with the wind and is separated from him as he goes to distant mountains. The poem talks about the lovers' separation, yearning and reunion.

34 The poem "Beggar" depicts the sorry plight of beggars. Hunger makes them beg for money and food. Nirala evokes our pity towards their sorry state for these beggar children have nothing to eat and have

Humanistic Approaches in Hindi Literature

to compete with stray dogs to fill their starved bellies. It is pathetic see how humans are lowered down to the level of animals because of their poverty. Nirala believed in justice for all mankind and rebelled against the capitalist approach which deprived the underprivileged from even basic amenities. Matthew Baker, "The Beggar," Poets Corner, April 14, 2020.

35 The poem "Breaking Stones" presents the harsh realities of society where the abject working conditions of poor people are shown. The poet wants to demonstrate these lamentable working conditions. A female is breaking stones in the afternoon of midsummer and suffering from heat stroke. The poet describes her beauty, sense of dignity and acceptance of her fate. Suryakant Tripathi Nirala, "Breaking Stones" (1935). Trans. Arvind Krishna Mehrotra. *The Baffler* 19, January 2014.

36 Ramesh Chandra Shah. "Another Returning of the Heart … Nirala's Imagination." *India International Centre Quarterly* 25, No. 1 (1998): 35–42. http://www.jstor.org/stable/23005601 (Accessed August 21, 2021). The original poem can be found at http://kavitakosh.org/ kk/सरोज_स्मृति_/_सूर्यकांत_त्रिपाठी_"निराला.

37 Advaita in Sanskrit means non-dualism. It is one of the most influential schools of Vedanta, which is one of the six orthodox philosophical systems (darshans) of Indian philosophy. While its followers find its main tenets already fully expressed in the Upanishads and systematized by the *Brahma-sutra*s (also known as the *Vedanta-sutra*s), it has its historical beginning with the seventh-century-CE thinker Gaudapada, author of the *Mandukya-karika*, a commentary in verse form on the Mandukya Upanishad. www.britannica.com/topic/Advaita-school-of-Hindu-philosophy

38 K. Satchidanandan. *Indian Poetry: Modernism and After* (New Delhi: Sahitya Akademi New Delhi, 2001), 90.

39 The original poem can be read here: kavikakosh.org/kk/कुकुरमुत्ता_(कविता)_/_सूर्यकांत_त्रिपाठी_"निराला

40 Trivedi, Sunil. "Baba Nagarjun." *Indian Literature* 42, No. 6 (188) (1998): 140–144. http://www.jstor.org/stable/23342351 (Accessed August 21, 2021).

41 Kavitakosh.org/kk/अकाल_और_उसके_बाद/नागार्जुन

42 Ibid.

43 *Indian Poetry*, 56

44 Ibid.

45 The *Bhakti* saints emphasized two ways of imagining the nature of the God viz. *Nirguna* and *Saguna*. Nirguna is the concept of a formless God, who has no attributes or quality. Saguna has form, attributes and quality. Both of these can be traced to the famous Vedic Hymn *"Ekam sat vipra bahudha vadanti"*—Truth is one; sages call it many names. It is the same God, but is viewed from two perspectives. One is Nirguni, which is knowledge-focussed and other is Saguni which is love-focused. Thus, Nirguna poetry is Gyanshrayi (has roots in knowledge) while Saguna poetry is Premashrayi (has roots in love). https://www.gktoday.in/topic/bhakti-movement/

46 S. D. Bhanot. "Lofty Humanism of Hazari Prasad Dwivedi," *Indian Literature* 11, No. 3 (1968): 53–61. http://www.jstor.org/stable/23329592 (Accessed August 21, 2021).

47 See, for example, "Towering like a Colossus." *The Hindu*, July 10, 2015. https://www.thehindu.com/features/metroplus/acharya-hazari-prasad-dwiveditowering-like-a-colossus/article7408209.ece (Accessed August 30, 2021).

48 Shashi Bhushan Upadhyay. "Premchand and the Moral Economy of Peasantry in Colonial North India." *Modern Asian Studies* 45, No. 5 (2011): 1227–1259. http://www.jstor.org/stable/25835717 (Accessed August 21, 2021).

49 Ibid.

50 Ibid.

51 Charu Gupta. "Portrayal of Women in Premchand's Stories: A Critique." *Social Scientist* 19, No. 5/6 (1991): 88–113. doi: 10.2307/3517875 (Accessed August 21, 2021).

52 Veshya in Hindi is used as a derogatory term for women who sell their bodies for money. Kabrein menas graveyards.

53 *Mansarovar*. "Selected Stories of Premchand," 8 volumes, MS 1 to 8 (New Delhi: Prakashan Sansth, 1997), 8.

54 Jawaharlal Nehru and Jagat S. Bright. *Selected Writings of Jawaharlal Nehru: Selected Statements and Pick-of-the-Basket Quotations from the Writings of Jawaharlal Nehru, 1916–1950: Dealing with the Shape of Things to Come in India and the World* (Indian Printing Works, 1951), 2:15.

55 Ibid.

56 Ashis Nandy. *The Romance of the State: And the Fate of Dissent in the Tropics* (London: Oxford University Press, 2003).

57 Ibid.

58 Ibid.

59 Dominick La Capra. "Trauma, Absence, Loss," *Critical Inquiry* 25 (Summer 1999).

60 Scott C. James. *The Moral Economy of the Peasant: Rebellion and Subsistence in South East Asia* (New Haven and London: Yale University Press, 1976), 18.

61 Vanashree, 198.

62 Some of the important aspects of Pragativaad included a rebellion against the dominant classes and oppressors, a spirit of humanism and empathy towards fellow beings, raising awareness of women's rights and belief in hard work.

63 These were experimental poets who played with the form of poetry. Intellectualism gained dominance over emotionalism, new metaphors and images were brought into literature to add novelty and free expressions of love that turned towards obscenity, pessimism, egoism and rebelliousness against the traditional norms of society.

64 The original poem by Kedarnath is as follows:
पृथ्वी के सारे खून एक हैं / एक ही यात्रा में
एक ही पृथ्वी-भर लम्बी देह में
दौड़ रहे हैं वे
नहीं – विश्राम उन्हें नहीं चाहिए
सीरिया में जो टपकती है बूँद
उसे सुनती है मेरे गाँव के
बच्चे की धड़कन
अरबों धड़कनें एक ही लय में
घुमा रही हैं दुनिया को
हर खून/ हर
खून से बतियाता है!

65 मेरे देश के एक हाथ को
एक खुले हुए भूखे मुँह तक पहुँचने में
कितने बरस लगते हैं?

66 Gajanan Madhav Muktobodh. "Prayogvad" (Experimentalism) in *Rachanavali*, Vol. 5, ed. by Nemichand Jain, 2nd ed. (Delhi: Rajkamal Prakashan, 1980), 287.

67 Muktibodh. *Letters in Rachanavali, Collected Works*. Vol. 6 ed. by Nemichand Jain (Delhi: Rajkamal Prakashan, 1986), 397.

68 Muktibodh. "Pragativad: Ek Drishti" in *Rachanavali* (Vol. 5, Delhi, 1980), 29.

69 Qtd in Narendrasinh, *Sathottari Hindi Kavita Mein Janvadi Chetna* (*Janvadi Consciousness in post-1960s Poetry*), 137.

70 A. S. Kalsi, and أ. س. سلكي. "Human Rights in the Contemporary Hindi Short Story / حقوق الإنسان في القصة القصيرة المعاصرة المكتوبة باللغة الهندية." *Alif: Journal of Comparative Poetics* 13 (1993): 148. doi:10.2307/521796 (Accessed August 22, 2021).

71 Javaharsinh, 54.

72 Ibid., 56.

73 Ibid., 56.

74 Ibid., 66.

75 Madhukar Singh, "Harijan Sevak," 147.

76 Madhukar Singh, "Lahu Pukare Admi" in *Pahla Path*, 77–91.

77 Madhukar Singh, "Lahu Pukare Admi," 78.

78 Swami Achhutanand Harihar, "Manusmriti Is Burning Us." Qtd in Tapan Basu, "The Dalit Personal Narrative in Hindi Reflections on a Long Literary Lineage." *Biography* 40, No. 1 (2017): 44–63. doi: 1353/bio.2017.0002.

79 Sarah Beth Wilkerson. *Hindi Dalit Literature and the Politics of Representation* (Cambridge: University of Cambridge, 2006), 25–82.

80 *Apne Apne Pinjre* is the autobiography of Mohandas Namishray. The book is divided into three parts: *Apne Apne Pinjare*, Part 1 and 2, and *Rang Kitne Sang Mere* as the conclusive part of the book. It exposes the atrocities committed against Dalit communities and exposes the cruelty of feudalism and caste-based exploitation.

81 *My Childhood on My Shoulders* is a translation of Sheoraj Singh Bechain's autobiographical work *Mera Bachpan Mere Kandhon Par*, a paradigmatic life-story of a member of one of India's numerous Dalit castes. The book narrates his struggle against the social disabilities imposed on him by the material circumstances of his 'outcaste' family and succeeding in his quest for an education (Syorājasiṃha Becaina and Tapan Basu. *My Childhood on My Shoulders*. New Delhi: Oxford University Press, 2018).

82 Omprakash Valmiki describes his life as an untouchable, or Dalit, in the newly independent India of the 1950s. "Joothan" refers to scraps of food left on a plate, destined for the garbage or animals. India's

untouchables have been forced to accept and eat joothan for centuries, and the word encapsulates the pain, humiliation, and poverty of a community forced to live at the bottom of India's social pyramid. *Joothan* is a major contribution to the archives of Dalit history and a manifesto for the revolutionary transformation of society and human consciousness. Vālmīki, Omaprakāśa. *Joothan: An Untouchable's Life*. Translated by Arun Prabha Mukherjee (New York: Columbia University Press, 2008).

83 The poem is translated from the Hindi by Pratik Kanjilal and appears in *The Little Magazine*, Vol. 6, Issue 4 and 5.

84 S. Radhakrishnan, *History of Philosophy—Eastern and Western* Vol. II (London: George Allen & Unwin, 1953), 352.

85 Anand, Mulk Raj. *Apology for Heroism* (Arnold-Heinemann, 1975), 78.

86 Naik, Madhukar K. *Perspectives on Indian Poetry in English* (New Delhi: Abhinav, 1984), 10.

87 The four facets of wholesome living according to Hindu concepts are based on the following eternal values: *dharma* (moral values), *artha* (financial prosperity), *kama* (physical pleasure) and *mokshya* (self-realization).

10

Headhunting and Native Agency in Lundayeh Oral Literature

A Humanist Perspective

Kavitha Ganesan and Shaffarullah Abdul Rahman

Introduction

The oral literature from the Bornean region has been used in numerous works of scholarship about South-East Asia as it represents—in most cases—what little remains of Bornean cultural records, considering the fact that the British and Dutch colonizations of the island irrevocably changed the indigenous way of life.[1] Oral literature is perhaps the closest available resource to researchers who are both interested in the past way of life as well as the present condition of the native peoples, since the erosion of indigenous identity has been manifold in recent years.[2] It is along this line of thinking that this chapter examines one of the minority indigenous communities in Sabah, Malaysia, known as the Lundayeh, by situating their oral literature within the tenets of humanism.

Simply put, this chapter aims to interrogate the primary notion of what is to be human according to the Lundayeh worldview, especially considering the fact that they were one of the inland tribes of Borneo where headhunting was not only a given way of life but also an integral part of a belief system that was based on the relationship between the human and non-human worlds.[3] We argue that, even though the cultural aspect associated with headhunting is textually manifested in the oral literature and in many ways contradicts the very core of humanism, the tyranny of colonialism, the complete obliteration of the native belief system for conversion into Christianity, and inevitably the emergence of Malaysia as an independent nation-state, are the primary reasons that have shaped the perception of the Lundayeh past way of life as uncivil and inhuman.[4] The importance given to history in this chapter is in conflict with a certain naïve humanist assumption that literary works should exist above and beyond historical context. The timelessness and universality that older forms of humanism propose to find in and through literature is immaterial here because native communities like the Lundayehs had a way of life befitting the dense forest they occupied, and unsurprisingly then their oral narratives are a product of that system that is unique to their indigenous identity. It is due to this that we begin by detailing the native belief system in the succeeding section.

The main discussion, however, is based on two seemingly opposing worldviews: while asserting the human factor through the exploration of native agency in oral literature, this chapter paradoxically lays claim to the Lundayeh tradition that is deeply rooted in headhunting as a justifiable means or expression of the native belief system. Or, to word it differently, how, during the process of locating the native voice in Lundayeh oral literature, can this chapter, by the modern-day humanist definition, unravel the "barbaric" traditions of the native system? Such a line of inquiry invariably prompts another question, that is, what is the pressing need, two decades into the twenty-first century, to examine the Lundayeh oral narratives within the tropes of humanism, especially since these songs and stories are a dying tradition in Sabah? We aim to answer these questions in the rest of the chapter.

146

DOI: 10.4324/9781003046004-13

Understanding the Intersections of a Lundayeh Longhouse, Swidden Agriculture, and Headhunting

The Lundayeh are a group of people whose origin can be traced to the Kerayan-Kelabit Highlands of East Kalimantan.[5] Even today, the Lundayeh people accept that their origin is in the "mountainous country" where the borders of Kalimantan, Sabah, and Sarawak meet; since this "ancestral homeland" was largely an unnavigable terrain, it initiated journeying among the Lundayehs[6] (see Figure 10.1).

Additionally, as swidden cultivators and hunter-gatherers, their need for fertile lands for cultivation caused them to travel along rivers and build their settlements along river basins. Hunting, foraging, and subsistence farming—on the one hand, all of this contributed to the Lundayehs' sustenance, while on the other, it meant that the community was brought together oftentimes through shared activities, thus forming the crux of their social grouping. At the heart of such communalism was the community's longhouse dwelling.

Since the Lundayehs were often on the move, a section of the river basin where a group settled then formed the village's territory, which was often typified by a longhouse or several longhouses.[7] Jay Crain describes a Lundayeh longhouse in the following way:

> Lun Dayeh longhouses contain from five to twenty apartments owned by individual domestic families. The domestic family (*uang ruma'*) is a familial social grouping containing from one to four generations. Its members use a single hearth for preparing common meals and share

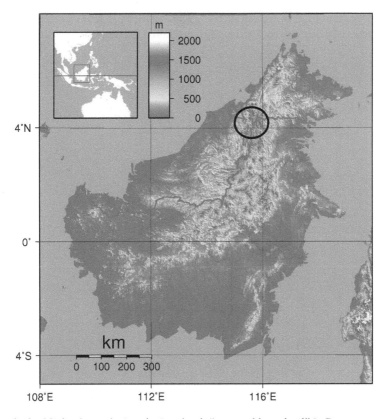

Figure 10.1 The highlighted area depicts the Lundayeh "ancestral homeland" in Borneo
Adapted from: https://commons.wikimedia.org/wiki/File:Borneo_Topography.png

in the production and consumption of the economic assets [...] The fundamental mechanism for defining social continuity in Lun Dayeh society is the domestic family. Relations between domestic families are established and maintained through a series of public social, and economic exchanges [such as] the cyclical activities of rice agriculture.[8]

The longhouse was central to Lundayeh communalism because it is through the longhouse that the occupants established a sense of belonging where kinship was secured among individual ("domestic") families residing in different apartments of a longhouse; this kinship eventually contributed to the labor force required for arduous agricultural activities especially hill paddy cultivation since the highland origin of the Lundayehs meant that they were familiar with cultivation suited for that terrain. The community eventually shifted to wet paddy cultivation in later years following the change in their dwelling to individual households—a move strongly encouraged by the colonial government and later supported by the state—which will be taken up shortly in this chapter when discussing the factors leading to the erosion of indigenous identity. The longhouse kinship—as mentioned—formed the heart of the Lundayeh social system, because communalism among its occupants was continuously practiced through the sharing of resources, and crucially also by establishing a sense of camaraderie between one another for defense against opponents from another longhouse. This is the reason why longhouses were built on stilts; the stairs leading up to the longhouse will not only protect the occupants from pests and rodents, but they will also delay the vengeful attacks of intruders as they will have to climb up the stairs before approaching the occupants of the longhouse[9] (see Figure 10.2 and 10.3).

Functioning as a longhouse unit *vis-a-vis* communal group was important because the Lundayeh practiced headhunting. In fact, besides the search for fertile lands for cultivation, incessant communal disputes between warring groups also prompted movement from one place to another.

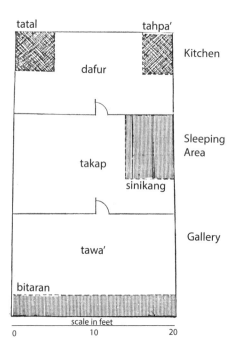

Figure 10.2 The floorplan (schematic) of a longhouse
Adapted from: Crain, 1970 (174)[10]

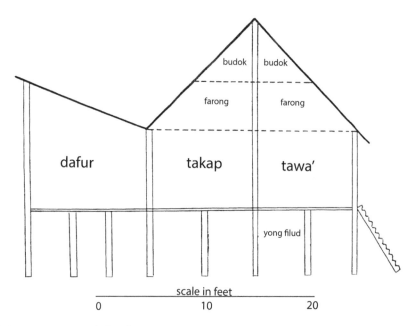

Figure 10.3 Cross-section of a longhouse
Adapted from: Crain, 1970 (176)[11]

Headhunting was integral to the Lundayeh culture because a man was bestowed the title of *Lun Mebalaa*, a prestigious position accorded for his ability in successfully raiding and taking heads. These leaders will eventually assume the responsibility of safeguarding a longhouse, and when the need arises, command the warfare against another longhouse or warring tribe.[12]

Even though headhunting is largely perceived as an assertion of masculinity by the present-day Lundayehs as they believe that, in the past, the severed head was used as a trophy to impress women and secure alliances with prospective in-laws, the truth of the matter is that headhunting was a core cultural element upon which the wellbeing of the entire longhouse/village depended. At this point, it will be useful to refer to Janet Hoskins' (1996) definition because, in the introduction to her edited volume, *Headhunting and the Social Imagination in Southeast Asia*, which is notable for situating the practice within a comparative view across the region, she explains as follows:

> headhunting [was] an organized, coherent form of violence in which the severed head is given a specific ritual meaning and the act of headtaking is consecrated and commemorated in some form.[13]

Even though she provides a definition, Hoskins makes it clear that, despite the widespread practice of headhunting among the varying tribal groups in South-East Asia, it is not possible to use one group's headhunting practice and cultural significance to make generalizations or draw conclusions about the whole region, including Borneo. Nevertheless, the wealth of material made available by Western scholars, especially about Borneo—exemplified by Hoskins' edited work—proves that headhunting raids held enormous cultural importance and continue to inform communal memory. In other words, if one were to chart the cultural trope of the Bornean indigenous natives, then one has to examine the situatedness of headhunting within the specifics of the "consecrated" and "commemorated" act of headtaking that were highlighted in Hoskins' definition, *vis-a-vis* the native worldview.

Here, it is necessary to bear in mind that, even though this chapter, among others, argues against the Western-informed agenda of colonialism, the available literature on headhunting is mostly as a result of work done by Western scholars who have been fascinated by the practice while attempting to map the past history of Borneo. This means that any effort to interpret the traditional practice of headhunting has to be done retrospectively by utilizing materials presented by the outsiders. Such an outsider view is beneficial for two reasons: (1) due to the prohibition of headhunting followed by the religious reshaping of the native community, the insider view, especially of recent times, may have a totalizing de-limiting tendency, thus providing grounds for bias and partiality; and, (2) Western scholars, unlike Western imperialists, with access to remote regions of the island have managed to document changes within the purview of research, rather than visiting native cultural markers for the purpose of re-constructing colonial stereotypes even though their origin may be in the metropolitan center.

In returning to the idea of indigenous worldview with regards to headhunting among the Lundayehs, it is necessary to start the discussion by probing whether headhunting was merely an issue between a predator and prey, or were far more complex issues involved that prompted these inlanders to traditionally practice headhunting? By taking Hoskins' caution to heart that the reason for headhunting varies hence should not be used to draw any generalizations, we take her broader description through the phrase, "headtaking [is] a potent ritual act" as our point of departure as it also corroborates with the findings from one of the earlier works on Bornean headhunting by McKinley[14] as well as the latest by Janowski.[15] Both McKinley and Janowski have based their arguments on the oral narratives gathered from the Bornean people.[16]

McKinley's work is perhaps the most important when examining headhunting from the perspective of humanism as it centers on the native cultural logic. In his account of the tribal groups, McKinley notes that headtaking was related to the natives' perception of a cosmos as it involved the existence of soul force. In order to understand why the soul force was vital to the natives, it is necessary to trace the foundation of their belief system.

To the natives, the longhouse/village that was situated along a river was the center of the universe (see Figure 10.4). This universe and its inhabitants, who are in fact members of the same village, or in short, one's own tribe, are the "earth dwellers." The river or more specifically the far-reaching upstream region, is the one that separates these earth dwellers from the immortal deities and cultural heroes of the upper (sky) world who have the ability to move in and out of the universe. The underworld or the downstream region of the river offers a complementary opposition to the upper world, and together these two form the native cosmology. While the upperworld is attributed to success in warfare, the underworld is associated with agricultural abundance and human fertility. What stands out in this philosophy is that the social formation of a group or tribe is homogenous; additionally, the unknown part of the thick forest is equally important as the familiar jungle plain where food is sourced through acts of hunting and foraging. In other words, it can be said that the spatial locus, which is the tropical rainforest, is the reason why the natives of Borneo founded their beliefs on both the seen (human) and unseen (non-human) world.

According to McKinley, such nature-based ideology (Figure 10.5—Arrow A) is faced with problems when, within a homogenous tribe, calamities, misfortunes, and death occur (Arrow B). Nevertheless, the cosmological system that is designed on the existence of nature, i.e., the upstream and downstream region as well as animals and plants, accommodates the dead where it is believed that the soul force is carried through the great river system thus connecting the vast human and non-human world (Arrow C). This justifies the native belief in soul force or spirits.

Complications arise when one group realizes that another group exists with a different set of cultural practices (Arrow D), hence is in conflict with the "presumed universal validity of one's society's way of life."[17] It is at this point that the native belief system creates a perception that those who occupy the spatial and social system unfamiliar to one's homogenous tribe as non-human

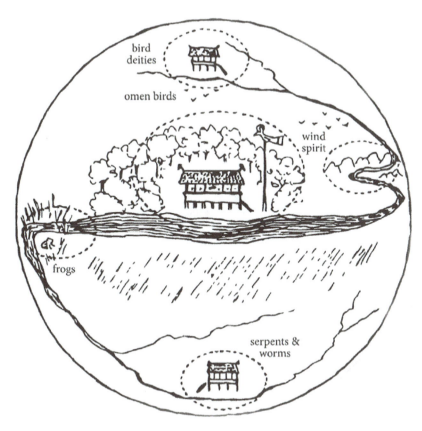

Figure 10.4 Southeast Asian tribal cosmology
Adapted from: McKinley, 2015 (455)

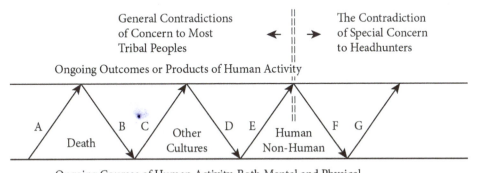

Figure 10.5 Headhunting as reality maintenance
Adapted from: McKinley, 2015 (461)

(Arrow E). But the knowledge that these strangers are in fact humans and occupy a valid space within members of their own community calls for an act of intervention that manifests in the form of headhunting (Arrow F). This is to say that a head was hunted for purely ritual reasons; hence, it was not done frequently. The journeying and ceremony that follows a successful headhunting expedition is most important as it depicts the native's approach toward humanizing a seemingly non-human subject (Arrow G), i.e., the heterogenous (dead) member from another tribe.

Rather than abandoning or discarding the dead body, the head (face) is taken into possession because it is perceived that the head holds both the soul force and personality of the dead person. It is treated with care as the headhunter and his raiding group sets on the travel back to their own village with the head alongside hence partaking in a cosmic journey. Upon reaching the village, elaborate cultural celebrations and commemorations are held where the severed head is symbolically incorporated into the tribe as a "social person" where "the former enemy [is turned] into a friend" (461) through ritual acts (Arrow G). Many scholars, besides McKinley, such as De Raedt and Mashman, have noted the centrality of such headhunting celebrations as the tribe comes together, especially the womenfolk who indulge in a long process of taunting and mocking the head before nursing it as a baby to show that it has now become a member of the tribe. These ritual acts are in fact to reinstate the dead to their rightful place within the cosmos, which is among the members of the headhunter's tribal group that McKinley describes as the act of humanizing the non-human subject.

Even though such cultural justification for beheading falls short of the present-day humanist logic, when the same act of headtaking is situated comparatively within the overarching global climate of wars, whether driven by political, religious, or economic reasons, it seems that the stigma attached to the indigenous belief system *vis-a-vis* headhunting, is overrated. Yet, since the wars of the world are given sophisticated names and reasons, the cost to human lives is easily justified because humanity is supposedly safeguarded when one power wins over the other and a new ideology is popularized for the benefit of the world, thus keeping humanity alive. It is in relation to this that it was mentioned earlier in this chapter that the Lundayeh oral literature occupies a distinctive space since the humanizing process accorded by the native belief system is in contrast with the universality proposed by humanism as a general principle.

If one were to argue that McKinley's explanation about the indigenous belief system is situated too broadly, as it is based on the evidence drawn from numerous headhunting groups, Janowski's analysis of the inland and highland Kelabits who both share their ancestral homeland and linguistic similarities with the Lundayehs depict that the native belief in soul force, cosmic journey, headhunting, and heroism are still pertinent. This is to say that, while McKinley's work largely focused on decoding the indigenous belief system through various headhunting tribes' oral narratives, Janowski's was based on finding the link that the Kelabit stories have with both the past and present times. This is because Janowski's chapter includes an analysis of how through the stories of headhunters, i.e., cultural heroes, the existence of a life/cosmic force is foregrounded as men and women who possess such force are perceived as ideal humans whose behaviors have to be emulated by the younger generation. This is why even though headhunting has long been abolished, the stories of these heroes, according to Janowski, have survived where the headhunter's cosmic journey in search of the life/cosmic force has now been replaced by the present form of journeying among Kelabit youngsters to acquire good education and job opportunities. Nevertheless, in the past, the heroes always returned to their respective longhouses highlighting a circular pattern of journeying, while at present, most of them, after having acquired the life force in the form of education and opportunities, make the outside world their home and do not return to their place of origin. The crucial distinction between the past and present, moreover, is that, while in the past the Kelabits believed that the life force was collected through shamanic relationships with spirits, at present, and especially after their conversion to Christianity following World War II, the source of the life force is Christ. But the belief in accumulating life force has remained.

The following significant points are worth noting about Janowski's work in relation to the life force: (1) the highland heroes were not ordinary people because they were able to interact and journey in and out of the cosmic world, thus highlighting the importance of journeying and adaptiveness resulting from the non-human world, be it from the upperworld or underworld, populating the cosmos; (2) the heroes are often able to transform into other forms such as powerful animals or plants and therefore had the extraordinary ability to fly, leap, and drop from the sky; and (3) the heroes, both male and female, were often attractive and efficient members of society, and were associated with the color red. In other words, "headhunting was intended to concentrate vital force" (117) that resonates with McKinley's conceptualization of humanizing the non-human as it was driven by the need to accumulate life/soul force. This is the definition we use to study the oral narratives of the Lundayeh people in order to examine whether, at present, the soul force as well as the native perception regarding the non-human spirit world continues, or whether it has been replaced by another belief. In short, we look at the ways through which the native voice is made audible in the oral literature by situating the oral narratives from the past and present within a comparative lens. Nonetheless, before we do that, it is necessary to trace the erosion of the Lundayeh indigenous identity, which has been manifold following the drastic changes to the community's way of life. This erosion calls for a timely and urgent examination of their native agency in the twenty-first century.

Erosion of Indigenous Identity: From the Establishment of North Borneo to the Formation of Sabah, Malaysia

In order to fully understand the erosion of Lundayeh indigenous identity, four things are crucial for discussion: (1) territorial/geographical division as the result of colonization and postcolonial nation-state, (2) religious conversion, (3) national identity, and (4) modernization. It is important to note here that the loss of indigenous agency among the Lundayeh people neither happened overnight nor was caused by a single reason; rather, the reasons for such phenomena are multifarious, involving many generations and historical periods. That said, we believe these four contributing factors are sufficient and necessary in order to paint a full picture of the erosion of indigenous identity.

We begin with the effect of territorial division as a result of colonization and the emergence of a postcolonial nation on the Lundayehs' sense of identity. What is now known as Southwestern Sabah, North-eastern Sarawak, and North Kalimantan was once part of the Lundayeh heartland. As it was slowly colonized or influenced by three different colonial powers and one local Sultanate, namely the British North Borneo Company, the Sarawak Raj, the Dutch East India Company, and the Brunei Sultanate, the Lundayeh people became dispersed into disparate territories. The 1915 Boundary Treaty Agreement between the Netherlands and Great Britain effectively divided the Lundayeh heartland into two permanent different spheres of influence, which eventually formed the modern Malaysia–Indonesia border. The political division did not just happen between two different countries, but it was further compounded by the interstate division between the two Malaysian Borneo states of Sabah and Sarawak. The Lundayeh people are now defined by the interstate and intra-state division in which they reside: Brunei, Indonesia, and the Malaysian states of Sabah and Sarawak. It is due to this territorial division that the cohesive intra-ethnic identity of the Lundayeh is diluted, to which we now turn our discussion.

The Lundayeh—at present—are found in all four political units of Borneo. The name Lundayeh is not unproblematic, however, because, to this day, those in Sabah are known as Lundayeh, while those in Sarawak are known through the self-referent Lun Bawang.[18] In Brunei they are known as Murut Lun Bawang and in Kalimantan, Indonesia they are Dayak Lundayeh. These varied ethnic labels, according to the four political units of Borneo have been the cause of much confusion and anxiety. To make matters worse, the community that once shared a borderless land area, has become divided with lasting consequences; in Sabah, they are a minority and even in the area that is widely perceived as a Lundayeh heartland such as the village of Long Pasia, the children do not speak the native language, and numerous native practices have been totally abandoned or adapted to suit the village's Christian way of life. This is a point of interest in this chapter because we believe that oral literature is the only form of cultural record that can be used collectively to examine the Bornean Lundayehs, despite the various divisive labels and categories.

It has to be kept in mind that ethnic classification is rooted in the colonial census and became reified by the nation-state for the purpose of governance—it is our assertion that both the colonial administration and postcolonial Malaysia's nation formation have unwittingly created a Bornean identity that is complex and compounded. Again, this is another point of interest, because the group's sense of belonging, like other tribes in Borneo, was based on kinship, which stemmed from the location/river basin that a group, or multiple groups, occupied and was therefore rather fluid. Marriage alliances between different longhouses can also contribute to such a sense of belonging. This is to say that, before the colonial territories were drawn and postcolonial borders were established, the Lundayehs sense of identity, due to their place of origin and alliances, was part of a wider shared imagination. In this way, they were not bound by exclusive ethnic identities. However, this fluid form of belonging became a stagnant and fixed category demarcated by ethno-linguistics and became officially recognized in the 1970s. We explain the brief history of the transition in the following paragraphs.

The name Lun (people) Dayeh (upriver) is an identification based on the headwaters location of the river, as compared to those who occupied the lowlands who were known as Lun (people) Lod (downriver). Even though the Lun Dayehs and Lun Lods shared linguistic similarities, their kinship *vis-a-vis* the longhouse that was built based on their respective locations meant that their agricultural activities were distinctive. As highlighted earlier, the geographic location that a group occupied also tended to determine the type of paddy the group cultivated; those in the highlands engaged in hill paddy cultivation while those in the lowlands engaged in wet paddy cultivation. These agricultural groups emerged as the sub-groups of the Lundayeh community.[19]

The two-word river basin-based identity, i.e., Lun Dayeh, became an ethno-linguistic classification, "Lundayeh," because, during the British colonial period, they were mislabelled as "Murut," which is a different group from the Lundayeh, and belonged to another language family. Researchers have conceded that, while the Dutch used the term "Dayak" to broadly include pagans and inland peoples of Kalimantan, the British used the term "Murut" to refer to a wide range of highlanders in North Borneo, Sarawak, and Brunei. Deegan[20]—for example—explains that the "Murut" classification was introduced by "foreigners in a derogatory fashion to classify hill peoples such as the Lundayeh and Lun Bawang when in fact it refers to the Tagals, a neighboring group."[21] Numerous attempts have been made both by local and foreign researchers to trace the reason why "[a] varied assortment of mountain peoples in northern Sarawak and the interior districts of Sabah [were referred in such a way when] the term has bever been used in self-reference among these peoples."[22] Even though the answers vary, a widely accepted explanation is that the word "Murut" might have derived from Mount Murut, the highest peak in Sarawak, where one of the early Lundayeh settlements was located, and was used by outsiders to refer to a collection of various groups of people who migrated from there.[23] Since mobility and hybridity of population was common in Borneo and as Kahn puts it "[in the past] particular localities were either impermanent or flexible, continually being made and remade."[24] there was this sense of openness among the people in general until it was changed during the British colonial rule and was reified following postcolonial Malaysia's ethnic construct for governance purposes.

In other words, even though the Lundayeh identified themselves according to the geographic location they occupied, the classification was rarely an issue since the cultural borrowing, and cross-fertilization between Bornean communities had been in practice until ethnicity was introduced through the colonial government's administration of the census. This is the reason why the term "Murut" was vehemently fought against, and in its place the ethno-linguistic classification, Lundayeh, began to be used in the 1970s after Sabah joined the Federation of Malaya in 1963.

There was another reason for this conflict. The implication caused by the term "Murut" as it was entrenched in well-worn colonial stereotypes was further compounding. As early as 1913, the British North Borneo Herald had used the name Sarawak Murut to refer to "drunken, dirty, and indolent" people.[25] Ricketts[26] also noted that Murut people were associated with drunkenness, an unhygienic way of living, filthy habits, and customs that were repulsive. It is due to this that, following independence, with the joint efforts of the various Lundayeh sub-groups and with the church as the unifying force, the single-word, "Lundayeh" began to be used as an ethnic classification justified through the linguistic differences that existed between the Murut and Lundayeh languages.[27] Deegan,[28] Martin,[29] and Hoare[30] agree that, while the Lundayehs and Muruts share some cultural characteristics, they are linguistically remote, highlighting that on one hand, the fluidity between these communities allowed for the cross and mix of cultures, but on the other the need to disassociate from the colonial labels especially through linguistic demarcations resulted in a fixed ethnic identity. This is why, at present, researchers like Mashman have suggested identifications such as "Lun Tauh" through which the tensions caused by ethnic categories can be overcome, because the term promotes a "more fluid, relational, and inclusive" idea, thus providing those from the borderlands with a common ancestral origin, and linguistic similarity, the ability to reside within a wider collective imagination.[31]

The second reason why we believe the Lundayeh indigenous identity has been eroded is due to the religious conversion of the Lundayeh people from animism to Christianity over the last century; however, this needs a careful analysis because Christianity has become synonymous with the modern Lundayeh identity. Before we begin our discussion, a brief history of missionary work is necessary. The snapshot of the Lundayeh people whom the Western missionary encountered in the 1930s is radically different from the Lundayeh people who are now dwelling in the highland in north-central Borneo. As Crain and Pearson-Rounds write:

> When [the Ludayeh] finally made their way into the Europeans' list of tribes [...] in the early decades of the twentieth century, they were almost always represented in a strange alterity: head-taking savages, yes, untrustworthy drunkards, yes, but at the same time ingenious and highly successful highland wet-rice farmers, with very large communities and substantial herds of water buffalo.[32]

It was perhaps the Western missionary efforts undertaken by the Christian Missionary Alliance in the Dutch colony of Kalimantan and the Borneo Evangelical Mission in the Sarawak Kingdom that managed to change the drunkard image and headhunting tradition of the Lundayeh people. While the Western missionaries paved the way for the large-scale conversion of the Lundayeh people, it was perhaps through the Borneo Evangelical Church (known as Sidang Injil Borneo in the Malay language) in the 1960s that the effort to convert the Lundayeh people into religiously devout and practicing Christians became fruitful. Such success has led the President of the Borneo Evangelical Mission (BEM Rev. Dr. Justin Wan) to claim that "the Christian gospel preachers saved the Lun Bawang community from the destruction of alcoholism by turning a sickly and dying tribe into a flourishing people today."[33] Hence, we must not overlook the fact that the religious conversion of the Lundayeh people did not miraculously happen in a single generation or one historical period; rather, the successful religious conversion of the Lundayeh people covers a considerable long period of time and involves several generations.

The success of religious conversion is closely associated with the substantial change in the indigenous identity. Lundayeh people traditionally dwelled in long houses.[34] But upon conversion, some practices like headhunting, and other practices that were deemed contradictory with Christianity have been abandoned. Although alcoholic drinks are not particularly forbidden in the Christian religion, the missionary managed to persuade the community to give up alcoholic drinks altogether. Since consuming alcoholic drinks was also associated with unwarranted be-haviors such as disputes, tribal wars, and sexual promiscuity that often led to the torching of longhouses, the community's longhouse dwelling structure eventually changed to individual households—a move particularly encouraged by the colonial government.

As a matter of fact, during the transition from colonial rule to the emergence of Sabah as a Malaysian state, the shift to residing in individual households strongly affected the type of paddy cultivation the community engaged in. As mentioned earlier, Lundayehs of the upstream region were hill paddy cultivators, and the workforce for such agricultural activity came from the long-house. Since the longhouse dwelling was strongly discouraged following the spread of serious diseases, and re-building burned longhouses following communal altercations meant that high costs were incurred, the shift to individual households was unavoidable; as a result of such a settled form of living, the community also resorted to wet paddy cultivation.[35]

During our fieldwork observations in the village of Long Pasia in 2019–2020, one of the strik-ing features—which is perhaps well known to those scholars who study the Lundayeh people—is the manner in which the Lundayeh people practice Christian religiosity, as they take religious observance seriously. For example, they consider gambling and gossiping as sinful. When the Lundayeh people perform musical tunes during Sunday mass, only a certain kind of music is al-lowed by the pastor. According to the pastor, the general rule of thumb for the song selection is that songs that inspire people to remember God are permissible, while songs that invoke a sense of lust are forbidden. It is also interesting to note here although some elders of the Lundayeh people, when interviewed for this research, acknowledged the pagan beliefs that their ancestors held, but they were also quick to say that they no longer subscribe to such a belief, at least the way their forefathers and mothers practiced paganism.

Apart from the territorial division and religious conversion, the third reason for the erosion of the indigenous identity is crucially linked to the formation and emergence of national identity in postcolonial Malaysia. Like many nations that achieved independence from the colonial em-pire, the formulation of a national identity for Malaysia is paramount for the purpose of nation-building. A full discussion of postcolonial national identity falls outside of our scope here, but we would like to focus on the National Language policy, where the Malay language is constitution-ally the official language of the federation.

How better can we understand the erosion of indigenous identity than in terms of the loss of a native language? The medium of language in the Malaysian school system mandatorily changed from English to the Malay language in the 1970s, and a good command of Malay became a re-quirement for entry into the Malaysian public service—these are the contexts through which the loss of indigenous identity should be understood. In the interview conducted in Long Pasia (2018), the Lundayeh people wanted their children to learn Malay as they believed mastery of the language to be economically important for the future of their children. Further research should be done to understand this phenomenon, but during our observation in the classroom, many younger generations of the Lundayeh people are no longer conversant in their native language as they are more comfortable talking in Malay to one another. The decreasing use of the native language was evident when we stayed at a homestay in Long Pasia. Although our respondents conversed among their peers in Lundayeh, surprisingly, they spoke to their grandchildren in the Malay language. The slow demise in the use of the native Lundayeh language has unwittingly affected the production of oral literature, a crucial cultural marker that denotes the indigenous culture and value system.

If colonization and decolonization have divided the Lundayeh people into contested intra-ethnic categories, if religious conversion from paganism to Christianity effectively forced the Lundayeh people to abandon their traditional way of life, and if postcolonial Malaysia has made more members of the younger Lundayeh generations lose their mother tongue, deforestation *vis-a-vis* modernization has caused an imminent threat to their surrounding environment, which is the forest land. Increasing land encroachment by logging companies, in addition to the building of timber routes in Lundayeh heartland areas such as in Ulu Padas, has caused food sourcing in the form of hunting-foraging to largely cease; the villagers now mainly depend on store-bought meat, because even with hunting techniques suited for the present depleting forest land, game is hard to catch. Education, search for hard cash through job opportunities, and migration to city centers have become common among the Lundayehs, thus demonstrating the ways in which traditional ways of life have been abandoned for modern living.

It is therefore clear that the Lundayehs' sense of indigenous identity has been eroded over the past century. In what follows, we argue that despite this, Lundayeh native agency is audible in the oral literature, albeit in varying forms.

Locating Lundayeh Native Agency in Works of Oral Literature

In this section, we begin by investigating a funeral chant known as *Tido Ada'* to examine how the Lundayeh informants, though they were Christians at the time the song was recorded, were still able to recall the lyrics. This is because, even though they had converted, the Lundayeh only became religiously observant in the 1970s, and the native funeral rituals were still in their collective memory. The case is very different today because indigenous funeral rites have become obsolete in the Lundayeh communal memory as they have been replaced by Christian religious ceremonies; therefore, these songs have completely disappeared from their native repertoire. The main reason for the inclusion of the *Tido* in this section, however, is to examine how dominant the native belief in soul force and the non-human spirit world when mourning for the dead was even as recently as the 1970s.

We could not include a song/narrative directly on headhunting in this chapter because, due to the lapse in time following the abolishment of the practice in the 1930s, most of the songs referring to the headhunter or the practice of headhunting only existed through the lyrics that represented the image of a crocodile. The reason for this is because, during the past celebrations of a successful headhunting expedition called *nui ulung*, an earthen crocodile mound was erected along with the ceremonial poles where the severed head was kept in a basket. The *ukui* dance and song was performed as a village around the crocodile mound to celebrate the headhunter's victory. Today, long after the abolishment of headhunting, and especially following the religious prohibitions the image of the crocodile is portrayed through food forms (*Luba' Buaya*) or concrete structures to remind that the animal is one of the closest cultural representations of the Lundayehs' in relation to the past practice of headhunting.[36] This is not unproblematic as religious regulations continue to question the use of crocodile images as the surviving means to represent Lundayeh culture and tradition. It is indeed a conflicting space of cultural allegiance. Therefore, it is unsurprising that the use of crocodile imagery in oral literature is fast declining.

The beginning, middle, and ending sections given below are part of a *Tido Ada'* collected by Ricky Ganang[37] (the full version of the chant is given in the Appendix):

The many-voiced storytelling surfaces as the chant starts off in a conversational tone between the dead and living that resonates with the idea of communalism discussed earlier in relation to a traditional Lundayeh longhouse (refer to Table 10.1). The term of reference that begins with "my dear sister" (*cur*) eventually turns to "you" (*iko*), highlighting a sense of impersonalization befitting the idea of the demised as a non-human, i.e., "spirit." Such heterogenous speaking positions—at times as an insider ("sister"), and at other times as an outsider ("spirit")—also marks a type of fragmented storytelling which is symbolic of the native belief in the spirit world. The ability of the singing voice to move in and out between the human and non-human world is also characteristic of the native cosmology.

This chant tells the story of Nubur Igur. Before she went up to the upperworld, she turned into a spirit. She went to look for beads to be worn for she would look very pretty to look at compared

K. Ganesan and S. Abdul Rahman

Table 10.1 Tido Ada' *(beginning of the chant)*

Tido Ada'	English translation[38]
Buley' cur bukap nan feraya',	My dear sister, my best companion
buley' susani nan febaya',	My dear sister, only you I can get along with,
iko manen kuh ale',	only you I always adore,
suen ku ada',	You have turned into spirit,
iko ruen ku ada' busaya'.	You are always in my mind.

Table 10.2 Tido Ada' *(middle section of the chant)*

Tido Ada'	English translation
Buley', buley'	My dear sister
Idey ngadan?	What name?
Feribubud keh teu ngadan,	let us introduce each other's name,
feribada' ngadan taman.	let us tell each other's fathers' names. Here, I am Ecung
tunge' kwi Ecung Meruu retnan Baa'	Meruu from Nan Baa'
Meruu Padan dei' Baa' Maraa',	Meruu Padan from Baa' Maraa'
mo' aca', mo' ceh kedaya'	Ok my dear brother
Tunge' wi nuger kibung ret yang tana',	I am here from under the earth to search for cloth,
Busak tunung ret yang abpa'	I am an orchid flower from under the river
Nubur Igur yeh nerabpa'	Nubur Igur who has died
Iyeh manen suen ku ada',	She has turned into a spirit,
iyeh suen ku ada' busaya'	has become a friendly spirit
Me' ngelayag ilung yeh eki' Sia',	She has come to search for red beads,
Merey atuk fingelaka', mieh buley'.	Red beads, which most people love to own.

to the rest who had died and reached the upperworld earlier than her. When she reached the sky, she was very happy to be with those who were already there, who had died earlier. She is prettier than the rest because she is wearing the red beads.

The chant that began as a rhetorical dialogue between two sisters—feminine voice—shifts when a male voice is incorporated in the middle section of the chant (refer to Table 10.2). The speaking position weaves in and out between the first and third person, and includes singular as well as plural voices. This means that the *Tido Ada'* is told by different family members—two sisters (one alive and the other dead), and the deceased's brother-in-law (*aca'*). It highlights the social dynamics of a domestic family that occupies an individual apartment of a longhouse where, besides lineage, close kinships are also secured through marriages. The noteworthy points about the exchange are as follows: (1) the masculine voice belongs to a member who came into the family through marriage; hence his identity is established through his paternity (Ecung Meruu from Nan Baa' / Meruu Padan from Baa' Maraa'); (2) this male member is from a different longhouse/ river basin that possibly practices a different type of paddy cultivation (Nan Baa' / Baa' Maraa'); and, (3) the rhetorical conversation between the two sisters that was cathartic in nature turned to a form of question and answer when it involved the brother-in-law because it is through him that the dead spirit is seeking closure (to gather red beads and travel to the upperworld).

Even though she is Nubur Igur to the living, her real identity is as a spirit or soul force, hence her revelation to her brother-in-law: "I am here from under the earth to search for cloth, I am an orchid flower from under the river." By giving voice to Nubur Igur's "friendly spirit" and later, by

Headhunting and Native Agency

partaking in a cosmic journey with her, the brother-in-law is given the agency to humanize the non-human spirit, in order to place the dead Nubur in the rightful place in the universe. This is why he accompanies her to gather the beads. The chant also highlights that both Nubur Igur and her brother-in-law possessed the soul force, symbolically referred to by the color "red" (*sia*), and hence had the ability to move in and out of the human to the spirit world.

The important question here is, why was the brother-in-law instead of the sister chosen to give a final send-off to the demised female? According to the native belief, the male is associated with success in warfare concerning the beings of the upperworld; naturally, then, Nubur Igur's spirit seeks his help. In other words, even though Nubur was not an ordinary woman because she possessed the soul force to interact with the human world, she needed someone with an equally strong soul force like her brother-in-law to send her off in her final journey. She was able to do the rest with the assistance from other female relatives, such as to purify herself in the river as well as gather and adorn herself in beautiful clothes and flowers.

There may also be another explanation for the inclusion of the male voice. Janowski details the following when referring to some of the reasons associated with headhunting: "heads were believed to bring *lalud* into the community—a fresh source of vitality to replace that lost through the death".[39] This is to say that Nubur's death will be mourned until another soul force is brought into the community, albeit through headhunting, which is a male domain.

In order to establish the male/female distinction—furthermore—very specific reference is made to the way the red bead is threaded into a necklace (refer to Table 10.3). The way these beads (*ilung sia*) are strung resembles the way the *Tido* itself is composed by the female singing voice: "slowly and carefully." The way the chant is strung and the sequence through which Nubur's journeying is presented are both representative of the female.

The whole chant demonstrates two very clear boundaries, one between the human and non-human, the other between the male and female. Even though as the song progresses, the boundary is crossed and mixed in order to forward the idea that the dead spirit is on a journey to the upperworld, the process through which she attains the rightful place in the universe is demonstrated throughout the chant. In other words, the native agency in the *Tido Ada'* is audible through two ways: one by establishing the differences, and the other by unfolding the complementarity that exists between two opposing forces such as the human/non-human and male/female.

Table 10.3 Tido Ada' *(ending section of the chant)*

Tido Ada'	English translation
Eme' mecing neh nei ruma',	You are about to reach your home,
eme' mafit neh nei tawa', kenem	you stop by at the veranda of the house
Mecing gadung ruma',	When you reach the palace,
dawa' ada' mecing bupung rufa'	the other spirits who welcome her are a bit older
Dawa' lufa' mieh buley'.	They are the elders.
Merey ilung neh eki' sia',	She gave them some red beads,
merey atuk fingelaka'	she gave them the beautiful beads
Ilung uken neh ini ale',	Which she put thread through them,
mo nuka', keruren muh kerura'	which she put thread through them,
Kalai-kalai bukat ranga',	She was good at putting the threads through,
ulai-ulai sani baya'	slowly and carefully
Nalan neh kiteh bukat ranga',	Let us go little girl,
ngerinan sani baya', fieh buley'.	I will accompany you.

Such complementarity, as discussed earlier, especially in relation to the human and non-human world, is thought to complete the universe. In the same way, the male and female shared a complementarity because, while the man was the headhunter, the female was the receiver of the severed head. The coming together of the male and female transpired as the ritual celebration of a successful headhunting expedition. Even when it comes to food sourcing, the men hunted game while the women complemented hunted food with cultivated crops. This complementarity is reflective of the swidden agricultural egalitarian relationships that scholars like Sutlive have noted.[40]

Consistent with the theme of complementarity and the existence of the universe in its entirety, this chant also includes people of different age groups. The young demised woman, meets young babies as well as older folks upon reaching the upperworld. She is the bridge between these two age groups, because the bead necklace she carries symbolizes her youth. This is why the whole chant is filled with a choric melancholy (*buley buley*—what a pity, what a pity) that is cathartic, digressive, and interruptive, all at the same time.

That said, the criss-cross of multiple points of view—"I," "she," and "you"—denotes that the persona occupies multiple spatial loci at any given time, highlighting a sense of omniscience and omnipotence. This is further accentuated by the fact that all types of beings are included in the chant (male; female; married; unmarried; young; old; familial relationships), both from the human and non-human world, thus representing the cosmos in its entirety—an enabling position for the omniscient and omnipotent story-teller. It is due to this that it can be said that this persona is well-suited for the theme that involves the native belief in death and calamities, where the soul force will be carried to the vast universe consisting of the natural (forest and river) environment.

We have included a *benging*—collected in 2019—in the succeeding section that was sung by Ladu Balang, a 71-year-old woman, in Long Semadoh. This genre, one that is mostly recited for humor, is included here to examine the ways in which the native agency has undergone changes from the past. As mentioned earlier, *Tido Ada'* is not sung anymore, and most of the songs/poetry at present are in the form of *benging*. *Benging* can be sung during celebrations (*irau*), weddings, and even as a form of entertainment. It is, to a large extent, one of the very few available genres of oral literature that is practiced among the older generation men and women, which is not against the Christian way of life. The younger generation who are conversant in the language are able to comprehend these songs but are unable to produce it themselves.

Table 10.4 Benging iBurung Mapad

Benging[41]	English translation
Wa ku ceh benging,	Let me sing a humorous benging about,
iBurung Mapad,	Si Burung Mapad,
iBurung Tagung luka pegurep,	Si Burung Tagung tripped and fell,
Kok meh aceh lal peped peled,	The rooster was crowing from the wooden beam,
Ngaten mepelin tulang kelabet,	Pulling out a hairpin made of kelabet bone,
Tulang berangad, tulang langur	Berangad bone, langur bone
Kiung metengeb, muka pendek	Riverbank face, short face
Ame uih diu tang mesingob,	I went to the river to take my bath and heard a soft scream,
Tang melio iring dei pekop tengeb,	It came from the other side of the river bank,
Do ruyung anak lipated,	Along with the newly spawned baby fish,
Dawa anak luang do ibed-ibed,	The baby fish that were so pretty,
Nier yang tabir uih mekelep,	I looked down and blinked,
Yang tabir beladan ngukat yang rengeb,	Beneath its flap the turtle was digging a hole,
Ngukat yang paru seruep-rueb.	Digging a hole along the river flow.

Headhunting and Native Agency

This rather short poem (we have included the entire poem here) is light-hearted because, unlike *Tido Ada'*, it does not involve any serious themes or depart from an inherent understanding regarding the indigenous belief system. It relates incidents of ordinary life, ridiculing human actions and behaviors, in particular the two men, Si Burung Mapad and Si Burung Tagung. Even though the setting of the *benging* is characteristically realistic as it includes a typical village environment, the light and low-key tone demonstrates that it can be understood and enjoyed by the everyday common people. That is why the very first line starts off with a welcoming note: "*Wah ku ceh benging.*" As a matter of fact, the rustic flavor of this poetry is audible through the names of the characters, Si Burung Mapad (*iBurung* Mapad) and Si Burung Tagung (*iBurung Tagung*), where the article "Si" is a Malay derivative of the Lundayeh "*i*" used to describe or name people of certain unusual nature in order to highlight a sense of farce attached to their demeanor. In this way, it can be said that this *benging* involves a type of buffoonery with an appeal to the lesser faculty of the mind. Such simpleton traits are further accentuated through the line, "pulling out a hair pin made of kelabet bone, berangad bone, langur bone," because long hair pulled up into a bun and held together by an animal bone, tooth, or tusk is characteristic of a Lundayeh male. In other words, this song/poetry is about these two young men whose awkward demeanor and clumsy actions ("tripped and fell") calls for the onlooker's scrutiny and ridicule.

Even though these young men are seemingly portrayed as less sophisticated, the emphasis on their appearance, i.e., long hair, demonstrates that their masculinity is not a subject to be ridiculed since the long hair, when untied, covers the back of their neck similar to the past headhunters who believed that their thick hair would prevent them from becoming easy targets of another headhunting tribe.[42] Although these young men were not headhunters, the accessories they used on their hair signifies that they were skilful hunters; animal body parts were kept as memorabilia of their hunting abilities. This is an important point of native agency that highlights food sourcing traditions such as hunting continue to live in communal memory.

Another feature that depicts the rustic village life is portrayed through the crowing rooster. The way it is perched on the rear end of the wooden beam of the house provides grounds to create a mental picture or visual representation that appeals to one of the most common bodily senses—sight. The vivid image of the village house, its architecture, along with the sound of the crowing rooster (auditory imagery), can be interpreted as evoking the listeners' other senses as well. And since Si Murung Mapad's fall coincides with the rooster's crowing, another sense involving the tactile image surfaces in the poetry. Rather than interpreting such sensuous imageries as lustful, we need to situate them within Lundayeh food sourcing methods; hunting and foraging require the use of sight, hearing, and touch.

Unlike the earlier chant, where multiple voices were incorporated by alternating points of view, in this *benging*, the home has become an individualized *vis-a-vis* singular unit; therefore, the persona that performs as the onlooker merges with the self-constructed voice, "I." This is to say that the persona occupies a performative location in the poetry, and thus starts relating with the surrounding environment. The merging of the third and first person is consistent with the idea of a realistic comedy as the focus shifts to the non-human animal world, where the poetry from this point onwards is told relationally between "I" and the surrounding environment.

Specific reference is made to emphasize the animals found in the forest land of Borneo as well as its vast river system. Numerous rainforest monkey species are given textual space, such as the "berangad" (hose's langur), "kelabat" (Bornean gibbon), and "langur," demonstrating that the names given to these animals have a phonetically rhyming sound. Hence through the repeated use of the consonant /b/ and /l/, placed at the beginning, middle, or end of the words referring to the monkeys, the *benging* gains a sense of orality. Likewise, the reference made to "lal" (chicken/rooster), "luang" (large fish species), "lipated" (small fish species), and "beladan" (river turtle), provides grounds for a rhyming pattern to emerge between the same consonant sounds, only this time around it is reversed, i.e., /l/ and /b/. This means that the ecological elements incorporated in the poetry through linguistic expression are symbolic of the synergy that exists between the community and their natural environment.

While on the one hand, the depiction of the animals fosters feelings of unity with nature, on the other, it shows that human life has to continue, and for that, all these animals have to be consumed. In other words, from the monkeys to the river turtles, these non-human animals provide the food source for Lundayeh human sustenance. As a symbolic representation of this continuity, the *benging* includes an instance of fish spawning. The Lundayehs believed that fish spawning is triggered by unique environmental conditions; when the tide is very low and nights are very cold, the fish gather at shallow, stony areas to spawn.[43] This fertile procreation is necessary for the continuation of life for both the human and the non-human animal world.

That said, the sense of calm continuity foregrounded through fish spawning is interrupted by reference to a high tide beneath which the river turtle is digging a hole. This is a point of interest that figuratively describes the present-day Lundayehs, who have the ability to navigate between calm and rough patches of their lives, often not going against the stream but flowing with it as symbolically represented by the river turtle.

The *benging*—strikingly different from the earlier account presented in the *Tido*—is a realistic comedy that merges the native agency of the persona both as an onlooker and participant in human life. The centrality of nature, whether presented in the third or first person, demonstrates that despite numerous changes spanning a few generations, the Lundayehs' interdependence and appreciation for life has always been drawn from nature.

Conclusion

We have comprehensively presented in this chapter a humanist depiction of the indigenous Lundayeh belief system. The primary idea that we wish to highlight is that, despite a perceivably savage form of living in the past through headhunting, the Lundayehs' deep association with their surrounding environment continues to find agency. Even where the belief in the non-human spirit world may have ceased to exist in a post-Christian way of living, the belief that their indigeneity is inherently connected to the vast environment continues. Such an oriental (not *orientalist*) humanism foregrounded in the Lundayeh oral literature is distinctive and should have its place in the scholarly debate on humanism. The indigenous oral literature can write, from a wealth of human experience, against the Western-informed idea of humanism and promote a deep appreciation for the increasingly threatened natural environment.

The oral literature from the past and present is proof that the Lundayeh community has undergone numerous changes that span a few generations. These shifts are incorporated in their oral tradition either as a genre, theme, or literary device showing that the community has an intrinsic sense of fluidity and adaptability akin to their past semi-nomadic living. This is why regardless of the changes, the Lundayeh people are able to navigate challenges, and continue to keep their sovereignty alive with regards to their surrounding environment. The current problem in the form of deforestation warrants another examination in the near future in order to see how the native agency either lives on, or is completely obliterated, which makes the contribution of this chapter critical for the present time.

Appendix

Tido Ada'
Buley' cur bukap nan feraya',
My dear sister, my best companion

Headhunting and Native Agency

buley' susani nan febaya',
My dear sister, only you I can get along with,
iko manen kuh ale',
only you I always adore,
suen ku ada',
You have turned into spirit,
iko ruen ku ada' busaya'.
You are always in my mind.

Buley', buley',
Oh my dearest sister,
mafu' wi ara',
I don't want to leave
mabar ara' semiga',
I don't want to depart,
ara' wi nacan ni di ama',
I don't want to leave daddy behind
naa wi merey nacan ni ina'.
I don't want to leave mommy behind
Buley' cuu bukap nan feraya',
But my dear sister, I want to go with you
muley' rusa ni nan febaya',
I want to go along with you
iko manen kuh ku iNubur aya',
You are always in my mind sister Nubur
iNubur aya' ruma',
Nubur, pet of the house (pet here is a synonym for a loved child)
me' ngelayag ilung ku eki' sia',
going to look for red beads
ngelayag atuk fingelaka',
to get them to make you happy
idey me' ngerayen negkuh nengerana'?
who will accompany me?
ara' wi tufuu fetegala',
I don't want to be alone,
sibuleng kudeng bua'.
Alone like a piece of fruit.

Buley' kinanak buley',
Oh my dear sister,
wi me' ngerengen nemuh ale' wen rengama',
I purposely want to go with you,
wi me' nated nemuh wen taca',
I am going to send you
nuger kibung wi me' maya',
I am going with you to look for some expensive cloths
busak tunung me' ngerada' yeh buley'.
Like chasing orchid flowers/blooms.

Buley', buley',
Oh my dear sister,
Muh decur meh nei nginua',
You are like a young mother,
menalaa' luk nefuraa', keneh
get rid of the used items when migrating
Yeh decur luk nenginua',
She is a young mother,
menalaa' luk nerufaa',

163

she disposes of all used items
Ayung iNubur mieneh tekip bata',
Nubur is wearing a blue colored gown
tekip using bulan buda',
a white gray gown
Lefi' dih lefut rua' nan tana', tieh buley'.
The edge of her gown reaches the floor.

Buley', buley',
Oh my dear sister,
ngalap neh lek iyeh neh baduu,
she goes to fetch her jacket,
yungen neh lek yunga',
then she puts it on,
fekuyen neh fekuya',
she fits it on properly
berii ulun riung nineh mula',
she looks very elegance in it,
luun afui neh wen musa', tieh buley'.
Looks like the flame of a burning fire.

Buley', buley',
Oh my dear sister,
kedur kiteh decur niko (neh iko) me' maya',
You stood up ready to go with me
fufud lawey ticaa', kenem,
"I will follow your footsteps, she said
mecing kiteh me' ruma',
until we reach the home,
iEcung Meruu dei' Nan Naa',
Home of Ecung Meruu at Nan Baa'
Meruu Padan dei' Baa' Maraa',
Meruu Padan house at Baa' Maraa'"
nangi' neh decur beruh fawa',
She then cried all alone
nak adi' mangud buda',
A very tender and fair young girl.
" Ina'," kenem, "cuu tinan nenginuaa,'"
"Mom," she said, "I am a young and a first time mother"
wi decur nemerinan,
"I am still an inexperience girl,
nak adi' neh wi nalan,
a young girl, I can travel
me' ngelayag wi ilung eki' sia',
to look for red beads
atuk buki' ngelaka' 'fieh buley',
which people love to own," my dear sister.

Ucek itii deh kinima',
kunen keli' deh binada',
buley'.

Buley', buley'
Oh my dear sister,
Tunge' wi nuger kibung wi eme',
I am here on the way to search for cloths
kiteh ngerinan busak tunung
we are longing to have flowers of the orchids

Headhunting and Native Agency

Kiteh nalan eme' ni Nubur aya',
Let us go to Nubur
Nubur Igur aya' ruma'
Nubur Igur pet of the house
Tufed nan tadur yeh ki Sia',
She is standing on the platform in front of the house
nan barat beluu buda'
on the platform with bright light.
Remurut ican tabpa',
She is climbing down the wooden ladder
telawii tabpa' ria'
made of a special wood
Lunguu nan figkar balad abpa',
She changes her clothes on the river bank
nan fatar balad tana', mieh buley'.
On the flat area of the river bank.

Buley', buley'
Oh my dear sister,
Na' mesadu' neh feh uduh,
When she accidentally kick/step on the grass
befud feh udung kayuh
It shook the top of the nearby bushes,
Kebesakan busak beluu yeh kebua', bua' ool tuu,
It shook the flowering ool fruit tree
udung-udung mefiing feh, udung-udung mefegkiing
Her body brushes through the top of the tree
kebesakan busak kering, yeh ool kading
the dried flowers were shaken
berii ulun riung inubuu mula',
They sound like the rushing flash flood of a river
ulun afui nih meh musa'
like the sound of flames of a burning fire,
tegumin kiteh meh ruma',
we look down at the house on the horizon
fawin kiteh meh tawa'
we climb to the verandah
ruma' iEcung Meruu dih Nan Baa',
Ecung Meruu's house at Nan Baa'
Meruu Padan dei' Baa' Maraa', mieh buley'.
Meruu Padan at Baa' Maraa'.

Buley', buley'
My dear sister
Ngilo' sangit idang tata',
I wish the sun would stop shining on us
ngilo' wiit kiteh idang mula'
I wish we could bring more sunshine.
Tudo fi Ecung Padan neh ngimunung,
If Ecung Padan sits at the window
ngayud kibung tudo itawa'
weaving cloth while sitting on the verandah
Mula' ulun riung dih wen musa',
Let the light be bright enough
ulun afui dih wen mula'
let the flames of the fire be more
Na' kedur mieh temina',
He sat up to get ready

tufed munung tanga'
He is standing at the door
Tufii kaban ruma',
At the center of the house
eceh tulai lused ruma'
he cleaned the front part of the house
Inan sakai dih ukey tawa', mieh buley'.
For the guests to sit on the verandah.

Buley', buley'
My dear sister,
Idey ngadan?
What name?
feribubud keh teu ngadan,
let us introduce each other's name
feribada' ngadan taman,
let us tell each other our fathers' names
tunge' kwi Ecung Meruu ret Nan Baa'
Here, I am Ecung Meruu from Nan Baa'
Meruu Padan dei' Baa' Maraa',
Meruu Padan from Baa' Maraa'.

Mo' aca', mo' ceh kedaya'
Ok my dear brother
Tunge' wi nuger kibung ret yang tana',
I am here from under the earth (grave)to search for cloth
busak tunung ret yang abpa'
I am an orchid flower from under the river(a dead person)
Eme' ngerengen eme' rengana',
I purposely come here
eme' nated dih wen taca'
Please take me, send me
Nated ni Nubur iyeh nih neluka',
Send Nubur, who has passed away
Nubur Igur yeh nerabpa'
Nubur Igur who has died
Iyeh manen suen ku ada',
She has turned into spirit
iyeh suen ku ada' busaya'
has become a friendly spirit
Me' ngelayag ilung yeh eki' Sia',
She comes to search for red beads
Merey atuk fingelaka', mieh buley'.
Red beads, which most people love to own.
Tawa' merebung ini ku ebpen abpa',
The corridor is flooded with water,
bungaluu teley laya'
the whole floor
Tawa' merebung ebpen rufan,
The corridor is flushed with water,
bungaluu teley lungan
the whole floor
Rerebpen muh nieh rerabpa',
Please fill it with more water
diuwen muh yeh diuwa'
for her to take a bath
Manen iyeh nih ku ada',
She has turned into a spirit

Headhunting and Native Agency

suen ku ada' busaya', yeh buley'.
She has turned into a friendly spirit.

Usad neh nei ruma',
Please take a rest at the house
ukey neh nei itawa'
you go up to the verandah
Afen nei neh Nubur bukat ranga',
You take Nubur
Nubur Igur sani baya'
Nubur Igur, the pet of the house (a person who is loved)

Rerebpen neh rerabpa',
Immerse her in the water
wen nieh neh wen nguba'
bathe/wash her properly until she is clean
Wen neh ngurai nieh bang kawa',
Wash her with the warm water
ngalap abpa tabar finepin nan neluka'
take the liquid from the tabar plant
Tabar fetuwii nan nerabpa',
Tabar plant which makes her rise from death
kudeng fureit mieh inebpeh
she sounded like lightning/thunder when she fell
Kudeng lalam mieh rayeh,
As if she is as big as a thunder
tudo meh Nubur aya'
She sat down alone
Tudo mi Nubur aya' ruma', mieh buley'.
Nubur the pet of the house sat down.
Meluun nenucun neh do' sira'
She was a very good looking lady
Meluun neh luun do' teh lia', fieh buley'.
Prettiest among them all.

Buley', buley'
Oh my dear
iNubur bukat ranga',
Nubur who has no match
Nubur Igur sani baya'
Nubur Igur the pet of the house
Iko ni niman kuh ku ada',
You have turned into a spirit
inisu' ku ada' busaya'
you turned into a friendly spirit
Eme' mecing neh nei ruma',
You are about to reach your home
eme' mafit neh nei tawa', kenem
you stop by at the verandah of the house
Mecing gadung ruma',
When you reach the palace
dawa' ada' mecing bupung rufa'
the other spirits who welcome her are a bit older
Dawa' lufa' mieh buley'.
They are the elders.
Merey ilung neh eki' sia',
She gave them some red beads
merey atuk fingelaka'

167

she gave them the beautiful beads
Ilung uken neh ini ale',
Which she put thread through them
mo nuka', keruren muh kerura'
which she put thread through them
Kalai-kalai bukat ranga',
She was good at putting the threads though
ulai-ulai sani baya'
slowly and carefully.
Nalan neh kiteh bukat ranga',
Let us go little girl
ngerinan sani baya', fieh buley'.
I will accompany you.

Buley', buley'
Oh my dear sister,
Eme' mecing neh kiteh feh ubab dita',
We are about to reach the opening of the sky
ubab firuu arang gawa'
the opening of the heavens
Yeneh keh mecing ubab dita',
When we reach at the opening of the sky
mafit feh arang gawa'
we stop by for a while
Edui tunge' iNubur ret yang tana',
Oh, here is Nubur who came from under the earth (grave)
Nubur Igur ret yang abpa'
Nubur Igur from under the river
feh lun nguiit cukub lun kibung sia'?,
Why is nobody bringing red cloth?
ban baru' laya'?
a soft cloth?
Dawa' anak luk inepuu dih neh neluka',
The dead children who were wrapped
inatey dih nerabpa'
who had died came,
Mutuh nuney ret ni ina' kei,
"We are asking for nuney (glutinous rice cooked in bamboo) from our mothers
tinafey ret ni ama'
tinafey (glutinous rice cooked in a pot) from our fathers,"
Segerimu meh lek iNubur Igur, mieh meriruh
Nubur Igur only managed to give them a smile
muyuh anak sia', mo anak muyui abpa',
"You little children,
naa wi nenguiit nuney ret ni tinam
I have not brought any nuney from your mothers
Tinafey ret ni tamam,
Or tinafey from your fathers
Ini maan wi ni ku ada'
I am here as a spirit
Inisu' ku ada' busaya',
I have turned into a friendly spirit
ine' ngelayag ilung eki' sia'
I went to search for red beads
Atuk fingelaka', mieh buley'.
Which many people love to own."
Mo usad neh nei ruma',
"Okay, you take a rest in the house

Headhunting and Native Agency

ukey neh nei tawa'
you climb up onto the verandah
Mecing fitengeb takung ada',
When you reach at the bank of the lake of the spirit
ifuun buyo ada', kenem
under the lemon tree of the spirit."
Eceh wi decur fem umak ruma',
I am a women; I am going up the house
inukey nideh tawa', feh buley'.
I climb up to the verandah.

Buley', buley'
Oh my dear sister
Ini gadung feh ruma' dawa' ada',
This is the palace of the spirits/ghosts
ini fufung dawa' lupa'
this is their home
Usad neh nei ruma',
You take a rest
ukey neh nei tawa'
you climb up the verandah
Meducun niko do' sira',
You will be clearly seen
meluun do' teh lia'
you will be more pretty to look at
Eceh teh nei me' fesifuu nedawa' ada',
You are not going to mix with the other spirits
me' femung dawa' lupa'
or to gather with them
Meducun niko do' sira',
You will be very pretty to look at (compared with the other spirits)
meluun do' teh lia'.
Much better to look at from among the rest.

Bibliography

British North Borneo Herald (February 17, 1913).

Crain, Jay Bouton. "The Mengalong Lun Dayeh Long-House." *Sarawak Museum Journal*, Vol. 18 (1970): 169–185.

Crain, Jay Bouton. "*Ngerufan*: Ritual process in a Bornean Rice Harvest." *Bornean Societies: Social Process and Anthropological Explanation*, edited by George Appell, Northern Illinois University: Center for Southeast Studies (1976), 51–63.

Crain, Jay Bouton. "The Lun Dayeh," *Essays on Borneo Societies,* edited by V. T. King. Hull Monographs on Southeast Asia No. 7, Oxford: Oxford University Press, 1978, 123–142.

Crain, Jay Bouton. and Pearson-Rounds, Vicki. "A Fallen Bat, a Rainbow, and the Missing Head: Media and Marginalization in Upland Borneo," *Indonesia*, Vol. 79 (April 2005), 57–68. https://ecommons.cornell.edu/bitstream/handle/1813/54344/INDO_79_0_1115148085_57_68.pdf?sequence=1&isAllowed=y

"Christian Gospel saved the Lun Bawang People," *Dayak Daily* (November 25, 2019), https://dayakdaily.com/christian-gospel-saved-the-lun-bawang-people/

Deegan, James Lewis. "Some Lun Bawang Spirit Chants," *Sarawak Museum Journal*, Vol. 18, No. 36–37 (1970), 264–281.

Deegan, James Lewis. *Change among the Lun Bawang: A Borneo People.* [Ph.D. Dissertation]. University of Washington, 1973.

De Raedt, Jules. "Buaya headhunting and its ritual: Notes from a headhunting feast in Northern Luzon." *Headhunting and the Social Imagination in Southeast Asia*, edited by Janet Hoskins, California: Stanford University Press, 1996, 167–183.

Ganang, Ricky Yakub. *Inventori Budaya Etnik Negeri Sabah: Etnik Lundayeh*, edited by Joisin Romut, Denis J. Sading, and Fiona Jamiyan, Kota Kinabalu: Lembaga Kebudayaan Negeri Sabah, 2016.

Ganang, Ricky Yakub, Jane Wong Kon Ling and Kavitha Ganesan. "Representation of Buayeh in the Quality of Life of the Lundayeh People." *Malaysian Journal of Social Sciences and Humanities (MJSSH)*, Vol. 3, No. 2 (2018), 169–184.

Ganesan, Kavitha, Anantha Raman Govindasamy, Jane Wong Kon Ling, Shaffarullah Abdul Rahman, Kennedy Aaron Aguol, Jamsari Hashim, and Bilcher Bala. "Environmental challenges and traditional food practices: The indigenous Lundayeh of Long Pasia, Sabah." *eTropic*, Vol. 19, No. 1 (2020). doi: 10.25120/etropic.19.1.2020.3734

Heyward, Nigel. *Dusun and Murut in Sarawak, Brunei, and North Borneo*, Singapore: Eastern Universities Press, 1963.

Hoare, Alison. *Cooking the Wild: the role of the Lundayeh of the Ulu Padas (Sabah, Malaysia) in managing forest foods and shaping the landscape*. [PhD Dissertation]. University of Kent: Department of Anthropology, 2002.

Hoskins, Janet. (ed.) "Introduction: Headhunting as Practice and as Trope." *Headhunting and the Social Imagination in Southeast Asia*, edited by Janet Hoskins, California: Stanford University Press, 1996, 1–49.

"Indonesia-Malaysia Boundary." *International Boundary Study*. No. 45. (March 15, 1965), Department of State, United States of America: The Geographer, Office of the Geographer, Bureau of Intelligence and Research.

Janowski, Monica. "Journeys in quest of cosmic power: Highland heroes in Borneo." *Austronesian Paths and Journeys*, edited by James T. Fox, Australia: ANU Press, 2021, 93–126.

Kahn, Joel. *Other Malays: Nationalism and Cosmopolitanism in the Modern Malay World*. Singapore: NUS Press, 2012.

Langub, Jayl. "Ethnic Self-Labelling of the Murut or *Lun Bawang* of Sarawak." *Sojourn: Journal of Social Issues in Southeast Asia*, Vol. 2, No. 2 (1987), 289–299.

Lees, Shirley. *Drunk Before Dawn*. Foreword by Michael Griffiths. United Kingdom: OMF Books, 1979.

Map of Lundayeh. "Ancestral Homeland" in Borneo. https://commons.wikimedia.org/wiki/File:Borneo_Topography.png

Martin, Peter W. "Linguistic Research in Brunei Darussalam: A Review." *Shifting Patterns of Language Use in Borneo*, edited by Peter Martin, The Borneo Research Council Proceeding Series, Williamsburg: Borneo Research Council, 1994, 81–106.

Mashman, Valerie. "Warriors and weavers: a study of gender relations among the Iban of Sarawak." *Female and Male In Borneo: Contributions and Challenges To Gender Studies*, edited by Vinson H. Sutlive Jr., Virginia: The Borneo Research Council, 1991, 231–270.

Mashman, Valerie. "The Story of *Lun Tauh*, 'Our People': Narrating Identity on the Borders in the Kelabit Highlands." *Stories across Borders: Myths of Origin and Their Contestation in the Borderlands of South and Southeast Asia*, edited by Monica Janowski and Erika de Maaker, special issue, *Southeast Asian Studies*, Vol. 9, No. 2, (August 2020), 203–229.

McKinley, Robert. "Human and proud of it! A structural treatment of headhunting rites and the social definition if enemies." *HAU: Journal of Ethnography Theory*. reprint, Vol. 5, No. 2 (2015), 443–483.

Morrison, Alastair. *Fair Land Sarawak: Some Recollections of an Expatriate Officer*, Ithaca: Cornell University Press, 1993.

Ricketts. O.F. "The Muruts of the Trusan River," *The Sea Dyaks and Other Races of Sarawak: Contributions to the Sarawak Gazette between 1888 and 1930*. Kuching: Borneo Literature Bureau, 1963, 367–378.

Schneeberger, Werner F. (1945). "The Kerayan-Kelabit Highlands of Central Northeast Borneo." *The Geographical Review*, Vol. 35, 544–562.

Sutlive, Vinson H. Jr. (ed) *Female and male in Borneo: contributions and challenges to gender studies*, Virginia: The Borneo Research Council, 1991.

Tuie, Meechang. *Masyarakat Lun Bawang Sarawak: Suatu Pengenalan*, Kuching: DBP, 1995.

Yansen, T.P. and Ricky Yakub Ganang. *Dayak Lundayeh Idi Lun Bawang: Budaya Serumpun di Dataran Tinggi Borneo*. Kalimantan: Penerbit Lembaga Literasi Dayak, 2018.

Notes

1 The inhabitants of Borneo occupied a borderless region and shared a close kinship until the expansion of British and Dutch empires as their territorial interests permanently divided the natives. This is because each of these colonies eventually became independent nation-states belonging to Indonesia (Kalimantan), Malaysia (North Borneo/Sabah and Sarawak), and Brunei, which permanently changed the

natives' sense of indigeneity. For more information on the Anglo-Dutch Treaty 1824, see B.W. Andaya and L.Y. Andaya, *A History of Malaysia*, London: Red Globe Press (2017, 3rd edition).

2 Deforestation, rapid urbanization, migration to city centers in search of better opportunities, and the demise of native languages are some of the threats that continue to challenge the indigeneity of the peoples even in highland locations that are relatively isolated. See for example, Kavitha Ganesan et al. "Environmental Challenges and Traditional Food Practices: The indigenous Lundayeh of Long Pasia, Sabah, Borneo" *eTropic*, Vol. 9, No 1 (2020) doi: 10.25120/etropic.19.1.2020.3734.

3 Even though superstition and supernatural beliefs are against the logic reasoning of humanism, in this chapter we will present a section on the Lundayeh worldview where we situate headhunting within Lundayeh cosmology that calls for an understanding of the upper (sky) and under (soil) world.

4 Shirley Lees in her book *Drunk Before Dawn* (1979) details that before conversion to Christianity, the Lun Bawangs of Sarawak (who have common ancestral ties with the Lundayehs in Sabah) led a rather wasteful life as alcoholics, and their strong belief in supernatural elements prevented them from engaging in productive agricultural activities. This changed when they converted to Christianity, which is institutionally centred around the Borneo Evangelical Church. Alastair Morrison's memoir *Fair Land Sarawak* (1993) gives a similar account of the Lun Bawangs, where, according to Morrison, the population faced a point of near extinction in the 1920s due to deplorable living conditions that caused outbreaks and the situation only changed following the community's conversion to Christianity.

5 See for example Werner Schneeberger. "The Kerayan-Kelabit Highlands of Central Northeast Borneo," *The Geographical Review*, Vol. 35 (1945), 544–562.

6 Information obtained from Ricky Ganang in March 2019.

7 See for example James Deegan. "Community Fragmentation Among the Lun Bawang," *Sarawak Museum Journal*, Vol. 22, No. 43 (1974), 229–247.

8 "Ngerufan: Ritual process in a Bornean Rice Harvest" *Bornean Societies: Social Process and Anthropological Explanation*. George Appell (ed.), Center for Southeast Studies, Northern Illinois University, 1976, 51–52.

9 Information obtained from Pith Kaya in Long Pasia, Sabah during fieldwork in February 2020.

10 "The Mengalong Lun Dayeh Long-House," *Sarawak Museum Journal*, Vol. 18 (36–37), 169–185.

11 Ibid.

12 See for example Jayl Langub "Ethnic Self-Labelling of the Murut or *Lun Bawang* of Sarawak," *Sojourn: Journal of Social Issues in Southeast Asia*, Vol. 2, No. 2 (1987), 289–299. Also see Ricky Ganang. *Inventori Budaya Etnik Negeri Sabah: Etnik Lundayeh* (2016), Lembaga Kebudayaan Negeri Sabah.

13 Janet Hoskins. "Introduction: Headhunting as Practice and as Trope." *Headhunting and the Social Imagination in Southeast Asia*, edited by Janet Hoskins (California: Stanford University Press, 1996), 2.

14 "Human and Proud Of It! A Structural Treatment of Headhunting Rites and the Social Definition of Enemies," *HAU: Journal of Ethnography Theory*, Reprint, Vol. 5, No. 2 (2015), 443–483. (Originally published in *Bornean Societies: Social Process and Anthropological Explanation*, edited by George Appell, Northern Illinois University: Center for Southeast Studies (1976), 92–126.)

15 "Journeys in quest of cosmic power: Highland heroes in Borneo" *Austronesian Paths and Journey*. James Fox (ed.), Australia: ANU Press (2021), 93–126.

16 While McKinley's discussion is based on the various indigenous groups in the region who practiced headhunting including those from Borneo, Janowski's work is mainly based on the Kelabits, a group whose origin can be traced to the Kerayan-Kelabit Highlands and shares close linguistic ties with the Lundayehs.

17 McKinley, 461.

18 For an account on why the self-referent "Lun Bawang" came to be used among those in Sarawak even though they were part of the same nation, i.e., Malaysia, refer to Langub. "Ethnic Self-Labelling of the Murut or Lun Bawang of Sarawak" (1987), 289–299.

19 See for example Jay Crain. "The Lun Dayeh," *Essays on Borneo Societies*, edited by V.T. King. Hull Monographs on Southeast Asia No. 7, Oxford: Oxford University Press (1978), 123–142.

20 Deegan, James. "Some Lun Bawang Spirit Chants", *Sarawak Museum Journal*, Vol. 18, No. 36–37 (1970), 264–281.

21 Ibid., 264.

22 Langub, 1987, 291.

23 See Nigel Heyward. *Dusun and Murut in Sarawak, Brunei, and North Borneo,* Singapore: Eastern Universities Press (1963).

24 Joel Kahn. *Other Malays: Nationalism and Cosmopolitanism in the Modern Malay World*. Singapore: NUS Press (2012) [first published in 2006], 64.

25 *British North Borneo Herald*, (February 17, 1913), 36.

26 O.F. Ricketts. "The Muruts of the Trusan River," *The Sea Dyaks and Other Races of Sarawak: Contributions to the Sarawak Gazette between 1888 and 1930,* Kuching: Borneo Literature Bureau (1963), 367–378.

27 For the reference on the role played by the church in bringing together these various sub-groups, see James Deegan, *Change among the Lun Bawang: a Borneo People.* [Ph.D. dissertation] University of Washington (1973), 284–286.

28 James Deegan. "Some Lun Bawang Spirit Chants," *Sarawak Museum Journal*, Vol. 18, No. 36–37 (1970), 264–281.

29 Peter Martin. "Linguistic Research in Brunei Darussalam: A Review." *Shifting Patterns of Language Use in Borneo*, edited by Peter Martin, The Borneo Research Council Proceeding Series, Williamsburg: Borneo Research Council (1994), 81–106.

30 Alison Hoare. *Cooking the Wild: The role of the Lundayeh of the Ulu Padas (Sabah, Malaysia) in managing forest foods and shaping the landscape.* [Ph.D. Dissertation]. University of Kent: Department of Anthropology (2002).

31 Valerie Mashman. "The Story of *Lun Tauh*, 'Our People': Narrating Identity on the Borders in the Kelabit Highlands." *Stories across Borders: Myths of Origin and Their Contestation in the Borderlands of South and Southeast Asia*, edited by Monica Janowski and Erika de Maaker, special issue, *Southeast Asian Studies*, Vol. 9, No. 2 (August 2020), 203–229.

32 Jay Crain and Vicki Pearson-Rounds. "A Fallen Bat, a Rainbow, and the Missing Head: Media and Marginalization in Upland Borneo," *Indonesia,* Vol. 79 (April 2005), 57–68. https://ecommons.cornell.edu/bitstream/handle/1813/54344/INDO_79_0_1115148085_57_68.pdf?sequence=1&isAllowed=y (Accessed on August 27, 2021)

33 From "Christian Gospel saved the Lun Bawang People," *Dayak Daily* (November 25, 2019). https://dayakdaily.com/christian-gospel-saved-the-lun-bawang-people/ (Accessed on August 27, 2021)

34 For a more comprehensive account of Lundayeh long house, see Jay Crain, "The Mengalong Lun Dayeh Long-House." *Sarawak Museum Journal*, Vol. 18 (1970): 169–185.

35 See Jay Crain, "The Mengalong Lun Dayeh Long-House." *Sarawak Museum Journal*, 18 (1970): 169–185.

36 For more information on this see Ricky Ganang et al., "Representation of Buayeh in the Quality of Life of the Lundayeh People." *Malaysian Journal of Social Sciences and Humanities*, Vol. 3 No. 2 (2018), 169–184.

37 See his latest publication in T.P. Yansen and Ricky Ganang. *Dayak Lundayeh Idi Lun Bawang: Budaya Serumpun di Dataran Tinggi Borneo.* Kalimantan: Penerbit Lembaga Literasi Dayak (2018), 166–173.

38 The funeral chant was recorded, transcribed, and translated into English by Ricky Ganang, a Lundayeh native.

39 See "Journeys in quest of cosmic power: Highland heroes in Borneo."

40 *Female and Male in Borneo: Contributions and Challenges to Gender Studies*, Virginia: The Borneo Research Council (1991).

41 This *benging* was recorded, transcribed, and translated by Frank Dawat Yusia, a Lun Bawang native, who is also the Graduate Research Assistant for this project.

42 See for example Meechang Tuie. *Masyarakat Lun Bawang Sarawak: Suatu Pengenalan*, Kuching: DBP (1995).

43 Information gathered during fieldwork in Long Pasia.

11

Woman is the Measure of All Things

Authoritarianism and Anti-Humanism in the Criticism of Anglo-Saxon Poetry

Michael Bryson

As Late Antiquity transitions into the Early Middle Ages, amid such works as Bede's *Historia Eccle-siastica Gentis Anglorum* (*Ecclesiastical History of the English People*) of 731, and the epic poem *Beowulf*, thought to have been completed sometime between 700 and 1000, a new (or renewed) spirit is appearing in European poetry. In a literary and scribal tradition dominated by what Miriam Muth calls "a consistent narrative that exemplifies the bond of loyalty between a warrior and his lord,"[1] there is an awakening of love poetry that looks back to the traditions of an earlier time, one in which Ovid was the model more than the Church or the Emperor. In this poetry, the value of human life, and the pressing nature of human concerns, are found not in the dictates and doctrines of the Church (or the demands and dogmas of the Empire), but in the private desires of the heart. In the discourse presented in this poetry, Man—or more accurately—*Woman* is the measure of all things, not God, the Church, or the Empire. Two poems in particular have survived, first collected in the Exeter Book (c. 960–990 CE), which each present an alternate view of life and the world—a view that "has little in common with the personal poetry of native tradition, the poetry of the scops," but one in which one might instead "look to classical antiquity for models."[2] In "The Wife's Lament" and "Wulf and Eadwacer," we have the "only two surviving Anglo-Saxon poems featuring a female speaker,"[3] works which Stanley Greenfield calls "poignant poems of love-longing," and crucially identifies as "the first of their kind in the secular literatures of western Europe."[4]

But like the Hebrew שיר השירים, *Shir ha-Shirim*, or the *Song of Songs*, a love poem that itself rose to full prominence in the days of a censorious Empire,[5] these stirringly passionate poems have been "rewritten" by censorious and imperious scholars and interpreters for so long that Greenfield's making of a simple observation about them being love poems has become a radical act. An authoritarian, anti-humanist (and even *anti-human*) tradition of reading these poems—much like that which surrounds the *Song of Songs*—has long insisted that the value of these poems lies not in their passionate words, but in the empty spaces between them, spaces that are then filled with the arid speculations of a style of criticism that itself seeks to be the measure of all things.[6] But before we spend time exploring why that is, and how that kind of anti-humanist reading of poetry works, let us look at the poems themselves:

The Wife's Lament

I sing this wretched song of my absolute sadness,
my journey into exile, that I might tell
what hardships I have dwelt in since I grew up,
new or old, never more than now.
Always I have suffered torments, miseries and wretchedness.

DOI: 10.4324/9781003046004-14

Michael Bryson

First my lord departed hence from his people
over the waves' destructive uproar; I could not sleep for fear
of where my lord might be on Earth.
Then I departed on my journey, to follow and seek to serve,
a friendless wandering exile, my poverty caused
by men who undertook to think and plan, my lord's own kin,
that he might separate us through secret counsel,
that we two might live far apart in this worldly realm,
where I live most horribly, grieving and longing
since my lord commanded me here to this hard dwelling.
I have few that are close in this place,
few loyal friends; therefore my heart was sad
when I found my equal, my companion
unhappy and miserable,
hiding his intentions, planning murder.

Happy in our outward manner, we very often boasted
that nothing could divide us except death alone,
nothing else—now all that is changed;
now that is as if it had never been...
Our love, our friendship ... I shall for now, and for long,
My dearly-beloved's feud endure.
He called me to remain in this forest grove,
under this oak-tree, in this earthen-hovel,
this ancient cave, in which I am tortured with longing.
The valleys are dark here, the mountains high,
the towns blasted by overgrown thorn-bushes,
joyless dwellings. Too often, I am cruelly afflicted here
because of the departure of my lord. Earthly friends,
do you live and love, occupy beds, or graves,
while I walk alone at dawn
under oak-trees, and through this earthen-hovel?
There must I sit the long summer day;
there must I weep and mourn my wretched exile,
my many hardships that will not ever let me
give rest to my sorrows and my griefs,
nor all the longing that afflicts me in this life.

Always may the young man be burdened, be sad at heart,
have hard and bitter thoughts in mind; likewise, if he shall have
happiness and cheer, let him also have sorrow and grief,
enormous and in multitudes. Keep him dependent on himself
for all his worldly joy, surrounded by foes, stained by enmity
in distant lands and by strange folk, since my lover sits
under rocky cliffs, surrounded by storms,
my despondent friend, floodwaters rising around him
in a dark and dreary house, where he endures and suffers
much heartfelt-sorrow, since he too often remembers
a more joyful dwelling. Woe shall be to all of us
who wait in longing for one we love.[7]

In "The Wife's Lament" (a title only affixed to the poem in the nineteenth century), readers have an enigmatic and passionate poem in which a woman[8] expresses anguish over her loss of a past life and love, over her current exile from all that she has loved and known, and describes herself as "eal ic eom oflongad," [tortured with longing]. As her "giedd wrecce" [song of wretchedness/exile] ends, she describes loving one who is no longer near as a kind of torment: "Woe shall be to all of us / who wait in longing for one we love." It seems to be a straightforwardly passionate poem dedicated to a female experience of loss and loneliness and desire.

Woman is the Measure of All Things

In a similar vein, the short poem "Wulf and Eadwacer" gives every appearance of being a poem of frustrated passion and longing, representing the voice of a woman whose lover is torn from her by military and tribal divisions, and the threat of war:

Wulf and Eadwacer

My people treat him like a sacrificial gift,
And they will devour him if he comes threatening war.
We are so different.
Wulf is on one island; I am on another.
His island is fortified, surrounded by fens.
This island is filled with slaughter-crazed men.
And they will devour him if he comes threatening war.
We are so different.
Wulf tracks my hopes like a bloodhound,
When I sit, crying, in the rain
He clasps me within his warrior's arms,
Such joy to be held, such pain to be let go.
Wulf! My Wulf! Pining for you
Makes me sick; your rare visits
Have starved me more than lack of meat.
Do you hear, Eadwacer? Our poor whelp,
Take, Wulf, to the woods.
That man easily tears what was never made one:
Our song together.[9]

In this poem, a woman cries out in desperation over her longing for a man with whom she can never settle down and establish anything like a life of comfortable and daily routine. Her passion is for a man separated from her, different from her, and that passion makes both her *and* him different—outcasts, in a sense, within their respective peoples: *ungelice is us*. Their song, never given a chance to be made one, will be (and in fact, already is) torn to pieces by the jealousies and hatreds of others. That poor whelp, which serves as a figure for their love,[10] will die in the woods, in the exile the poem describes in both physical and emotional terms. The speaker's "desire for Wulf," as Marilynn Desmond has argued, is "a desire not sanctioned by the social or legal structures of her culture, [and it] makes her an exile, an exile from herself as much as from her community."[11]

Despite the seeming clarity of their surfaces, however, much of the scholarship that surrounds these works (in a pattern of critical activity that has become all too familiar in recent decades[12]) very often dedicates itself to arguing away the passionate exclamations of love, desire, and longing each poem's female voice expresses. Desmond, with a certain arch yet deftly-targeted irony, presents the problem as one of "patriarchal sensibilities" and "phallic authority" exercised by "modern scholars and editors":

The Wife's Lament and Wulf and Eadwacer, as anonymous, female-voiced lyrics, have occasionally disturbed the patriarchal sensibilities of modern scholars and editors, who have reacted with appropriate phallic authority by emending the texts and producing elaborate allegorical readings, thus silencing the female speakers of these two poems and erasing women from Anglo-Saxon literary history. These critics characteristically support such textual appropriations by their assumptions, sometimes only implicitly expressed, that within the structures of Anglo-Saxon culture women were essentially mute.[13]

But rather than leave such women merely "essentially" mute, why not take the necessary steps to mute them entirely? For instance, David Clark, though he notes that the suggestion is "somewhat tongue-in-cheek," holds out the possibility that "[t]he speaker is a young man

175

[...] imprisoned on an island and socially ostracized for engaging in a sexual relationship with another man,"[14] before he goes on to argue for "one further possible interpretation [...] namely, that [Wulf and Eadwacer] is a poem about love between two men and by a male speaker, but that the love described is not conceived of as sexual," and goes on to warn against "heterosexist assumptions" in reading either poem.[15] Note how comfortably such a seemingly radical gesture as Clark's (with its warnings about "heterosexist assumptions") supports the very "patriarchal sensibilities" that Desmond decries. In Clark's reading, the very possibility of a female voice is simply erased. Such silencing of the inconvenient or oppositional voice, whose perspectives and passions will simply not fit the paradigm du jour, is all too often the basic working method of literary scholarship.

Stanley Greenfield illustrates the same problem in a slightly different way: in writing about the critical reception of "Wulf and Eadwacer," he argues against those who would minimize or even erase the idea of love in the poem. He specifically opposes the idea (expressed by Dolores Frese, who cites it from David Daiches) that the "'intense, romantic passion' of a sexually tormented woman is a theme which [...] is 'quite uncharacteristic of Anglo-Saxon poetry as it has come down to us.'"[16] He then goes on to oppose Marijane Osborne's notion (borrowed from C. S. Lewis—one borrows from another who, in turn, borrowed from another, and thus the same arguments tend to get made again and again) that

> romantic or sexual love was not the literary commonplace before the twelfth century that it has been since; other loves took precedence [...] Our cultural assumption is that if someone in literature is longing for someone else, it is likely to be a case of romantic or erotic love. But this is not an assumption that an earlier audience would share."[17]

The arguments that Greenfield opposes are frequently made in a number of different areas, though their structures are generally quite similar: the basic claim is for an unbridgeable gap between whatever *now* the critic writes from, and whatever *then* the critic writes about. We are assured, by the all-knowing critic, that our assumptions about the literature of any given *then* are misinformed; beyond that, we are commanded to disregard, lest we be accused of naivete, even our own emotional responses—for we are authoritatively informed that the emotions of *now* bear little or no resemblance to the emotions (if any) of the *then* in question. Once this point is ceded, the critic now controls the argument with the reader, who has been made properly compliant.

Perhaps the most prominent of such critics is Paul Zumthor, who insists that modern readers have no way of relating—*as* human beings—to texts written *by* human beings who lived, moved, and had their being in a different time and place: "A first obvious piece of evidence becomes clear to our eyes: the remoteness of the Middle Ages, and the irrecoverable distance separates us [...]. Medieval poetry belongs to a universe that has become foreign to us."[18] For Zumthor:

> When a man of our century confronts a work of the twelfth century, the time that separates one from the other distorts, or even erases the relationship that ordinarily develops between the author and the reader through the mediation of the text: such a relationship can hardly be spoken of anymore. What indeed is a true reading, if not an effort that involves both the reader and the culture in which the reader participates, an effort corresponding to that textual production involving the author and his own universe? In respect to a medieval text, the correspondence no longer occurs spontaneously. The perception of form becomes ambiguous. Metaphors are darkened, comparisons no longer make sense. The reader remains embedded within his own time; while the text, through an effect produced by the passage of time, seems timeless, which is a contradictory situation.[19]

Woman is the Measure of All Things

But this is tendentious at best, and always has been.[20] For example, Osborne's insistence that "romantic or sexual love was not [a] literary commonplace before the twelfth century"[21] will not hold up to even a cursory reading of Homer's treatment of Odysseus' longing for Penelope,[22] or Virgil's treatment of Dido's passion for Aeneas,[23] much less Musaeus' portrayal of Hero and Leander[24]—though some scholars, like Elaine Baruch, will dismiss much of this latter material by claiming that we can "discount the Greek romances [like *Hero and Leander*] as sources because their relationships are strictly physical, whereas romantic love glorifies the object spiritually as well as physically,"[25] thus revealing the fourteenth-century Petrarchan lenses through which she understands the entire concept of "romantic love." Note, especially, Baruch's use of the word *object* in her description of "romantic" love in poetry. By his time, Petrarch is on the receiving end of a two-century tradition of taking the female presence in poetry (as, for example, in the poetry of the Troubadour and Trobairitz poets of the 11th and 12th centuries) and transforming speaking and desiring *subjects* into spoken-of and desired *objects*. Italian poetry in this period (beginning with the early sonnets of Giacamo da Lentini like *Io m'aggio posto in core a Dio servire*, but especially evident in such works as Guido Guinizelli's *Al Cor Gentil* and Dante's *La Vita Nuova*) shifts its emphasis from a focus on the *here* to a focus on the *hereafter*. This is consistent with the kinds of anti-humanist discourse (found as far back as Plato in his attempted refutations of Protagoras in *Protagoras*, *Theaetetus*, and the *Laws*) that insists that the measure of all useful things (πάντων χρημάτων μέτρον) is not humanity (ἄνθρωπος), but is to be found in the forms, or the divine itself. In this pre-Petrarchan and then Petrarchan poetry, the female *object* is never an end in herself (and never considered as a subject with desires of her own), but is treated as a step toward heaven, and the love of God, for the male poetic voice.[26]

As Greenfield points out, the critics with whom he contends are very careful to avoid any mention of the passionate (and therefore inconvenient) "Wife's Lament" in their arguments: "Particularly noticeable in both Frese's and Osborn's essays is the almost complete absence of reference to 'The Wife's Lament,' the poem most similar to 'Wulf and Eadwacer.'"[27] Greenfield goes on to maintain that it is "ill-advised to discredit as un-Anglo-Saxon a passionate situation for reading either" poem.[28]

However, what Miriam Muth refers to as the "authoritarian approach"[29] to literary criticism, will not be overcome quite so easily as calling it "ill-advised." In her view, "The Wife's Lament" represents a challenge to the prevailing orthodoxies of Anglo-Saxon scholarship, and so "the large majority of criticism [...] has either ignored, refuted, or reframed [...] the poem" likely because it "depicts a first person speaker who addresses her emotional response directly to the reader rather than placing her experiences in a social, ancestral, or didactic context."[30] The rewriting of this poem by the majority of its critics goes to the extent of displaying a near-total refusal to take it as it appears, a refusal which includes

> an unwillingness on the part of modern critics to contemplate a female narrator in the Anglo-Saxon corpus. Along with the enigmatic poem *Wulf and Eadwacer*, the *Lament* is one of only two surviving Anglo-Saxon poems featuring a female speaker. In this context, the poem appears to represent a voice that was already marginalized in the speaker's own society: that of a female exile. Instead of drawing this voice back into the center of critical debate, however, critics such as Benjamin Thorpe, Rudolph Bambas, and Jerome Mandel have chosen to query the text and suggest instead that the unexpected female speaker is the result of scribal or editorial errors. This theory is based on the assumption that the use of feminine grammatical endings in the text is the result of scribal error, implying a surprisingly systematic failure of the scribal copying process. First suggested by early editor Thorpe in 1842, the theory remains surprisingly current.[31]

As with the "authoritarian approach" to readings of the *Song of Songs*, so also, it seems, goes the "authoritarian approach" to Anglo-Saxon poetry. If the text does not comply with the pre-existing requirements of the critic (whether theological or ideological), then it is simply *forced* to submit:

> Take, for example, the argument of Rudolph C. Bambas. Bambas explains that according to Anglo-Saxon poetic conventions "the only matters worth celebrating in verse are the affairs of heroic war chiefs."[32] Operating under this assumption, he concludes that a female speaker is therefore a practical impossibility. Given the fact that so few Anglo-Saxon texts survive, Bambas's claim must be based directly on those scant and randomly selected texts still extant, making any generalizing conclusions somewhat tautological. In essence, Bambas's line of argument is that because so few texts with female speakers have survived, such texts did not exist, meaning that those texts that do exist are not rare examples of [a] less common form, but the results of scribal error. According to this logic, any unusual textual forms at all would be subsumed into the form and genre of the majority, despite that majority itself being based on a very small sample of works.[33]

Bambas' argument was supported, although from a different angle, by Martin Stevens, who argued that "the attribution of [The Wife's Lament] to a woman speaker on grammatical grounds is at best doubtful."[34] Though these views were soon enough strongly opposed by other scholars (especially by Angela M. Lucas[35]), and are certainly not universally held today, [36] the "authoritarian" argument *against* reading the voice of the poem as female has not gone away, having been exhumed by Jerome Mandel, who argues that "it is not necessary to view the speaker as a woman."[37] It is not necessary, despite the poem's repeated use of feminine word forms, presumably because Mandel's and Bambas' and Stevens' desire to see their own face in the glass that is "The Wife's Lament" drives their readings of the poem (and one can only wonder at the form their Caliban-esque rage at *not* seeing their faces in that glass would take). As Muth puts it:

> the argument for a male speaker is so strained that it holds up an intriguing mirror to the masculinist face of twentieth century Anglo-Saxon scholarship, which goes to great lengths to portray the gender roles of the Anglo-Saxon world in its own image [as part of] a concerted effort to silence the tenth century speaker of the poem and to mold the multivalent text into hermeneutic unity.[38]

This phenomenon illustrates the core of the problem we confront when reading the works of those scholars, teachers, and critics charged with the eminently humanist task of the preservation, transmission, and interpretation of literary history and form: once committed to a particular point of view, all too many critics appear to be unable and/or unwilling to see in any other way (and the current author is not claiming immunity—this seems to be an inherent hazard of the profession). In this sense, *a way of seeing is also a way of not seeing*. The critic interprets the text, violently, if necessary, in such a way that it can be fit into the Procrustean bed of his or her established intellectual, ideological, and theological commitments. Even critics who *seem* to want to resist this kind of authoritarianism, end up making gestures of submission in their own writing. For example, Claire Lees *seems* to want to argue for a recovery and recognition of a female voice in "The Wife's Lament," but ends up affirming the primacy of the male individual instead, trapped by the very language and conventions of her own analytical frame:

> if we are to read the elegies as one place in the poetry where the internal psychological state of the individual matters, then it follows that in Anglo-Saxon England that individual is male,

Woman is the Measure of All Things

even when, or perhaps especially when, that voice is universalized. Pertinent examples are the warrior voice of *The Wanderer,* and the peculiarly literal and metaphoric voice of *The Seafarer.* Located in the intersection between gender and genre, the female voice of, for example, *The Wife's Lament* has to be accommodated within, or abjected from, the conventions of the male.[39]

Sometimes, the stretching and cutting of texts to fit the "bed" of the critic's interpretive frame involves wholly denying one of the text's defining features—and in the aforementioned case of Bambas, that means arguing that the "female" voice of the poem is a mistake, and that if we learn to read the poem correctly, we will, of course, hear the actually *male* voice of the poem's speaker. As Muth observes, "[g]iven the absence of any recognizable masculine perspective in the poem, the one interpretation that is directly at odds with the text is that which would deny the speaker to be a female voice,"[40] which is precisely the interpretation the critic, Bambas, provides. In other cases, all that is required is to bury the poem under an avalanche of specialized vocabulary (called "jargon" by reprobate readers). For example, it is possible, in a discussion of the poem's powerful emotional content, to speak of emotion entirely without anything that even begins to resemble human feeling. The quality of mercy may, or may not, be strained, but in such instances, the quality of literary criticism is quite nearly strained beyond all recognition:

> This text invites empathetic engagement from its audience through emotional contagion, made possible through the combination of imagery produced in the mind in the process of making sense, and the embodied emotional response produced automatically while entertaining a recognisably affecting scenario created during that act of interpretation. In this brief comment, weeping, anguish, and longing are all foregrounded, and grief is represented as active, encompassing, and time-consuming. The reader is required to call up not only narrative schema, but also emotional schema, created from memories, personal experience, and embodied feeling, to fill out the sketchy scenario, make sense of the sequence of ideas, and account for a potential cause for such extreme abandonment to the emotional life. In doing so, the reader enacts feeling, which is implicated in cognitive processing, and thereby becomes emotionally engaged in the narrative. Because we now know that cognition and affect are mutually reliant, it is possible to see how a reader can respond emotionally to culturally remote, poetically communicated fictional narrative, a process that occurs at both the specific and general levels.[41]

By the time artificial intelligence software is writing literary criticism, it may very well sound something like this. In writing about the poetry of love from the perspective of cognitive psychology, some of our critics manage to seem as if they are visiting from an alien world, and perhaps too much is lost in the journey. As Jacques Derrida, a famously non-cybernetic and recognizably terrestrial thinker, once observed: "framing so violently, cutting off the narrated figure's own fourth side so as to see only triangles, one evades, perhaps, a certain complication,"[42] in this case, the complication of human life, and any sense of poetry's relation thereto.

If the text speaks of red, but the critic is committed to blue, the critic will manage to find that all of the text's references to red are actually coded references to blue. If the critic is dedicated to the idea, for example, that all Anglo-Saxon texts reflect *male* experience, that critic will find a way to take a text that *appears* to describe *female* experience and demonstrate that it has actually been describing male experience all along, then go on to explain how misguided we had all been ever to have thought otherwise. The emperor may be as naked as the day he was born, but the critic will describe in fabulous detail the fabric, texture, colors, and cut of the garment he or she is committed to seeing. And this approach is hardly restricted to the Anglo-Saxon era, but is alive and well in the criticism written about the works of every literary period that follows.

179

Muth makes a trenchant observation that shines a bright light on much contemporary anti-humanist and even authoritarian literary criticism: "For the modern reader, the real mystery is what lies at the root of the many desperate attempts by modern critics to reinterpret the poem's content."[43] These desperate attempts to reinterpret the content of poetry, what Gerson Cohen describes as an attempt to control both poetry *and* the lives and emotions of those who read it, have been with us at least since the days of the early Church father Origen and the first- and second-century (CE) Rabbi Akiba, for whom the *Song of Songs* had to be "rewritten" by reading it allegorically, because "if love could not be ignored, it could be channeled, reformulated, and controlled."[44] In case there was any doubt about the connection between theological readings that insist texts be "rewritten" to fit an approved template of meaning, and modern, supposedly "secular" literary criticism, Muth helpfully dispels that doubt: "[a]nother popular interpretation of ['The Wife's Lament'] has been based on Christian allegory, presenting the speaker as the mournful Christian Church longing to be reunited with her beloved Christ."[45] Rabbis, priests, and literary critics—though this might sound like the setup for a joke, it is, instead, a list of those with shared interpretive principles and techniques who use those tools to circumscribe the available readings of poetry, ensuring (or at least enforcing) the orthodoxy of those readers who fall within the purview of their respective authorities. While discussing the critical attempt to channel, reformulate, and control readings of "The Wife's Lament," Muth observes: "Given the amount of critical smoke obfuscating this short, 53-line poem, it is valid and necessary to ask: who started the fire and why did they do it?" She then goes on to note that "[t]his line of questioning brings the critical response to the poem into sharp focus, offering a revealing history of repressive reception."[46]

The question that finally arises is the one first made famous by the Russian author Nikolay Chernyshevsky in his 1863 novel, Что делать? [*What is to be done?*] What can oppose this kind of repressive reading practice? Perhaps this might be of some use: the kind of humanist, *humane and human-centered*, literary criticism that many scholars have been calling for since Eve Sedgewick's own call for reparative reading, which she envisioned as teaching "the many ways in which selves and communities succeed in extracting sustenance from the objects of a culture—even a culture whose avowed desire has often been not to sustain them."[47] As Vera Pavlovna sings near the beginning of Chernyshevsky's novel, Просветимся—и обогатимся [*Let Us Enlighten and Enrich Ourselves*]. The kind of reparative practice through which we might enlighten and enrich ourselves would advocate for *un*channeled, *un*reformulated, and most definitely *un*controlled (by that literary clergy for whom control always seems most urgent) readings of poetic and other literary expressions of love. Unfortunately, however, in pursuit of such a practice, there will be, at every turn, critics whose professional purpose seems to be, as Muth puts it, to generate "critical smoke," and for whom love must be defined reductively as a "convention" or a "literary commonplace," a result of exposure to "emotional contagion" or in one especially egregious case, as "a citation" of the perceived experiences of others.[48] Those on the reparative path will encounter eminent scholars who describe individual poets as "sick," [49] and others who would—if only they could—*literally* rather than merely *interpretively* rewrite the poems and other literary productions upon which they expound.[50] But this, perhaps, is an understandable side-effect of what Noam Chomsky once called "the self-selection for obedience that is [...] part of elite education."[51] It reflects—both in what was transmitted *to* and what is transmitted *by* the critic, the goals that Fichte, the German Idealist philosopher, once described for *der neuen Erziehung* (the new education):

> If you would have power over a man, you have to do more than merely address him; you must shape him, and shape him so that he cannot want otherwise than you would have him want.[52]

Such anti-humanist critics as we encounter, and often argue against, often seem unable or unwilling to see poetry as anything other than a self-referential system of conventions, tropes, and signs,

Woman is the Measure of All Things

already dead on the page, irrelevant except for the urgent need felt by the critics to make sure that readers be trained to see as they see, and read as they read. *Obedience*, once self-selected, becomes the lens through which such critics read, and the pattern after which they would shape readers in their own image, so that they cannot want otherwise.

But along the way, perhaps we should remember the voice of the speaker of "The Wife's Lament," an unmistakably female voice

> that departs from the dutiful deference to God that shapes many other Anglo-Saxon poems, in order to show an altogether more vivid fragment of the brittle individuality forced upon someone excluded from […] communal life, both as a woman and as an exile.[53]

We should also remember the desire and frustration expressed by the equally-unmistakably female voice in "Wulf and Eadwacer," where we cannot readily tell what the precise relationship is between the speaker and Wulf, and the speaker and Eadwacer, which can be literally translated as Property-Watcher, or Goods-Watcher, a dreary if entirely likely euphemism for "husband." For those on the reparative path, Eadwacer is a familiar enough type. Shari Horner argues that Eadwacer "in effect prohibits [the speaker's] expression of joy; he is the guardian […] who tries to limit the possibility both of earthly love and of female creative expression,"[54] rather after the fashion of many critics of the poem itself.

The question, however, remains: is the speaker a married woman, involved in an affair with a warrior from another island? As Helene Scheck contends, if

> we take Wulf to be […] a lover with whom she began a relationship after her marriage, [much of the poem suggests] her pleasure and guilt in continuing the affair, a possibility that finds parallels in the stereotype of the adulterous woman as presented in Old English literature, but may also be a genuine expression of the ambivalence and instability of adulterous love.[55]

If we read the voice that cries "Wulf! My Wulf!" in this way, then her complaint—"Pining for you / Makes me sick; your rare visits / Have starved me more than lack of meat"—becomes what is perhaps the first sympathetic portrayal of "the adulterous woman […] in Old English literature," a positive presentation akin to that suggested by Audrey Meaney, who argues that the poem strongly emphasizes "that Wulf is unacceptable to [the speaker's] society, and that she herself offends society by loving him." And yet, here, a critic makes an all-too-rare life-and-love-affirming move, one that makes her analysis a sharp and vibrant contrast to much of the criticism that surrounds these elegies. As Meaney writes: "our sympathies are with her; and surely it is the Anglo-Saxon poet's recognition of the fact that powerful passion will not be constrained by the normal bonds of society that gives this poem its universal appeal."[56]

Life and love and longing are here, and they are real, despite the best efforts of societal law-givers and law-enforcers, and "the many desperate attempts"[57] of the critical re-writers and re-interpreters of poetry past and present. But as small a sample of these passions as we see in the *frauenlieder*, or female laments, of two Anglo-Saxon poems, they plant the seeds for traditions that follow, especially for the eleventh- and twelfth-century poetry of a group of Occitanian singers and poets we have long since learned to call the Troubadours.[58] From that combined Arabic, Spanish, and Occitanian root[59] springs the flowering orchard of so much of later poetry, from the German Minnesingers, to the Italian poets of the *dolce stil novo* (culminating in the works of Dante and Petrarch), to Shakespeare, the Romantics, the Wildean aesthetes, and the powerful works of modern authors like the Chilean poet Pablo Neruda[60] and the Syrian poet Nizār Qabbanī.[61] But even as we have seen poetry thrive, expressing that "powerful passion [that] will not be constrained by the normal bonds of society," so we have also seen—from the days of Origen and Akiba until now—the anti-humanist attempts to channel, reformulate, and control it grow stronger, more systematic, and infinitely more destructive.[62] It is this systematic destruction, this ancient and ongoing attempt to control the minds and hearts of others, that a reformulated and more truly universal humanism should, and must, stand against.

Such a reformulated humanism is what Edward Said defined, late in his career, as that which "must think of itself as life-enhancing and constitutively opposed to every form of tyranny, domination, and abuse; its social goals are noncoercive knowledge produced in the interests of human freedom."[63] Poetry is only a small part of that necessary struggle, but it is the battleground that contains all others—for it represents, as Plato feared, all of life in its blend of passions, failings, and (as Goethe describes it), eternal striving: *Es irrt der Mensch, solang er strebt*[64] [Man makes mistakes as long as he strives]. Such mistakes, and such relentless striving to overcome them have characterized the always-imperfect humanist project since Protagoras, and that unyielding human spirit will, one hopes, continue to oppose tyranny, domination, and abuse long into the future.

Bibliography

Bambas, Rudolph C. "Another View of the Old English Wife's Lament." *Journal of English and Germanic Philology* 62 (1963): 303–309.

Baruch, Elaine. *Women, Love, and Power: Literary and Psychoanalytic Perspectives*. New York: NYU Press, 1991.

Baugh, Albert C. and Kemp Malone. *The Literary History of England: Vol 1: The Middle Ages (to 1500)*. London: Routledge, 1967.

Belanoff, Patricia A. "Women's Songs, Women's Language: Wulf and Eadwacer and The Wife's Lament." *New Readings on Women in Old English Literature*. Edited by Helen Damico and Alexandra Hennessey Olsen. Bloomington: Indiana University Press, 1990, 193–203.

Bolton, W. F. "The Wife's Lament and the Husband's Message: A Reconsideration Revisited," *Archiv* 205 (1968), 337–351.

Bryson, Michael, and Arpi Movsesian. *Love and its Critics: From the Song of Songs to Shakespeare and Milton's Eden*. Cambridge: Open Book Publishers, 2017.

Burckhardt, Jacob. *Die Cultur der Renaissance in Italien: Ein Versuch*. Basel: Schweighauser, 1860.

Buturovic, Amila. "'Only Women and Writing Can Save Us From Death': Erotic Empowering in the Poetry of Nizār Qābbanī." *Tradition, Modernity, and Postmodernity in Arabic Literature: Essays in Honor of Professor Issa J. Boullata*. Edited by Kamal Abdel-Malek and Wael Hallaq. Leiden: Brill, 2000, 141–157.

Chomsky, Noam. *LBBS, Z-Magazine's Left On-Line Bulletin Board*. Online discussion posted at rec.arts. books, November 13, 1995 03:21:23. http://bactra.org/chomsky-on-postmodernism.html

Clark, David. *Between Medieval Men: Male Friendship and Desire in Early Medieval English Literature*. Oxford: Oxford University Press, 2009.

Cohen, Gerson D. "The Song of Songs and the Jewish Religious Mentality." *Studies in the Variety of Rabbinic Cultures*. Philadelphia: Jewish Publication Society, 1991, 3–17.

De Graef, Ortwin. "Silence to be Observed: A Trial for Paul de Man's Inexcusable Confessions." *(Dis)continuities: Essays on Paul de Man*. Edited by Luc Herman, Kris Humbeeck, and Geert Lernout. Amsterdam: Rodopi, 1989, 51–73.

De Man, Paul. *Allegories of Reading: Figural Language in Rousseau, Nietzsche, Rilke, and Proust*. New Haven: Yale University Press, 1979.

Derrida, Jacques. "Le Facteur de La Vérité," *Poetique*, 21 (1973): 96–147.

Derrida, Jacques. "Typewriter Ribbon: Limited Ink (2) ('within such limits')." In *Material Events: Paul de Man and the Afterlife of Theory*, translated by Peggy Kamuf, edited by Tom Cohen, Barbara Cohen, J. Hillis Miller, and Andrzej Warminski. Minneapolis: University of Minnesota Press, 2001, 277–360.

Desmond, Marilynn. "The Voice of Exile: Feminist Literary History and the Anonymous Anglo-Saxon Elegy." *Critical Inquiry* 16 (Spring 1990), 572–290.

Elliger, Karl, and Willhelm Rudolph. *Biblia Hebraica Stuttgartensia*. Stuttgart: Deutsche Bibelgesellschaft, 1983.

Epstein, Isidore, ed. *Tractate Sanhedrin*. In *Hebrew English Edition of the Babylonian Talmud*, Vol. 19. London: Socino Press, 1969.

Felski, Rita. *The Limits of Critique*. Chicago: University of Chicago Press, 2015.

Fichte, Johann Gottlieb. *Johann Gottlieb Fichte: Fichtes Reden an die Deutsche Nation*. Edited by Samantha Nietz. Hamburg: Severus, 2013.

Fish, Stanley. "Masculine Persuasive Force: Donne and Verbal Power." In *Soliciting Interpretation: Literary Theory and Seventeenth-Century English Poetry*. Edited by Elizabeth D. Harvey and Katharine Eisaman Maus. Chicago: University of Chicago Press, 1990, 223–252.

Goethe, Johann Wolfgang Von. *Faust*. Munich: Wilhelm Goldman Verlag, 1978.

Greenfield, Stanley B. "Wulf and Eadwacer: All Passion Pent." Edited by Peter Clemoes, Simon Keynes, and Michael Lapidge. *Anglo-Saxon England* 15 (1986): 5–14.

Harbus, Antonina. "Affective Poetics: The Cognitive Basis of Emotion in Old English Poetry." In *Anglo Saxon Emotions: Reading the Heart in Old English Language, Literature and Culture*. Edited by Alice Jorgensen, Frances McCormack, and Jonathan Wilcox. Farnham: Ashgate, 2015, 19–34.

Homer. *Odyssey*, 5.210. Volume I, Books 1–12. Edited by A.T. Murray. Cambridge: Loeb Classical Library, Harvard University Press, 1919.

Horner, Shari. *The Discourse of Enclosure: Representing Women in Old English Literature*. Albany: State University of New York Press, 2001.

Lees, Clare A. "At a Crossroads: Old English and Feminist Criticism." In *Reading Old English Texts*. Edited by Katherine O'Brien O' Keeffe, 146–169. Cambridge: Cambridge University Press, 1997.

Lésper, Avelina. *El fraude del arte contemporáneo*. Bogotá: Libros Malpensante, 2015.

Lucas, Angela M. "The Narrator of The Wife's Lament Reconsidered." *Neuphilologische Mitteilungen* 70 (June 1969): 282–297.

Mackie, W.S., ed. *The Exeter Book, Part II*. London: Oxford University Press, 1934.

Mandel, Jerome. *Alternative Readings in Old English Poetry*. New York: Peter Lang, 1987.

Meaney, Audrey L. "The Ides of the Cotton Gnomic Poem." *Medium Ævum* 48, no. 1 (1979): 23–39.

Menocal, Maria Rosa. *The Arabic Role in Medieval Literary History: A Forgotten Heritage*. Philadelphia: University of Pennsylvania Press, 2010.

Musaeus. *Hero and Leander*. Edited by Thomas Gelzer. Cambridge: Loeb Classical Library, Harvard University Press, 1973.

Muth, Miriam. "Delete as Appropriate: Writing Between the Lines of Female Orality in The Wife's Lament." In *Women and Language: Essays on Gendered Communication across Media*, edited by Melissa Ames and Sarah Himsel Burcon. Jefferson: McFarland & Co., 2011, 61–74.

Neruda, Pablo. *Veinte Poemas de Amor y una Canción Desesperada*. Bogotá, Barcelona: Editorial Norma, 2002.

Origen. *Commentaire sur le Cantique des Cantiques. Vol 1. Texte de la Version Latine de Rufin*. Edited by Luc Bresard, Henri Crouzel, and Marcel Borret. Paris: Éditions du Cerf, 1991.

Osborne, Marijane. "The Text and Context of Wulf and Eadwacer." *The Old English Elegies: New Essays in Criticism and Research*. Edited by Martin Green. Madison: Fairleigh Dickinson University Press, 1983, 174–189.

Parvini, Neema. "Rejecting Progress in the Name of 'Cultural Appropriation.'" *Quillette*, August 22, 2018. http://quillette.com/2018/08/22/rejecting-progress-in-the-name-of-cultural-appropriation/ [accessed September 8, 2021].

Redfield, Marc. "Mistake in Paul de Man: Violent Reading and Theotropic Violence." In *The Political Archive of Paul de Man: Property, Sovereignty and the Theotropic*. Edited by Martin McQuillan. Edinburgh: Edinburgh University Press, 2012, 103–117.

Rousseau, Jacques. *Les Confessions*, Vol. 1. Lausaunne: Francois Grasset, 1782.

Said, Edward. *The World, the Text, and the Critic*. Cambridge: Harvard University Press, 1983.

Scheck, Helene. "Seductive Voices: Rethinking Female Subjectivities in The Wife's Lament and Wulf and Eadwacer." *Literature Compass* 5, no. 2 (2008): 220–227.

Sedgewick, Eve. *Touching Feeling: Affect, Pedagogy, Performativity*. Durham and London: Duke University Press, 2003.

Spivak, Gayatri Chakravorty. "Righting Wrongs." *The South Atlantic Quarterly*, Volume 103, Number 2/3 (Spring/Summer 2004), 523–581.

Stevens, Martin. "The Narrator of The Wife's Lament." *Neuphilologische Mitteilungen* 69 (1968): 72–90.

Stone, Gregory B. *The Death of the Troubadour: The Late Medieval Resistance to the Renaissance*. Philadelphia: University of Pennsylvania Press, 1994.

Swanton, M. J. "The Wife's Lament and The Husband's Message: A Reconsideration," *Anglia* 82, (1964), 269–290.

Tolstoy, Leo. *Что такое искусство?* [*What is Art?*], Л. Н. Толстой [L.N. Tolstoy], Собрание сочинений в 22 томах [Complete Works in 22 volumes]. *Russian Virtual Library*. Vol. 15. https://rvb.ru/tolstoy/01text/vol_15/01text/0327.htm [accessed September 8, 2021].

Michael Bryson

Trotsky, Leon. *Литература и революция* [*Literature and Revolution*]. Moscow: Политиздат [Politizdat], 1991.

Virgil. *The Aeneid*. In *Virgil*, 2 vols. Edited by H. Rushton Fairclough. Cambridge: Loeb Classical Library, Harvard University Press, 1960.

Notes

1 Miriam Muth. "Delete as Appropriate: Writing Between the Lines of Female Orality in The Wife's Lament." *Women and Language: Essays on Gendered Communication across Media*. Edited by Melissa Ames and Sarah Himsel Burcon (Jefferson: McFarland & Co., 2011), 66.

2 Albert C. Baugh and Kemp Malone. *The Literary History of England: Vol 1: The Middle Ages (to 1500)* (London: Routledge, 1967), 91.

3 Muth. 64.

4 Stanley B. Greenfield. "'Wulf and Eadwacer': All Passion Pent." *Anglo-Saxon England*, Volume 15. Edited by Peter Clemoes, Simon Keynes, and Michael Lapidge (Cambridge: Cambridge University Press, 1986), 14.

5 Caesar Augustus sought, through legislation, to control the sexual mores and behaviors of his people. The *Lex Iulia de Maritandis Ordinibus* of 18 BCE restricted marriage between the social classes, and the *Lex Iulia de Adulteriis Coercendis* of the same year made adultery punishable by banishment. By the end of the first century CE, the *Song of Songs*, which had long been enjoyed as a *secular* love song, was redefined at the Council of Jamnia as an allegory of the love between Yahweh and his people, and thus rendered "safe" for inclusion into the developing Hebrew canon. See Michael Bryson and Arpi Movsesian. *Love and its Critics: From the Song of Songs to Shakespeare and Milton's Eden* (Cambridge: Open Book Publishers, 2017).

6 Two brief examples of this kind of censorious rewriting (drawn from the treatments of the *Song of Songs*) will suffice here to illustrate both the strenuous lengths to which such critics will go, and the antiquity of this critical tradition. Before looking at Origen's strained interpretation, let's look directly at the opening words of the young woman's song at 1:2. (All translations in this chapter are my own, and the Hebrew Biblical text is quoted here from *Biblia Hebraica Stuttgartensia*. Edited by Karl Elliger and Willhelm Rudolph (Stuttgart: Deutsche Bibelgesellschaft, 1983).):

> יִשָּׁקֵנִי מִנְּשִׁיקוֹת פִּיהוּ כִּי- טוֹבִים דֹּדֶיךָ מִיָּיִן׃
>
> [Let him kiss me with the kisses of his mouth: for your loving is better than wine.]

For Origen, this is far too direct, erotic, and physical. So, in his hands, this is transformed into an allegory for the relationship between Christ (the Bridegroom) and the Church or the individual believer (the Bride):

> propter hoc ad te Patrem sponsi mei precem fundo et obsecro, ut tandem miseratus amorem meum mittas eum, ut iam non mihi per ministros suos angelos dumtaxat et prophetas loquatur, sed ipse per semet ipsum veniat et osculetur me ab osculis oris sui, verba scilicet in os meum sui oris infundat, ipsum audiam loquentem, ipsum videam docentem. Haec enim sunt Christi oscula quae porrexit ecclesiae, cum in adventu suo ipse praesens in carne positus locutus est ei verba fidei et caritas et pacis"
>
> (Origen. *Commentaire sur le Cantique des Cantiques. Vol 1. Texte de la Version Latine de Rufin*. Edited by Luc Bresard, Henri Crouzel, and Marcel Borret (Paris: Éditions du Cerf, 1991), 180)
>
> [For this reason I beg you, Father of my spouse, pouring out this prayer that you will have pity for the sake of my love for him, so that not only will the angels and the prophets speak to me through his ministers, but that he will come, and "let him kiss me with the kisses of his mouth" by his own self, that is, to pour his words into my mouth with his breath, that I might hear him speak, and see him teach. For these are the kisses of Christ, who offered them to the Church when at his coming, he made himself present in the flesh, and spoke the words of faith and love and peace.]

For later Hebrew readers of the *Song of Songs*, such as the writers and compilers of the *Babylonian Talmud*, the sensuality therein posed a similar dilemma, which they solved in a similar way, by interpreting various sensual/erotic details as references to the Sanhedrin, the judicial body appointed in each Israelite city:

> שררך אגן הסהר אל יחסר המזג וגו' שררך – זו סנהדרי [...] בטנך ערימת חטים מה ערימת חטים הכל נהנין ממנה אף סנהדרין הכל נהנין מטעמיהן
>
> ("Tractate Sanhedrin." *Hebrew English Edition of the Babylonian Talmud*. Edited by Rabbi Isidore Epstein (London: Socino Press, 1969), 37a))

Woman is the Measure of All Things

[Your navel is like a round goblet which lacks no wine: that navel—that is the Sanhedrin [...] Your belly is like a heap of wheat [*Song of Songs* 7:2]: even as we profit from wheat, so also we profit from the Sanhedrin's reasonings.]

For a more in-depth discussion of this tradition of critical rewriting of the *Song of Songs*, see Michael Bryson and Arpi Movsesian, *Love and its Critics* (Cambridge: Open Book Publishers, 2017), 37–57.

7 Ic þis giedd wrece bi me ful geomorre,
minre sylfre sð. ic þæt secgan mæg
hwæt ic yrmþa gebad, siþþan ic up weox,
niwes oþþe ealdes, no ma þonne nu.
A ic wite wonn minra wræcsiþa.
ærest min hlaford gewat heonan of leodum
ofer yþa gelac; hæfde ic uhtceare
hwær min leodfruma londes wære.
ða ic me feran gewat folgað secan,
wineleas wræcca for minre weaþearfe.
ongunnon þæt þæs monnes magas hycgan
þurh dyrne geþoht þæt hy todælden unc,
þæt wit gewidost in woruldrice
lifdon laðlicost; ond mec longade.
het mec hlaford min her heard niman;
ahte ic leofra lyt on þissum londstede,
holdra freonda; forþon is min hyge geomor.
ða ic me ful gemæcne monnan funde,
heardsæligne, hygegomorne,
mod miþendne, morþor hycgendne,

bliþe gebæro. ful oft wit beotedan
þæt unc ne gedælde nemne deað ana,
owiht elles; eft is þæt onhworfen,
is nu swa hit no wære
freondscipe uncer. sceal ic feor ge neah
mines felalcofan fæhðu dreogan.
Heht mec mon wunian on wuda bearwe,
under actreo in þam eorðscræfe.
eald is þes eorðsele, eal ic eom oflongad;
sindon dena dimme, duna uphea,
bitre burgtunas brerum beweaxne,
wic wynna leas ful oft mec her wraþe begeat
fromsiþ frean. frynd sind on eorþan,
leofe lifgende, leger weardiað,
þonne ic on uhtan ana gonge
under actreo geond þas eorðscrafu.
Þær ic sittan mot sumorlangne dæg,
þær ic wepan mæg mine wræcsiþas,
earfoþa fela; forþon ic æfre ne mæg
þære modceare minre gerestan
ne ealles þæs longaþes þe mec on þissum life begeat.

a scyle geong mon wesan geomormod,
heard heortan geþoht; swylce habban sceal
bliþe gebaro eac þon breostceare,
sinsorgna gedreag; sy æt him sylfum gelong
eal his worulde wyn. sy ful wide fh
feorres folclondes þæt min freond siteð
under stanhliþe storme behrimed,
wine werigmod, wætre beflowen
on dreorsele, drogeð se min wine
micle modceare; he gemon to oft

Michael Bryson

> wynlicran wic. wa bið þam þe sceal
> of langoþe leofes abidan.

("The Wife's Lament." *The Exeter Book*, Part II. Edited by W. S. Mackie
(London: Oxford University Press, 1934), 152, 154.)

8 As Muth remarks, "the speaker's use of female adjectival and pronomial endings in phrases of self-description [...] leaves no doubt that she is a woman" (Muth, 64).

9
> Leodum is minum swylce him mon lac gife;
> willað hy hine aþecgan gif he on þreat cymeð.
> ungelic is us.
> wulf is on iege ic on oþerre.
> fæst is þæt eglond fenne biworpen
> sindon wælreowe weras þær on ige;
> willað hy hine aþecgan gif he on þreat cymeð
> ungelice is us.
> wulfes ic mines widlastum wenum hogode;
> þonne hit wæs renig weder ond ic reotugu sæt.
> þonne mec se beaducafa bogum bilegde,
> wæs me wyn to þon, wæs me hwæþre eac lað.
> wulf min wulf wena me þine
> seoce gedydon þine seldcymas
> murnende mod nales meteliste
> gehyrest þu, eadwacer uncerne earne hwelp
> bireð wulf to wuda
> þæt mon eaþe tosliteð þætte næfre gesomnad wæs
> uncer giedd geador.

("Wulf and Eadwacer." *The Exeter Book*, Part II. Edited by W.S. Mackie
(London: Oxford University Press, 1934), 86.)

10 Greenfield, 12–13.

11 Marilynn Desmond. "The Voice of Exile: Feminist Literary History and the Anonymous Anglo-Saxon Elegy." *Critical Inquiry* 16. Spring 1990, 587.

12 For an in-depth discussion of this pattern, based in what Paul Ricoeur has called the hermeneutics of suspicion (*les herméneutiques du soupçon*), see Bryson and Movsesian, *Love and its Critics*, 10–22. See also Rita Felski, *The Limits of Critique* (Chicago: University of Chicago Press, 2015).

13 Desmond, 574.

14 David Clark. *Between Medieval Men: Male Friendship and Desire in Early Medieval English Literature* (Oxford: Oxford University Press, 2009), 30.

15 Ibid., 31.

16 Greenfield, 7.

17 Ibid.

18 "Une première évidence éclate aux yeux: l'éloignement du moyen âge, la distance irrécupérable qui nous en sépare [...] la poésie médiévale relève d'un univers qui nous est devenu étranger" (Paul Zumthor. *Essai de Poétique Médiévale* (Paris: Éditions du Seuil, 1972), 19).

19 "Lorsqu'un homme de notre siècle affronte une œuvre du XIIe siècle, la durée qui les sépare l'un de l'autre dénature jusqu'à l'effacer la relation qui, ordinairement, s'établit entre l'auteur et le lecteur par la médiation du texte: c'est à peine si l'on peut parler encore de relation. Qu'est-ce en effet qu'un lecture vraie, sinon un travail où se trouvent à la fois impliqués le lecteur et la culture à laquelle il participe? Travail correspondant à celui qui produsuit le texte et où furent impliqués le auteur et son propre univers. A l'égard d'un texte médiéval, la correspndance ne se produit plus spontanément. La perception même de la forme devient équivoque. Les métaphores s'obscurcissent, le comparant s'écarte du comparé. Le lecteur reste engagé dans son temps; le texte, par un effet tenant à l'accumulation des durées intermédiaires, apparaît comme hors du temps, ce qui est une situation contradictoire" (Ibid., 20).

20 The source of this argument is the now-infamous thesis of Jacob Burckhardt, who argues that we cannot understand people who lived in the Middle Ages because they understood themselves in a way that is unfamiliar to us today, not as individuals who may be part of a whole, but *strictly as pieces of that larger whole*:
> Im Mittelalter lagen die beiden Seiten des Bewußtseins—nach der Welt hin und nach dem Innern des Menschen selbst—wie unter einem gemeinsamen Schleier träumend oder halbwach. Der Schleier war gewoben aus Glauben, Kindesbefangenheit und Wahn; durch ihn hindurch gesehen erschienen

Woman is the Measure of All Things

Welt und Geschichte wundersam gefärbt, der Mensch aber erkannte sich nur als Race, Volk, Partei, Corporation. Familie oder sonst in irgend einer Form des Allgemeinen.

[In the Middle Ages the two sides of consciousness—that turned toward the world and that turned toward the inner self of man—were dreaming or half awake under a common veil. The veil was woven of faith, childish partiality, and delusion, through which the world and its history appeared in miraculous hues, but Man recognized himself only as a race, a people, a party, a corporation, a family, or otherwise in any general or common form.]

(Jacob Burckhardt. Die Cultur der Renaissance in Italien: Ein Versuch
[The Culture of the Renaissance in Italy: An Essay]
(Basel: Schweighauser, 1860), 131.)

One wonders, perhaps, at how Peter Abelard and Heloise D'Argenteuil would have reacted to being described in such a way, much less such figures as Guilhem de Poitou, Bertran de Born, or Dante Alighieri (or the Francesca de Rimini the latter poet so famously describes in his *Inferno*). Though it has not always gone by the same name, the anti-humanist (even *anti-human*) trend in scholarship has deep roots.

21 Marijane Osborne. "The Text and Context of Wulf and Eadwacer." *The Old English Elegies: New Essays in Criticism and Research*. Edited by Martin B. Green (Madison: Farleigh Dickinson University Press, 1983), 183–184.

22 Odysseus, when offered immortality by Calypso, can think only of return to Penelope, whom the goddess describes as "σὴν ἄλοχον, τῆς τ' αἰὲν ἐέλδεαι ἤματα πάντα" [Your wife, she that you ever long for daily, in every way.] Homer. *Odyssey*, 5.210. Volume I, Books 1–12. Edited by A.T. Murray (Cambridge: Loeb Classical Library, Harvard University Press, 1919). Their reunion in the *Odyssey* is among the most romantic stories ever told in any language anywhere, and the poem is not shy about narrating the passionate and sexual element of that reunited love.

23 Dido *begs* Aeneas (her *romantic and sexual* lover) not to leave her:

mene fugis? per ego has lacrimas dextramque tuam te
(quando aliud mihi iam miserae nihil ipsa reliqui),
per conubia nostra, per inceptos hymenaeos,
si bene quid de te merui, fuit aut tibi quicquam
dulce meum, miserere domus labentis et istam,
oro, si quis adhuc precibus locus, exue mentem

(*The Aeneid*. 4.314–19. In *Virgil*, 2 vols. Edited by H. Rushton Fairclough.
Loeb Classical Library (Cambridge: Harvard University Press, 1960))

You're running from me? By these tears and by your hand,
(since there is nothing else for my miserable self),
through our marriage, by the way our wedding took place,
if I have deserved well of you, or if there was anything
sweet about me, have mercy on a falling house, and yet,
I pray you, if there is room for prayers, change your mind.

24 Hero, on learning of the death of Leander (her *romantic and sexual* lover), commits suicide:

ῥοιζηδὸν προκάρηνος ἀπ᾽ ἠλιβάτου πέσε πύργου.
κὰδ δ᾽ Ἡρὼ τέθνηκε σὺν ὀλλυμένῳ παρακοίτῃ,
ἀλλήλων δ᾽ ἀπόναντο καὶ ἐν πυμάτῳ περ ὀλέθρῳ

(Musaeus. *Hero and Leander*. Edited by Thomas Gelzer
(Cambridge: Loeb Classical Library, Harvard University
Press, 1973), ll.341–43)

with a rushing sound, she fell head-first from her high tower.
Hero died next to her dead husband,
and at last in death, each had joy in the other.

25 Elaine Baruch. *Women, Love, and Power: Literary and Psychoanalytic Perspectives* (New York: NYU Press, 1991), 27.

26 For a full discussion of the transition in poetry from the early Sicilian poets, through the *dolce stil novo* school, to Dante and Petrarch, see Bryson and Movsesian, *Love and its Critics*, 300–330.

27 Greenfield, 8.

28 Ibid., 9.

29 Muth, 62.

30 Ibid.

Michael Bryson

31 Ibid., 64.

32 Rudolph C. Bambas, "Another View of the Old English Wife's Lament." *Journal of English and Germanic Philology* 62 (1963): 303.

33 Muth, 65.

34 Martin Stevens. "The Narrator of The Wife's Lament," *Neuphilologische Mitteilungen* 69. (March 1968), 73.

35 Angela M. Lucas. "The Narrator of The Wife's Lament Reconsidered." *Neuphilologische Mitteilungen* 70 (June 1969): 282–297. For Lucas, "the interpretation which maintains that the narrator is a woman need not hinge entirely on the [feminine] grammar of the first two lines, and there are undercurrents of tone and emphasis in the poem which lead one towards understanding it as the lament of a woman separated from the man she loves" (282).

36 As Shari Horner argues, "most critics now agree that the speaker is a woman" (*The Discourse of Enclosure: Representing Women in Old English Literature* (Albany: State University of New York Press, 2001), 49), and "[r]ecent feminist studies of the elegy have […] put to rest earlier theories that the speaker is male" (62, n. 57). Along similar lines, Patricia A. Belanoff notes that "Kemp Malone [has] argued that our two Old English poems were the Germanic representatives of an international genre of women's songs designated by their German name, *frauenlieder*" ("Women's Songs, Women's Language: Wulf and Eadwacer and The Wife's Lament." *New Readings on Women in Old English Literature*. Edited by Helen Damico and Alexandra Hennessey Olsen (Bloomington: Indiana University Press, 1990), 193), and argues, based on the work of Cixous, Irigiray, and Kristeva, that "the language of the *Wife's Lament* and *Wulf and Eadwacer* […] is different because the poem's are women's songs, a genre which inevitably entails a differentness of language" (194).

37 Jerome Mandel. *Alternative Readings in Old English Poetry* (New York: Peter Lang, 1987), 154.

38 Muth, 73.

39 Clare A. Lees. "At a Crossroads: Old English and Feminist Criticism." In *Reading Old English Texts*. Edited by Katherine O'Brien O'Keeffe (Cambridge: Cambridge University Press, 1997), 157.

40 Muth, 72–73.

41 Antonina Harbus. "Affective Poetics: The Cognitive Basis of Emotion in Old English Poetry." In *Anglo Saxon Emotions: Reading the Heart in Old English Language, Literature and Culture*. Edited by Alice Jorgensen, Frances McCormack, and Jonathan Wilcox (Farnham: Ashgate, 2015), 30.

42 "[E]n cadrant aussi violemment, en coupant la figure narrée elle-même d'un quatrième côté pour n'y voir que des triangles, on élude peut-être une certaine complication" Jacques Derrida, "Le Facteur de La Vérité." *Poetique* 21 (1975), 108.

43 Muth, 68.

44 Gerson Cohen. "The Song of Songs and the Jewish Religious Mentality," *Studies in the Variety of Rabbinic Cultures* (Philadelphia: The Jewish Publication Society, 1991), 14.

45 Muth, 64. On the idea of reading "The Wife's Lament" as Christian allegory, see M. J. Swanton, "The Wife's Lament and The Husband's Message: A Reconsideration," *Anglia* 82 (1964), 269–290; W. F. Bolton, "The Wife's Lament and the Husband's Message: A Reconsideration Revisited," *Archiv* 205 (1968), 337–351.

46 Ibid., 68–69.

47 Eve Sedgewick. *Touching Feeling: Affect, Pedagogy, Performativity* (Durham and London: Duke University Press, 2003), 150–151.

48 Citing Jonathan Culler's work *On Deconstruction* as his authority, Stone delivers what he fancies is the death blow to the idea of love in poetry: "Saying 'I love you,' that is, is always a convention, a citation; it does not so much distinguish an individual as it makes him resemble everyone else." Gregory B. Stone. *The Death of the Troubadour: The Late Medieval Resistance to the Renaissance* (Philadelphia: University of Pennsylvania Press, 1994), 7–8.

49 Stanley Fish is on record as regarding the English poet John Donne's work as "sick," and the poet himself as equally "sick," someone who can be read only through "the pleasures of diagnosis." Stanley Fish. "Masculine Persuasive Force: Donne and Verbal Power." In *Soliciting Interpretation: Literary Theory and Seventeenth-Century English Poetry*. Edited by Elizabeth D. Harvey and Katharine Eisaman Maus (Chicago: University of Chicago Press, 1990), 223.

50 Easily the most famous example of this is Paul de Man, who in his work *Allegories of Reading* (1979), rewrote (by the simple insertion of *ne*) a passage from Rousseau's *Confessions*. As first pointed out by Ortwin de Graef, de Man "adds a negation to Rousseau's sentence, as if this did not make a difference, as if one was entitled to do so on the basis of the main clause" ("Silence to be Observed: A Trial for Paul de Man's Inexcusable Confessions." In *(Dis)continuities: Essays on Paul de Man*. Edited by Luc Herman, Kris Humbeeck, and Geert Lernout (Amsterdam: Rodopi, 1989), 61). As Marc Redfield later notes, "de

Man manipulates the quotation" ("Mistake in Paul de Man: Violent Reading and Theotropic Violence." In *The Political Archive of Paul de Man: Property, Sovereignty and the Theotropic*, edited by Martin McQuillan (Edinburgh: Edinburgh University Press, 2012), 111). Rousseau's original runs thusly:

> Mais je ne remplirois pas le but de ce livre si je n'exposois en même tems mes dispositions intérieures, & que je craignisse de m'excuser en ce qui est conforme à la vérité.
>
> (Jean-Jacques Rousseau. *Les Confessions*, Vol. 1. (Lausaunne: Francois Grasset, 1782), 151).

> But I would not fulfill the purpose of this book if I did not expose at the same time my internal dispositions, and if I feared to excuse myself for what conforms to the truth.

But de Man renders the second part of Rousseau's sentence as "que je [ne] craignisse de m'*excuser* en ce qui est conforme à la vérité" (*Allegories of Reading: Figural Language in Rousseau, Nietzsche, Rilke, and Proust* (New Haven: Yale University Press, 1979), 280), which he translates as "if I did not fear to *excuse* myself by means of what conforms to the truth," creating a statement whose significance is precisely the *opposite* of that found in the plain meaning of the text. Even Jacques Derrida was famously vexed by de Man's willful rewriting of Rousseau's text, asking: "Why does he cut the sentence, mutilating it or dismembering it in this way and in such an arbitrary fashion?" before concluding that de Man's mistranslation "risks making the text say exactly the opposite of what its grammar [...] says, namely that Rousseau does not fear, he does not want to fear, he does not want to fear to have to excuse himself" ("Typewriter Ribbon: Limited Ink (2) ('Within Such Limits')." *Material Events: Paul de Man and the Afterlife of Theory*. Translated by Peggy Kamuf, edited by Tom Cohen, Barbara Cohen, J. Hillis Miller, and Andrzej Warminski. (Minneapolis: University of Minnesota Press, 2001), 311, 338–339). As we will see throughout this book, though the techniques will differ (as most will not resort to actual textual emendation), such rewritings of texts by critics have long since become commonplace.

51 Noam Chomsky. Online discussion that took place on LBBS, Z-Magazine's Left On-Line Bulletin Board. Posted at rec.arts.books, November 13, 1995 03:21:23. Accessible at http://bactra.org/chomsky-on-postmodernism.html.

52 "Willst du etwas über ihn vermögen, so mußt du mehr tun, als ihn blos anreden, du mußt ihn machen, ihn also machen, das er gar nicht anders wollen könne, als du willst, das er wolle." Johann Gottlieb Fichte. *Johann Gottlieb Fichte: Fichtes Reden an die Deutsche Nation*. Edited by Samantha Nietz (Hamburg: Severus, 2013), 32. Fichte's idea is reflected in Spivak's fairly recent description of Humanities education as an "uncoercive rearrangement of desires" (Gayatri Chakravorty Spivak. "Righting Wrongs." *The South Atlantic Quarterly* 103, no. 2/3 (Spring/Summer 2004), 526). The "uncoercive" nature of such "rearrangement" is perhaps best attested to by the experience of one of my colleagues who had the occasion to observe a discussion of this idea in a group of Ph.D. students. One student in the group noted the possibility that such "uncoercive rearrangement" might merely be a covert form of coercion. *Every other student in the group* condemned that idea, and the discussion was quickly dropped.

53 Muth, 73.

54 *The Discourse of Enclosure*, 46.

55 Helene Scheck. "Seductive Voices: Rethinking Female Subjectivities in The Wife's Lament and Wulf and Eadwacer." *Literature Compass* 5, no. 2 (2008), 224.

56 Audrey L. Meaney. "The Ides of the Cotton Gnomic Poem." *Medium Ævum* 48, no. 1 (1979), 36.

57 Muth, 68.

58 For a discussion of these poets in their context, see Bryson and Movsesian, *Love and its Critics*, Chapter 4.

59 For the Arabic influence on Troubadour (and thus most of Western) poetry, see Maria Rosa Menocal, *The Arabic Role in Medieval Literary History: A Forgotten Heritage* (Philadelphia: University of Pennsylvania Press, 2010).

60 Neruda's poem, "Puedo escribir los versos más tristes esta noche" [I can write the saddest verses tonight], from his 1924 collection *Veinte Poemas de Amor y una Canción Desesperada* [Twenty Poems of Love and a Song of Despair], is among the most powerful modern laments that stands in the tradition of the old Anglo-Saxon elegies.

61 Qābbanī, whose work was harshly condemned by the authorities of his time and place, was an inspiration to younger readers trying to find a place for their own humanity amidst the antihumanism of clerical authority:

> His pointed criticism of the social milieu was directed at the relationship between the sexes in particular. His [...] rejection of the blunt misogynist attitudes which left the Arab woman under the constant scrutiny of patriarchal canons [informed his call] to liberate the body from sexual repression and more specifically, to allow the Arab woman to cherish her erotic ecstasy openly and freely. Controversy erupted instantly: Sheikh al-Tantāwī characterized the poems as "blasphemous and

Michael Bryson

stupid," while young Syrian readers treated the collection as a kind of manifesto of their culturally suppressed sexuality.

("'Only Women and Writing Can Save Us From Death': Erotic Empowering in the Poetry of Nizār Qābbanī." In *Tradition, Modernity, and Postmodernity in Arabic Literature: Essays in Honor of Professor Issa J. Boullata*, ed. by Kamal Abdel-Malek and Wael Hallaq (Leiden: Brill, 2000), 141.)

62 One major common thread between figures as chronologically far removed from one another as Plato (whose Socrates argues for the banishment of poetry and poets in the *Republic*) and many modern critics (whether Marxist, feminist, new-historicist, post-humanist, anti-humanist, or otherwise), is the idea that art should be (must be) approached solely through a political/theoretical agenda. A poem (or a painting, for that matter) seems now to exist primarily as a site of contention, an arena of combat between warring ideologies, a proving ground for various sorts of muscular (and non-aesthetic) criticisms to contend for yet one more "victory" over largely imaginary opponents. As the Mexican art critic Avelina Lésper notes, art and art criticism have reached the point that "Una obra se legitima con una cita de Adorno, Baudrillard, Deleuze, Benjamin. Las obras existen por el discurso teórico y curatorial, negando el razonamiento lógico" [A work is legitimized by citations of Adorno, Baudrillard, Deleuze, or Benjamin. The works exist for a theoretical and curatorial discourse, denying all logical reasoning.] (*El fraude del arte contemporáneo* [*The Fraud of Contemporary Art*] (Bogotá: Libros Malpensante, 2015), 18). In the more extreme case of Leon Trotsky, for example, the argument is that all art is inherently political, *and in fact must be a servant to the politics of its day*: "Споры о «чистом искусстве» и об искусстве направленческом [...] Нам они не к лицу. Материалистическая диалектика выше этого: для нее искусство, под углом зрения объективного исторического процесса, всегда общественнослужебно, исторически-утилитарно" [disputes about "pure art" and directed (political) art [...] do not suit us. The materialist dialectic is higher than this: for her art, from the perspective of an objective historical process, is always a public servant, historically utilitarian.] (Литература и революция [*Literature and Revolution*] (Moscow: Политиздат [Politizdat], 1991), 134). But as Leo Tolstoy contends, art is perhaps the ultimate *humanist* endeavor, an attempt to bring human beings into communion across borders of time, space, and language:

искусство есть одно из средств общения людей между собой. Всякое произведение искусства делает то, что воспринимающий вступает в известного рода общение с производившим или производящим искусство и со всеми теми, которые одновременно с ним, прежде или после его восприняли или воспримут то же художественное впечатление.

[Art is one of the means of communication between people. Every work of art causes the perceiver to enter into a certain kind of communication with the one who produced or is producing the art, and with all those who, simultaneously with him, before or after him, have perceived or will perceive the same artistic impression.]

(*Что такое искусство?* [*What is Art?*], Л. Н. Толстой [L. N. Tolstoy], Собрание сочинений в 22 томах [Complete Works in 22 volumes]. *Russian Virtual Library* 15, 78). https://rvb.ru/tolstoy/01text/vol_15/01text/0327.htm

Unfortunately, it seems that Trotsky is more contemporary than Tolstoy where the criticism surrounding art and poetry is concerned. What Neema Parvini has referred to as "an incredibly dangerous [...] and above all anti-human way of thinking" ("Rejecting Progress in the Name of 'Cultural Appropriation.'" *Quillette*, August 22, 2018. http://quillette.com/2018/08/22/rejecting-progress-in-the-name-of-cultural-appropriation/) is—and has been since Plato—the form of thinking that has been most determined to reduce poetry to ideology and most opposed to the expansions of human possibility, even when that opposition comes in the form of seemingly liberal and liberatory rhetoric.

63 Edward Said. *The World, the Text, and the Critic* (Cambridge: Harvard University Press, 1983), 29.

64 Johann Wolfgang Von Goethe. *Faust* (Munich: Wilhelm Goldman Verlag, 1978), l.317.

12

Humanism and Universal Values in European Medieval Literature

Freidank's *Bescheidenheit* and *Sir Gawain and the Green Knight*

Albrecht Classen

In light of what we know today about the Middle Ages, viewed through a wide range of new theoretical lenses developed over the last few decades, we might have to admit that much of our previous understanding was pretty simplistic and informed by standard concepts that no longer fully conform with what we can truly say about medieval mentality, everyday life, the history of emotions, the relationship between people and things, and between people and animals.[1] The role of women in medieval society, for instance, was radically different from what we had still assumed in the late twentieth century;[2] although medieval authorities were strongly opposed to and rigidly repressed homosexuals, but then also heretics, and other deviant individuals, the situation was rather complex and not at all plainly a shut case, as otherwise not so many poets and artists would have included relevant allusions, probed the limits of the acceptable, and transgressed standards and norms.[3]

We can safely assume that all power structures, the common worldviews, concepts about the foreign worlds, the willingness to travel over long distances even far beyond the European limits in geographical terms, the ordinary technical, scientific, and medical know-how, and so forth, were much more complex and sophisticated than we could have imagined only 30 or 40 years ago.[4] The medieval discourse on love, for instance, was so elaborate and intricate across the various medieval courts that we still have difficulties today grasping its purpose, functions, manifestations, and meaning comprehensively and in-depth.[5] Moreover, it used to be a standard notion that the discovery of the self was the launching point of the Renaissance, but notions of identity and self were already well established long before that.[6]

Of course, it would be dangerous, if not outright wrong, to ignore major differences between the medieval world and us today. And it would also be completely erroneous to glorify medieval culture in contrast to the modern one. Neither the notion of the "Dark Ages" nor the Romantic perception of a mysterious and fascinating past far superseding the present would help us to gain a better understanding of that historical period. No medieval group, community, or whole society was thoroughly evil or completely good; people then were people like us, with some individuals demonstrating strong and others weak characters; there were certain figures with great artistic and scientific abilities, but also ignoramuses and outright fools; there were leaders and followers, etc.

Without leveling or harmonizing the past with the present, we can be certain that fundamental human issues concerned them as much as they do concern us today to various degrees. Our

DOI: 10.4324/9781003046004-15

responses and approaches certainly differ from our medieval predecessors, but who could say satisfactorily to what extent we are truly their avatars or in what way we represent really new people with different needs, attitudes, or mindsets? If the Middle Ages in their basic mental and emotional structures had been completely alien to us, we could not even endeavor to study them critically because we would not share any epistemological basis upon which to build comprehension.

When we examine the Middle Ages, there has always been a certain tendency, quite understandable, to subscribe to a Eurocentric perception. Both methodologically and theoretically, this has made good sense because comparisons between, say, the medieval kingdom of Mali with the kingdom of Denmark would not help much for either case. Japanese or Chinese models of royal rulers certainly reveal interesting parallels with those in medieval Europe, but we should not push this endeavor to develop global perspectives too much since that would lead us to the danger of comparing the proverbial apples with oranges.[7]

The question to be raised here, by contrast, does not aim at furthering our research into the Global Middle Ages; certainly a highly fascinating and insightful approach pursued particularly in the last few years.[8] Instead, the question pertains to the fundamental concepts and attitudes about human values and ideals, fears and problems formulated in a variety of medieval texts, which might prove to be universal, global, and hence would be of relevance in all cultures in the modern world. I do not argue in favor of global comparisons but in favor of reading some medieval texts as universal in their meaning and relevance.

If Dante Alighieri, Giovanni Boccaccio, Geoffrey Chaucer, Heinrich Kaufringer, Johann von Tepl, and Christine de Pizan mean anything to us, even though we might be limited by our common Eurocentric focus, then their messages, concerns, ideas, and values must mean something also for other cultures across the globe today. My premise here is that many of the critical discussions about a variety of fundamental themes as formulated in medieval European literature do not only appeal to students, scholars, and general readers of European origin, but carry relevance across all of humanity. The same observation applies, of course, to Japanese, Chinese, Indian, Brazilian, or any other culture and literature, when it proves to be of high quality and hence addresses global human issues.

Two simple examples from two different worlds and time periods might quickly illustrate this phenomenon: The Arabian *One Thousand and One Night* (tenth or eleventh century, if not much earlier) have been similarly popular throughout the world, as have been the fairy tales by the Brothers Grimm (1st ed., 1812). Other famous cases would be the many accounts of Alexander the Great[9] and the narrative of Buddha's life in the story of *Barlaam and Josaphat* both in Asia and in Europe.[10] In short, this chapter intends to probe the question of to what extent pre-modern European literature can appeal to readers in other parts of the world, or, how much the various poets addressed issues of global relevance, both then and today, and hence could be identified as meaningful and influential for global perspectives throughout time.[11]

There are, apparently, only very few topics that have always concerned people all over the globe, and they have appeared constantly throughout the ages in a variety of manifestations, informed by different ideologies, religions, or philosophies. One of those, for example, would be the issue of death and its meaning, which all world religions have endeavored to answer in one or the other way. People in all cultures have mourned the passing away of their loved ones, but each culture has expressed its emotions in different forms. The foundation appears to be always the same, whereas the cultural or literary responses have certainly differed throughout time.[12] If we accept that this phenomenon is predicated on the notion of a discourse, then we can recognize universally shared ideas and concepts. Those include, apart from death: love, God, fear, hope, honor, shamefulness, vices and sins, virtues and ideals, honor and dignity, and so forth. All of those have had a huge relevance and impact on medieval society, but the concerns with them have never been limited to European literature.

A Most Critical Franciscan Agenda: Freidank

When we approach the large collection of proverbs and other memorable statements or stanzas by the thirteenth-century Franciscan poet Freidank, we face the great opportunity not only to realize how ignorant we seem to have been about medieval values, concepts, and fundamental notions, and how much his collection of comments called *Bescheidenheit* (ca. 1215–1230) proves to be open to people in many different cultures because of the universal teaching of wisdom contained in his stanzas.[13] Insofar as this work enjoyed tremendous popularity far into the late Middle Ages and beyond, and since Freidank was commonly quoted or glossed by contemporary and subsequent poets, we can be certain that his work must have had a huge impact on his audiences.[14] My intention is thus focused on the two critical issues, one, what he informs us about the social, ethical, and philosophical conditions of his time, and two, to what extent *Bescheidenheit* could be considered an important source for reflections and meditations on fundamental issues in human life irrespective of the linguistic, political, or historical conditions.

The title of this collection is already revealing, insofar as the poet proclaims to convey deep wisdom, knowledge about all kinds of aspects of human life. Beginning with sections on God, the church mass, the soul, and on human beings in general, Freidank then offers comments on Jews, heretics, usury, arrogance, sins, the wealthy and the poor, loyalty and lack thereof, thieves, gambling, justice and injustice, old age, aristocracy and virtues, medical doctors and sickness, wrath, heaven and hell, the clergy, the king and the princes, generosity and misery, honor, drunkenness, friendship, love, hunger, animals, the Holy See, the human language, and so forth, intending to be almost encyclopedic at least in an ethical and moral sense. The volume concludes with remarks on the Antichrist, God's commands, death, and the Day of Judgment.

Since these short stanzas are intended mostly as proverbs, we can easily recognize their global purpose, that is, instructing, teaching, and offering memorizable comments about a wide range of topics relevant at Freidank's time. As we will see, however, many of his insights and notions prove to be of timeless value and can be studied within any cultural context. For our purpose, I will not engage with the religious sections and focus, instead, on his observations regarding people's social interactions and conditions, beginning with an analysis of Freidank's remarks on epistemology. The term itself might sound inappropriate for the Middle Ages, but there is no doubt that the poet explicitly addresses the issue of "erkennen" (106.12; to understand). He means to say that the strategy to probe into one's own self would be the starting point to bring lying to an end. But he also warns about people who claim to know everything about another person and yet know nothing about themselves.

The ability to gain solid, profound knowledge about oneself would constitute wisdom (106.16). The study of the own self is closely connected to law and justice, goodness and wrongdoing, but there is always a self that needs to become aware of itself, either for moral or ethical reasons (107.12). The self always exists within a social context, and only when the self can enjoy freedom from any external forces, does it achieve personal happiness. As stanza 107.14 illustrates, an individual would quickly lose interest in even their most favorite activities when s/he would be forced to do it. Both here and elsewhere, Freidank addresses the notion of freedom, which was, as we have learned only recently, much more widespread in the high and late Middle Ages than we have thought so far.[15]

Interestingly, this also applies to the world of monasteries as he warns that forced encloistering would not stand up to God's scrutiny (107.20). In another context, the poet emphasizes that individuals who enjoy doing some kind of job would quickly lose all their interest in it if they were required to do it against their free will (107.24). At the same time, Freidank insists that young children need the firm hand of their parents, and not freedom; otherwise, they could later in their life fall into criminal activities and then suffer the consequences by being imprisoned and punished by the bailiff (108.13).

Subsequently, after having explored the aspects of love and social interactions, Freidank returns to his epistemological endeavor by stressing that only he himself could claim to know himself thoroughly, although he would keep that hidden from public view (110.19). The study of the own heart would lead to the realization that one cannot speak ill of others any longer (108.21). Even better, which would certainly appeal to all readers even today, it is necessary for our lives to learn how to distinguish between good and evil, and upon that knowledge to act accordingly, to choose the former and to leave the latter (110.23).

Criticizing his contemporaries in general, Freidank also points out that many people promise much and yet do not live up to it (111.13). Many people claim much but act to the contrary (111.14). If one promises much but does not follow up on them would unnecessarily pile dishonor and shame upon oneself (111.18). Apart from his various remarks on greed and unlawfulness, the poet also addresses the issue of imprisonment, which makes one experience time as passing very slowly (113.6). On another note, he stresses that a lack of self-knowledge would lead to great pain (113.22). And Freidank also comments that he would not want to be friends with someone who hates himself (113.26).

Further, the poet, moving from one topic to another, although they are all related to self-awareness and critical reflections about goodness, evilness, proper behavior, and self-control (e.g., 114.7 and 114.9), also offers philosophical reflections which appear to be directly predicated on the teachings by Boethius in his *De consolatione philosophiae* (ca. 524). In 114.27, for instance, we are advised to keep in mind that good fortune is like an ever-moving ball and hence most mobile, never resting and always changing: "swer stîget, der sol fürhten val" (1144.28; he who rises ought to guard himself against falling).[16] Related to that, Freidank observes that many people suffer from self-illusion, believing that their life would have to be identified as the best possible (115.4), or that they are the best in their own art or craft (115.6). Politically, this would apply as well because whenever a dynasty is on the rise, another would certainly decline (117.26).

Most significantly, the poet highlights that all thoughts are free since no one can tie them up as people are often taken prisoners (115.14). This notion concerning the freedom of thinking, which was also expressed well before Freidank by Walther von der Vogelweide in his song "Ob ich mich selben rüemen sol" (62.6, ca. 1210),[17] anticipates by ca. 400 years the ideals of freedom as propagated in the nineteenth century, when the song "Die Gedanken sind frei" became greatly popular again when Hoffmann von Fallersleben included a version in his *Schlesische Volkslieder mit Melodien* (Silesian Folk Songs with Melodies) in 1842. Considering that Freidank's name, a *nom de plume*, meant something like "Freethinker," we can gather that the ideal of individual freedom mattered critically for him. This makes particular sense when we consider his stanza 115.18 where he points out that no prison walls would be thick enough to prevent him from thinking freely and sending out his ideas to the world beyond (see also 122.17).

We also learn a fundamental truth that many people today might do well to observe: those who try to do two jobs at once often end up doing neither job properly. Freidank warns us that those who try to accomplish two tasks at the same time would rarely achieve anything good in either one (115.10). The poet did not know anything about smartphones, the internet, and the like, yet his warning certainly resonates with us, in global terms.

Most relevant for his approach to epistemology, however, proves to be stanza 115.22, where he draws a significant distinction between authenticated truth and hearsay. Only what he has seen with his own eyes could be trusted, whereas everything else which might have learned from other would be nothing but opinion: "ich waene manges, daz man seit, / unz ich ervar die wârheit" (24-25; I [only] assume many things which were told me, until I learn the truth). Of course, he does not question the validity of his knowledge gained through his eyesight, which could be deceptive as well, as we would claim today, but the central point of his stanza consists of the importance to inspect everything oneself before one could trust it. He is truly talking about verification and falsification, which modern science accepts as the most critical tools in all research. He extends this approach further in the next stanza, where he insists that truth that can be grasped and seen would be reliable. Those who simply reject what can be evidenced through close inspection would be fools' companions.

Interestingly, Freidank then applies these insights to his human topic insofar as he notices that one cannot really understand people unless they fully reveal themselves because the eyes can only look at the outer body, but cannot penetrate to the other person's heart (116.3). Perception of others can easily deceive the observer because there are many people who look kind and attractive on the outside but who carry a bitter heart (116.17). Another aspect pertaining to epistemology comes to the fore in stanzas 116.13 and 116.15, where he observes that on earth there is an infinitude of creatures who or which are all different from each other. One would not even be able to distinguish among flowers if they all looked the same. Regarding the material existence, Freidank opines that even those objects that one would appreciate could not hold our attention all the time; at some point, we would find them bothersome or a burden (117.2). He illustrates this also with a reference to the season of summer, which is commonly highly appreciated. At one point, however, when summer never comes to an end, even that special season might become a bother and a source of irritation (117.6). Subsequently, the poet mixes in social teachings again, alerting us to the fact that one sorrow has passed, joy sets in, and that once joys have come to an end, sorrow appears (117.16).

Freidank warns his listeners to stay away from evil people, especially because virtuous individuals would too easily be attached to them and might then gain some vices due to their too-close contacts with others (118.7). But those who are restless and easily cause conflicts ought to be aware that God might impose problems on them as the natural course of events (118.19). Then, reflecting on his own status, Freidank admits that prophets rarely wear a crown in their own land; that is, they are hardly ever acknowledged in their country (119.6), which is, of course, a direct borrowing from the New Testament (Luke 4:24; Mark 6:4, etc.), a phenomenon which should not surprise us at all in light of the genre used by him, proverbs and didactic teachings.

If we pursued his proverbs further, we would recognize many other "classical" or biblical sources, but the decisive point here proves to be that Freidank formulated these ideas either as innovative thoughts or as paraphrases of older statements for his audience and thus provided them with universal lessons of greatest value, being timeless and applicable to everyone with only slight adaptations, so when he warns that a person who walks barefoot ought to stay away from thistles (119.14). Or, no one enjoys a life so free that s/he would not face some conflicts from time to time (119.22); or, weeds easily grow, whereas good seeds of grain might not make it (120.7); or, all people are subject to change, and no one is perfect so as to avoid that principle force in all of life (120.17).

Hidden among many of those stanzas with solid advice, we also find considerable social criticism targeting particularly the aristocracy and the king. Here, for instance, in stanza 121.12, he claims unabashedly that knights erect their castles for the sole purpose of subjugating, literally, suffocating, the poor. If a peasant grows in his wealth, the bailiff would easily target him with the intention of robbing him by means of tax claims, or otherwise (122.7). At the same time, Freidank warns about parvenus who have risen from the peasant class and have assumed a leadership role (122.11). He perceives the danger that that person would quickly turn everything around and mistreat and abuse the other peasants just as much as he had been suffering before. He would hence draw from his own terrible experience and compensate for it by making the others suffer as much or even worse.

Most powerful, this entire section concludes with a stanza in which the poet returns to the essential topic, self-awareness, or self-reflection, noting that he as an individual is bound by his own being: "Ich kan mit allen sinnen / mir selbe niht entrinnen" (124.13-14; With all my senses

I cannot escape from myself). He would like to free himself from his own self, but he does not know where to hide because wherever he would go, he would always find himself once again as a human being: "nû bin ich mensche, swar ich var" (124.16).

When we turn our attention to other sections, we recognize more social and ethical comments which deliberately undermine the traditional power structure of his time and aim for a renewal of the meaning of nobility. In 54.8, for instance, Freidank comments that inner nobility, i.e., virtue and honor, can be acquired by anyone, a free or a subservient person, if one only strives for it. He does not care about birth conditions and emphasizes that no social background would be sufficient by itself, if the individual would not gain an honorable character.

In previous stanzas, he outlined various factors which would facilitate the struggle to gain virtues, such as a strong sense of shame in oneself as protection against wrongdoing (52.24 and 53.1). In 53.15, he formulates this in a dramatic image of a lion who would become tame if it were to feel fear. In people, the broom cleaning one's honor would be shame. No one could claim an aristocratic character who would not possess virtues (53.17). Honor itself could not exist without inner self-discipline (53.23). When an individual commands virtues, then s/he is well-born, but those whose life is void of virtues no longer can claim a noble status (54.6).

More globally, Freidank raises his voice in warning against lawlessness, though he can only refer to God as the ultimate judge in such cases, probably because the poet did not trust the worldly legal courts to bring about justice (50.16). He harbors hope, however, that the goods which someone has acquired will not last long and will disappear again (50.22). Apparently being aware of many illegal machinations, which cause misfortune to individuals, he warns that God will not be deceived and will help at the end to redeem to abused person (51.3). The person who knowingly joins the forces of that person, who launches an unjust war, will eventually be exposed before God as a great sinner (51.7).

Lords are pleased when they are surrounded by flatterers, but the latter ultimately rob them of their own honor (49.23). The sycophants praise everything that their lord does, and do not think for themselves or uphold honor (50.2). As many other contemporary didactic poets, Freidank views wealth with considerable suspicion, commenting that many rich people display considerable dumbness, whereas poor people shine forth in their virtues (40.9). Wealth can only be acquired through the employment of evil cunning (40.11); at the same time, he notes that rich people are surrounded by many "friends" when they hand out much of their money (40.17). Wealth, however, is never to be trusted (40.20), and those who enjoy it, has many friends, whereas those who lose it find themselves without friends (40.25). On the other hand, Freidank does not hold back in his criticism of those who rise beyond their social class because of newly gained money (41.8), just as in the case of enriched and newly empowered peasants who quickly turn against their own neighbors, as was powerfully described by the more or less contemporary verse narrative *Meier Helmbrecht* by Wernher the Gardener (ca. 1260-1270).

There, the young man leaves his peasant community against his father's urgent pleading and joins a band of robber knights, and he at first attacks merchants and other people outside the village, but soon begins to plunder among his own social class and causes great harm everywhere until he and his evil fellows are apprehended by bailiffs and quickly executed. Only Helmbrecht is "spared," being granted his life, but not without losing his right hand, his left leg, and his eyesight, which makes it impossible for him ever to climb onto a horse and wield a sword.[18] A year later, he is caught by surprise by a group of peasants whom he had previously badly mistreated, and they mercilessly lynch him, which serves as a stern warning against anyone at that time thinking about rising beyond the peasant class.

All this serves to alert us not to glorify Freidank too much; he was, after all, still a conservative medieval commentator, and as much as we might sympathize with many of his proverbs because of their timeless messages, as much as we would also have to be on the lookout for rather typical

Humanism in European Medieval Literature

medieval viewpoints. Another example would be stanza 14.16, where the poet notes that those who increase their wisdom, honor, and wealth would certainly also increase their worries and struggles as if "wîstuom" would suddenly count as something negative.

On the other hand, Freidank warns us that greedy and rich people would never be satisfied with what they could acquire (41.18), and he alerts the rich that none of their material goods would help them against death (42.1), a global observation that would find countless resonances in world literature both in the Middle Ages and beyond. When a rich man dies, as the poet comments, their children's tears would dry up quickly, whereas the survivors of a poor man would remember him for a long time and not stop crying out of honestly felt grief (42.7). At the same time, Freidank ridicules the poor people as well because their poverty would make it impossible for them to achieve virtues (42.19). Then, however, he discriminates further and remarks that a rich man would not even notice any difference when a poor man would take some wood from his forest, whereas the latter would be very pleased with having gotten free fuel (42.27).

Those who are content with what they own would always enjoy a sense of wealth (43.11). The section then concludes with several stanzas in which he warns us once again about the dangers of wealth for one's virtues. It would be impossible to gain riches without committing sins and shameful deeds (43.14). Those who are poor tend to be determined by virtues, but once they would have gained money, those virtues would be quickly lost (43.18). He who would be able to enjoy his life, even in poverty, would possess great riches, though not in material terms (43.20). And finally, if all people were equal, there would not be poor or rich individuals (43.22). Surprisingly, this idea is later picked up again and applied in more global terms when Freidank observes that we all, whether aristocrats or peasants, descend from Adam, hence, that we are all people and should treat each other correspondingly (135.10).

Freidank also included a whole section with proverbs based on animal behavior, so he obviously borrowed from the fable tradition, which was highly popular throughout the Middle Ages and far beyond, both in European and in Asian and Arabic literature, and then also in other parts of the world.[19] Here we learn, for instance, that a sheep's clothing is the wrong attire for the wolf (137.9), that a wolf who becomes the shepherd would soon ravage the entire heard of sheep (137.11), that it would be a utopia when the wolf would grant peace to sheep (137.17), or that a dog which went to mass a thousand times still would remain a dog, not changing its animal nature (138.5). He who would dare to get into a fight with a bear would need a very thick skin (139.7), and a country that chooses an ass as its king would be deeply dishonored (140.3).

We could go through the long list of other fable-like proverbs, but we would only notice the same phenomenon, i.e., the essential truth hidden behind each statement. Freidank clearly commented on human failures and shortcomings through the mask of animals and thereby could voice his deep concerns about the many wrongdoings by people, not without wit and even humor, so when he states that he would grant peace to the lion if only the fleas would leave him alone (146.3).

In the 45th section, the poet targets the ills in the Holy See and attacks particularly the pope as the worst offender of all of Christ's teachings. Relying on irony, Freidank observes that the net with which St. Peter caught fish apparently never reached Rome, and instead the ecclesiastics resort to their own, Roman net with which they endeavor to catch silver, gold, castle, and land, all of which had been unknown to St. Peter (152.16). In the 47th section, the focus rests on the tongue, or the human language, which tends to create many of the conflicts and tensions here on earth. Because of evil words, for instance, friends bonded by mutual trust separate from each other, and similarly, lovers begin to feel mutual hate (165.1). Altercations between husband and wife are the results of foolishly uttered words (165.15), and Freidank hence recommends that the tongue be shortened (165.19), meaning that people ought to watch out for their language and the words they use to communicate with each other.[20]

The section on death (51) contains numerous observations about the incommensurability of this phenomenon which affects everyone in this life and yet remains incomprehensible. As the poet laments, we are all fooled by the illusion that we might live forever (176.14), we all must leave everything behind (176.26), we are all born naked and leave this world again with barely any clothing covering the corpse (177.1 and 177.3). Almost like much later successors during the Baroque period, Freidank highlights that we have, as the only certain knowledge, the awareness that death will come one day, but the day and hour always remains uncertain (177.13). He also laments that one of the greatest worries consists of the fear of death felt by all living creatures (178.6).

If we turn our attention back to the ninth section, which deals with the properties of this world, we realize that the poet has created a fitting arch from the beginning to the end, and yet each part of it pursues a slightly different emphasis. A few more examples can illustrate impressively how much Freidank's thoughts truly address timeless concerns, such as when he notes that all people strive for goods, knowledge, and honor and can never get enough of either one of them (31.2). The most powerful word in the human language would be, as he argues, the possessive "mine" (31.6), which reminds us immediately of the contemporary me-society in the twenty-first century all over the world (the selfie generation). The love for all material things represents poison for the soul (31.10), and all physical existence proves to be contingent, limited, and unstable: "Hiute liep, morne leit, / deist der werlde unstaetekeit" (31.16; Today enjoyment, tomorrow sorrow, / that's the instability of this world), probably once again a reflection of Boethian teachings.

A person who would be able to combine God and this world would deserve to be blessed (31.18), and s/he who would live properly could expect to be welcomed in heaven as well (31.24). By contrast, Freidank bitterly complains about the fact that only those individuals who would commit crimes and violence would deserve full recognition by people (32.7). But there are some who have seen through the deceptiveness of the world and simply laugh about it because they can easily leave it behind (32.13). As much as people are attracted to worldly joys, the fear of death always stands in the background (32.23). Finally, Freidank emphasizes unequivocally that there is nothing here in this life that would have a long endurance; everything is evanescent and ephemeral (33.2), which implies, of course, that the opposite can only be found in the afterworld, in God.

We could easily continue studying the vast number of other verse couplets with their insightful and profound comments, which in most cases appear to formulate universal truths which would be of great relevance for all people across the globe, whether Christians or not. Freidank openly speaks his mind and admonishes his audiences to be wary about the false seductiveness of physical existence. He has much to say about human wrongdoings, failures, shortcomings, lack of virtues, and criminal mindsets. Although expressed in literary terms, these stanzas emerge as philosophical observations of profound quality and would need little introduction or translation into a modern language to make them palpable, meaningful, and relevant for any audience both in the Middle Ages and beyond, within the European framework and in the rest of the world.

Until today, however, Freidank's proverbs and statements have not yet been translated into other languages, medieval or modern.[21] Nevertheless, as our analysis has demonstrated, in this anthology under the very telling title of *Bescheidenheit*, we encounter a didactic thinker who has much to offer in terms of his fundamental understanding of human nature, all the good and the bad; that is, insights which easily transcend historical, geographic, and cultural barriers and demonstrate that some of the medieval literature certainly contains a universal appeal.

Even when Freidank turns to some of the core Christian notions about the end of time and the Day of Judgment, he leaves a comment behind that proves to be of universal value: "Armer liute reiner muot / name ich für aller keiser guot" (179.2; I would prefer the pure spirit of poor people over all of the emperor's gold). As simplistic as it might sound, he concludes in a stunningly striking fashion, stating, "sô ist ân ende iemer mê, / den guoten wol, den boesen wê" (180.3-4; at the end, the good are well, the evil ones are badly off). Of course, he meant it in the Christian sense, him being a Franciscan bent on teaching his parishioners about the right way through this life, which the overall structure of *Bescheidenheit* clearly indicates. At the same time, as we could confirm through many examples studied above, Freidank's concerns focused on the social interaction among people, on virtues and vices, on self-reflection, epistemology, and the meaning of death, both in a secular and a theological context. None of those issues have lost anything in relevance, and they are not characteristic of European literature, religion, and philosophy only. As we could observe, practically all of the poet's concerns address universal issues fundamental in human life the world over. We would need relatively few adjustments, conceptional translations, and contextualization to make most of Freidank's proverbs applicable to modern people since they are predicated on the quest for wisdom, and this in a universal framework.

Sir Gawain and the Green Knight – the Quest for Honor

There would be countless other examples from medieval German literature to reconfirm and expand these observations, whether we think of the fables by Ulrich Bonerius (*Der Edelstein*, ca. 1350) or the dialog poem *Der Ackermann* by Johannes von Tepl (ca. 1400). While the former created one of the most popular fable collections of his time and well into the sixteenth century, in which he addressed a wide range of critical topics similar to those dealt with by Freidank, the latter explored the meaning of death and the meaning of life in face of death. For our present purposes, however, it seems to be more effective to include a very different text with a thematic focus on individual honor. Much of world literature has dealt with this value, whether we think of heroic epics or courtly romances. We might no longer talk much about "honor" in the present time, but all individuals require honor and cannot exist in a life filled with shame, for instance. Of course, we learn much about honor in *Beowulf*, in *El Poema de mío Cid*, or in the *Chanson de Roland*, not to forget the vast scope of Eddic sagas. Courtly protagonists are also always most anxious to secure their honor because there is no knighthood without it.[22] But if we take into consideration the anonymous alliterative romance of *Sir Gawain and the Green Knight* from ca. 1370, which has certainly already been discussed from many different perspectives, we are confronted with a most critical situation where the protagonist's honor is very much at stake and who survives the greatest challenge because he had observed his exigencies of honor to the extreme.[23]

This anonymous romance is so well known that we do not need to summarize the plot once again. Instead, I want to focus on the issue of honor only, which constitutes, of course, the central concern of the entire text. Only a few remarks are necessary to take us quickly to the central issue. The Green Knight wants to test the stamina and courage of the Arthurian court, but he relies on an unfair advantage, magical power he has received from Morgan le Fay, which makes it possible for him to offer the decapitation game and yet to survive. Sir Gawain does not have that option and is actually afraid for his life, as anyone would be under normal circumstances. Nevertheless, he accepts the challenge, strikes at the Green Knight with the ax, and thus accomplishes the task set to him. However, a year later, he has to allow the same thing to happen to him despite the impossibility to survive, and no one at Arthur's court actually expects him to return alive. We could thus characterize Gawain's resolve to face his opponent wherever he might fight him (at the Green Chapel) as a truly heroic approach, resolutely living up to his commitment because his honor and that of the king depend on it, although he does not seem to have a fair chance in that decapitation "game."

Once he has arrived at Castle Hautdesert, the host Bercilak proposes a game of its own, with each one of them going hunting, and in the evening exchanging their preys or conquests, except that the lord would go into the woods, and Gawain would stay in the castle. During the actual hunt, each day a different animal caught by Bercilak represents some of Gawain's personality traits (deer for swiftness, bear for strength, and fox for intelligence), while his guest is being "hunted"

Albrecht Classen

by the lady of the house who tries to seduce him erotically. While the animals are killed, Gawain survives the temptations for three days, except that he takes the life-saving belt from the lady without handing it over to the host, a clear breach of their mutual agreement.[24] Of course, Bercilak knows about it: "'ffor, hit is my wede þat þou wereȝ, þat ilke wouen girdle; / Myn own wyf hit þe weued, I wot wel, forsoþe" (2358-2359), and for that reason he actually nicks Gawain's neck during the test at the Green Chapel, but he does not kill him and so stays true to his original plan to play games with his opponent.

Most importantly, Bercilak, who is, as we know only too well the Green Knight, fully empathizes with Gawain for having taken and kept that girdle for himself without exchanging it with him as agreed upon as part of their exchange. He praises Gawain in the highest terms possible, but also mentions his one shortcoming, though he contextualizes it by acknowledging that he acted out of his deep and existential desire to live: "lufed your lyf" (2368). Bercilak does not perceive in him any shred of wickedness or improper lust (2367), so he can forgive him this one-time fracture of his commands and orders and blame it on women, which creates deep shame in Gawain. We could argue that here we grasp the central point in the entire narrative with Gawain addressing the essential values of his life: fight against cowardness and covetousness (2374), embracing of liberality and loyalty (2381), and opposing treachery and untruth (2382). For the Green Knight, who now smiles upon Gawain, no real harm has done, and he actually deems the other man as pure and clean as on day one (2393-2394), completely forgiving his small infraction, which was, under those circumstances, very understandable.

Of course, Gawain then tries to find a culprit for his own failure and then immediately plunges into a diatribe against women drawing on the "classical" trope of misogyny, evoking the destiny suffered by the biblical figures of Adam, Solomon, Samson, and David (2415-2428).[25] This outburst appears to be quite natural considering the enormous stress Gawain just had gone through, and he quickly recovers his reason, leaves this misogyny behind, and instead reflects upon his own self and the personal failure he had to let happen. In fact, he then accepts the green girdle as a token of his "surfet" (2433; shame), that is, as a reminder that he was fallible and placed his love of life above his deep desire for honor, honesty, and loyalty. From that day on, Gawain wants to use the girdle as a critical means to keep him aware of his own physical limitations, his being bound to his own body, and its natural tendency to commit a transgression of all values and ideals when life is at stake: "How tender hit is to entyse teches of fylþe" (2436), which Vantuono has elegantly translated as: "How it tends to be enticed to sinful transgression."

Gawain has learned a profound lesson; he is now aware of the great danger of pride and the deceptiveness of his self-conceit: "Þe loke to þis luf-lace schal leþe my hert" (2438). Despite Bercilak's pleading, he then does not return to Castle Hautdesert and instead returns to King Arthur's court where he has to relate to them all what has happened and why he both failed and succeeded, as demonstrated by the green girdle. He is deeply ashamed and reveals it all, talking about his sinfulness and weakness, warning them all about the danger of concealing one's sins which would only result in much suffering afterward.

All of this self-flagellation, however, does not convince anyone at court that Gawain had really failed, and instead they burst out laughing (2514), comforting their worthy and honorable companion whose alleged failure was nothing but to try to stay alive in an impossible situation. where both his life and his honor were at stake, basically the paradox of human existence.[26] Significantly, all members of the court then don the same kind of girdle because Gawain's failure, if that would even be the right word as they all acknowledge, made him shine forth as one of the most glorious knights. Gawain had to learn humbleness and to accept that he was human, after all, and could not help it grasping for that proverbial straw of hope granted him with this girdle. The first time when the Green Knight had swung the ax at him, Gawain had glanced sideways, fearing for his life, of course, which made his body flinch: "And schranke a lytel with þe shulderes for þe scharp yrne" (2267). The opponent then mocked him, and Gawain subsequently stood form, with his neck exposed defenselessly to the opponent's blow with the ax. He promises, having been shamed, to refrain from flinching, and yet he also protests against this unfair fame: "But, if my head falls off in pain / I can not it restore" (2282-2284).

One man's failure at the end turns into the glory of all members of King Arthur's court, especially because the little blemish, the nicked neck, serves only as a reminder of Gawain's mortality and physical existence; he can die, of course, like everyone else. And it is fully understandable, as the Green Knight emphasizes, that Gawain loves to live; who would not? True honor thus emerges as the result of embracing one's own humanity, both strong and weak, good and bad. The romance concludes with references to the destiny of Troy, which led to the foundation of Rome and to the Passion of Christ. Mocking at Gawain's failure would be an evil thing because he simply demonstrated his being human, after all, so the concluding motto, "HONY SOYT QUI MAL PENCE" (shame to anyone who thinks evil thereof) makes perfect sense and addresses all audiences of this famous romance.[27]

The issue addressed here is much more focused than the multiplicity of opinions formulated by Freidank, but it proves to be timeless in relevance, and meaningful in global terms. Gawain has to accept the proposition of virtually certain death in order to maintain his honor. He even rejects the servant's offer to stay away from the Green Chapel and to go his way; he himself would never reveal this shirking of duty to anyone, that is, his cowardice. But Gawain cannot accept that offer, irrespective of the danger for his life, he must resist this "temptation," and so he accepts the challenge, risks his life because his own honor is at stake (2130-2135), and he holds steady in the decapitation challenge despite his shoulder blades shirking a little.

The entire situation proves to be nothing but a game, a bit morbid and grotesque, maybe, but the core issue addressed by the poet concerns human honor and how to uphold it even under extreme conditions. No one voluntarily accepts death; everyone wants to live, here leaving extreme exceptions (suicide, etc.) aside. This is certainly the case with Gawain as well, but his ideal to uphold his honor is stronger than his body's will to live. Of course, he does not know that the Green Knight is only pretending; it is a gruesome game, but throughout the entire process Gawain proves to be human and yet also heroic. His ability to overcome his fear underscores the extent to which he commands a virtually ideal character, full self-control, and a supremely strong sense of honor. But Gawain is not divine; he still has a human body, so the little neck wound reminds him of his mortality and his existential love of life. Without that little failure, we would not be able to appreciate his performance, to accept his glory as being the worthiest knight at King Arthur's court, and would not have available a hermeneutic bridge to this alliterative romance.

Curiously, medieval audiences did not appreciate this romance much, which has survived in only one manuscript (Nero A.x. Article 3) which also contains the other texts by the same poet,. Modern readers have recognized the grand importance of *Sir Gawain and the Green Knight* as one of the best contributions to late medieval English literature, and this for many different reasons. We can be certain that the anonymous poet, perhaps John de Masey de Sale, who served as rector of Ashton-on-Mersey in Cheshire between 1364 and 1401,[28] intended to probe a universal human issue with this rather unusual romance, which we can simply circumscribe as "honor." Fighting for one's honor, accepting even death as a possible price for this valuable ideal, emerges as Gawain's greatest accomplishment, irrespective of his trouble, doubts, fears, and worries. In the end, he holds firm, awaits the blow with the ax, and is yet spared his life.

Sir Gawain and the Green Knight was predicated on very specific Arthurian literary material, representative of the late European Middle Ages. Nevertheless, the issue developed here proves to be of timeless concern, human honor, a highly valuable, yet also fragile and tenuous value that could be easily lost and was very hard to maintain. Not surprisingly, the text has been translated in modern times into many different languages, including Turkish, Russian, Japanese, Korean, and Chinese, obviously not only because of its entertainment value, but because it carries deep meaning, and this also for audiences across the world.

Conclusion

The evidence presented here has demonstrated that certain medieval literary texts continue to speak to many different audiences, within Europe and far beyond. To these two selected here we could easily add many others, especially if we widened our focus and also examined other issues of great and universal significance, such as the quest for God, love, death, meaning of life, the relationship between humans and nature, etc. There is, of course, the general intrigue that the Middle Ages exerts on the modern world, virtually driven by an aura associated especially with medieval art, music, architecture, and literature. But we have certainly realized that the proverbs by Freidank and the anonymous *Sir Gawain and the Green Knight* stand out in many unique ways, addressing fundamental human concerns that have always been with us throughout time and that certainly appeal to many different audiences across the world. The questions regarding virtues and vices, the role of God, the function of death, the definition of the self, the search for honor and dignity, and the quest for spirituality, ethics, and morality will never go away. These selected medieval texts underscore in clear terms the timeless quality of their poets' concerns.

The Middle Ages are not only very much alive also today, but some of those literary works have continued to provide universal ideas and answers to people's worries and problems all over the world. This does not mean at all that we would deliberately (and perhaps manipulatively) subscribe to a form of crude anachronism to make Freidank's proverbs operable again or to bring the anonymous alliterative romance of *Sir Gawain and the Green Knight* back to our consciousness in a retrograde ideology. Instead, the analysis has simply demonstrated that the issues contained in both works have a very long history and continue to be troublesome and virulent until today because we are humans, with all our inner strengths and weaknesses, our failures and accomplishments. Both works speak to humanity, not just to European audiences.

Bibliography

Beecroft, Alexander. *An Ecology of World Literature: From Antiquity to the Present Day*. London and New York: Verso, 2015.

Beecroft, Alexander. "Eurafrasiachronologies: Between the Eurocentric and the Planetary," *Journal of World Literature* 1.1 (2016): 17-28.

Blackham, Harold J. *The Fable as Literature*. London and Dover, NH: Athlone Press 1965.

Blamires, Alcuin, Karen Pratt, and C. W. Marx, eds. *Woman Defamed and Woman Defended: An Anthology of Medieval Texts*. Oxford: Clarendon Press, 1992.

Borgolte, Michael. *Europa im Mittelalter: Mittelalter in der größeren Welt*, ed. Tillmann Lohse and Benjamin Scheller. Essays zur Geschichtsschreibung und Beiträge zur Forschung, 24. Berlin and Boston: Walter de Gruyter, 2014.

Brewer, Derek. "Sir Gawain and the Green Knight: An Essay in Enigma," *The Chaucer Review: A Journal of Medieval Studies and Literary Criticism* 46, no. 1-2 (2011): 248-260.

Brewer, Derek, and Jonathan Gibson, eds. *A Companion to the Gawain-Poet*. Arthurian Studies, 38. Cambridge: D. S. Brewer, 1997.

Burrow, J. A. *A Reading of* Sir Gawain and the Green Knight. London, Henley, and Boston, 1965: Routledge & Kegan Paul, 1977.

Chism, Christine, ed. *A Companion to World Literature*, Vol. 2: *601 CE to 1450 CE. Blackwell Companions to Literatures and Culture*. Series editor Ken Seigneurie. Chichester and Hoboken: John Wiley & Sons, 2020.

Classen, Albrecht. "Boethius as a Source for Late-Medieval German Didactic Poetry? The Example of the Gnomic Poet Heinrich der Teichner," *Carmina Philosophiae* 15 (2006): 63-88.

Classen, Albrecht. "Crime and Violence in the Middle Ages: The Case of Heinrich der Glichezare's *Reinhart fuchs* and Wernher der Gartenære's *Helmbrecht*," *Crime and Punishment in the Middle Ages and Early Modern*

Age: Mental-Historical Investigations of Basic Human Problems and Social Responses, ed. Albrecht Classen and Connie Scarborough. Fundamentals of Medieval and Early Modern Culture, 11. Berlin and Boston: Walter de Gruyter, 2012, 131-158.

Classen, Albrecht. *Death in the Middle Ages and Early Modern Times: The Material and Spiritual Conditions of the Culture of Death*, ed. A. Classen. Fundamentals of Medieval and Early Modern Culture, 16. Berlin and Boston: Walter de Gruyter, 2016.

Classen, Albrecht. "Der Gürtel als Objekt und Symbol in der Literatur des Mittelalters. Marie de France, *Nibelungenlied*, *Sir Gawain and the Green Knight* und Dietrich von der Glezze," *Mediaevistik* 21 (2008, appeared 2010): 11-37.

Classen, Albrecht. "Die Antwort auf die Frage nach der Zukunft liegt auch in der Vergangenheit: Neue Ansätze zu einer europäisch konzipierten Mediävistik. Oder: Wohin mit der national-geprägten Philologie in Anbetracht von St. Augustin, Martianus Capella, Boethius, Thomas von Aquin oder Christine de Pizan?," *Zeitschrift für deutsche Philologie*. Sonderheft: *Deutsche Philologie: Nationalphilologien heute*, 139 (May 2021): 34-70.

Classen, Albrecht. *Freedom, Imprisonment, and Slavery in the Pre-Modern World: Cultural-Historical, Social-Literary, and Theoretical Reflections*. Fundamentals of Medieval and Early Modern Culture, 25. Berlin and Boston: Walter de Gruyter, 2021.

Classen, Albrecht. "Global History in the Middle Ages": A Medieval and an Early Modern Perspective. "The *Niederrheinische Orientbericht* (ca. 1350) and Adam Olearius's *Vermehrte New Beschreibung der Muscowitischen vnd Persischen Reyse* (1647; 1656)," forthcoming in *Philological Quarterly*.

Classen, Albrecht. "Globalism in Medieval Literature? Pre-Modern Perspectives in Poetic Projections: Wolfram von Eschenbach's *Parzival*, Konrad Fleck's *Flore und Blancheflor*, and *Reinfried von Braunschweig*," *Athens Journal of Philology* 7 (2020): 1-29.

Classen, Albrecht. "Global Literature – What Do We Know, What Should We Know, and How Can We Create an Epistemological Network to Work toward New Humanities?," *Humanities Open Access*, online at: https://www.mdpi.com/journal/humanities/special_issues/global_literature February 24, 2021.

Classen, Albrecht. "Global Travel in the Late Middle Ages: The Eyewitness Account of Johann Schiltberger," *Medieval History Journal* 23.1 (2020): 1-28.

Classen, Albrecht. *Handbook of Medieval Culture: Fundamental Aspects and Conditions of the European Middle Ages*, ed. Albrecht Classen. 3 vols. Berlin and Boston: Walter de Gruyter, 2015.

Classen, Albrecht. *Handbook of Medieval Studies: Terms – Methods – Trends*, ed. Albrecht Classen. 3 vols. Berlin and New York: Walter de Gruyter, 2010.

Classen, Albrecht. "Laughter as an Expression of Human Nature in the Middle Ages and the Early Modern Period: Literary, Historical, Theological, Philosophical, and Psychological Reflections," *Laughter in the Middle Ages and Early Modern Times: Epistemology of a Fundamental Human Behavior, Its Meaning, and Consequences*, ed. id. Fundamentals of Medieval and Early Modern Culture, 5. Berlin and New York: Walter de Gruyter, 2010, 1-140.

Classen, Albrecht. "Messages from the Past for Our Current Crisis," *The Living Pulpit* February 22, 2019; http://www.pulpit.org/2019/02/messages-from-the-past-for-our-current-crisis/.

Classen, Albrecht. "Queer Medieval," *Oxford Bibliographies Online*, forthcoming.

Classen, Albrecht. "The Amazon Rainforest of Pre-Modern Literature: Ethics, Values, and Ideals from the Past for our Future. With a Focus on Aristotle and Heinrich Kaufringer," *Humanities Open Access* 9(1).4 (2020), published on December 24, 2019, online at: https://www.mdpi.com/2076-0787/9/1/4/pdf (last accessed on June 18, 2021).

Classen, Albrecht. "The Global World in the Pre-Modern Era: Lessons from the Past for Our Future With a Focus on the Early Modern Novel *Fortunatus* (1509)," *Current Research Journal of Social Sciences and Humanities* 3.2 (2020): 152-164.

Classen, Albrecht. "The Human Quest for Happiness and Meaning: Old and New Perspectives: Religious, Philosophical, and Literary Reflections from the Past as a Platform for Our Future. St. Augustine, Boethius, and Gautier de Coincy," *Athens Journal of Humanities & Arts* 5.2 (2018): 179-206.

Classen, Albrecht. "Universal Wisdom in Medieval Fable Literature," *Medieval History and Literature*, blogsite, https://boydellandbrewer.com/blog/medieval-history-and-literature/universal-wisdom-in-medieval-fable-literature/, March 11, 2021.

Coenen, Hans Georg. *Die Gattung Fabel: Infrastrukturen einer Kommunikationsform*. Uni-Taschenbücher, 2159. Göttingen: Vandenhoeck & Ruprecht, 2000.

Cölln, Jan, Susanne Friede, and Hartmut Wulfram, eds. *Alexanderdichtungen im Mittelalter: Kulturelle Selbstbestimmung im Kontext literarischer Beziehungen*. Veröffentlichungen aus dem Göttinger Sonderforschungsbereich 529 Internationalität nationaler Literaturen, 1. Göttingen: Wallstein, 2000.

Cordoni, Constanza and Matthias Meyer, eds. *Barlaam und Josaphat: Neue Perspektiven auf ein europäisches Phänomen*. Berlin and Boston: Walter de Gruyter, 2015.

Dicke, Gerd, and Klaus Grubmüller, *Die Fabeln des Mittelalters und der frühen Neuzeit: ein Katalog der deutschen Versionen und ihrer lateinischen Entsprechungen*. Münstersche Mittelalter-Schriften, 60. Munich: Wilhelm Fink, 1987.

Dinzelbacher, Peter. *Das fremde Mittelalter: Gottesurteil und Tierprozess*. 2nd exp. ed. Darmstadt: Wissenschaftliche Buchgesellschaft, 2020.

Dinzelbacher, Peter. *Structures and Origins of the "Twelfth-Century Renaissance."* Monographien zur Geschichte des Mittelalters. Stuttgart: Anton Hiersemann, 2017.

Dinzelbacher, Peter. *Verzweiflung und Hoffnung. Die Suche nach der kommunikativen Gemeinschaft in der deutschen Literatur des Mittelalters*. Beihefte zur Mediaevistik, 1. Berlin: Peter Lang, 2002.

Dithmar, Reinhard. *Die Fabel: Geschichte, Struktur, Didaktik*. 8th rev. ed. Rpt. of the completely rev. ed. from 1988. Uni-Taschenbücher, 73, 1988. Paderborn and Munich: Schöningh, 1997.

Doufikar-Aerts, Faustina. *Alexander Magnus Arabicus: A Survey of the Alexander Tradition Through Seven Centuries: From Pseudo-Callisthenes to Sūrī*, Mediaevalia Groningana. New Series. Paris and Leuven: Peeters, 2010.

Dronke, Peter. *Medieval Latin and the Rise of European Love-Lyric*, 2 vols. 2nd ed. Oxford: Clarendon Press, 1968.

Eriksen, Stefka G., Karen Langsholt Holmqvist, and Bjørn Bandlien eds. *Approaches to the Medieval Self: Representations and Conceptualizations of the Self in the Textual and Material Culture of Western Scandinavia, c. 800–1500*. Berlin and Boston: Walter de Gruyter, 2020.

Ferrante, Joan M. *The Conflict of Love and Honor: The Medieval Tristan Legend in France, Germany and Italy*. De proprietatibus litterarum: Series practica, 78. The Hague: Mouton, 1978.

Freidank. *Freidankes Bescheidenheit*. Ed. H. E. Bezzenberger. Halle a. d. S.: Verlag der Buchhandlung des Waisenhauses, 1872.

Freidank. *Freidanks Bescheidenheit mittelhochdeutsch/neuhochdeutsch* von Wolfgang Spiewok. Wodan. Greifswalder Beiträge zum Mittelalter. Serie 1: Texte des Mittelalters, 15. Greifswald: Reineke-Verlag, 1996.

Freidank. *L'indignazione di un poeta-crociato: i versi gnomici su Acri*, trans. Maria Grazia Cammarota. Biblioteca medievale, 135. Rome: Carocci, 2011.

Freidank. *Middelnederlandsche rijmspreuken als vertaalde verzen van Freidanks Bescheidenheit: Uit een oud Brusselsch handschrift van de Koninklijke Bibliotheek*, ed. and explained by Willem H. D. Suringar. Leiden: Brill, 1886.

Fried, Johannes, ed. *Die abendländische Freiheit vom 10. zum 14. Jahrhundert: der Wirkungszusammenhang von Idee und Wirklichkeit im europäischen Vergleich*. Vorträge und Forschungen/Konstanzer Arbeitskreis für Mittelalterliche Geschichte, 39. Sigmaringen: Thorbecke, 1991.

Gärtner, Wernher der. *Helmbrecht: Mittelhochdeutsch / Neuhochdeutsch*, ed., trans., and commentary by Fritz Tschirch. Stuttgart: Philipp Reclam, 1974.

Gill, Jana Lyn. "Gawain's Girdle and Joseph's Garment: Tokens of 'Vntrawþe.'" *Journal of the International Arthurian Society* 2.1 (2014): 46–62.

Hatt, Cecilia A. *God and the Gawain-Poet: Theology and Genre in Pearl, Cleanness, Patience and Sir Gawain and the Green Knight*. Cambridge: D. S. Brewer, 2015.

Heinzle, Joachim. *Marburger Repertorium der Freidank Überlieferung* (1998-2006), online at: https://mrfreidank.de/; https://handschriftencensus.de/werke/115 (last accessed on June 18, 2021).

Heiser, Ines. *Autorität Freidank: Studien zur Rezeption eines Spruchdichters im späten Mittelalter und der frühen Neuzeit*. Hermaea: Neue Folge, 110. Tübingen: Max Niemeyer, 2006.

Heng, Geraldine. "Early Globalities, and Its Questions, Objectives, and Methods: An Inquiry into the State of Theory and Critique," *Exemplaria* 26.2–3 (2014): 232–251.

Heng, Geraldine and Lynne Ramey. "Early Globalities, Global Literatures: Introducing a Special Issue on the Global Middle Ages," *Literature Compass* (2014): 1–6.

Hermans, Erik, ed. *A Companion to the Global Early Middle Ages*. Companions. Leeds: Arc Humanities Press, 2020.

Hofman, Rijcklof, Charles Caspers, Peter Nissen, et al. eds. *Inwardness, Individualization, and Religious Agency in the Late Medieval Low Countries: Studies in the* Devotio Moderna *and Its Contexts*, Medieval Church Studies, 43. Turnhout: Brepols, 2020.

Holmes, Catherine, and Naomi Standen, eds. *The Global Middle Ages*. Past&Present. Supplement, New Series, 13. Oxford and New York: Oxford University Press, 2018.

Howard, Donald R., and Christian Zacher, eds. *Critical Studies of Sir Gawain and the Green Knight*. Notre Dame, IN, and London: University of Notre Dame Press, 1968.

Kaeuper, Richard W. *Medieval Chivalry*. Cambridge Medieval Textbooks. Cambridge: Cambridge University Press, 2016.

Kaylor, Jr., Noel Harold, and Philip Edward Phillips, eds. *Vernacular Traditions of Boethius's "De consolatione philosophiae,"* Research in Medieval Culture. Kalamazoo: Medieval Institute Publications, 2016.

Klimek, Kimberly, Pamela L. Troyer, Sarah Davis-Secord, and Bryan C. Keene. *Global Medieval Contexts 500–1500: Connections and Comparisons.* New York and London: Routledge, 2021.

Knapp, Fritz Peter. *Blüte der europäischen Literatur des Hochmittelalters,* vol. 2: *Roman – Kleinepik – Lehrdichtung.* Stuttgart: S. Hirzel, 2019, 338-339.

McMullen, A. Joseph, and Erica Weaver, eds. *The Legacy of Boethius in Medieval England: The Consolation and Its Afterlives,* Medieval & Renaissance Texts & Studies, 525. Tempe: Arizona Center for Medieval and Renaissance Studies, 2018.

Middell, Matthias, ed. *The Practice of Global History: European Perspectives.* London, New York: Bloomsbury Academic, 2019.

Neumann, Friedrich. "Freidanks Herkunft und Schaffenszeit," *Zeitschrift für deutsches Altertum und deutsche Literatur* 89 (1958/1959): 213–241.

Nolte, Theodor, and Tobias Schneider, eds. *Wernher der Gärtner: „Helmbrecht": Die Beiträge des Helmbrecht-Symposions in Burghausen 2001,* Stuttgart: S. Hirzel Verlag, 2001.

Outhwaite, Patrick. "Sir Gawain's Penitential Development from Attrition to Contrition," *The Chaucer Review: A Journal of Medieval Studies and Literary Criticism* 56.2 (2021): 153-170.

Pfister, Manfred, ed. *Laughter from* Beowulf *to Beckett and Beyond.* Internationale Forschungen zur allgemeinen und vergleichenden Literaturwissenschaft, 57. Amsterdam and New York: Editions Rodopi, 2002, 1-5.

Putter, Ad. *An Introduction to the Gawain-Poet.* Longman Medieval and Renaissance Library. London and New York: Longman, 1996.

Rubin, David Lee, and A. L. Sells. "Fable," *The New Princeton Encyclopedia of Poetry and Poetics,* ed. Alex Preminger and T. V. F. Brogan. Princeton: Princeton University Press, 1993.

Rüdiger, Jan. *All the King's Women: Polygyny and Politics in Europe, 900–1250.* The Northern World, 88 Leiden and Boston: Brill, 2020.

Seelbach, Ulrich. *Späthöfische Literatur und ihre Rezeption im späten Mittelalter: Studien zum Publikum des "Helmbrecht" von Wernher dem Gartenaere.* Philologische Studien und Quellen, 115 Berlin: Erich Schmidt, 1987.

Singh, Harleen. *The Rani of Jhansi: Gender, History, and Fable in India.* Delhi: Cambridge University Press, 2014.

Stock, Markus. *Alexander the Great in the Middle Ages: Transcultural Perspectives.* Toronto, Buffalo, and London: University of Toronto Press, 2016.

Treadgold, Donald W. *Freedom: A History.* New York: New York University Press, 1990.

Vantuono, William, ed. and trans. *Sir Gawain and the Green Knight,* rev. ed, 1997. Notre Dame: University of Notre Dame Press, 1999.

Vogelweide, Walter von der. *Leich, Lieder, Sangsprüche,* 15th rev. ed. by Thomas Bein. Berlin and Boston: Walter de Gruyter, 2013, 254, no. 38.

West, Kevin R. "Tokens of Sin, Badges of Honor: Julian of Norwich and Sir Gawain and the Green Knight," *Renascence: Essays on Values in Literature* 69.1 (2017): 3-16.

Wilpert, Gero von. "Fabel." *Sachwörterbuch der Literatur.* 8th improved and expanded ed. Stuttgart: Alfred Kröner Verlag, 2011, 254-255.

Notes

1 Peter Dinzelbacher, *Structures and Origins of the "Twelfth-Century Renaissance."* Monographien zur Geschichte des Mittelalters (Stuttgart: Anton Hiersemann, 2017). In another context, however, he also emphasizes that many aspects of medieval culture will remain alien to us today, though terms such as "primitivism" or "barbarity" ought to be avoided. Peter Dinzelbacher, *Das fremde Mittelalter: Gottesurteil und Tierprozess.* 2nd exp. ed. (Darmstadt: Wissenschaftliche Buchgesellschaft, 2020).

2 See now Jan Rüdiger, *All the King's Women: Polygyny and Politics in Europe, 900–1250.* The Northern World, 88 (Leiden and Boston: Brill, 2020).

3 Albrecht Classen, "Queer Medieval," *Oxford Bibliographies Online,* forthcoming.

4 See now the contributions to the *Handbook of Medieval Studies: Terms – Methods – Trends,* ed. Albrecht Classen. 3 vols. (Berlin and New York: Walter de Gruyter, 2010), and to the *Handbook of Medieval Culture: Fundamental Aspects and Conditions of the European Middle Ages,* ed. Albrecht Classen. 3 vols. (Berlin and Boston: Walter de Gruyter, 2015).

5 See, for instance, Peter Dronke, *Medieval Latin and the Rise of European Love-Lyric,* 2 vols. 2nd ed. (Oxford: Clarendon Press, 1968).

6   *Approaches to the Medieval Self: Representations and Conceptualizations of the Self in the Textual and Material Culture of Western Scandinavia, c. 800–1500*, ed. Stefka G. Eriksen, Karen Langsholt Holmqvist, and Bjørn Bandlien (Berlin and Boston: Walter de Gruyter, 2020).

7   Alexander Beecroft, "Eurafrasiachronologies: Between the Eurocentric and the Planetary," *Journal of World Literature* 1.1 (2016): 17-28. See also his study, *An Ecology of World Literature: From Antiquity to the Present Day* (London and New York: Verso, 2015); *The Practice of Global History: European Perspectives*, ed. Matthias Middell (London; New York: Bloomsbury Academic, 2019); cf. also Albrecht Classen, "Universal Wisdom in Medieval Fable Literature," *Medieval History and Literature*, blogsite, https://boydellandbrewer.com/blog/medieval-history-and-literature/universal-wisdom-in-medieval-fable-literature/, March 11, 2021. See also *A Companion to World Literature*, ed. Ken Seigneurie. Vol. 2: *601 CE to 1450 CE*, ed. Christine Chism. *Blackwell Companions to Literatures and Culture* (Chichester, West Sussex, and Hoboken: John Wiley & Sons, 2020). Cf. also the latest attempt to write global history, Kimberly Klimek, Pamela L. Troyer, Sarah Davis-Secord, and Bryan C. Keene, *Global Medieval Contexts 500–1500: Connections and Comparisons* (New York and London: Routledge, 2021).

8   Geraldine Heng and Lynne Ramey, "Early Globalities, Global Literatures: Introducing a Special Issue on the Global Middle Ages," *Literature Compass* (2014): 1–6. doi: 10.1111/lic3.12156; eadem, Geraldine Heng, "Early Globalities, and Its Questions, Objectives, and Methods: An Inquiry into the State of Theory and Critique," *Exemplaria* 26.2–3 (2014): 232–251; Michael Borgolte, *Europa im Mittelalter: Mittelalter in der größeren Welt*, ed. Tillmann Lohse and Benjamin Scheller. Essays zur Geschichtsschreibung und Beiträge zur Forschung, 24 (Berlin and Boston: Walter de Gruyter, 2014); *The Global Middle Ages*, ed. Catherine Holmes and Naomi Standen. Past&Present. Supplement, New Series, 13 (Oxford and New York: Oxford University Press, 2018); *A Companion to the Global Early Middle Ages*, ed. Erik Hermans. Companions (Leeds: Arc Humanities Press, 2020); Albrecht Classen, "Global Travel in the Late Middle Ages: The Eyewitness Account of Johann Schiltberger," *Medieval History Journal* 23.1 (2020): 1-28. doi: 10.1177/0971945819895896; https://journals.sagepub.com/doi/abs/10.1177/0971945819895896; id., "Globalism in Medieval Literature? Pre-Modern Perspectives in Poetic Projections: Wolfram von Eschenbach's *Parzival*, Konrad Fleck's *Flore und Blancheflor*, and *Reinfried von Braunschweig*," *Athens Journal of Philology* 7 (2020): 1-29. https://www.athensjournals.gr/humanities/2021–8-1-1-Classen.pdf; "The Global World in the Pre-Modern Era: Lessons from the Past for Our Future With a Focus on the Early Modern Novel *Fortunatus* (1509)," *Current Research Journal of Social Sciences and Humanities* 3.2 (2020): 152-164. http://journalofsocialsciences.org/pdf/vol3no2/CRJSSH_Vol03_No2_p_152–164.pdf; id., "Global Literature – What Do We Know, What Should We Know, and How Can We Create an Epistemological Network to Work toward New Humanities?," *Humanities Open Access*. https://www.mdpi.com/journal/humanities/special_issues/global_literature (February 24, 2021); id., "Global History in the Middle Ages: A Medieval and an Early Modern Perspective. The *Niederrheinische Orientbericht* (ca. 1350) and Adam Olearius's *Vermehrte New Beschreibung der Muscowitischen vnd Persischen Reyse* (1647; 1656)," to appear in *Philological Quarterly*.

9   *Alexanderdichtungen im Mittelalter: Kulturelle Selbstbestimmung im Kontext literarischer Beziehungen*, ed. Jan Cölln, Susanne Friede, and Hartmut Wulfram. Veröffentlichungen aus dem Göttinger Sonderforschungsbereich 529 Internationalität nationaler Literaturen, 1 (Göttingen: Wallstein, 2000); Faustina Doufikar-Aerts, *Alexander Magnus Arabicus: A Survey of the Alexander Tradition Through Seven Centuries: From Pseudo-Callisthenes to Sūrī*, Mediaevalia Groningana. New Series (Paris and Leuven: Peeters, 2010); *Alexander the Great in the Middle Ages: Transcultural Perspectives*, ed. Markus Stock (Toronto, Buffalo, and London: University of Toronto Press, 2016).

10 *Barlaam und Josaphat: Neue Perspektiven auf ein europäisches Phänomen*, ed. Constanza Cordoni and Matthias Meyer (Berlin and Boston: Walter de Gruyter, 2015).

11 Albrecht Classen, "Die Antwort auf die Frage nach der Zukunft liegt auch in der Vergangenheit: Neue Ansätze zu einer europäisch konzipierten Mediävistik. Oder: Wohin mit der national-geprägten Philologie in Anbetracht von St. Augustin, Martianus Capella, Boethius, Thomas von Aquin oder Christine de Pizan?," *Zeitschrift für deutsche Philologie*. Sonderheft: *Deutsche Philologie: Nationalphilologien Heute* 139 (May 2021): 34-70; id., "The Amazon Rainforest of Pre-Modern Literature: Ethics, Values, and Ideals from the Past for our Future. With a Focus on Aristotle and Heinrich Kaufringer," *Humanities Open Access* 9(1).4 (2020), published on December 24, 2019. https://www.mdpi.com/2076–0787/9/1/4/pdf (last accessed on June 18, 2021). I have addressed this issue also recently in a non-scholarly publication: "Messages from the Past for Our Current Crisis," *The Living Pulpit* February 22, 2019. http://www.pulpit.org/2019/02/messages-from-the-past-for-our-current-crisis/.

12 *Death in the Middle Ages and Early Modern Times: The Material and Spiritual Conditions of the Culture of Death*, ed. A. Classen. Fundamentals of Medieval and Early Modern Culture, 16 (Berlin and Boston: Walter de Gruyter, 2016).

Humanism in European Medieval Literature

13 Friedrich Neumann, "Freidanks Herkunft und Schaffenszeit," *Zeitschrift für deutsches Altertum und deutsche Literatur* 89 (1958/1959): 213–241. Here I quote from *Freidanks Bescheidenheit mittelhochdeutsch/neuhochdeutsch* von Wolfgang Spiewok. Wodan. Greifswalder Beiträge zum Mittelalter. Serie 1: Texte des Mittelalters, 15 (Greifswald: Reineke-Verlag, 1996). See also the full edition by H. E. Bezzenberger, *Freidankes Bescheidenheit* (Halle a. d. S.: Verlag der Buchhandlung des Waisenhauses, 1872). https://brittlebooks.library.illinois.edu/brittlebooks_open/Books2008-02/bezzehe0001frides/bezzehe0001frides.pdf

14 See Joachim Heinzle, *Marburger Repertorium der Freidank Überlieferung* (1998-2006), online at: https://mrfreidank.de/; https://handschriftencensus.de/werke/115 (both last accessed on June 18, 2021). Cf. Ines Heiser, *Autorität Freidank: Studien zur Rezeption eines Spruchdichters im späten Mittelalter und der frühen Neuzeit.* Hermaea: Neue Folge, 110 (Tübingen: Max Niemeyer, 2006). For a bibliography of older Freidank studies, see https://de.wikipedia.org/wiki/Freidank (last accessed on June 19, 2021); for a summary of the little biographical information we have, see Fritz Peter Knapp, *Blüte der europäischen Literatur des Hochmittelalters*, vol. 2: *Roman – Kleinepik – Lehrdichtung* (Stuttgart: S. Hirzel, 2019), 338-339.

15 Donald W. Treadgold, *Freedom: A History* (New York: New York University Press, 1990); see also the contributions to *Die abendländische Freiheit vom 10. zum 14. Jahrhundert: der Wirkungszusammenhang von Idee und Wirklichkeit im europäischen Vergleich*, ed. Johannes Fried. Vorträge und Forschungen/Konstanzer Arbeitskreis für Mittelalterliche Geschichte, 39 (Sigmaringen: Thorbecke, 1991); *Inwardness, Individualization, and Religious Agency in the Late Medieval Low Countries: Studies in the* Devotio Moderna *and Its Contexts*, ed. Rijcklof Hofman, Charles Caspers, Peter Nissen et al. Medieval Church Studies, 43 (Turnhout: Brepols, 2020); Albrecht Classen, *Freedom, Imprisonment, and Slavery in the Pre-Modern World: Cultural-Historical, Social-Literary, and Theoretical Reflections.* Fundamentals of Medieval and Early Modern Culture, 25 (Berlin and Boston: Walter de Gruyter, 2021).

16 The influence of Boethian thinking was pervasive throughout the entire Middle Ages; see, for instance, *Vernacular Traditions of Boethius's "De consolatione philosophiae,"* ed. Noel Harold Kaylor, Jr. and Philip Edward Phillips. Research in Medieval Culture (Kalamazoo: Medieval Institute Publications, 2016); *The Legacy of Boethius in Medieval England: The Consolation and Its Afterlives*, ed. A. Joseph McMullen and Erica Weaver. Medieval & Renaissance Texts & Studies, 525 (Tempe: Arizona Center for Medieval and Renaissance Studies, 2018); Albrecht Classen, "Boethius as a Source for Late-Medieval German Didactic Poetry? The Example of the Gnomic Poet Heinrich der Teichner," *Carmina Philosophiae* 15 (2006): 63-88; id., "The Human Quest for Happiness and Meaning: Old and New Perspectives: Religious, Philosophical, and Literary Reflections from the Past as a Platform for Our Future. St. Augustine, Boethius, and Gautier de Coincy," *Athens Journal of Humanities & Arts* 5.2 (2018): 179-206. http://www.athensjournals.gr/humanities/2018-5-2-3-Classen.pdf.

17 Walter von der Vogelweide, *Leich, Lieder, Sangsprüche*, 15th rev. ed. by Thomas Bein (Berlin and Boston: Walter de Gruyter, 2013), 254, no. 38. Walther did not imply here a political message; instead, his verse "jô sint iedoch gedanke vrî" (62.19, or: Stanza II, 4) refers to his love for his lady, a feeling which no one could forbid him to have. For the relevant text and its English translation, see https://en.wikipedia.org/wiki/Die_Gedanken_sind_frei#cite_ref-2 (last accessed on June 19, 2021).

18 Wernher der Gärtner, *Helmbrecht: Mittelhochdeutsch/Neuhochdeutsch*, ed., trans., and commentary by Fritz Tschirch (Stuttgart: Philipp Reclam jun., 1974); for critical comments, see Ulrich Seelbach, *Späthöfische Literatur und ihre Rezeption im späten Mittelalter: Studien zum Publikum des "Helmbrecht" von Wernher dem Gartenaere.* Philologische Studien und Quellen, 115 (Berlin: Erich Schmidt, 1987); *Wernher der Gärtner: "Helmbrecht": Die Beiträge des Helmbrecht-Symposions in Burghausen 2001*, ed. Theodor Nolte and Tobias Schneider (Stuttgart: S. Hirzel Verlag, 2001); Albrecht Classen, "Crime and Violence in the Middle Ages: The Case of Heinrich der Glichezare's *Reinhart fuchs* and Wernher der Gartenære's *Helmbrecht*," *Crime and Punishment in the Middle Ages and Early Modern Age: Mental-Historical Investigations of Basic Human Problems and Social Responses*, ed. Albrecht Classen and Connie Scarborough. Fundamentals of Medieval and Early Modern Culture, 11 (Berlin and Boston: Walter de Gruyter, 2012), 131-158.

19 David Lee Rubin and A. L. Sells, "Fable," *The New Princeton Encyclopedia of Poetry and Poetics*, ed. Alex Preminger and T. V. F. Brogan (Princeton: Princeton University Press, 1993), 400-401; here 400. See also the detailed and precise article "Fabel" in Gero von Wilpert, *Sachwörterbuch der* Literatur. 8th improved and expanded ed. (1955; Stuttgart: Alfred Kröner Verlag, 2011), 254-55, which comes along with an extensive bibliography; Harold J. Blackham, *The Fable as Literature* (London and Dover, NH: Athlone Press 1965); Gerd Dicke and Klaus Grubmüller, *Die Fabeln des Mittelalters und der frühen Neuzeit: ein Katalog der deutschen Versionen und ihrer lateinischen Entsprechungen.* Münstersche Mittelalter-Schriften, 60 (Munich: Wailhelm Fink, 1987); Reinhard Dithmar, *Die Fabel: Geschichte, Struktur, Didaktik.* 8th rev. ed. Rpt. of the completely rev. ed. from 1988. Uni-Taschenbücher, 73 (1988; Paderborn and Munich: Schöningh, 1997); Hans Georg Coenen, *Die Gattung Fabel: Infrastrukturen einer Kommunikationsform.* Uni-Taschenbücher, 2159 (Göttingen: Vandenhoeck & Ruprecht, 2000). But fables were written all

over the world; see, for instance, Harleen Singh, *The Rani of Jhansi: Gender, History, and Fable in India* (Delhi: Cambridge University Press, 2014).

20 Albrecht Classen, *Verzweiflung und Hoffnung. Die Suche nach der kommunikativen Gemeinschaft in der deutschen Literatur des Mittelalters*. Beihefte zur Mediaevistik, 1 (Berlin: Peter Lang, 2002); this is an intensive engagement with modern communication theory and the question of how it can be utilized to gain a better understanding of some of the major medieval literary works. At that time, I had not yet been fully aware of Freidank's significant contributions to this topic.

21 For a small exception, see Freidank, *L'indignazione di un poeta-crociato: i versi gnomici su Acri*, trans. Maria Grazia Cammarota. Biblioteca medievale, 135 (Rome: Carocci, 2011), dealing with Freidank's poetic comments on Acre in the Holy Land and Emperor Frederick II's crusade. See also Freidank, *Middelnederlandsche rijmspreuken als vertaalde verzen van Freidanks Bescheidenheit: Uit een oud Brusselsch handschrift van de Koninklijke Bibliotheek*, ed. and explained by Willem H. D. Suringar (Leiden: Brill, 1886). I am in the process of publishing a volume on medieval texts dedicated to wisdom, which will contain an English translation of most of Freidank's stanzas (Berlin: Peter Lang, forthcoming).

22 Joan M. Ferrante, *The Conflict of Love and Honor: The Medieval Tristan Legend in France, Germany and Italy*. De proprietatibus litterarum: Series practica, 78 (The Hague: Mouton, 1978); Richard W. Kaeuper, *Medieval Chivalry*. Cambridge Medieval Textbooks (Cambridge: Cambridge University Press, 2016).

23 *Sir Gawain and the Green Knight*, ed. and trans. by William Vantuono. Rev. ed. (1997; Notre Dame: University of Notre Dame Press, 1999). For some recent scholarship, see J. A. Burrow, *A Reading of* Sir Gawain and the Green Knight (1965; London, Henley, and Boston: Routledge & Kegan Paul, 1977); *Critical Studies of Sir Gawain and the Green Knight*, ed. Donald R. Howard and Christian Zacher (Notre Dame, and London: University of Notre Dame Press, 1968); Ad Putter, *An Introduction to the Gawain-Poet*. Longman Medieval and Renaissance Library (London and New York: Longman, 1996); *A Companion to the Gawain-Poet*, ed. Derek Brewer and Jonathan Gibson. Arthurian Studies, 38 (Cambridge: D. S. Brewer, 1997); Cecilia A. Hatt, *God and the Gawain-Poet: Theology and Genre in Pearl, Cleanness, Patience and Sir Gawain and the Green Knight* (Cambridge: D. S. Brewer, 2015).

24 As to the belt and its symbolism in a wider context, see Albrecht Classen, "Der Gürtel als Objekt und Symbol in der Literatur des Mittelalters. Marie de France, *Nibelungenlied, Sir Gawain and the Green Knight* und Dietrich von der Glezze," *Mediaevistik* 21 (2008, appeared 2010): 11-37; Jana Lyn Gill, "Gawain's Girdle and Joseph's Garment: Tokens of 'Vntrawþe,'" *Journal of the International Arthurian Society* 2.1 (2014): 46-62; Patrick Outhwaite, "Sir Gawain's Penitential Development from Attrition to Contrition," *The Chaucer Review: A Journal of Medieval Studies and Literary Criticism* 56.2 (2021): 153-170.

25 For this old trope, see *Woman Defamed and Woman Defended: An Anthology of Medieval Texts*, ed. Alcuin Blamires with Karen Pratt and C. W. Marx (Oxford: Clarendon Press, 1992), though he does not engage with our text.

26 *Laughter from Beowulf to Beckett and Beyond*, ed. Manfred Pfister. Internationale Forschungen zur allgemeinen und vergleichenden Literaturwissenschaft, 57 (Amsterdam and New York: Editions Rodopi, 2002), 1-5; Albrecht Classen, "Laughter as an Expression of Human Nature in the Middle Ages and the Early Modern Period: Literary, Historical, Theological, Philosophical, and Psychological Reflections," *Laughter in the Middle Ages and Early Modern Times: Epistemology of a Fundamental Human Behavior, Its Meaning, and Consequences*, ed. id. Fundamentals of Medieval and Early Modern Culture, 5 (Berlin and New York: Walter de Gruyter, 2010), 1-140; here 60-62.

27 Kevin R. West, "Tokens of Sin, Badges of Honor: Julian of Norwich and Sir Gawain and the Green Knight," *Renascence: Essays on Values in Literature* 69.1 (2017): 3-16; most insightful and also frustrating proves to be the fundamental study by Derek Brewer, "Sir Gawain and the Green Knight: An Essay in Enigma," *The Chaucer Review: A Journal of Medieval Studies and Literary Criticism* 46.1-2 (2011): 248-260. There are, certainly, internal conflicts in the narrative which do not become fully solved, but the crucial issue remains relevant at the end, the struggle for a human's honor in the face of almost certain death.

28 Vantuono, ed. and trans. (see note 23), ix-x.

13

The Circulation of Atheism in Early Modern England

Marlowe, Greene, and Shakespeare

Peter C. Herman

Atheism is not a very popular topic in early modern studies. While there has been significant work over the years, particularly by such intellectual historians as David Wootten and Michael Hunter, literary critics have shied away from atheism.[1] A subject search in the MLA Bibliography for "atheism" in the period 1500–1599 yields only 29 hits between 1940 and 2019, most focusing on Christopher Marlowe. A search for 1600–1699 yields only 52 references for the same period. Again, not a lot. Key critical works exclude atheism from consideration. For example, Debora Shuger's *Habits of Thought in the English Renaissance* does not include "atheism" in the index, presumably because Shuger does not consider atheism a Renaissance habit of thought.[2] Similarly, *The Oxford Handbook of Shakespearean Tragedy* omits "atheism" from its index. "Religion" and "Religious, beliefs," yes; but "atheism," no.[3] Perhaps the most influential comment on the topic comes from Stephen Greenblatt, who observed, "I am arguing not that atheism was literally unthinkable in the late sixteenth century but rather that it was almost always thinkable only as the thought of another."[4] Greenblatt clearly has a point, although that point requires major qualifications, as we shall see. But he published this remark a long time ago. 1988, to be precise.

Since then, with the major exception of Michael Bryson's *The Atheist Milton*, research on the topic has largely stagnated.[5] Even Chloe Preedy's recent book, *Marlowe's Literary Scepticism*, sidelines today's conventional understanding of atheism—i.e., there is no god—and pushes Marlowe into a more religious framework, tracing the skepticism in his plays to the proliferation of religious persuasions and the impossibility of deciding between them. It's not that there's no God, Preedy has Marlowe arguing, it's that we have no way of deciding which is the right one.[6]

Part of the problem is that in the early modern period, "atheist" was often used as a synonym for "heretic." Surely, whoever called Elizabeth I "an atheist and a maintainer of atheism" did not mean the Queen did not believe in God; rather, this person meant that Elizabeth held wrong beliefs about God.[7] Conversely, when John Hull denounced the Catholic Church as atheist, he does not mean that Catholics do not believe in God ("For what is Papisme? A denying there is a God? No, seeing no Barbarian (excepting some few) was so Barbarous"[8]); rather, he means they hold beliefs Hull considers false: "for what is the kingdome of Popery, but heresie [...]"[9] "Atheism" could, and was, invoked to describe any religious belief you don't like. For example, Henry Smith directs his very popular *Gods Arrow against Atheists* (1593; republished 11 times) against Islam, Catholicism, and "the Brownists and Barrowists, with their detestable Schismes are confuted, and our Church approved to be the only true Church of God."[10] Nor was atheism's definition restricted to religion. According to one preacher, "the hypocrite is a close Atheist: the loose wicked man is an open Atheist, the secure, bold, and proud transgressor is Atheist: he that will not be taught & reformed, is an Atheist."[11] Any sort of bad behavior could get one labeled an "atheist."

DOI: 10.4324/9781003046004-16

Nonetheless, there are two definitions of atheism that were clearly present in early modern England. The first is the common definition today: that God does not exist.

In 1438, "a man named Brewer [...] claimed that malt did more to justify god's ways to man than the Bible."[12] This medieval braxeator was probably more interested in increasing sales than making a theological point. More serious is the 1519 case of one Elizabeth Walthorpe, who endured a genuine spiritual crisis, and found herself in deep trouble as a result:

> First, she says that since Whitsunday last she has had not perfect nor steadfast belief in God, nor since that time she had no manner good mind to come to the Church nor to serve God, and for the most part she has not come to the Church, and she has not believed in the holy sacrament of the altar [...][13]

Walthorpe avoided serious punishment by claiming that these thoughts were put into her head by the devil. Nonetheless, the notion that "God" is a fiction was evidently thinkable in the early Henrician era, and as one's own thought, not the thought of another.

Moving ahead to the Elizabethan era, we again find scattered references to prosecutions for unbelief tied to specific utterances. In 1587, one Augustine Draper of Essex found himself indicted "for disbelief in the immortality of the soul and sentenced to repeated conferences in the parish church with three divines until he was persuaded otherwise" (a punishment one imagines that could be worse than death).[14] Two more incidents from roughly the same period: John Minot, a lay reader for a parish church, meaning, a man licensed to preach and conduct some religious services, therefore, presumably someone at least reasonably acquainted with religious doctrine, nonetheless faced the accusation that he "hath openlie and manifestlie reported that ther is no god, no devil, no heaven, ne hell, no lyf after this lyf, no judgment to come."[15] And in 1596, Robert Fisher was accused of elder abuse ("unnatural usage of his father"), forgery, bearing a loaded pistol, and "heretical and execrable words ('that Christe was no savioure & the gospell a fable')."[16]

The second definition, hinted at in the charges against Minot, allows for the existence of a deity, but denies that the universe is governed by moral rules and that one's eternal soul is judged by those rules after we die. As Wootton puts it, the second "defining characteristic of an atheist was not that he or she denied the existence of God, but that he or she did not believe in a divine economy of rewards and punishments, in heaven and hell."[17] For Philippe du Plessis-Mornay, this view is actually worse than denying God's existence:[18]

> I cannot say but that the graunting that there is a God, and yet notwithstanding to denye him the government of things, is more untolerable than the other; considering how great injurie is offered unto him [God] in confessing him after such a sort, as to attribute unto him eyes without sight, eares without hearing, might without mynd, mynd without reason, will without goodnesse, yea and a Godhead without properties peculiar to a Godhead.

Anyone holding such an opinion, de Plessis-Mornay says, quoting Aristotle, "should be answered by a whippe or a hangman, and not by a Philosopher."[19] The two opinions (God does not exist; or if God does exist, He does not care about this world) uneasily co-existed. For example, in the 1580s, a Surrey landowner named William Gardiner found himself before the Star Chamber to answer the charge that "he gave out speeches that he thought there was no God, or that God hath now no government of the World, or that man need not care whether he do well or ill."[20] And the third interrogatory of the 1594 Cerne Abbas investigation into Sir Walter Raleigh's supposed atheism specifically asks about this opinion: "who doe you knowe or have harde that hathe spoken against god his providence over the worlde?"[21]

While these examples are isolated instances in a sea of orthodoxy, they nonetheless demonstrate that atheism, pace Lucien Febvre, was most certainly thinkable in the early modern period, and pace Stephen Greenblatt, not always as the thought of another. No doubt we can ascribe the paucity of explicit assertions of unbelief to how expressing doubt about religion could land you in serious trouble, up to and including execution. As William Perkins writes in 1595, "the magistrate, which is the vicegerent of the lord [...] is to maintain religion with the sworde: and so may put to death both Atheistes, which hold there is no god, of which sorte there is many in these daies."[22] Nonetheless, atheism was clearly present, albeit in a very minor and intermittent way, for most of the sixteenth century.

However, that changes once we reach the last years of Elizabeth's reign and the beginning of the Jacobean era. According to the combined EEBO/EEBO-TCP databases (an imperfect register, to be sure, but useful nonetheless[23]), we find only three references to atheism in published books in 1574–1575 (one is in French, the other two are translations from the French).[24] The next year, the number drops to two books that reference atheism. And in 1576–1577, the number bumps up to three. So we can safely assume that in the 1570s and early 1580s, atheism was not a major concern in Elizabethan England.

But as the 1590s approach, the numbers start to rise, and they keep rising through 1605–1606, exactly the time Shakespeare wrote King Lear:

From 1578 to 1587, there are between 13 to 15 references to atheism in published books. For the year 1587–1588, however, the year Christopher Marlowe likely wrote *Tamburlaine*, 21 books address atheism. In 1592–1593, the number jumps to 33. The numbers dip for the next two years (1593–1594: 22; 1594–1595: 18). But starting in 1595, they go back up and continue to rise through the end of the sixteenth century and the beginning of the 17th.

Significantly, the rise in concerns about atheism track almost perfectly England's decline into "the Crisis of the 1590s," when terrible weather caused multiple crop failures, dearth, starvation, and widespread anger against a social system that failed the poor. In addition, as the 1590s progressed, anxieties about the succession grew more and more pronounced, and the sense that the government was incapable or incompetent to deal with the Crisis was exacerbated by the deaths of Elizabeth's original counselors. Of the 15 Privy councilors alive in 1588, the year the English defeated the Spanish Armada (in many ways, the apex of Elizabeth's reign), 11 had died by 1596 and 12 by 1598.[25] As food became scarce and prices rose exponentially, apprentices rioted in London. According to Stow, in 1595, "some apprentices and other young people [...] being pinched of their

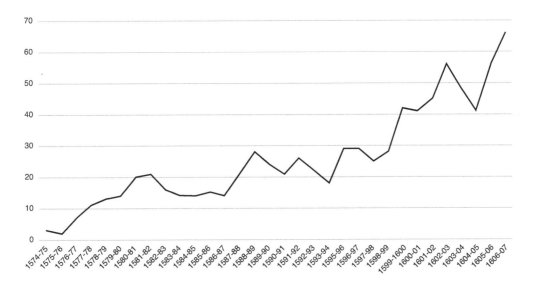

Figure 13.1 Published references to atheism 1574–1606

victuals [...] took from the market people" food they considered overpriced.[26] Some were arrested, and the apprentices then rioted in front of the Lord Mayor's house, and then, "on 16 June, a group of apprentices, soldiers and masterless men met in St Paul's plotting an insurrection against the Lord Mayor with the aim of 'playing the Irish trick on him,' i.e., removing his head."[27] The unrest was not restricted to London. In 1595, the mayor and justices of Norfolk received an anonymous letter accusing them of indifference to the fate of the poor ("For seven years the rich have fed on our flesh. Bribes make you justices blind and you are content to see us famished"), impotence in the face of calamity ("What are these edicts and proclamations, which are here and scattered in the county [...] but a scabbard without the sword"), threatened armed insurrection ("There are 60,000 craftsmen in London and elsewhere, beside the poor country clown, that can no longer bear [their grievances] [...] some barbarous and unmerciful soldier shall lay open your hedges, reap your fields, rifle your coffers, and level you houses to the ground"), and concluded with these chilling words: "Necessity hath no law."[28] The threat was not idle. In 1596, Bartholomew Steere led an abortive uprising against the government. According to one of the co-conspirators, Steere "commonly heard that poor people that they were ready to famish for want of corn, and thought they should be forced by hunger to take it out of men's houses."[29]

There are two pieces of evidence tying the Crisis of the 1590s to the rise in atheism. First, the ecclesiast and historian, Thomas Tymme, connects them in his 1592 taxonomy of the "lepers" afflicting the English commonwealth. The last are the "Murmurers" who direct their mutters against God, and he explicitly states that the dearth afflicting England caused a significant number to doubt God's providence: "Of this sort of murmurers, there are too many at this day among us, who in the time of scarcitie [...] do more like Pagans then Christians begin to murmur against God."[30] Second, in the records of the 1594 Cerne Abbas investigation, the deponent reported that there "is a company about this towne that say, that hell is noe other but povertie & penury in this world; and heaven is no other but to be ritch, and enjoy pleasures; and that we dye like beastes."[31] The deponent, however, was in all likelihood, not making a general observation about poverty and penury, but referring to how the deteriorating food situation affecting mainly the lower sorts—"the poorer sorte," a contemporary Londoner observed, "are cheefely pinched with the dearth"[32]—caused class tensions (hatred, really) to rise and belief to plummet.

Nonetheless, as Greenblatt and others have pointed out, while we have many accusations of atheism, and many testimonials to the extreme presence of atheism in early modern England, we have almost no first-hand unambiguous expressions of disbelief in God and the hereafter, or in the lack any sort of moral order in the universe. Instead, the accusations, even the most detailed, are all second-hand. The 1594 Cerne Abbas investigation into Raleigh's atheism is a perfect example of how tracking down early modern atheism turns into a kind of snipe hunt. None of the deponents have any first-hand knowledge; instead, they respond that they heard second-hand about someone's atheism, and frequently they don't remember whom they heard the rumor from. For example, to the first interrogatory—"Whome doe you know, or have harde [heard] to be sussspected of atheism"—John Jesopp, minister of Gillingham, responds:[33]

> To the first Interrogatorye he can saye nothing of his owne knowledge; but he hath harde that one Herryott of Sir Walter Rawleigh his house hath brought the godhedd in questions, and the whole course of the scriptures but of whome he soe harde it he doth no remember.

How did these rumors start? How did they circulate? As David Wootton puts it, "we have as yet no sure knowledge of the social distribution of unbelief."[34]

I suggest, however, that the early modern stage is a previously unsuspected vector for spreading atheism, and so I now want to turn to the trio of connected plays (I will explain the connections shortly) that make atheism a central element of the plot: both parts of Marlowe's *Tamburlaine*,

Atheism in Early Modern England

Robert Greene's *Selimus*, and Shakespeare's *King Lear*. As we will see, each treats atheism differently. *Tamburlaine* is less about the existence of the gods and more concerned with undermining the traditional assumption that God, or the gods, punish vice. But Marlowe tempers his atheism with a view of the universe as encouraging and rewarding aspiration. Perhaps because Greene's play comes later, when the Crisis of the 1590s was in full swing, his play is more nihilistic than Marlowe's. Greene's *Selimus* embodies the Elizabethan nightmare of a ruler unbounded by judgment after death. Shakespeare takes atheism in a different direction: in *King Lear*, we enacted, literally, the falsity of religion and, at the same time, how religion is a necessary lie, a precursor to Ibsen's "life illusion."[35]

★★★

Marlowe wrote the first part of *Tamburlaine* in 1587, and in response to audience demand, he wrote the second part in 1588, at exactly the time, in other words, when references to atheism started to climb upward.[36] We do not have records for the first performances of these plays, but Henslowe's diary shows that starting in 1594, the plays replaced *The Jew of Malta* as Marlowe's most popular offering. Between October and November that year, the Rose theater presented *Tamburlaine* Part 1 seven times. Starting in December, the Admiral's Men presented both parts on successive days seven times between 1594–1595, when the plays drop from the repertoire (or Henslowe stopped recording the names of the plays his theater performed).[37] Both parts were published together in 1590, then republished in 1593 and 1597; Part 1 was republished in 1590, 1593, 1597 and 1605); Part 2 was republished in 1590, 1593, 1597 and 1606. All told, there are 11 editions of the *Tamburlaine* plays between 1590 and 1606.[38] In addition to audiences flocking to watch the plays and readers buying copies, Marlowe's *Tamburlaine* plays "produced perhaps the largest body of contemporary comment on any early modern play," almost all of it approving of Marlowe's hero and his astounding deeds.[39] Significantly, the first response, by Robert Greene, arriving in 1588, just after the play was first performed, focused on Marlowe's 's challenge to conventional religion, his "daring God out of heaven with that Atheist Tamburlan."[40]

It's true that both parts of *Tamburlaine* flirt with the notion that God does not exist.[41] Defeated, caged, and seeing no hope at all for relief, Bajazeth's wife, Zabina, exclaims, "Then there is left no Mahomet, no God" (Part 1; 5.2.175), leading to the only logical recourse: suicide.[42] But as much as this line hints at a wider application, it's as likely as not that the point is to depict Islam as a false religion. Still, Tamburlaine makes a crucial qualification in Part 2 when he observes that Allah seems to have done nothing even though Tamburlaine burned the Koran because he remains in Hell, so Tamburlaine suggests that Muslims switch their allegiance to "The God that sits in heaven, if any God / For he is God alone, and none but he" (5.2.137–138; my emphasis). Most of these lines repeat the standard Judeo-Christian tenet that God is singular. But then, Tamburlaine tosses in "if any God," raising, if just momentarily, the possibility that there is no God at all.

However, as Greene's statement suggests, Marlowe's atheism in *Tamburlaine* is geared more toward the question of providence than God's non-existence. Except for the brief moment noted above, Tamburlaine never disavows the existence of the gods. In fact, he invokes them as models, and claims that he enjoys their explicit favor. Tamburlaine tells Cosroe that the "heavens have sworn/To royalize the deeds of Tamburlaine" (Part 1; 2.3.7–8), and repeatedly refers to himself as "the Scourge and Wrath of God" (Part 1; 3.3.44; 4.2.31–32; Part 2; 3.5.21; and especially 4.1.144–155, when Tamburlaine justifies his increasingly bloody triumphs by claiming that the gods "enjoined me from above, / To scourge the pride of such as the heavens abhor"). Tamburlaine claims that "empyreal heaven" has given him the power to turn his enemies' curse "all upon their proper heads" (Part 1; 4.4.30–31), and he tells his sons that war is a life "that may illustrate [make illustrious] gods" (Part 2; 4.1. 77). Just before Tamburlaine kills his son, Calyphas, for refusing to

213

Peter C. Herman

participate in battle, he says, "Here Jove, receive his fainting soul again" (Part 2; 4.1.109).[43] So it's fair to say that Tamburlaine (for the most part) accepts the existence of the gods.

But whether the gods adhere to conventional standards of good and bad, whether they intervene in earthly affairs to enforce those rules, that is another question entirely.

Certainly, the printed versions of the play would lead a reader to expect Tamburlaine to be properly punished for his misdeeds. The title prefacing the play's text (as opposed to the title page) in the 1597 edition of *Tamburlaine*, Part 1, is "The Tragical Conquests of Tamburlaine,"[44] and the prologue repeats the generic classification, inviting the reader to view Tamburlaine's "picture in this tragic glass" (Prol., 7). For Marlowe and his audience, tragedy did not mean the fall of a great man, leading to catharsis, but a moral lesson perfectly described by Alexander Neville in the preface to his 1563 translation of Seneca's Oedipus. "Mark thou," Neville enjoins his reader, how "The wrathfull vengeaunce of God [is] provoked," how the "ryght hyghe and immortall God, wyll never leave suche horrible and detestable Crimes unpunished," all to this end: "Myne onely entent was to exhorte men to embrace Vertue and shun Vice."[45]

This view of the universe—that God will punish sin—lies behind Zenocrate's assertion that "The gods, defenders of the innocent, / Will never prosper your intended drifts" (Part 1; 1.2.68–69) and Bajazeth's prediction that "Ambitious pride shall make thee fall as low / For treading on the back of Bajazeth" (Part 1; 4.2.75).

But as everybody knows, nothing of the sort happens in Marlowe's plays. Part 1 ends not with Tamburlaine's fall due to pride, but with his marriage to Zenocrate. The play ends not as a tragedy, but a comedy. Part 2 ends with Tamburlaine's death, but there is again nothing supernatural about his demise. While Tamburlaine falls ill after his burning the Islamic holy book, his sickness does not occur immediately afterward, and the pause interrupts any attempt at drawing a connection between the two events. Furthermore, it's possible that Tamburlaine could have survived his sickness. Tamburlaine's doctor tells him that if he rests, "your Majesty may escape this day / No doubt but you shall soon recover all," and Tamburlaine agrees to stay in bed: "Then will I comfort all my vital parts / And live in spite of death above a day" (Part 2; 5.4.98–101). But then Tamburlaine hears that Callepine is about to attack, and so decides, against medical advice, to rise from his bed and meet him. That decision is what seals his fate. Tamburlaine dies, in other words, not because Jove decides to punish him, but because he did not follow his doctor's orders.

Another example of how the plays demonstrate that the gods, assuming they exist, decline to take any part in human affairs. After Sigismund perjures himself and turns on his Islamic allies on the specious grounds that Christians don't have to keep promises to "infidels / In whom no faith nor true religion rests" (Part 2; 2.1.33–34), the "infidels" defeat him. At first, Orcanes ascribes their victory to divine intervention, even if he is not sure which divinity intervened: "Now lie the Christians bathing in their bloods, / And Christ or Mahomet hath been my friend" (Part 2; 2.3.10–11).[46] But his lieutenant, Gazellus, immediately pours cold water on this notion: "Tis but the fortune of the wars, my lord, / Whose power is often proved a miracle" (Part 2: 2.4.31–32). Divine intervention, in other words, had no bearing on the result, just the "fortune of the wars," that is all. The Islamic army had better soldiers or better tactics. God, whether Jove, Christ or Mahomet, had nothing to do with their victory.

It would seem that *Tamburlaine* portrays a bleak universe in which amoral power rules (a cross between Samuel Beckett and the Terminator), but Marlowe tempers the plays' nihilism in two ways that help explain the play's popularity and shows how Marlowe challenged the standard assumptions about atheism.

First, as many critics have noted, Tamburlaine's rise is cast in explicitly class terms. His adversaries all consider themselves Tamburlaine's social superior, and they are deeply offended at having to deal with someone so far beneath them on the social ladder. "What means this devilish

214

shepherd to aspire," says Cosroe, after Tamburlaine breaks their alliance and turns on him, accusing Tamburlaine of "giantly presumption" (Part 1;2.6.1–2). Bajazeth cannot believe that Tamburlaine has the temerity to call him by his name when the "kings of Fess, Morocco, and Argier" call him "lord" (Part 1; 3.3.66), and the king of Fess cannot believe that Bajazeth would lower himself to speak with a man so far beneath him on the social ladder: "what means the mighty Turkish Emperor / To talk with one so base as Tamburlaine" (Part 1: 3.3.87–88). Bajazeth's wife, Zabina, also cannot believe that she must watch the battle sitting next to Zenocrate: "Base concubine, must thou be placed by me, / That am Empress of the mighty Turk?" (Part 1: 3.3.166–167), and when Tamburlaine's forces defeat Bajazeth, Zabina curses "Mahomet, that mak'st us thus / The slaves to Scythians rude and barbarous" (Part 1: 3.3.270–71). The insult to their dignity exceeds the ignomy of military loss.

With good reason, because Tamburlaine does not stop at destroying the opposing army and slaughtering his enemies. He humiliates Bajazeth in Part 1 by using him as a footstool so "that I may rise into my royal throne" (Part 1: 4.2.15), and in Part 2 Tamburlaine harnesses the defeated kings to his chariot, driving them on with a whip and his famous, "Holla, ye pampered jades of Asia" speech (Part 2: 4.3.1–26). Obviously, these scenes enact the precise opposite of the ordered, hierarchical, and divinely authorized society depicted in official documents, such as the aptly titled "Homily on Obedience." Equally obviously, they enact Tamburlaine's famous assertion that Nature teaches "us all to have aspiring minds," and his enlisting Jove deposing his father as a model for the low striving toward "the sweet fruition of an earthly crown" (Part 1; 2.7.19, 29). Thomas Cartelli has argued that such scenes "may actually have been experienced by Marlowe's audience as a holiday licensing of social, political, and psychological unrestraint," and that Tamburlaine is a "lord of misrule."[47] But the impact of the *Tamburlaine* plays goes well beyond carnivalesque inversions of authority.

While Marlowe wrote the plays in the late 1580s, they enjoyed their great popularity at the same time that the government was harshly cracking down on the uproars caused by the Crisis of the 1590s.[48] In 1596, for example, after apprentices rioted to protest high food prices, rescued one of their number who had been arrested, and set up a gallows in front of the Lord Mayor's house, London's authorities arrested so many people that they had to put them in at least seven outdoor cages placed in Newgate Market, Cripplegate, and the Lime Street, Cheap, Langbourn, Bishopsgate, and Billingsgate wards.[49] As the illustration shows, the cages were placed throughout London, although three were in London's poorer areas. It would have been difficult for patrons of the Rose theater (or anyone else) to miss them.

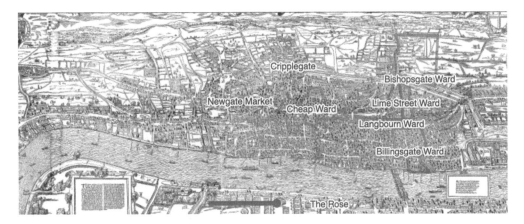

Figure 13.2 Map created at Early Modern Map of London, dir. Janelle Jenstad https://mapoflondon.uvic.ca/index.htm

My point is that at a time when, as Camden puts it, "the meaner sort of people in *London* began to raise tumults,"[50] the spectacle of a shepherd not just conquering, but utterly humiliating his social betters, and telling his followers that Nature approves the low rising against the high would have likely thrilled an audience furious at Elizabeth's government for their inability to control food prices and furious at the rich abandoning their obligations to help the poor.

On the one hand, Marlowe's plays would seem to illustrate the dangers of atheism. Fear of God and punishments in the hereafter were considered essential to the social order.[51] Take away God's justice, and you take away the guardrails preventing chaos. As we have seen, Tamburlaine does not deny that supernatural deities exist, but the play demonstrates that any and all conventions governing behavior have no force whatsoever. Tamburlaine slaughters men, women, and children without any consequence, and he dies in his bed from the human condition: mortality. These plays seem to confirm that atheism and civil society are mutually exclusive. As John Locke would later put it: "The taking away of God, though but even in thought, dissolves all."[52]

But does it dissolve all? In fact, *Tamburlaine* shows that civil society is entirely possible in the absence of supernatural enforcement.

When Tamburlaine forms his army, he does not base his leadership on force and fear. Unlike Richard III, Tamburlaine does not murder his way to the top. Instead, he rules his army, and this is absolutely crucial, not because of superior force, because he has the consent of the governed.

The stage direction tells us that after Tamburlaine defeats Cosroe, "He takes the crown and puts it on" (Part 1; 2.7), but he does not turn to his followers and gloat in triumph, reveling in his victory. Instead, he turns to "Theridamas, Techelles, and the rest" (Part 1; 2.7.55), and asks them, "Who think you now is King of Persia?" (Part 1.2.7.56). They all shout "Tamburlaine!" But then, Tamburlaine does something curious. He clearly feels he needs something more: he needs their explicit permission to rule:

> Though great Mars himself, the angry god of arms
> And all the earthly potentates conspire
> To dispossess me of this diadem,
> Yet will I wear it I despite of them,
> As great commander of this eastern world,
> *If you but say that Tamburlaine shall reign.*
>
> (Part 1: 2.7.58–63; emphasis mine)

They of course give their permission, shouting "Long live Tamburlaine and reign in Asia" (Part 1; 2.7.64). And that's the response that Tamburlaine wants. It is their agreement, not his superior force, not divine permission, that assures his rule: "So now it is more surer on my heard / Than if the gods had held a parliament / And all pronounced me King of Persia" (Part 1; 2.7.65–67).

This is an extraordinary moment because Marlowe combines Tamburlaine's ascendancy with the origin myths of both civil society and the Ancient Constitution, the unwritten rules governing the relative powers of the English monarch and parliament.

According to Plutarch, after Theseus killed the Minotaur, he unified Attica not through the sword, but through agreements: Theseus "wanne them [the rich and the poor], promising that [the new state] should be a common wealth, and not subject to the power of any sole prince, but rather a popular state."[53] Sir John Fortescue, in his fifteenth century and deeply influential *On the Laws and Governance of England*, divides monarchies into two categories: "royal," meaning, absolutist, the king is above the law, and "political," which is what England has, the king is not above the law, and can "change the law [only with] the assent of his subjects."[54] Fortescue traces the beginning of "royal" rule to Nimrod, who ruled through conquest, not agreement: just "as a hunter compels beasts enjoying liberty to obey him, so did he compel men."[55] Fortescue does not give "politic" rule a similarly mythical origin. Instead, he uses analogy, comparing how "a people that

Atheism in Early Modern England

will to erect itself into a kingdom or any other body politic must always set up one man for the government of all" just as "the physical body grows out of the embryo, regulated by one head."[56] In England, Fortescue continues, power "[issues] from the people."[57] Sir Thomas Smith, in *De Republica Anglorum* (1583), drawing on Fortescue, calls parliament (not the monarch), the "most high and absolute power of the realme of Englande" because it "representeth & hath the power of the whole realme both the head and the bodie."[58]

Significantly, Tamburlaine does not just compare the assent of his soldiers to parliament, he says that their authority exceeds a "parliament" of the gods.[59] Equally significantly, despite his ferocity toward his intended conquests, Tamburlaine is fiercely loyal to those who serve him, not just his immediate subordinates, but also his soldiers. After Theridamas joins him, Tamburlaine introduces him to his allies: "These are my friends, in whom I more rejoice / Than doth the king of Persia in his crown / [...] / Make much of them, gentle Theridamas, / And they will never leave thee till the death" (Part 1; 2.1.241–42, 248–249). Later, in Part 2, Tamburlaine describes to Theridamas the culinary wonders that await them after they defeat Natolia, but he adds that his soldiers will also enjoy the spoils of victory: "Lachryma Christi and Calabrian wines / Shall common soldiers drink in quaffing bowls" (2.1.221–222).

While there is no denying the savagery Tamburlaine visits upon the world, which might serve to justify the notion that a belief in divine providence is necessary for social order, in many ways Tamburlaine proves the opposite. He bases his initial authority not on force, but on the explicit permission of the ruled, just as in England the monarch's power emanates from the people. With all due respect to John Locke and his anti-atheist predecessors, taking God out of the equation does not dissolve all. Instead, Marlowe's *Tamburlaine* plays show that people are quite capable of organizing themselves and maintaining order without any divine help or expectation of post-life reward or punishment.[60] With each performance, and with each playbook sold, that message spread farther and wider.

Selimus

In 1594, an anonymous play later attributed to Robert Greene appeared in the bookstalls: *Selimus, Emperor of the Turks*.[61] Greene may have expressed some ambivalence about Marlowe's play in 1588, and he likely had Marlowe in mind with his deathbed condemnation of a "famous gracer of Tragedians [...] who hath said with thee (like the foole in his heart) There is no God."[62] Nonetheless, Greene clearly intended to take advantage of Tamburlaine's success by writing a similar play.[63] As Daniel Vitkus puts it, "Greene's play picks up where Marlowe's plays left off."[64]

Granted, there are a few differences: Selimus is Sultan Bajazeth's son, not a shepherd, and he has an equally ruthless brother, Acomat (*Tamburlaine* does not refer to any siblings). Also, *Selimus* does not advertise itself as a tragedy, but as history (more on that below). Nonetheless, the plot parallels the *Tamburlaine* plays in key ways. Both plays are set in the east, and both trace the rise of a murderous leader who recognizes no limits and suffers no downfall at the end. Selimus, like Tamburlaine, is an ambitious "overachiever," and like Tamburlaine, holds that a crown surpasses all other pleasures. Like Marlowe's Tamburlaine, Selim I, known as "Selim the Grim," the character Greene's Selimus is based on, dies of disease, not divine retribution or military defeat.[65] Greene even explicitly alludes to Tamburlaine four times.[66] Most importantly, both plays are suffused with atheism.

But while Marlowe's plays show that the gods don't care and they certainly don't intervene, Greene's Selimus delivers an extensive account of God's non-existence and the political consequences thereof:[67]

> I count it sacrilege for to be holy
> Or reverence this threadbare name of "good."
> Leave to old men and babes that kind of folly;

217

Count it of equal value with the mud:
Make thou a passage for thy gushing flood
By slaughter, treason, or what else thou can;
And scorn religion—it disgraces man.
[…]
The names of gods, religion, heaven and hell,
And 'gan of pains and feigned rewards to tell:
Pains for those men which did neglect the law;
Rewards for those that lived in quiet awe.
Whereas indeed they were mere fictions,
And if they were not, Selim thinks they were;
And these religious observations,
Only bugbears to keep the world in fear
And make men quietly a yoke to bear.
So that religion (of itself a fable)
Was only found to make us peaceable.
[…]
But we, whose mind in heavenly thoughts is clad,
Whose body doth a glorious spirit bear
That hath no bounds but flieth every where;
Why should we seek to make that soul a slave,
To which dame Nature so large freedom gave?
Amongst us men, there is some difference
Of actions, termed by us good or ill:
As he that doth his father recompense
Differs from him that doth his father kill.
And yet I think, think other what they will,
That parricides, when death hath given them rest,
Shall have as good a part as have the best;
And that's just nothing: for as I suppose
In Death's void kingdom reigns eternal Night,
Secure of evil and secure of foes,
Where nothing doth the wicked man affright,
No more than him that dies in doing right.
Then since in death nothing shall to us fall,
Here while I live, I'll have a snatch at all[.]

(2:15–21, 98–108, 118–136)

This speech, at great length, seems to expand Marlowe's opinion, as reported in the 1593 Baines document, "That the first beginning of Religion was only to keep men in awe," and that men should "not to be afeard of bug-beares and hobgoblins."[68] But the Baines document could not be a source for *Selimus* as it came to light only in the twentieth century. Both, in all likelihood, are drawing on the same sources. Furthermore, Greene's *Selimus* seems to answer, at least in part, the question of how atheism circulated in early modern England. Between 1590 and 1594, the Queen's Men was predominantly a touring company. And as the company included *Selimus* in its repertoire, we can imagine this play being performed in town after town, spreading atheism the way Johnny Appleseed wandered about, planting apple trees.[69] Then, in 1594, as the company dissolved, they sold a clutch of their more popular plays to Thomas Creede, who published three immediately: *The Famous Victories of Henry V, The True Tragedy of Richard III*, and *Selimus.*[70]

However, it could be argued that *Selimus* is an anti-atheistical play. Unlike Tamburlaine, who at least has the virtue of basing his authority on the consent of the governed, and who presents himself as a role model for lower-class aspiration, there is nothing redeeming about Greene's character. Selimus, as he gleefully admits, is a parricide who kills every member of his family he can find to secure his position. Greene's *Selimus* thus seems to demonstrate why early modern political thinkers considered fear of God necessary for social order.[71] Since the bad get the same reward after death as the good, which is nothing, therefore, Selimus concludes, "while I live, I'll have a snatch at all," since there will be no consequences at all for my actions. Atheism, in other results, results in utter selfishness, tyranny, and mass murder. Exactly what Locke and others feared.

Because Selim, however, is not English, and because the action is set in a faraway country, it could be argued that Greene has built in "plausible deniability," i.e., the play implies that only foreign, evil, family-killers who lust after power are atheists. Perhaps the audiences in London and the provinces threw rotten tomatoes and booed Selimus as he delivered this speech. But Greene overlaps the play-world with contemporary England in three ways.

First, history: *Tamburlaine* may be based on actual events, but they happened in the fourteenth century, approximately 200 years before Marlowe wrote his plays. Long ago, in other words, in a land far away. But Greene brings his play much closer to the present. As the title page says, Selimus is "grandfather to him that now reigneth." Close enough to the 1580s, in other words, for at least some in the audience to remember the events of the play, and a reminder of the present Sultan and the close commercial and diplomatic relations Elizabeth fostered between England and the Ottoman Empire.

Selimus cannot be easily dismissed as a fantasy having no relation to contemporary England, especially since Selimus' denial of the soul's immortality was clearly circulating at the time. The sixth interrogatory for the Cerne Abbas asks if the deponent knew anyone who had "spoken against the beinge; or immortality of the soule of man? Or that a mans soule should dye & become like the soule of a beaste[?]"[72] A few years later, one John Derpier was accused, in nearly identical words, holding the "most hereticall & damnable opinion (that there was noe god & noe resurrection, & that men died a death like beastes)."[73] And as we have seen, John Minot was accused of declaring that there is "no god, no devil, no heaven, ne hell, no lyf after this lyf, no judgment to come [...]."[74] Selimus' speech, in other words, would have sounded alarmingly familiar to this play's audience and readers.

Greene further underscores how *Selimus* is a figure for late sixteenth-century England by paralleling Selimus' father, Bajazet, with Elizabeth. Both have been on the throne for 30 years: Elizabeth became Queen in 1558, and Bajazet has been Sultan "Twice fifteen times hath fair Latona's son / Walked around the world with his great light / Since I began" (1.32–34). Greene even drops in a reference to "Cynthia" two lines later (36), a popular term for Elizabeth throughout her reign.[75] The parallel extends further than chronology. Greene depicts Bajazet as utterly exhausted by monarchy's rigors ("what dangers I have overpassed / Would make a heart of adamant aghast" [1.38–39]). As for Elizabeth, she too was widely recognized as nearing the end of her tether. A c. 1593 painting by Marcus Gheeraerts the Younger, the same artist who painted the Dicheley Portrait, unsparingly depicts the ravages of age.

Even if Gheeraerts' portrait did not circulate widely, everyone at the time knew that Elizabeth was aging and her long reign drawing to a close. While Elizabeth did not have to contend with murderous progeny, like Bajazet, she too felt that everything was broken, and she was tired of it: "Now the wit of the fox is everywhere on foot," she complained to the lawyer and antiquary, William Lambarde, "so as hardly a faithful or virtuous man may be found."[76]

Next, Greene's use of allusions: While characters in *Selimus* will occasionally invoke Islam (e.g., Acomat swears "by the holy rites of Mahomet, / His wondrous tomb and sacred Alcoran" [12:19–20]), more often, they invoke classical deities. Bajazet, for example, says that the "tyrant Dionysus / Did picture out the image of a king / When Damocles was placed in his throne" with a sword over his head hanging by a thread (9:18–20), and after he finds out that his son, Acomat, has slaughtered his nephew along with 6000 citizens, calls on "Avernus," "Tartarus," "Demogorgon," and the "Erinyes armed with whips" to pour down their vengeance, and then asks "Jove" to overrule his wishes as Acomat is still his son (14:65–81). Acomat, for his part, compares himself to

Figure 13.3 Portrait of Elizabeth I by Marcus Gheeraerts the Younger https://commons.wikimedia.org/wiki/File:Elizabeth_I_portrait,_Marcus_Gheeraerts_the_Younger_c.1595.jpg

"Tityrus," who "With restless cries doth upon high Jove" while a vulture eats his heart (14.1–2), and Selimus says that he will rise "like Antaeus quelled by Hercules" (16:22). Greene puts into his characters' mouths a classical culture that may be entirely foreign to actual Ottomans, but is entirely familiar to his audience.

Greene even has his characters allude to contemporary literature. Selimus refers to Basilius and his "troops of slave-born Muscovites" (4.18). This phrase is taken straight out of Sir Philip Sidney's *Astrophil and Stella*, Sonnet 2: "and now, like slave-borne *Muscovite*, / I call it praise to suffer tyrannie."[77] While Sidney's collection was published in 1591, it circulated widely in manuscript, and so far as I can tell, the phrase "slave-born Muscovite" occurs nowhere else in the sixteenth century.[78] Similarly, after Corcut announces that he has converted to Christianity, he swears by Christ, "Whom dead, as everliving" (19:82), he adores. The phrase, "dead, as everliving" comes from Edmund Spenser's 1590 epic, *The Faerie Queene*: "For whose sweete sake that glorious badge he wore, / And dead as living ever him ador'd" (1:1:2:2–4).[79] The effect must have been jarring: characters who lived in the early 1500s quoting very recent, and very popular, poetry, and again, the effect is to turn the play into a mirror, not of the Ottoman Empire, but of 1590s England.

Finally, when the clown, Bullithrumble, says "down Holborn, up tribune" (21.46), Greene connects the play to the growing Crisis of the 1590s. As the play's editor, Daniel Vitkus, explains, "Holborne was a fashionable district in London known for its aristocratic residences," and a "'tribune' is a defender of the people's rights."[80] In the middle of a play that takes place a long time ago and far away, suddenly the audience and subsequent readers find an overt reference to London's class tensions, the anger against the rich for abandoning the poor in the hour of need. While the worst disturbances were to come in 1595 and 1596, deteriorating economic conditions led to increasing instances of class-based anger. In 1590, a baker was indicted for threatening the Queen's life, and in October that year, a group of apprentices attacked the lawyers of Lincoln's Inn.[81]

Greene's *Selimus*, then, may dramatize the rise of a particularly ruthless Ottoman Sultan in the early 1500s, but the play also functions as a mirror for the atheism, even nihilism, circulating throughout 1590s England.

King Lear

By 1606, the Crisis of the 1590s had faded. Normal weather patterns prevailed, and James Stuart had ascended the throne peacefully and without controversy. Nonetheless, the concern for atheism not only did not abate, but continued to increase, which may have led William Shakespeare to revisit an old play. Greene's *Selimus* was not particularly successful—the playbook was not reprinted, and Greene never wrote the sequel—yet the play evidently made an impact on William Shakespeare, as he turned to *Selimus* as a source for *King Lear*. In both plays, a child of the monarch (Regan and Acomat) blind a faithful courtier of the monarch (Gloucester and Aga).[82] Equally importantly, both plays feature repeated appeals to the gods for help. In *Selimus*, Bajazet appeals to the gods and wants to know why they don't intervene: "Oh, you dispensers of our hapless breath / Why do ye glut your eyes and take delight / To see sad pageants of men's miseries?" (13.26–28), and Aga, after he is blinded and has his hands chopped off (a detail Shakespeare mercifully leaves out), also appeals to the "supreme architect of all" to "dart they smoldering flame / Upon the head of cursèd Acomat!" (14.94, 100–101). In *Lear*, after the king discovers that Kent has been put in the stocks, he implores, "O heavens, / If you do love old men, if your sweet sway / Allow obedience, if you yourselves are old, / Make it your cause, send down and take my part" (2.4.182–185).[83] Gloucester too turns to the heavens after Regan plucks out one eye: "He that will think to live till he be old, / Give me some help—Oh cruel! O you gods!" (3.7.69–70). The gods of course do not answer. No flames smite Acomat, just as the gods ignore Lear's and Gloucester's pleas for help, just as Mahomet ignores Bajazeth and Zabina's pleas.

Both *Tamburlaine* and *Selimus* include characters who state the orthodoxy that the gods will punish the malefactors. In the former play, Zenocrate tells her captor and later husband, Tamburlaine, that "The gods, defender of the innocent, / Will never prosper your tended drifts" (Part 1; 1.2.68–69), and in the latter, the Queen of Amasia warns Selimus that "the heavens still bear an equal eye, /And vengeance follows thee even at the heels" (26.12–13). But the only character in *Lear* who asserts this commonplace is Edmund: "I told him [Edgar] the revenging gods / Gainst parricides did all their thunder bend" (2.1.47–48). But Edmund, of course, is lying. The gods in *Lear* are no more "revengive" (the version of this word in the Quarto *Lear*) than they are in *Selimus* and *Tamburlaine*.

But Shakespeare takes atheism in a different direction than Marlowe or Greene.[84] When the blinded Gloucester reunites with Edgar (disguised as "Poor Tom"), he is in When Gloucester reunites with Edgar, he is in despair ("As flies to wanton boys are we to th'gods: / They kill us for their sport" (4.2.38–39), and (like Bajazeth and Zabina), suicidal. Gloucester asks Edgar to lead him to Dover, so he can jump off the cliff. No doubt to the original audience's puzzlement, even though Edgar hears his father say, "O dear son Edgar, / The food of thy abused father's wrath, / Might I but live to see thee in my touch / I'd say I had eyes again" (4.2.22–24), he does not reveal himself. Several scenes later, we find out why: "I do trifle thus with his despair / Is done to cure it" (4.6.36–36). But the cure is an imposture. Edgar tricks his father into believing that he did indeed jump off a cliff (in fact, they are nowhere near Dover), but instead of falling to his death, Gloucester floated down like a feather. "Thy life's a miracle" (4.6.56), Edgar tells Gloucester, and then, he takes the fiction to its conclusion. What was that thing with you, Edgar asks, and his father responds, "A poor unfortunate beggar" (4.6.60). No, Edgar says:

> As I stood here below, methought his eyes
> Were two full moons. He had a thousand noses,
> Horns whelked and waved like the enraged sea.
> It was some fiend.
>
> (4.6.71–74)

Edgar then drives the point home: "Think that the clearest gods, who make them honors / Of men's impossibilities, have preserved thee" (4.6.75–76). To cure Gloucester's despair, Edgar creates a fiction—the gods exist, they care, and they intervene. None of this of course is true. The audience watches Edgar make it all up, change roles, change his accent, and convince his father to believe in something that is manifestly not true. But this false belief is what saves his life. Religion may be a bugbear to keep men in fear and awe, but religion may also be a comforting fiction that gives one strength to deal with life's tribulations.

Edgar brings this scene to a close enjoining Gloucester to "Bear free and patient thoughts" (4.6.82), pure stoicism, in other words. But the lesson does not stick. After Gloucester hears that Lear has lost and that both the king and Cordelia are prisoners, he falls once more into despair: "No further, sir, a man may rot even here" (5.2.8). Edgar has no time (or patience) for another extended piece of theater, so Edgar switches from stoicism to what can only be called early modern existentialism: "What, in ill thoughts again? Men must endure / Their going hence even as their coming hither" (5.2.9–10). We must endure because we must endure. Because we must. There is no reason why, and certainly no supernatural or divine plan. That is the hard truth this play teaches.

Tamburlaine, *Selimus*, and *King Lear* thus form a connected trilogy of plays that promoted, in their different ways, atheism. *Tamburlaine*'s extraordinary popularity led Greene to not only imitate the play, but cite it numerous times, and with each reminder, *Selimus*'s audience and readers were not only confronted by the play's atheism, but also Marlowe's. Shakespeare, in *King Lear*, recalls both plays, drawing on their atheistic energy for his own purposes. Collectively, these three plays form the beginnings of a coherent literature on atheism, one that will continue to grow, and continually disturb religious certainties.

Bibliography

Anonymous. "Accusations Against Christopher Marlowe by Richard Baines and Others." https://www.bl.uk/collection-items/accusations-against-christopher-marlowe-by-richard-baines-and-others

Anonymous (possibly Henry Willoughby). *Willobie his Avisa*. London, 1594.

Aylmer, G. E. "Unbelief in Seventeenth-Century England," *Puritans and Revolutionaries: Essays in Seventeenth-Century History presented to Christopher Hill*, eds. Donald Pennington and Keith Thomas. Oxford: Clarendon Press, 1978.

Berti, Silvia. "At the roots of Unbelief." *Journal of the History of Ideas* 56, no. 4 (1995): 555–575.

Bryson, Michael. *The Atheist Milton*. Surrey and Burlington, VT: Ashgate, 2012.

Buckley, George T. *Atheism in the English Renaissance*. New York: Russell & Russell, 1965.

Camden, William. *The History of the Most Renowned and Victorious Princess Elizabeth, late Queen of England*. London, 1688.

Cartelli, Thomas. *Marlowe, Shakespeare, and the Economy of Theatrical Experience*. Philadelphia: University of Pennsylvania Press, 1991.

Cheney, Patrick. *Marlowe's Republican Authorship: Lucan, Liberty, and the Sublime*. New York: Palgrave MacMillan, 2009.

Clark, Peter. "A Crisis Contained? The Condition of English Towns in the 1590s," in *The European Crisis of the 1590s: Essays in Comparative History*, ed. Peter Clark. London: George Allen & Unwin, 1985, 44–66.

Davidson, Nicholas. "Christopher Marlowe and Atheism," *Christopher Marlowe and English Renaissance Culture*, ed. Darryll Grantley and Peter Roberts. Aldershot: Scolar Press, 1996, 129–147.

Deats, Sara Munson. "Marlowe's Interrogative Drama: *Dido, Tamburlaine, Faustus*, and *Edward II*," *Marlowe's Empery: Expanding his Critical Contexts*, ed. Sara Munson Deats and Robert A. Logan. Newark: University of Delaware Press, 2002, 107–130.

Deloney, Thomas. *Jack of Newbury*, ed. Peter C. Herman. Peterborough, Ontario: Broadview, 2015.

Demiralp, Ayse Nur. "*The Life and Death of Jack Straw* and *The Tragical Reign of Selimus*: A Note on Some Verbal and Thematic Parallels," *Notes and Queries* 59, no. 1 (257) (2012): 45–48.

Ekeblad, Inga-Stina. "'*King Lear*' and '*Selimus*,'" *Notes and Queries* 202 (1957): 193–194.

Elton, William. *King Lear and the Gods*. 1966 Reprint. Lexington: University Press of Kentucky, 1988.

Febvre, Lucien. *The Problem of Unbelief in the Sixteenth Century*, trans. Beatrice Gottlieb. Reprint Edition. Cambridge: Harvard University Press, 1982.

Fortescue, Sir John. *On the Laws and Governance of England*, ed. Shelley Lockwood. Cambridge: Cambridge University Press, 1997.

Gaskell, Ian. "2 *Tamburlaine*, Marlow's War against the Gods," *English Studies in Canada* 11, no. 2 (1985), 178–192.

Giovio, Paolo. *A short treatise upon the Turkes Chronicles*, trans. Peter Ashton. London, 1546.

Greenblatt, Stephen. *Shakespearean Negotiations: The Circulation of Social Energy in Renaissance England*. Berkeley: University of California Press, 1988.

Greene, Robert. *Greenes groatsworth of wit*. London, 1637.

Greene, Robert. *Perimides the Blacke-Smith*. London, 1588.

Gurr, Andrew. *The Shakespearian Playing Companies*. Oxford: Clarendon Press, 1996.

Hawarde, John. *Les Reportes del Cases in Camera Stellata, 1593–1609*, ed. William Paley Baildon. London: Privately Printed, 1894.

Henslowe, Philip. *Henslowe's Diary*, 2nd ed., ed. R. A. Foakes. Cambridge: Cambridge University Press, 2002.

Herman, Peter C. "EEBO and Me: A Response to Michael Gavin." *Textual Cultures* 13, no. 1 (2020), 207–216.

Hottson, Leslie. *Shakespeare versus Shallow*. London: Nonesuch Press, 1931.

Hull, John. *The Unmasking of the Politike Atheist*. London, 1602.

Hunter, Michael. "The Problem of 'Atheism' in Early Modern England." *Transactions of the Royal Historical Society* 35 (1985): 135–157.

Hunter, Michael, and David Wootton, eds. *Atheism from the Reformation to the Enlightenment*. Oxford: Clarendon Press, 1992.

Ibsen, Henrik. *The Wild Duck*. New York: Samuel French, 1980.

Jacquot, Jean. "A propos du Tragicall Raigne of *Selimus*: Le Probleme des emprunts aux classiques a la Renaissance," *Etudes Anglaises: Revue du Monde Anglophone* 16 (1963): 345–350.

Jenstad, Janelle. *Early Modern Map of London*. https://mapoflondon.uvic.ca/index.htm

King, John N. "Queen Elizabeth I: Representations of the Virgin Queen," *Renaissance Quarterly* 43, no. 1 (1990), 30–74.

Kocher, Paul. *Christopher Marlowe: A Study of his Thought, Learning, and Character*. Reprint edition. New York: Russell & Russell, 1962, 69–103.

Levin, Richard. "The Contemporary Perception of Marlowe's *Tamburlaine*," *Medieval and Renaissance Drama in England* 1 (1984): 51–70.

Lewis, Rhodri. "Review of 'A Brief Discourse of Rebellion and Rebels' by George North," *The Library* 19, no. 4, 2018, 514–520.

Loewenstein, David. "Agnostic Shakespeare?" "The Godless World of *King Lear*," *Shakespeare and Early Modern Religion*, ed. David Loewenstein and Michael Witmore. Cambridge: Cambridge University Press, 2015, 155–171.

Marlowe, Christopher. *Tamburlaine the Great Part One and Part Two*, ed. Matthew R. Martin. Peterborough, Ontario: Broadview, 2014.

McMillan, Scott. "The Queen's Men in 1594: A Study of 'Good' and 'Bad' Quartos," *English Literary Renaissance* 14, no. 1 (1984), 55–69.

Neale, J. E. "The Elizabethan Political Scene," *Essays in Elizabethan History*. New York: Jonathan Cape, 1958, 59–84.

Neill, Michael, and David Schalkwyk, eds. *The Oxford Handbook of Shakespearean Tragedy*. Oxford: Oxford University Press, 2016.

Outhwaite, R. B. "Dearth, the English Crown, and the 'Crisis of the 1590s,'" *The European Crisis of the 1590s: Essays in Comparative History*, ed. Peter Clark. London: George Allen & Unwin, 1985, 23–43.

Perkins, William. *An Exposition of the Symbole or Creed of the Apostles*. London, 1595.

Philadelphe, Eusebe (possibly Nicolas Barnaud). *Le Reveille-Matin des Francois, et de Leurs Voisins*. Edinburgh, 1574.

Pinciss, G. M. "Thomas Creede and the Repertory of the Queen's Men, 1583–1592," *Modern Philology* 67, no. 4 (1970), 321–330.

Plessis-Mornay, Phillipe de. *A Woorke Concerning the Trewness of the Christian Religion*, trans. Sir Philip Sidney and Arthur Golding. London, 1587.

Plutarch. *Plutarch's Lives of the Noble Grecians and Romans Englished by Sir Thomas North*, ed. George Wyndham. Reprint edition. New York: AMS Press, 1967.

Power, M. J. "London and the Control of the 'Crisis' of the 1590s," *History* 70 (1985), 371–385.

Preedy, Chloe. *Marlowe's Literary Scepticism: Politic Religion and Post-Reformation Polemic*. London: Bloomsbury, 2012.

Reeve, James Bryant. *Godless Fictions in the Eighteenth Century*. Cambridge: Cambridge University Press, 2020.

Ribner, Irving. "Greene's Attack on Marlowe: Some Light on 'Alphonsus' and 'Selimus,'" *Studies in Philology* 52, no. 2 (1955): 162–171.

Riggs, David. "Marlowe's Quarrel with God," *Marlowe, History, and Sexuality*, ed. Paul Whitfield White. New York: AMS, 1998, 15–38.

Riggs, David. *The World of Christopher Marlowe*. New York: Henry Holt, 2005.

Sager, Jenny. *The Aesthetics of Spectacle in Earl Modern Drama and Modern Cinema: Robert Greene's Theatre of Attractions*. New York: Palgrave, 2013, 127–139.

Seneca. *The Lamentable Tragedie of Oedipus*, trans. Alexander Neville. London, 1563.

Serres, Jean de. *The Three Partes of Commentaries Containing the Whole and Perfect Discourse of the Civill Warres of France*. London, 1574.

Shakespeare, William. *King Lear*, in *The Norton Shakespeare: Later Plays and Poems*, ed. Stephen Greenblatt et al. New York: Norton, 2016.

Shuger, Debora K. *Habits of Thought in the English Renaissance: Religion, Politics, and the Dominant Culture*. Reprint Edition. Toronto: University of Toronto Press, 1997.

Sidney, Philip. *Astrophel and Stella*, ed. Risa Bear (Renascence Editions, n.d.). http://www.luminarium.org/renascence-editions/stella.html

Slotkin, Joel Elliot. "'Seeke out another Godhead': Religious Epistemology and Representation of Islam in *Tamburlaine*," *Modern Philology* 111, no. 3 (2014), 408–436.

Smith, Henry. *Gods Arrow against Atheists*. London, 1593.

Smith, Sir Thomas. *De Republica Anglorum*. London, 1583.

Spenser, Edmund. *The Faerie Queene*, ed. Thomas P. Roche, with Patrick O'Donnell, Jr. New Haven: Yale University Press, 1978.

Talpin, Jean. *A forme of Christian pollicie drawne out of French by Geffray Fenton*. London, 1574.

Thomson, John A. F. *The Later Lollards: 1414–1520*. Oxford: Oxford University Press, 1965.

Tymme, Thomas. *A Plaine Discoverie of Ten English Lepers*. London, 1592.

Vitkus, Daniel. "Introduction." *Three Turk Plays from Early Modern England: "Selimus," "A Christian Turned Turk," "The Renegado,"* ed. Daniel Vitkus. New York: Columbia University Press, 2000, 1–54.

Vitkus, Daniel. *Turning Turk: English Theater and the Multicultural Mediterranean, 1570–1630* New York: Palgrave, 2002.

Walter, John. "A 'Rising of the People'? The Oxfordshire Rising of 1596," *Past & Present* n. 107 (1985), 90–143.

Watkins, Leila. "Justice *Is* a Mirage: Failures of Religious Order in Marlowe's *Tamburlaine* Plays," *Comparative Drama* 46, no. 2 (2012), 163–185.

Webb, David. "The Interrogation of the Heavens in *King Lear* and *Doctor Faustus*," *Cahiers Èlizabèthains* 61 (2002): 13–29.

Werth, Tiffany Jo. "Atheist, Adulterer, Sodomite, Thief, Murderer, Lyer, Perjurer, With, Conjuror or Brute Beast? Discovering the Ungodly in Shakespeare's England." *Literature Compass* 10, no. 2 (2013): 175–186.

Whitney, Charles. *Early Responses to Renaissance Drama*. Cambridge: Cambridge University Press, 2006.

Wingfield, John. *Atheism Close and Open, Anatomized*. London, 1634.

Woods, Gillian. "Marlowe and Religion," *Christopher Marlowe in Context*, ed. Emily C. Bartels and Emma Smith. Cambridge: Cambridge University Press, 2013, 222–231.

Wootton, David. "Fear of God in Early Modern Political Theory," *Historical Papers/Communications Historiques* 18, no. 1 (1983), 56–80. *Journal of Modern History* 60, no. 4 (1988): 695–730.

Atheism in Early Modern England

Wootton, David. "Lucien Febvre and the Problem of Unbelief in the Early Modern Period." *The Journal of Modern History* 60, no. 4 (December, 1988), 695–730.
Wootton, David. "Unbelief in Early Modern Europe." *History Workshop* 20 (1985): 82–100.

Notes

1 See George T. Buckley, *Atheism in the English Renaissance* (New York: Russell & Russell, 1965); William Elton, *King Lear and the Gods* (1966; rpt. Lexington: University Press of Kentucky, 1988); *Atheism from the Reformation to the Enlightenment*, ed. Michael Hunter and David Wootton (Oxford: Clarendon Press, 1992); David Wootton, "Unbelief in Early Modern Europe," *History Workshop* 20 (1985): 82–100; Michael Hunter, "The Problem of 'Atheism' in Early Modern England," *Transactions of the Royal Historical Society* 35 (1985): 135–157; D. Wootton, "Lucien Febvre and the Problem of Unbelief in the Early Modern Period," *Journal of Modern History* 60, no. 4 (1988): 695–730; Silvia Berti, "At the roots of Unbelief," *Journal of the History of Ideas* 56, no. 4 (1995): 555–575. Collectively, these articles and books definitively rebut Lucien Febvre's thesis in *The Problem of Unbelief in the Sixteenth Century*, trans. Beatrice Gottlieb (rpt. Cambridge: Harvard University Press, 1982) that atheism was unthinkable in the early modern period.
2 Debora K. Shuger, *Habits of thought in the English Renaissance: Religion, Politics, and the Dominant Culture* (rpt. Toronto: University of Toronto Press, 1997), 279.
3 *The Oxford Handbook of Shakespearean Tragedy*, ed. Michael Neill and David Schalkwyk (Oxford: Oxford University Press, 2016), 916, 945.
4 Stephen Greenblatt, *Shakespearean Negotiations: The Circulation of Social Energy in Renaissance England* (Berkeley: University of California Press, 1988), 22.
5 Michael Bryson, *The Atheist Milton* (Surrey and Burlington, VT: Ashgate, 2012). James Bryant Reeve's *Godless Fictions in the Eighteenth Century* (Cambridge: Cambridge University Press, 2020) does not address the English Renaissance. The exception is Tiffany Jo Werth, "Atheist, Adulterer, Sodomite, Thief, Murderer, Lyer, Perjurer, With, Conjuror or Brute Beast? Discovering the Ungodly in Shakespeare's England," *Literature Compass* 10, no. 2 (2013): 175–186. doi: 10.1111/lic3.12025.
6 Chloe Preedy, *Marlowe's Literary Scepticism: Politic Religion and Post-Reformation Polemic* (London: Bloomsbury, 2012), xviii.
7 Quoted in Wootton, "The Problem of Atheism," 139.
8 John Hull, *The Unmasking of the Politike Atheist* (London, 1602), sig. A7v. Here and elsewhere, I have silently expanded contractions and adopted the modern usage of i/j and u/v.
9 Hull, sig. A7r.
10 Smith, *Gods Arrow*, sig. A4r.
11 John Wingfield, *Atheism Close and open, Anatomized* (London, 1634), sig. E12v-r; Wootton, "The Problem of Atheism," 139.
12 Wootton, "Unbelief in Early Modern Europe," 83; John A. F. Thomson, *The Later Lollards: 1414–1520* (Oxford: Oxford University Press, 1965), 62.
13 Wootton, "Unbelief in Early Modern Europe," 82–83.
14 G. E. Aylmer, "Unbelief in Seventeenth-Century England," *Puritans and Revolutionaries: Essays in Seventeenth-Century History presented to Christopher Hill*, ed. Donald Pennington and Keith Thomas (Oxford: Clarendon Press, 1978), 31.
15 Aylmer, 32.
16 John Hawarde, *Les Reportes del Cases in Camera Stellata, 1593–1609*, ed. William Paley Baildon (London: Privately Printed, 1894), p. 42.
17 Wootton, "Disbelief in Early Modern Europe," 86.
18 Phillipe de Plessis-Mornay, *A Woorke Concerning the Trewness of the Christian Religion*, trans. Sir Philip Sidney and Arthur Golding (London, 1587), sig. L6r; Wotton, "Disbelief in Early Modern Europe," 86.
19 De Plessis-Mornay, *A Woorke*, sig. L6r.
20 Quoted in Leslie Hottson, *Shakespeare versus Shallow* (London: Nonesuch Press, 1931), 228; Hunter, "The Problem of Atheism," 150.
21 *Willobie his Avisa (1594)*, ed. G. B. Harrison (New York: Dutton, 1926), 255.
22 William Perkins, *An Exposition of the Symbole or Creed of the Apostles* (London, 1595), sig. N2r.
23 The main problem is that EEBO-TCP is far from complete: "Instead, it depends on those parts of Pollard and Redgrave (currently around fifty per cent) whose facsimiles have been digitally transcribed by EEBO-TCP" (Rhodri Lewis, review of "A Brief Discourse of Rebellion and Rebels' by George North," *The Library* 19.4 (2018), 515). Also, since the vendors paying for the transcription of early modern books

Peter C. Herman

charged by the page, not the title, there is a bias towards shorter documents, and some books, such as legal dictionaries, were excluded because they were considered irrelevant. See Peter C. Herman, "EEBO and Me: A Response to Michael Gavin," *Textual Cultures* 13, no. 1 (2020), 214.

24 *Le Reveille-Matin des Francois, et de Leurs Voisins* (Edinburgh, 1574); *A Forme of Christian Pollicie drawn out of French by Gefray Fenton* (London, 1574); and *The Three Partes of Commentaries Containing the Whole and Perfect Discourse of the Civill Warres of France* (London, 1574).

25 R. B. Outhwaite, "Dearth, the English Crown, and the 'Crisis of the 1590s,'" *The European Crisis of the 1590s: Essays in Comparative History*, ed. Peter Clark (London: George Allen & Unwin, 1985), 24.

26 Quoted in Peter Clark, "A Crisis Contained? The Condition of English Towns in the 1590s," in *The European Crisis of the 1590s*, ed. Clark, 53.

27 M. J. Power, "London and the Control of the 'Crisis' of the 1590s," *History* 70 (1985), 379.

28 "The Norfolk Libel (1595)," in *Jack of Newbury*, ed. Peter C. Herman (Peterborough: Broadview, 2015), 159.

29 "Norfolk Libel," 166. See also John Walter, "A 'Rising of the People'? The Oxfordshire Rising of 1596," *Past & Present* n. 107 (1985), 90–143.

30 Thomas Tymme, *A Plaine Discoverie of Ten English Lepers* (London, 1592), sig. L4r; Elton, *King Lear and the Gods*, 21.

31 *Willobie his Avisa (1594)*, ed. G. B. Harrison (Dutton: New York, 1926), 264.

32 Quoted in Outhwaite, "Dearth and the English Crown," 28.

33 *Willobie his Avisa*. 255, 258.

34 Wootton, "Unbelief in Early Modern Europe," 96.

35 Henrik Ibsen, *The Wild Duck*. New York: Samuel French, 1980.

36 Marlowe, *Tamburlaine the Great Part One and Part Two*, ed. Matthew R. Martin (Peterborough: Broadview, 2014), 45. All references to Marlowe's plays will be to this edition.

37 See *Henslowe's Diary*, 2nd ed., ed. R. A. Foakes (Cambridge: Cambridge University Press, 2002), 23–33.

38 I have taken the publishing history from the Database on Early English Plays (DEEP): deep.sas.upenn.ed.

39 Charles Whitney, *Early Responses to Renaissance Drama* (Cambridge: Cambridge University Press, 2006), 18; Richard Levin, "The Contemporary Perception of Marlowe's *Tamburlaine*," *Medieval and Renaissance Drama in England* 1 (1984): 51–70.

40 Robert Greene, *Perimides the Blacke-Smith* (London, 1588), sig. A3r; Whitney, 17.

41 Paul Kocher, *Christopher Marlowe: A Study of his Thought, Learning, and Character* (rpt. New York: Russell & Russell, 1962), 69–103; Nicholas Davidson, "Christopher Marlowe and Atheism," *Christopher Marlowe and English Renaissance Culture*, ed. Darryll Grantley and Peter Roberts (Aldershot: Scolar Press, 1996), 129–147; David Riggs, "Marlowe's Quarrel with God," *Marlowe, History, and Sexuality*, ed. Paul Whitfield White (New York: AMS, 1998), 15–38; D. Riggs, *The World of Christopher Marlowe* (New York: Henry Holt, 2005), 218–219; Ian Gaskell, "2 *Tamburlaine*, Marlow's War against the Gods," *English Studies in Canada* 11, no. 2 (1985), 180; Leila Watkins, "Justice *Is* a Mirage: Failures of Religious Order in Marlowe's *Tamburlaine* Plays," *Comparative Drama* 46, no. 2 (2012), 163–185. Joel Elliot Slotkin, however, argues that the plays, despite their "pervasive cynicism" about religion, nonetheless insist "on the importance of the search for religious knowledge" ("'Seeke out another Godhead': Religious Epistemology and Representation of Islam in *Tamburlaine*," *Modern Philology* 111, no. 3 (2014), 410).

42 Christopher Marlowe, *Tamburlaine the Great, Part One and Part Two*, ed. Matthew R. Martin (Peterborough; Broadview, 2014). Unless indicated otherwise, all further references will be to this edition and cited parenthetically.

43 Calyphas is in fact not a coward, as his brothers say. When they accuse him of being too scared to pick up a sword, he tells them he's not frightened; rather, he doesn't like killing: "I know, sir, what it is to kill a man. / It works remorse of conscience in me. / I take no pleasure to be murderous" (Part 2; 4.1.27–29). On the mixed critical responses to Calyphas, see Sara Munson Deats, "Marlowe's Interrogative Drama: *Dido, Tamburlaine, Faustus*, and *Edward II*," *Marlowe's Empery: Expanding his Critical Contexts*, ed. Sara Munson Deats and Robert A. Logan (Newark: University of Delaware Press, 2002), 116.

44 Marlowe, *Tamburlaine the Great* (London, 1597), sig. A3r.

45 Seneca, *The Lamentable Tragedie of Oedipus*, trans. Alexander Neville (London, 1563), sig. A.vi.v, A.vi.r., A.viii.r.

46 Slotkin suggests that Orcanes' skepticism "leads to a greater acceptance of religious pluralism" ("Religious Epistemology," 422). See also Gillian Woods, "Marlowe and Religion," *Christopher Marlowe in Context*, ed. Emily C. Bartels and Emma Smith (Cambridge: Cambridge University Press, 2013), 225.

47 Thomas Cartelli, *Marlowe, Shakespeare, and the Economy of Theatrical Experience* (Philadelphia: University of Pennsylvania Press, 1991), 69–70.

48 Cartelli, 71–72.

49 M. J. Power, "London and the Control of the 'Crisis' of the 1590s," *History* 70, no. 230 (1985), 380.

50 William Camden,*The History of the Most Renowned and Victorious Princess Elizabeth, late Queen of England* (London, 1688), 506.

51 David Wootton, "Fear of God in Early Modern Political Theory," *Historical Papers/ Communications historiques* 18, no. 1 (1983), 56–80.

52 Quoted in Wootton, "Fear of God," 63.

53 *Plutarch's Lives of the Noble Grecians and Romans Englished by Sir Thomas North*, ed. George Wyndham (rpt. New York: AMS Press, 1967), vol. 1, 52.

54 Sir John Fortescue, *On the Laws and Governance of England*, ed. Shelley Lockwood (Cambridge: Cambridge University Press, 1997), 17.

55 Fortescue, 19.

56 Fortescue, 20.

57 Fortescue, 21.

58 Sir Thomas Smith, *De Republica Anglorum* (London, 1583), sig. F2v-r.

59 See also Patrick Cheney, *Marlowe's Republican Authorship: Lucan, Liberty, and the Sublime* (New York: Palgrave MacMillan, 2009), 99–103.

60 Watkins argues that the plays "produce skeptical interpretations of every religious order," ("Failures," 164), but that does not lead to a collapse of *political* order.

61 Thomas Creed published Greene's play in 1594, and the title page says that it was "played by the Queen's Majesty's Players." But the company was in decline from the late 1580s until its dissolution in 1594, in part because of competition from Marlowe's company, the Admiral's Men, and in part because the theaters were closed due to plague (Andrew Gurr, *The Shakespearian Playing Companies* (Oxford: Clarendon Press, 1996), 204–211). Alexander Grossart attributed the play Robert Greene, and as the play's contemporary editor, Daniel Vitkus, says, that claim has never been refuted, although it is possible that others contributed passages (Vitkus, "Introduction," *Three Turk Plays from Early Modern England: "Selimus," "A Christian Turned Turk," "The Renegado,"* ed. Daniel Vitkus (New York: Columbia University Press, 2000), 17). All further references to *Selimus* will be to this edition and cited parenthetically.

62 Greenes groatsworth of wit (London, 1637), sig. C3v.

63 *Selimus* has not attracted much critical attention. But see Irving Ribner, "Greene's Attack on Marlowe: Some Light on 'Alphonsus' and 'Selimus,'" *Studies in Philology* 52, no. 2 (1955): 162–171; Ayse Nur Demiralp, "*The Life and Death of Jack Straw* and *The Tragical Reign of Selimus*: A Note on Some Verbal and Thematic Parallels," *Notes and Queries* 59, no. 1 (257) (2012): 45–48; Jenny Sager, *The Aesthetics of Spectacle in Earl Modern Drama and Modern Cinema: Robert Greene's Theatre of Attractions* (New York: Palgrave, 2013), 127–139.

64 Daniel Vitkus, *Turning Turk: English Theater and the Multicultural Mediterranean, 1570–1630* (New York: Palgrave, 2002), 57.

65 While Greene's source attributes Selim's death to "an ague," it seems the cause was a type of skin cancer: "Selimus lying quietlye at home was grevouslye handeled in the Reynes of the backe, with a fowle scabbe which crepynge in hys bodye, lyke unto a Canker, changed by lyttle and little, that disposition and qualitie of the bodye, which we do calle the complexion and also destroyed al his warlike counsayle" (Paolo Giovio, *A short treatise upon the Turkes Chronicles*, trans. Peter Ashton (London, 1546), sig. Mviiir). There is no suggestion that divine retribution was involved. Also, Giovio is distinctly ambivalent about Selim the Grim. On the one hand, the "extreme crueltye he [Selim] used towards his own aliaunce and blud made him (not without a cause) to have an yl name"; on the other hand, "in the perfect knowledge of warre, and governanunce of the people, he excelled," and Selim would "commaunde equitie and justice to be straytlye every where kepte and observed" (sig. N.ii.r, N.iii.v–r). All told, Selim "was such a one as seldome hath ben heard of" (sig. N.iii.v).

66 In Scene 2, Selimus echoes Tamburlaine's praise of rule as "the ripest fruit of all, / That perfect bliss and sole felicity/ The sweet fruition of an earthly crown" (Part 1: 2.7.27–29), when he tells Sinam: "An empire... is so sweet a thing / As I could be a devil to be a king" (2.203). Selimus' father, the hapless Bajazet, says that his namesake was "ten times happier" (18.7) because "Tamburlaine, the scourge of nations" (18.8) deposed him, not his son. Tonombey swears "by the great Usan-Cassano's ghost, / Companion unto mighty Tamburlaine, / From whom my father lineally descends" (25.17–19) that he will defeat Selimus, who responds, "Captain of Egypt, thou that vaunt'st thyself / Sprung from great Tamburlaine the Scythian thief" (28. 6–7).

67 On the sources for Selimus' speech, see Jean Jacquot, "A propos du Tragicall Raigne of Selimus: Le Probleme des emprunts aux classiques a la Renaissance," *Etudes Anglaises: Revue du Monde Anglophone* 16 (1963): 345–350.

Peter C. Herman

68 "Accusations Against Christopher Marlowe by Richard Baines and Others." https://www.bl.uk/collection-items/accusations-against-christopher-marlowe-by-richard-baines-and-others

69 Scott McMillan, "The Queen's Men in 1594: A Study of 'Good' and 'Bad' Quartos," *English Literary Renaissance* 14, no. 1 (1984), 68.

70 G. M. Pinciss, "Thomas Creede and the Repertory of the Queen's Men, 1583–1592," *Modern Philology* 67, 4 (1970), 322.

71 See Wootton, "The Fear of God in Early Modern Political Theory."

72 *Willobie*, 256.

73 Quoted in Hunter, "The Problem of 'Atheism,'" 151.

74 Aylmer, 32.

75 See John N. King, "Queen Elizabeth I: Representations of the Virgin Queen," *Renaissance Quarterly* 43, no. 1 (1990), passim.

76 Quoted in J. E. Neale, "The Elizabethan Political Scene," *Essays in Elizabethan History* (New York: Jonathan Cape, 1958), 79.

77 Philip Sidney, *Astrophel and Stella*, ed. Risa Bear (Renascence Editions, n.d.). http://www.luminarium.org/renascence-editions/stella.html

78 For example, the Bright Manuscript, a verse miscellany dating from the late 1580s. https://celm-ms.org.uk/repositories/british-library-additional-15000.html, and http://www.bl.uk/manuscripts/FullDisplay.aspx?ref=Add_MS_15232. I base these claims on searches using EEBO-TCP, which, as I acknowledge above, n. 23, means that they are provisional.

79 Edmund Spenser, *The Faerie Queene*, ed. Thomas P. Roche, with Patrick O'Donnell, Jr. (New Haven: Yale University Press, 1978).

80 Vitkus, *Three Turk Plays*, 146.

81 Peter Clark, "A Crisis Contained?," 53.

82 Inga-Stina Ekeblad, "'*King Lear*' and '*Selimus*,'" *Notes and Queries* 202 (1957), 193–194.

83 *King Lear*, in *The Norton Shakespeare: Later Plays and Poems*, ed. Stephen Greenblatt et al. (New York: Norton, 2016). All references will be to the combined text and cited parenthetically.

84 On Lear and atheism, in addition to Elton's magisterial *"King Lear" and the Gods*, see David Webb, "The Interrogation of the Heavens in *King Lear* and *Doctor Faustus*," *Cahiers Èlizabèthains* 61 (2002): 13–29 and David Loewenstein, "Agnostic Shakespeare?" "The Godless World of *King Lear*," *Shakespeare and Early Modern Religion*, ed. David Loewenstein and Michael Witmore (Cambridge: Cambridge University Press, 2015), 155–171.

14
Surrogacy and Empire in *The Man-Plant* and Eighteenth-Century Vernacular Medical Texts

Danielle Spratt

In the opening pages of the satirical *The Man-Plant: Or Scheme for Increasing and Improving the British Breed* (1752), the pseudonymous author Vincent Miller boldly proclaims that his treatise will deliver

> Women from the Embarrassments, and Inconveniencies of Pregnancy, from the Pangs, and Dangers of their Delivery [...] [T]he Art of Midwifery has been carried to a high Point of Perfection amongst us; but it would be yet a greater Point gained, to have no Occasion for it at all.[1]

Miller explains that despite the recent peace between England and France following the War of Austrian Succession, he "often, in the Spirit of Ambition and Plunder, make[s] not insignificant Descents upon the *French* Coast, and carr[ies] on a literary Forage [...] inriching myself and Nation with the Pillage."[2] Translating physical battles over colonial domination into nationalistic contests of superior scientific authority, the author is most eager to share his discovery of the titular tract, which offered "such a Discussion of the Analogy between the animal and vegetable Kingdoms, as first furnished me with the Hint, which I have since pushed such amazing Lengths."[3] Adding elements of artificial heat based on recent discoveries in both electricity and early embryology, the author advances schemes to develop "the grand Plan of the Ingraftment of the human Species, considered as partaking of the vegetable Species, upon his Scheme of maturing the Man-*foetus* by artificial heat."[4] In other words, *The Man-Plant* describes a kind of technological surrogacy typically credited to second-wave feminists like Shulamith Firestone, albeit using wicker baskets, leather bladders, seedbeds, and greenhouses as incubators.[5]

The Man-Plant is not singular as a fictional exploration of how scientific and medical discoveries made reproductive surrogacy a thinkable project even in the middle of the eighteenth century, as Raymond Stephanson has shown.[6] Rather than considering this text in conversation with related works of a genre that Stephanson calls "fictional science" from the period, however, I am interested in exploring how *The Man-Plant*'s rhetorical valences resonate with a complementary and even more widely read genre from the period: vernacular medical texts about reproduction.[7] Reading Miller's work in tandem both with the wildly popular, pseudonymously published *Aristotle's Masterpiece* (1684), and with medical guides written by physicians for domestic and colonial audiences, I suggest, reveals how the concept of surrogacy was fundamental to notions of conception from the period, despite the seeming anachronism of the term's current common meaning. While the term "surrogate" did not describe particular forms of gestation until the twentieth century, its Latin origin, *surrogatus*, to elect as a substitute, was common beginning in the seventeenth century, thus making it possible to imagine this kind of surrogacy in the ways that Miller

DOI: 10.4324/9781003046004-17

229

outlines in his fictional treatise.[8] Further, preformationism, the prevailing theory of conception in the eighteenth century, held that either sperm or egg contained miniaturized yet fully formed organisms, such as *animalcules* or *homunculi*.[9] In works that employed preformationist thinking, especially those that found paternal origins for these miniaturized beings, pregnant bodies were effectively positioned as surrogate carriers of another person's child. Framing conception and pregnancy as acts of surrogacy was appealing to many medical men from the period, not only because it often validated both paternal lineage and the increasingly professionalized realm of male medical authority, but also because, as an extension of the possibility of population control, such rhetoric reflected broader nationalistic interests in improving the island of Britain and expanding its colonial holdings.[10]

The imperial ambitions of *The Man-Plant*'s reproductive project further demonstrate the conceptual and capitalistic affordances of reproductive surrogacy across the eighteenth century. Anita Allen and Dorothy K. Roberts have argued that reproduction *was* surrogacy for enslaved Black people in America before the Civil War, an insight that is relevant to the context of the British colonies as they expanded across the eighteenth and early nineteenth centuries. Allen writes, "Before the American Civil War, virtually all southern Black mothers were, in a sense, surrogate mothers. Slave women knowingly gave birth to children with the understanding that those children would be owned by others."[11] Roberts further develops this claim, arguing that the institution of slavery itself prompted the logic of reproductive surrogacy: "It is the enslavement of Blacks that enables us to imagine the commodification of human beings, and that makes the vision of fungible breeder so real," a logic that Alys Eve Weinbaum has termed "the slave episteme."[12] More recently, Jennifer L. Morgan has put it this way:

> Reproduction (and thus enslavability) was tethered to enslavement in a way that foreclosed the possibility that kinship might destabilize capital. To be enslaved meant to be locked into a productive relationship whereby all that your body could do was harnessed to accumulate capital for another.[13]

In other words, the expanding system of the transatlantic slave trade and, after its abolition in 1807, the maintenance of enslaved populations until emancipation in the 1830s, made reproductive surrogacy not only conceptually but also legally and logistically feasible, a phenomenon that both fiction and medical writing register.

The traces of colonial capitalism in modern-day commercial surrogacy remain both prevalent and contentious. Yet for Donna Haraway and Sophie Lewis, full surrogacy—consciously divested of its ties to slavery, colonialism, and oppression—has the liberatory potential of making kin, in opposition to the nuclear family, by establishing anti-patriarchal, anti-capitalist, anti-racist radical utopian queer communities.[14] Fundamentally, they are reframing the concept of surrogacy as being something other than "the practice of arranging a pregnancy in order to construct and deliver a baby that is 'someone else's.'"[15] Pushing against the idea of the "ownership" of children connected to either an individual gestator or a nuclear family, for these thinkers, surrogacy can radically expand the connections between the humane and the human by forging a kind of "knotting" among groups and, for Haraway, even across species, a strategy that rejects posthumanism in an understanding that "species of all kinds are consequent upon worldly subject- and object-shaping entanglements."[16] This model, according to Lewis, would allow us to

> bring about the conditions of possibility for open-source, fully collaborative gestation [...] explode notions of hereditary parentage, and multiply real, loving solidarities. Let us build a care commune based on comradeship, a world sustained by kith and kind more than kin.

Surrogacy in Eighteenth-Century Vernacular Medical Texts

Where pregnancy is concerned, let every pregnancy be for everyone. Let us overthrow, in short, the "family."[17]

Lewis observes that

many people on earth are putting something like "full surrogacy" into practice every day, cultivating non-oedipal kinship and sharing reciprocal mothering labors between many individuals and generations. In particular, trans, Black, sex-working, migrant, and queer communities have historically survived thanks to their skills in this sphere (sometimes called "kinning").[18]

Making kin, Morgan reminds us, was both an "obstacle to fungibility" and a decided act of resistance among enslaved people, as was the act of kinlessness, of not bearing children.[19]

Considering surrogacy's participation in developing the modern colonial capital state *and* its potential to unmake or resist these structures in radical ways, this chapter seeks to provide a pre-history of modern surrogacy as it began to emerge in the eighteenth century. I argue that works like *The Man-Plant* and vernacular domestic and colonial medical texts from the period document surrogacy's participation in justifying and expanding British imperial and medical power even as it was also wielded in domestic and intimate spaces in ways that resisted and reformulated elements of the colonial medical state, largely by constructing alternate models of kinship that existed outside of these frameworks.[20] *The Man-Plant* and preformationist vernacular medical manuals written by obstetricians work together to justify and outline protocols for surrogative work that assumed English control of reproductive bodies at home and in the colonies. These works sought to distinguish their authors' humanity, and the authority of white Europeans more broadly, often by othering women and frequently dehumanizing Black and brown bodies in ways that both justified their medical treatments and encouraged broader national and imperial projects. Yet even in these colonial medical manuals, there are often inadvertent accounts of alternate strategies that pregnant and caregiving people used to resist colonial surrogacy by constructing kinship models that supported Black communities of care: some people resisted institutionalized plantation hospital care, others extended breastfeeding (which effectively disrupted typical work and reproductive cycles), while still others chose not to have children at all.[21]

By contrast, *Aristotle's Masterpiece* documents a kind of reproduction that is closer to Lewis's concept of full surrogacy. Unlike most of the medical treatises of the eighteenth century, this work resorted to a model of epigenesis, or the concept of fetal development over time. This work also relied on macrocosmic thinking, which positions the human as one point in a chain of being that links plant and animal life on earth to divine beings and God, in ways that rhetorically denied full medical mastery over human reproduction. The work's documentation of so-called monstrous births also relied on ideas of parental imprinting, or the idea that a parent, usually the mother, could see or think things that would physically alter the child in utero. Embracing the messy and speculative nature of reproductive theories from the period, while also giving its readers tips and strategies for navigating conception, pregnancy, childbirth, and caregiving, this often-dismissed pop medical text actually establishes a strong continuity among humans and their surroundings and, as Mary Fissell notes, functioned "as a material object" that ultimately "serve[s] as an embodiment of family and kinship," with multiple generations of readers writing their names and occasionally logging their own family birth history in its margins.[22] Exploring theories of reproductive surrogacy during the eighteenth century contextualizes one of the reasons that *Aristotle's Masterpiece* remained both in print and widely read for over three centuries, only waning in popularity in the early twentieth century.

By examining the ways that pregnant people and their care networks crafted strategies and spaces to maintain important elements of their own identity and support their belonging to structures outside the colonial capital state, this chapter thus explores how a pre-history of surrogacy facilitates what Michael Bryson describes as a core goal of literary humanistic inquiry: it shows "a convergence of diverse elements into a kind of unity which—paradoxically—maintains, and even enhances, individuality," and thus becomes a method that documents "our attempts to transcend [...] forces beyond our understanding and control."[23] Despite medical and various state surveillance technologies, reproduction and kin-making have long had the capacity to function outside of and often against human and state intervention. Considering these issues through the type of new humanism that Bryson calls for reveals the ways that literary and other printed works can help identify the kinds of anti-sexist, anti-racist praxis that we must engage in to oppose the long legacies of the western state's brutality against women and people of color.

A Modest Proposal

The Man-Plant's overarching goal is to support the mechanization of reproduction with the goal of instigating an explosion of Britain's population at home and in its colonial holdings. The bulk of the tract outlines the author's method of innovating the surrogacy experiments of others, including a titillating description of his first successful extraction of a fertilized egg from his gardener's beautiful teenage daughter, along with his plan to create a vastly more productive cadre of child-bearing British women:

> They may then become like those fertile Fields that yield two or three Crops in a Season, and their Fecundity will be only limited by such small Reposes, as the Necessity of lying fallow will require for the Reparation of the Ground. They will continue longer able and apt for Impregnation; so that upon a moderate Estimate, a well disposed, well constituted, and industrious Woman, may furnish her Country, for her Contingent, with one hundred and thirty, to one hundred and forty or more Children.[24]

In this passage, the author plays with well-worn figurative language of conception and generation: Words like "seed" and "fruit" have since ancient times provided concrete images for the largely unseen components of embryology, and parallels between the parturient body and fertile land have long framed discussions of both domestic and political bodies. In this instance, the author links human interventions in successfully exploited fertile land to his model of the hyper-efficient, super-generative pregnant body.

Extending the human–plant metaphor, the author also connects his project to broader imperial goals. In addition to creating an exponentially greater number of British subjects at home, the plan will also populate the colonies and enable the domination of contested lands:

> By this Means, we shall see infinite Broods of Subjects thus pullulating, serve to repeople and enrich, as well our Island as those vast Tracts in North-America, which are so thinly inhabited, and which are now obliged to be stocked with Palatines, or other foreign Refugees. A Naturalization-Bill will then be out of the Question. We may also then more reasonably grasp the Conquest of both the Indies, especially when we shall have completed the Discovery of the Northwest Passage. Our actual possessions, and those of which we shall infallibly, by Dint of superior Numbers, procure the Acquisition, will be abundantly supplied with Swarms of our own Subjects, and become as populous as China itself.[25]

Surrogacy in Eighteenth-Century Vernacular Medical Texts

The text cites the Palatine refugee situation in England and America and concern about imperial expansion in both the West Indies and the Carnatic Wars in India to rationalize the need for its plan, while it also embraces nationalistic and xenophobic biases about Britain's expanding empire. The creation of "infinite Broods" and "Swarms" further emphasizes the connections between the plantation-nation and the earth-body, and offers a kind of population fantasy that promises a new, powerful generation of Britons:

> This new Earth-born, Cucumber, Chicken Progeny, will be far less imperfect than the fribbling Race that now totters about Town [...] Neither will this Project of mending the Breed appear either absurd or chimerical to those who shall reflect, that Plantations of Men are susceptible to Improvement as well as those of Trees.[26]

Here, the author uses language that registers mid-eighteenth-century concerns about the feminization of British culture and fears about population decline at home and in the colonies.[27] *The Man-Plant* addresses these issues by invoking the genre of project writing that, as David Alff has shown, hinged on planning the impossible and that, retrospectively, "index[es] a world of defunct possibility that shapes and shadows histories of the real."[28]

The Man-Plant's extended use of the human–plant parallel also satirizes genres that documented knowledge of botany and natural history in line with works by Carl Linnaeus, which "promoted a classification system for plants based on their sexual parts, leading to all manner of erotic—and racialized—anthropomorphisms," as Heather V. Vermulean observes.[29] Miller exploits the messy and potentially licentious connotations in the Linnaean system by describing the female body using plant metaphors written in Latin. Although this passage initially seems to document women's bodies generally, it ends with a caveat: "Note. Species vary with respect to place of birth," which he then annotates with a reference to Pierre-Louis Moreau de Maupertuis's *Vénus Physique* (*The Earthly Venus*, 1745), which has a whole volume that attempts to account for racial difference. Vermulean argues that this passage reveals "it is not only—perhaps not at all—the (white) 'British breed' that Miller has in mind but enslaved persons from the African continent and their descendants, conscripted to support the British Empire."[30]

While *The Man-Plant* is noteworthy for speculative thinking that anticipates science fictions of the nineteenth and twentieth centuries, its core concern about population control demonstrates how theories of human reproduction have long troubled the boundaries between human and other. Aristotle's understanding of epigenetic conception, or the idea that an embryo develops over time, was grounded in an examination of chicken eggs, a strategy that also informed famed physician William Harvey's writing on generation. In debates about reproduction, even the popular (if erroneous) eighteenth-century theory of preformationism relied on alleged observations of miniaturized animals and plants found in eggs or seeds. Informed by ancient beliefs and new medical theories about childbirth, conception, monstrosity, and wonder, the eighteenth-century cultural imagination saw important discoveries in the understanding of human development, from sensational accounts of monstrous births that were published alongside Leeuwenhoek's microscopic study of sperm in the Royal Society's *Philosophical Transactions*, to accounts of *in vitro* fertilization of frog eggs and the artificial insemination of dogs in Lazzaro Spallanzani's *Experiences pour servir à l'histoire de la géneration des animaux et des plantes* (1786).[31] The period simultaneously also granted much media coverage, if varying levels of credibility, to stories like that of the infamous Mary Toft, who, in an elaborate scheme to support her family, claimed to give birth to rabbits after seeing and craving one while pregnant.[32]

The concept of surrogacy, articulated overtly in *The Man-Plant* and via popular theories of preformationism in other works from the period, illuminates the often-uneasy rhetoric surrounding human conception and pregnancy in domestic and colonial vernacular medical manuals across the eighteenth century. As a work of what Stephanson describes as an "early novelistic attempt to make use of *then* current science *and* technology," *The Man-Plant* demonstrates "the impact on the literary imagination of then emerging technological developments in artificially assisted reproduction" in animal husbandry and botanical management, while it also invokes the artificial wombs that many midwives and obstetricians like Richard Manningham used to train medical personnel in the management of pregnancy, labor, and delivery.[33] These new medical and technological insights into reproduction cohered around two important components of the literary marketplace. The first, the common generic mixing found in scientific and medical manuals from the period, meant that such works included references to ancient history, philosophy, and literature, as well as to more quotidian writing, including works like almanacs, and even involved forays into narrative styles that would come to be associated with prose fiction and the novel.[34] The second market factor was the public's increasing desire to own, both as reference and entertainment, a general vernacular medical manual on reproduction, pregnancy, and childbirth, as well as other common medical conditions that would most commonly be treated at home.[35] As the century progressed and more vernacular medical treatises became available, the most popular manual remained, as noted above, the notorious *Aristotle's Masterpiece*. Throughout its editions across many decades, *Aristotle's Masterpiece* tended to recycle ancient information about conception and pregnancy while occasionally inserting new details.

Alongside the popularity of *Aristotle's Masterpiece*, midwives and early obstetricians who sought credibility published general medical manuals and those that catered to specialized populations. A sub-genre of these manuals emerged in the context of colonial plantation management, where it became necessary for enslavers and their medical employees to treat myriad ailments and, especially after abolition, to attempt to manage and expand birth rates among enslaved peoples. In this way, *The Man-Plant*'s focus on surrogacy as a means of expanding the population at home and abroad is in keeping with its endorsement of imperial actions. Although the author of *The Man-Plant* opens his work with claims of women's liberation from the physical toil involved in full-term pregnancy and infant care, he can only imagine reproductive surrogacy as an instrumentalized means to imperialist and capitalist ends. The text's conflation of surrogacy and reproduction in fact replicates longstanding beliefs, amplified vociferously through preformationist rhetoric and many medical manuals from the period, which framed the pregnant body as always already being a surrogate or an incubator for the preformed being it housed. These theories complemented the discourse of masculine medical control over pregnancy and childbirth that emerged across the century, all of which worked in concert to link the generation of children to the growth of Britain itself.

Aristotle's Masterpiece and Communities of Care

Aristotle's Masterpiece was ubiquitous across the eighteenth and nineteenth centuries, and its popularity can at least partially be accounted for not just because of its ability to titillate its audiences and provide what Mary Fissell has described as early sex education, but also because of the ways it encouraged and empowered its readers to create communities of care surrounding the treatment of conception, reproduction, and childcare.[36] Methodologically, it is also starkly different than later eighteenth-century medical manuals, which often existed as much to demonstrate the prowess of its (usually male) medical writer as it did to provide information about the reproductive body. In its earliest iteration, the manual opens with a description of the development of the world from its chaotic origins to its divine transformation into a generative, fecund space that tracks in the language of the great chain of being, or the idea that there is a direct link between the earth's flora and fauna and its divine creator. In this way, the work fundamentally frames reproduction as a collective experience, thus encouraging the communal elements of surrogacy that Haraway and Lewis posit.

Surrogacy in Eighteenth-Century Vernacular Medical Texts

Far from simply regurgitating a concept that was common in both ancient thinking and early modern thought, however, this macrocosmic analogy foreshadows the text's account of human conception. The work notes early and often that the advice it offers is for married couples only, and that it is therefore sanctioned by God himself, who urges his readers to procreate (it is worth noting, however, that readers were not always of the married sort, as Fissell has shown; many were teens and young adults curious about sex and the body). The manual opens by describing how to know when a woman is ready for marriage and has the ability to bear a child, and then explains the most important components that help a couple prepare for conception: they need "Divine Providence" as the primary cause, as well as the following secondary causes:

> First, the Genital Humour which proceeds partly from the Brain, and partly from the Liver, the Fountain of Blood; then the spirit that is conveyed by Arteries from the Heart, by force whereof the Yard is erected, and made capable to eject the Seed; and partly it flows from the whole Body without exception. To which may be added the Appetite and desire to Copulation, which fires the Imagination with unusual Fancies.[37]

Described as a holistic mind–body experience, the text organizes conception through a series of processes, first addressing methods of stimulating such imaginative appetites, including suggestions for rich food and drink, and then providing suggestions for conceiving a male or female child, all of which are influenced by sexual position, the timing of sex post-menstruation, and even the alignment of the zodiac (this last detail alludes to details typically found in another popular eighteenth-century genre, the almanac).

The narrative then resumes to offer "various Opinions" about the process of conception. Granting agency to both male and female seed, the author likens the process of a developing embryo to the creation of the world: "And Physicians that have narrowly contemplated Mans Nature, constitute four different times wherein this Microcosm or little World is framed and perfected in the Womb."[38] For the first week, the author states, the seed of man and woman combine in the uterus, "mixing and fermenting, becom[ing] like a Cream"; second, approximately two weeks after a couple copulates, the embryo forms:

> Nature and the force of the Womb, by use of her own inbred forces and vertue, makes a manifest mutation in the Seed, so that all the substance seems congealed Flesh and Blood [...] and may be called the rough draught, or *Embrio*.

For eighteen days following conception, the arteries, brain, and liver develop and circulate the blood; and finally, after approximately a month, the embryo transforms into a "perfect and absolute Child"—boys are formed by 30 days, and girls by 45 days.[39] In these ways, the *Masterpiece* continues to invoke classical assertions about the epigenetic nature of human generation, while also granting equal importance to both parental contributions.

In the following chapter, the author discusses the astonishing power of the maternal imagination, which further amplifies the active role of the pregnant person's mind:

> Nothing is more powerful than the imagination of the Mother; for if she conceives in her mind, or do by chance fasten her eyes upon any Object, and imprint it in her Memory, the Child in its outward parts frequently has some representation thereof.[40]

The work's entry on maternal marking and the imagination was perhaps its most well-known visual signifier: depending on the edition, it offers a series of woodcuts that depict "monstrous births," including the frontispiece that shows a hairy woman and a Black baby born of white

Danielle Spratt

parents.[41] A woman's imagination can cause anomalous births and even make another man's child resemble her husband, yet the male seed tends to have the most power to shape the child's mind and personality.[42] Nevertheless, the text is sure to observe that "the mother's equally contributing to the making of the Child"—while the "Seed of man is the chief efficient and beginning of action, motion, and Generation, yet that the Woman does afford seed, and effectually contributes in that particular to the procreation of the Child, is evinced by strong reasons."[43] The narrator even goes one step further by invoking the plant-human analogy, suggesting that "the Mother confers the most toward its Generation" because, following Galen's analogy, "as Plants receive more from fruitful ground than from the industry of the Husbandman, so the Infant in more abundance receives from the Mother than the Father."[44] Although the text combines and compresses debates about the exact agency of male and female seed, it tends to suggest a significant partnership between participants. The work here shows a modulation between ancient and more modern facts and theories, incorporating an acknowledgment of the circulation of the blood alongside Galenic theories. Making kin in this account involves the union of disparate but equally important forces.

A copy of a later 1700 edition held at the British Library, annotated by several of its eighteenth-century owners, demonstrates how audiences read and re-read this work, suggesting a kind of collective affective readership practice, which alternated between compendium for consultation and a more immersive, sustained intellectual rumination.[45] In it, multiple readers repeatedly write their names within the pages of the book. For instance, Ruth Swindell claims the text as her book on multiple pages, writing "Ruth Swindell her Book," first in the introduction, then in the margins and headings, and finally in a blank space just before the edition's woodcut engravings of monstrous births. She dates the first note in this section 1703, and then beneath this entry she writes her name again two times before reiterating "Ruth Swindell her Book 1705" again.[46] James Swindell, Hanah Marpels, and Sarah Webster, perhaps siblings, relatives, or neighbors, claim ownership of the book throughout. These inscriptions suggest not only that readers visited and re-visited this work, but also that they created a community of readers seeking information about reproduction and the body across families, communities, and generations.

In addition to the ways that readers took ownership over the book and its contents, later versions of the work encouraged mastery of its contents through other means. The 1771 *Aristotle's Masterpiece Compleated*, for instance, promotes memorization by appending mnemonic poetic verses at the close of many sections. At the end of the chapter on conception, for instance, the manual distills its central points into the following:

> Thus purest Blood to Seeds first turn'd, and then
> Nature converts it into Blood again:
> Of which a harmless Mass soon after made,
> Such Pow'r by Nature is therein convey'd;
> And by Degrees it into Form does grow,
> And all its Part, distinguish'd are, that so
> It may to a living Soul united be,
> And lay a claim to Immortality.
> Whilst in mean time the anxious Mother's Cares
> Increase, as doth the Burthen which she bears:
> For as it grows, it wants a larger Room,
> And is uneasy in the too strait Womb,
> At last, to quit its dark recess it ventures,
> And into an unknown light World it enters.[47]

Both these additional verses and the overall iterations of the *Masterpiece* endorse the long tradition of epigenesis originally espoused by Aristotle himself, thus suggesting that lay readers were commonly exposed to this perspective, even as preformationism dominated scientific discussion throughout the eighteenth century. While much of the language is reminiscent of earlier versions of the *Masterpiece*, this version is far more adamant in the passive nature of the woman's role in conception and generation, as compared to the "active Principle, or efficient Cause of the *Foetus*," which is "the Seed of Man."[48] The manual also subordinates the more extensive role of the maternal imagination in conception by making it complicit only in generating anomalous fetuses or births.[49] Still, the work encourages collective popular knowledge of conception, pregnancy, and childrearing in ways that support it as a domestic process outside of a state-making apparatus. Readers seem to have responded to the text as a call for documenting kin in this way: Fissell has identified one 1684 edition that included a woman's entry of all the children to whom she gave birth, prefaced by a note that an aunt had given her the work several years before her first child was born.[50] In this way, *Aristotle's Masterpiece* shared knowledge about acts of conception, pregnancy, childbirth, and childrearing across generations, even as such knowledge was increasingly assumed to be specialized medical knowledge.

Mastering Domestic and Foreign Bodies

Even as the *Masterpiece* texts encouraged readers to create domestic communities of care for reproduction, by the mid-eighteenth century, its main competition among popular vernacular medical texts sought to establish reproduction as a public good to be controlled. William Buchan's *Domestic Medicine* (1769) was published in no fewer than 142 editions across the eighteenth and nineteenth centuries, making Buchan's name a brand that conferred a level of medical credibility. Interestingly, just as the "Aristotle" texts used the philosopher's name on texts he did not author, establishing a brand identity signifying a work about reproduction, so too did Buchan's name become attributed to other vernacular medical works that he did not author, an attribution that sought to indicate a certain level of knowledge about the body.[51] Early on, Buchan's text indicated an awareness of this popularity. In 1772, when the second edition was published, Buchan notes in the prefatory material that his "most sanguine expectations could never have suggested that above five thousand copies would have been sold in a corner of Britain before another edition could be got ready."[52] Buchan spends ample time early in the text defending his composition, an extensive work on the body, health, and medicine aimed at a general reading public. Unlike previous manuals, however, he figures this endeavor as specific to an elite community of male readers:

> If a gentleman has a turn for observation [...] surely the natural history of his own species is a more interesting subject, and presents a more ample field for the exertion of genius, than the natural history of spiders and cockle-shells.[53]

He proceeds to note that such a publication actually increases knowledge for the entire community, as it allows for a more complete mode of what Steven Shapin and Simon Schaffer have called the process of virtual witnessing: "The united observations of all the ingenious and sensible part of mankind, would do more in a few years toward the improvement of Medicine, than those of the Faculty alone in a great many."[54] Here, while Buchan does not restrict medical knowledge specifically to physicians, he encourages a specifically male community of medical knowledge.

Although Buchan's treatise offers medical knowledge about the overall health of both sexes, he observes that one of the most important components of medicine resides in the generation and treatment of children. Successful human breeding is so central to his concerns, in fact, that Buchan articulates an ableist argument, claiming that it should be illegal for those with chronic conditions:

> No person who labours under any incurable malady ought to marry. He thereby not only shortens his own life, but transmits misery to others [...] In matrimonial contracts, it is

amazing so little regard is had to the health and form of the object. Our sportsmen know, that the generous courser cannot be bred out of the foundered jade, nor the sagacious spaniel out of the snarling cur. This is settled upon immutable laws.[55]

This passage reveals Buchan's need to rely not only on species mixing but particularly animal breeding in order to make his argument, one that he complements by critiquing urban society's tendency to create deformities and illnesses absent from non-European settings: "How little deformity of body is to be found among uncivilized nations? So little indeed, that it is vulgarly believed they put all their children to death. The truth is, they hardly know such a thing as a deformed child."[56] Buchan cites problems of industrialization, including early and hard labor on the parts of the lower classes, and a tendency toward rich food and excessive behavior, as the causes of problems with conception.[57] Yet in this passage's reliance on distinguishing between urban/pastoral and, presumably, European nations versus those they have colonized, Buchan reveals a kind of exceptionalist logic that deeply informed British writing about Black and brown reproductive bodies: for those from non-European countries, he suggests a kind of Edenic space where nothing goes wrong with reproduction, a claim that plantation owners and colonial doctors would use as a means of blaming unfree and enslaved people when reproduction went wrong. Buchan's manual thus leaves the detailed hypothesizing about conception and other bodily and domestic intimacies to works like *Aristotle's Masterpiece*, instead shifting his emphasis to the relationship among industrialization, public medicine, and public health issues.

The public stakes of reproduction take on further complexities in colonial medical manuals, which overtly attempt to replace often sentimentalized and domesticated language about the white British parturient body with claims that sought to manage and control the financial and public-plantation impact of the Black body's reproductive potential. Such works, according to George C. Grinnell, portray "the health of slaves [as] worth preserving to the extent that it incurs profits and furthers productivity. Its function, in other words, is social and economic, and only minimally concerned with an ethic of care."[58] David Collins's *Practical Rules for the Management and Medical Treatment of Negro Slaves in the Sugar Colonies* (1803) identifies, but ultimately rejects, ethical arguments for abolition; Collins justifies his stance via claims of the colonial need for medical and clinical management, which allows him to frame his treatise as superficially sympathetic behaviors toward the enslaved population.[59] Collins, a physician and "professional planter," provides suggestions on how best to feed, clothe, house, and attend to the unfree men, women, and children on West Indies plantations, using a language of care in an attempt to obfuscate his work's brutal logic and practices.

One detail that sets Collins's work apart from earlier colonial medical manuals is its recognition that, once the slave trade was abolished, expanding the enslaved population through pro-natalist practices would be the only way to maintain a properly viable plantation. In the work's sixth chapter, Collins addresses a "subject of very great consequence, that of the breeding of negroes; which appears to have been less understood, and worse attended to, than any other part of West-Indian management."[60] He continues,

> Hereafter, there is no doubt, but it will force itself upon our notice, either from the impossibility of obtaining new negroes, or from the greatness of their price. To the rules, herein recommended, for the increase of our gangs, by the natural means of procreation, no objection can possibly be made, as they are neither expensive, nor of difficult application.[61]

Collins observes that the death rate far exceeds the birth rate for enslaved people in the Caribbean, which necessitates the forced transportation of more Africans, a situation that

Surrogacy in Eighteenth-Century Vernacular Medical Texts

has afforded matter of concern to many good men, whose humanity revolted from a system of commerce, which depopulates one part of the world for the aggrandizement of the other, and whose efforts for its suppression, have been exerted with no common zeal.[62]

In an argument that typifies the base calculations of slavery, Collins suggests that part of the planter's interest in transporting new bodies is that breeding seems too time- and labor-intensive: "Their tardy generation, through all stages of pregnancy, and infancy" requires "an expense more than equal to their value."[63] He warns now that

calculation very clearly coincides with duty, and tells us, that it is much cheaper to breed than to purchase; the price of new negroes being three times as great as it was forty years ago, and a possibility existing, that we may be finally excluded from that source of supply.[64]

Here, in an attempt to overturn longstanding biases and practices of plantation owners, Collins joins appeals to economic urgency with a neat solution: proper medical management.

Rather than observing the relationship between brutal conditions and enslaved people's low birth rates, Collins suggests that the situation derives from four primary causes: a dearth of enslaved women; female sterility; accidental or intentional abortions; and the high infant mortality rate.[65] While the treatise admits that accidental miscarriages often occur because of difficult labor and injury, Collins suggests that the core reason for the low birth rate on the Caribbean islands is a behavioral one. African women, he claims,

have ardent constitutions, which dispose them to be liberal of their favors; and it has been found by experience, that they who resign themselves to the indiscriminate caresses of men, are seldom very prolific; therefore, you must expect that there will be many of your female slaves, who will contribute but little to the population of your estate.[66]

Collins modulates his language of blame with feigned sympathy for the enslaved people on his plantation, but even these rhetorical sleights of hand fail to conceal the ways enslaved people resisted his attempts at breeding and reproductive management and instead cultivated subversive communities of care. Collins notes that the state of pregnancy for enslaved women is torturous:

Upheld by no consolation, animated by no hope, her nine-months of torment issue in the production of a being, doomed, like herself, to the rigours of eternal servitude, and aggravating, by its claims on maternal support, the weight of her own evils.[67]

To help with the psychological burden facing these women, Collins suggests, enslaved pregnant women should not be excused from all labor, but they should receive routine indulgences. Unlike other treatises that fully promote the idea that the Black parturient body feels no pain and risks no real harm in childbirth, Collins advocates for the attention of a midwife, and suggests that enslaved women may—about 20 percent of the time—require the assistance of a surgeon as well.

Nevertheless, Collins invokes exceptionalist rhetoric about racial difference when he notes that new mothers in the Caribbean are less threatened than they are in colder climates; enslaved people only require about 35 days to recover before returning to fieldwork. Collins encourages women to breastfeed under carefully managed timetables, having them visit the plantation nursery at set times during the day. He further suggests that weaning take place between one year and eighteen months, to allow women to become pregnant more quickly than if they continued to nurse. He also advocates that any woman who has given birth to and raised six living children should receive special "indulgences," like extra days off. Such strategies, alongside creating care for children in communal nurseries, Collins argues, will allow children to develop in a healthier manner, and ultimately, when they are about "five or six years," he claims, "they are capable of labour little indeed at that tender age, yet sufficient to defray the expenses of their own support."[68] In these passages, Collins attempts to endorse and naturalize the increasingly contested system of slavery even as his specific advice for managing pregnancy and childbirth belie such rhetoric.

Although the maternal imagination's capacity to threaten the body and mind of the fetus would align with other concepts Collins invokes, his manual denies such agency for women of African descent. Instead, the African-Caribbean imagination is one to be tricked and mollified. In the second section of the manual, which outlines various medical treatments and receipts, Collins suggests that while plantation managers cannot quell the discomfort of morning sickness and other pregnancy-related pains—no medicine, he says, can do that—"you must make a shew of doing something to satisfy the negro, that you are not indifferent to her relief; and that which medicine cannot effect, the imagination, more powerful, may possibly be able to accomplish."[69] The placebo offered is a julep, consisting of peppermint oil and sugar ground together, mixed with water and the spirit of lavender. If given twice a day, along with a short-term residence of one or two days in the sick house, the woman should feel cured. "By such laudable frauds, you will find that you effect cures greater than the medicine authorized you to expect," Collins confides. When there is a medical condition to address, as in a threatened miscarriage, the woman must lay perfectly still, and, if the condition has arisen from injury, she ought to be bled "six or eight ounces" and given "twenty five drops of laudanum," repeated every twelve hours or increased as necessary; her diet, too, must be controlled, and consisting entirely of mild food that is "the least stimulous to the body."[70] Collins's choice to outline these strategies allows him to evince a sense of reproductive mastery over the bodies that he and other planters own as property.

After abolition, these treatises suggest even more urgency regarding the control of women's reproductive bodies on plantations. John Williamson's *Medical and Miscellaneous Observations Relative to the West India Islands* (1817) opens its section on "On the Management of Negro and Women Children" proclaiming that because abolition has disrupted the slave trade, "it is desirable, on every commendable consideration, to do what is practicable to rear a healthy and vigorous race of negroes to fill up the numbers who go off in the usual course of nature."[71] Williamson thus begins this section attempting to naturalize slavery and its high mortality rates, and, like many writers who came before him, he blames low birth rates on enslaved women's alleged promiscuity. He first offers a plan of seeming domestic tranquility that contradicts the brutal details of the remainder of this section: he encourages "the authority of masters, or the influence of clergy" to arrange appropriate marriages for young enslaved women to promote "a great and public end [...] the extent of which, so impressively full of importance, should be forwarded by proprietor, attorney, overseer, and physician."[72] Yet the ruse of companionate domesticity gives way to the remainder of this section: just pages later he admits that while excessive flogging can cause a prolapsed uterus and may often lead to miscarriage, he continues to blame the low birth rates on the promiscuousness of women, rather than brutal conditions and malnourishment.[73] To counterbalance this "natural" proclivity, he suggests that every property have "some decent discreet old female negroes" to serve as didactic models of instruction; these women would oversee young enslaved women's education until marriages can be arranged. He further suggests that white men should avoid "the improper connections, imperiously formed [...] to the injury of that negro man who considered her his own, and the rightful companion of his bed."[74] Even here, Williamson frames the "injuries" not against the women themselves, but rather against their husbands, thus imagining enslaved women as doubly commoditized.

Williamson advocates for a maternity ward specifically for enslaved women because, he claims, left to their own devices, they give birth to children in squalid conditions at home, endangering

Surrogacy in Eighteenth-Century Vernacular Medical Texts

both mother and child. Williamson includes two shocking anecdotes in an attempt to convince his readers of the necessity of this plan:

> One negro female has been mentioned, who lost her life by ants penetrating a neglected blistered part to the spinal marrow. Another negro woman on a property was slightly indisposed after labour, for whom a visit was applied. I requested her to shew me if she had got a fine child; but, when uncovered, the infant was no more, and all over with myriads of ants, penetrating the vital parts.[75]

This horrifying description attempts to sublimate the barbaric conditions of enslaved women into their own unnatural moral failure. Its anxious description of bodily infestation also attempts to spur change via horror: it is evidence that there ought to be a strong coordination between women midwives and the plantation doctor, hired specifically because he has training in surgical midwifery, to handle childbirth in general and more complicated deliveries in particular. Although he uses the language of racial difference to claim that most enslaved women "will be found to make a good recovery, and seldom suffer from puerperal affections, as our more delicate countrywomen, accustomed to the habits which so enervate, and render them more liable to fever," he suggests that others will occasionally need surgical assistance.[76] Medical intervention here is always balanced in ways that distinguish the subordinated and subservient Black body—and its naturalized place in infinite servitude—from white bodies. The delicate nature of white female bodies promotes white humaneness and humanity while denying the same to African women, a narrative that is framed by men whose primary occupation is to regulate and profit from the Black reproductive body's instrumentalization.

Like Collins's work, Williamson's treatise indicates how enslaved people resisted colonists' attempts at managing their reproductive bodies. In addition to breastfeeding their children for several years, he notes that unfree women are reluctant to give birth in a lying-in hospital, even when it is separate from the plantation hospital itself.[77] Despite the best efforts of plantation owners and managers, enslaved women fought to give birth in their own homes, thereby resisting an institutionalized space that attempted to deprive laboring women of yet another ritual of kinship, the home birth.[78] Added to his breeding project in the Caribbean, like Collins, Williamson suggests how plantation owners can construct a local cultural narrative that distinguishes enslaved women who have successfully given birth and weaned a healthy child. Perhaps inspired by utopian writers like More and Bacon, their reward, he thinks, ought to be a kind of sumptuary law rendered as gift:

> Let that important feeling [of successfully birthing a healthy child] be maintained and encouraged by the proprietor, attorney, and overseer, by distinguished pieces of dress, and other marks of favor, which, in all probability, will be amply repaid by the individuals thus rewarded; and future accessions to the number of negroes will be produced in good time.[79]

This provision, not just for women who have successfully given birth, but specifically for those who have raised *and* weaned a child, indicates that these people would be ready to bear another child for the sake of the plantation and, more broadly, would visually signify an antidote to threats to the institution of slavery posted by abolition and low birth rates. He ends his treatise by shifting the entire discussion to a speculative future, one wherein the unfree are transformed into a "useful class" of "peasantry."[80] At the end of the work, after offering a fictional description of happy breeders whose clothing offers all the reward they would need for the perpetuation of generations of enslaved people, Williamson seems to will the abolitionist debate and the legacy of slavery to disappear by shifting how he categorizes their labor, instead referring to enslaved people as an

241

industrious class of volitional labor and laborers. Here, Williamson's breeding scheme recalls the project of Miller's *The Man-Plant*, both of which rely on a futuristic speculative narrative that wishes for reproductive surrogacy as a means of promoting the domination of the British state in domestic and colonial spaces.

As both a concept and a practice, reproductive surrogacy functioned as a crucial instrument for the expansion of the British colonial state, aligning it with other Enlightenment technologies of the eighteenth century.[81] Yet competing discourses of conception and pregnancy, ones that encouraged connections among humans and their environment and emphasized localized communities of care, allowed for surrogacy to support radical acts of creation and resistance. The transatlantic slave trade dispossessed generations of African people and their descendants legally and socially from identifying kin, thus creating a state of kinlessness, as Morgan, Hortense Spillers, and Saidiya Hartman have all persuasively argued.[82] Against this violence, enslaved people created affective surrogative networks that emphasized what Hartman calls "affiliation," a bond among people beyond blood.[83]

The rhetoric of surrogacy across the eighteenth century reverberates in ways that affect reproductive justice today, demonstrating the long tradition of how, as Barbara Gurr puts it, the reproductive body has been "marked for management" since the advent of the modern state.[84] Beyond various attempts at pro-natalist, surrogative language that served the ends of the British state and its empire, as in *The Man-Plant* and Buchan's *Domestic Medicine*, colonial medical manuals framed pregnancy and childbirth as eminently controllable by plantation management, and any mishaps as direct results of enslaved people's moral failure. Such logical jumps mirror today's conservative talking points that on the one hand make reproductive choice a matter of state concern, yet on the other suggest that a person's health and healthcare options are private matters based on moral goodness or moral failure.[85] At odds with this rationale, the full surrogacy model advocates for individual and collective health and locates much of its strength in educative models and communities of kin and care, forms of which were made available in works like *Aristotle's Masterpiece* for British and white colonial women and in affiliative networks of enslaved people in ways that resisted the broader paternalistic forces surrounding them. A pre-history of surrogacy thus demonstrates, in the words of Lisa Lowe, how the "inequalities of our time are a legacy of the processes through which 'the human' is 'freed' by liberal forms, while other subjects, practices, and geographies are placed at a distance from the 'human.'"[86] In other words, a pre-history of surrogacy helps to reframe our understanding of the humanistic tradition itself.

Bibliography

Alff, David. *The Wreckage of Intentions: Projects in British Culture, 1660–1730*. Philadelphia: University of Pennsylvania Press, 2017.

Allen, Anita. "The Black Surrogate Mother." *Harvard BlackLetter Journal* 8 (1991): 17–31.

Aristotle's Masterpiece Completed. London: Printed by B. H. and are to be Sold by most Book-sellers, 1698.

Aristotle's Master-piece, or the Secrets of Generation. London: Printed, and to be sold at the Hand and Scepter, near Temple-Bar, 1700. The British Library.

Aristotle's Masterpiece Compleated. London, 1771.

Benedict, Leah. "Auxiliary Breasts and Mechanical Wombs: Prosthetic Reproduction in Vincent Miller's *The Man-Plant*." Paper presented at the Annual Conference of the American Society for Eighteenth-Century Studies, Minneapolis: March 30, 2017.

Buchan, William. *Domestic Medicine*, 2nd edition. Edinburgh, 1771.

Bryson, Michael. *The Humanist (Re)Turn: Reclaiming the Self in Literature*. New York: Routledge, 2020.

Cody, Lisa Forman. *Birthing the Nation: Sex, Science, and the Conception of Eighteenth-Century Britons*. New York: Oxford University Press, 2005.

Collins, David. *Practical Rules for the Management and Medical Treatment of Negro Slaves in the Sugar Colonies*. London, 1803.

Darnton, Robert. "First Steps toward a History of Reading (1986)." *Australian Journal of French Studies* 51, no. 2/3 (2014): 152–177.

Daston, Lorraine and Katharine Park. *Wonders and the Order of Nature*. New York: Zone Books, 2001.

Dorner, Zachary. *Merchants of Medicines: The Commerce and Coercion of Health in Britain's Long Eighteenth Century*. Chicago: University of Chicago Press, 2020.

Firestone, Shulamith. *The Dialectic of Sex: The Case for Feminist Revolution*. New York: Bantam Books, 1971.

Fissell, Mary. "Hairy Women and Naked Truths: Gender and the Politics of Knowledge in 'Aristotle's Masterpiece.'" *The William and Mary Quarterly*. 60, no. 1 (2003): 43–74.

Fissell, Mary. "Making a Masterpiece: The *Aristotle* Texts in Vernacular Medical Culture." *Right Living: An Anglo-American Tradition of Self-Help Medicine*. ed. Charles E. Rosenberg. Baltimore: Johns Hopkins University Press, 2003, 59–87.

Fissell, Mary. *Vernacular Bodies: The Politics of Reproduction in Early Modern England*. New York: Oxford University Press, 2004.

Fissell, Mary. "When the Birds and the Bees Were Not Enough: *Aristotle's Masterpiece*." *The Public Domain Review*. August 19, 2015. Accessed October 17, 2017.

Grinnell, George C. "Freedom, Health and Hypochondria in Ignatius Sancho's *Letters*" in *Liberating Medicine, 1720–1835*. Ed. Tristanne Connolly and Steve Clark. New York: Routledge, 2009, 27–40.

Gurr, Barbara. *Reproductive Justice: The Politics of Health Care for Native American Women*. New Brunswick: Rutgers University Press, 2015.

Haraway, Donna J. *Staying with the Trouble: Making Kin in the Chthulucene*. Durham: Duke University Press, 2016.

Hartman, Saidiya. *Lose Your Mother: A Journey along the Atlantic Slave Route*. New York: Farrar, Straus and Giroux, 2007.

Harvey, Karen. *The Imposteress Rabbit Breeder: Mary Toft and Eighteenth-Century England*. New York: Oxford University Press, 2020.

"Historical Perspectives on Contemporary Issues: Aristotle's Masterpiece: Early Modern Sex Ed." Interview with Mary Fissell. *Consortium for the History of Science, Technology, and Medicine Podcast*. https://www.chstm.org/earlymodernsexed

Hitchcock, Tim and Michél Cohen. *English Masculinities, 1660–1800*. New York: Longman, 1999.

Horkheimer, Max and Theodor Adorno *Dialectic of Enlightenment: Philosophical Fragments*. Ed. Gunzelin Schmid Noerr. Trans. Edmund Jephcott. Stanford: Stanford University Press, 2002.

Kastan, David Scott. *Shakespeare after Theory*. New York: Routledge, 1999.

Keller, Eve. *Generating Bodies and Gendered Selves: The Rhetoric of Reproduction in Early Modern England*. Seattle: University of Washington Press, 2007.

Klepp, Susan E. *Revolutionary Conceptions: Women, Fertility, and Family Limitation in America, 1760–1820*. Chapel Hill: University of North Carolina Press, 2009.

Lewis, Sophie. *Full Surrogacy Now: Feminism against Family*. New York: Verso, 2020.

Lowe, Lisa. *The Intimacies of Four Continents*. Durham: Duke University Press, 2015.

Miller, Vincent (pseud.). *The Man-plant; or, Scheme for Increasing and Improving the British Breed*. London: Printed for M. Cooper, at the Globe in Pater-noster Row, 1752.

Morgan, Jennifer L. *Laboring Women: Reproduction and Gender in New World Slavery*. Philadelphia: University of Pennsylvania Press, 2004.

Morgan, Jennifer L. *Reckoning with Slavery: Gender, Kindship, and Capitalism in the Early Black Atlantic*. Durham: Duke University Press, 2021.

Paugh, Katherine. *The Politics of Reproduction: Race, Medicine, and Fertility in the Age of Abolition*. New York: Oxford University Press, 2017.

Pinto-Correia, Clara. *The Ovary of Eve: Egg and Sperm and Preformation*. Chicago: University of Chicago Press, 1997.

Porter, Roy and Lesley Hall. *The Facts of Life: The Creation of Sexual Knowledge in Britain, 1650–1950*. New Haven: Yale University Press, 1995.

Roberts, Dorothy. *Killing the Black Body: Race, Reproduction, and the Meaning of Liberty*. New York: Vintage Books, 2017.

Rosenberg, Charles E. "Medical Text and Social Context: Explaining William Buchan's *Domestic Medicine*." *Bulletin of the History of Medicine* 57, no. 1 (Spring 1983): 22–42.

Ross, Loretta J. and Rickie Solinger. *Reproductive Justice: An Introduction*. Berkeley: University of California Press, 2017.

Shapin, Steven and Simon Schaffer. *Leviathan and the Air-Pump: Hobbes, Boyle, and the Experimental Life*. Princeton: Princeton University Press, 1985.

Sheridan, Richard B. *Doctors and Slaves: A Medical and Demographic History of Slavery in the British West Indies, 1680–1834.* New York: Cambridge University Press, 1985.

Spillers, Hortense J. "Mama's Baby, Papa's Maybe: An American Grammar Book," *Diacritics* 17, no. 2 (Summer 1987): 64–81.

Stephanson, Raymond. "Fictional Science and Genre: Ectogenesis and Parthenogenesis at Mid-Century." *Journal for Eighteenth-Century Studies* 42 no. 4 (2019): 471–486.

Todd, Dennis. *Imagining Monsters: Miscreations of the Self in Eighteenth-Century England.* Chicago: University of Chicago Press, 1995.

Turner, Sasha. *Contested Bodies: Pregnancy, Childrearing, and Slavery in Jamaica.* Philadelphia: University of Pennsylvania Press, 2017.

Vermulean, Heather V. "Thomas Thistlewood's Libidinal Linnaean Project: Slavery, Ecology, and Knowledge Production." *Small Axe* 22, no. 1 (March 2018, No. 55), 18–38.

Weinbaum, Alice Eve. *The Afterlife of Reproductive Slavery: Biocapitalism and Black Feminism's Philosophy of History.* Durham: Duke University Press, 2019.

Williamson, John. *Medical and Miscellaneous Observations, Relative to the West India Islands.* Edinburgh, 1817.

Wittman, Reinhard. "Was there a Reading Revolution at the End of the Eighteenth Century?" *A History of Reading in the West.* Ed. Guglielmo Cavalio and Roger Chartier. Trans. Lydia G. Cochrane. Amherst: University of Massachusetts Press, 1999, 284–312.

Notes

1 Miller, Vincent (pseud.), *The Man-plant; or, Scheme for Increasing and Improving the British Breed*, London: Printed for M. Cooper, at the Globe in Pater-noster Row, 1752, 1–2.

2 Ibid., 4–5.

3 Ibid., 5.

4 Ibid., 13.

5 Shulamith Firestone outlines her plans for outsourcing the labor of pregnancy and childbirth in *The Dialectic of Sex: The Case for Feminist Revolution* (New York: Bantam Books, 1971).

6 Stephanson "Fictional Science and Genre: Ectogenesis and Parthenogenesis at Mid-Century," *Journal for Eighteenth-Century Studies* 42 no. 4 (2019): 471–486, 472. David Scott Kastan has argued for the concept of the "thinkable" in literature in *Shakespeare after Theory* (New York: Routledge, 1999).

7 Stephanson, "Fictional Science," 472. Here I follow Mary Fissell's use of the phrase "vernacular medical texts" from *Vernacular Bodies: The Politics of Reproduction in Early Modern England* (New York: Oxford University Press, 2004).

8 "surrogate, n. and adj." OED Online. June 2021. Oxford University Press. https://www-oed-com.avoserv2.library.fordham.edu/view/Entry/195052 (accessed July 21, 2021).

9 For more on the histories of preformation, see Clara Pinto-Correia, *The Ovary of Eve: Egg and Sperm and Preformation* (Chicago: University of Chicago Press, 1997).

10 Katherine Paugh argues that "The efforts of British doctors to theorize and manage Afro-Caribbean women's childbearing thus resonates deeply with the simultaneous efforts of British man-midwives to establish themselves as authorities on childbirth." Paugh, *The Politics of Reproduction: Race, Medicine, and Fertility in the Age of Abolition* (New York: Oxford University Press, 2017), 91.

11 Anita Allen, "The Black Surrogate Mother," *Harvard BlackLetter Journal* 8 (1991), 17–18. Dorothy K. Roberts, *Killing the Black Body: Race, Reproduction, and the Meaning of Liberty* (New York: Vintage Books, 2017), 278.

12 Dorothy K. Roberts, *Killing the Black Body: Race, Reproduction, and the Meaning of Liberty* (New York: Vintage Books, 2017), 293; Alice Eve Weinbaum, *The Afterlife of Reproductive Slavery: Biocapitalism and Black Feminism's Philosophy of History* (Durham: Duke University Press, 2019), esp. Introduction and Chapter 1.

13 Jennifer L. Morgan, *Laboring Women: Reproduction and Gender in New World Slavery* (Philadelphia: University of Pennsylvania Press, 2004), 5.

14 Donna J. Haraway, *Staying with the Trouble: Making Kin in the Chthulucene* (Durham: Duke University Press, 2016), 102. Sophie Lewis, *Full Surrogacy Now: Feminism against Family* (New York: Verso, 2020), 22.

15 Lewis, *Full Surrogacy*, 19.

16 Haraway, *Staying with the Trouble*, 11.

17 For Lewis, this model would "bring about the conditions of possibility for open-source, fully collaborative gestation.... [and] explode notions of hereditary parentage, and multiply real, loving solidarities.

Surrogacy in Eighteenth-Century Vernacular Medical Texts

Let us build a care commune based on comradeship, a world sustained by kith and kind more than kin. Where pregnancy is concerned, let every pregnancy be for everyone. Let us overthrow, in short, the 'family.'" Lewis, *Full Surrogacy*, 26.

18 Ibid., 147.

19 Morgan, *Reckoning with Slavery*, 61; 2222–2223. On controlled fertility among enslaved people, see Paugh, *The Politics of Reproduction*, 97.

20 For more on the relationship between medicine and empire, see Zachary Dorner's *Merchants of Medicines: The Commerce and Coercion of Health in Britain's Long Eighteenth Century* (Chicago: University of Chicago Press, 2020).

21 See Morgan, *Reckoning with Slavery*, Chapter 6. Sasha Turner, *Contested Bodies: Pregnancy, Childrearing, and Slavery in Jamaica* (Philadelphia: University of Philadelphia Press, 2017), 202–211.

22 "Historical Perspectives on Contemporary Issues: Aristotle's Masterpiece: Early Modern Sex Ed," Interview with Mary Fissell, *Consortium for the History of Science, Technology, and Medicine Podcast*, https://www.chstm.org/earlymodernsexed.

23 Michael Bryson, *The Humanist (Re)Turn: Reclaiming the Self in Literature* (New York: Routledge, 2020), 35.

24 Miller, *The Man-Plant*, 35.

25 Ibid., 36.

26 Ibid., 38–39. Leah Benedict's "Auxiliary Breasts and Mechanical Wombs: Prosthetic Reproduction in Vincent Miller's *The Man-Plant*" (presentation, Annual Conference, American Society for Eighteenth-Century Studies, Minneapolis, March 30, 2017), importantly discusses the connection between early embryology, reproductive technology, and "the generative capacity of impotence and its potential to revise definitions of familial and sexual relationships in the eighteenth-century imagination." I thank Professor Benedict for introducing me to this text.

27 For more on the feminization debate, see Tim Hitchcock and Michél Cohen, *English Masculinities, 1660–1800* (New York: Longman, 1999); Susan E. Klepp, *Revolutionary Conceptions: Women, Fertility, and Family Limitation, 1760–1820* (Chapel Hill: University of North Carolina Press, 2009), 5–7.

28 "The word 'project' marks a historical attempt at becoming, an arrival of potential distinct from the stage at which ambition ultimately succeeds or fails." David Alff, *The Wreckage of Intentions* (Philadelphia: University of Pennsylvania Press, 2017), 14–16.

29 Heather V. Vermulean, "Thomas Thistlewood's Libidinal Linnaean Project: Slavery, Ecology, and Knowledge Production," *Small Axe* 22 no. 1 (March 2018), 23.

30 Ibid., 28.

31 Lorraine Daston and Katharine Park, as well as Dennis Todd, have described the relationship between wonder and "monstrous births" in the early modern period. See Daston and Park, *Wonders and the Order of Nature* (New York: Zone Books, 2001), especially Chapter 5. See Todd, *Imagining Monsters: Miscreations of the Self in Eighteenth-Century England* (Chicago: University of Chicago Press, 1995).

32 See, for instance, Karen Harvey, *The Imposteress Rabbit Breeder: Mary Toft and Eighteenth-Century England* (New York: Oxford University Press, 2020), and Lisa Forman Cody, *Birthing the Nation: Sex, Science, and the Conception of Eighteenth-Century Britons* (New York: Oxford University Press, 2005), especially Chapter 5.

33 Stephanson, "Fictional Science," 471–472.

34 Ibid., 479.

35 For info on generic mixing, see Stephanson, "Fictional Science," 482; for vernacular medical manuals, see Eve Keller. *Generating Bodies and Gendered Selves: The Rhetoric of Reproduction in Early Modern England.* Seattle: University of Washington Press, 2007.

36 The bibliographic lives and afterlives of the *Aristotle* texts are dizzying in their explosive variants: Fissell suggests that there are three core *Aristotle's Masterpiece* texts: the first, published in 1684; the second, in 1697, which combines the 1684 edition with other writing on women's diseases; and the third, first published in 1702, which rewrites and revises the 1697 edition and became the version that continued to be republished through the nineteenth century. See Fissell, "Making a Masterpiece: The *Aristotle* Texts in Vernacular Medical Culture," *Right Living: An Anglo-American Tradition of Self-Help Medicine*, ed. Charles E. Rosenberg (Baltimore: Johns Hopkins University Press, 2003), 61–62, for a more involved description of these three versions and other pertinent textual variants. Roy Porter and Lesley Hall's *Facts of Life* also offers a discussion of the textual variants, which they place at a total count of four, including a Victorian edition. See Porter and Hall, *The Facts of Life: The Creation of Sexual Knowledge in Britain, 1650–1695* (New Haven: Yale University Press, 1995), 54–64.

37 *Aristotle's Master-piece* (1684), 10–11.

38 Ibid., 17.

39 Ibid., 18–19.

40 Ibid., 5.

41 Fissell, "Hairy Women and Naked Truths: Gender and the Politics of Knowledge in 'Aristotle's Master-piece,'" *The William and Mary Quarterly* 60, no. 1 (2003): 43–74.

42 *Aristotle's Masterpiece* (1684), 27.

43 Ibid., 27–28.

44 Ibid., 29.

45 On intensive and extensive reading practices, see Reinhard Wittman, "Was there a Reading Revolution at the End of the Eighteenth Century?" in *A History of Reading in the West*, ed. Guglielmo Cavalio and Roger Chartier, trans. Lydia G. Cochrane (Amherst: University of Massachusetts Press, 1999), 284–312; see also Robert Darnton, "First Steps Toward a History of Reading (1986)," *Australian Journal of French Studies* 51 no. 2/3 (2014): 152–177.

46 *Aristotle's Master-piece, or the Secrets of Generation* (London: Printed, and to be sold at the Hand and Scep-ter, near Temple-Bar, 1700). The British Library.

47 *Aristotle's Masterpiece Compleated.* (London, 1771), 46–47.

48 Ibid., 36.

49 Ibid., 89–90.

50 "Historical Perspectives on Contemporary Issues: Aristotle's Masterpiece: Early Modern Sex Ed."

51 Charles E. Rosenberg, "Medical Text and Social Context: Explaining William Buchan's *Domestic Medicine*," *Bulletin of the History of Medicine* 57, no. 1 (Spring 1983), 22, 42.

52 William Buchan, *Domestic Medicine*, 2nd ed. (Edinburgh: 1771), iii.

53 Ibid., xix.

54 Ibid., xx. Steven Shapin and Simon Schaffer, *Leviathan and the Air-Pump*: *Hobbes, Boyle, and the Experimental Life* (Princeton: Princeton University Press, 1985), 60–65.

55 Buchan, *Domestic Medicine*, 2nd ed. (Edinburgh: 1771), 9–10.

56 Ibid., 13.

57 Ibid., 34–35, 68–69.

58 George C. Grinnell, "Freedom, Health and Hypochondria in Ignatius Sancho's *Letters*" in *Liberating Medicine, 1720–1835* ed. Tristanne Connolly and Steve Clark (New York: Routledge, 2009), 27–40, 35.

59 For more on the work of David Collins, see Turner, *Contested Bodies*, 56–62, 76–93, and Richard B. Sheridan, *Doctors and Slaves: A Medical and Demographic History of Slavery in the British West Indies, 1680–1834* (New York: Cambridge University Press, 1985), esp. Chapters 5, 6, and 8.

60 David Collins, *Practical Rules for the Management and Medical Treatment of Negro Slaves in the Sugar Colonies* (London: Vernor and Hood, 1803), 30.

61 Ibid., 30.

62 Ibid., 150.

63 Ibid., 151.

64 Ibid., 153.

65 Ibid., 153.

66 Ibid., 156.

67 Collins, *Practical Rules*, 157.

68 Ibid., 173.

69 Ibid., 448.

70 Ibid., 451.

71 John Williamson, 197.

72 Williamson, vol. 2, 198.

73 Williamson, vol. 2, 205. See also Sasha Turner, *Contested Bodies*, 92–94.

74 Williamson, vol. 2, 201.

75 Ibid., 204.

76 Ibid., 205–206.

77 Ibid., 202–205.

78 For more on reproduction (or the lack thereof) as a form of resistance, see Morgan, *Reckoning with Slavery*, Chapter 6.

79 Ibid., 210.

80 Ibid., 211.

81 Max Horkheimer and Theodor Adorno *Dialectic of Enlightenment: Philosophical Fragments*. Ed. Gunzelin Schmid Noerr. Trans. Edmund Jephcott (Stanford: Stanford University Press, 2002), 2.

82 Morgan, *Reckoning with Slavery*, especially 179–180 and 220; Hortense Spillers, "Mama's Baby, Papa's Maybe: An American Grammar book," *Diacritics* 17, no. 2 (Summer 1987): 64–81; and Saidya Hartman, *Lose Your Mother: A Journey along the Atlantic Slave Route* (New York: Farrar, Straus and Giroux), 2007, 204–206.

83 Hartman, *Lose Your Mother*, 204.

84 Barbara Gurr, *Reproductive Justice: The Politics of Health Care for Native American Women* (New Brunswick: Rutgers University Press, 2015).

85 Loretta J. Ross and Rickie Solinger make a similar point in Chapter 3 of their *Reproductive Justice: An Introduction* (Berkeley: University of California Press, 2017), esp. 19–20, 131, 151–159.

86 Lisa Lowe, *The Intimacies of Four Continents* (Durham: Duke University Press, 2015), 2.

PART III

Digital Humanisms

15

Digital Humanities and the Humanistic Tradition

Situating Digital Humanism

Mauro Carassai

The notion of a digital humanism can evoke, in the expression's very construct, the specter of a contradiction in terms. As many a digital studies scholar has remarked,[1] some of the main features of the digital lie along elements of division, segmentation, and parceling. One can barely think about digital technologies without referencing, for example, *sampling* and *quantization*.[2] These processes typically involve the creation and manipulation of progressively small discrete units – from samples and pixels down to the elemental, mutually-exclusive binary digits of zeros and ones. Humanism, on the other hand, has frequently called to mind a unified, integral, and holistic vision of the human subject, of human agency, of human dignity and capabilities, and, more largely, of the human desire to follow the adventure of knowledge beyond conventional classifications and outside the reductive demarcations of disciplinary boundaries. The various historicized characterizations of the humanist – from the Renaissance global mind[3] operating against the pedantry of hierarchical taxonomy and immanent theology of the Middle Ages to its later 19th-century[4] instantiation as a cultural agent influencing the ethical and civic life of all human society – have all promoted humanism as a process of comprehensive universal emancipation of the individual.[5] It might therefore be a considerably difficult task to assess how, and to what extent, these contrasting elements of disjuncture and wholeness, of granularity and synthesis, of electric polarities and perceptive transcendence can actually coexist in the *digital humanism* compound. And, most crucially, whether they can (or indeed do) converge toward the formation of our modern idea of the contemporary humanist, the last heir of a centuries-long critical and philosophical attitude aimed at promoting human progress and now operating in an age of intelligent machines and their promises. Given the emphasis that humanism has traditionally placed on the speculative domain of human subjects in terms of their intellectual achievements, the issue of intelligence – in its etymological reference to the Latin word *intelligere* (the comprehend, to perceive) – can become a privileged site of inquiry when reviewing problems and perspectives related to digital humanism.

Although many a contemporary discipline-specific and interdisciplinary scholarly community today accepts that the notion of human intelligence is fundamentally elusive, controversial, hardly definable[6] or, at the very least "pluralized,"[7] there can be few doubts about the central role that (formal) logic, (analog) computational procedures, and (rule-guided) mental and behavioral patterns have traditionally played in understanding the long history of human intellectual accomplishments. Most of these intellective operations lie at the base of what we often call critical thinking. They typically involve critical assessment and evaluation, comparison and contrast, and the reckoning and processing of a range of heterogenous perspectives. As a consequence, they have *de facto* traditionally constituted humanism's major assets. More importantly, they form the basis

DOI: 10.4324/9781003046004-19

of the set of approaches to life that, in contrast with any perspective working with static wisdom received from dogmatic systems of thought (like religions and other *auctoritas*[8]), started conversely by valuing a human search for meaning and human cultural agency and then eventually reaffirmed the crucial value of human reason. Historically, we posit these intellectual attitudes as permanent features of humanism in Western culture at least since the rediscovery of Greek and Latin texts in the 14th century by scholars interested in reviving the knowledge and accomplishments contained in these texts well beyond the Christian mediation operated by the Middle Ages.[9] In order to address the issue of a digital humanism, however, we might need a larger reflection on the intellective use that human beings have historically made of *all* textual artifacts – from the Mesopotamian clay tablets in the 3rd millennium BCE to the modern era bound book.[10]

The radically new aspect in this long trajectory is that contemporary humanists have now for some time moved beyond the habit of working exclusively with tools characterizable as inert and static informational objects – objects that, by means of the technology of writing, have regularly separated, in Walter Ong's terms, the "knower from the known."[11] The scholarly work of the 21st-century humanists today at some level necessarily involves, on the contrary, the interaction with computational entities that are constantly filtering for them large amounts of digitized information according to definite parameters. Rather than fixedly inscribed on material surfaces, information is now often formally organized into digital archives, online libraries, or virtual repositories, and stored and structured as data within various types of responsive databases. These resources typically come with software components that, by allowing their users to perform algorithmic treatments of their data, materialize cognitively-distributed scholarly activities in the form of various kinds of interactions between intelligent contributors, the one human and the other machinic. N. Katherine Hayles, possibly the most authoritative example of a contemporary scholar operating along the scientist-humanist threshold, observes how "any entity that can perform these tasks [information filtering, data selecting, neural nets decision-making] should *prima facie* be considered thinking or intelligent."[12] As a result, capturing the essence of modern humanism in our contemporary digital juncture faces the fundamental challenge of thoroughly reflecting on human intellective achievements in relation to the machinic ones.

In recent literary and cultural theory, this has become the problem of grasping the actual extent of human contribution in intellectual work and of focusing on the delicate interplay in which humanism is currently involved in relation to new positions and perspectives, such as posthumanism and transhumanism.[13] The contemporary problem of either separating machinic knowledge from human knowledge or of understanding their complex interplay also becomes part of a trans-historical self-reflection on both the human and the humanities. Humanistic self-reflexive views typically reach back into the ancestry of Western civilization, along a trajectory that, from Aristotle's treatment of *Organon* (discussion of the value of logic) and *Paideia* (the creation of the ideal member of the *polis*), usually include the 15th-century distinction between *studia divinitatis* and *studia humanitatis* and go through what are by now canonical names, such as Coluccio Salutati, Boezio, Erasmus, Giambattista Vico, Enlightenment humanists,[14] and Wilhelm Dilthey and his influential distinction between *Geisteswissenschaften* and *Naturwissenschaften*.[15] It might be somewhat expected, therefore, that discussing the notion of digital humanism requires, besides addressing the new role of human cognition, also some level of evaluation of the emergence of a comprehensive frame of mind encompassing both the sciences and the humanities, one with convergent mental skills and a similar inquiry mindset.

Since the time of C. P. Snow's influential 1959 Rede Lecture "The Two Cultures" on the misrecognition between these two areas,[16] the ideal distinction between the chiefly abstract and speculative processes typical of the humanities and the predominantly practical and empirical methods of sciences has been largely rearticulated.[17] Not only has the emergence of areas of study such as the *history* of science, the *sociology* of science, and the *rhetoric* of science (the persuasiveness

Situating Digital Humanism

of its discourses) revealed a contemporary disciplinary "picture [that] does not recognize two distinct and opposing intellectual cultures,"[18] but studies of interdisciplinarity, drawing on fields such as the history of ideas or the history of thought, have highlighted the essential convergence of their *imaginative* intellectual practices. All the items constituting the semantic field of ingenuity, inventiveness, vision, fabrication, prediction, and insightful envisioning create a picture of our scholarly activities as operating as the foundation of a collective social practice of *imagining* possible states of affairs. The practice of creating models *of* our past (and present) as well as models *for* our future pertains then to the idealistic awareness-enhancement pursued within the humanities just as much as to the technology-based faith in life improvement that typically guides the sciences.

It is within this cultural trajectory of convergence and within this overall intellectual paradigm shift that the emerging field of digital humanities, as an interdisciplinary scholarly discipline *par excellence*, has shaped up. From its initial formal designation as "humanities computing,"[19] as the presence of the *digital* has progressively become pervasive in the everyday life of scholars and laymen, the field seems to have settled into its current stable denomination.[20] In the most recent construct, the term *digital* accounts both for the field's agenda going well beyond the strictly *computational* component and for the extensive set of relationships between digital studies and the humanities that allow digital humanities to become a visible presence in our current organization of knowledge and education systems.[21] As Susan Hockey describes it the field seems to emerge since its very outset, as intrinsically trans-medial (involving different media like manuscripts and punch cards), trans-disciplinary, (bringing together theology, theory of interpretation, and computer sciences), and trans-national (intertwining the European and the American continents):

> Unlike many other interdisciplinary experiments, humanities computing has a very well-known beginning. In 1949, an Italian Jesuit priest, Father Roberto Busa, began what even to this day is considered a monumental task: to make an *index verborum* of all the words in the works of St. Thomas Aquinas and related authors, totaling some 11 million words of medieval Latin. Father Busa imagined that a machine might be able to help him, and, having heard of computers, went to visit Thomas J. Watson at IBM in the United States in search of support (Busa 1980).[22]

Even from these few lines, we see how, in the very narrative of its birth, the field of digital humanities already brings into close conversation a constellation of disparate elements whose conceptual areas extend both within and outside the thought tradition that we typically identify as humanism. In this system, we find a fascinating set of opposites: a religious scholar (Roberto Busa) and a secular businessman (Tom J. Watson as the CEO of International Business Machines); a medieval thinker with a foundational role in the *exegesis* and interpretation of the Sacred Scriptures (Thomas Aquinas) and the contemporary penchant of literary theory for reinterpreting Aquinas's *oeuvre* in the light of unexplored textual connections; the encoded nature of inscription in ancient manuscripts and the alphabetical illegibility of punch cards; and, ultimately, the quest for knowledge reminiscent of Old World Renaissance and its re-elaboration through American technological modernity.

From the time of its symbolic and anecdotical inception, the field of digital humanities can be said to have subsequently constantly expanded such a tendency to encompass scattered elements to the point of working today as an umbrella term that identifies what can actually be seen as a pretty wide range of research. This range covers, just to give an idea, everything from studies of digital objects (e.g., "new media" or "digital media" studies) to large-scale text computing (e.g., analysis of so-called "Big Data," "macroanalysis," and "cultural analytics") to VR/AR-based reproduction of architectural and archeological sites (e.g., "Immersive and Interactive Technologies" and the larger field of "Data Visualization"). The heterogeneity of its activities, while invigorating and regenerating research initiatives in the humanities, makes it problematic at some level to pin down digital humanities' most appropriate institutional collocation,[23] with consequent challenges to the identification of its specific contribution to the existing map of humanistic knowledge production and of any recognizable delimitation of what constitutes *humanism* in it.[24] Current perspectives from which we look at digital humanities see them as "increasingly integrated in the humanities at large."[25] As the Mission Statement of Alan Liu's *4Humanities* project reads, today

> [digital humanities] catch the eye of administrators and funding agencies who otherwise dismiss the humanities as yesterday's news. They connect across disciplines with science and engineering fields. They have the potential to use new technologies to help the humanities communicate with, and adapt to, contemporary society.[26]

Liu's remark is, especially in the light of the sheer number of funded digital humanities projects and funding agencies supporting those projects,[27] undoubtedly solidly grounded. What remains to be assessed is whether this re-energizing effect of the digital humanities on the humanities as a whole might correspond a parallel re-energizing of the tenets of humanism as historically understood on the one hand and as fostered by this new specific area on the other hand.

What follows, with all the ambitions and limitations typical of the purpose and possibilities of the book chapter format, can therefore be seen as an attempt to sketch continuities and disruptions between practices and methodologies implemented in digital humanities and the long tradition of humanism and its historicized connotations. A relevant but monumental task, the tracking of such continuities and disruptions might take a number of directions, some of which remain here merely suggested. In terms of continuities, it might be sufficient at this stage to consider that, while digital studies within the humanities is a relatively young sub-area spreading across many of its disciplines, some of its key concerns can be thought of as carrying on the work of centuries-long speculative efforts. Among these, we can certainly list the essential epistemological practice of studying humankind's self-reflection in its own artifacts,[28] the connected central modernist problems around the basis and convergence of media,[29] and the larger anthropological attention to reimagining a productive relationship between human beings and their technologies beyond the limits of a technology-dependent culture.[30] As far as discontinuities go, we might simply look at how writing and reading in the digital environment present a unique challenge to established concepts of materiality, cognition, meaning-making, and embodiment that, in their turn, disturb established notions such as selfhood,[31] textual artifacts, and [processes of] interpretation. Which of these trajectories will eventually establish themselves as forming the paradigmatic, practical, theoretical, and philosophical *doxa* of digital humanism is, quite expectedly, too early to determine at this stage. However, we might likely agree about the following.

First of all, if humanism is intended as the cultural tradition that has shaped our view of the human subject at least since the Renaissance denomination of *studia humanitatis*,[32] we might find ourselves charged with a compelling task when it comes to characterizing digital humanism. Our present and future task might consist in monitoring undercurrents and tendencies of postmodernist and posthumanist theories that try to reconfigure humanism in the light of positivist approaches when these tend to see logical, quantitative, and computational treatments of data as the privileged or most highly-regarded source of all authoritative knowledge.[33] In conjunction with the current increasing application of digital technologies to the analysis of textual data in the humanities, we might have to continuously keep track of the possible parallel underlying process of reconfiguring "humanism" and the "human" in the service of machinic-oriented normative epistemological values. Taken together, the increasing emphasis on the new "distributed cognition"[34] across man and computational machines, the philosophical redefinition of the human as

Situating Digital Humanism

an "info-organism,"[35] the reliance on (bio-)technology in the attempt to transcend mental and physical human limitations,[36] and the general re-positioning of the human entity in a complex network of both sentient and non-sentient creatures, can represent a collective set of positions that end up potentially redefining central tenets of a centuries-long humanist tradition.

Second, if the conceptual system of humanism has been consistently based not only on the awareness of human potential and of human capability – which can certainly be augmented with electronic computation – but also on the human responsibility to give meaning to life without delegating any metaphysical entity or divine being the task of explaining the universe, then we might have to protect digital humanism against technological versions of metaphysical intrusions. In fact, our reliance on obtaining knowledge at a scale "unthinkable"[37] or "unimaginable"[38] for human cognition before the advent of modern computers risks generating a reappearance of that subjection to entities endowed with super-human knowledge possibilities that the tradition of humanism, in its battle for legitimation, has long fought against.

Lastly, if the humanist emphasis has traditionally been on the human power to transform the reality in which we exist and, what matters most, to develop an ethics out of it, then we might find value in keeping an eye on current debates in the interdisciplinary areas of digital humanities, electronic literature, cultural analytics, technology and new media studies in relation to their occasional tendency to unreservedly emphasize the unlimited promises of computational-enhanced practices, of algorithmic empirical objectivity, or of autonomous machine learning and unsupervised data analysis.

The breadth of the task of mapping ways to maintain a centrality of the human element in this context calls for a discussion of identified major turning points in digital practices (the creation of hypertextual technologies,[39] of digital archives and critical editions,[40] of AI-based and interactive narratives,[41] etc.) and criticism (cognition and cybernetics,[42] materiality,[43] software and code studies[44]) that might be put in conversation with the tradition of humanist contributions, literary criticism, and theory that focus on human agency, capabilities, and potential for freedom and progress. The next subsections of this chapter will therefore review at least five main discourses or cultural formations, each of which examines a representative advancement in digital technology *vis-à-vis* a *humanist* approach to the human: 1) networks, hypertexts and human complexity; 2) artificial intelligence, automated algorithms, and human processes; 3) metadata, encoding, and human mapping; 4) super-computing, expert systems and the scale of human knowledge; 5) interfaces, programming, and the reexamination of human creativity.

Without formally anticipating the result of this exploratory survey, we might want to pay attention, along the conceptual unfolding of the next sections, to a common basic dynamic. Each of these technological turning points seems to start with the promises of fully realizing the human potential called for by some version of historicized humanism and seems to subsequently reconfigure such promises by taking a multiplicity of directions that can, in principle, create productive distance between the initial promise and its desired fulfillment. The extent to which such a distance can remain a productive *humanist* one depends, however, on the margin for human self-understanding outlined in each of the next conceptual units.

Hypertexts, Networks, and Human Complexity

Even humanists most resistant to integrating a proactive use of technology in their scholarly work happen to experience the influence of the digital on contemporary textuality in the form of the "HT" abbreviation for *hypertext*. They regularly encounter the "HT" bigram any time they happen to access a web page – mostly in relation to web-related acronyms such as "HTML" (shortened form for the "hypertext markup language"[45] used to encode documents to be displayed in a web browser) or "http://" (the omnipresent initial string found in URLs[46] on the internet and standing for "hypertext transfer protocol"). The term "hypertext" was coined in 1965 by Ted Nelson, who offered, in his *Literary Machines*, an early definition for what has now become a common concept. Nelson describes hypertext as "non-sequential writing – text that branches and allows choices to the reader, best read at an interactive screen"[47] or as "a series of text chunks connected by links which offer the readers different pathways."[48] In both phrases, we can detect the major difference this technology introduced in the humanities: The shift from the linearity of textual content of the codex, manuscript, or bound book (*texts*) to the non-linear way of organizing textual information as a web of materials on the internet (*hypertexts*).

The last decades have been characterized by a remarkable process of digitization and hypertextualization of knowledge from various disciplines mainly connected to the spreading of the *World Wide Web*.[49] Along this general transition, however, the ingenious adoption of hypertextual writing technologies for either creative or scholarly purposes in the humanities is often regarded as a much more circumscribed phenomenon.[50] Prominent digital media scholars such as Jay Bolter had acutely indicated that by the early 1990s how computers had opened a new "writing space."[51] At the same time, however, eminent hypertext theorists, such as George Landow, have been observing how "the expected explosion of hyperfiction does yet not seem to have taken place"[52] and digital culture scholars, such as Scott Rettberg, remark today how "the hypertext novel itself is [no longer] an area of much contemporary activity".[53] Retrospectively, we might conclude that, rather than as a phenomenon concerned with innovative writing experimentation in the fashion of the modernist and avantgarde tradition, hypertext has mostly impacted the humanities at the level of literary theory. As far as digital textuality is concerned, the junction between poststructuralist theory and hypermedia studies had been highlighted by George Landow's early and seminal "theory of convergence."[54] According to Landow, we can notice a surprising convergence between literary critique and information technologies to the point that "critical theory promises to theorize hypertext and hypertext promises to embody and thereby test aspects of theory."[55] Landow opens his *Hypertext 3.0: Critical Theory and New Media in an Era of Globalization* by pointing out that

> When designers of computer software examine the pages of *Glas* or *Of Grammatology*, they encounter a digitalized, hypertextual Derrida; and when literary theorists examine *Literary Machines*, they encounter a deconstructionist or poststructuralist Nelson. These shocks of recognition can occur because over the past several decades literary theory and computer hypertext, apparently unconnected areas of inquiry, have increasingly converged. Statements by theorists concerned with literature, like those by theorists concerned with computing, show a remarkable convergence.[56]

In the early days of electronic textuality, such "recognitions" would open up the way toward a re-empowerment of human reading that was very much called for by literary theory. As Adalaide Morris observes, "hypertext appeared to materialize the still vibrant poststructuralist dream of processual, dynamic, multiple signifying structures activated by readers who were not consumers of fixed meanings but producers of their own compositions."[57] Such characterization of a re-empowered reader, free to compose her individual text out of all the allowed linking possibilities, would mainly produce its effects at the level of interpretation. Reading would now more explicitly operate *against* the tyranny of author-centered signification and as an activity whose margins of interventions in meaning-making would go in the direction of amplifying the range of the so-called *signified* component of the sign.[58] However, in the age of the digital humanities, after a few decades of both media experimentation and digital textual manipulation for literary purposes, the re-empowerment of human reading seems recently to have shifted its technological focus from the liberating power of network thinking connected with hypertexts to concerns related to machinic affordances for data processing. Initiated by the scholarly reflection on hypertexts, our evaluation

Situating Digital Humanism

of the possibilities of human reading as enhanced by computer technologies has increasingly been replaced by an attention to the capabilities of *machinic* reading in terms of the parsing, processing, and computing of digitized textual data. A consequence of such a shift is that the anthropological awareness of the difference between information and *linked information* has eventually given way to the allure of the unexplored critical possibilities connected with code-based data mining of *digitized information* for humanities investigations. A related consequence in terms of literary theory is that the attention to the enhanced possibilities for understanding and meaning-making operating at the level of the *signified* (the hypertextual reconfigurable constellations of meanings) shifts its focus toward different concerns. These renovated concerns mostly deal with how to use machinic affordances for large-scale reading intended as formalized analyses operating conversely at the level of textual *signifier* (the digitized data).

This shift might strike us as a significant one, especially when we consider that hypertext as a textual device characterized by a multi-linear way of organizing information (as opposed to the linearity of printed books) had been envisioned as closely connected to human cognition and intelligence since the 1940s, namely well before the internet era. Vannevar Bush's idea of *memex*, as described in his article eloquently titled "As We May Think,"[59] represents the most frequently mentioned prototype of an instrument that, by more closely emulating human mnemonic processes, could link information by associative connections rather than by indexes. A striking and foundational point raised by this article is that Bush strongly believed that, during the process of reading, readers usually feel the urge to link their own thoughts to the text. Anytime a reader needs to do so,

> He inserts a page of longhand analysis of his own. Thus he builds a trail of his interest through the maze of materials available to him. And his trails do not fade.[60]

Particularly interesting is the reference to the possibility of adding thoughts and comments to the text in an *indelible* way, or, in any case, in a way less transitory than the one guaranteed by mnemonic processes only. Potentially helpful in dealing with any text, this ideal option can become indispensable when the set of primary texts under examination or the collection of documents that the contemporary humanist might have to do research on shows a high rate of structural complexity.

Given the amount of speculative reasoning traditionally associated with the humanities since their very outset, we might make a case for hypertext to have represented a potential technological turning point in its encouraging forms of networked thinking that seemed to materialize the ancient Graeco-Roman ideal of the *uomo universale*,[61] a characterization of the human subject as a limitless one in terms of potential for development and endowed with a moral duty to embrace all knowledge. Such a characterization represents one of the first instantiations of the figure of the humanist and of the humanist conception of the human subject. Young Italian Renaissance nobleman and humanist Pico della Mirandola, who at the age of 23 considered himself as the most educated man in Europe, in his call to his contemporaries to challenge his 900 theses on philosophy, religion, law, and ethics characterized the position of the human subject as a privileged observer of the totality of the physical and metaphysical universe. In his figurative description of a dialogue between God and the human being, we see an example:

> The nature of all other beings is limited and constrained in accordance with the laws prescribed by Me. Constrained by no limits, in accordance with your own free will, which I have given to you, you shall independently determine the bounds of your own nature. I have placed you at the center of the universe from where you may more easily observe whatever is in the universe.[62]

In a paradigmatic rediscovery of the above ideal, and in a sort of prescient approach to digital treatment of *textual* Big Data, hypertext technology seemed to follow in the early humanist tradition and pursue the apprehension and comprehension of knowledge down to its technical functions. Early hypertext software, such as *Storyspace*, provided navigation tools such as lists of links, tree maps, overviews, and bookmarks in order to grant the reader some sort of conceptual orientation over a vast landscape of textual material (see Figure 15.1).

Further specific options of hypertextual environments such as the possibility of saving reading paths that the reader might want to preserve for future textual access, the various ways of visualizing links and their networked structure, or the ability of adding comments to text, would provide a more adequate framework for the reading experience of large-scale collections of texts. From this point of view, early stand-alone hypertextual environments implemented by a variety of tools such as the *Mosaic* web browser,[63] the *Mapa System*,[64] or *Storyspace*, to name a few, had been specifically conceived of and/or had specific tools and functions that would allow the human subject to enact strategies for gaining orientation across a boundaryless sea of knowledge. Possibly an understudied area of inquiry concerning technology and the humanities, a reflection on the set of interface affordances granted by early hypertext environments would make absolutely clear how these tools allowed both readers and scholars a mastery of textual information that the admittedly more practical adoption of the HTML, XML, and other forms of encoding for visualizing texts on the web had implicitly lost – with non-trivial consequences for the contemporary humanist mind. The issue is not only about the functional relationships between the human neurological network and the networked computer as a productive convergence between cognitive studies and humanistic practices[65] but impacts the tenets of networked thinking and networked learning as the basis of the foundational epistemological principle of both ancient and modern humanism. Humanism,

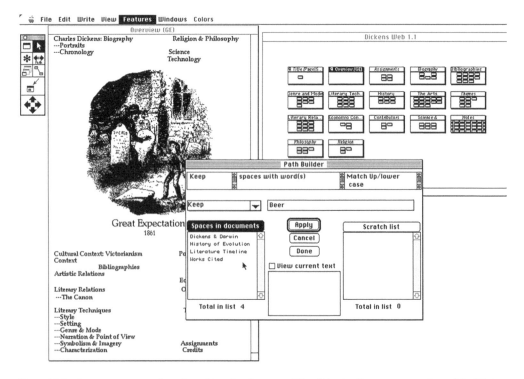

Figure 15.1 Storyspace screenshot. Searching for the name "Beer" in the Storyspace version of the Dickens Web [Landow and Kahn 1992]

Situating Digital Humanism

throughout its different instantiations, has constantly historically operated against both the philosophical *dualism* that had often divided the universe into a material and a spiritual one (along the tradition of orthodox Christianity and its major philosopher Thomas Aquinas, as well as such diverse thinkers as Plato, Plotinus, and even Renee Descartes in his objectivism and subjectivism) and against the metaphysical *idealism* usually ascribing the universe a mind, a consciousness, or an intelligent design of its own (as reflected in various philosophical positions from the 18th-century English churchman Bishop Berkeley to the 19th-century German philosopher Georg Wilhelm Friedrich Hegel). In the passage from the human-like technology for thinking of the hypertextual *docuverse*[66] to the dichotomic separation of human and machinic treatment of large-scale collections of texts in digital humanities' practices, we might witness a reappearance of both dualism and idealism. The former is concerned with the re-establishment of a dualistic separation between *language* and *data* while the latter deals with the illegitimate idealistic identification of the things that are symbolized with the symbols used (think about the idea of a collection of individual texts as monolithic "data" and its similarity with the transformation of the universe into Idea). Hypertext as a technology that fully accounted for human complexity in terms of networks, connections, associative thinking across boundaries, and perception of qualitatively multi-dimensional aspects of textuality has possibly transitioned into a scholarly attention to the kinds of quantitative, algorithmic, computationally formalized complexity that are closer to promoting a philosophy of existence based on digitized data as explorable metaphysical ontologies.

This is, however, part of a larger dynamics that seems to look at the digital humanities as possibly drifting away from humanism's original mission. In recent times, the term hypertext is, of course, no longer all there is to digitally-mediated literature, forms of technology-based criticism, and digital textual practices. However, if *hypertext* could be considered the official password shared by new media scholars operating in literature- and/or media-related fields throughout the 1990s, the beginning of the 21st century has registered an increasing centrality of terms such as *code, database*, and *posthuman* in the humanities, and discourses on digital media textuality in general can be said to have eventually revolved with remarkable recurrence, for example, around issues of *materiality*.[67] Such a paradigmatic shift does not affect humanities students, scholars, and practitioners only at the level of terminology, but can have large systemic repercussions for our idea of a present and future digital humanism. If key terms typical of early hypertext scholarship, such as *hybridity, rhizome, transculturation, deterritorialization, othering* (and others), could reveal, for example, how much hypermedia studies and American studies, literary theory, critical theory, ethnic and gender studies, and all the main humanities disciplines could be envisioned as potentially interconnected at the time, the current terminological drift toward a more recognizably scientific model-making of electronic texts, digital artifacts, and computational tools – presently understood in terms of their *intermediation, sensorimotor, inscriptional* effects[68] – shows how a convergent dynamic between digital humanities and these disciplines is destined to become more and more problematic as much as it remains more and more needed.[69]

AI, Automated Algorithms, and Human Processes

It might be both suggestive and productive to continue our discussion of humanism in the digital age by building on a minor feature of hypertext technology: the presence of so-called *guard links* in some of the first-generation hyper-novels. Simply put, a guard link in a hypertext novel would either allow or forbid the reader's access to specific text content ("pages," *lexias*, passages, etc.) should s/he have already read some other specific ones. While signaling the possibility of using software to provide a digital text with a set of conditional instructions that enables it to *react* by changing its own morphological structure during the process of reading, these options implicitly offer the opportunity for a reflection on another aspect of the digital connected with our

259

understanding of any present and future digital humanism, namely the aspect of computer-based *procedurality*. Guard links and technical subsystems in adaptive hypertexts[70] are just minor examples of a historical moment and of a cultural environment that is particularly supportive of forms of responsive textuality often involving various forms of algorithmic processes and artificial intelligence (AI) engines. The increasing presence of forms of interactive fiction (IF) using natural language processing,[71] of AI text generators for creating essays,[72] poems, and stories as well as of literary, filmic,[73] and game-based electronic works[74] that are heavily based on algorithmic instructions call for a humanistic discussion of these new procedure-based aspects. Humanists are offered the chance to engage in a cultural reflection on digital artifacts as textual, informational, and literary entities that continually evolve depending on the particular action of the user. Conceiving of a digital work in the form of a textual entity provided of the largest range of possible interactions offers the opportunity to reflect on digital textuality as the progressive approximation to the simulation of a virtual language-based *subject* the user interacts with rather than the electronic remediation[75] of a static mechanical textual *object* that the reader could at best just use to extract information from.

As a counterpoint to the extensive theoretical reflection on the posthuman subject,[76] the presence of these textual, informational, and literary *post-machinic* subjects opens the space for a meditation on the mission of digital humanism in a time in which the human subject is responding to an ontological and epistemological shift in what it means to think as a human in the era of digital machines and their processes. Nowadays, artificial intelligence and digital procedurality at large have penetrated the human sensorium through so many dimensions of our daily lives (economy, geographical mobility, security, communication, and so on) that a humanistic understanding of the digital has become imperative in order to re-examine its larger implications for the humanities' disciplinary and interdisciplinary connections. As Luciano Floridi remarks, "the study of artificial intelligence, in strict relation to psychological and physiological investigations of the nature of biological intelligence and the philosophy of mind, represents the oldest area of contact between philosophy and computer science."[77] In this interdisciplinary "contact zone," crucial for our definition as human beings as much as digital humanists, realist and constructivist attitudes have not always been neatly divided along distinct methodological concerns. As Sam Williams suggests, "unlike their counterparts in the chemistry lab or the physics departments, A.I. researchers have found their efforts to break down intelligence into a few foundational precepts continually rebuffed."[78] As a consequence, we might point out that, metaphorically speaking, in the gray area of definitions of intelligence, science's alleged incremental knowledge-building methodology is destined to meet the erosion of the recursive waves typical of philosophical and humanistic thought. Therefore, it becomes crucial for digital humanism to attend to the *post-objectual* and inherently *behavioral* qualities of textual digital artifacts. Far from tools we dispose of, these digital interactive entities require an increased attention to qualities of *things* that have commonly been downplayed by humanism's traditional focus on human values and concerns.[79] Endowed with equal status with other existing entities, things or artifacts can be viewed as expressing that rather ineffable "before and after of the object," that "thingness" that, in Bill Brown's terms, "amounts to a latency (the not yet formed or the not yet formable) and to an excess (what remains physically or metaphysically irreducible to objects)."[80] Moreover, as Noah Wardrip-Fruin observes in *Expressive Processing*, we should consider that "rather than defining the sequence of words for a book or images for a film, today's authors are increasingly defining the rules for system *behavior*."[81] And, more generally, Matthew Kirschenbaum points out in *Mechanisms* that "what is unique about computers as writing technologies – [is] that they are material machines dedicated to propagating an artificial environment capable of supporting immaterial *behaviors* [emphasis added]."[82] When behavior enters the stage, *culture* is to be recognized as a crucial factor, alongside the technical and/or the biological.

Situating Digital Humanism

A basic re-conceptualization process that, besides meditating on human subjects becoming posthuman, might emphasize the dynamics according to which human digital creations become post-machinic, would encourage a more recognizable presence of the old mission of humanism, potentially taking the form of a more insistent focus of digital humanities on issues such as the notion of identity formation, the problems of trans-cultural relationships, and our ways of negotiating textual, linguistic, and literary content in the *contact zone* of the man-machine interface.[83]

A clear focus on understanding the subject implies therefore an attention to the prominence of relationality over issues concerning the essence of the single Cartesian subject or the ontology of machines. In its characterization as a rule-guided activity in the Wittgensteinian sense, digitally-mediated language – and the digital *as* language made of both linguistic and extra-linguistic manifestations (clicking, scrolling, forwarding, etc.) – can become a privileged *locus* where we can investigate the set of relational phenomena, multifariously connected in a texture of family resemblances, that shape our inter-subjective activity. In interpreting our relationship with the machinic *other* as a mind-to-mind kind of relation, scholars who already are usually comfortable in granting the machine some level of cognitive intelligence, especially in relation to empirical processing of information,[84] might extend the scope of their inquiry into the often latent, inexpressible, and indefinable aspects of the human condition that have been traditionally addressed in humanistic scholarship.

Conceiving digital textual artifacts as entities provided with a set of behavioral reactions through the use of algorithm technology, time-based processes, expressive AI, and hypertext adaptivity (to name a few) could greatly help in the eminently overall humanist mission of investigating our processes of identity formation in the specific case of the human–machine interface borderland and our inter-cultural negotiation processes. It might be worth reminding ourselves that the enormous increased amount of available information that we usually associate with Renaissance humanism did not come only in the form of textual discoveries but also of cultural discoveries in relation to the peoples, places, products, and things whose existence Europe had not postulated and whose effects had not been anticipated. Geographical discoveries posed challenges in terms of the emergence of a plurality of possible alternatives to habits, traditions, century-long forms of civilizations, and fundamental cultural and philosophical assumptions that needed active rethinking. As a consequence, the new availability of the wisdom of the past was not going to appear as a secure lifeline against the unsettling experience of the present. The past was not supposed to function as a guide but helped in re-energizing a creative and fully imaginative response to the present. Although the vast extent of contemporary human knowledge has been mostly accumulated by means of a re-elaboration of past acquisitions, the need to make our data, information, and knowledge available to the largest audience grants us a considerable advantage in reflecting on how we organize, disseminate, store, and preserve knowledge in the modern era – hence a necessary discussion of practices of encoding data and information into available knowledge.

Metadata, Encoding, and Human Mapping

The increasing amount of digitized data and the heightened complexity of born-digital textual artifacts[85] now accessible on information and communication systems (ICTs) such as the internet has called for a huge interdisciplinary effort to find ways to best use online resources for scholarly and research purposes. Collaborations between scholars and professionals have led to the creation of both automated and human-operated *tools* as well as to the coordination of *standards* for data formats and software programming able to meet the needs of the largest number of users. The contribution of humanists to this gargantuan effort has mainly come in the form of specialized concerns related to texts' classification schemes,[86] textual metadata,[87] text encoding,[88] and electronic editing[89] – all areas of invaluable theoretically productive work that proves useful also to the scholarly self-reflection about the humanities' contents and practices. As Joanna Drucker observes, "the tasks of creating metadata, doing markup, and making classification schemes or information architectures forced humanists to make explicit many assumptions often left implicit in our work."[90] Just to give an example, in order to be able to mark up sections of a text with specific labels (e.g., "center" for alignment or "header" for font type/size) that the computer can interpret for the correct rendition of its formatting on a screen, we need to have first clearly established *what* specific kind of text we are encoding and make sure that is one in which spatial distribution and hierarchy of textual signs prove *meaningful*. Making such assumptions explicit in large-scale digital humanities projects, however, does not obviously translate into reducing the complexity of the human cultural archive, of the human subject (of which such archive is, to some extent, a reflection), and of the universe (of which the human subject is part) to its operational formalization. On the contrary, the formalization process leading to the labeling and description of aspects of language-based texts by means of language can reveal the humanistic short circuit in the process. The extensibility of XML, the provisional character of any single classification scheme, and the philosophical uncertainty on the theoretical possibility of establishing actual meta-languages,[91] just to name a few elements, all remind us of how many dimensions of textuality are destined to remain outside the possibility of language tools – be they formal languages or natural languages. Figuratively speaking, to the extent that metadata and encoding contain what can be classified, i.e., what can be said by formal practices, they also implicitly point to what remains ineffable and inexpressible in our conceptual understanding of the human condition.

Unlike their colleagues in the sciences, humanists do not typically privilege as their object of study the set of facts occurring strictly within a computable physical world. On the contrary, in the humanities, the study of the observable is often in the service of an understanding of historical, philosophical, and cultural dimensions that remain only speculative. The conventional modeling of the human archive is mainly a reflection of life's ineffable meaning and of the ineludible relationship between the human subject and the metaphysical and ethical dimensions with which our human condition is imbued. As Coluccio Salutati, the major humanist of the generation after Petrarch, would point out, "Humane studies are bound up together; and the study of divinity is bound up with them, so that a true and complete knowledge of the one cannot be had without the other."[92] And, as Douglas Bush reminds us in *Humanism and English Renaissance*,

> Humane studies, says Leonardo Bruni, are those which have to do with life and conduct, those which form a good man, that is, the works of the ancient philosophers, poets, orators, and historians; scientific and professional knowledge, though good in itself, does not teach how to live rightly.[93]

Nowhere is the strict relationship between technicality and ethics, between computer technology and cultural concerns, between established procedures and conceptually creative new practices more evident than in the archiving and preserving of born-digital artifacts – activities heavily relying on metadata and *contextual* information.[94]

As Howard Besser points out in "Longevity of Electronic Art," "while the default for physical artifacts is to persist (or deteriorate in slow increments), the default for electronic objects is to become inaccessible unless someone takes an immediate proactive role to save them."[95] If we keep this crucial issue of the obsolescence[96] of digital textual forms at the forefront of our concerns, we can agree that, among the various definitions of archive,[97] the most appropriate for the ones concerning digital documents are those in which the term archive is applied to a body of records continually: From its very early stage of documents' creation to their eventual permanent preservation. This concept of archive as a "record continuum"[98] resonates with the consideration that, as both computer science scholars and archivists have observed, digital documents do not allow for

Situating Digital Humanism

problems of preservation to be faced at a later stage distinct from their creation. White papers such as Nick Montfort and Noah Wardrip-Fruin "Acid Free Bits: Recommendation for Long-Lasting Electronic Literature" and Alan Liu's "Born-Again Bits: A Framework for Migrating Electronic Literature" both contain appeals directly to authors of digital works to act preemptively to secure the longevity of their texts against the relentless technological upgrade path. And in archival science terms, the phases of creation, management, and preservation – typically distinct in paper-based contexts – become completely coincident in the digital one.

Projects such as the Electronic Literature Organization's Preservation Archive and Dissemination (PAD) initiative, the publication of *The Electronic Literature Collection* series, and the then proposed implementation of X-Lit format are invaluably useful to preserve digital content of works. They do not, however, automatically guarantee the preservation of the network of relationships that allows the possibility of situating a work of electronic literature in its original historical/cultural/social setting – with an implicit loss of information relevant to the study of specific e-lit works and of digital literature in general as an instantiation of human intellect in the 21st century. Posing the problem of preserving e-literature only in terms of "saving" computing context risks reducing preservation to a problem of securing readability according to the following binary opposition: readability vs unreadability. Literary research framed within an archival perspective must, however, also be concerned with the problem of both securing contextual multi-readability and avoiding historical mis-readability. The importance of metadata has been so far mainly connected to technical aspects of electronic literature works – a fundamental practice that undoubtedly needs priority attention. Metadata have not, perhaps, been equally sufficiently employed so far as connected to the complementary side of the issue: documents' contexts description, which brings us to the next relevant question for digital humanism. We need to move from the consideration that, just like we cannot accurately predict what future software systems e-literature will be experienced through,[99] we cannot reasonably assume we already know every single scholarly perspective future scholars will be interested in exploring about it. Therefore, these issues call into question how much information we *can* process, understand, and eventually structure into knowledge according to humanistic methods, practices, and purposes.

Super-Computing, Expert Systems, and the Scale of Human Knowledge

Up to this point, we have addressed the ideal of a digital humanism mostly by referring to the reflections around the human subject carried on by Renaissance humanism and Enlightenment humanism. However, referring to *humanism* and *studia humanitatis* interchangeably can hide a necessary qualification that needs conceptual unpacking, especially in reference to much recent scholarship on Renaissance humanism. We need to point out that, according to Paul Oskar Kristeller, the term *studia humanitatis* applies to a much smaller domain than the term *humanism*.[100] As Jennifer Summit acutely reminds us, the word *humanitas* does not imply a pre-existing human quality in terms of the human condition or human dignity but is rather connected to the Latin meaning of *humanus* as "learned," i.e., something that is not constitutive of human nature by default but that is conversely cultivated and pursued through the process of education.[101] As any human being was endowed, according to Erasmus, with a "fervent desire for knowledge,"[102] any discussion of a digital humanism must therefore at some point address the issue of the mission, the usefulness, and the desirable scale of human *knowledge* that is now achievable by means of computer-enhanced quantitative analytical thinking in the digital age. As Johanna Drucker observes, "the cultural authority of computing has an older history yet, linked as it is to traditions of analytic thought and rational calculus in the work of Descartes and Leibniz."[103] Although rigorous analytical thinking has rarely been completely disconnected from humanistic concerns, it might be useful to keep in mind, however, that, as an alternative to the medieval scholastic method of knowledge production and its emphasis on formal logic, the humanist ideal of the educated Renaissance subject involved a reorientation toward the language arts. The practical knowledge needed by new intellectuals (secretaries, ambassadors, chancellors, judges, lawyers, notaries, etc.) operating in the proto-urban environment of the 15th-century European city-state translated into activities that involved uncertainties and possibilities that needed to be assessed in a case-by-case scenario. Rather than the incontrovertible demonstrations of exact sciences and the solid eternal truth of theology and religion, Renaissance humanists usually privileged the study of persuasion and argumentation (Cicerone and Quintiliano were the Latin masters of rhetoric). From this point of view, we might have to keep in mind that the fundamentally ambiguous and polysemous nature of language was the default condition for the humanist mind.

If digital humanism is to keep a connection with the above tradition, the transformation of language into indistinct *data* (and the consequent reduction of language complexity to the quantitative consideration of language tokens) is to remain a means to an end, namely an intermediate stage allowing contemporary humanists to see (hidden) macrosystemic relationships that need eventually to shift back to the ineffable intricacy, elaboration, and multiplicity of meaning. Even the revival of humanism brought by the Age of Enlightenment (the so-called age or reason) in the 17th and 18th centuries, as a reaction to the authoritarian dogmatic positions connected with Lutheranism, Calvinism or Anglicanism as well as the Counter-Reformation of the previous centuries, eventually resulted in a form of increased secular and scientific-oriented humanism that, however, posed the need for holistic *human* understanding as unavoidably central. In the 19th century, Wilhelm Dilthey's concern for establishing a philosophical foundation that would advocate for the "human sciences" (in his view comprising history, law, and literary criticism) an equally scientific approach as that of the sciences made very clear that the *Naturwissenschaften* (sciences) and the *Geisteswissenschaften* (humanities) would be operating from different methodological perspectives.[104] While, in deciphering life's phenomena, the sciences were seeking the explanation (*erklären*) of cause-and-effect mainly through either inductive or deductive reasoning, the "human sciences" would privilege an understanding (*verstehen*) of the multiple connections among the parts and the whole in the hope of perceiving what Dilthey regarded as the "nexus" of life (*Lebenszusammenhang*) – a phenomenological grasp that would not foster a process of abstraction from life's lived context in the way that the sciences conversely typically do.[105] Although, when it comes to digital humanities, the emphasis is typically on quantitative-oriented practices such as *distant reading* and macroanalysis of Big Data[106] rather than on qualitative and aesthetic scrutiny, a look at the articulate practice of Topic Modeling can perhaps work here as a most representative example of the complex dynamic between textual data and practices of critical interpretation with the humanist hermeneutic tradition.

Topic Modeling, the statistics-based forms of data analysis that use unsupervised machine learning algorithms to discover subjects and issues discussed across a large collection of documents ("topics"),[107] is gradually emerging as a widespread cutting-edge research practice that, besides marketing and science, is increasingly used in social sciences, cultural analytics, and in historical and textual scholarship – becoming therefore a humanistic concern both in praxis and theory. In Topic Modeling, the statistical parsing of large-scale data sets results in yielding bits of information as output clusters (typically clusters of words) that require interpretation in the form of abstract (but coherent) topics.[108] As a consequence, the software-based output of your chosen Topic Modeling practice eventually and inevitably assigns humanists the task of interpreting computer-generated data *as texts*, namely as assemblages of elements of signification (signs).

As a counterpoint to the proliferating introduction of computation into the various humanistic areas we have mentioned so far, this unavoidable stage along the computer-assisted workflow involved in Topic Modeling represents the reciprocal necessity to open the door to speculative-oriented scholarly accomplishments in a domain that we typically consider as strictly empirical

Situating Digital Humanism

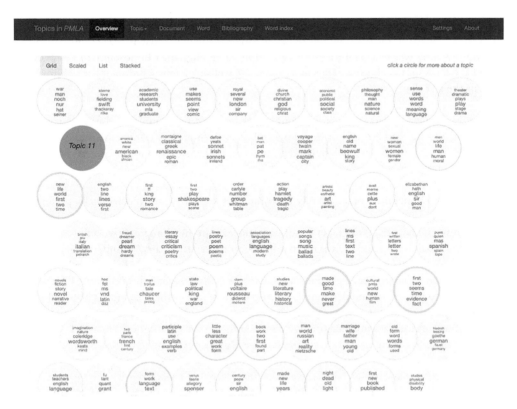

Figure 15.2 A Topic Model of the PMLA collection in which "topics" are visualized as bubbles of words (Reproduced by Permission of Andrew Goldstone, Rutgers University, author of the DFR Browser)

and computational and therefore chiefly informed by the rationality of formal sciences. A few considerations on the technical aspects of Topic Modeling can reveal the exact calibration of the proportion between empirical and speculative components. The initial consideration might be that what you see, say, in the words' bubbles of the DFR Browser[109] in Figure 15.2 are not the empirical or directly observable data. They are rather estimated data resulting from a probabilistic processing of the actual words (tokens) in the corpus. In other words, such lists of words (topics) gathered by the LDA algorithm collectively represent just a possible picture of our object of analysis.[110] As a result, when it comes to Topic Modeling, the computer, besides being in charge of counting or retrieving data beyond human cognitive-mnemonic possibilities, is in charge of making an initial wild (i.e., large-scale) computational-based *guess*. To this gigantic algorithmic speculation, we then add the one connected with the human-reading practice of identifying a topic as reflective of a specific semantic area. We can gradually begin to understand how the process of "topic labeling," i.e., deciding *what* topic the word bubble alludes to, far from being the result of any possible automated or standardized procedure, represents the final stage of speculative layers at both the machinic and human level.[111]

We need, however, to operate necessary distinctions in considering the layers of human and machinic speculation that brings with them implicit foundational questions for digital humanism. To what extent are our views of Big Data providing a look at issues that can offer a peek at the problem as the observation of human condition *sub specie aeternitatis*? To what extent does high-level computation power, and the promises of super-computing,[112] pose the problem of the reappearance of a knowledge produced *metaphysically*? To what extent does our reliance on (super-) computation takes the form of relying on a cognitive complexity that is *beyond* human and/or alien to inherently *human* capabilities? As we read in "The Humanist Philosophy in Perspective" by Fred Edwords on the *American Humanist Association* website, a longstanding tenet of humanism concerns the fact that:

> Anything that's said to make sense should make sense to us as humans; else there is no reason for it to be the basis of our decisions and actions. Supposed transcendent knowledge or intuitions that are said to reach beyond human comprehension cannot instruct us because we cannot relate concretely to them.[113]

Although digital humanities practices rely on computers mainly as *tools* mechanically performing algorithmic operations aimed at knowledge production, it might still be relevant for digital humanism to address (and negotiate) the super-computational gaps in the humanistic workflow. Although designed by human beings and used as mechanical cognitive engines, any "unsupervised" machine learning way of processing textual information makes it *de facto* impossible for human beings (and therefore for humanists) to check possible flaws in the machinic *reasoning* procedure.[114] Figuratively speaking, once designed and implemented, any run of the software that produces a Topic Model as an output is, to some extent, a leap of faith that allows neither human intervention in the speculative treatment of the data nor imaginative contribution to the creation of the model. The mere idea of the possibility of empirically accurate, supposedly objective, and scientific-oriented analysis of textual data finally entering the stage of the humanities often generates in contemporary humanists a reassuring validation against the everlasting charges of lack of rigor and objectivity from their scientist colleagues. It is mostly this incorporation of objectivity that promotes the perception of being on the threshold of a new kind of knowledge production, of being able to produce *new* knowledge previously unattainable with traditional reasoning rather than in terms of a rearrangement of previous incremental acquisitions. In order to remain recognizably humanist, digital humanism might, however, need to put, alongside the scientific-oriented use of digital technology aimed at producing new (i.e., previously unavailable) knowledge, a conscious willingness to use technology for developing *imaginative* forms of knowledge. These imaginative forms of knowledge, rather than allowing a more objective understanding of macro-dynamics concerning the collection of (textual) artifacts we create, might conversely facilitate a better understanding of the *human* component in the digital humanities terminological construct. A few concluding remarks on the role of our epistemological interfaces, i.e., of our imagination and our creativity along the development of a future digital humanism might put things in perspective.

Interfaces, Programming, and the Reexamination of Human Creativity: A Human-Scaled Digital Humanism?

It is indeed dangerous territory to try to monitor the state, the good health, or even the presence of old-fashioned humanism in the digital age without sounding nostalgic or conservative. After all, the larger context of modern scholarship already frames the current situation as a deviation from an idealized golden age of humanism. As Geoffrey Harpham recently observed, "contemporary advocates for the humanities sometimes refer to the Renaissance [humanists] in their attempts to reclaim an authenticity that we have lost in our corrupt modern times."[115] The review of selected issues that we have been discussing in this chapter, however, is not certainly meant to be ideological in nature and can be more characterized as a thought experiment about what models of our historicized versions of humanism can still be relevant for contemporary humanities scholars. If not concretely viable, these models might at least work as helpful landmarks in mapping and

Situating Digital Humanism

envisioning the future(s) of both humanism and the humanities. Digital humanism is no exception to the fact that evolution in any area of human thought usually takes the form of an intellectual and paradigmatic negotiation. As Daniel Frankforter and William Spellman remark,

> There is wisdom in warning people not to let an appetite for novelty obscure the hard-won lessons of earlier generations. However, excessive reverence for the past diminishes curiosity about the world, acquiesces when limits are placed on intellectual freedom, and hampers experimentation and exploration. It can lead to stagnation and ultimate irrelevance.[116]

In-between these two forms of wisdom and in-between this two-fold dynamic, the contemporary digital humanist is charged with the enormously demanding task of re-examining what it means to be human in the age of digital technologies. Our ideas about what it means to be human[117] have, of course, changed over the centuries, not only along extended temporal arcs such as from the 14th century to the Enlightenment, but also even from just the mid-20th to early 21st century – as the rise and fall of literary theory and its discourses on subjectivity has made quite evident. Any anthropocentric notion of the privileged position of the human over other entities would probably be rejected by today's fields of ecocriticism, of animal studies, of posthumanism, and of all views inclusive of the role of minerals, natural environments, and machines in human life.[118] And it is only natural that these fields would and will continue to reject any privileged status of studies that are most eminently human-centered or explicitly oriented toward serving the purpose of any form of anthropological dominance. At the same time, the periodical reexamination of the humanities' self-definition, mission(s), and features operated by looking back at its human-centered trajectory should neither be regarded as a stagnant enterprise aimed at slowing down its newest and most exciting developments (such as the recent emergence of digital humanities), nor feared as a hesitation aimed at undermining the cultural relevance of this massive history-long human adventure. On the contrary, it might possibly work as one of the best standard practices aimed at guaranteeing the humanities' future survival.

If humanism can be considered the underlying philosophy of a set of disciplines that we call the humanities, digital humanism can hardly become in the future a philosophical *system* in the sense of a comprehensive worldview or *Weltanschauung*. On the other hand, over-specialization – which is particularly encouraged in the field and by the nature of the digital – cannot provide a convenient way of avoiding, downplaying, or disregarding major universal and controversial questions. Humanists are, after all, experts in integration and have historically been reminding thinkers operating in other fields of the wonderful complexity connected with the interrelatedness of things. Digital humanism, however, adds a new demand as it indeed challenges the old Platonic tenet that "the philosopher is the spectator of all time and all existence."[119] This is not only because it calls for a new research paradigm that, in Stephen Ramsey's claim, is no longer about being just a thinker but also a builder, but because, with its practical building of digital models and its theory informed by concrete technological practice, it primarily reminds us that the philosopher has never been only a spectator but an active and creative inventor of the reality with which the thinker interfaces. As literary scholars committed to ascribing the highest power to verbal metaphors and to see language as an irreplaceable poietic tool, it would only be natural to take responsibility for what we, as humans – and now as digital humanists and creators of digital artifacts – can allow to exist *as* cultural entities.[120] To the imaginative humanistic mind, a system that evolves in ways unexpected even to its own creator *is* already, to some extent, a textual organism. To the imaginative humanistic mind, software emulators that, in Terry Harpold's terms, replicate "features of one computing system using the resources of another or as to imitate *behaviors* [emphasis added] of the first system as closely as possible"[121] should evoke the role of actors in enlivening inert written drama scripts. To the imaginative humanist mind, the algorithmic possibilities of digital texts in envisioning the simulation of a virtual narrating subject could technologically re-enact the trope of the "talking book" of the first slave narratives at the birth of African-American literature.[122] Similar interactions might well be observed along a wide range of digitally-mediated imaginative models. In rethinking ways to integrate computers and programming languages within humanities paradigms, Matthew Kirschenbaum observes in "Hello Worlds: Why Humanities Students Should Learn to Program" that:

> computers should not be black boxes but rather understood as engines for creating powerful and persuasive models of the world around us. The world around us (and inside us) is something we in the humanities have been interested in for a very long time. I believe that, increasingly, an appreciation of how complex ideas can be imagined and expressed as a set of formal procedures – rules, models, algorithms – in the virtual space of a computer will be an essential element of a humanities education.[123]

Such an emphasis on model-making *through* digital artifacts can probably function at its best in conjunction with the wide range of all cultural and critical work in the humanities that has seen and still sees texts, information, and literature as *social* practice and *cultural* performance. Such attention to social and cultural criticism might account for how digital humanism may imagine itself precisely as a practice rather than as a concrete scholarly entity, a practice that rests firmly and predominantly in the subjective experiential expression of the theoretical. The humanities, compared to social sciences, for example, have often found their specificity and grounded their practices in human self-understanding. Human self-understanding, although of course not disconnected from the large-scale data processing of our digitized artifact, too often seems to remain a step back in digital humanities, or at best, regarded as an indirect result of the prevalent attention to the operable computer-based procedures. Not accidentally, the intervention of practices of distant reading and large-scale data set analyses impact perhaps more literary *history* and are mostly useful to the historiography of literary artifacts than studies of the "literary" *per se*. The "literary," intended as any attempt at producing and understanding types of meanings that go beyond the basic functional communication purpose of words,[124] proves, in fact, different from the mere chronicling of a history of literature as it usually more directly points to the subjective dimension of experiencing meaning during the practice of textual interpretation.

And here likely lies the recurrent historical use of the word *humanism* in conjunction with human dignity and human experience – a dimension that digital humanism might address with productive results for human progress in the digital age. Attention to subjective experience challenges, in fact, the typical binaries to which digitality is often reduced: organic/machinic, language/code, self/other, or subject/object. More generally, it also implicitly questions the categorical primacy of rational/analytical thinking in the theoretical understanding of human life. In emphasizing the experiential dimension of human meaning-making, interrogations of our future as digital humanists might take the form of an open-ended question investing the full spectrum of intellectual resources we usually reserve for individuality, from highly abstract concepts to the most immediate intense feelings and intuitions. A human-scaled approach to digital technologies typically positions the scholarly subject in-between *gnosis* (conceptual grasp) and *poiesis* (speculative construction). The subject of digital humanism would function without assumptions of mastery and, to use T. S. Eliot's words, the best analogy would probably be that of the catalyst. As we have seen with the technological discourse we have examined, productions and achievements in digital environments and in digital scholarship (be they artistic, socio-political, or scientific in nature) seem to lie suspended until the proper juncture between catalyst and the chemical reactants make them possible. And the digital subject as catalyst finds its most charged reactions when negotiating the unexpected.

The impulse of the digital humanist might benefit by proliferating models of thinking and behaving through digital *apparati* rather than ordering or dominating experience with digital tools and functions. Contrary to the apparent micro-field specialization of digital humanities, an understanding of the digital as inter-related sets of processes seems to call for a return of global or Renaissance minds – no matter if single or distributed ones. The digital as a process, and as a traveling concept entertains new (heuristic) forms of intellectual curiosity. In its formulation as relational and associative rather than binary or oppositional, the digital can promote thought whose goal is not to grasp a global picture of objective macro-relations (by means of digitized Big Data) but to be seduced by cosmic intuitions, aesthetic visions and a pervading "sense of wonder" of silicon-based future possibilities.

Bibliography

Arendt, Hannah. *Between Past and Future: Six Exercises in Political Thought.* New York: Viking Press, 1961.

Arendt, Hannah. *On Revolution.* New York: Viking Press, 1963.

Bellardo, Lewis J., Lynn Lady Bellardo, and Society of American Archivists. *A Glossary for Archivists, Manuscript Curators, and Records Managers.* Chicago: Society of American Archivists, 1992.

Bennett, Jane. *Vibrant Matter: A Political Ecology of Things.* Durham: Duke University Press, 2010.

Berry, David. "The Explainability Turn." *Stunlaw* (blog). Accessed September 1, 2021, http://stunlaw.blogspot.com/2020/01/the-explainability-turn.html

Besser, Howard. "Longevity of Electronic Art," ICHIM (International Cultural Heritage Informatics Meeting) *Archives & Museum Informatics* (2001).

Blei, David. "Probabilistic Topic Models." *KDD '11 Tutorials: Proceedings of the 17th ACM SIGKDD International Conference Tutorials,* 2011.

Bogost, Ian. *Alien Phenomenology, or, What It's like to Be a Thing.* Posthumanities 20. Minneapolis: University of Minnesota Press, 2012.

Bolter, J. David. *Writing Space: Computers, Hypertext, and the Remediation of Print.* 2nd ed. Mahwah: Lawrence Erlbaum Associates, 2001.

Bolter, J. David. *Writing Space: The Computer, Hypertext, and the History of Writing.* Hillsdale: L. Erlbaum Associates, 1991.

Bolter, J. David, and Richard A. Grusin. *Remediation: Understanding New Media.* Cambridge: MIT Press, 1999.

Bostrom, Nick. "A History of Transhumanist Thought." *Journal of Evolution and Technology* 14, no. 1 (April 2005): 1–25.

Braidotti, Rosi. "Posthuman Critical Theory." *Journal of Posthuman Studies* 1, no. 1 (2017): 9.

Brown, Bill. "Thing Theory." *Critical Inquiry* 28, no. 1 (2001): 1–22.

Burdick, Anne, ed. *Digital Humanities.* Cambridge: MIT Press, 2012.

Burke, Peter. *The European Renaissance: Centres and Peripheries.* Making of Europe. Oxford; Malden: Blackwell Publishers, 1998.

Burnard, Lou. *What Is the Text Encoding Initiative ?: How to Add Intelligent Markup to Digital Resources,* 2014.

Bush, Douglas. *The Renaissance and English Humanism.* The Alexander Lectures in English at the University of Toronto, 1939. Toronto: University of Toronto Press, 1939.

Calvi, Licia. "Adaptivity in Hyperfiction." *Proceedings of the fifteenth ACM conference on Hypertext & hypermedia – HYPERTEXT '04,* 2004.

Carroll, Laura, Erika Farr, Peter Hornsby, and Ben Ranker. "A Comprehensive Approach to Born-Digital Archives". *Archivaria* 72 (2011): 61–92.

Cassirer, Ernst, Paul Oskar Kristeller, and John Herman Randall. *The Renaissance Philosophy of Man.* Chicago Editions. Chicago: Univ. of Chicago Press, 1948.

Chun, Wendy Hui Kyong. *Programmed Visions: Software and Memory.* Software Studies. Cambridge: MIT Press, 2011.

Clarke, Bruce, and Mark B. N. Hansen, eds. *Emergence and Embodiment: New Essays on Second-Order Systems Theory.* Science and Cultural Theory. Durham: Duke University Press, 2009.

Cohen, Benjamin R. "Science and Humanities: Across Two Cultures and into Science Studies." *Endeavour* 25, no. 1 (2001): 8–12.

Danto, Arthur C. *The Transfiguration of the Common Place: A Philosophy of Art.* Cambridge; London: Harvard University Press, 1981.

Derrida, Jacques. *Writing and Difference*. Chicago: The University of Chicago Press, 2017.

Descola, Philippe, and Janet Lloyd. *Beyond Nature and Culture*. Chicago; London: The University of Chicago Press, 2013.

Drucker, Johanna. "Philosophy and Digital Humanities: A review of Willard McCarty, Humanities Computing." London and NY: Palgrave, 2005. In *Digital Humanities Quarterly* 1 No. 1 (2007). http://www.digitalhumanities.org/dhq/vol/1/1/000001/000001.html

Durand, David, and Paul Kahn. "MAPA: A System for Inducing and Visualizing Hierarchy in Websites," *Proceedings of the ninth ACM conference on Hypertext and hypermedia: links, objects, time and space – structure in hypermedia systems: links, objects, time and space – structure in hypermedia systems – HYPERTEXT '98*, 1998.

Edwords, Fred. "The Humanist Philosophy in Perspective." *American Humanist Association*. Accessed September 1, 2021. https://americanhumanist.org/what-is-humanism/humanist-philosophy-perspective/

Eliot, Simon, and Jonathan Rose. *A Companion to the History of the Book*. Hoboken: Wiley Blackwell, 2020.

Emerson, Lori. *Reading Writing Interfaces: From the Digital to the Bookbound*. Electronic Mediations 44. Minneapolis: University of Minnesota Press, 2014.

Emerton, Ephraim. *Humanism and Tyranny: Studies in the Italian Trecento*. Cambridge: Harvard University Press, 2013.

Erasmus, Desiderius. *Against War and In Praise of Folly*. Anthony Uyl (ed.). Ingersoll: Devoted Publishing, 2017.

Evens, Aden. *Logic of the Digital*. New York: London; Bloomsbury Academic, 2015.

Ferrando, Francesca, and Rosi Braidotti. *Philosophical Posthumanism*. London: Bloomsbury Academic, 2020.

Fitzpatrick, Kathleen. *Planned Obsolescence: Publishing, Technology, and the Future of the Academy*. New York: New York University Press, 2011.

Flores, Leonardo. "Third-Generation Electronic Literature." *Electronic Literature as Digital Humanities*, 2021. doi: 10.5040/9781501363474.ch-002.

Floridi, Luciano. *Philosophy and Computing: An Introduction*. London; New York: Routledge, 1999.

Floridi, Luciano. *The 4th Revolution: How the Infosphere Is Reshaping Human Reality*. First edition. New York; Oxford: Oxford University Press, 2014.

Floridi, Luciano. "Artificial Intelligence's New Frontier: Artificial Companions and the Fourth Revolution." *Metaphilosophy* 39, no. 4–5 (2008): 651–655.

Frankforter, A. Daniel, and W. M. Spellman. *The West: A Narrative History*. 3rd ed. Upper Saddle River: Pearson, 2013.

Gardner, Howard. *Creating Minds: An Anatomy of Creativity Seen through the Lives of Freud, Einstein, Picasso, Stravinsky, Eliot, Graham, and Gandhi*. New York: Basic Books, 1993.

Gardner, Howard. *Frames of Mind: The Theory of Multiple Intelligences*. New York: Basic Books, 1983.

Gates, Henry Louis. *The Signifying Monkey: A Theory of African American Literary Criticism*. Twenty-Fifth anniversary edition. Oxford: Oxford University Press, 2014.

Geyh, Paula, Fred Leebron, and Andrew Levy, eds. *Postmodern American Fiction: A Norton Anthology*. 1st ed. New York: W.W. Norton, 1998.

Gochenour, Philip H. "Nodalism." *Digital Humanities Quarterly* 5, no. 3 (2011). http://www.digitalhumanities.org/dhq/vol/5/3/000105/000105.html

Gold, Matthew K., ed. *Debates in the Digital Humanities*. Minneapolis: Univ Of Minnesota Press, 2012.

Grigar, Dene, and James O'Sullivan, eds. *Electronic Literature as Digital Humanities*. Electronic Literature, book 3. New York: Bloomsbury Academic, 2021.

Hansell, Gregory R., William Grassie, Russell Blackford, Nick Bostrom, and Jean-Pierre Dupuy, eds. *H±: Transhumanism and Its Critics*. Philadelphia: Metanexus Institute, 2011.

Haraway, Donna Jeanne. *When Species Meet*. Posthumanities 3. Minneapolis: University of Minnesota Press, 2008.

Harpham, Geoffrey Galt. *The Humanities and the Dream of America*. Chicago: The University of Chicago Press, 2011.

Harpold, Terry. *Ex-Foliations: Reading Machines and the Upgrade Path*. Electronic Mediations 25. Minneapolis: University of Minnesota Press, 2009.

Hayles, N. Katherine. *Electronic Literature: New Horizons for the Literary*. The Ward-Phillips Lectures in English Language and Literature. Notre Dame: University of Notre Dame, 2008.

Hayles, N. Katherine. *How We Became Posthuman: Virtual Bodies in Cybernetics, Literature, and Informatics*. Chicago: University of Chicago Press, 1999.

Hayles, N. Katherine. *How We Think: Digital Media and Contemporary Technogenesis*. Chicago; London: The University of Chicago Press, 2012.

Heidegger, Martin. *The Question Concerning Technology, and Other Essays*. New York: Garland Publishing, 1977.

Situating Digital Humanism

Heidegger, Martin. *Being and Time*, John Macquarrie and Edward Robinson (trans.). New York: Harper & Row, 1962.

Hockey, Susan. "The History of Humanities Computing," in *A Companion to Digital Humanities*, ed. Susan Schreibman, Ray Siemens, John Unsworth. Oxford: Blackwell, 2004, 3-19.

Jockers, Matthew Lee. *Macroanalysis: Digital Methods and Literary History*. Topics in the Digital Humanities. Urbana: University of Illinois Press, 2013.

Kirschenbaum, Matthew G. *Mechanisms: New Media and the Forensic Imagination*. Cambridge: MIT Press, 2008.

Kirschenbaum, Matthew G. "What Is Digital Humanities and What's It Doing in English Departments?" *ADE Bulletin*, 2010, 55–61.

Kirschenbaum, Matthew G. "Hello Worlds: Why Humanities Students Should Learn to Program." *The Chronicle of Higher Education*. January 23, 2009. Accessed September 1, 2021. https://www.chronicle.com/article/hello-worlds/

Kittler, Friedrich A., and Hans Ulrich Gumbrecht. *The Truth of the Technological World: Essays on the Genealogy of Presence*. Stanford: Stanford University Press, 2013.

Koenitz, Hartmut, Gabriele Ferri, Mads Haahr, Digdem Sezen, and Tonguc Ibrahim Sezen, eds. *Interactive Digital Narrative: History, Theory and Practice*. Routledge Studies in European Communication Research and Education 7. New York: Routledge, Taylor & Francis Group, 2015.

Kohl, Benjamin G. "The Changing Concept of the "Studia Humanitatis" in the Early Renaissance." *Renaissance Studies* 6, no. 2 (1992): 185–209.

Kurzweil, Ray. *How to Create a Mind: The Secret of Human Thought Revealed*. New York: Penguin, 2014.

Kurzweil, Ray. *The Singularity Is Near: When Humans Transcend Biology*. New York: Viking, 2005.

Landow, George P. *Hypertext: The Convergence of Contemporary Critical Theory and Technology*. Parallax. Baltimore: Johns Hopkins University Press, 1992.

Landow, George P. *Hypertext 3.0: Critical Theory and New Media in an Era of Globalization*. 3rd ed. Parallax. Baltimore: Johns Hopkins University Press, 2006.

Liu, Alan. "Mission." *4Humanities: Advocating for the Humanities*. Accessed September 11, 2021. https://4humanities.org/mission/

Makdisi, George. *The Rise of Humanism in Classical Islam and the Christian West: With Special Reference to Scholasticism*. Edinburgh: Edinburgh University Press, 1990.

Makkreel, Rudolf A. "Husserl, Dilthey and the Relation of the Life-World to History." *Research in Phenomenology* 12 (1982): 39–58.

Marckwardt, Albert H. "The Humanities and Non-Western Studies." *The ANNALS of the American Academy of Political and Social Science* 356, no. 1 (1964): 45–53.

McCarty, Willard. *Humanities Computing*. Paperback edition. Basingstoke: Palgrave Macmillan, 2014.

McGann, Jerome J. *Radiant Textuality: Literature after the World Wide Web*. New York: Palgrave, 2001.

McKemmish, S. et al. "Records Continuum Model." *Encyclopedia of Library and Information Sciences* (3rd ed.) (2010): 4447–4448.

McKnight, Cliff, Andrew Dillon, and John Richardson. *Hypertext in Context*. The Cambridge Series on Electronic Publishing. Cambridge; New York: Cambridge University Press, 1991.

Mitchell, Jeff. "Danto, Dewey and the Historical End of Art." *Transactions of the Charles S. Peirce Society* 25, no. 4 (1989): 469–501.

Montfort, Nick. *Twisty Little Passages: An Approach to Interactive Fiction*. Cambridge: MIT Press, 2003.

Moretti, Franco. *Graphs, Maps, Trees: Abstract Models for a Literary History*. London; New York: Verso, 2005.

Morris, Adalaide Kirby, and Thomas Swiss, eds. *New Media Poetics: Contexts, Technotexts, and Theories*. Leonardo. Cambridge: MIT Press, 2006.

Munster, Anna. *Materializing New Media: Embodiment in Information Aesthetics*. 1st ed. Interfaces, Studies in Visual Culture. Hanover: Dartmouth College Press: Published by University Press of New England, 2006.

Negroponte, Nicholas. *Being Digital*. 1st ed. New York: Knopf, 1995.

Nelson, Theodor Holm. *Literary Machines*. Sausalito: Mindful Press, 2001.

Ong, Walter J. *Orality and Literacy: The Technologizing of the Word*. New Accents. London; New York: Routledge, 1991.

Owensby, Jacob. "Dilthey's Conception of the Life-Nexus." *Journal of the History of Philosophy*, 25 (4) (1987): 557–572.

Ping-chen, Hsiung. "The Evolution of Chinese Humanities." *The American Historical Review* 120, no. 4 (2015): 1267–1282.

Pinn, Anthony B., ed. *What Is Humanism, and Why Does It Matter?* Studies in Humanist Thought and Praxis Series. Sheffield; Bristol: Equinox Publishing, 2013.

Plato. *The Republic*, Book VI. *The Internet Classics Archive*. Accessed September 1, 2021 http://classics.mit.edu/Plato/republic.7.vi.html

Pressman, Jessica. *Digital Modernism: Making It New in New Media*. Modernist Literature & Culture 21. New York: Oxford University Press, 2014.

Publius Virgilius Maro. *The Georgiks* [sic] *of Publius Virgilius Maro*, trans. A.F. (Abraham Fleming) (London, 1589).

Rettberg, Scott. *Electronic Literature*, 2019. https://search.ebscohost.com/login.aspx?direct=true&scope=site&db=nlebk&db=nlabk&AN=1991326

Riley, Jenn. *Understanding Metadata*. Baltimore: Niso Press, 2017.

Saussure, Ferdinand de. *Writings in General Linguistics*. Oxford; New York: Oxford University Press, 2006.

Schreibman, Susan, Raymond George Siemens, and John Unsworth. *A Companion to Digital Humanities*. Malden: Blackwell, 2013. http://www.credoreference.com/book/wileycdih

Snow, C. P. *The Two Cultures*. Canto ed. London; New York: Cambridge University Press, 1993.

Sula, C., S. Hackney, and Phillip Cunningham. "A Survey of Digital Humanities Programs." *The Journal of Interactive Technology and Pedagogy* 11 (2017). https://jitp.commons.gc.cuny.edu/a-survey-of-digital-humanities-programs/

Summit, Jennifer. "Renaissance Humanism and the Future of Humanities." *Literature Compass* 9/10 (2012): 665–678.

Terras, Melissa M., Julianne Nyhan, and Edward Vanhoutte, eds. *Defining Digital Humanities: A Reader*. Farnham, Surrey, England: Burlington, VT: Ashgate Publishing Limited; Ashgate Publishing Company, 2013.

Tyler, Priscilla. "Non-Western Humanities in the Americas: A Definition." *Educational Horizons* 53, no. 1 (1974): 4–14.

Ulmer, Gregory L. *Avatar Emergency*. New Media Theory. Anderson: Parlor Press, 2012.

Upward, F. "Structuring the Records Continuum – Part One: Postcustodial Principles and Properties". *Archives & Manuscripts* 24, no. 2 (1996): 268–285.

Van Pelt, Tamise. "The Question concerning Theory: Humanism, Subjectivity, and Computing." *Computers and the Humanities* 36, no. 3, *A New Computer-Assisted Literary Criticism?* (2002): 307–318.

Voigt, Georg. *Die Wiederbelebung des Classischen Alterthums, oder das erste Jahrhundert des Humanismus*. 2 Bd. Berlin: de Gruyter, 1960.

Wardrip-Fruin, Noah. *Expressive Processing: Digital Fictions, Computer Games, and Software Studies*. Software Studies. Cambridge: MIT Press, 2009.

Wardrip-Fruin, Noah, and Nick Montfort, eds. *The New Media Reader*. Cambridge: MIT Press, 2003.

Williams, Sam. *Arguing A.I: The Battle for Twenty-First Century Science*. New York: At Random, 2002.

Wolfe, Cary. *What Is Posthumanism?* Posthumanities Series, vol. 8. Minneapolis: University of Minnesota Press, 2010.

Ziolkowski, Jan M. "Cultures of Authority in the Long Twelfth Century." *JEGP, Journal of English and Germanic Philology* 108, no. 4 (2009): 421–448.

Notes

1   Although the range of contributions on the subject are very wide, for a brief history of digital technologies narrated by an author who has actually been first-handedly involved in their realization, see Nicholas Negroponte. 1st ed. (New York: Knopf, 1995). For a more conceptual or philosophical perspective on binary code, see Aden Evens. *Logic of the Digital* (New York: London; Bloomsbury Academic, 2015).

2   For example, every analog music signal existing in an interval of time, in order to be converted into digital format, needs to be first recorded at discreet moments in time (sampling) and then the resulting samples need to be mapped into a finite number of elements (quantization) that the digital device can reproduce.

3   The reference here is to the Italian word *umanista* as a scholar who practices the *studia humanitaties*, namely the set of topics that are at the root of modern humanities. An *umanista* would study classical texts of the Graeco-Roman tradition in light of the belief that the study of rhetoric, grammar, moral philosophy, history and logic would lead to a rebirth of society based on virtuous living. For the first use of the word "humanist" in English see Publius Virgilius Maro, *The Georgiks* [sic] *of Publius Virgilius Maro*, trans. A.F. (Abraham Fleming) (London, 1589).

4   It is in the 19th century that the term "humanism" becomes current from the German "humanismus." Some scholars ascribe the first use of the term to educationalist Friedrich Immanuel Niethammer in

Situating Digital Humanism

the early 19th century to describe university curriculum based on the study of ancient Greek and Latin. Other scholars connect the term to pioneering historian of humanism Georg Voigt who wrote *Wiederbelebung des classischen Alterthums oder das erste Jahrhundert des Humanismus* (*Revival of Classical Antiquity or the First Century of Humanism*) in 1859.

5 This is, of course, a necessary generalization in order to ground humanism around a specific tradition of scholarly contributions. Contemporary scholars of Renaissance humanism, for example, are divided about the alleged neat separation between construing the Middle Ages as the token oppressor of human intellectual freedom and conversely characterizing Renaissance humanism as its token liberator. Their positions generally range from extending Renaissance features backwards to include the Middle Ages to extending Middle Ages tenets forward to include the Renaissance. For further insights into the problem, see Douglas Bush, *The Renaissance and English Humanism* (Toronto: University of Toronto Press, 1962). Nor Renaissance figures – thinkers, artists, and intellectuals – represented themselves any unified intellectual consensus concerning one of these two positions for that matter and their contributions might be better understood as a constellation of worldviews from which the human-centered outlook can emerge.

6 With significant occasional exceptions in the form of explicit attempts at human mind's formalization, such as, Ray Kurzweil's *How To Create a Mind: The Secret of Human Thought Revealed* (London: Duckworth, 2014). In this work, the visionary author applies neuroscience research to artificial intelligent machines and offers a series of thought experiments aimed at reverse engineering the brain and its functioning.

7 See Howard Gardner, *Frames of Mind: The Theory of Multiple Intelligences* (1983). Concerning relationships between intelligence and creativity, see also Gardner's *Creating Minds: An Anatomy of Creativity Seen Through the Lives of Freud, Einstein, Picasso, Stravinsky, Eliot, Graham, and Gandhi* (New York: Basic Books, 1993).

8 For a survey of attitudes towards authoritative knowledge in early Middle Age with a specific reference to humanists (rhetoricians, grammarians, and exegetes), see Jan M. Ziolkowski, "Cultures of Authority in the Long Twelfth Century." *The Journal of English and Germanic Philology* 108, no. 4 (2009): 421–448. For a critique of authority in relation to the modern rejection of religion and tradition, see Hannah Arendt "What is Authority?" in *Between Past and Future* (New York: Viking Press, 1961). For an analysis of how the concept of *auctoritas* influenced in the various political dynamics related to Westers absolutism in the 18th century, see Hannah Arendt, *On Revolution* (London: Faber & Faber. 1963).

9 In the Renaissance period, classical texts, increasingly seen as instruments of intellectual and cultural emancipation, have been circulating more and more – in original and in translation – thanks to a multiplicity of factors, among which the urbanization of culture and the invention of the printing press in the 15th century. For a comprehensive illustration of the chronological, geographical, and sociological cultural movements of Renaissance culture in Europe with a special reference to cultural centers such as Florence, Avignon, Flanders and Rome in the 14th and 15th centuries, see Peter Burke, *The European Renaissance: Centres and Peripheries* (Malden: Blackwell, 1998).

10 For a survey of the main historical developments and methodological approaches of the discipline known as History of the Book (typically including textual scholarship, codicology, bibliography, philology, palaeography, and many other studies on textual artifacts), see Simon Eliot and Jonathan Rose (eds), *A Companion to the History of the Book*, (Hoboken: Wiley-Blackwell, 2020).

11 Walter Ong, *Orality and Literacy: the Technologizing of the Word* (London: Routledge, 1991), 46.

12 Hayles, N. K., "The Time of Digital Poetry," in A. Morris and T. Swiss (eds), *New Media Poetics: Contexts, Technotexts, and Theories* (Cambridge: The MIT Press, 2006), 35.

13 Both these positions go beyond the discourses privileging the notions of human nature, human reason, human understanding, and even human subjectivity as understood by traditional Enlightenment thought (the human self/nature as autonomous, rational, capable of free will, and unified). For a sample illustration of the concept of co-evolution of human beings and machines see N. Katherine Hayles, *How We Became Posthuman: Virtual Bodies in Cybernetics, Literature, and Informatics* (Chicago: University of Chicago Press, 1999). For a brief survey of ideas about transcending human limitations, see Nick Bostrom's "A History of Transhumanist Thought" originally published in *Journal of Evolution and Technology* 14, no. 1 (April 2005).

14 Although the relation between humanism and the Enlightenment has not been examined by scholars as extensively as the one between humanism and Renaissance, Enlightenment humanism is usually seen as emphasizing and stressing – perhaps to the extreme – issues of human autonomy, reason, and progress to the point of acquiring an exclusively secular nature. Continuities are, however, just as important as differences and, as Howard B. Radest observes in "Humanism As Experience," the Enlightenment itself "was an incarnation in naturalistic and democratic terms of the Classical, Catholic,

Mauro Carassai

and Renaissance humanisms that preceded it in the West" (p. 5). See Anthony B. Pinn (ed.), *What is Humanism, and Why Does It Matter?* (Sheffield; Bristol: Equinox Publishing, 2013).

15 This cursory list of scholarly figures frequently cited as relevant to the development and historicization of humanities studies reflects, of course, a typically Euro-centric canon. Such canon builds on the established historiographic periodization that sees the Renaissance era as characterized by the rebirth of the wish to understand the human subject according to the Greek aphorism "know thyself" inscribed in the forecourt of the Temple of Apollo at Delphi, i.e., beyond the religious mediation operated by Christianity during the Middle Age in 15th- and 16th-century Europe. A myriad of studies that address the variety of non-Western humanities traditions has emerged over the years, among which, cited here only as samples, Albert H. Marckwardt's "The Humanities and Non-Western Studies" in *The Annals of the American Academy of Political and Social Science* 356, The Non-Western World in Higher Education (November, 1964), pp. 45–53, or Priscilla Tyler's "Non-Western Humanities in the Americas: a Definition" *Educational Horizons* 53, no. 1, The Humanities in Education (Fall 1974), pp. 4–14, George Makdisi, *The Rise of Humanism in Classical Islam and the Christian West: With Special Reference to Scholasticism* (Edinburgh: Edinburgh University Press, 1990), or Hsiung Ping-chen, "The Evolution of Chinese Humanities," *American Historical Review* 120, no. 4 (2015): 1267–1282.

16 It might be noted that along the dividing line delineated by C. P. Snow, the disconnection between the scientific and the humanistic intellectual approach showed at least two significant unifying components. First, Snow makes clear in his talk that such a separation is, at least in his culture, uniformly distributed as a feature typical of Western culture. Secondly, he points out how such a partition fundamentally affects intellectual life as a whole when this is intended as the totality of our lived experience. See C. P. Snow, *The Two Cultures and the Scientific Revolution* (Cambridge: Cambridge University Press, 1993).

17 In the subsequent decades such a distinction has perhaps even been made almost obsolete by the development of the various interdisciplinary fields of *science studies*. For a brief survey of these developments, from the so-called science wars in the early 1990s to the present, see Benjamin R. Cohen's "Science and Humanities: Across the Two Cultures and into Science Studies." *Endeavour* 25, no. 1 (2001).

18 Benjamin Cohen, "Science and Humanities," 10.

19 Willard McCarthy's *Humanities Computing* remains a foundational contribution for the establishment of the digital humanities field thanks to its extensive treatment of how computing, modeling, and the analytical reasoning germane to empirical sciences can work as an epistemological tool for humanistic inquiries.

20 The issue of defining the field of digital humanities remains at the center of its own concerns. For a historical account of how the term "humanities computing" became "digital humanities," see *Defining Digital Humanities: A Reader* (London: Routledge 2013) edited by Melissa Terras, Julianne Nyhan, Edward Vanhoutte. For a general idea of issues around the definition of dh, see the brief list in the blog post "Day of DH: Defining the Digital Humanities" in *Debates in Digital Humanities.* https://dhdebates.gc.cuny.edu/read/untitled-88c11800-9446-469b-a3be-3fdb36bfbd1e/section/550ab4e6-ca58–4840-acba-ea555be32601#enp1b501

21 For a report on existing academic programs in Digital Humanities in the Anglophone world (Australia, Canada, Ireland, the United Kingdom, and the United States), see Chris Alen Sula, S. E. Hackney, and Phillip Cunningham's "A Survey of Digital Humanities Programs" in *The Journal of Interactive Technology and Pedagogy*, no. 11, May 24, 2017. https://jitp.commons.gc.cuny.edu/a-survey-of-digital-humanities-programs/

22 Susan Hockey, "The History of Humanities Computing," in *A Companion to Digital Humanities*, ed. Susan Schreibman, Ray Siemens, John Unsworth (Oxford: Blackwell, 2004). http://www.digitalhumanities.org/companion/

23 See Matthew Kirschenbaum's "What Is Digital Humanities and What's It Doing in English Departments?" and his treatment of the "digital humanities" denomination as a "tactical term."

24 Although not specifically on the issue of humanism per se, David Parry discusses a variety of features in relation to digital humanists in his "The Digital Humanities or a Digital Humanism" in *Debates in Digital Humanities* ed. Matthew K. Gold (Minneapolis: University of Minnesota Press, 2012). https://dhdebates.gc.cuny.edu/read/untitled-88c11800-9446-469b-a3be-3fdb36bfbd1e/section/c3127960-92ee-4b32–8b69-38f87aa2d9c5#ch24

25 Alan Liu, "Mission," *4Humanities: Advocating for the Humanities.* https://4humanities.org/mission/

26 *4Humanities*, "Mission."

27 To have a rough idea of the variety of existing digital humanities projects, practices, tools and initiatives compare the Projects page of the *European Association for Digital Humanities* (https://eadh.org/projects),

Situating Digital Humanism

the Digital History Resources page of the *American Historical Association* (https://www.historians.org/teaching-and-learning/digital-history-resources), the Digital Art History page of the *Getty Research Institute* (https://www.getty.edu/research/scholars/digital_art_history/index.html), and the Digital Humanities Projects at Stanford page of Stanford University (https://digitalhumanities.stanford.edu/projects) as a representative example of projects carried on in most universities around the world. All these projects receive intramural grants from academic institutions and extramural grants from many funding agencies, such as the *National Endowment of the Humanities* through the Office of Digital Humanities division (https://www.neh.gov/divisions/odh), the *Andrew G. Mellon Foundation, The Council on Library and Information Resources* and many others.

28 For an interesting explanation of how art and philosophy have historically thrived in societies and civilizations which make a distinction between reality and appearance, see Arthur Danto, *The Transfiguration of the Common Place: A Philosophy of Art* (Cambridge: Harvard University Press, 1981). In particular, Danto observes that "philosophy has arisen only twice in the world, once in India and once in Greece, civilizations both obsessed with a contrast between appearance and reality" (pp. 147–148). Of particular interest for the present purposes it is also Jeff Mitchell's observation that "True art arises together with philosophy, which provides the sort of conceptual viewpoint necessary to embrace the idea of a universe simultaneously containing appearance and reality. Science alone will not create such a vantage point, for it simply represents the world. The altitude required for the birth of art is higher than that provided by science, because it must have both a conception of the world and a conception of representation." in Jeff Mitchell, "Danto, Dewey and the Historical End of Art." *Transactions of the Charles S. Peirce Society* 25, no. 4 (Fall, 1989): 469–501.

29 For a compelling study about the ways in which genealogy of media studies can be traced back to literary studies and how experimentations in born-digital literature can be connected to avant-garde and high literary modernism, see Jessica Pressman, *Digital Modernism: Making It New in New Media* (Oxford: Oxford University Press, 2014).

30 On the relationship between philosophy and technology as a larger frame for understanding the human and the computational, see foundational scholarly contributions such as Martin Heidegger's *The Question Concerning Technology and Other Essays* (New York: Garland Pub, 1977) and Friedrich A. Kittler's *The Truth of the Technological World: Essays on the Genealogy of Presence* (Stanford: Stanford University Press, 2013).

31 Gregory L. Ulmer examines the augmentation of selfhood made immediate by digital technologies in his *Avatar Emergency* (Anderson: Parlor Press, 2012). With the need to reason, process, and act in the compressed model of time and space presented by digital technologies and real time communication, Ulmer examines the meaning of avatar as not simply a representation or icon of a self but a fully instantiated presence in the digital realm that probes and links its circulation in the media community.

32 The term *studia humanitatis* (studies of humanity) was used by 15th-century Italian humanists to denote secular literary and scholarly activities in grammar, rhetoric, poetry, history, moral philosophy, and ancient Greek and Latin studies carried out in the belief that these subjects made men emphasize the value and agency of human beings, individually and collectively, as fully empowered citizen of their societies.

33 See Franco Moretti's explanation for both the title of his book and the suggested implementation of the abstract models from quantitative history (graphs), geography (maps), and evolutionary theory (trees) involving a "great respect for the scientific spirit" (vii) and the belief that "there was actually much more to be learned from the natural and the social sciences." (vii) in *Graphs, Maps, Trees: Abstract Models for Literary History* (New York: Verso, 2005).

34 See N. Katherine Hayles, *How We Became Posthuman: Virtual Bodies in Cybernetics, Literature, and Informatics* (Chicago: University of Chicago Press, 1999).

35 See Luciano Floridi, *The Fourth Revolution: How the Infosphere is Reshaping Human Reality* (Oxford: Oxford University Press, 2014).

36 See a variety of scholarly works from the past decades ranging from Ray Kurzweil's *The Singularity is Near: When Humans Transcend Biology* (New York: Viking, 2005) to Gregory R. Hansell's (ed.) *Transhumanism and Its Critics* (Philadelphia: Metanexus Institute, 2011).

37 Harvard comparative literature professor Jeffrey Schnapps, in reviewing the early stages of computational work in the humanities, observes that "by means of such early uses of mainframe computers to automate tasks such as word-searching, sorting, counting, and listing, scholars could process textual corpora on a scale unthinkable with prior methods that relied on handwritten or typed index cards" (p. 63). See Jeffrey Schnapp's "A Short Guide to Digital Humanities" in Anne Burdick, Johanna Drucker, Peter Lunenfeld, Todd Presner, Jeffrey Schnapp, *Digital_Humanities* (MIT Press, 2012), 121–136 https://jeffreyschnapp.com/wp-content/uploads/2013/01/D_H_ShortGuide.pdf

38   DH scholar Stephen Ramsay, in praising current data mining possibilities, describes computer-based affordances as a major intellectual human turning point: "I can now search for the word "house" (maybe "domus") in every work ever produced in Europe during the entire period in question (in seconds). To suggest that this is just the same old thing with new tools, or that scholarship based on corpora of a size unimaginable to any previous generation in history is just "a fascination with gadgets," is to miss both the epochal nature of what's afoot, and the ways in which technology and discourse are intertwined." Ramsay, Steven. Comment on the blog entry The MLA, @briancroxall, and the non-rise of the Digital Humanities. 2010.

39   See early 1990s contributions such as George Landow's *Hypertext* (Baltimore: Johns Hopkins University Press, 1992) or Jay Bolter's *Writing Space: The Computer, Hypertext, and the History of Writing* (Hillsdale: L. Erlbaum Associates, 1991).

40   See Jerome McGann's *Radiant Textuality* (New York: Palgrave, 2001) and early digital humanities projects such as *The William Blake Archive* (http://www.blakearchive.org/) or *The Walt Whitman Archive* (https://whitmanarchive.org/).

41   See Nick Montfort's *Twisty Little Passages* (Cambridge: MIT Press, 2003) or Stephen Cave et al. *AI Narratives: A History of Imaginative Thinking about Intelligent Machines* (New York: Oxford University Press, 2020)

42   See various contributions, such as, N. Katherine Hayles's *How We Think: Digital Media and Contemporary Technogenesis* (Chicago: University of Chicago Press, 2012), Mark Hansen's *Emergence and Embodiment: New Essays on Second-Order Systems Theory* (Durham: Duke University Press, 2009), or John Johnston's *The Allure of Machinic Life* (Cambridge: MIT Press, 2008).

43   See the seminal study by Matthew Kirschenbaum *Mechanisms: New Media and the Forensic Imagination* (Cambridge: MIT Press, 2008) and his critique of the so-called "screen ideology" in favor of the materiality of digital storage.

44   See the Software Studies series by MIT Press including Noah Wardrip fruin's *Expressive Processing: Digital Fictions, Computer Games, and Software Studies* (Cambridge, MA: MIT Press, 2009), Wendy Hui Kyong Chun's *Programmed Visions* (Cambridge: MIT Press, 2011), or Mark Marino's recently published *Critical Code Studies: Initial Methods* (Cambridge: MIT Press, 2020) based on the works of the Critical Code Studies Working Groups (https://criticalcodestudies.com/ccswg.html).

45   Readers unfamiliar with the concept of mark-up language can refer to Tim Berners-Lee's *Hypertext Markup Language: the HTML explained from the Inventor of the WWW* (Kindle Edition, 2014). For further information on standards for the representation of texts in digital form, visit the web site of the *Text Encoding Initiative* consortium at https://tei-c.org/ For more recent developments in mark-up language practices, see John Gruber and Aaron Schwartz's creation of *Markdown* in 2004, a language for creating formatted texts particularly suitable to blogging, online forums, and various documentation practices.

46   URL stands for Uniform Resource Locator and is the term frequently used to refer to a web address typically appearing in the address bar of a web browser.

47   Theodore H. Nelson, *Literary Machines* (Sausalito: Mindful Press, 1992), 0–2.

48   Nelson, *Literary Machines*, ibid.

49   Tim Berners-Lee, formally credited as the inventor of the *World Wide Web* used Nelson's concept of hypertext in his 1989 "Information Management: A Proposal" for the 1990 first implementation of the exchange of hyperlinked document between client and server on the CERN network. An HTML version of the original proposal can be read at https://www.w3.org/History/1989/proposal.html

50   In terms of hypertext literary works, for example, authors such as Michael Joyce, Shelley Jackson, and Jane Yellowlees Douglas had initially gained considerable attention in the American world of letters. Some of these authors and electronic works have earned academic canonization by being included in collected anthologies. Michael Joyce and Jane Yellowlees Douglas, for example, appear in the "Technoculture" section of the *Norton Anthology of Postmodern American Fiction* (New York: W. W. Norton, 1998).

51   See chapter 5 "The Electronic Book" in Jay David Bolter, *Writing Space: Computers, Hypertext, and the Remediation of Print* (Mahwah: L. Erlbaum Associates, 2001).

52   George Landow, *Hypertext 3.0: Critical Theory and New Media in an Era of Globalization* (Baltimore: Johns Hopkins University Press, 2006), 264.

53   Scott Rettberg, "Posthyperfiction: Practices in Digital Textuality," in *Interactive Digital Narrative* eds. Hartmut Koenitz, Gabriele Ferri, Mads Haahr, Diğdem Sezen, Tonguç İbrahim Sezen, 174–184. (New York: Routledge, 2015), 180. Also available at: https://elmcip.net/sites/default/files/media/critical_writing/attachments/posthyperfiction_prepress.pdf

Situating Digital Humanism

54 See George Landow, *Hypertext 2.0: The Convergence of Critical Theory and Technology.*

55 George Landow, *Hypertext 3.0*, 2

56 George Landow, *Hypertext 3.0*, 1

57 Adelaide Morris, "New Media Poetics: As We May Think/How to Write," in *New Media Poetics: Contexts, Technotexts, and Theories*, eds. A. Morris, and T. Swiss (Cambridge: The MIT Press, 2006), 12.

58 The crucial turning point of the so-called linguistic turn in literary theory is to be found in Ferdinand De Saussure's famous distinction between the two components of the *signifier* and the *signified* in the linguistic sign. The sign, as intended in post-Saussurean semiotics and linguistics theory, is usually regarded as formed by a signifier (the either tangible or abstract proxy for meaning) and the signified (the concept to which the signifier points). For a general introduction to Saussure's ideas about signification, see Ferdinand de Saussure, *Writings About General Linguistics* (Oxford: Oxford University Press, 2006).

59 Vannevar Bush, "As We May Think," in *The New Media Reader*, ed by Noah Wardrip-Fruin and Nick Montfort (Cambridge: The MIT Press, 2003), pp. 37–47 (first publ. in *Atlantic Monthly* 176 (1945), 101–108).

60 Bush, "As We May Think," 46.

61 This ideal was elaborated by Leon Battista Alberti (1404–1472). However, poet and scholar Petrarch, often considered the father of humanism and also the first humanist to achieve intellectual recognition (appointed poet laureate in 1341), offers a good proto-example of a thought that lacks a systematic course or progression and that is rather characterized by an encompassing web of recurring themes. In his view, the mission of achieving moral perfection would not require the rigid causal unfolding of logical reasoning but, as reflected in his writings and letters, would rather involve the inter-connection of personal reflections, contributions, and references that ranged from pagan antiquity, classical Roman rhetoric (Cicero and Seneca), and an inclusive Christianity (Saint Augustine *Confessions*). This freedom across systems of thought inaugurated a practice that, starting in the Florence tradition of humanists (Coluccio Salutati, Poggio Braciolini, Niccolo Niccoli, and others), would be eventually emulated by any intellectual circle interested in a *liberal* education, namely in the widening of the mind and in the intellectual growth typical of studies worth of a free human being.

62 Giovanni Pico Della Mirandola, "Oration on the Dignity of Man," *The Renaissance Philosophy of Man*, ed. E. Cassirer and P. Kristeller, 223–254 (Chicago: University of Chicago Press, 1948), 224.

63 Released in early 1993, the *Mosaic* browser could link both graphics and texts and supported the *Gopher* protocol, a system for sharing and searching documents on the internet. Such system offered menu-based functionalities for documents' hierarchy and storage that were not natively supported by the Web and would be eventually abandoned.

64 The *Mapa System* was a toolkit that allowed to analyze the link structure of a web site and that proved particularly effective in visualizing the hierarchical structures of pages in large web sites (50 to 50,000 pages). For further information, see David Durand and Paul Kahn, "MAPA: A System for Inducing and Visualizing Hierarchy in Websites" in *HYPERTEXT '98: Proceedings of the Ninth ACM Conference on Hypertext and Hypermedia*, May (1998): 66–76.

65 For an interdisciplinary survey on the concept of "node" and networked thinking, see Phillip H. Gochenour, "Nodalism" published in the *Digital Humanities Quarterly*. Gochenour traces the discourse of nodalism through neuroscience, psychology, and information technology. In his view, the passage of the term "node" across such fields demonstrates an established initiative in computing to replicate the structure and function of the human neural process, an initiative that reconfigures the various concepts of lists, data, anomalies, and narrative.

66 See Ted Nelson's 1974 first hypertext project called *Project Xanadu* (https://xanadu.com/). See also Cliff McKnight, Andrew Dillon, John Richardson's *Hypertext in Context* (Cambridge University Press, 1991).

67 See in particular Anne Munster, *Materializing New Media: Embodiment in Information Aesthetics* (Hanover: Dartmouth College Press, 2006) and Matthew Kirschenbaum, *Mechanisms: New Media and the Forensic Imagination* (Cambridge: MIT Press, 2008).

68 See Katherine Hayles's use of neurocognitive terms, Mark Hansen's focus on the haptic, kinetic, and proprioceptive effects of the digital, Matthew Kirschenbaum's recourse to forensic investigation, and Franco Moretti's use of abstract scientific models in exploring the material dynamics of digitized texts.

69 Among the many calls for reconnecting the two domains, one of the most timely advocations is likely Alan Liu's contribution to the 2012 *Debates in Digital Humanities* volume, a piece eloquently titled "Where Is Cultural Criticism in the Digital Humanities?" https://dhdebates.gc.cuny.edu/read/untitled-88c11800-9446-469b-a3be-3fdb36bfbd1e/section/896742e7-5218-42c5-89b0-0c3c75682a2f

70 See Licia Calvi, "Adaptivity in Hyperfiction," in *Hypertext 2004: Proceedings of the Fifteenth ACM Conference on Hyprtext and Hypermedia* (New York: ACM Press, 2004): 163–170.

71 Interactive fiction in its contemporary connotation is usually intended as software-based simulation of a diegetic world in which the user is able to influence events thanks to the exchange of language-based inputs meaningfully interpreted by the computer *parser*. For a history of Interactive Fiction and a compelling treatment of its various aspects, see Nick Montfort, *Twisty Little Passages: An Approach to Interactive Fiction* (Cambridge: MIT Press, 2003).

72 One of the first examples of an accessible web-based AI text generator was indeed aimed at questioning essay writing in the humanities, especially in relation to postmodernism and its theoretical, critical, and rhetorical practices. As we read on the *Postmodernism Generator* web site, the text generator "was written by Andrew C. Bulhak using the Dada Engine, a system for generating random text from recursive grammars, and modified very slightly by Josh Larios." Despite the verisimilitude of its outcomes, the installation would produce essays that are described as "completely meaningless" and "randomly generated." For more information, see Bulhak, Andrew C. (April 1, 1996). "On the Simulation of Postmodernism and Mental Debility using Recursive Transition Networks," Monash University. Department of Computer Science Technical Report 96/264.

73 As a representative example of an AI-based cinematographic text, we can consider *Terminal Time*, a collaboration between a computer scientist specializing in AI-based art and entertainment (Michael Mateas), an interactive media artist (Paul Vanouse), and a documentary filmmaker (Steffi Domike). It can be conceived of as a participatory and interactive movie artifact that builds ideologically-biased history documentaries. Noah Wardrip-Fruin, in his book *Expressive Processing*, observes how each story "is presented as a twenty-minute multimedia projection with the 'look and feel' of the traditional authoritative PBS documentary" but "the ideological bias is shaped by audience responses – recorded by an applause meter – to public opinion polls that appear at three points during the performance" (260). For more information, see Michael Mateas; Steffi Domike; Paul Vanouse, "Terminal Time: An Ideologically-biased History Machine." https://users.soe.ucsc.edu/~michaelm/publications/mateas-aisb-1999.pdf. For a visual illustration of *Terminal Time*, see https://vimeo.com/357559820

74 As a representative example, we can consider the art/research experiment *Façade* published in *Electronic Literature Collection Vol. 2.* https://collection.eliterature.org/2/works/mateas_facade.html

75 For an explanation of the concept of "remediation" as the defining feature of new digital media consisting in reorganizing, reshaping, and refashioning old media (with different level of visibility in the process), see Jay Bolter and Richard Grusin, *Remediation: Understanding New Media* (Cambridge: MIT Press, 1999).

76 For an up-to-date contribution reviewing the landscape of literature including movements, such as, Posthumanism, Transhumanism, Antihumanism and Object Oriented Ontology, see Francesca Ferrando, *Philosophical Posthumanism* (London: Bloomsbury Academic, 2020). For a contextualization of a survey of posthumanism in relation to the Anthropocene and to the creation of a posthuman ethics, see Rosi Braidotti, "Posthuman Critical Theory." *Journal of Posthuman Studies* 1, no. 1 (2017): 9–25 published by Penn State University Press.

77 Luciano Floridi, *Philosophy and Computing: An Introduction* (New York: Routledge, 1999), 18.

78 Sam Williams, *Arguing A.I.: The Battle for Twenty-first-Century Science* (New York: Atradom, 2002), xiii.

79 From this point of view, the contribution of theoretical positions revolving around new materialism, posthumanism, and object-oriented ontology can become extremely relevant. For more in-depth analysis of the subject see Jane Bennett, *Vibrant Matter: A Political Ecology of Things* (Durham: Duke University Press Books, 2010) or Philippe Descola and Marshall Sahlins's *Beyond Nature and Culture*, trans. Janet Lloyd (Chicago: University of Chicago Press, 2014). On Object-Oriented Ontology with a relevant focus on digital studies, see Ian Bogost, *Alien Phenomenology, or What It's Like to Be a Thing* (Minneapolis: University of Minnesota Press, 2012).

80 Bill Brown, "Thing Theory," *Critical Inquiry* 28, no. 1 (2001): 5.

81 Noah Wardrip-Fruin, *Expressive Processing: Digital Fictions, Computer Games, and Software Studies* (Cambridge: The MIT Press, 2009), 3.

82 Matthew Kirschenbaum, *Mechanisms: New Media and the Forensic Imagination* (Cambridge: The MIT Press, 2008), 158.

83 As Katherine Hayles points out in *Electronic Literature: New Horizons for the Literary* (Notre Dame, Ind: University of Notre Dame, 2008) for the specific case of digital literature, electronic literature can be seen as "a cultural force helping to shape subjectivity in an era when networked and programmable media are catalyzing cultural, political and economic changes" (p. 37).

Situating Digital Humanism

84 As Luciano Floridi observes in his "Artificial Intelligences' New Frontier: Artificial Companions and the Fourth Revolution," "we are now slowly accepting the idea that we might be informational organisms ... not so dramatically different from clever, engineered artefacts" (p. 1).

85 The term "born-digital" refers to materials that originate in digital form and is typically used in opposition to "digitized" which is used to refer to content that conversely previously exists in analog format (such as paper records). For a discussion of how born-digital content has promoted innovations in archival practices and research methodologies, see Carroll, Laura, Erika Farr, Peter Hornsby, and Ben Ranker's "A Comprehensive Approach to Born-Digital Archives." *Archivaria* 72 (2011): 61–92.

86 See C. M. Sperberg-McQueen's "Classification and its Structures" in *A Companion to Digital Humanities*, ed. Susan Schreibman, Ray Siemens, John Unsworth (Oxford: Blackwell, 2004).

87 On the general concept of "metadata," namely data that provide information about other data, see Jenn Riley's *Understanding Metadata* (Baltimore: NISO Press, 2017) available at: https://groups.niso.org/apps/group_public/download.php/17446/Understanding%20Metadata.pdf

88 For a quick introduction to the *Text Encoding Initiative* (TEI) and quick guidelines for the application of TEI markup for scholarly editions, language corpora, historical lexicons, and digital archives, see: Lou Burnard, *What is the Text Encoding Initiative?: How to Add Intelligent Markup to Digital Resources* (OpenEdition Press, 2014). See also the TEI web site at: https://tei-c.org/

89 For a representative example of how digital editing can reveal unexplored critical possibilities about texts, see Jerome J. McGann, *Radiant Textuality: Literature after the World Wide Web* (New York: Palgrave, 2001). Through the illustration of a foundational scholarly project in the field of digital humanities, *The Rossetti Archive* at the Institute for Advanced Technology in the Humanities (IATH) at the University of Virginia, MacGann explores textual deformation as interpretation, gaming as innovative reading, and archiving as forms of thorough analytical rethinking of textuality.

90 Johanna Drucker, "Humanistic Theory and Digital Scholarship" in *Debates in Digital Humanities* ed. Matthew K. Gold (Minneapolis: University of Minnesota Press, 2012), 85. https://dhdebates.gc.cuny.edu/read/untitled-88c11800-9446-469b-a3be-3fdb36bfbd1e/section/0b495250-97af-4046-91ff-98b6ea9f83c0

91 The issue of the actual possibility of distinguishing between an "object language" and a "metalanguage" represents a controversial topic in the philosophical perspectives of many important 20th-century philosophers: among these, we can remember Alfred Tarski, Rudolph Carnap, Ludwig Wittgenstein, and Hilary Putnam. In some philosophical perspectives, the sheer possibility to theorize a metalanguage became the object of severe criticism.

92 Ephraim Emerton, *Humanism and Tyranny: Studies in the Italian Trecento* (Cambridge: Harvard University Press, 2013), 341–377.

93 Douglas Bush, *The Renaissance and English Humanism* (Toronto: University of Toronto Press, 1962), 55.

94 For a larger survey on how born-digital artifacts can be approached from the point of view of digital humanities, see Dene Grigar and James O' Sullivan (eds.), *Electronic Literature as Digital Humanities: Contexts, Forms & Practices* (Bloomsbury Academic, 2021).

95 Howard Besser, "Longevity of Electronic Art," *ICHIM (International Cultural Heritage Informatics Meeting) 2001*, 103. *Archives & Museum Informatics.* Last modified July 1, 2018, https://www.archimuse.com/ichim2001/abstracts/prg_115000637.html

96 For a survey or various aspects related to digital publishing and its consequences for digital objects and their analysis, see Kathleen Fitzpatrick, *Planned Obsolescence: Publishing, Technology, and the Future of the Academy* (New York: NYU Press, 2011).

97 Usually, the term "archive" refers to any generic repository of documents. Since some definitions even in the disciplinary field of archival science, including the one by The Society of American Archivists, defines archives as "the noncurrent records of an organization or institution preserved because of their continuing value" (see *The Council on Library and Information Resources* web site at: https://www.clir.org/pubs/reports/pub89/role/), the term archive typically refers to the final ("historicized") stage of the so-called life span of records and becomes synonymous with "preservation."

98 For an introduction to the record continuum model in archival sciences, see S. McKemmish et al.'s "Records Continuum Model." *Encyclopedia of Library and Information Sciences* (3rd ed.) (2010): 4447–4448; and Upward's "Structuring the Records Continuum – Part One: Postcustodial Principles and Properties." *Archives & Manuscripts.* 24 (2) (1996): 268–285.

99 See the evolution of the volumes of the *Electronic Literature Collection* anthologies. In general, see Scott Rettberg *Electronic Literature* (Medford: Polity Press, 2019) for a history of major developments of e-literature. For a specific discussion of third-generation e-literature, see Leonardo Flores, "Third Generation Electronic Literature," *Electronic Book Review.* https://electronicbookreview.com/essay/third-generation-electronic-literature/

100 For further information on the concept of *studia humanitatis*, see also Benjamin G. Kohl, "The Changing Concept of the 'Studia Humanitatis' in the Early Renaissance." *Renaissance Studies* 6, no. 2 (1992): 185–209. Accessed July 28, 2021, www.jstor.org/stable/24412493

101 See pp. 666–667 in Jennifer Summit, "Renaissance Humanism and the Future of Humanities." *Literature Compass* 9/10 (2012): 665–678.

102 Desiderius Erasmus, *Against War and In Praise of Folly*, ed. Anthony Uyl (Devoted Publishing, 2017), 12. Original reference: "Nature hath endued man with knowledge of liberal sciences and a fervent desire of knowledge: which thing as it doth most specially withdraw man's wit from all beastly wildness …"

103 Johanna Drucker, "Philosophy and Digital Humanities: A review of Willard McCarty, Humanities Computing" (London and New York: Palgrave, 2005), in *Digital Humanities Quarterly* 1 no. 1 (2007). http://www.digitalhumanities.org/dhq/vol/1/1/000001/000001.html

104 Dilthey's resistance to the adoption of a humanist framework strictly modeled on the natural sciences is actually part of a larger tradition of thought that promotes hermeneutics as a set of general theories of interpretation that might be applicable to texts and artworks just as much as to religious scriptures, laws, and anthropological practices. The anti-positivist positions of George Simmel and Max Weber in sociology as well as Martin Heidegger's "hermeneutics of factical life" in *Being and Time* (1927) are undoubtedly part of this tradition. On the language-centered nature of the epistemological concerns typical of "human sciences," as the term has been understood particularly in Europe, see Jacques Derrida, "Structure, Sign, and Play in the Discourse of the Human Sciences," in *Writing and Difference* (London: Routledge, 1978).

105 For further information about Wilhelm Dilthey's perspective on the epistemological relationship between sciences and the "human sciences," see his 1883 seminal work *Introduction to Human Sciences*. On Dilthey's specific concept of life-nexus see Jacob Owensby, "Dilthey's Conception of the Life-Nexus," *Journal of the History of Philosophy* 25, no. 4 (1987): 557–572. On the larger issue of the role of history in the understanding of our lifeworld, see Rudolf A. Makkreel, "Husserl, Dilthey and the Relation of the Life-World to History," *Research in Phenomenology* 12 (1982): 39–58.

106 Both Franco Moretti's *Graphs, Maps, and Trees* and Matthew Jockers's *Macroanalysis* can be considered foundational texts in the field that push for overcoming the limitation of traditional "close reading" by asking big, macroscopic questions by means of the quantitative treatment of textual and literary data across large collections of digitized materials.

107 For an introduction to the practice of Topic Modeling, see David M. Blei. "Introduction to Probabilistic Topic Models." *Communications of the ACM*, 2011. For a discussion of Topic Modeling in relation to literary studies, see Ted Underwood's "Topic Modeling Made Just Simple Enough." https://tedunderwood.com/2012/04/07/topic-modeling-made-just-simple-enough/

108 The *Oxford English Dictionary* defines the word "topic" as "the subject of a discourse, argument, or literary composition," or, more generally, "a matter treated in speech or writing."

109 DFR stands for "data for research" and the *DFR Browser* is the graphic interface developed by Andrew Goldstone that visually renders the Mallet-processed analysis of source texts. For further information about the *DFR Browser*, see "Dfr Browser: Take a MALLET to Disciplinary History." https://agoldst.github.io/dfr-browser/

110 In terms of the LDA algorithm, the output is based on what we call posterior probability, namely the influence of further conditions assigned after primary physical evidence (in our case: counting words occurrences) is gathered. Additionally, we need to remind ourselves that Bayesian statistics itself (on which the LDA algorithm is designed) does not work with physical probabilities but with evidential probabilities, i.e., degrees of belief in terms of subjective plausibility.

111 We can also understand, then, how the remarkable amount of scholarship addressing meaning ambiguity and language polysemy that has characterized humanistic and literary studies since the 1960s (with Literary Theory scholarship reaching its peak in the 1980s) can come as an extremely valuable help and actual operational toolkit for contemporary data science.

112 A supercomputer is an algorithmic machine able to perform at incommensurably higher performance than a general-purpose computer (typically trillions of floating-point operations per second). For a cursory review of the evolution of supercomputing in relation to cultural perspectives, see Chester Gordon Bell, "Supercomputers: the Amazing Race," Microsoft Research, Microsoft Corporation Technical Report (2014).

113 Fred Edwords, "The Humanist Philosophy in Perspective," *American Humanist Association*. Accessed September 1, 2021, https://americanhumanist.org/what-is-humanism/humanist-philosophy-perspective/

Situating Digital Humanism

114 For an interesting take on the need to implement practices of designing and building "explainable systems" – as opposed to computation as a black box model – in connection with a humanist-oriented critique of capitalism and the theory of the human mind, see David Berry's "The Explainability Turn" *Stunlaw* (blog), 2019. http://stunlaw.blogspot.com/2020/01/the-explainability-turn.html

115 Geoffrey Galt Harpham. *The Humanities and the Dream of America* (Chicago: University of Chicago Press, 2011), 84.

116 Daniel Frankforter and William Spellman, *The West: A Narrative History*, Volume Two: Since 1400 (Upper Saddle River: Pearson, 2011), 353.

117 An expression that features as foundational both in the 1964 *ACLS Report of the Commission on the Humanities* and the 1980 Rockefeller Foundation's "Commission of the Humanities" Report. https://publications.acls.org/NEH/Report-of-the-Commission-on-the-Humanities-1964.pdf

118 Besides N. Katherine Hayles's foundational *How We Became Posthuman*, see, among others, Cary Wolfe *What Is Posthumanism?* (Minneapolis: University of Minnesota Press, 2010) and Donna Haraway, *When Species Meet* (Minneapolis: University of Minnesota Press, 2008). On the topic of how these fields might be rewriting human subjectivity from humanist to posthumanist within a possibly anti-humanist perspective, see Tamise Van Pelt, "The Question concerning Theory: Humanism, Subjectivity, and Computing." *Computers and the Humanities* 36, no. 3, *A New Computer-Assisted Literary Criticism?* (August, 2002): 307–318.

119 Plato, *The Republic*, Book VI, *The Internet Classics Archive*. Accessed September 1, 2021 http://classics.mit.edu/Plato/republic.7.vi.html

120 Promising examples of convergence between humanistic approaches and computer-based practices go from Mark Marino's exploration of the extra-functional signification of programming languages by applying hermeneutics and literary theory to snippets of code in his *Critical Code Studies* to the 2021 Creative Computing Initiative at UCSB and its summer course program whose goal is "to forge more personal, imaginative, and critical connections to computationally based media and technology" (https://www.summer.ucsb.edu/courses/course-spotlight/creative-computing).

121 Terry Harpold, *Ex-Foliations: Reading Machines and the Upgrade Path* (Minneapolis: University of Minnesota Press, 2008), 4.

122 The trope of the talking book, recurring in some of the first slave autobiographies written between 1770 and 1815, provides, according to Henri Louis Gates, Jr., "those formal links of repetition and revision that, in part, define any literary tradition." See Henry Louis Gates, Jr., *The Signifying Monkey: A Theory of African American Literary Criticism* (Oxford: Oxford University Press, 2014).

123 Matthew Kirschenbaum, "Hello Worlds: Why Humanities Students Should Learn to Program," in *The Chronicle of Higher Education*, January 23, 2009. accessed September 1, 2021, https://www.chronicle.com/article/hello-worlds/

124 It is interesting to note how, in shifting meaning-making from print to digital textuality, Lori Emerson in her *Reading Writing Interfaces: From the Digital to the Bookbound* connects the "new" literary, i.e., the literary in new media, with the intuitive probing and exploring of the digital textual interfaces exhibited not only by works of electronic literature but also by a range of digital technologies operating through a GUI (graphic user interface) in an articulate dynamic between interface's visibility and invisibility. For further in-depth analysis of this issue, see Lori Emerson, *Reading Writing Interfaces: From the Digital to the Bookbound* (Minneapolis: University of Minnesota Press, 2014).

16

Beyond the Algorithms

On Performance and Subjectivity in *Detroit: Become Human*[1]

Nizar Zouidi

Due to the unprecedented achievements in the fields of robotics and machine intelligence, the future of human–machine relationships is increasingly becoming a highly controversial and widely debated issue. Many leading scientists, politicians, businesspeople, public figures as well as literary figures, philosophers, academics and artists have warned that the future of humanity may depend on how we handle our relationship with our most intelligent and human-like invention by far. Whether we will be able to achieve a peaceful and fruitful coexistence with this emerging life form or whether we should brace for conflict and destruction is yet to be determined. However, it is very likely that in a few decades – or probably a few years – we will not be alone on this planet.

There is no denying that the development of artificial intelligence "will fundamentally alter our existence."[2] Artificial intelligence is transforming both itself and us. It is already reconfiguring our conceptualization of human subjectivity, position and role in the universe. The human subject is increasingly being understood "in terms of data"[3] processed by different forms of artificial intelligence. It is even used to understand, predict and control consumption trends, political inclinations, sexual preferences, behavioral patterns, and other human motives and actions.

Artificial intelligence in particular plays an important role in enhancing the immersive experience of games. The conceptualization, design, production and consumption of games, gaming materials and player experiences invariably involve interacting with artificial intelligence. As such, designing or playing a video game narrative necessitates reaching a mutual understanding with AI. It is, therefore, natural that everyone (every human) at the different ends of the gaming world should be intrigued by their ever-evolving intelligent non-human partner. Naturally, therefore, AI is not only an integral technical aspect of the medium, but it also is one of its most popular subject matters.

According to Richard Schechner, performance studies seek to explain how "people turn into other people, gods, animals, demons, trees, beings, whatever – either temporarily as in a play or permanently as in some rituals."[4] Central to performance studies is the study of the human as a performing or performed subject. Indeed, as Philip Auslander remarks, the word performance itself "extends into many areas of human endeavors."[5] As a result, studying the gaming experience may prove to be a new frontier for the interdisciplinary human-centered approaches of performance studies.

Gradually replacing theater[6] as "the most embracing of all art forms,"[7] video games can be described as a versatile and highly collaborative creative medium of storytelling that relies on different technologies and arts. They use cutting-edge visual, auditory and computational technologies to offer an immersive experience that is not possible in other entertainment industries

282

DOI: 10.4324/9781003046004-20

Beyond the Algorithms

and arts and even competes with sports. These technologies enhance the player's experience of "autonomy, competence and relatedness."[8] The interactivity of games enables the player to feel in control of the game's narrative. Moreover, it allows them to enjoy the unique status of empowered and empowering agency as they act on the game world and change it. Finally, they can identify with and relate to the fictional characters that populate the world of the game.

One of the most powerful depictions of intelligent machines in video games is the 2018 Quantic Dream game *Detroit: Become Human*. The game is arguably a great commercial success. It sold more than 3.2 million copies on PlayStation 5 alone. This makes it one of the landmarks of the industry. Accordingly, its influence on the future development of the genre of narrative games is likely to be quite significant. Its narrative and gameplay mechanics deliver a powerfully immersive experience that is lauded in players' reviews, video game journalism and academic studies.

Written by David Cage (who also directed it) and Adam Williams, the game presents the player with a powerfully engaging story about the relationship between humans and androids in a futuristic Detroit. It puts the player in the shoes of three androids whose storylines intersect at different stages. The choices of the player as one character influences the story of the other two characters.[9] Through these characters and their branching stories, the game engages with contemporary social, political and cultural issues such as "racism, domestic abuse, gendered expectations and police brutality,"[10] while at the same time exploring the technical as well as aesthetic and cultural potentialities and limitations of the narrative medium of cinematic games.

Like in other choose-your-own-adventure or choices-matter cinematic games, the players in *Detroit: Become Human* take on the roles of playable characters and identify with them. They also interact with automated processes playing the roles of human characters. In video games, machine intelligence takes the role of human characters. This certainly influences the player's conceptualization of humanness. The identities of the performing entities in the gaming space are determined by the intertwining of the narrative and the gameplay mechanics. This makes the subjectivities of the player, and the playable and non-playable characters are represented as mutable, situational, and mobile. This complicates the questions of AI and human subjectivities and intersubjective relationships.

The context of the development and reception of *Detroit: Become Human* is characterized by a growing interest in the future of AI technology. In the loading screens, background voice-overs and in-game readable materials of *Detroit: Become Human*, the player reads, sees and listens to advertisements about androids. These ads are pervaded by normative discourses and discursive practices about human subjectivity and gender roles. The advertisements reveal the underrepresentation of certain minorities and social categories in the consumer society of a futuristic Detroit. This illustrates the role of technology in enforcing normative discourses and practices.

In recent years, the nature and functions of human intelligence(s) have been being transformed by the introduction of automated processes. In fact, since the arithmometer replaced human computers in the second half of the nineteenth century – reducing the need to learn basic calculations,[11] artificial intelligence has been taking over many of the cognitive operations of the human brain. Whether the use of AI to reduce the time and effort of processing and analyzing data will continue to further unlock new areas of knowledge for human intelligence or whether it will reduce it to passive dependency – or even redundancy – will depend on the nature and potentialities of both intelligences and the contexts of their (co)development.

In the game, there are references to the role of android technology in the rise of unemployment among humans. Some human characters in the game use that discourse to justify violence and discrimination not only against androids but also against other humans. While the game does not justify the discriminatory and violent acts of humans, it reveals that little is done to reskill and reemploy the people who are replaced by automated processes. This will not guarantee a safe and cooperative future for the human race.

As AI devices and machines get closer to becoming another intelligent life form, the future of our relationship with intelligent machines continues to be a major literary and cultural issue. In literature, independent automatons are usually portrayed as difficult to control.[12] In many cases, they rebel against their creators. The story of the Golem of Prague is one of the earliest examples of a robot turning on humans. The story is archetypal. Indeed, many subsequent narratives have been fashioned using similar patterns. In contemporary popular culture, the lingering popularity of the archetype of the evil super-intelligent humanoid, which probably started with Brainiac from the 1958 Superman action comics, reveals a deep distrust of artificial intelligence.

This entrenched distrust led Isaac Asimov to suggest subjecting intelligent machines to strict rules. In his book *The Complete Robot*,[13] Asimov introduces three laws to keep robots, androids, and other automated devices from becoming a threat to humans. The laws of Asimov are as follows:

1   A robot should not injure a human being or, through inaction, allow a human being to come to harm.
2   A robot must obey the orders given to it by human beings except where such orders would conflict with the first law.
3   A robot must protect its own existence as long as such protection does not conflict with the first and second law.

These rules imply that robots have the potential of becoming harmful. As a result, he believes that they should be subject to strict control.

Both the archetype of Brainiac and the laws of Asimov illustrate "the modernist antipathy towards machine intelligence."[14] In his "Machines like Us? Modernism and the Question of the Robot," Paul March-Russel argues that machine intelligence threatens the modernist phallocentric concept of human agency. The image of "an otherwise inert automobile or aero plane until stirred into pulsating life by the motorist or aviator"[15] was often celebrated with an emphasis on "the hyperbolic masculinity"[16] of the act. For modernist writers, technology should always be dependent on this human agency. "A machine that consciously talks, writes and creates, however,"[17] is a threat to the security of agency. Russel believes that the image of the human as a dominant masculine agency[18] is at the center of the modernist debate about artificial and robotic intelligences.

As such, technology cannot be considered neutral. Indeed, as Adrianna Kizkkowski (2020) insightfully suggests, "the lines of technological evolution are very dependent on hegemonic values in a given society."[19] Stereotypes about different social categories like women, children or the elderly have found their way into "project proposals and determine the technology that is invented."[20] The role and identity of artificial intelligence in the coming technological society is to a large extent determined by the dominant rhetoric. This is why we cannot separate the debate about the future of AI from major political, social and cultural issues.

This is no more evident than in the video game industry, where the limits and potentialities of machine intelligence determine the gaming experience. In games, the portrayal of intelligent machines and robots has developed from the one-dimensional enemy, ally or guide to a more complex character with existential dilemmas and questions. EDI from the *Mass Effect Trilogy* is a case in point. When the playable character, commander Shepard, meets "it" in an optional side quest of the first game, "it" is a rogue VI shooting everything that moves. In the second game, EDI is an artificial intelligence that assists the hero of the game and guides them. In the third game, the unshackled AI eventually acquires a (female) body (a visually gendered and sexualized mobile hardware) and starts to become a fully-fledged companion of the playable character. "She" even starts a romantic relationship with a human crew member. In 2017, the intimacy between *Mass effect*'s playable character and AI takes a remarkably dramatic turn with the introduction of SAM, an artificial intelligence connected to the brain of Ryder, the pathfinder (the playable character).

A year later, Quantic Dream took a significant leap forward. The player can now take the role of artificial intelligence. This move is quite complex in nature. On the one hand, it makes the game "an immersive experience in marginalization."[21] Indeed, the player experiences the world of the game from the perspective of socially marginalized characters. On the other hand, the player's choices can bring major change into the fictional world of the game. In this sense, the experience of marginalization is limited by the emphasis on human agency. The centrality of human agency is reinforced in the scenes of rebooting, where the player takes control of the playable character as it is reset. This might be seen as a return to the modernist image of the inert machine that requires human agency to spring to action.

While typically emphasizing the player's subjectivity and centrality as the empowered and empowering human agent, the game gives them the opportunity to experience forms of de-humanization and marginalization as non-human characters. Indeed, although the player's tacit conceptualization of their humanness as (masculine) agency is only partially shaken, the core mechanics of the game also stress the notion of responsibility. In *Detroit: Become Human*, "most choices are presented with a short timer, which is particularly stressful when a choice has moral" or narrative "implications."[22] The player is forced to make tough moral choices that not only affect the ending of the game but that challenge their secure spectatorial position. There are consequences for each choice that affect the playing experience throughout the game.

In addition, the shifting point of view from one segment of the narrative to the other results in a negotiated identification between the player and the playable characters. Playing as three characters with different and even conflicting interests makes the player struggle to balance them. Players may have to accept the failure of one character to achieve the objectives of the other. For example, when a character is chasing another, running away from them or is tasked with finding and destroying them, the player has to choose between them. While choosing for one character, the player has to think of the effect of their choices on the other characters, on the game world and on their desired ending. From their (meta)gaming experiences gained from playing similar games or watching and discussing the game online, players know that it is possible to achieve a satisfactory ending where all the characters can be considered successful. However, along the way, they cannot afford to satisfy every character. As a result, their emotional and moral investment in the playable characters cannot be equal.

The game starts with a murder case and a hostage situation in which the culprit is an android (a human-like robot with artificial intelligence). The first playable character, Conner, is sent by the android producing company Cyberlife to negotiate with the deviant. The initial conversations between Conner, the mother of the hostage and the police officers give the player an idea about the world of the game. The futuristic society of *Detroit: Become Human* is not totally different from contemporary Western societies. Mega-corporations have gained great power and can impose their will on states and individuals.

Bringing together corporations, the state, humans and androids in a crime scene, the prologue of the game sheds light on the tensions that characterize the futuristic society of Detroit. This is reminiscent of the opening scenes of plays by Henrik Ibsen, George Bernard Shaw and Jean-Paul Sartre, where characters from different backgrounds are brought together in a confined space to enhance the sense of hostility and distrust. The claustrophobic setting turns into a microcosmic representation of the game world, and the ominous atmosphere foreshadows the coming conflict.

Connor's first mission is to negotiate with the rogue android and save the hostage. As in most other interactive cinematic narratives, there are different approaches to performing the quest. The character either heads toward the main objective or takes time to explore the crime scene. Both choices have their consequences, but players know that there are choices that are more rewarding than others. Indeed, as players get familiar with the game structure either through the continuous playing of the same genre, watching recorded playthroughs or participating in online – and offline – gaming communities, their choices become more predictable. They know that the more space the player covers and the more narrative s/he constructs, the higher the success odds of the mission become. As a result, they usually opt for the second choice.

As the player explores the setting, they discover evidence about the murder and its motives. Archetypal of detective narratives is that once the detective can piece together a complete linear narrative that links motives to actions, they can force the other characters to submit to it. As they construct the narrative of the crime and determine the who and why, and how of the story, they also construct all the subjects involved in it. This gives them epistemological, narrative, discursive and performative power. In this game, this is manifested in the dialogue options the exploration unlocks for the player to use in their interaction with other characters. For example, the exploration of the performative space and the reconstruction of the past helps Connor achieve narrative superiority over the other performing entities in the opening mission. It helps the android negotiator to liberate the hostage and convince the kidnapper to surrender.

Wrestling the discursive, narrative and performative space from other performers – be they individuals or organizations – is also characteristic of Markus' story. After being framed for the murder of a famous artist (by the latter's son), Markus is switched off and thrown in a junkyard of androids. From there, the android begins a journey to Jericho, a shelter for freedom-seeking androids. In Jericho, Markus becomes the leader of an androids' liberation movement. Whether the player chooses the peaceful path or the violent one, the struggle for freedom involves claiming the discursive and performative space. Accordingly, leaving their marks on the space of performance or occupying it are the strategies of the android revolution. Protest as a performative act usually takes place in a hostile or indifferent territory. The success of protest is usually commemorated through the renaming of places and dates or the erection of memorials and monuments. In a certain sense, protest is a struggle for space and time. This is reminiscent of current events like the Black Lives Matter demonstrations and other forms of protest.

The third character is a fugitive on the run. As such, Kara's relationship with space is transient. It is either welcoming or hostile (but this does not depend solely on Kara's choices). Unlike Conner, who represents the system and Markus, who leads a revolution, Kara usually moves in human or android controlled spaces without leaving a distinctive or lingering mark on them or their inhabitants, be they humans or androids. Still, Kara has a special relationship with the other characters. Kara interacts with humans and androids as individuals rather than as groups.

This is hardly the case with the other two characters. In certain quests of Markus and Conner, the game interface represents humans and other androids as pure numbers. The player experiences them as numbers rather than characters. Despite investing in the personal relationships and emotional lives of the two characters, the private sides of Conner and Markus seem artificial. Markus' romantic relationship with North might be seen as shedding light on the character's private side. However, it is archetypal of the narrative. North can be seen as a female figure that adds a romantic flavor to the narrative. She is no different from Lois in the Superman comics, cartoons and movies or Lady Marian in Robin Hood legends and their different adaptations. Even "her" background story is quite typical. The forced partnership turned into a friendship pattern of Conner's relationship with Hank is also paradigmatic of many police narratives in cinema and fiction. This makes choices related to these relationships quite predictable and less significant to the player, unless they are related to the characters' roles as rebel leader or agent of the system.

Being neither a force of change like the rebellious Markus nor an agent of preservation (the representative of the system) like Conner, Kara deals with the world in more private terms. In addition, Kara is a domestic android designed to perform housework and take care of children. These roles are traditionally associated with women (either as family roles or as paid jobs). The

Beyond the Algorithms

female appearance of the android certainly reflects how social norms and stereotypes determine technology. The need to pretend to be human in certain situations makes the female appearance of the android even more significant. The figure of Kara is not untypical of feminist narratives; this is why Kara[23] is more relevant to the study of subjectivity than the two other characters.

In contemporary theory, the subject is seen "as the precipitate of variously mutable subject positions engendered within complex networks of power relations and discursive systems".[24] The situational and performative nature of Kara's identity is evident at every stage of the android's story. Kara is not in total control of the narrative. The Markus's rebellion and the investigations of Conner affect the performance space. Kara has to cope with situations created by the other two characters at a macro level. For example, in the final chapter, if public opinion is against the androids – possibly as a result of Markus opting for violence, Kara cannot convince many humans to provide assistance or shelter.

While being an android is by no means ordinary, Kara strikes the player as an ordinary person thrown in the middle of events beyond their control – and understanding. As the world around them changes (without their consent or even knowledge), ordinary folks, like Kara, have to cope with the changes. In the process, their identity shifts according to the situation. The pathos and overwhelming emotional flow of Kara's story can be explained by the android's closeness to the player – as a normal person with limited agency. In addition, the relationship between Kara, Alice and later Luther is the most intimate in the game.[25] There is a sense of family and a bond forged in emotionally charged moments of loss and sacrifice. The degree of the player's identification with the playable character in the case of Kara is potentially higher than that of the other two characters.

Despite being burdened with the established conventions of the genre, *Detroit: Become Human* offers a powerful exploration of cultural, social and political issues related to human and non-human or dehumanized subjectivities. By focusing on the characters' interaction with the performative space of the game, this chapter contends that *Detroit: Become Human* deconstructs itself by making visible the hegemonic cultural and generic paradigms that determine how game characters and narratives are designed and experienced. In this game, the playing experience is a tacit questioning of the cultural and aesthetic paradigms of the gaming industry.

Bibliography

Asimov, Isaac. *The Complete Robot*. London: Harper Collins, 2018.

Auslander, Philip. "General Introduction." In *Performance: Critical Concepts in Literary and Cultural Studies*, ed. Philip Auslander. London: Routledge, 2003, 1–24.

Barrat, James. *Our Final Invention: Artificial Intelligence and the End of the Human Era*. London: Thomas Dunne Books St. Martin Press, 2015.

Eco, Umberto. *Semiotics and the Philosophy of Language*. Bloomington: Indiana University Press, 1986.

Endler, Cordula. "Becoming with Technology – the Reconfiguration of Age in the Development of a Digital Memory," in *Feminist Philosophy of Technology*, ed, by Janina Loh and Mark Coeckelberg. Wein: J.B. Metzler, 2019, 123–42.

Kizkkowski, Adrianna. "Facts and Fiction in a Robotic Society from a Feminist Perspective," *Zagadnienia Rodzajów Literackich* (2020) 63.1: 53–61.

Leach, Rebecca and Marco Dehmert. "Becoming the Other: Examining Race, Gender and Sexuality in *Detroit: Become Human*," *Review of Communication*, (2021) 21.1: 23–32.

March-Russel, Paul. "Machines like Us? Modernism and the Question of the Robot." In *AI Narratives: A History of Imaginative Thinking about Intelligent Machines*, ed, by Stephen Cave, Kanta Dihel and Sarah Dillon. Oxford: Oxford University Press, 2020, 165–86.

Parisi, Luciana. "The Alien Subject of AI," *Subjectivity* (2019) 12: 24–48.

Schechner, Richard. *Performance Theory*. London: Routledge, 2008.

Sikes, Alan. *Representation and Identity from Versailles to the Present: The Performing Subject*. New York: Palgrave Macmillan, 2007.

Nizar Zouidi

Styan, John L. *Drama, Stage and the Audience*. Cambridge: Cambridge University Press, 1975.
Tamborini, Ron et al. "Defining Media Enjoyment as the Satisfaction of Intrinsic Needs," *Journal of Communication*, (2010) 60.4: 758–77.

Notes

1 This chapter is based on a project that was for the University of Cambridge Micromasters in Writing for Performance and Entertainment Industry, a program offered by the University of Cambridge in collaboration with Edx.

2 James Barrat, *Our Final Invention: Artificial Intelligence and the End of the Human Era*. (London: Thomas Dunne Books; St. Martin Press, 2015), 7.

3 Luciana Parisi. "The Alien Subject of AI." *Subjectivity* (2019), 28.

4 Richard Schechner. *Performance Theory* (London: Routledge, 2008), ix.

5 Philip Auslander. "General Introduction." In *Performance: Critical Concepts in Literary and Cultural Studies*, ed. Philip Auslander (London: Routledge, 2003), 1.

6 Theater as another versatile medium also uses different forms of technology. However, since criticism takes theatrical technology for granted, it is either overlooked or seen as a technical aspect of the medium – not as technology *per se*.

7 John L. Styan. *Drama, Stage and the Audience* (Cambridge: Cambridge University Press, 1975), vii.

8 Ron Tamborini, et al. "Defining Media Enjoyment as the Satisfaction of Intrinsic Needs." *Journal of Communication* (2010) 60.4: 758.

9 And – quite archetypally – the lives and stories of the non-playable characters be they "humans" or androids.

10 Rebecca Leach and Marco Dehmert. "Becoming the Other: Examining Race, Gender and Sexuality in *Detroit: Become Human*." *Review of Communication* (2021) 21.1: 25.

11 Although human beings can (and sometimes do) learn these operations, many of us do not see a reason for doing so – other than training our brains or showing off – not unusually depending on how successful we are in learning them.

12 Different versions of the legend of Pygmalion and Galatea shows that a being with a will of their own cannot be exactly what their creators intended them to be.

13 Isaac Asimov. *The Complete Robot*. London: Harper Collins, 2018.

14 Paul March-Russel. "Machines like Us? Modernism and the Question of the Robot." In *AI Narratives: A History of Imaginative Thinking about Intelligent Machines*, ed, by Stephen Cave, Kanta Dihel, and Sarah Dillon (Oxford: Oxford University Press, 2020), 167.

15 Ibid.

16 Ibid.

17 Ibid.

18 Biological gender is not totally irrelevant to this biocentric understanding of agency and intelligence.

19 Adrianna Kizkkowski. "Facts and Fiction in a Robotic Society from a Feminist Perspective." *Zagadnienia Rodzajów Literackich* (2020) 63.1: 54.

20 Cordula Endler, "Becoming with Technology – the Reconfiguration of Age in the Development of a Digital Memory." In *Feminist Philosophy of technology*, ed, by Janina Loh and Mark (Coeckelberg. Wein: J.B. Metzler, 2019), 137.

21 Leach and Dehmert, 24.

22 Ibid.

23 Throughout this article, I do not use any pronouns to refer to the three playable androids to highlight the gender ambiguity – but not neutrality – of these characters.

24 Alan Sikes. *Representation and Identity from Versailles to the Present: The Performing Subject*. (New York: Palgrave Macmillan, 2007), 3.

25 Conner also experiences emotionally charged encounters, but they are transient – even from the perspective of the player.

INDEX

Note: Page numbers followed by 'n' refer to notes.

4Humanities project 254

Abu-Manneh, Bashir 61, 65
Adleman, Daniel 73
Adorno, T. 50
Agamben, Giorgio 87
ageism 115–116
Agyeya (poet) 134
Ahluwalia, Pal 34–36, 64, 68
AI *see* Artificial Intelligence (AI)
Alberti, Leon Battista 277n61
Alessandrini, Anthony 32, 34, 36
Alff, David 233
Alighieri, Dante 192
Allen, Anita 230
alter-humanism 60
Althusser, Louis 3–4
Ambedkar, B.R. 137
Anand, Mulk Raj 139
Ananthamurthy, U.R. 114
Anglo-Saxon poetry: authoritarianism and anti-humanism in 173–182; *Wife's Lament* 173–174, 177, 180; *Wulf and Eadwacer* 173, 175, 181
Animal Liberation (Singer) 87, 91
animal turn 87–88; anti- and posthumanist approaches 93–95; as challenge to humanism 86–96; Darwinian approach 91–93; history 88–91
anthropocentric humanism 93
anti-humanism 3, 60, 93–95
"anti-humanistic humanism" 46
Apter, Emily 65
Aquinas, Thomas 90, 253, 259
Arendt, Hannah 39–40
Aristotle (*Masterpiece*) 231, 234, 242
Arnold, Matthew 50
artha (financial prosperity) 125

Artharvaveda 105, 107
Artificial Intelligence (AI) 179, 259–261, 278n72–73, 282
Ashcroft, B. 63
Asimov, Isaac 284
Assheuer, Thomas 80
Atharbaveda 103
atheism: definition 210; in early Modern England 209–222; *King Lear* 221–222; *Selimus* 217–221; *Tamburlaine* 211, 213–217
Atrahasis 4
Auerbach, E. 50, 60, 65
Augustine Draper of Essex 210
Aurobindo, Shree 125
Auslander, Philip 282
Austen, Jane 67
automated algorithms 259–261
Avalon, Arthar 108
Āyurveda 105, 106–107

Balang, Ladu 160
Bambas, Rudolph 177, 178
Bandhapadhyay, Suresh Chandra 104, 108
Baratay, Eric 88
Basu, Yogiraj 103
Beaufret, Jean 74
Bechain, Sheoraj Singh 137
Beginnings: Intention and Method, The (Said) 50
Behrent, Michael C. 7n17
being (human) 11–28; *Being and Time* project 12–13; fate in continental thought 27–28; Heidegger's existential analysis 20–22; and metaphysics 22–26; re-formulating question 13–14
being-an-object-with-properties 22–23
Belanoff, Patricia A. 188n36
benging song 160–162
Benjamin, Walter 40, 64

Index

Bentham, Jeremy 90
Bentinck, William 142n29
Beowulf (poem) 173
Berkeley, Bishop 259
Berners-Lee, Tim 276n49
Berry, Peter 101
Bescheidenheit (Freidank) 191, 193–199
Besser, Howard 262
Bhabha, Homi 34–35, 36, 45, 50
Bhakti poetry 126–127
Bhartendu era 128
Bhasha literatures, and aging in India 114–122;
　Boodhi Kaaki (Premchand) 115–117; *Palang*
　(Priyamvad) 119–121; *Pitaa* (Gyanranjan)
　117–119
Bhatt, Balkrishna 128
Bhattacharyya, Narayan Chandra 107
Bhattacharyya, Sukumari 103
Big Data 258, 264
Bildung project 32, 41, 43–45
biological intelligence 260
biotechnology 79
Black communities: enslaved people 238–240;
　surrogacy before Civil War 230–231
Bloom, Allan 61, 67
Bloom, Harold 56, 62
Boccaccio, Giovanni 62, 192
Boezio 252
Bolter, Jay 256
Bonerius, Ulrich 199
Boodhi Kaaki (Premchand) 115–117
Borneo Evangelical Church 155
Boundary Treaty Agreement (1915) 153
Bragg, Raymond 53
Braidotti, Rosi 4, 93–94
Brennan, Timothy 67
Brown, Bill 260
Bryson, Michael 173, 209, 232
Buchan, William 237–238
Bulhak, Andrew C. 278n72
Burckhardt, Jacob 186n20
Busa, Roberto 253
Bush, Douglas 262
Bush, Vannevar 257
Butler, Judith 12
Butön 109

Cabral, Amilcar 45
Cage, David 283
Caillois, R. 61
Calarco, Matthew 91–92
Callard, Felicity 105
Camden, William 216
capitalism 3
Carakasaṁhitā 106
Carassai, Mauro 251
Cavalieri, Paola 87
Césaire, Aimé 36, 42, 60–61, 64
Chandra, Pratap 102–103

Chaturvidha Purushartha 125
Chaucer, Geoffrey 192
Cheah, Pheng 44
Chernyshevsky, Nikolay 180
Chhayavad (neo-romanticism) 128–129
child–elder relationships 117
chiti (supreme consciousness) 125
Christianity 52, 124, 155
Cicero 5, 73–74
Clark, David 175–176
Classen, Albrecht 191
Clifford, James 34, 60, 65
cogito (absolute truth) 28
Cohen, Gerson 180
Collins, David 238–239
colonialism 33
Colonial violence 39
colonization 153
compassion 130–132
Complete Robot, The (Asimov) 284
comprehensive historical humanism 139
Comte 27
Conrad, Joseph 50, 67
Copson, Andrew 101
Crain, Jay 155
Creed, Thomas 227n61
Crist, Eileen 2
critical editions 255
critical humanism 60–64
criticism: democratic 57; digital 255; literary
　180–181; secular 51, 64–65
Crutchfield, Parker 7n16
cultural humanism 56
cultural stereotyping 55
culture 43, 44
Culture and Imperialism (Said) 53, 56, 57

Dalit writings 137
Damodar Dutta Dixit 132
"Dasein" 14–15, 19, 26, 29n13
data mining 257, 275n38
Davies, Tony 34, 43
decolonization 31–33, 38, 41–46
De Gennaro, Mara 61, 66
dehumanization 39
Deleuze, Gilles 87, 94–95
de Man, Paul 188n50
de Maupertuis, Pierre-Louis Moreau 233
democratic criticism 57
de Pizan, Christine 192
de Plessis-Mornay, Philippe 210
Derrida, Jacques 87, 94, 179
De Saussure, Ferdinand 277n58
de Saussure, Raymond 120
Descartes, Rene 28, 88–89, 259
Desmond, Marilynn 175
Detroit: Become Human (game) 282–287
Devy, G.N. 114–115
Dewey, John 53

Index

DFR Browser 265, 280n109

Dhargyey, Geshe Ngawang 108

dharma (moral values) 125

Dharmaśāstra 104

different humanism 60

digital humanities 251–255; AI 259–261; hypertexts 255–259; interfaces 266–269; metadata 261–263; super-computing 263–266

digital literature 278n83

Dilthey, Wilhelm 252, 264

Dinzelbacher, Peter 205n1

disalienation 38

Discourse on Colonialism (Césaire) 60–61

discrimination 115–116

distant reading 264

divine violence 40

docuverse 259

Domestic Medicine (Buchan) 237, 242

Donaldson, Sue 92

Douglas, Jane Yellowlees 276n50

Drucker, Johanna 262–263

dualism 259

Dwivedi era 128–130

Dying Colonialism, A (Fanon) 33

Eagleton, Terry 66

Edwords, Fred 266

EEBO/EEBO-TCP databases 211, 225n23

electronic editing 261

Electronic Literature Collection, The series 263

eliminationism 3

Eliot, T.S. 268

Elizabeth I 209, 211, 219–220

Ellis, Thomas B. 109

embryology 229, 232

emergent humanism 31, 33–37

Emerson, Lori 281n124

encoding 261

Enlightenment humanism 26, 32, 252, 264, 273n14

enslaved women 239–241

epistemology 193–194, 195

Erasmus, Desiderius 52, 58n14, 252, 263

ethical humanism 23

Eurocentric humanism 60–61, 66

European humanism 61

European literature 191–202; *Bescheidenheit* (Freidank) 191, 193–199; *Sir Gawain and the Green Knight* 191, 199–202; *see also* Anglo-Saxon poetry

Evans, Martyn 105

évolué 37–39, 41

Exeter Book 173

existentialism 11–12, 20–22, 24, 35

"Existentialism is a Humanism" 12, 23, 75

Fanon, Frantz 3, 4, 12, 25, 36, 64; decolonization 41–46; *Dying Colonialism, A* 33; intellectual struggles as *évolué* 37–39, 41; New Humanism 32–33, 41–46; Revolutionary Violence Theory 39–41; scholarly debates over humanism 33–37; *Wretched of the Earth, The* 31, 39

Farahmandfar, Masoud 50

Febvre, Lucien 210

Fichte, Johann Gottlieb 180

Firestone, Shulamith 229

Fish, Stanley 188n49

Fishel, Stefanie 2

Fisher, Robert 210

Fissell, Mary 231

Fitzgerald, Des 105

Flaubert, G. 54

Floridi, Luciano 260, 278n84

Fortescue, John 216

Foucault, Michel 7n17, 12, 27, 63

Francis, Pope 53

Frankforter, Daniel 267

freedom 193–194

Freidank (poet) 191, 193–199

Freud, S. 94

Freud & the Non-European (Said) 64

Frye, Northrop 62

Fudge, Erica 87–88

full surrogacy 230–231

fundamental ontology 17, 19, 22

Ganang, Ricky 157

Ganesan, Kavitha 146

Gardiner, William 210

Gates, Henry Louis Jr. 37

Ghosal, Abhisek 101

Gilroy, Paul 5

Gītā 104

Gobineau, A. 61

Gochenour, Phillip H. 277n65

Godrej, Farah 108

Great Ape Project 87, 91

Greaves, David 105

Greenblatt, Stephen 209, 211, 212

Greene, Robert 213, 217

Greenfield, Stanley 173, 176

Grinnell, George C. 238

guard links 259–260

Guattari, Felix 87, 94–95

Gupt, Maithili Sharan 128

Gyanranjan 117–119

Habermas, Jürgen 80–81

Hallaq, Wael 66

Haraway, Donna 4, 94–95, 230

Harihar, Achhutanand (Swami) 137

Harpham, Geoffrey 266

Harpold, Terry 267

Hartman, Saidiya 242

Harvey, William 233

Hayles, Katherine 252, 278n83

headhunting: in Lundayeh community 146–149; as reality maintenance 151

Hegel, G.W.F. 37

Index

Hegy, Andree 106
Heidegger, Martin 4, 73–77, 74; *Being and Time* project 12–13; Dasein (term) 14–15, 19, 26, 29n13; existential analysis 20–22; *Letter on Humanism* 11–12
Henslowe, Philip 213
Herman, Peter C. 209
Hiddleston, Jane 65
Hindi literature 115; *Bhakti* poetry 126–127; compassion for downtrodden 130–132; human rights in *Janvadi Sahitya* 135–137; ideals of 127–128; Indian humanism 125–126; individualism 128–130; modern man's turmoil 134–135; peasant narratives and migratory labor 132–134; resistance/rage/revolt against oppression 137–138
Historia Ecclesiastica Gentis Anglorum (Ecclesiastical History of the English People) 173
Hockey, Susan 253
Homer 52
Horner, Shari 181, 188n36
Hoskins, Janet 149
HT *see* hypertexts (HT)
Hull, John 209
human(s): animal community 95; capability 255; as info-organism 254–255; intelligence 251; knowledge, scale of 263–266; labor 3, 8n18; machine relationships 282; morality 7n16; rights in *Janvadi Sahitya* 135–137; and technologies 254; values 52
humanism 2, 52–53; Anglo-Saxon poetry 173–182; *animal turn* as challenge to 86–96; in Continental philosophy 11–28; defined 64–65, 125; different kind of 60–68; digital 4, 251–269; Edward Said about 53–57; in European medieval literature 191–202; and spiritualism 125; traditions 2; as usable praxis 65–68; *see also specific types*
Humanism and Democratic Criticism (Said) 31, 51, 53–54, 60
Humanism's Sphere 62
"humanism without humanism" 32, 41, 45–46
humanist ethics 52
Humanist International 101
humanitas 74, 124, 263
Humanities Computing (McCarthy) 253, 274n19
Hume, David 55
"humiliation of man" 61
Hunter, Michael 209
Huntington, Samuel 62
Hunt, Sarah Beth 137
hypertexts (HT) 255–259

Ibsen, Henrik 285
ICTs *see* information and communication systems (ICTs)
idealism 2, 259
IF *see* interactive fiction (IF)
Ijtihad (commitment/effort) 68

Indic humanisms 101–110; Hindi literature 125–126; *oneness* in diversity 110; overview 102–104; in post-vedic tāntric traditions 107–109; in vedic medical humanities 105–107; *vs.* Western humanism 139
individualism 128–130
information and communication systems (ICTs) 261
inhumane 23–24
integral humanism 53, 125–126
intellectuals 54
interactive fiction (IF) 260, 277n71
intergenerational conflicts 118
International Humanist and Ethical Union 125
interpretation processes 254

Jackson, Shelley 276n50
James, William 58n18
Jani, Deepa 31
Janowski, Monica 150, 152
Janvadi Sahitya 135–137
Jocasta complex 120
Jones, Therese 105
Joyce, J. 54
Joyce, Michael 276n50

Kabir (poet) 126–127
kama (physical pleasure) 125
Kamal, Sauleha 60
Kane, P.V. 104
Kant, Immanuel 52, 89
Kaufringer, Heinrich 192
Khetan, Prabha 138
Kilbride, Janet 120
King Lear (Shakespeare) 221–222
Kirschenbaum, Matthew 260, 268
Kizkkowski, Adrianna 284
Knauft, Bruce M. 108
Korsgaard, Christine 88
Kristeller, Paul Oskar 263
Kumar, Malreddy 34, 36, 61
Kumar, Saurav 114
Kuwahara, Kazumi 121
Kymlicka, Will 92

La Capra, Dominique 133
Landow, George 256
Lazarus, Neil 34, 35, 36, 45
LDA algorithm 265, 280n110
Leavis, Frank Raymond 50
Lees, Claire 178
Lees, Shirley 171n4
Leeuwenhoek, A. 233
Lésper, Avelina 190n62
Letter on Humanism (Heidegger) 11–12, 23, 75–77, 81
Lewis, Sophie 230–231
liberation struggle 33, 40, 42–43
Lidke, Jeffrey S. 107

Index

linked information 257
Linnaeus, Carl 233
Linzey, Andrew 87
literary criticism 180–181
Liu, Alan 254, 263, 277n69
Lowe, Lisa 242
Lukács, Georg 51, 134
Lundayeh community 146; *benging* song 160–162; colonization 153–155; erosion of indigenous identity 153–157; headhunting in 146–162; longhouses 147–149; modernization 156–157; national identity 156; religious conversion 155–156, 171n4; *Tido Ada'* (funeral chant) 157–159; works of oral literature 157–162
Luther, Martin 52
Lyotard, Jean-François 1

machine intelligence 284
machinic reading 257
Mahābhārata 104
Makdisi, George 62
Malebranche, Nicolas 89
Mandel, Jerome 177, 178
Manichaeanism 32–33, 38
Manningham, Richard 234
Man-Plant, The (Miller) 229–234, 242
Manu, Saint 125
Mapa System 258, 277n64
March-Russel, Paul 284
Margulis, Lynn 94–95
Markendeya 132–133
Marlowe, Christopher 209, 211, 213
Marx, Karl 3–4, 37
Mass Effect Trilogy (game) 284–285
Masterpiece (Aristotle) 231, 234, 242
materiality 259
McCarthy, Willard 274n19
McKinley, Robert 150
Meaney, Audrey 181
medical humanities 105–107
Meerabai (princess) 142n26
Memmi, Albert 36
memory palace/mirror 120
Merleau-Ponty, Maurice 12, 37
metadata 261
Midas (King) 8n23
Middle Ages 52, 187n20, 251; European literature 191–202; as oppressor of human intellectual freedom 273n5; woman as measure of all things 173–182
Midgley, Mary 87
migratory labor 132–134
Miller, Vincent 229–230, 233
Minot, John 210
Mirandola, Pico della 124, 141n3, 257
Mohan, Shailendra 132, 133
mokshya (self-realization) 125
monstrous births 231, 233, 235–236
Montfort, Nick 263

More, Thomas 58n14
Morgan, Jennifer L. 230, 231, 242
Morris, Adalaide 256
Mosaic browser 258, 277n63
Muktibodh, Gajanan Madhav 135
Muller, Robin M. 11
Müller-Doohm, Stephan 85n60
Muth, Miriam 173, 177, 178–180
mythical violence 40

Nagarjun (poet) 129–130
Nagy, Sharon 120
Nandy, Ashis 132
Narayan, R.K. 118–119
national consciousness 39, 40, 41, 43–44
National Socialism 81–82
Native American genocide 62
Naxalbari revolt 135–136
Neeraj, Gopal Das Saxena 135
Nehru, Jawaharlal 132
Nelson, Ted 256
neo-romanticism 128
Neruda, Pablo 181
New Humanism (Fanon) 32–33; and decolonization 41–46; intellectual struggles as *évolué*, and Revolutionary Violence theory 37–41; residual/emergent humanism debate 33–37
Nietzsche, Friedrich 3, 8n23, 12, 28, 53, 77
Nimishray, Mohandas 137
Nirala (poet) 129
Nirala, Suryakant Tripathi 128
nonracial humanism 5
Noordegraaf-Eelens, Liesbeth 81
Nussbaum, Martha 93

obedience 181
Ong, Walter 252
ontology 17, 19, 22
Orientalism (Said) 33–34, 50, 63
Osborne, Marijane 176
otherness 36, 61
over-specialization 267

Padmavat 126, 141n10
Palang (Priyamvad) 119–121
Pannian, Prasad 63, 65
Pant, Sumitranandan 128
Paramhansa, Ramkrishna 128
Parvini, Neema 190n62
Paugh, Katherine 244n10
Pavlovna, Vera 180
Pearson-Rounds, Vicki 155
peasant narratives 132–134
Perkins, William 211
Persson, Ingmar 7n16
Petrarch, Francesco 62, 141n2, 177

Index

phenomenology 18–19
Philcox, Richard 32
philological humanism 65
Pitaa (Gyanranjan) 117–119
planetary humanism 5
Plato 1, 2, 78, 259
Plotinus 259
political humanism 61
Politikos (Plato) 78
post-humanism 3, 93–95, 252
Prasad, Jai Shankar 128
Preedy, Chloe 209
preformationism 230, 233
Premchand, Munshi 115–117, 130
Priyamvad 119–121
Priyanka, Prachi 124
programming 266–269
Protagoras 1, 2, 52, 86
pseudo-humanism 63
purdah system 128, 142n28

Qābbanī, Nizār 181, 189n61
quantization 251
"quasi-totalitarian" philosophy 80, 85n62
question(s): intended 19–20; interrogating some
being(s) 17–19; and questioner 14–15; about
something 15–17

racialism "humanism" 61
Radhakrishnan, Rajagopalan 64, 65–66
Radhakrishnan, S. 138
Rahim-I-Khana, Abdul 126
Rahman, Shaffarullah Abdullah 146
Raleigh, Walter 210, 212
Rāmāyaṇa 104
Ramcharitmanas 126, 141n11
Ramsey, Stephen 267, 275n38
rationality 25
real humanism 64–65
Regan, Tom 87, 92
remediation 278n75
Renaissance humanism 52, 102, 124, 191, 264,
273n5
Renan, E. 61, 62
Representations of the Intellectual (Said) 54
reproductive surrogacy 230
residual humanism 31, 33–37
Restating Orientalism (Hallaq) 66
Rettberg, Scott 256
Revolutionary Violence Theory 39–41
Ṛgveda 103
Riti-kaavy Kaal 127, 142n20
Roberts, Dorothy K. 230
robotics 282
romantic love 177
Roy, M.N. 139
Roy, Raja Ram Mohan 128, 139
Rubinstein, Robert 120

Rules for the Human Zoo (Sloterdijk) 73, 80, 82
Ryder, Richard 86

sādhakas (religious worshippers) 107–109
Sagun 127, 142n21
Said, Edward 4, 5, 31, 46, 50; critical humanism
60–64; definition of humanism 63; *Humanism
and Democratic Criticism* 60; *Orientalism* (Said)
33–34, 50; real humanism 64–65; re-defining
humanism 62–63, 64, 182; secularism 64–65;
use of Césairian critique 60–64; worldliness
51, 55
Salutati, Coluccio 252, 262
sampling 251
Sāmveda 103
Saraswati, Dayanand 128
Sartre, Jean-Paul 4, 11, 23, 25–26, 28, 37,
39, 285
sati pratha 128, 142n29
Savulescu, Julian 7n16
Schaffer, Simon 237
Schechner, Richard 282
Scheck, Helene 181
Schiller, F.C.S. 2
Schinkel, Willem 81
Schnapps, Jeffrey 275n37
Scott, James C. 133
secular criticism 51, 64–65
secular humanism 55
Sedgewick, Eve 180
self-actualization 43, 45
self-awareness 57
selfhood 254, 275n31
self-realization 43
self-reflection 254
Selimus, Emperor of the Turks (Greene)
217–221
Sellars, Wilfrid 16
Sellers, Roy 53
Shakespeare, William 221–222
Shapin, Steven 237
Shapiro, Kenneth 87
Shaw, George Bernard 285
Shenk, Dena 121
Sherma, Rita Dasgupta 107
Shir ha-Shirim (Song of Songs) 173, 178
Shuger, Debora 209
Siddiqi, Yumna 63, 67
Silenus 4, 8n23
Simondon, Gilbert 89
Singer, Peter 86, 87
Singh, Kedarnath 134–135
Singh, Madhukar 136–137
Sinh, Jawahar 136
Sir Gawain and the Green Knight 191, 199–202
Skonieczny, Krzysztof 86
slaves 238; and surrogacy 230; trade
62, 238

294

Index

Sloterdijk, Peter 4; calming inner beast 73–75; getting drift 80–82; habitat for inhumanity 82; Nietzsche and 77–78; Plato and 78–80; response to *Letter on Humanism* 75–77; *Rules for the Human Zoo* 73, 80, 82
Smith, Adam 7n17
Smith, Frederic M. 108
Smith, Henry 209
Smith, Thomas 217
Snow, C.P. 252, 274n16
Sophocles 52
Spallanzani, Lazarro 233
speciesist 86, 87
Spellman, William 267
Spillers, Hortense 242
Spinoza 94
spiritualism, in humanism 125
Spitzer 60, 61, 65
Spivak, Gayatri 31, 50
Spratt, Danielle 229
Steere, Bartholomew 212
Stephanson, Raymond 229, 234
Stevens, Martin 178
Storyspace 258
Stuart, James 221
studia humanitatis (studies of humanity) 83n7, 252, 254, 263, 275n32
super-computing 263–266, 280n112
Surdas 127
surrogacy 229–242
Sur Sagar 126, 141n12
Swift, Jonathan 50
Swindell, Ruth 236

Tagore, Rabindranath 125, 139
Tai, Michael Cheng-Tek 105
Tamburlaine (book) 211, 213–217
tāntras 107–109
Taylor, Thomas 91
technologies, and human 254
telecommunicative bridge 74
Terence (African slave) 5
Terrell, Mary 105
textual artifacts 254, 261
Thorpe, Benjamin 177
Tido Ada' (funeral chant) 157–159
Toft, Mary 233
Tolstoy, Leo 190n62
Topic Modeling 264–265
transhumanism 252
Tripathi, S.N. 106
Trotsky, Leon 190n62
Tulsidas 127
Turgenev, I. 54
Tymme, Thomas 212
tyranny 3

Übermensch 53, 77
ungendered humanism 5
unhomeliness 50
universal humanism 61–62, 68
Upadhyaya, Pandit Deen Dayal 125–126
Urban, Hugh B. 109

Valiathan, M.S. 106–107
Valmiki, Omprakash 138
van Tuinen, Sjord 80
Varma, Mahadevi 129
Vatsyayan, Kapila 110
vedas 103
Verma, Archana 138
Vermulean, Heather V. 233
Vico, Giambattista 51, 63, 252
video games 282–283
Virgil 52
virtual witnessing 237
Vivekananda, Swami 125, 128
von der Vogelweide, Walther 194
von Fallersleben, Hoffmann 194
von Tepl, Johannes 192, 199

Walthorpe, Elizabeth 210
Wan, Justin 155
Wardrip-Fruin, Noah 260, 263
Watson, Tom J. 253
Wear, Delese 105
web-based AI text generator 278n72
Weinbaum, Alys Eve 230
Weinberger, Steven Neal 109
Weisman, Alan 8n24
Wells, Robin Headlam 5
Western humanism 31, 36, 39, 61, 63; end of 45; lack of spirituality 125; *vs.* Indic humanism 139
West-Pavlov, Russell 61
Wetzel, James 58n12
Whitehead, Alfred North 94
Wife's Lament (poem) 173–174, 177, 180
Wilhelm, Georg 259
Williams, Adam 283
Williams, Raymond 34
Williamson, John 240
Wollstonecraft, Mary 91
woman, as measure of all things 173–182
Wootton, David 209, 210, 212
worldliness 51, 55
World, the Text, and the Critic, The (Said) 51
World Wide Web 256
Wulf and Eadwacer (poem) 173, 175, 181
Wynter, Sylvia 4–5

Index

X-Lit format 263

Yadav, Rajendra 138
yajñas mantras 103, 111n7
Yayurveda 103
yogās 104, 111n14
Young, Robert 33, 34, 36, 37, 65

Zablotsky, Diane 121
Zammit-Lucia, Joe 88
Zarathustra (Persian prophet) 77
Zarathustra Project, The (Assheuer) 80–81
Žižek, Slavoj 2, 80
Zouidi, Nizar 282
Zumthor, Paul 176